WITHDRAWN
JUL 29 2024
RICKS COLLEGE
DAVID O. McKAY LRC
REXBURG, IDAHO 83440

INTRODUCTION TO THE CRIMINAL JUSTICE SYSTEM

KF 9223 .R6 1984 c.2
Robin, Gerald D., 1936-
Introduction to the criminal
justice system

INTRODUCTION TO THE CRIMINAL JUSTICE SYSTEM

Principles · Procedures · Practice

SECOND EDITION

Gerald D. Robin
University of New Haven

1817

HARPER & ROW, PUBLISHERS, New York
Cambridge, Philadelphia, San Francisco,
London, Mexico City, São Paulo, Sydney

Photo Credits Page 1, Freed, Magnum; 10, Glinn, Magnum; 28, Lucas, Rapho Photo Researchers; 29, Bikar, *Mansfield News Journal;* 31, from *Equal Justice Under Law,* courtesy Foundation of the Federal Bar Association; 35, reprinted from *U.S. News & World Report,* © 1977, U.S. News & World Report, Inc.; 40, reprinted from *U.S. News & World Report,* © 1975, U.S. News & World Report, Inc.; 57, Powers, *Corrections* Magazine; 54–55, O'Brien, *Police* Magazine; 75, Wide World; 77, UPI; 81, UPI; 83, Lustig, *Washington Star;* 86, Gatewood, Magnum; 89, Dain, Magnum; 92, Copyright Normon Y. Lono/*Philadelphia Daily News;* 98, Seattle Times Co.; 102, Hausner, The *New York Times;* 108, Daniels, Photo Researchers; 113, *Psychology Today* Magazine; 114, Wide World; 117, courtesy Maui, Hawaii, Police Department; 119, Bikar, *News Journal;* 120, Galyn, Photo Researchers; 122, Wide World; 123, courtesy New York Police Department; 124, Don Dornan; 125, Hamilton, Cornell University; 125, *Boston Globe;* 129, Dain, Magnum; 131, O'Brien, *Police* Magazine; 134, Powers, *Police* Magazine; 141, Dain, Magnum; 145, Wide World; 146, UPI; 149, Levick, Black Star; 154, Manheim, Photo Researchers; 157, O'Brien, *Police* Magazine; 161, Beckwith; 163, UPI; 166, courtesy Henry Lee, Univ. of New Haven; 174, Wide World; 180, O'Brien, *Police* Magazine; 182, courtesy White House Information Office; 188, UPI; 189, Providence Journal Bulletin Photo; 197, Powers, *Corrections* Magazine; 200, Roberts, Rapho/Photo Researchers; 201, Texas Highway Departments; 213, from *Equal Justice Under Law,* Courtesy Foundation of the Federal Bar Assoc.; 218, UPI; 223, Mark, Archive Pictures; 224, Wide World; 232, *Corrections* Magazine; 245, Wide World; 253, Powers, *Police* Magazine; 256, UPI; 257, UPI; 260, courtesy Henry Lee and New Haven Public Defender Assoc.; 269, UPI; 277, Palermo, N.Y. *Daily News;* 286, Stapleton, Anchorage *Daily News;* 292, Wide World; 295, UPI; 299, Church, *The New York Times;* 303, Medford Taylor; 307, Wide World; 308, Wide World; 309, Wide World; 310, UPI; 318, Wide World; 319, *Law Enforcement Communication;* 320, UPI; 322, Harris, *Cleveland Plain Dealer;* 327, Mark, Archive Pictures; 329, Levick, Black Star; 338, Wide World; 340–341, Dominique Strandquist; 350, Wide World; 357, UPI; 358, Schiller, Photo Researchers; 359, Wide World; 365, Davidson, Magnum; 373, courtesy Rita Gold, Boulder County Justice Center; 377, Wide World; 379, Hausner, *The New York Times;* 383, Powers, *Corrections* Magazine; 386, Powers, *Corrections* Magazine; 388, Giles, Photographic; 391, courtesy William D. Leeke, South Carolina Department of Corrections; 395, UPI; 405, O'Brien, *Corrections* Magazine; 407 (top) Powers, *Corrections* Magazine; 407 (bottom) Courtesy Texas Department of Corrections; 412, Wolff, Black Star; 416, Powers, *Corrections* Magazine; 423, Powers, *Corrections* Magazine; 427, *Corrections* Magazine; 429, reprinted from *U.S. News & World Report,* © 1975, U.S. News & World Report, Inc.; 431, Gruzen & Partners; 432, Koltz, Black Star; 434, Springmann, Black Star; 437, Wide World; 443, UPI; 446, Powers, *Corrections* Magazine; 456, Powers, *Corrections* Magazine; 459, Powers, *Corrections* Magazine; 467, courtesy Pearl S. West, California Department of Youth Authority; 470, Powers, *Corrections* Magazine; 471, Powers, *Corrections* Magazine; 477, Forsyth, Monkmeyer; 480, Image; 482, Manheim, Photo Researchers; 483, courtesy LEAA Newsletter; 488, Mara Platsky, New York; 491, Powers, *Corrections* Magazine; 494, and 497, Powers, *Corrections* Magazine; 507, *Pacifici, The New York Times;* 509, reprinted from *U.S. News & World Report,* © 1978, U.S. News & World Report, Inc.; 515, Ken Love; 522, Wide World; 524, Wide World.

Sponsoring Editor: Jean Hurtado
Project Editor: Holly Detgen
Designer: Michel Craig
Production Manager: Willie Lane
Photo Researcher: Mira Schachne
Compositor: Progressive Typographers
Printer and Binder: R. R. Donnelley & Sons Company
Art Studio: Vantage Art, Inc.

INTRODUCTION TO THE CRIMINAL JUSTICE SYSTEM
Principles, Procedures, and Practice, Second Edition

Library of Congress Cataloging in Publication Data

Robin, Gerald D., 1936–
Introduction to the criminal justice system.

Includes bibliographical references and index.
1. Criminal justice, Administration of—United States. 2. Criminal procedure—United States.
I. Title.
KF9223.R6 1983 345.73'05 82-21174
ISBN 0-06-045512-8 347.3055

To my father, Jack Robin,
the greatest man I know,
and to my loving
and wise mother, Sylvia.

Contents

Preface xvii

Chapter 1
CRIME

THE LEGAL FOUNDATION OF CRIME 2

Close-up 1.1: Insanity as a Defense to Criminal Responsibility 3

STATUTORY AND PROCEDURAL CRIMINAL LAW 5
THE LAW IN ACTION AND DISCRETION 7
REASONABLENESS AND THE LAW 9
THE CLASSIFICATION OF CRIME 11
THE *UNIFORM CRIME REPORTS* 13
Index Crimes 13

Close-up 1.2: Coming to Grips with the Problem of Arson 14

The Amount of Crime 18
Crimes Cleared by Arrest 19
Persons Arrested 20
Recidivism 21
VICTIM SURVEYS 23

Close-up 1.3: The "Shrinkage" of Crime from Reporting to Conviction 24

THE FEAR OF CRIME 27
SUMMARY 29

Chapter 2
THE CRIMINAL JUSTICE SYSTEM: AN OVERVIEW

THE PROCESSING STAGES IN FELONY CASES 33
Arrest 33
Initial Court Appearance 36
Preliminary Hearing 37
Grand Jury 38

Close-up 2.1: Should the Grand Jury be Abolished? 41

Arraignment 43
Pretrial Motions 45
Trial 45
Sentencing 46
Probation 47
Correctional Institutions 48
Parole 48
CRIMINAL JUSTICE ADMINISTRATION AS SYSTEM AND NONSYSTEM 49
Jurisdictional and Operational Problems 52
Differences in Roles and Goals 52
People Problems 53
Substantive Issues 53
THE FEDERAL ROLE IN IMPROVING STATE AND LOCAL CRIMINAL JUSTICE SYSTEMS 53
The President's Crime Commission 54
Law Enforcement Assistance Administration (LEAA) 56
The Standards and Goals Commission 57
SUMMARY 58

Chapter 3
THE POLICE ROLE

LAW ENFORCEMENT AND ORDER MAINTENANCE 62
THE WORKING PERSONALITY OF THE POLICE 65
Police Prejudice and Authoritarianism 66
THE EXERCISE OF DISCRETION 67
Full Enforcement of the Law Versus Selective Enforcement 68
Factors Influencing the Decision to Arrest 70
The Control of Discretion 71
CRIME CONTROL AND THE POLICE 73
Do the Police Deter Crime? 73
Special Approaches to Crime Control 76

Close-up 3.1: Supreme Court Decisions on Entrapment 79

VICTIMLESS CRIME AND DECRIMINALIZATION 84
SUMMARY 86

Chapter 4
THE POLICE AND THE COMMUNITY

"POLICE BRUTALITY" 90
DEADLY FORCE 93

Close-up 4.1: The Fyfe Study of Deadly Force 97

CIVILIAN REVIEW BOARDS 100
SUING THE POLICE 103
POLICE-COMMUNITY RELATIONS 107
DOMESTIC CRISIS INTERVENTION 112

Close-up 4.2: Thomas Promised 116

COMMUNITY CRIME PREVENTION 119
Neighborhood Crime Watches 119
Citizen Patrols 120

Close-up 4.3: The Guardian Angels 121

Citizens as Police Auxiliaries 123
Technology, Private Security Personnel, and Students 123
Citizen Court Watchers 125
SUMMARY 126

Chapter 5
THE PROFESSIONALIZATION OF THE POLICE

COLLEGE EDUCATION 130
TRAINING 137
ETHNIC MINORITIES IN POLICE DEPARTMENTS 140
POLICEWOMEN ON PATROL 147
OPERATING POLICE DEPARTMENTS MORE EFFICIENTLY 150

Close-up 5.1: Homosexuals as Police Officers 151

The Consolidation of Police Services 152
Civilians in Police Departments 153
One-person Patrol Cars 154
New Arraignment Procedures for Police 155
NEIGHBORHOOD TEAM POLICING 155
SUMMARY 159

Chapter 6
THE POLICE AND THE CONSTITUTION

THE EXCLUSIONARY RULE 163
Mapp v. *Ohio* (1961) 165
Viability of the Exclusionary Rule 166

Close-up 6.1: The Dropsy Defense 168

CUSTODIAL INTERROGATION AND CONFESSIONS 169
The Prompt Arraignment Rule 171
Escobedo v. *Illinois* (1964) 172
Miranda v. *Arizona* (1966) 174
STOP AND FRISK: STREET INTERROGATION 177
Terry v. *Ohio* (1968) 179
DECISIONS OF THE SUPREME COURT UNDER BURGER 181
The Retreat from the Exclusionary Rule 182
The Erosion of *Miranda* 185
The Expansion of Stop and Frisk 190

Close-up 6.2: Reasonable Suspicion and the Drug Courier Profile 192

Other Decisions Compatible with Police Interests 191
SUMMARY 194

Chapter 7
THE COURTS

THE STATE COURT SYSTEM 198
Lower Courts 198
Trial (Felony) Courts 202
Appellate Courts 203

Close-up 7.1: Two Successful Appeals 205

THE FEDERAL COURT SYSTEM 208
The Supreme Court 211

Close-up 7.2: Women on Juries 214

COURT REFORM 215
Judicial Discipline Commissions 215

Merit Selection of Judges 217
Court Administrators and Court Unification 218
SUMMARY 220

Chapter 8
THE BAIL SYSTEM

THE RIGHT TO BAIL 224
THE ADMINISTRATION OF BAIL BEFORE THE 1960s 225
PRETRIAL DETENTION 228
THE MANHATTAN BAIL PROJECT 231

Close-up 8.1: The Manhattan Bail Project in Action 233

TEN PERCENT CASH BAIL 235
CONDITIONAL RELEASE 236
THE BAIL REFORM ACT OF 1966 237
BAIL: A CURRENT PERSPECTIVE 240
SUMMARY 242

Chapter 9
THE PROSECUTOR AND DEFENSE COUNSEL

THE ROLE OF THE PROSECUTOR 246
THE MANAGEMENT OF PROSECUTION 250
The Bronx Major Offense Bureau 252

Close-up 9.1: The Major Offense Bureau at Work 255

THE RIGHT TO COUNSEL 256
PUBLIC DEFENDERS AND COURT-ASSIGNED COUNSEL 259
SUMMARY 266

Chapter 10
PLEA BARGAINING AND SPEEDY TRIAL

PLEA BARGAINING 270
The Prosecutor's Incentive to Plea Bargain 271
Defense Counsel's Incentive to Plea Bargain 274
The Plea Bargaining Process 275

Close-up 10.1: Plea Bargaining in Homicide Cases—Getting Away with Murder 276

The Case for Plea Bargaining 279
The Case Against Plea Bargaining 280

Close-up 10.2: Assembly Line Justice 282

RESTRUCTURING THE PLEA BARGAINING PROCESS 283
The Pretrial Conference 284
Restricting the Scope of Plea Bargaining 286
SPEEDY TRIAL 288
The Speedy Trial Act of 1974 290

Close-up 10.3: Should Murderers Go Free Because the Prosecutor Has Blundered? 294

SUMMARY 296

Chapter 11
TRIAL
THE ADVERSARY METHOD OF JUSTICE 300
PUBLIC ACCESS TO TRIAL 301
SELECTION OF THE JURY 304

Close-up 11.1: Pretrial Publicity, Freedom of the Press, and Gag Orders 307

Scientific Jury Selection: The Joan Little Case 310
SIX-PERSON JURIES 313
NONUNANIMOUS VERDICTS 316
VIDEOTAPED TRIALS 318

Close-up 11.2: Supreme Court Gives Go-Ahead to Televising of Trials 320

CHARGING THE JURY 323
SUMMARY 324

Chapter 12
SENTENCING
THE OBJECTIVES OF SENTENCING 329
Retribution 329
Incapacitation 330
Deterrence 330
Rehabilitation 331

THE PRESENTENCE REPORT 332
DISPARITY IN SENTENCING 335
SENTENCING INSTITUTES, COUNCILS, AND GUIDELINES 340
Sentencing Institutes 340
Sentencing Councils 340
Sentencing Guidelines 341
APPELLATE REVIEW OF SENTENCES 343

Close-up 12.1: Connecticut's Sentence Review Board 345

THE MODEL PENAL CODE AND THE MODEL SENTENCING ACT 346
The Model Penal Code 346
The Model Sentencing Act 347
ALTERNATIVES TO THE INDETERMINATE SENTENCE 348
THE DEATH SENTENCE 351
Furman v. *Georgia* (1972) 352
Gregg v. *Georgia* (1976) 354

Close-up 12.2: The Course of Capital Punishment in California 357

Close-up 12.3: Have Judges Made the Death Penalty an Idle Threat? 360

SUMMARY 362

Chapter 13 JAILS

THE NATIONAL JAIL SURVEY 367
CONTEMPORARY JAIL PROBLEMS 370
Local Administration of Jails 371
The Concern with Security 374

Close-up 13.1: The Federal Metropolitan Correctional Center 374

THE MANHATTAN HOUSE OF DETENTION 376
SUMMARY 381

Chapter 14
PRISONS

TYPES OF PRISONS 384
The Reception and Diagnostic Center 385
THE OVERCROWDED PRISONS 387

Close-up 14.1: Double Celling Passes Constitutional Muster 390

IMPRISONMENT AS CRUEL AND UNUSUAL PUNISHMENT 392
James v. *Wallace* (1976) 393

Close-up 14.2: The Tucker Prison Farm 394

Ruiz v. *Estelle* (1980) 396
THE CUSTODIAL STAFF 398
Restructuring the Role of Guards 401

Close-up 14.3: The Stanford Prison Experiment: College Students as Prisoners and Guards 402

WORK, EDUCATION, AND TREATMENT PROGRAMS 404
Vocational Training 405
Education 411
Treatment 413

Close-up 14.4: The Therapeutic Community 414

THE PAROLE DECISION 416
Parole Board-Determined Release 419
Parole Contracts (Mutual Agreement Programming) 425
The Abolition of Parole 427
Mandatory Release and Discharge 430
THE FUTURE OF IMPRISONMENT 431
SUMMARY 434

Chapter 15
PRISONERS' RIGHTS

THE CONDITIONS OF INCARCERATION 438

Close-up 15.1: Section 1983 of the Civil Rights Act 440

The Attica Riot of 1971 441
SEEKING PRISONERS' RIGHTS THROUGH THE COURTS 444
Access to Courts and Counsel 444
Religion 446
Prisoners' Labor Unions 447
Medical Services 448
The Right to Rehabilitative Treatment 449
The Right Not To Be Treated 451
Discipline 452
Inmate Safety 458

Close-up 15.2: Necessity as a Defense for Crime 460

Legal Rights of Jail Inmates 462
SEEKING PRISONERS' RIGHTS BY NONJUDICIAL MEANS 464
Formal Grievance Procedures 465
The Ombudsman 468
Inmate Councils 471

Close-up 15.3: Inmate Self-Government at Walpole Prison 473

SUMMARY 474

Chapter 16
COMMUNITY CORRECTIONS

DIVERSION 478
PROBATION 482
DEINSTITUTIONALIZATION: THE MASSACHUSETTS EXPERIMENT 488
COMMUNITY-BASED RELEASE PROGRAMS 490
Work Release 490
Education Release 493
Furloughs 494
HALFWAY HOUSES 496
PAROLE 500

Close-up 16.1: Methadone Users Cannot Work for the New York City Transit Authority 502

The Parole Function 504
AIDING THE VICTIMS OF CRIME 507
Victim Compensation Programs 507
Victim Assistance Programs 508
Victim-Witness Assistance Programs 509

Close-up 16.2: The Federal Witness Security Program 510

Rape Crisis Centers 512
SUMMARY 512

Chapter 17
THE JUVENILE JUSTICE SYSTEM

THE JUVENILE COURT UNTIL THE 1960s 516
EXTENDING THE CONSTITUTION TO THE JUVENILE COURT 521
Kent v. *United States* (1966) 521
In re Gault (1967) 523
In re Winship (1970) 525
Breed v. *Jones* (1975) 527
THE CONTEMPORARY JUVENILE COURT SYSTEM 527
Intake 529
The Adjudication Hearing 530
The Disposition Hearing 531
REFORMING THE JUVENILE COURT 533
SUMMARY 535

REFERENCES 537
GLOSSARY OF TERMS 594
GLOSSARY OF LEGAL CASES 607
THE CONSTITUTION OF THE UNITED STATES: SELECTED AMENDMENTS AFFECTING CRIMINAL LAW 615
INDEX 616

Preface

As a professor who has taught "An Introduction to the Criminal Justice System" for several years, I felt there was a critical need for a textbook on the subject that was uniquely designed to meet the special needs of undergraduate students in community colleges, junior colleges, and four-year institutions. Equally important was the need for a professional text that instructors with varying backgrounds could feel comfortable teaching from or could use as a point of departure to accommodate their individual approaches to the introductory criminal justice course. In striving to realize these goals, the present text reflects my philosophy of criminal justice education as it pertains specifically to the basic orientation and overview course on the criminal justice system.

By nature, the introductory criminal justice course must be concrete, substantive, and comprehensive in order to provide students with the necessary building blocks for more specialized and advanced coursework while "doing justice" to the field of criminal justice education. Students must come away from their initial contact with criminal justice education with the conviction that they have acquired valuable knowledge about the operation, issues, and problems besetting the criminal justice system. Accordingly, I consider it essential that the introductory text present a large amount of information, touching all bases in a manner that is clear, concise, stimulating, well balanced, free of bias, and reflective of the ideals (principles) and realities (practices) of the criminal justice system.

I consider it essential that the introductory text describe the status quo of the contemporary criminal justice system as well as the ways in which it is changing, improving, and experimenting. The major controversies, innovations, themes, and moving forces are interwoven and reinforced throughout the text: decision making, discretion, reasonableness, new roles for criminal justice personnel, rehabilitation versus punishment, the gap between principle and practice, the Supreme Court decisions, and the impact of the crime commissions and the LEAA. The criminal justice system is presented as a related series of processing stages, personnel, principles, practices, and problems. This approach guarantees an accurate and dynamic picture of the contemporary criminal justice system, and it should make the course more interesting and relevant to students and instructors alike.

The introductory course should present the material in a logical, readable, tightly conceptualized, well-structured format that escorts the student on a sequential tour through the criminal justice system. This demanded a careful selection of chapters, comprehensive and up-to-date coverage of material, a uniformly academic quality of topics, unambiguous explanations of legal concepts and related social issues, the continuity of material and its reinforcement, and a constant sensitivity to the nature of the learning process. I felt strongly that the text for the introductory criminal justice system course should not rely heavily on lengthy quotations, crime commission excerpts, and other documentary material that tends to be excessively detailed, dry, and redundant, belabors points, and adds little to the student's interest in and knowledge of the criminal justice system. Such material should instead be thoughfully and succinctly paraphrased, tersely interwoven throughout the text, and omitted entirely where it has become outdated.

Given the voluminous amount of material, the rapidity with which "conventional wisdom" becomes obsolete, and the shifting emphasis on the "important" elements of the criminal justice system, I was convinced of the need to summarize large quantities of information, to place material in perspective, and to reflect the "laws" of human nature that account for differences between the system in principle and in practice and which shape the law in action. Without declining to draw cautious, responsible, tentative conclusions supported by the "totality of the circumstances" surrounding controversial issues, an introductory text of this type should strive for rigorous objectivity, leaving instructors a free hand to utilize the material as they see fit as part of the challenge of criminal justice education in a free society. Thus the book is extensively documented and draws generously upon social science research and a broad scope of legal literature sources. The only intentional frame of reference in the text is a "sociolegal" approach to criminal justice education.

A number of special pedagogical aids have been incorporated into the text. Each chapter opens with a concise chapter outline that can be used as an effective study and teaching guide. Marginal notes cue the reader to the content of the accompanying sections. The Close-ups expand on the text, clarifying terms or concepts and reinforcing material previously presented, and convey an action dimension to the administration of the criminal justice system. By providing this added dimension, the Close-ups may be utilized by instructors as flexible points of departure in a variety of ways congruent with their varying interests and backgrounds and the needs of their students. Content footnotes at the bottom of the page are used occasionally to communicate information not important enough to place in the body of the text but too important to omit. The book also contains many topics not discussed elsewhere: Chapter 4, The Police and the Community; Chapter 5, The Professionalization of the Police; Chapter 7, The Courts; Chapter 10, Plea Bargaining and Speedy Trial; Chapter 11, Trial; Chapter 12, Sentencing; Chapter 13, Jails; Chapter 14, Prisons; Chapter 15, Prisoners' Rights; and Chapter 16, Community Corrections.

The preparation of the manuscript was basically a one-man operation, a labor of love with which I have been obsessed for five years. From the outset, I was determined to produce the "perfect" introduction to the criminal justice system. While such an aspiration, like "perfect justice" itself, may be unattainable in practice, I never considered that sufficient reason to waver in my pursuit of this elusive and worthy goal.

Gerald D. Robin

Acknowledgments
I wish to thank the following reviewers whose guidance has been helpful in both the first and second editions.

Gary Adams
California State University at Long Beach

Richard Ansen
Memphis State University

Stan Barnhill
University of Nevada, Reno

Harry Barrineau, III
University of South Carolina

Clemens Bartollas
Sangamon State University

William J. Bopp
Florida Atlantic University

Robert G. Culbertson
Illinois State University

Fred De Francesch
Louisiana State University

Dr. Vern L. Folley
University of Texas, Tyler

Charles W. Forester
Eastern Kentucky University

Brian Forschner
University of Dayton

Michael J. Grant
Monmouth College

Joel Hartt
John Abbott College, Quebec

Frederick Hussey
The Pennsylvania State University

Alphonso Jackson
University of Missouri, St. Louis

Edward J. Kane
Green Community College
Greenfield, Massachusetts

Victor Kowalewski
University of Wisconsin, Platteville

Raymond J. Lavertue, Sr.
Bristol Community College

Lawrence Lynch
Onondaga Community College

Richard A. McCullough
Modesto Junior College

John P. Matthews
Sam Houston University

Richter H. Moore, Jr.
Appalachian State University

Timothy F. Moran
Northeastern University

Edward Peoples
Northern California Criminal Justice Training and Education System,
Santa Rosa Center

Thomas Phelps
California State University, Sacramento

Carl Pope
The University of Wisconsin, Milwaukee

Donald T. Shanahan
Unviersity of Texas, Dallas

Richard Snarr
Eastern Kentucky University

Margaret de Stefano
Ulster Community College

Professor James D. Stinchcomb
Virginia Commonwealth University

Calvin Swank
Youngstown State University

Mary Synal
Temple University

Robert Tegarden
St. Petersburg Junior College

Mark Tezak
Illinois State University

Claude Thormalen
Sul Ross University

Frederick E. Whitmore
Long Beach City College

Joseph Wilson
Flint Community College

Craig A. Zendzian
Tunxis Community College

Alvin Zumbrum
Catonsville Community College

INTRODUCTION TO THE CRIMINAL JUSTICE SYSTEM

Chapter 1

CRIME

The Legal Foundation of Crime
Mens rea / Free will and reasonableness

Close-up 1.1: Insanity as a Defense to Criminal Responsibility

Statutory and Procedural Criminal Law
Criminal statutes / Procedural criminal law / Case law / The appellate process

The Law in Action and Discretion
Limits of the written law / Discretion / Limits to discretion

Reasonableness and the Law
The Constitution / Changing standards of reasonableness

The Classification of Crime
Mala in se and *mala prohibita* crimes / Common law and statutory crime / Felonies and misdemeanors

The *Uniform Crime Reports*
Index Crimes
Crimes known to police / Arson as a new index crime

Close-up 1.2: Coming to Grips with the Problem of Arson

Unfounded complaints / Counting index offenses
The Amount of Crime
Crime rates
Crimes Cleared by Arrest
Multiple clearances / National clearance rates
Persons Arrested
Recidivism

Victim Surveys
Interviewing victims / NORC victim surveys

Close-up 1.3: The "Shrinkage" of Crime from Reporting to Conviction
The National Crime Panel survey / Reasons for not reporting crime / Validity of the victim surveys
The Fear of Crime
Concern for personal safety / The Figgie Report
Summary

THE LEGAL FOUNDATION OF CRIME

Crimes are specific acts, or failures to act, defined by state legislatures or Congress as being socially injurious to society.* Upon conviction, crimes are punishable by a sentence of death, incarceration, a fine, or conditional freedom in the community (probation). The definition of particular acts as crimes reflects, although imperfectly, the values of various groups in society at a particular time. As the values, the distribution of power, and other features of society change, so may the designation of behavior defined as criminal. The criminal law is based on the belief that criminal acts are an injury to all citizens of the state or nation because they are detrimental to social and political stability, civilized nationhood, and economic survival. The criminal law is also an expression of the state's desire to discourage individuals from taking personal revenge against offenders—which would only increase the chaos, instability, and unpredictability of the socioeconomic order.

Every crime may be described according to some combination of three main elements.

The conduct itself, or *actus rea.* Possessing one ounce of marijuana is different conduct from possessing one pound of pot; unarmed robbery and armed robbery are two different acts. "Conduct" refers to the commission of a specific act or the failure to act where there is a legal duty to do so. With minor exceptions, the criminal justice system deals with acts of commission rather than omission.

Mens rea

The mental state of the offender. For an individual to be subject to criminal penalties, criminal intent or *mens rea* (guilty mind) must be present at the precise moment the crime was committed. *Mens rea* means that,

* *Failure to act.* The law requires citizens to act in a prescribed manner. For example, parents are required to provide adequate medical care for their children, construction workers must take necessary precautions not to injure passersby, and physicians must use proper medical procedures. The failure to do something that is required by law is a crime of omission. (Most offenses are crimes of commission: specific acts that are prohibited by law.)

in the eyes of society, the offender acted wrongfully, almost invariably by his or her own choosing. Since individuals have or should have control over their own behavior, offenders are fully responsible for transgressing the law.

The outcome of the crime. This embraces the result of the act and the harm done to the victim and to society.

Free will and reasonableness

The criminal law assumes the existence of "free will": that human beings have the capacity to choose between right and wrong, that their actions are voluntary, and that if they violate the law it is because they *intended* to do so. The free will doctrine is a legal philosophy of personal responsibility for one's behavior, which is the basis of criminal accountability and punishment. It maintains that the individual who breaks the law could or should have acted otherwise. If a person's conduct—even if it causes serious injury—is not "voluntary" and an expression of free will, it is unreasonable to expect that person to have acted differently. Under such circumstances, there is no criminal intent or *mens rea,* which is required for the act to be considered a crime and for the offender to be held criminally responsible.

"Reckless driving," for example, is usually considered a voluntary and free will matter, because the motorist chose to drive in a way that endangered pedestrians and other drivers; it is reasonable to expect motorists to drive more carefully. However, the reckless driving of a motorist who suffers a heart attack and thereby unavoidably kills a child is not considered voluntary. Under these exceptional circumstances, the motorist did not possess the free will to avoid driving recklessly. Therefore, in this case no criminal intent or *mens rea* existed at the time of the event.

In the case of "ordinary" crimes, *mens rea* is rarely a contested issue: it is assumed that the offenders intended to do what they did or that they could and should have acted otherwise. But individuals who are "insane" (see Close-up 1.1), are under 7 years of age, or who violate the law in self-defense, while under duress, or through necessity, are not held criminally responsible for their acts because they did not possess free will and *mens rea* at the time of the act.

Close-up 1.1 INSANITY AS A DEFENSE TO CRIMINAL RESPONSIBILITY

The landmark insanity case originated in England in 1843 when Daniel M'Naghten shot Prime Minister Peel's secretary, mistaking the secretary for the intended victim Peel. Psychiatric testimony presented at trial established that at the time M'Naghten shot the secretary he was "under the influence of a form of mental disorder symptomized by delusions of persecution, in which Peel appeared as one of the persecutors."[a] The jury found M'Naghten not guilty on the ground of insanity; afterwards, M'Naghten was committed to a hospital where he remained until his death 22 years later. The test of insanity established in the case—the M'Naghten Rule—requires the defense to prove that, at the time of the crime, the accused was laboring under a "mental disease" (defect of reason) such that he or she did not know the difference between right and wrong.[b] In practice, cases invoking the M'Naghten Rule often rested upon resolution of the right-wrong issue.

In 1869, New Hampshire became the first state to reject completely the M'Naghten right-wrong test of insanity. The state based rejection upon a case in which the defendant, Joseph Pike, was charged with killing his victim with an axe during the course of a robbery. In charging the jury, Chief Justice Perley stated that "if the killing was the offspring or product of mental disease in the defendant" the verdict should be not guilty by reason of insanity.[c] This "product test" of insanity was subsequently adopted by Judge David Bazelon in 1954 in Washington, D.C., stemming from a case in which the accused, Monte Durham, was convicted of housebreaking.[d] Like the Pike case which laid the foundation for it, the Durham Rule held that "an accused is not criminally responsible if his unlawful act was the product of mental disease or mental defect." The intent behind the Durham Rule (product test)—which eliminates the right-wrong question—was to make the determination of insanity more compatible with the realities of mental illness and principles of psychiatry.

The most liberal definition of insanity is the "substantial capacity" test recommended in the Model Penal Code: "A person is not responsible for criminal conduct if at the time of such conduct as a result of mental disease or defect he lacks substantial capacity either to appreciate the criminality (wrongfulness) of his conduct or to conform such conduct to the requirements of law."[e] The Model Penal Code proposal tries to avoid a narrow litigation of terminology rather than underlying behavioral issues, to make the insanity decision more responsive to modern psychiatric knowledge and changes in the field of mental illness (even more so than the Durham Rule), and to allow the judge and jury to consider a broader spectrum of factors justifying exemption from criminal responsibility. Notably, both the Durham Rule and substantial capacity test take the position that a mentally ill person may be able to distinguish right from wrong, yet be incapable of rational behavior or unable to refrain from committing crime.

Critics of the Durham Rule and substantial capacity test, however, contend that these definitions of insanity are more ambiguous than the M'Naghten Rule, have the practical effect of reducing the threshold of criminal responsibility, and make it easier for normal individuals to escape punishment on the pretext of insanity. In particular, critics allege the rules cause the jury to be more dependent upon expert testimony in reaching a verdict, and divert the jury's attention from the only question which is intrinsically meaningful and about which they can exercise their own judgment in arriving at an informed decision: whether the accused knew the difference between right and wrong at the time of the act. These considerations may account for the fact that the M'Naghten Rule has been adopted by the overwhelming majority of states and has rarely been entirely rejected by any court or legislature.

[a] John Biggs, *The Guilty Mind* (Baltimore: Johns Hopkins University Press, 1967), p. 97.
[b] *Ibid.*, p. 105.
[c] *Ibid.*, p. 114.
[d] *Ibid.*, p. 153.
[e] *Model Penal Code* (Philadelphia: American Law Institute, 1962), p. 66.

STATUTORY AND PROCEDURAL CRIMINAL LAW

Criminal statutes

The state documents that define the various crimes and their penalties are *criminal statutes* or *penal codes.* Statutes are criminal (and civil) laws enacted by the legislative body in each state. Criminal statutes are a governmental response to community concern over behavior that threatens public safety, social existence, and the orderly pursuit of economic activity. Because these are basic human needs that characterize all community life, the conduct defined as crime tends to be similar in all states. The criminal statutes are also referred to as the *substantive* or *statutory* criminal law. The substantive (statutory) criminal law applies directly to those who commit crimes.

Procedural criminal law

Procedural criminal law is concerned with *how* the substantive criminal law is enforced and administered by agents of the criminal justice system: the police, prosecutors, courts, probation officers, institutional personnel, parole board, and parole officers. Procedural criminal law applies directly to the government officials who operate the criminal justice system. In principle, the activities and decision making of all criminal justice practitioners are subject to the control of the procedural criminal law. Procedural criminal law regulates the methods used by the police in making arrests, conducting searches, and interrogating suspects; the courts in trying defendants; and corrections officers in disciplining prisoners. An arrest made without "probable cause," the denial by the court of free counsel to an "indigent" defendant, and the physical abuse of an inmate as a disciplinary measure are violations of procedural criminal law.

The highest source of procedural criminal law is the United States Constitution, especially the Fourteenth Amendment's *due process* and *equal protection* clauses. The Fourteenth Amendment provides that no state shall "deprive any person of life, liberty, or property, without due process of law; nor deny to any person within its jurisdiction the equal protection of the laws." The idea behind due process is to guarantee citizens fair and proper treatment by government officials. The legal protections covered by the due process clause apply to persons who are arrested, accused of crime, convicted, sentenced, and incarcerated. Theoretically, society as represented by the "state" becomes the legal victim of all crime. The terms used in criminal prosecution reflect the adversary relationship between the government and the defendant: *the State* v. *the Accused.*

Case law

The basis of procedural criminal law is also found in state constitutions, and it is "created" by the courts in their rulings on specific cases ("case law"). Ultimately, all procedural law is case law. Even the Constitution must be interpreted by the Supreme Court in the context of specific cases that involve "substantial federal issues" or constitutional questions. Thus, in procedural criminal law, the interpretation of each case by the judiciary is all-important. Judicial interpretation of cases is influenced by a variety of factors: the principle of *stare decisis;** "what the law says"; politics; public pressures and expectations; ethical and humanitarian considerations; and the personality and philosophy of the judge.

The appellate process

Sometimes the judicial interpretation of similar cases or the "same" case seems to be or is inconsistent. However, because no two cases are ever identical, the inconsistency may be more apparent than real. Also, inconsistency in judicial interpretation of procedural criminal law may be the result of an explicit change of policy, values, or political administration. For various reasons, the procedural criminal law is in a constant state of flux, unlike the substantive criminal law. Even when the substantive criminal law is revised, it is usually the penalties that are changed rather than the basic definition of the crime itself. Procedural criminal law is established primarily through the *appellate process:* the appeal of criminal convictions to a court of higher jurisdiction, until all of the remedies for appeal have been exhausted.† The highest level of appeal is the

* The principle of *stare decisis* is the policy of following the rules of law decided in previous judicial rulings. Prior decisions on points of law become binding on future cases if substantially the same issue is involved. Where the facts of the individual case—the "totality of the circumstances"—are not basically the same, *stare decisis* does not apply.

† An appeal is an application to a higher court to correct or modify the judgment (the conviction or sentence) of a lower court.

United States Supreme Court, which accepts only cases that involve "substantial federal questions" and particularly issues requiring interpretation of the Constitution. The manner of taking appeals, and the cases which may be appealed, are regulated by various state and federal statutes. The statutory criminal law is rarely appealed, unless it is alleged that a penal code provision is itself unconstitutional.* Through the voice of the Supreme Court, the Constitution defines the use of certain methods and procedures as unlawful in and of themselves, regardless of the actual or legal guilt of the individuals involved.

THE LAW IN ACTION AND DISCRETION

The substantive and, to a lesser extent, procedural criminal law are imperfect blueprints for administering the criminal justice system. Criminal statutes, for example, are phrased in generalities, without reference to the problems of implementation. The statutory and procedural law are often silent on such issues of the enforcement of the *law in action* as:

The feasibility and desirability of "strict" (total) law enforcement, or whether certain statutes should be more rigorously enforced than others;
when the police should arrest, release in the field or at the stationhouse, issue a warning, or simply overlook an on-sight violation;
whether a youth who forcibly steals a basketball from children in a playground should be charged with robbery, disorderly conduct, malicious mischief, or youthful indiscretion;
the factors the prosecutor should consider in deciding whether to press charges and which charges to press;
the weight given by the court to the various purposes of the criminal law in imposing sentence;
the rights of prisoners.

The list is as long as the number of different decisions that the various practitioners must make in their respective roles in the criminal justice system. The enforcement of the law in action requires flexibility in decision making. It must take into account the seriousness of the crime, responsiveness to community needs and the victim's attitude, political factors, and so on. Substantive and procedural criminal law provide few answers to the questions that these considerations raise. Thus the *written*

Limits of the written law

* Statutes must define each crime with sufficient clarity so that the ordinary person is given fair warning ("notice") of the specific acts to be avoided. If a statute is so vague that the average person cannot identify what specific conduct is involved in the violation, the substantive criminal law can be appealed on the basis that it should be invalidated because it is too vague. Upon appeal, vagrancy statutes have occasionally been declared "void for vagueness."

law does not adequately meet the needs of those responsible for enforcing it; at times the law on the books is in conflict with the law in action. The written law in most jurisdictions, for example, gives the police the legal *right* to shoot "fleeing felons." But the written law does not tell the officer *when* to shoot. The written law does not identify those situations in which it is better to let a fleeing felon escape rather than risk a stray bullet's injuring an innocent bystander.

To some extent the gap between the written law and the law in action cannot be avoided. No matter how well constructed, no abstract legal (or administrative) rule can take into account the totality of the circumstances of the specific encounters and issues routinely faced by criminal justice workers. The guidelines of the criminal statutes and case law are like road maps that provide a general direction for its user but may quickly become outmoded. The administration of justice in the street, in the prosecutor's office, in the courtroom, and in prison presents innumerable problems that are not covered by "the book." In the daily operation of the criminal justice system, its practitioners constantly make decisions that negotiate justice, contribute to social order, and reinforce the implied consent of citizens to be governed. Like the motorist who comes to a detour that is not indicated on the map, the criminal justice practitioner who confronts an uncharted situation for which there is no codified response must use *discretion* in deciding what to do.

Discretion enters the picture whenever the legal (or administrative) rules do not make clear the most appropriate course of action or the practitioner cannot rely exclusively upon such rules in deciding what to do. Discretion, then, is used to resolve practical problems in running the system when there are no rigid or binding rules available to follow, or when there are discrepancies between a strict interpretation of the written law and the enforcement of the law in action. Discretion is a common resource used extensively by all major workgroups in the criminal justice system. "Everyone in the system has broad discretion—cops on whether to arrest, district attorneys on whether and how hard to prosecute, judges on the length of the sentence, and penal and parole authorities on when to award freedom."[1]

Discretion

Thus "shortcomings" in the substantive and procedural law with respect to implementation make lawful discretion necessary. The intent behind the enabling legislation and consideration of the purposes of the criminal sanction further support discretion. Absolutely uniform law enforcement eliminating discretion would not be possible or acceptable in a democratic society.[2] Additional reasons for criminal justice workers to exercise discretion in enforcing the law in action include: the large number of different offenses, the amount of crime, its complexity, individual differences among offenders, and conflicting judicial interpretations on the same issue. And as a tax-supported institution, the criminal justice system's financial resources are severely limited. Thus *efficiency* may be the most convincing reason for the public to accept discretionary law enforcement and for all criminal justice agencies to rely upon it in performing their functions. It costs up to $20,000 a year to keep a criminal in prison; at this price, society cannot afford to lock up everyone who commits a crime for which the written law authorizes incarceration.

Limits to discretion

Although discretion is routinely used by all criminal justice professionals to "individualize" the law, no official has the discretion to break the law. Discretion is authorized as a partial solution to the limitations of the substantive and procedural criminal law only so long as its exercise is not clearly illegal. When the Supreme Court, for example, issues a ruling that provides specific rights to suspects, defendants, or prisoners, criminal justice employees do not have the discretion to discard or circumvent the law of the land, for such actions would be blatantly illegal. *Within* the framework of the substantive and procedural criminal law, all criminal justice workers must function as diplomats by striking a workable balance in enforcing and abiding by the written law, in the process sometimes modifying but not mutilating the law on the books.

REASONABLENESS AND THE LAW

Reasonableness is the yardstick for much of the law. The definition of those acts defined as crimes and their penalties is largely determined by what seems "reasonable." This concept is the touchstone of judicial interpretation and the procedural criminal law. Much of the procedural law holds all operators of the criminal justice system accountable *to act reasonably* in administering the substantive law. The principle of reasonableness is a lawful restraint on uninhibited emotional acts, irresponsible judgments, and arbitrary and capricious decisions.

The Constitution

The Constitution is a document of reasonable guarantees to all citizens, as evidenced by the language in the amendments to the Constitution. The Fourth Amendment prohibits *unreasonable* searches and seizures. The Fifth Amendment prohibits police from "forcing" suspects to confess to crimes because such tactics are considered unreasonable in a democratic society. The Eighth Amendment prohibits "excessive" bail, which is by definition unreasonable bail. The same amendment also prohibits "cruel and unusual" punishment because in a society that values humaneness, the infliction of "cruel and unusual" punishment is unreasonable. The Fourteenth Amendment's due process clause is based upon a reasonableness standard. Before allowing citizens to be deprived of life or liberty, it is reasonable to inform the accused of the charges against them and to allow them the opportunity to prepare a defense with the assistance of counsel, to confront their accusers, and to be tried by an impartial jury. To secure a conviction at trial, the prosecutor must prove that the accused is guilty of the crime "beyond a *reasonable* doubt." Per-

The "reasonable person" standard is the legal yardstick for much of the procedural criminal law

sons whose injurious acts are not the result of *mens rea* and free will are not held criminally responsible because it would be unreasonable to do so under the circumstances.

Reasonableness is measured by the conduct and standards of "the reasonable person." When the ordinary person is acting reasonably, his or her behavior is not supposed to be a direct expression of raw emotions, human nature, and pure self-interest. Instead, the reasonable person should be guided by the capacity to reason and to think, even to the point of reacting moderately and fairly in an emergency or under highly emotional circumstances. In part, how the reasonable person should act in a given situation is an ideal that the court uses (a) to evaluate the appropriateness and legality of acts committed by alleged offenders, that is, to determine whether the substantive criminal law has been violated, and (b) to evaluate actions taken by criminal justice personnel in relation to offenders, that is, to determine whether state officials violated the procedural criminal law. In effect, the amendments to the Constitution protect the individual—whether suspect, defendant, or inmate—against unreasonable procedures, actions, and decisions by the government officials who operate the criminal justice system.

Changing standards of reasonableness

Obviously, what is considered reasonable changes over time. Some states no longer consider it reasonable to authorize incarceration for such "victimless" offenses as marijuana use, drunkenness, prostitution, and gambling. In the past many types of severe corporal punishment have been considered reasonable penalties for crime that would be considered unreasonable and illegal today. Reasonableness in complying with the procedural criminal law is especially changeable: it involves striking a delicate and constantly shifting balance between the rights of the individual and the right of society to be protected from crime.

A persistent problem in the administration of criminal justice is that reasonable people cannot always agree on what is reasonable in applying the law to the individual case. There is occasional disagreement over what is a reasonable deviation between the written law and the law in action, and in identifying the thin line between discretion and the abuse of discretion. The nature of the reasonable balance between the protection of individual civil rights and the rights of society and the needs of the state is forever changing.

THE CLASSIFICATION OF CRIME

Mala in se and *mala prohibita* crimes

Various attempts have been made to describe criminal acts in terms of a few general categories or classifications. Acts such as murder and rape have been described as "wrong in themselves" or inherently evil (*mala in se*). Public intoxication, driving over the speed limit, and carrying a concealed weapon are acts that are *made* wrong (*mala prohibita*) only because they are prohibited by legislation. Acts of the *mala in se* type are universally treated as crimes, not tolerated by any society, and have their origins in unwritten tribal mores of early cultures. In contrast, there is no such consensus that acts of the *mala prohibita* type are actually "wrong," should be defined as crimes, or should be controlled by the state. In highly developed and pluralistic societies in particular, *mala prohibita* crimes may express the values of the dominant group, the protection of their economic interests, and their control of the political process. The reasonableness of prohibiting *mala in se* crimes is taken for granted by everyone, but many individuals and groups may consider it unreasonable for the state to regulate certain *mala prohibita* acts, especially those of the "victimless crime" variety.

Common law and statutory crime

A related classification is that of *statutory* crimes versus *common law* crimes. Historically, the first step in identifying and punishing criminal behavior was taken by the English courts, which created a few important "common law" crimes that everyone would consider inherently wrong behavior. The *judicial* creation of such crimes was based upon "the law" as decided by the courts of the time on an individual case basis. This practice led to the expression "case law," which denotes the common law as evolved and shaped by the court. In the United States the legislatures gradually began to assume responsibility for creating, defining, and punishing new crime by statute—a procedure that differs from the historical origin of the common law, which was "person-made" in private by the individual judge responding to the particular case before him. In America today virtually all crimes are defined by legislatures and contained in their penal codes.

The relevant legal classification of crimes is that of misdemeanors and felonies. *Felonies* are crimes punishable by death or incarceration in a state prison or penitentiary, ordinarily for more than one year. *Misdemeanors* are crimes punishable by a fine or imprisonment in a local or county jail, generally for less than one year. The classification of acts as felonies or misdemeanors is not uniform across states; the same conduct may be defined as a misdemeanor in one state and a felony in another. The felony-misdemeanor distinction is the most useful classification of crime. It is the one most used and most uniformly applied in the administration of the criminal justice system. It clearly and directly identifies distinct types of violations and offending conduct. The felony-misdemeanor identification has action implications and a permanent relationship to the operational justice system. Such clarity and practicality is missing from the historical classification of crime.

Felonies and misdemeanors

The felony-misdemeanor classification is critical because so many aspects of the administration of justice and processing of offenders are related to this distinction. Whether a felony or misdemeanor was committed will affect:

The conditions under which the police can make an arrest and the degree of force that will be authorized;
the "charges" which the prosecutor will ultimately press;
the care exercised by the trial judge in accepting a guilty plea and admitting evidence into the record;
the availability of procedural and constitutional safeguards;
the quality of counsel and the conduct of the court;
the determination of the court that will retain trial jurisdiction;
the sentence that can be imposed;
the type of institution to which an offender may be committed;
the conditions of release from incarceration;
the size of the jury;
whether a jury verdict must be unanimous.

Each of these factors can have enormous consequences on the lives and opportunities of the individuals involved, and sometimes they are a matter of life or death. Many of the landmark decisions of the Supreme Court have made the Constitution applicable depending upon whether the crime was a felony or misdemeanor, or the severity of punishment authorized. The High Court has rarely rendered such far-reaching decisions based upon any other classification. The effect that the misdemeanor-felony indicator has upon all legal agents who have contact with the offender is enormous. Greater leniency—formally authorized, informally permitted, and illegally practiced—is shown toward misdemeanants than felons, beginning with the police decision to arrest.

THE *UNIFORM CRIME REPORTS*

From 1930 until the early 1970s, the only official, nationwide source of crime statistics was the *Uniform Crime Reports* (*UCR*). The *UCR* is the outgrowth of a need for a uniform national compilation of law enforcement statistics—"police statistics." It is a voluntary national program for the collection of crime counts, initiated in 1930 by the International Association of Chiefs of Police (IACP). In that same year, the Federal Bureau of Investigation was authorized by Congress to serve as the national clearinghouse for statistical information on crime, and the *Uniform Crime Reports* has been published annually by the FBI since 1958.

Offenses in the *Uniform Crime Reports* are divided into two groups, designated as index (Part I) and nonindex (Part II) offenses. Offense and arrest information is reported for the index offenses on a monthly basis; only arrest information is reported for nonindex offenses.

Index Crimes

Crimes known to police

In an effort to provide as complete a picture as possible of crime in the United States, the IACP chose to obtain data on offenses known to police. A meaningful overview of the crime problem was available through examination of seven offenses that were selected for their seriousness, their frequency, and the likelihood of their being reported to the police. These seven offenses—known as the Crime Index Offenses—are willful homicide, forcible rape, robbery, aggravated assault, burglary, larceny-theft, and motor vehicle theft. The first four make up the violent crime category; the last three constitute the property offense category. As a group, the index offenses are the crimes that the public fears most, that represent the problem of "crime in the streets," and that involve serious stranger-to-stranger victimizations.

1. *Willful homicide.* Murder and nonnegligent manslaughter; all willful felonious homicides, as distinguished from deaths caused by negligence. Excludes attempts to kill, assaults to kill, suicides, accidental deaths, justifiable homicides, and manslaughter by negligence.
2. *Forcible rape.* The carnal knowledge of a female, forcibly and

against her will, in the categories of rape by force, assault to rape, and attempted rape. Excludes statutory offenses (no force used or victim under age of consent).

3. *Robbery.* Stealing or taking anything of value from the care, custody, or control of a person by force or violence or by putting in fear through such acts as strong-arm robbery, stickups, armed robbery, assaults to rob, and attempts to rob.
4. *Aggravated assault.* Assault with intent to kill or for the purpose of inflicting severe bodily injury by shooting, cutting, stabbing, maiming, poisoning, scalding, or by the use of acids, explosives, or other means. Excludes simple assaults.
5. *Burglary; breaking or entering.* Burglary, housebreaking, safecracking, or any breaking or unlawful entry of a structure to commit a felony or a theft; attempted forcible entry.
6. *Larceny-theft* (except auto theft). The unlawful taking, leading, or riding away of property from the possession or constructive possession of another; thefts of bicycles, auto accessories; shoplifting, pocket picking, or any stealing of property or article other than by force or violence or by fraud. Excludes embezzlement, "con games."
7. *Motor vehicle theft.*
8. *Arson.* Any willful or malicious burning. Excludes fire of suspicious or unknown origin.

Arson as a new index crime

Arson was designated an index offense by Congress in October 1978, and the FBI began developing a data collection strategy that will eventually lead to an accurate description of the arson problem (see Close-up 1.2). The strategy is also designed to protect the historical integrity of *UCR* data by tabulating the arson count separately, as well as including the arson statistics within the original seven index offenses in computing the national crime rate.[3] It is expected that the cases of arson known to police nationwide will be published in the 1980 *Uniform Crime Reports,* which were released in the latter part of 1981. According to statistics published by the National Fire Protection Association, there were an estimated 187,000 arsons in 1974 and perhaps as many as half a million in that year, depending upon how the crime is calculated.[4]

Close-up 1.2 COMING TO GRIPS WITH THE PROBLEM OF ARSON

Arson is the fastest growing, most expensive, and most socially destructive crime in America. Each year, arson increases at a rate of 25 percent, causes $1.8 billion in direct property loss (more than any other index offense), is responsible for 1,000 deaths and 10,000 injuries, and leaves an untold number of persons homeless and ravaged.[a] Its main victims are minorities, the poor, and the elderly, groups who live in neighborhoods and buildings where most arson occurs. Of the five major reasons for arson—revenge, vandalism, mental disturbance (pyromania), crime concealment, and arson-for-profit—the last is by far the most disturbing, potentially dangerous, and, ironically, preventable. Arson-for-profit is a thriving business because landlords can make much more money by deliberately burning their buildings and collecting on inflated fire insurance policies than they can by renting or selling their property. As a case in point, Charles R. purchased the Ellis Hotel in Chicago for only $2,000 down and "sold" it to an associate in 1974 for an inflated $126,000 on paper; that is, no money actually changed hands in the transaction. In 1977, the new owner took out a $150,000 fire insurance policy on the hotel. In February 1979 a four-alarm fire broke out in the hotel, the sixth fire to occur there since Charles R. purchased the place! Eight months after the blaze (which killed two people) the insurance company gave $145,000 to the beneficiaries, including the present owner and Charles R.[b] A Senate subcommittee report issued in 1979 found that insurance companies unwittingly encourage arson-for-profit schemes by failing to challenge suspicious fire claims, to investigate the backgrounds of policy applicants, and to ascertain the real value of the insured property.[c]

A number of factors account for the low rate of arrests, convictions, and incarcerations in arson cases.[d] Arson is one of the most difficult crimes to detect and to solve: Legally, fires are assumed to be accidental until proven otherwise. Usually an investigation must first be conducted in order to determine whether a crime was committed; if traces of fire accelerants, such as gasoline or other flammable materials, or multiple points of fire origin are found (the *corpus delecti*), arson is indicated.[e] Evidence of the crime is often destroyed by the fire or in the process of extinguishing it, and there are usually no witnesses because the crime is committed surreptitiously. As a result, the prosecution of arson cases depends heavily upon circumstantial evidence (much of it physical in nature), expert scientific testimony, and extensive trial preparation by experienced prosecutors. Seasoned prosecutors, though, are in short supply and have little incentive to incur the high work demands and risk of failure associated with arson cases. The investigation and prosecution of arson is further hampered by a shortage of trained investigators (including fire insurance adjusters), confusion and conflict over whether arson investigation is a responsibility of the police or the fire department, privacy laws that keep insurance companies from divulging certain information to law enforcement authorities, and the prominent role of organized crime in arson-for-profit.[f]

Despite the above problems, there are some encouraging new developments which suggest that the nation might be turning a corner in the battle against arson. Special antiarson programs and task forces have been established at all levels of government. Congress officially recognized the scope and severity of arson by recently classifying it as an index crime. The FBI, as well as state and local prosecutors, have targeted arson as a major impact ("white collar") crime warranting innovative and aggressive prosecution. Agencies are coordinating their efforts in order to provide more systematic and effective investigation and prosecution of arson cases.[g] Arson laws are being revised to facilitate the successful prosecution of arsonists and to ensure stiffer sentences upon conviction. The goal of the nationwide program sponsored by the U.S. Fire Administration is to develop greater local capacity to combat arson.[h] And other federal agencies, such as the Economic Development Administration, are funding a variety of programs in which diverse citizen action groups and activities are emerging as the cutting edge in arson control.[i]

Insurance companies are tightening up their procedures and practices, determining the real value of the insured property, and settling claims, as well as subsidizing model antiarson projects. For example, under a $140,000 grant from Aetna Life & Casualty (an insurance company), the California District Attorneys' Association is developing a manual on how to prosecute arson cases more successfully, which will be distributed nationally.[j] Made possible in part by a $10,000 grant from another insurance company, New Haven's Arson Warning and Prevention Strategy utilizes a "fire incidence file" to identify arson-prone buildings on the basis of four variables: tax delinquency, previous structural fires, housing code violations, and liens and other claims against the property.[k] Unlike other cities, where the approach to arson control is fragmented, New Haven's Arson Squad includes police detectives, fire department investigators, and prosecutorial personnel. Hopefully, the collective impact of these developments will reverse the epidemic growth of arson, which for too long has been placed on the back burner of crime control priorities.

[a] John F. Boudreau et al., *Arson and Arson Investigation: Survey and Assessment* (Washington, D.C.: Government Printing Office, October 1977), p. xiv.

[b] "Arson for Profit," *ABC Newsmagazine 20/20,* broadcast February 7, 1980, Media Transcripts, pp. 7–8.
[c] *New York Times,* February 18, 1979, p. 19.
[d] Nine persons are arrested, 2 convicted and less than 1 incarcerated per 100 fires classified as incendiary or of suspicious origin. This compares with 21 arrests, 6 convictions and 3 incarcerations per 100 index offenses, excluding arson.
[e] Boudreau, p. 60.
[f] *Ibid.,* pp. xv, 35.
[g] Richard L. Madden, "Arson Fight Heats Up," *New York Times,* February 18, 1979, Connecticut Weekly section, p. 1.
[h] Frank Logue, "Combating Arson," *New York Times,* June 26, 1980, p. A19.
[i] Jack Canavan, "How One Neighborhood Foils Arsonists," *Parade Magazine,* October 1, 1978, p. 5.
[j] *U.S. News & World Report,* May 26, 1980, p. 69.
[k] Logue, op. cit.

Law enforcement agencies report to the FBI the number of index offenses that become known to them each month. This count is taken from a record of all complaints of crime received by the law enforcement agency from victims and other sources or discovered by officers. Participating law enforcement agencies are wholly responsible for compiling their own crime reports and submitting them to the FBI. During 1974, crime reports were received from law enforcement agencies in over 11,000 jurisdictions covering 94 percent of the total U.S. population. The crimes tabulated by the FBI are violations of the criminal laws of the individual states. Because of the differences among the state penal codes, however, the offenses listed in the *UCR* are not distinguishable according to the felony-misdemeanor classification. Violations of federal statutes per se are not included within the *Uniform Crime Reports.* The crime counts used in the *UCR* Crime Index are based on actual offenses verified by police investigation. When the law enforcement agency receives a complaint of a criminal matter and the follow-up investigation discloses that no crime occurred, the complaint is declared *unfounded.* All unfounded complaints are eliminated from the official crime counts. The number of actual (founded) offenses known to police in the seven index crime categories is reported to the FBI regardless of whether anyone is arrested for the crime, whether the stolen property is recovered, whether prosecution is undertaken, and regardless of the outcome of prosecution or any other consideration.

Unfounded complaints

In the case of a single criminal event that involves several separate crimes, only the most serious index offense is counted. The *eight index offenses are arranged in order of decreasing seriousness.* Thus, in the course of a robbery in which the victim is unintentionally killed (a "fel-

Counting index offenses

ony homicide"), the crime known to police, submitted to the FBI, and included in the *UCR* would be murder. In the context of a robbery during which the female victim is also raped, the only crime counted in the *UCR* would be forcible rape. The hierarchy rule of counting only the most serious index offense does not apply to arson. All arsons, regardless of their occurrence in conjunction with another index offense, are to be included in the UCR. Thus, if a burglary and arson occurred at the same time and place, both crimes would be reported to the FBI.[5] Where disorderly conduct and simple assault are part of the same criminal event reported to the police, no crime would be counted by the FBI because neither one is an index crime. When the same crime is simultaneously committed upon several victims, each victim who is seriously injured is counted as a separate offense. But where multiple victims are present but not injured, each distinct operation is counted as one *UCR* offense.

The Amount of Crime

During 1979, an estimated 12,152,700 index offenses were reported to law enforcement agencies (see Table 1.1). The violent crime category increased by 11 percent from the previous year, while property offenses increased by 9 percent. From 1970 to 1979, the number of index offenses increased by 50 percent. Crime *rates,* which are based on the index offenses, relate the number of index offenses to population. A crime rate, therefore, is a victim risk rate. The crime (index) rate of the United States in 1979 was 5,521 per 100,000 inhabitants. The 1979 crime rate increased 8 percent over the 1978 rate. From 1970 to 1979, the national crime rate—the risk of being a victim of one of the seven index offenses—increased by 39 percent. Many factors influence the nature and extent of crime, but a crime rate takes into consideration only the numerical factor of population.

Crime rates

Table 1.1 National Crime Rate, 1979

CRIME INDEX OFFENSES	ESTIMATED CRIME 1979	
	Number	Rate per 100,000 Inhabitants
Total	12,152,700	5,521.5
Violent	1,178,540	535.5
Property	10,974,200	4,986.0
Murder (willful homicide)	21,460	9.7
Forcible rape	75,990	34.5
Robbery	466,880	212.1
Aggravated assault	614,210	279.1
Burglary	3,299,500	1,499.1
Larceny-theft	6,577,500	2,988.4
Motor vehicle theft	1,097,200	498.5

Source: Uniform Crime Reports, 1979, p. 37.

Crimes Cleared by Arrest

Law enforcement agencies *clear* a crime when they have identified the offender, have sufficient evidence to charge, and actually have the individual in custody. Crime solutions are also recorded in exceptional instances where some element prevents the known offender from being apprehended or charged: Cases in which (a) the victim refuses to cooperate in prosecuting after the offender has been arrested, (b) local prosecution is declined because the suspect is being held for prosecution elsewhere or is serving a prison term, and (c) the offender commits suicide are examples of *exceptionally cleared* crimes. The arrest of one person can clear several crimes, and several persons may be arrested in the process of clearing one crime. Crimes are counted as *cleared by arrest*—solved so far as the police are concerned—regardless of the outcome of prosecution. Thus defendants who are dismissed or acquitted are counted within the category of crimes cleared by arrest. However, suspects and persons who are merely questioned and released without technically being arrested and formally charged with a crime are not included in the cleared by arrest category.[6]

Multiple clearances

The *clearance rate* is the percentage of crimes reported to the police that the police claim to have solved. Any number of previously unsolved crimes may be cleared by a single arrest if the police determine that the arrested suspect was responsible for those offenses. For example, during the month a police department may receive 1,000 crime reports and make 50 arrests. If the detectives are able to link two additional previously unsolved crimes to each of the 50 suspects, then the police have solved 150 of the 1,000 known crimes—producing a cleared by arrest rate of 15 percent. Clearance rates are one of the indices used to evaluate the performance of police personnel and departments as a whole.

There are many factors involved in determining the clearance rate that may reduce the accuracy of clearance statistics. Since the decision as to when multiple cases have been cleared (through one arrest) is a matter of judgment, the decision to clear is not consistently applied across police units. The number of cases cleared by an arrest in any precinct is probably influenced by how important the unit commander believes the clearance rate is. A study published by the New York City Rand Institute in 1970 revealed great variation in the number of clearances claimed by 79 precincts in connection with burglary arrests.[7]

National clearance rates

In 1979 the nationwide clearance rate for index crimes was 20 percent. In other words, an offender was identified, taken into custody, held for prosecution, and stood a chance of being punished in only one out of every five crimes *known* to the police. Thus the chances were four out of five that lawbreakers would not be caught by the police for crimes officially reported and recorded by law enforcement agencies. As Figure 1.1 shows, the police were much more successful in clearing crimes against the person than crimes against property in 1979. The former are investi-

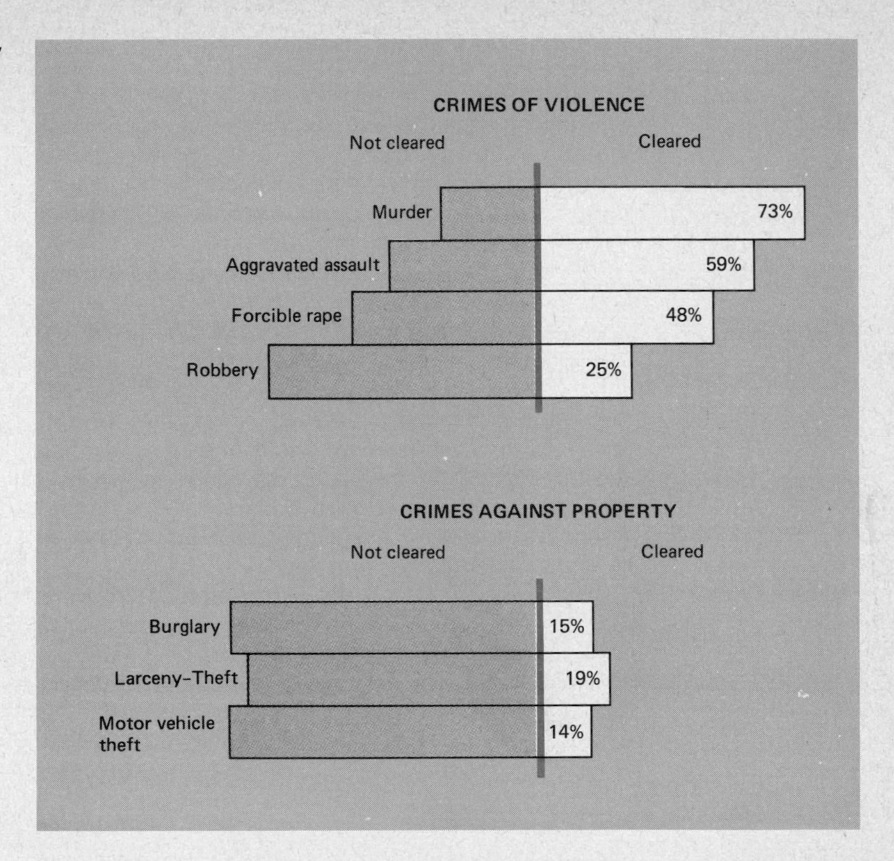

FIGURE 1.1 Crimes cleared by arrest, 1979. *Source: Uniform Crime Reports*, 1979, p. 178.

gated more thoroughly, and there are usually witnesses who can identify the perpetrators. Motor vehicle theft illustrates this point and highlights the difference between crimes known to police and crimes cleared by arrest. In order to collect insurance, automobile owners report virtually all motor thefts to the police. But of the 1.1 million motor vehicle thefts known to police in 1974—the crimes reported—only 14 percent were cleared by arrest. In that year, then, the chances were almost nine out of ten that a car thief would not be caught and exposed to punishment.

Persons Arrested

In 1979, law enforcement agencies made an estimated 10.2 million arrests nationally for *all* criminal acts (except traffic violations); about 2.3 million arrests were for index offenses. The arrest rate per 100,000 population was 5,046 in cities, 3,898 in suburbs, and 3,434 in rural areas. Thirty-nine percent of those arrested for index offenses were under 18 years of age, or juveniles. Since persons 10–17 years old constitute only 16 percent of the U.S. population, juveniles contribute disproportionately to the crime count.* The peak age for violent crime is 15 years, and more crimes are committed by children under 15 than by adults over 25. Between 1960 and 1974, the number of juveniles arrested nationwide increased 138 percent, compared with an increase of 16 percent in the arrests of persons 18 years and over. Most of the huge rise in juvenile arrests was for violent crimes.[8]

Recidivism

Recidivists—persons arrested two or more times—are largely responsible for the crime problem in urban America and the high crime rates. The role of repeaters in the national crime picture is revealed in the FBI's Careers in Crime program. Of the 255,936 offenders in their Computerized Criminal History File (CCHF) who were arrested in 1970–1975, 64 percent had been arrested at least twice. Members of this repeater group had been arrested an average of four times each and had an average "criminal career" of five years and three months between their first and last arrests. Based upon the last offense for which 78,143 offenders in the CCHF were arrested and released in 1972, Figure 1.2 shows the proportion of each group who were rearrested within four years. These figures understate the actual amount of crime committed by recidivists, however, because they are based upon crimes known to police, and there is reason to believe that crimes not reported to police are also primarily the work of repeaters.[9]

Virtually every study of the issue has confirmed the relationship between recidivism and the crime count. Of 14,214 adults arrested in Philadelphia in 1971, 69 percent had previously been arrested five times each.[10] About half of all felonies committed in Detroit were by persons with previous adult criminal records. In Washington, D.C., 80 percent of those charged with a felony had previously been *convicted*.[11] A study in a major metropolitan area found that within a single year more than 200 burglaries, 60 rapes, and 14 murders were committed by *10* individual offenders.[12] Marvin Wolfgang's classic study of 10,000 juveniles in Philadelphia found that a mere 627 "chronic offenders" committed 52 percent of all the offenses and two-thirds of the violent crimes. Nationally, 75 percent of the juveniles who are arrested are recidivists.[13]

Recidivism is a double-edged sword: it is responsible for the high crime counts and it is a bridge to crime prevention and deterrence. Most criminals are eventually arrested because they are repeaters. Consequently, their chances of permanently avoiding arrest are quite small. Yet a large

* A juvenile is counted as a person arrested when he or she is arrested for an offense for which an adult would have been arrested.

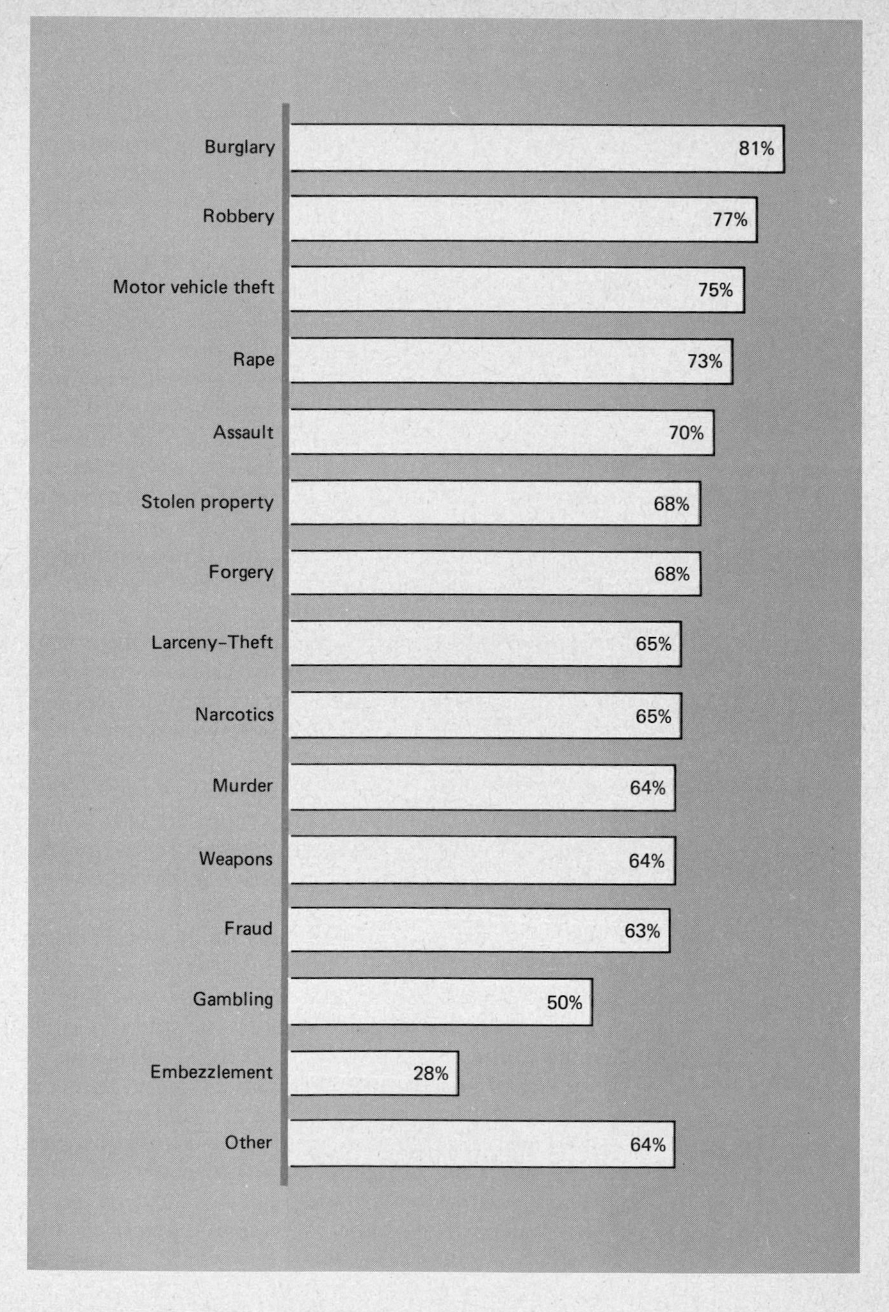

FIGURE 1.2 Persons released in 1972 and rearrested within four years, by type of crime in 1972. *Source: Uniform Crime Reports*, 1976.

proportion of recidivists are not punished by incarceration. Any efforts that increase the swiftness and certainty of punishment should be particularly effective in reducing recidivism and the crime rate.

VICTIM SURVEYS

Probably the most serious and most valid criticism of the *UCR* is that it does not reflect crimes known to citizens that are not reported to the police. This "dark figure" of crime had to be illuminated in order to determine the real trends of crime, the size of the "crime wave," and whether America is becoming a more violent society. To learn these and other effects of crimes not reported to police, in 1965 the President's Crime Commission introduced the *victim survey* technique of measuring crime.

Interviewing victims

Victim surveys measure the amount and study the characteristics of crime by going directly to the individual victims of crime rather than wait for them to call the police. Identifying the victims of crime is one of the main purposes of victimization surveys. Interviewers are sent to a sample of households to ask appropriate household members about their experience with crime. The interview begins with a brief series of "screening" questions to determine whether anyone in the household was a victim of crime within the previous year or six months, regardless of whether the crimes discovered were reported to the police. If victims are found, a full interview is conducted to learn more about the victims, the crimes that were committed, whether the crimes were reported to the police and if not, why not. In households without crime victims, the respondents may be asked about their attitudes, knowledge, and fear of crime.

In victim surveys, information about the extent of crime comes from the victim's recollection of the event rather than from the administrative records of police departments. No matter how good the *Uniform Crime Reports* system is, it provides only rough estimates of the extent of crime and crime trends. Their accuracy is questionable because the statistics are compiled by the police themselves. The comprehensiveness of the police crime count is doubtful because it omits crimes discovered by citizens which are not reported to the police. Victim surveys are conducted by members of scientific research groups who personally interview victims who do not report crimes to the police, as well as those who do. For this reason, victim surveys are considered to be a more reliable measure of the actual extent and trends of crime and a major step toward revealing the "dark figure" in crime.

NORC victim surveys

To determine the amount of unreported crime, the President's Crime Commission authorized the first national crime victimization survey. The University of Chicago's National Opinion Research Center (NORC) was commissioned to conduct interviews at 10,000 sample households

Table 1.2 Comparison of NORC Victim Survey and *UCR* Crime Rates

Index Crimes	NORC Victim Survey 1965–1966	*UCR* Rate for Individuals 1965
Willful homicide	3.0	5.1
Forcible rape	42.5	11.6
Robbery	94.0	61.4
Aggravated assault	218.3	106.6
Burglary	949.1	299.6
Larceny ($50 or more)	606.5	267.4
Motor vehicle theft	206.2	226.0
Violent crime	357.8	184.7
Property crime	1761.8	793.0
Total crime	2119.6	974.7

Sources: President's Commission on Law Enforcement and Administration of Justice: The Challenge of Crime in a Free Society (Washington, D.C.: Government Printing Office, 1967), p. 21. The "total crime" figure is from: Philip H. Ennis, "Crime, Victims, and the Police," *Trans-action,* June 1967, p. 37.

throughout the country during the summer of 1965. Among other things, the interviewers asked whether any member of the household had been a victim of crime in the preceding 12 months and whether the crime had been reported to the police.[14] As Table 1.2 indicates, the NORC victim survey revealed that, overall, *there was about twice as much major crime* as officially presented in the *UCR*. The frequency of forcible rape was four times greater than that stated in the *UCR*. More than three times as many burglaries were identified by the victims as by the *UCR* figures. Aggravated assault occurred twice as often and robbery 50 percent more often than those crimes were reported to the FBI. (The higher *UCR* car theft rate might reflect a tendency to report to the police "stolen" cars that had simply been misplaced or "borrowed"; or it may be related to the need to report stolen autos to the police for insurance purposes.) Close-up 1.3 describes the "shrinkage" between reporting index offenses to the police and the offenders' being convicted and punished.

Close-up 1.3 THE "SHRINKAGE" OF CRIME FROM REPORTING TO CONVICTION

In the NORC victim survey, there were 1,024 index offense situations in which the victims of crime notified the police. The police did not respond to the victims' requests for assistance in almost one-fourth of the cases. Of the 787 victimization situations in which the police did heed the victims' calls, they considered 25 per-

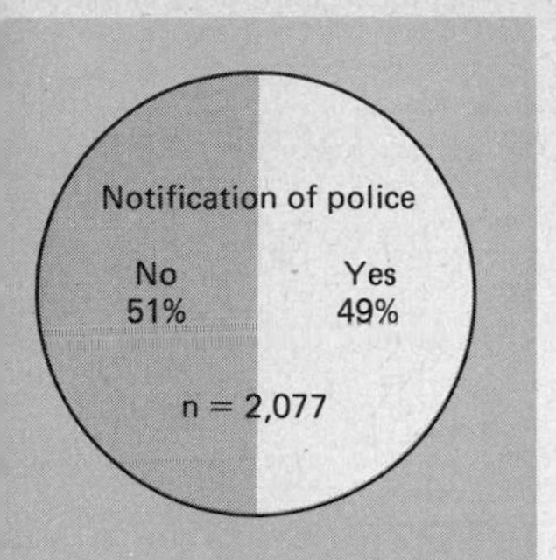

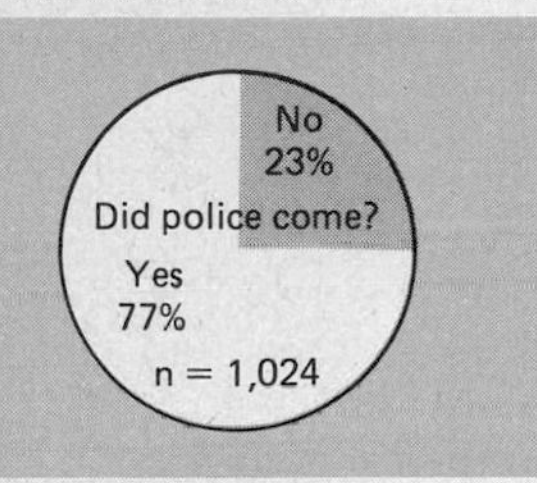

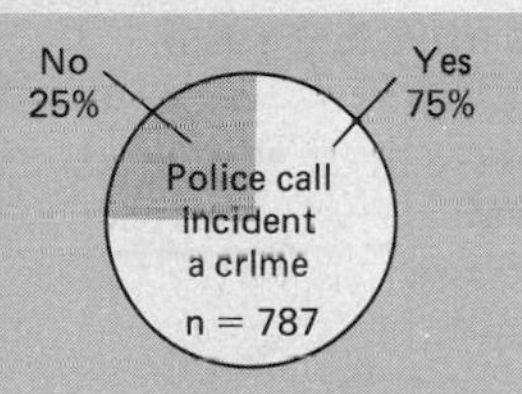

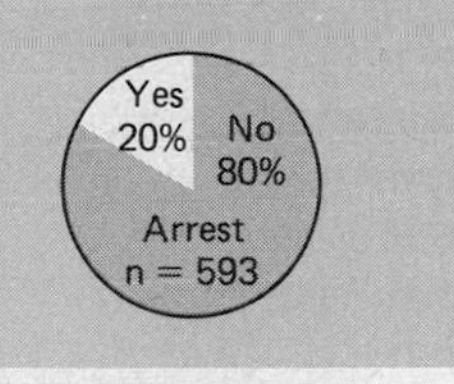

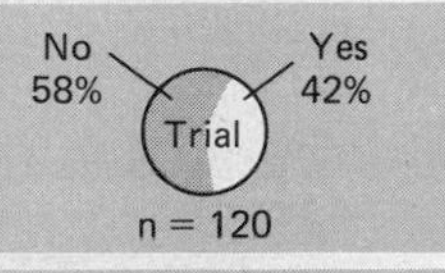

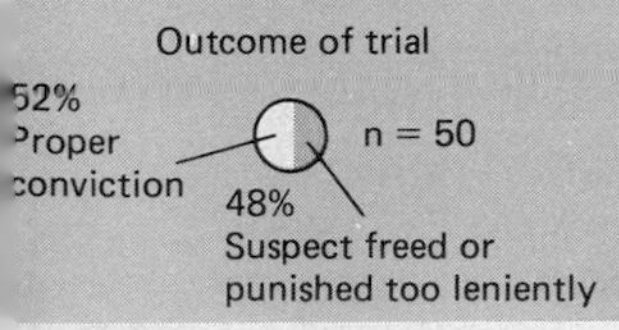

cent of the incidents "unfounded." Of the 593 incidents that the police considered crimes, an arrest was made (cleared by arrest) in 20 percent of the cases. Of the 120 persons arrested, 42 percent either pled guilty or went to trial. Of the 50 persons who pled guilty or went to trial, defendants were acquitted or given a "lenient" sentence in 48 percent of the cases. Thus there were only 120 persons arrested in connection with the almost 2,100 crime incidents known to victims—that is, about 5 percent of the total number of crimes known to victims were cleared by arrest. Only 50 persons were convicted at trial or through a guilty plea. Thus less than 2 percent of the offenders responsible for the 2,100 crime incidents faced criminal penalties. The offenders responsible for the 2,100 crimes had 98 chances out of 100 of avoiding punishment. Who says crime doesn't pay?

Source: Phillip H. Ennis, "Crime, Victims, and the Police," *Trans-action,* June 1967, p. 40. Information in the accompanying art is based on interviewed respondents; from the fourth circle on, the victim may simply have been ill-informed.

The victim surveys sponsored by the President's Crime Commission were the first of their kind and a one-time occurrence. It was left to the commission's successor, the Law Enforcement Assistance Administration (LEAA), to refine the victim survey technique and to conduct victim surveys on a regular, long-term basis. Only in this manner could the trends of crime be accurately plotted. The National Crime Panel (NCP) is a continuous, long-range program of victim surveys conducted by the U.S. Bureau of the Census for the LEAA, at a cost of $10 to $12 million per year. The NCP measures the extent to which individuals 12 years and over, households, and commercial establishments have been victimized by certain types of crime. In particular, the NCP collects information on whether or not the incident was reported to the police and why victims do not report crime.[15]

There are two parts to the NCP victim survey program. The major part consists of a nationwide victim survey conducted every six months at 60,000 households and 15,000 business concerns in hundreds of sampling areas throughout the country. The 135,000 persons interviewed at these places are the "panel" of respondents who are interviewed twice a year.* The second part of the NCP program involves victim surveys conducted in selected cities, where similar information is collected as in

* One-seventh of the NCP respondents are supposed to be dropped every six months and replaced with new respondents.

Table 1.3 Incidents from the National Crime Panel

Type of Crime	Total Incidents	Incidents Reported to the Police	Incidents from the *Uniform Crime Reports*
Rape	81,600	35,900	23,409
Robbery	600,600	318,100	179,478
Aggravated assault	637,200	314,500	198,560
Burglary	3,961,300	1,863,300	1,171,358
Larceny	11,085,800	2,406,500	1,980,007
Motor vehicle theft	586,100	381,700	429,492
Total	16,682,600	5,320,000	3,982,304

Victimization information may be compared with that collected from local police agencies by the FBI but such comparisons are inappropriate because of substantial differences in coverage between Panel surveys and police statistics.

Source: LEAA Newsletter, December 1974, p. 5.

The National Crime Panel survey

the national survey. The NCP program focuses upon those crimes that are of major concern to the general public, which generate the most "fear of crime" as a group, and which are roughly equivalent to the *UCR* index crimes.[16] NCP results for the first half of 1973 revealed that the total number of victim-recalled crimes was four times that known to police. Motor vehicle theft was the only crime not grossly underreported to the police. As Table 1.3 indicates, the National Crime Panel disclosed three times the number of index crimes reported to the police.

Reasons for not reporting crime

A particularly important section in victim survey questionnaires dealt with the reasons citizens gave for not reporting crimes to the police. The most common reason offered for not reporting crimes against the person to the police was that nothing could be done or there was no proof (34 percent). Twenty-eight percent said the event wasn't important enough to report.[17] Significantly, only about 6 percent of the victims mentioned police indifference—"police would not want to be bothered"—as the reason for concealing the crime from the authorities. Other victim surveys besides those conducted by the Bureau of the Census have confirmed that few persons are deterred from reporting crimes because of their skepticism toward the response of the police.[18] In the NORC victim survey, the reasons that assault victims didn't report the crime to police were analyzed separately. Although 14 percent of the assault victims mentioned "police indifference" as a reason for not calling the police, only 7 percent listed it as the "most important" reason for concealing the crime. Perceived police ineffectiveness was therefore a relatively minor reason for not notifying them. Almost one in five assault victims didn't report their attacks because *they believed the offenders, even if caught, would not be punished!* The public's desire for retribution and its lack of confidence in the courts to punish offenders properly are apparently serious obstacles to citizen involvement in the criminal justice system.

Validity of the victim surveys

The chief virtue of victim surveys is that they are not as subject or sensitive to changes that can artificially increase or decrease the crime *count* even though the number of crimes *committed* may not have changed. Victim survey results are not influenced by changes in the police command structure, the identity of the commissioner, reporting policy, size of police force, press coverage of crime, or racial issues or incidents—as are the *Uniform Crime Reports*. The interviewed victims have less reason and motivation to withhold or alter information about criminal events than do the police. Once the interviews are completed, the data are not subject to intentional and systematic irregularities and manipulations, as police statistics are.

Whether victim surveys will ever replace the *Uniform Crime Reports* remains to be seen. There is a developing consensus that the two sources of crime information are complementary rather than conflicting, each criminal event yardstick having unique functions for different groups with different purposes.[19] And despite their distinctive values, victim surveys produce rankings of the severity of crime which are the same as the decreasing order of seriousness in the *UCR* index offenses.[20] Another reason for directing major attention to reported crimes and to the *UCR* is that half of the victims interviewed felt that crime was not worth reporting.[21] The high cost of victim surveys is an additional factor to be considered in judging their benefits and future role in the criminal justice system.[22]

THE FEAR OF CRIME

The President's Crime Commission was responsible for bringing the fear of crime into the open, for popularizing the concept, and for encouraging research, scientific analysis and social commentary on the subject. The NORC national victim survey conducted in the summer of 1965 found that one-third of Americans felt unsafe walking in their own neighborhoods alone at night. Sixteen percent of the national sample said that the fear of crime had recently kept them from going someplace in town they wanted to. This reaction varied markedly by race: the fear of crime made one out of three black respondents, compared with one out of eight whites, "prisoners" in their own homes. Women were much more concerned about their safety than were men. The NORC survey also disclosed that one-fourth of the respondents always kept their doors locked in the daytime when family members were present, that 28 percent kept watchdogs, and that 37 percent had firearms in the house for protection.[23]

Concern for personal safety

Basically, the fear of crime hinges upon an anxiety concerning one's personal safety and, to a lesser extent, concern for one's personal property being stolen. The most intense expression of the fear of crime is the prospect of being attacked by a stranger while alone.[24] The fear of crime regularly manifests itself in the national Gallup public opinion polls and in the Louis Harris polls.[25] The nationwide Gallup poll conducted in March 1972 asked the question, "Is there any area right around here—that is, within a mile—where you would be afraid to walk alone at night?" Nearly six out of every ten women, compared with "only" 44 percent four years earlier, said there was. Among men the fear of crime increased from 16 percent to 20 percent.[26] The increase in the fear of crime seems to be keeping pace with the crime wave itself. Ironically, the fear of crime issue presents practical problems for the very research organizations who conduct field interviews on the fear of crime: many interviewers are reluctant to work in "bad" neighborhoods day or night because of *their* fear of crime.[27]

The Figgie Report

Based upon nationwide telephone interviews conducted with 1,047 adults in 1979, the *Figgie Report on Fear of Crime* concluded that the fear of crime has become so "alarmingly pervasive" that it has altered the way Americans live and adversely affected their quality of life.[28] The study found that four out of every ten citizens are "highly fearful" of becoming the victims of murder, rape, robbery, or assault and feel unsafe in their daily environments; and one-quarter do not go out at night alone. About half of the telephone respondents said that they dress inconspicuously to avoid drawing attention to themselves, that they would be willing to pay higher taxes for more police coverage, and that they keep guns in their homes for protection. The Figgie Report also revealed that, in response to the fear of crime and disillusionment with the courts and rehabilitation, the public's mood is becoming increasingly punitive: 45 percent of those surveyed support sterilization of habitual offenders; two thirds favor the death penalty; and nine out of ten endorse mandatory prison sentences for violent offenders.

The fear of crimes affects all groups but is especially prevalent among the elderly

It is difficult to minimize the reality and legitimacy of the fear of crime. The actual risks of becoming a victim of serious crime are between two and three times as great as the *UCR* statistics. In some cities the risks of being victimized during the year were three to ten times greater. One's chances of permanently avoiding becoming a victim of serious crime are rapidly dwindling. Depending upon where one lives and goes, social class, age, sex, race, and other factors, the odds may actually favor one's becoming a victim of a major crime sooner or later.[29]

The likelihood of victimization is so disturbing that even offenders are concerned about the prospect of becoming victims. A Chicago holdup man has acknowledged, "I myself walk light when I'm in the ghetto. I know the value of life has no weight. These younger criminals, they're sick. They have no motive for what they're doing."[30] A former New York City police commissioner has admitted that he doesn't walk alone anywhere after midnight.[31] At least one state supreme court has held that, under certain circumstances, employees who quit their jobs because of

enior citizens combat crime by elping police and prosecutor to uild strong cases

the fear of crime are entitled to collect unemployment compensation.[32] Citizens are beginning to outfit their homes as though they *were* castles; to protect themselves and their families, they are purchasing guns in unprecedented numbers. Some groups have demanded that the whipping post be restored. Nonetheless, society's main defense against the fear of crime, crime itself, and the challenge of crime in a free society is in the hands of the criminal justice system.

SUMMARY

Mens rea and free will are an integral part of the concept of crime and its legal foundation in the criminal law, which is divided into statutory and procedural criminal law. The administration of criminal law is heavily dependent upon discretion exercised by police, prosecutors, courts, and correctional personnel. "Reasonableness," the legal yardstick behind much of the criminal law, is reflected in the amendments to the Constitution and is the generic standard for determining the propriety of decisions made by criminal justice practitioners. While there are various classifications of crime, the relevant one is the distinction between misdemeanors and felonies. The national crime rate as measured by the FBI in the *Uniform Crime Reports* is based upon index offenses. Recidivism is a major factor in the nation's persistently high crime rates. Only a small proportion of the Part I crimes known to police are cleared by arrest. The major advantage of victim surveys over the *UCR* is its detection of crimes not reported to the police. The amount of crime and consequences of the fear of crime underscore the significance of the crime problem in America and invoke the government's response to the challenge of crime in a free society—the criminal justice system.

DISCUSSION QUESTIONS

1. What is the relationship between the substantive and procedural criminal law?
2. In what way is the *mala in se* versus *mala prohibita* crime classification related to the common law versus statutory law crime classification?
3. Is "drug addiction" a *mala in se* or *mala prohibita* crime? Why?
4. Identify some crimes of omission not mentioned in the text.
5. A wife comes home, finds her husband with another woman, and in a state of rage shoots both of them. Would the wife be exempted from criminal responsibility because she lacked *mens rea* or free will?

Chapter 2

THE CRIMINAL JUSTICE SYSTEM: AN OVERVIEW

The Processing Stages in Felony Cases

Arrest
Warrants and warrantless arrests / The prosecutor
Initial Court Appearance
Preliminary arraignment / Bail
Preliminary Hearing
Probable cause / Discovery / Plea bargaining / Waiving the hearing
Grand Jury
Indictment / Prosecutor's information

Close-up 2.1: Should the Grand Jury Be Abolished?

Arraignment
Pleas / Accepting guilty pleas
Pretrial Motions
Trial
Adversary proceeding / Verdict and judgment
Sentencing
Determinate and indeterminate sentences / Sentencing discretion
Probation
Probation officers / Revocation
Correctional Institutions
Parole
Parole rules / Parole officers / Violations of parole / Caseloads

Criminal Justice Administration as System and Nonsystem

Components of the system / Criticism of the nonsystem
Jurisdictional and Operational Problems
Differences in Roles and Goals

People Problems
Substantive Issues

The Federal Role in Improving State and Local Criminal Justice Systems

Riots of the 1960s
The President's Crime Commission
Recommendations of the commission / Events of 1967
Law Enforcement Assistance Administration (LEAA)
Law Enforcement Education Program (LEEP)
The Standards and Goals Commission

Summary

Crime and delinquency are most pronounced in the cities, each of which has its own justice system for processing offenders. While no two

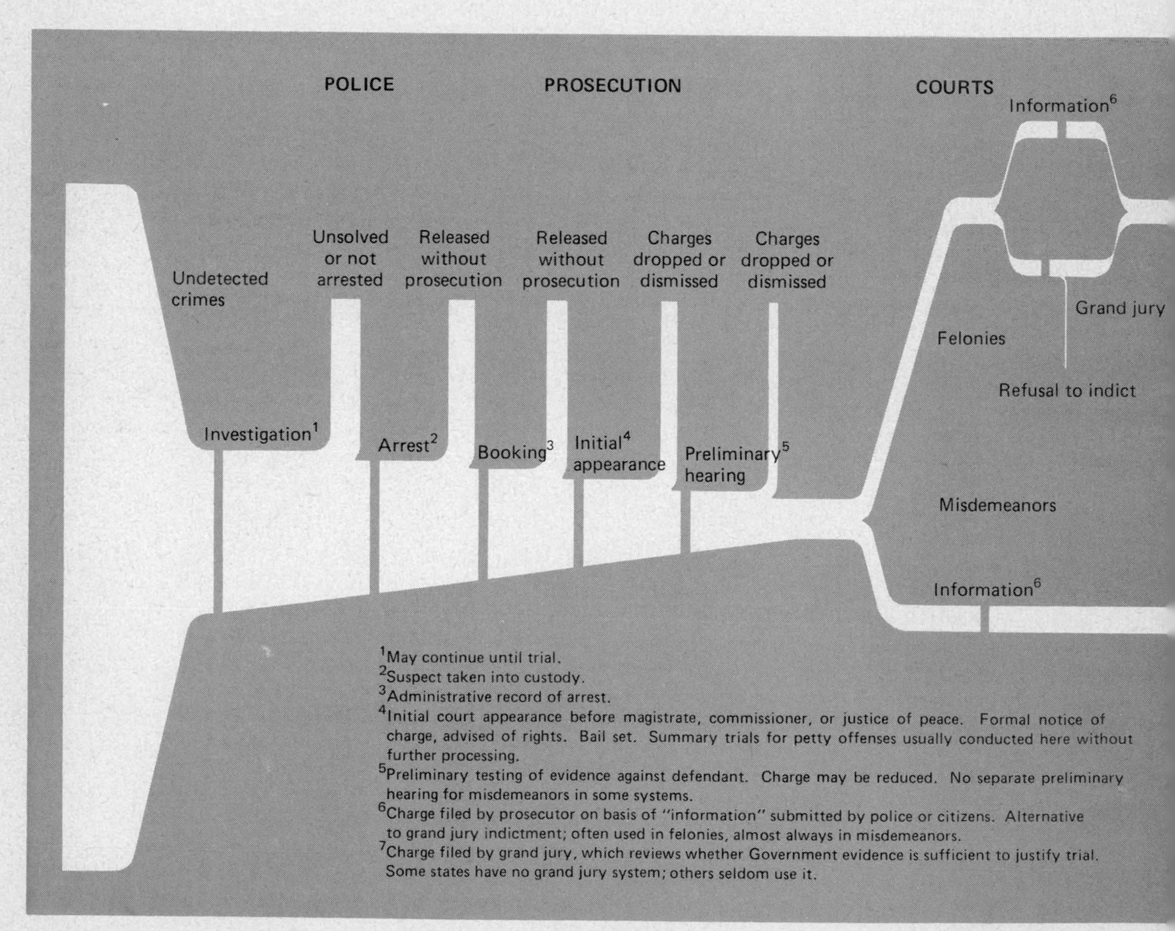

FIGURE 2.1 A general view of the criminal justice system. The chart shows the movement of cases through the system; the procedures in individual jurisdictions may vary from the pattern shown here. *Source:* President's Commission on Law Enforcement and Administration of Justice, *The Challenge of Crime in a Free Society*, Washington, D.C.: Government Printing Office, 1967, pp. 8–9.

such systems operate precisely alike, it is in these larger population centers that the administration of criminal justice is most similar and its common problems surface and converge. Therefore, the description of "the" criminal justice system that follows is a general one that is especially applicable to urban America (see Figure 2.1).

THE PROCESSING STAGES IN FELONY CASES

Arrest

With a few exceptions, suspected offenders enter the criminal justice system by *arrest:* being *taken into custody* to be formally charged in a court of law. An arrest can be accomplished verbally, without touching or physically subduing the suspect. As soon as and regardless of how the

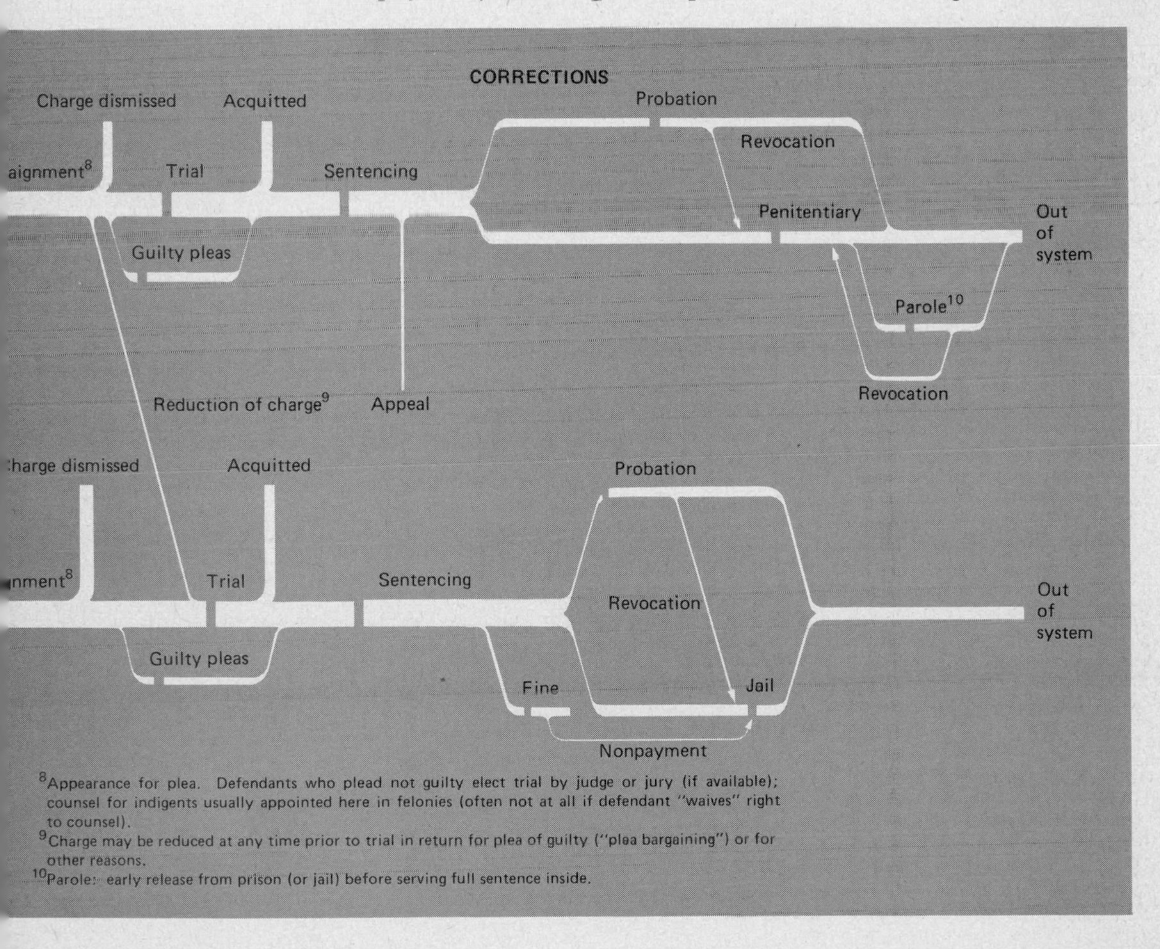

officer "takes control" and "restrains the liberty" of the suspect, an arrest has occurred. If the suspect does not resist being taken into custody (arrested), no force whatsoever should be used. Resistance authorizes the police to use *reasonable* force in self-defense and to effect the arrest. In a constitutional sense, an arrest is a "seizure" that occurs when the officer takes control of the suspect. Individuals suspected of committing specified petty offenses may enter the criminal justice system through a *citation* or *summons,* a written notice ordering subsequent appearance in court.

Some arrests are made on the basis of warrants issued to the police by the courts. A warrant is an order from the court that directs the police to arrest the person identified in the warrant. Based upon information contained in the complaint, the court has decided that there is *probable cause* (reasonable grounds) to believe that a crime has occurred and was committed by the person to be arrested. The majority of arrests are *warrantless;* that is, they are made without prior authorization by the court. When victims or witnesses report crimes, the police may make a warrantless arrest for felonies if there is probable cause—rather than mere suspicion or a hunch—to conclude that (a) a felony actually occurred and (b) it was committed by the individual to be taken into custody. The basic probable cause arrest doctrine is derived from the Fourth Amendment's prohibition against "unreasonable seizures." The probable cause requirement is a constitutional safeguard against government officials' depriving citizens of their liberty without good (reasonable) cause.

Warrants and warrantless arrests

In arresting suspected felons without a warrant, the officer's decision need only be *reasonable,* not one that is actually "right" in retrospect. It may subsequently turn out that a felony was not committed, that the arrested person was not the felon, or that the arrestee is acquitted of the felony charge. Nonetheless, so long as the "reasonable person" would have concluded at the time of the arrest that a felony had occurred and that the suspect taken into custody was the offender, the warrantless felony arrest is proper. In making a warrantless misdemeanor arrest in many jurisdictions, however, the officer must be *certain* that the suspect committed a misdemeanor. In other words, the officer's decision to make a warrantless misdemeanor arrest must be a "right" one. In misdemeanor cases, therefore, the law usually authorizes warrantless arrests only if they were committed in the presence of the police. The in-presence requirement—insisting upon certainty of guilt—for warrantless arrests in misdemeanor cases is a much higher standard of proof than the probable cause requirement for warrantless felony arrests.

The prosecutor

The *prosecutor* is the state's legal representative whose primary responsibility is to convict offenders. (The lawyer responsible for protecting the interests of arrestees and defendants is the *defense counsel.*) Entering the criminal justice system shortly after the police make an arrest, the prosecutor decides what specific criminal *charges* will be brought against arrested suspects and criminal defendants. In doing so, the prosecutor relies upon the information contained in police reports to determine the legal strength of the state's case. Often prosecutors are so overburdened that they do not have time to review the legal adequacy of the crimes identified in police reports, and they simply accept them automatically. Nonetheless, the identification of crime by the police as a basis for arrest and the offenses specified in police reports are not necessarily the formal or final criminal charges to be lodged against the defendant. The arrest crimes are immediately reviewable by the prosecutor, who has absolute discretion in deciding what crimes, if any, the suspect will be charged with. The formal charges brought by the prosecutor may differ from the arrest crimes listed by the police because warrantless arrests are made under conditions requiring quick decisions, when there is little time to analyze the fine points of the criminal law. The prosecutor, however,

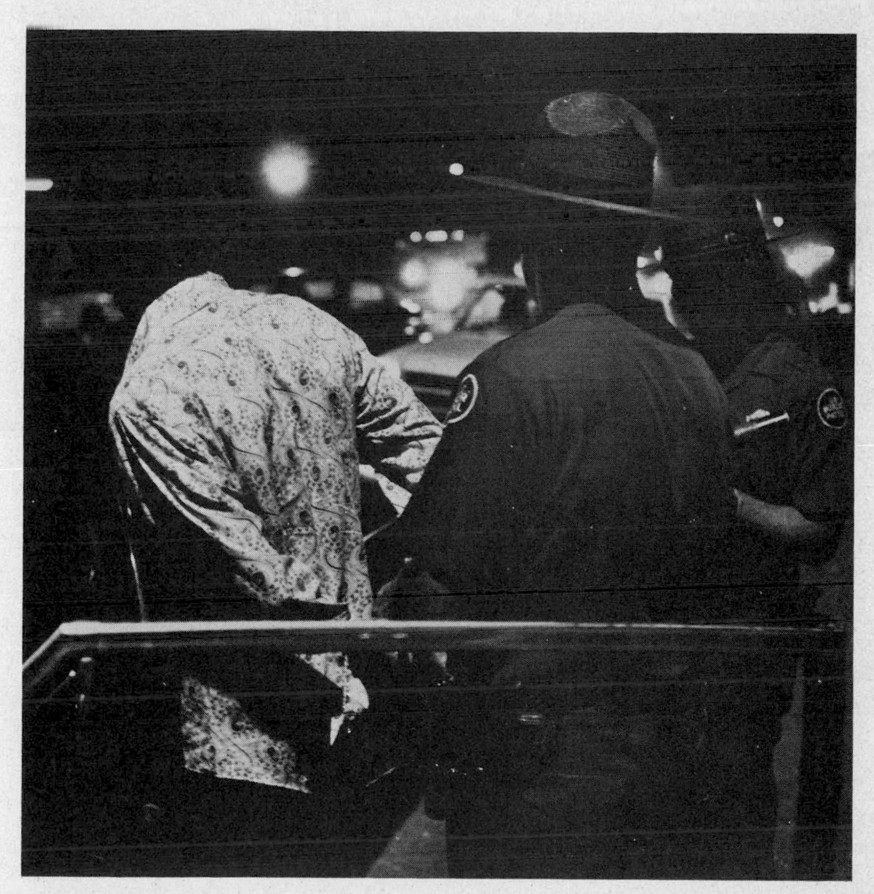

ıe authority of the police to
ake a felony arrest depends on
ırobable cause"

needs to make a more technical evaluation of the legal strength of the state's evidence, especially if the case is to go to trial. While the police are authorized to arrest upon probable cause, the standard of proof required for a conviction in court is "proof beyond a reasonable doubt" for each criminal charge.

Initial Court Appearance

The suspect must be presented (taken) before the nearest local magistrate or judge within a reasonable period after arrest.* The interval between arrest and the *initial court appearance*—the presentment, "first," or preliminary arraignment for felony cases—depends upon whether court is in session, the availability of the prosecutor, and allowing reasonable time for interrogation at the police station. Ordinarily, suspects are arraigned in court within 12 hours after their arrest.[1] This period could stretch to 72 hours for persons arrested on the weekend or on holidays, when the magistrate courts are not in session. Such individuals are placed in a police "lockup" while awaiting preliminary arraignment.

Preliminary arraignment

The *preliminary arraignment* (the initial court appearance) has two purposes. First, defendants are given formal notice of the tentative criminal charges against them. They are also advised of their constitutional rights to counsel and to remain silent. In most jurisdictions, felony defendants also have and are advised of their right to a *preliminary hearing,* which generally occurs within ten days after the preliminary arraignment. At the presentment, arrangements are made to supply indigent defendants with free defense counsel as soon as possible.† Some jurisdictions do not appoint state-supplied ("free") counsel until the preliminary hearing or until the formal arraignment stage.[2] The initial court appearance is a preliminary arraignment for felony defendants because at this stage they do not enter a formal plea of "guilty" or "not guilty" before the magistrate's court. Felony defendants enter a plea before a trial (felony) court at the arraignment stage, which occurs about four to six weeks after the preliminary arraignment. By the time of arraignment, felony defendants have had an opportunity to consult with their own or state-supplied attorneys concerning how they should plead to the charges against them.

Bail

The second principal purpose of the initial court appearance is to set *bail:* the financial or nonfinancial conditions under which defendants may be released while awaiting arraignment and trial. The amount or conditions of bail are usually determined by the seriousness of the initial charges and any previous criminal record of the accused. Those not released on bail are sent to jail in order to assure their appearance at further

* Without unreasonable, unnecessary, or undue delay.

† Indigent defendants are persons who cannot afford to hire their own private lawyer.

processing stages and at trial. These *unconvicted* defendants who are temporarily confined in jail awaiting further action are referred to as *pretrial detainees.* Such individuals are detained in the same jails as convicted and sentenced misdemeanants who are serving time for crimes carrying less than a one-year penalty. A trial date is also set for felony defendants at the preliminary arraignment. The interval between arrest and the trial stage is referred to as the pretrial period.

Preliminary Hearing

A *preliminary hearing* is often held in felony cases, usually within ten days after arrest.[3] The main purpose of the preliminary hearing is to protect defendants against unwarranted prosecution and detention; it is intended to operate for the exclusive benefit of the defendant. This is accomplished by requiring the prosecutor to establish *probable cause* at the preliminary hearing. The prosecutor must convince the magistrate that there are reasonable grounds for believing that the defendant committed a felony. To establish probable cause, the prosecutor must present evidence bearing on the defendant's likely guilt: testimony by a victim or witnesses, the results of police investigation, and so on. In doing so, the prosecutor discloses part of the state's case and the strategy for obtaining a conviction if it goes to trial.

Probable cause

Through the prosecution's "tipping its hand" in showing probable cause, the preliminary hearing has a secondary function as an informal *discovery* device for defense counsel. Defense counsel discovers (learns) something about the legal strength of the prosecutor's case should it go to trial. The preliminary hearing may be a mutual discovery tool if defense counsel reveals part of the defense while cross-examining state witnesses and introducing evidence to disprove probable cause. But the discovery feature of the preliminary hearing is of much greater benefit to defense counsel than to the prosecutor. This is because the prosecutor must present as much of the case as is necessary to establish probable cause, while defense counsel need do nothing or may choose to reveal little about its position to offset a finding of probable cause.

Discovery

Although defense counsel has the right to cross-examine prosecution witnesses and introduce evidence, he or she rarely does so in practice. This is because the prosecutor ordinarily has no difficulty in convincing the magistrate that there is a probable cause case against the accused. And establishing probable cause legally justifies holding the felony defendant for arraignment and trial. However, as a result of the preliminary hearing, the prosecutor may decide that the state's case would be legally weak if it went to trial—that the chances for an *adjudicated* (litigated in court) conviction are low. On the other hand, defense counsel may conclude that the chances for a conviction on the original charges are high. Thus expediency and the unpredictability of trial outcome often lead the

Plea bargaining

prosecutor and the defense counsel to decide to *plea bargain:* To work out a sentencing arrangement in exchange for a guilty plea. The result is an out-of-court conviction, which of course obviates the need for a trial.

If probable cause is not established at the preliminary hearing, the defendant is dismissed. This may occur because, by the time of the hearing, the victim wants to drop the matter completely. Witnesses may not want "to get involved" or to cooperate with the prosecutor. Or the state may simply be unable to establish a probable cause case in the judgment of the magistrate. If probable cause is established, the magistrate binds over the case for trial before a court of *general jurisdiction,* that is, a *trial* or *felony* court. Only courts of general jurisdiction have the authority to accept pleas in felony cases and to try them.

The preliminary hearing is not a trial. Its purpose is not to determine whether the defendant is in fact guilty or innocent but to determine whether it is *reasonable* to *believe* that the defendant committed a felony. The burden of proof at the preliminary hearing is probable cause rather than the higher standard of proof beyond a reasonable doubt required at trial. The preliminary hearing is a nonjury proceeding. The major function of defense counsel is to try to convince the magistrate that the prosecutor has not established probable cause, rather than to prove that the accused is innocent. Because the preliminary hearing is not a trial, dismissed cases may be reopened and prosecuted on the same charges later, when more evidence is available to establish probable cause. The constitutional protection against being exposed to punishment more than once for the same offense ("double jeopardy") applies to the trial stage.

Waiving the hearing

Finally, there is no constitutional right to a preliminary hearing, as there is to trial. Many jurisdictions do not offer a preliminary hearing; in those which do, many defendants *waive* their right to this hearing.* Waiver generally occurs when the defendant intends to plead guilty to the original or plea-bargained charges, thereby making a preliminary hearing unnecessary. States typically accord defendants the right to counsel and other due process safeguards at the preliminary hearing. In *Coleman* v. *Alabama* in 1970, the Supreme Court identified the preliminary hearing as a "critical stage" and, as such, it invokes the constitutional right to counsel.[4] Misdemeanor cases that carry penalties of one year or more and those in which jury trials are demanded follow the same procedures as felony cases.

Grand Jury

The final criminal charges against the defendant—each and every charge to which the defendant will plead guilty or not guilty at arraignment and face trial—are decided either by the grand jury through an in-

* *Waiver.* Relinquishment of a legal right.

dictment or by the prosecutor alone, using an "information" as the complaint vehicle.* State policy varies with respect to which of the two accusatory devices (grand jury or a prosecutor's information) will be used with different types of cases.

In many jurisdictions, the prosecutor's decision to charge felony defendants must be approved and formal criminal charges submitted to the trial court by a *grand jury,* who technically make the charging decision. In principle, the grand jury is another screening device intended to protect citizens against unwarranted prosecution and trial.† Accordingly, the grand jury's only function is to hear the state's case against the defendant and to determine whether there is probable cause to hold the accused for arraignment and trial. Some jurisdictions that have the preliminary hearing stage do not use a grand jury because their functions overlap; other jurisdictions require both processing and screening steps for felony defendants. A grand jury consists of from 16 to 23 citizens who are generally selected at random from voter registration rolls.[5] Qualifications for serving on the grand jury are minimal.

Grand jury proceedings are even less similar to a trial than the preliminary hearing. The grand jury meets in secrecy to review the evidence of the prosecutor. The defendant has no right to offer evidence in his or her behalf or to attend the inquiry, and defense counsel has no right to cross-examine prosecution witnesses subpoened by the grand jury. Some states keep no written record (transcript) of the body's proceedings, which everywhere are legally protected from public disclosure. In fulfilling their duties, grand jurors may ask questions, but the prosecutor normally dominates the proceeding. The only time the prosecutor is not present is during the grand jury's deliberations and voting sessions, when it decides whether or not to indict. The court's presence is restricted to giving the grand jury instructions on the law after it is empaneled and when jurors request a legal opinion. Grand jury proceedings are not covered by the rules of evidence applicable to trial. Under certain circumstances, hearsay and illegally obtained evidence is admissible. Some states allow the grand jury to compel witnesses to testify even though they may incriminate themselves by doing so (see Close-up 2.1).

Indictment

If a majority (usually 12) of the grand jurors find that the prosecutor has established probable cause, they issue an *indictment,* a written accusation prepared by the prosecutor and signed by the grand jury. The indictment charges the defendant with the commission of specified crimes. Each different criminal charge in the indictment is a separate *count* for which the defendant will be arraigned, must plead, and may be sentenced. Technically, the indictment document prepared by the prosecutor

* The Constitution requires the use of the grand jury only in capital cases.

† There is an increasing criticism that the grand jury has deviated from this historical mission and, unwittingly or intentionally, is being used as a repressive tool for the state.

In a confidential proceeding controlled by the prosecutor, the grand jury determines the final criminal charges against the defendant

is a *bill.* If the grand jury finds probable cause, it issues a "true bill"—it endorses the validity of the criminal charges specified in the bill—and returns an indictment. If the grand jury concludes that the criminal accusations against the defendant are unwarranted and not supported by probable cause, it refuses to endorse the bill. When this occurs the grand jury issues "no bill," it does not indict, and the defendant is dismissed.

Prosecutor's information

The alternative method to indictment by the grand jury is accusation by a prosecutor's *information.* Like the grand jury's indictment, the information document specifies the final criminal charges on which the defendant is arraigned, must plead, and may face sentencing. The main difference is that the information is prepared and executed entirely by the prosecutor, without the approval of a grand jury or any other group. The prosecutor prepares the information on the basis of the sworn complaint of the victim, supplemented by information from the police. Like the grand jury's indictment, the information is filed with the trial court of general jurisdiction, the court level that has the authority to arraign felony defendants, accept their pleas, and try them. Misdemeanor defendants who demand a jury trial or are subject to penalties exceeding one year are usually indicted by an information rather than by a grand jury. These defendants have the right to a preliminary hearing before having to stand trial. Prior to arraignment before a trial court, pleading to charges carrying a substantial penalty and adjudication, all defendants have the right to at least one probable cause proceeding, whether it be the preliminary hearing or the grand jury.

Close-up 2.1 SHOULD THE GRAND JURY BE ABOLISHED?

Dissatisfaction with various features of the grand jury and prosecutorial control of the proceeding has led its most severe critics to call for the institution's abolition. Grand juries were abolished in 1933 in England, where the grand jury originated in the twelfth century.[a] Most of the controversy concerns the procedures used by prosecutors in subpoening and questioning witnesses when the prosecutor decides that a grand jury investigation is needed to shed more light on the case. It is within the context of such inquiries that the prosecutor, acting on behalf of the grand jury, can invoke and allegedly misuse the jury's vast investigative powers. The situation is exacerbated by the fact that jurors seldom realize that they have the right to decide whom to subpoena, to question witnesses themselves, and to request that documents and other evidence be made available for their consideration. Instead, they relinquish these functions to the prosecutor and routinely acquiesce to the decisions and course of action taken by the jury's legal advisor.[b] Libertarians claim that the grand jury, whose historic American purpose was to protect the innocent against "hasty, malicious, oppressive prosecution," has evolved into an instrument for stifling legitimate dissent and political protest, chilling freedom of expression, and trapping unsuspecting witnesses on contrived perjury charges.[c]

Witnesses may be summoned from great distances to appear before the grand jury without adequate notice, any explanation of why they have been subpoened, or right to a transcript of their own testimony. Those subpoened to testify cannot refuse to do so on the grounds that it would violate their Fifth Amendment right against self-incrimination. They may be compelled to testify if the prosecutor grants them "use immunity" from prosecution, a device which theoretically eliminates the question of self-incrimination. Use immunity prevents the prosecutor from using the witness' testimony, or evidence derived therefrom, as a basis for indictment or at trial. However, witnesses granted use immunity who reveal details of crimes in which they were involved can still be prosecuted if the state obtains evidence which is independent of and not derived from their testimony before the grand jury. To resolve this problem, reform groups recommend that witnesses be given "transactional immunity," meaning that they cannot be prosecuted for any crime mentioned as part of their grand jury testimony.

Should witnesses granted either type of immunity still refuse to testify (be recalcitrant witnesses), they may be sent to jail for contempt of court for as long as the grand jury sits, which is usually up to 18 months. Their period of confinement can be extended for another 18 months if the witness again refuses to testify before a newly convened grand jury, ad infinitum, which in effect subjects a recalcitrant witness to indefinite incarceration. As for defendants,[d] they have no right to testify before the grand jury should they want to defend themselves against the charges levied against them, unless they are subpoened. Nor are they entitled to have the grand jury hear witnesses whose testimony would be favorable to them; and defendants are not allowed to be present when hostile witnesses testify against them.

Probably the most serious criticism of the grand jury system is that witnesses (and defendants) are usually not permitted to have counsel present in the grand jury chamber. A large majority of states allow counsel to wait outside, so that witnesses may leave the chamber to consult briefly with their lawyers.[e] Such procedures, however, are inconvenient and potentially prejudicial to witnesses because those who interrupt the proceeding to seek access to counsel may be perceived as uncooperative and attempting to delay the hearing.[f] Prosecutors contend that permitting lawyers to attend grand jury proceedings would transform the process into a minitrial and introduce another source of delay into a justice system already bogged down in inertia, a concern not entirely without foundation. Nonetheless, there is growing sentiment and expert opinion that witnesses should be allowed to have counsel by their side to advise them of their rights and liabilities and to be aware of any developments that might affect the outcome of trial. In this regard, Illinois and New York are among 12 states that have changed their laws to give witnesses, victims, and defendants a right to have counsel present in the grand jury room.[g] To prevent the presence of lawyers from turning the hearing into a time-consuming and full-fledged adversary event, these states typically regulate the role of counsel at the grand jury level: They can advise clients on how to respond to questions and on matters of law, but counsel cannot enter objections to the prosecutor's tactics, cross-examine hostile witnesses, or address the grand jury.

Other purported inequities associated with the grand jury are that prosecutors (a) are under no obligation to disclose exculpatory evidence concerning defendants, (b) may leak information to the press in order to discredit a defendant's character or to create an atmosphere in the community that is conducive to conviction at trial, (c) may seek to have defendants who were dismissed by one grand jury indicted by presenting the same or stronger case to a new grand jury, and (d) may rely exclusively on hearsay or illegally obtained evidence to obtain an indictment.[h]

Whether the above profile of grand jury shortcomings justifies abolishing the institution is of course debatable. At the federal level, abolition would require a constitutional amendment and possibly open a Pandora's box, a prospect most scholars of law adamantly oppose. Perhaps the most compelling argument for retaining the grand jury is that it provides one of the few opportunities for ordinary citizens to participate directly in governmental decision making, to monitor the activities of bureaucrats, to humanize the administration of justice, and to realize the ideals and values enshrined in the Bill of Rights.[i]

[a] Marvin E. Frankel and Gary P. Naftalis, *The Grand Jury: An Institution on Trial* (New York: Hill & Wang, 1977), p. 16.
[b] Joshua Eilberg, "A Proposal for Grand Jury Reform," *Judicature* (March 1977), p. 391.
[c] Richard Harris, "Annals of Law: Taking the Fifth," *New Yorker*, April 19, 1976, p. 43.
[d] Defendants are persons who are the subject of the grand jury investigation. By comparison, witnesses are subpoened by the prosecutor to establish a probable cause case against the defendant so that the grand jury will issue an indictment. Of course, by virtue of their own testimony, that of other witnesses, or questions raised during the investigation about their participation in crime, a witness appearing before one grand jury may subsequently become the subject of investigation by another grand jury.
[e] Dena Kleiman, "How Well Do Grand Juries Work?" *New York Times*, December 26, 1976, p. 4.
[f] "Reforming the Grand Jury," *Newsweek*, August 22, 1977, p. 46.
[g] *Judicature* (January 1976), p. 305.
[h] *Costello* v. *United States* 350 U.S. 359 (1956); *United States* v. *Calandra* 414 U.S. 338 (1974).
[i] Fred J. Solowey, "The Grand Jury and Post-Watergate America," *Trial* (November-December 1974), p. 34.

Arraignment

After the defendant is indicted by the grand jury or formally accused through an information, *arraignment* occurs: the accused is brought before a trial court to enter a plea. The charges in the indictment or information are read, and the accused is informed of his or her constitutional rights by the judge. They are then asked to plead to each of the criminal charges. Arraignment is the gateway to the trial process; it is the first opportunity that defendants have to respond to the final criminal charges lodged against them. Because the Supreme Court has defined the arraignment as a "critical phase" in the criminal justice system, the defendant is entitled to have counsel present before entering a plea.[6] Indigent defendants who were not previously given access to defense counsel will have an attorney appointed at this stage, and their arraignment will be postponed until they are able to consult with their lawyer on the matter.

Pleas

Defendants may plead guilty, not guilty, or *nolo contendere* at arraignment. *Nolo contendere* (no contest) is equivalent to a guilty plea; however, it protects defendants from having an admission of *criminal* guilt used against them in a *civil* court in the event they are subsequently sued by the victim. For example, in 1977 the motorcycle daredevil Evil Knievel pled *nolo contendere* to assaulting with a baseball bat his former press agent, who had written an uncomplimentary book about the stuntman.[7] By pleading *nolo contendere* instead of guilty, Knievel made sure that his conviction on the criminal assault charge could not be used against him if the agent were later to sue him for injuries, lost income resulting from the attack, and punitive damages. Defendants who "stand mute" (refuse to plead to the charges) have a not guilty plea entered for them by the court. Defendants who waive counsel at arraignment and those already represented ordinarily enter a plea at this time.

Accepting guilty pleas

The court must be certain that the defendant's decision to plead guilty is "intelligent, voluntary, and informed" before accepting it. Entering a guilty plea has substantial implications and consequences for the defendant. In doing so, the defendant relinquishes the constitutional right to trial, the right to confront witnesses, and the protection against self-incrimination. If the court is not diligent in accepting a guilty plea, the conviction and sentence may be appealed on the basis of procedural errors committed by the judge at arraignment.

The court can ascertain whether the defendant's guilty plea is made knowingly, is informed, and is voluntary by (1) asking defendants various questions to determine whether they understand the nature of the charges and their possible consequences, and (2) informing defendants of the possible sentences to which a guilty plea may expose them. These include:

The maximum term the charge carries;
consecutive sentences, where each count may carry a separate prison term, the several terms to be added together in arriving at the total length of imprisonment;
mandatory minimum sentences that may require minimum periods of incarceration as established by statute for the offense;
extended imprisonment that special statutes may provide for "habitual offenders," certain sex offenders, or persons with several prior felony convictions.

Such sentencing disclosure to defendants about to plead at arraignment also emphasizes the court's sentencing autonomy, for the court is not bound by any "promises" made by the prosecutor in plea bargaining. In practice, the court satisfies itself that the defendant's guilty plea is legally valid—made knowingly and voluntarily—by the presence of defense counsel at arraignment. If the court believes that the defendant's guilty plea is not valid, it will reject it and enter a not guilty plea for the record. Defendants who enter accepted guilty pleas are immediately scheduled for a sentencing date, when they will be informed of their criminal penalty.

Pretrial Motions

If the defendant pleads not guilty at arraignment, defense counsel may raise various procedural objections at *pretrial motions* before the trial court. The most important pretrial motions are those which (1) attempt to have the case dismissed, perhaps on the grounds of improper composition of the grand jury, violation of the defendant's right to a "speedy trial," expiration of the "statute of limitations," or (2) attempt to have illegally obtained incriminating evidence declared inadmissible at trial. Pretrial motions by defense counsel to suppress evidence obtained by police conduct in violation of the Fourth and Fifth Amendments are among the most significant and controversial issues in the administration of criminal justice. They include illegal arrests, searches, lineups, and interrogations. The court rules in pretrial motions on the legal admissibility of such evidence at trial. Resolving these kinds of procedural questions before the trial actually begins also reduces delays at trial.

Trial

Adversary proceeding

The constitutional right to a jury trial applies to crimes punishable by at least six months incarceration.[8] Felons and "high" misdemeanants who waive their right to a (petit) *jury* trial are given a *bench* trial in which a trial judge hears and tries the case alone. Trial is a full-fledged adversary proceeding: prosecution and defense counsel have opposite goals (conviction versus acquittal), and pursue them within the rules of evidence governing trial procedures. The adjudication of guilt or innocence through trial is also referred to as the *adversary model of justice.* The hallmarks of trial include (1) the presumption of innocence, (2) the requirement that the defendant's guilt be proven beyond a reasonable doubt, (3) the defendant's right not to take the stand in his or her own defense, without prejudice to their case, and (4) the exclusion of illegally obtained state evidence.

At the conclusion of a jury trial, the judge *charges* or *instructs* the jury. In its instructions to the jury, the court does not comment on the evidence presented during trial and does not express a personal opinion concerning the defendant's innocence or guilt. The jury is the sole decision maker in all matters of fact, interpretation, and reliability of the evidence in the case. In charging the jury the court explains the *principles of law* that are applicable in the case and should be considered by the jury in its deliberations and in reaching a verdict.

Verdict and judgment

The determination of guilt or innocence by a jury is a *verdict;* the same decision rendered by the court is a bench *judgment.* For a jury to convict or acquit, a unanimous verdict has traditionally been required. However, the Constitution contains no provisions regarding the size of juries or the number of votes needed to convict. Some jurisdictions have started to experiment with trial juries of less than 12 persons and with nonunanimous verdicts for certain crimes. When a jury cannot reach a verdict (a "hung" jury), the court may declare a mistrial. When this occurs the defendant may be retried on the same charges; or the prosecutor may decide that the case is legally weak and request that the charges be dropped.

Sentencing

Upon conviction at trial or by entering a guilty plea, the defendant faces *sentencing:* the imposition of criminal penalties for violating the law. Sentencing usually occurs between four and eight weeks after conviction. By then the judge is able to consider the recommendation in the presentence report in making a sentencing decision. While in principle there exist four types of sentences, in practice the sentencing decision becomes a choice between probation and prison. Today the death penalty is imposed and implemented so infrequently as to be virtually nonexistent. And fines, which go to the state rather than to the victim, are not considered adequate punishment for serious crimes; nor could indigent defendants afford to pay the fines attached to such crimes. Whatever the sentence imposed, it must be authorized by the penal code.

Determinate and indeterminate sentences

There are basically two types of prison sentences. In a *determinate, fixed,* or *flat* sentence, the offender is sentenced to a specific number of years, such as 2 years, 5 years, or 10 years. Fixed sentences are intended to punish offenders for their crimes—to give them their "just deserts"—and to deter recidivism. In an *indeterminate* or *indefinite* sentence, the offender is sentenced to a *range* of time in prison, such as 2–5 years, 5–10 years, or 10–20 years. The theory behind indeterminate sentences is that offenders should be viewed as "sick" individuals, offered treatment in prison, and released as soon as they are "rehabilitated."

Sentencing discretion

The court has tremendous *discretion* in sentencing. For most felonies, the court is authorized by statute to choose between penalties as different as probation and prison and, within statutory boundaries, to set the range in an indeterminate prison term. If a statute makes a crime punishable by probation or an indeterminate 10–30 year prison term, the court may set the range almost anywhere between the minimum and maximum, such as 10–25 years, 15–30 years, 12–20 years; or it may place the offender on probation instead. It is only when the statute requires the imposition of a fixed prison term—calls for a *mandatory* prison sentence—that the court is deprived of its sentencing discretion and must sentence the offender to the prescribed period of incarceration. Except in the case of mandatory prison sentences, the court may frequently impose a prison term, then "suspend" implementation of the sentence and place the offender on probation. The judge also has considerable discretion in attaching conditions to probation.

Probation

Probation is a sentence of conditional liberty in the community. While permitted to go about their regular activities, convicted defendants placed on probation remain under the supervision of a probation officer and are legally subject to the continued authority of the court. Probation is significant because it is the most common type of disposition and because of the role of the probation officer. In 1975 the estimated number of probationers in the United States exceeded one million, or about five times the number of inmates in prison. Compared with those sentenced to prison, individuals placed on probation are the less serious, low-risk offenders who stand a better chance of not recidivating while under the watchful eye and helping hand of their probation officer.

Probation officers

The probation officer is typically an employee of the court. In addition to supervising probationers, they are responsible for preparing *presentence reports* (PSR). Presentence reports are social history investigations of convicted defendants that contain sentencing recommendations to the court and a proposed plan for treatment, especially where probation is recommended. The court has enormous discretion in imposing conditions of probation, which in theory the probation officer must enforce. Failure to comply with these conditions may lead to the revocation of probation and commitment to prison. Probation officers have the opportunity to report violations of probationary conditions—and the *discretion* to overlook them.

Probation officers attempt to aid in the rehabilitation of offenders. But excessive caseloads and the time-consuming task of preparing PSRs make it impossible to provide intensive casework and counseling services. Their discretionary responsibility to enforce the conditions of probation also interferes with providing effective counseling and rehabilitation. As part of their custodial role, probation officers can initiate *revocation* of probation. Revocation of probation—for technical violation of the conditions imposed or for evidence of new crimes—is the first step to resentencing the offender to prison. Thus the surveillance role of probation officers interferes with their rehabilitation efforts and goals. For probationers are reluctant to trust counselors who are in a position to put them behind bars.

Revocation

Correctional Institutions

Correctional institutions are jails and prisons. Jails, which are operated under local auspices, house sentenced misdemeanants and pretrial detainees. Prisons, which are state-operated facilities, are responsible for the secure custody of sentenced felons. The most serious common problems of jails and prisons are related to overcrowded inmate populations, antiquated facilities located in remote areas, abuses of discretion by personnel, obstacles to proper supervision and effective treatment of inmates, and the dehumanization and anonymity that accompany incarceration. The administrative and political needs of institutional officials revolve around security and security measures. Their major concerns are to prevent riots, escapes, injury to staff, and rejection of formal authority. Constant attention to these possibilities determines the basic structure and function of "correctional" institutions.

Parole

Parole is the status of an offender who is released from prison after having served only part of his or her sentence inside.* The statutes of each jurisdiction specify the minimum periods that must be served in prison before an inmate is eligible for parole. Parole eligibility identifies the soonest time at which the law authorizes early release from prison. The *parole board* is the autonomous authority responsible for deciding precisely when or if eligible inmates will be granted parole. By exercising discretion, the parole board determines how much of the inmate's sentence must be completed in prison before the offender will be released to finish the remainder of the sentence in the community.

Parole rules

Inmates who are granted parole sign the board's rules or conditions of parole. The parole rules are a standard list of "dos and don'ts" that may also include special requirements in individual cases. The rules sensitize the parolee to potential problem areas, remind the parolee that he or she is still technically in the custody of the paroling authority. The rules are a tool used by the parole officer in supervising parolees. If the conditions of parole are violated, the parole board can revoke parole and reincarcerate the parolee. Despite their correctional similarities and the fact that both involve conditional liberty, parole and probation are legally distinct. Probation is a *sentence* of the court that returns convicted defendants directly to the community. Parole is not a sentence—no one is "sentenced to parole"—but is an early release from prison authorized by the parole board rather than the court.

Parole officers

Parole officers are responsible for supervising, helping, and controlling

* Parole is usually not available to misdemeanants in jail, most of whom are serving very short terms. Among other reasons, the brief length of their stays makes it impractical to rely upon parole release.

parolees assigned to their caseload.* Parole officers may also investigate prison release plans, develop employment opportunities for prisoners scheduled for parole, and occasionally conduct presentence investigations. Like probation officers, parole officers wear two hats. On the one hand, parole officers function as counselor and friend to parolees. They help parolees resolve personal problems and assist them in getting and keeping a job, and they facilitate the parolee's transition to the community and make his or her adjustment to freedom easier. On the other hand, parole officers have certain "law enforcement" responsibilities that interfere with their being trusted by parolees. They have great discretion in enforcing the conditions of parole, and the violation of those conditions could lead to revocation of parole and reimprisonment.

Violations of parole

Parole officers can report parolees to the parole board for technical or substantive violations of the parole rules. *Substantive* violations of parole refer to the commission of new crimes while on parole. *Technical* violations include all other types of failure to comply with the provisions of the parole rules. There are a large number of technical conditions attached to parole, such as not being permitted to drive a car, to associate with certain groups, or to change jobs or leave the state without permission. Consequently, the parole officer can usually find that something the parolee did was a technical violation. A parole officer who chooses to do so can initiate revocation of parole by reporting such technical (and substantive) violations to the parole board for consideration. The parole board makes the final decision on whether or not to revoke parole.

Caseloads

Besides the conflicting rehabilitation and surveillance demands made upon parole officers, their treatment efforts are limited by the size of their caseloads. Parole officers are responsible for supervising an average caseload of 68 parolees. One-fifth of parole officers have caseloads of 80 or more parolees. In contrast, research suggests that parole caseloads should be about 35 per officer.[9] The result of the case overload is that parole officers spend most of their time on administration and do very little personal counseling with parolees. The same basic problems are faced by probation officers: conflicting role demands, case overload, and excessive administrative burdens often take priority over treatment of the convicted offender.

CRIMINAL JUSTICE ADMINISTRATION AS SYSTEM AND NONSYSTEM

Criminal justice administration is a *system* in that all of its employees are concerned with the prevention, control, and reduction of crime and de-

* The caseload is the assignment of individual offenders to a correctional officer; it is the standard way of organizing the work of both probation and parole officers.

linquency. All justice personnel process individuals who have violated criminal statutes or the juvenile code. Criminal justice workers have a continuous responsibility for processing offenders, and they earn their livelihood in the same organization, business, or system. The system's total combined laborpower consists of 800,000 practitioners who are financed by and accountable to thousands of separate federal, state, county, city, town, and village jurisdictions.[10] The division of labor in the criminal justice system is represented by seven major functional components, as shown in Table 2.1. Each functional component is a distinct operational jurisdiction; each agency has a different job to do and is organized differently to perform its work. This division of labor makes it possible for the entire organization to function.

Components of the system

The seven functional components in the criminal justice process form a sequence such that (1) in order to reach the next department or agency it is usually necessary to have had contact with all the preceding ones, and (2) the work and accomplishments of each department are heavily influenced by the number and types of cases sent to it by the immediately preceding agency. Thus the criminal justice system can be thought of as an assembly-line operation. The police process suspects. Prosecutors proceed against defendants. Courts are concerned with cases to be litigated. Probation officers supervise low-risk, nonserious law violators. Correctional institutions control prisoners. The parole board selects inmates ready for early reentry to society. Parole officers counsel and supervise the more serious, recidivist, "hardened" criminal.

In varying degrees, each component in the criminal justice system is relevantly related to every other one. The greatest amount of cooperation, interdependence, and impact is found between adjacent agencies in the network. At the daily operational level, the personnel of adjacent processing stages simply need each other more in order to do their respective jobs. Their separate tasks are more directly dependent upon, immediately affected by, and interwoven into each other's activities; they have frequent and more visible contact with one another.

The police, for example, interact much more frequently with the prosecutor's office than they do with the court, to which they may be as much a stranger as the victim. In turn, the number of defendants prosecuted and the charges brought by the prosecutor affect judicial operations. The sentencing decisions of the court affect the size and composition of probation caseloads, prison populations, the management of institutions, and the work of the parole board. Decisions by the parole board concerning which inmates should be granted parole, and when, set the boundaries for what parole officers can accomplish. The effectiveness of parole officers with their caseloads affects the crime rate through recidivism, the public's fear of crime, and the activities of police officers who arrest the same offenders time and again. Nonadjacent workgroups are also interdependent in the administration of justice. This mutual dependence, im-

Table 2.1 Primary Activities of the Functional Components of the Criminal Justice System: Decisions, Decisions, Decisions

Functional Component	LAW ENFORCEMENT	COURTS			CORRECTIONS			
	Police	Prosecution	Lower Courts (magistrate courts)	Courts of General Jurisdiction (trial or felony courts)	Probation	Correctional Institutions	Parole Board	Parole
Decision-making Employees	Patrol officers Supervisors and administrators	States' attorney general District attorney and assistant DAs Chief prosecutor	Magistrates and judges	Judges	Probation officer	Administrators and supervisors Custodial staff (guards) Rehabilitation: professional correctional treatment staff	Members appointed by governor	Parole officers
Primary Activities	Crime control: arrest, investigation, searches, interrogation, prevention and deterrence Social service and order maintenance	Formal charging Nolees cases Securing convictions Plea bargaining	Issues warrants Preliminary arraignment: informs defendant of rights, appoints counsel Preliminary hearing: determines if probable cause exists Tries misdemeanor cases Sentences misdemeanants	Issues warrants Pretrial motions: rules on admissibility of evidence Arraignment: accepts pleas Conducts bench trial Presides over jury trial Charges jury Sentencing	Prepares presentence report Supervises and counsels probationer Enforces conditions of probation Initiates revocation of probation	Secure custody Preparation for release Treatment	Grants or denies parole Sets conditions of parole Revokes parole	Prepares presentence reports Supervises and counsels parolees Enforces conditions of parole Initiates revocation of parole

pact, and interlocking of each functional component in processing a common population of offenders identifies the system of criminal justice administration.

Criticism of the nonsystem

The administration of criminal justice has also been criticized as a *nonsystem.*[11] The nonsystem criticisms may be grouped into four categories which in practice interact and overlap.

Jurisdictional and Operational Problems

The four primary political bureaucracies—police, prosecution, courts, and corrections—are independent jurisdictions. Each superagency is in effect a separately operated entity; each has separate sources of authority, lines of communication, and accountability. Yet such independence and separation of power is a barrier to cooperation. It generates antagonisms between groups dependent upon each other and interferes with achieving the more general and common goals of the total criminal justice organization as well as individual objectives. Jurisdictional autonomy means that there is no recognized leader or level of leadership. No person, position, or body has the authority and power to act decisively in the name of all. There is no single group to whom all the various criminal justice agencies are responsible. The highest official in each jurisdiction has no formal control over the lowest echelon in a different criminal justice agency. Conflicting vested interests, longtime misunderstandings, and different community and political pressures on the various functional components also contribute to the nonsystem of criminal justice administration.

Differences in Roles and Goals

Basic differences in occupational performance and expectations contribute to the nonsystem quality of criminal justice. At the daily departmental and operational level, the common verbal allegiance to "prevent and control" crime is replaced with the need for "doing my job." Correctional administrators and parole boards, for example, are under considerable pressure to release inmates as early as possible. But given the high recidivism of ex-prisoners, law enforcement and public protection is made more difficult by a policy of early prisoner release. Parole board action and policy may also conflict with the court's role at sentencing. Judges sometimes give longer sentences than they actually want offenders to serve, knowing that prisoners will be paroled before the sentence expires.[12] Good policework involves keeping known offenders, such as probationers and parolees, under heightened surveillance. Correctional counselors, however, object to the practice because it interferes with treatment efforts and makes it more difficult for offenders to be accepted by the community. Some practitioners believe that the courts sentence too many convicted defendants to prison. The police and prosecutors, however, criticize the courts for sentencing too few offenders to prison, thereby returning to the streets on probation many serious offenders who go unpunished, undeterred, and untreated.

People Problems

Different types of people are employed in each of the seven functional components. Criminal justice practitioners differ in personality, social background, training and education, attitudes, and values. These factors —especially the individual's ideology with respect to the law, crime, and offenders—are the basis of "people problems" that contribute to the nonsystem. In practice, people problems have a tendency to revolve around whether the individual believes in punishment or treatment. This personal philosophy influences role performance and goal orientation. For beneath their official titles and formal roles, criminal justice employees are private citizens who bring their own philosophy of life with them to work each day. Their personal feelings and attitudes toward retribution, deterrence, incapacitation, and rehabilitation have a significant and continuous impact on what they do and the decisions they make. The result of such people problems can be strained relations, a failure to communicate, a reluctance to share information, and a nonsystem of criminal justice.

Substantive Issues

Everything that seems to be or is wrong in the administration of criminal justice has been identified as part of the reason for the nonsystem: undereducated and poorly trained police, low clearance rates, incompetent judges, ineffective defense counsel, limited sentencing alternatives, poorly managed courts, the abuse of bail, the denial of a speedy trial, too much discretion, and the absence of standards. Basically, there are too many cases to be processed, and there is not enough qualified personnel, technology, or consensus among practitioners to respond to them adequately.

THE FEDERAL ROLE IN IMPROVING STATE AND LOCAL CRIMINAL JUSTICE SYSTEMS

Riots of the 1960s

The frightening reality of domestic political life and governmental concern in the 1960s was "the riots." Riots began, almost unnoticed and unheeded, in 1964, and increased in frequency and severity through 1968. By then the nation had become preoccupied with their control and prevention. The impact of the civil disorders upon society created an unprecedented fear of crime and the demand that "law and order" be reestablished, both of which became significant issues in the 1968 presidential election. The federal government's response to the riots, the role of the police in precipitating them,[13] and the rising fear of crime was to establish "crime commissions" to study and analyze the riots, the police, and the fear of crime.

The President's Crime Commission

In his special message to Congress on March 8, 1965, President Lyndon B. Johnson noted that the crime rate had doubled since 1940. The president acknowledged that "crime in the streets" was the primary responsibility of local authorities but stressed the need for the federal government to assume a larger role in state crime control.[14] Sensitive to the public's growing fear of crime and to "law and order" as emerging political issues, President Johnson created the Commission on Law Enforcement and Administration of Justice (hereafter, the President's Crime Commission) on July 23, 1965.[15]

The alarming increase in the crime rate, the increasingly violent character of crimes, and the public's heightened awareness and fear of crime had made "crime in the streets" a national social crisis. While differing from the riots that were soon to follow, the upsurge in ordinary crime shared the quality and appearance of massive disobedience to the rule of law. But it was the riots that began shortly after the President's Crime Commission was created that compelled government officials and criminal justice administrators to take the commission's work and recommendations seriously. The riots increased in frequency and destructiveness during the commission's existence and while its reports were gaining national attention and being evaluated. Thus the riots gave the commission's recommendations to improve the criminal justice system a credibility, urgency, and real-life quality they might have otherwise lacked.

The President's Crime Commission was charged with investigating the causes of crime and delinquency and the adequacy of the existing system of law enforcement, judicial administration, the courts, and corrections. On the basis of these inquiries, it was responsible for reporting to the president by January 1967 on how federal, state, and local governments could make law enforcement and the administration of justice more effective and more fair. The studies and recommendations of the President's Crime Commission were published in February 1967 in its main volume, *The Challenge of Crime in a Free Society*. The commission's more detailed statements appeared in six separate task force reports. The reports of the commission are considered the most ambitious and most successful attempt in our nation's history to relate our knowledge of crime and delinquency to the administration of criminal justice.[16]

Recommendations of the commission

The commission's recommendations called for basic changes in the operation and management of the criminal (and juvenile) justice system, in the way Americans think about crime, and in the approach to crime control. The President's Crime Commission identified objectives to be accomplished in six major areas: (1) preventing crime, (2) dealing with offenders in new ways, (3) eliminating unfairness and providing dignified treatment to all persons in the arms of the law, (4) upgrading the quality and qualifications of criminal justice personnel, (5) expanding research in crime control, and (6) funding improvements in the criminal justice system.[17] To achieve this last, and in some ways the most important, goal the commission recommended a vastly enlarged program of federal financial assistance to strengthen the administration of criminal justice at the state and local levels.

The commission was also concerned about the possibility that its reports would be shelved and forgotten. To preclude that possibility, it urged the creation of a permanent federal agency for implementing its recommendations, its strategy for change, and its model for a more professional criminal justice system. This federal agency, it was hoped, would become the means for transforming the commission's proposals and principles into practice. Such a federal agency was subsequently created within the Department of Justice with the passage of the Omnibus Crime Control and Safe Streets Act of 1968.

Events of 1967

The two worst riots in the history of the nation occurred in Detroit and Newark, New Jersey, in the summer of 1967, just a few months after the publication of *The Challenge of Crime in a Free Society* and the distribution of the commission's more detailed task force reports. During the first nine months of 1967, there were 164 disorders officially recorded and as many as 217, according to some informed counts.[18] Thus, as the country emerged from the turmoil and breakdown of "law and order" in 1967, the commission's reports provided an appealing, ready-made framework for building a saner and safer society. The final straw, however, was yet to come. The assassination of Martin Luther King, Jr., in Memphis, Tennessee, on April 6, 1968, unleashed black rage and criminal opportunism that swept across 168 towns and cities in the following week. And two months later presidential candidate Senator Robert F. Kennedy was assassinated by a lone gunman.

There is no real connection between the increases in the number of "ordinary" crimes compiled in the *Uniform Crime Reports* and the civil disorders. The President's Crime Commission was created in 1965 to respond to the accelerating rate in traditional crime and especially the rapid increases in serious crime in major cities. But the subsequent events—the riots and the assassinations of national leaders—politicized the issue to the point that any federal legislation would have had to promise to reduce everyday crime in the streets as well as prevent riots, the two having become fused in the public and the congressional mind.[19] If there was ever a time that was politically right for the passage of federal legislation that promised to do both, it was in June 1968, when the Omnibus Crime Control and Safe Streets Act was passed and signed into law.

Law Enforcement Assistance Administration (LEAA)

The Safe Streets Act created a new federal agency, the Law Enforcement Assistance Administration (LEAA), to distribute funds to states wishing to improve their crime control capabilities and to upgrade the quality of their justice personnel.[20] By controlling the purse strings, the LEAA was to act as national coordinator for broad-based reforms in the management, organization, and operation of nonfederal criminal justice systems. The official recipient of LEAA funds was the State Planning Agency, a group of members appointed by the governor in each state to apply for and administer the federal grant.

To qualify for LEAA funds allocated on a population-based formula, the State Planning Agency (SPA) submitted to the LEAA a comprehensive plan explaining how the requested funds would be used to reduce crime and improve the criminal justice system in the commonwealth. These comprehensive plans consisted of descriptions of innovative *action projects,* rather than "more studies," that were the functional units of criminal justice system reform. The action projects were intended to bring about (1) concrete, meaningful, and measurable changes in the fight against crime and how it was waged, (2) operational and organizational improvements in the agencies charged with managing the crime problem, and (3) new working relationships and greater cooperation among the various components within the fragmented criminal justice "nonsystem." Action projects were submitted by a "unit of state or local government"—usually the police, prosecutor, courts and corrections—to the State Planning Agency for funding consideration. The project applications that the SPA approved and their cost were packaged into and became the basis of the comprehensive state plan that the SPA submitted to the LEAA in requesting federal crime control funds.

LEAA appropriations increased steadily from $60 million in fiscal 1969 to $895 million in 1975, then dropped to $811 million in 1976.[21] Over half of the 1970 LEAA budget was allocated to law enforcement, which used a substantial proportion of the funds to purchase police equipment and riot-control apparatus and to train officers for responding to civil disorders.[22] This early emphasis was not unusual or inappropriate in view of the riot-torn society of the 1960s, which gave rise to the LEAA and specific reference in the Safe Streets Act to the "purchase of equipment" and "prevention and control of riots." But with the passage of time the role of "hardware" in the LEAA agenda decreased and the agency became concerned exclusively with helping local criminal justice systems respond to ordinary crime under normal conditions.

Law Enforcement Education Program (LEEP)

LEAA's response to the educational deficiencies of criminal justice personnel was to establish the Law Enforcement Education Program (LEEP) as part of its internal structure. As the laborpower component of LEAA, LEEP subsidized the college education of persons who were pre-

e Law Enforcement Assistance
ministration distributed funds
r the improvement of local
minal justice systems

paring for a career in or were already employed by the criminal justice system. Through grants and loans, LEEP represented the first major federal effort on behalf of criminal justice education. The first LEEP funds, $6.5 million, were awarded in January 1969 to 485 schools for financing the education of some 20,000 students, the majority of whom were inservice police officers.[23] By 1975, well over a thousand colleges were participating in the annual $50 million LEEP program. And by 1980, some 300,000 had been recipients of LEEP assistance.[24]

The Standards and Goals Commission

In a speech in February 1971, Attorney General John Mitchell urged the creation of a Standards and Goals Commission to "establish concrete standards and goals to allow the dozens of State Planning Agencies and the hundreds of regional planning agencies to measure the problems in their own areas, and to see how and where they are ahead of or behind these suggested standards, and by how much."[25] Pursuant to the attorney general's directive, in October 1971 LEAA established the National Advisory Commission on Criminal Justice Standards and Goals (hereafter, the Standards and Goals Commission), which issued its reports two years later.

In broad outline, scope, and intent, the Standards and Goals Commission borrowed from and built upon the work of the President's Crime

Commission. Having accepted the challenge of crime proclaimed in 1967 by the President's Crime Commission, the Standards and Goals Commission determined to "do something about it," as indicated in its summary report, *A National Strategy to Reduce Crime,* released in January 1973. The *National Strategy* report specified the goal of reducing the high-fear, stranger-to-stranger crimes of burglary and robbery by at least 50 percent by 1983. By the same date, the incidence of the violent crimes of homicide, forcible rape, and aggravated assault was to be cut by at least 25 percent. To encourage and enable state and local criminal justice systems to achieve these objectives, the Standards and Goals Commission report contained proposals, policies, standards, and goals outlining the step by step procedures to be taken. More detailed comment was contained in its four task force reports on the police, courts, corrections, and community crime prevention. As strategies for reducing the above mentioned "target" crimes, the Standards and Goals Commission identified four general priorities: (1) preventing juvenile delinquency, (2) improving the delivery of social services, (3) reducing delays in the criminal justice process, and (4) obtaining greater citizen participation in the criminal justice system. The establishment of priorities, quantitative crime reduction goals, timetables for their achievement, and clear benchmarks for measuring progress and project effectiveness were hallmarks of the Standards and Goals Commission initiative.

By fiscal 1976, to qualify for LEAA funding every SPA had to adopt and demonstrate in its comprehensive plan the *process* of standard and goal setting pioneered by the Standards and Goals Commission. The new relationship between LEAA and the State Planning Agencies was clear-cut: If the SPAs—representing and reflecting the needs of state and local criminal justice agencies—wanted federal funds, they had to follow the lead of the Standards and Goals Commission.

For better or worse, the noble experiment in criminal justice reform begun in 1968 was on the verge of collapse by 1980. As part of President Carter's antiinflation drive, Congress voted to dismantle the entire LEAA program. LEEP was also scheduled for termination. It was transferred in May 1980 to the Department of Education, where it was temporarily surviving on funds left over from previous appropriations.[26] It is expected that by fiscal 1982 the LEAA will no longer exist as a distinct organizational entity, thus closing a unique chapter in the annals of criminal justice—one that, hopefully, has changed indelibly the course of the administration of justice in America.[27]

SUMMARY

As an overview of the criminal justice system and its administration, this chapter reviewed every processing stage and category of personnel and their basic functions. The criminal justice process usually begins when an arrest is made and ends with parole and discharge from sentence. The chapter also introduced many of the major concepts, problems, and issues that will be treated at length in subsequent chapters. While criminal justice administration is a "system" from one point of view, it has also been criticized as being a "nonsystem." The national effort to improve the administration of criminal justice began with the President's Crime Commission in 1965, was codified in the Safe Streets Act of 1968, was carried forward by the Standards and Goals Commission, and was financially nurtured by the Law Enforcement Assistance Administration until 1980, when the agency fell victim to President Carter's antiinflation drive. Many of the innovations and changes prompted by the two crime commissions, as well as the obstacles to progress caused by the nonsystem, are discussed thematically throughout the text.

DISCUSSION QUESTIONS

1. What is the relationship between the police and the prosecutor in the charging process?
2. Why are the police held to a higher standard of proof in making a warrantless misdemeanor arrest than in making a warrantless felony arrest?
3. In what ways is the administration of criminal justice a "system"?
4. In what ways are probation and parole alike and unlike?
5. Why do so many of the criminal justice stages require "probable cause" as a basis of decision making?
6. What is meant by the "nonsystem" of criminal justice administration?

Chapter 3

THE POLICE ROLE

Law Enforcement and Order Maintenance
Noncrime activities of police / Predominance of the law enforcement role

The Working Personality of the Police
Danger / Authority and isolation / The police subculture
Police Prejudice and Authoritarianism
Origins of authoritarianism

The Exercise of Discretion
Full Enforcement of the Law Versus Selective Enforcement
Factors That Influence the Decision to Arrest
Arrest for "disrespect" / Seriousness of the offense / Visibility of the decision to arrest
The Control of Discretion
Policy and guidelines / Objections to policy formulation

Crime Control and the Police
Do the Police Deter Crime?
Operation 25 and the Rand study / Crime in the subways / The Kansas City Experiment / The Rand detective study
Special Approaches to Crime Control
Special Weapons and Tactics squads / Police decoys / Undercover operations / Entrapment

Close-up 3.1: Supreme Court Decisions on Entrapment

The Sting / Abscam / Computer systems and 911 calls

Victimless Crime and Decriminalization
Forms of decriminalization / Rationale for decriminalization

Summary

The 1965 President's Crime Commission focused unprecedented attention on the role of the police in a free society. The status of the police function was also sharply underscored by the National Advisory Commission on Civil Disorders, which pointed an accusing finger at patrol officers for triggering many of the disorders of the 1960s. Finally, the major recommendations of the President's Crime Commission were reinforced and made operational by the Standards and Goals Commission in 1973. In large measure, emerging changes in the police role, the delivery of police services, and the administration of the police stem from the recommendations of the two crime commissions and the implementation of their proposals by the Law Enforcement Assistance Administration. In the expanded and enhanced role being carved out for them, the "new breed" police officers are envisaged as managers of conflict situations and social crises, providers of social services as well as crime fighters, professional bureaucrats with offices in the streets, and practical psychologists practicing without a license but preferably with a college degree. In some ways, the forces for change and the new expectations of the police have made policework more complex, diversified, demanding, stressful, and ambiguous.

The features of the contemporary police scene explored in this and the following chapters portray an occupation in hesitant transition. The degree to which police and the police department can operate successfully within a forever changing society—under pressure, conflicting demands, and the constant call for more efficient and effective performance—may be the best measure of their professionalism, responsiveness to community needs, sense of priorities, soundness of judgment, and their ability to endure.

LAW ENFORCEMENT AND ORDER MAINTENANCE

The many hats worn by patrol officers and the diversity of their activities are categorized as the "law enforcement" and "order maintenance" roles of the police.[1] The *law enforcement* or *crime control* role represents the traditional view of the police function that is emphasized by the public, the mass media, the courts, and the police themselves: preventing and deterring crime, making good arrests, obtaining confessions, building strong cases that result in convictions and stiff sentences, and increasing crime clearance rates. But in addition to law enforcement, there is an altogether different side to the work performed by the police: their *order maintenance* responsibilities.*

* The order maintenance role is also referred to as the social services, peacekeeping, or community services role of the police.[2]

Noncrime activities of police

When performing in an order maintenance capacity, the police are involved in noncrime assignments such as referring the disadvantaged to social agencies, furnishing information to citizens, providing emergency ambulance service, preventing suicide, aiding the physically disabled and mentally ill, giving shelter to drunks who might otherwise freeze to death on the streets, and assisting disaster victims. In their order maintenance role, the police provide immediate short-term relief in response to personal and interpersonal problems. They attempt to resolve conflicts by "handling" a situation with social skills and diplomacy instead of nightstick, gun, or the power to arrest. As community service agents, the police strive for orderly, tentative solutions in crisis situations and to requests for help that do not involve standard violations of the criminal law. When citizens call the police to intervene in such situations, their primary motivation is not to report a crime. Rather, they want to utilize the police officer's resources to get things done without making an arrest. Citizens call the police for social services because of their availability when needed, their dependability when called, and their ability to provide prompt resolution to the urgent interpersonal conflicts and crises to which they are summoned.

Order maintenance situations are not devoid of law enforcement implications or opportunities. While initially adopting a mediator's role in responding to a domestic disturbance (such as a family quarrel), an officer may subsequently don his or her law enforcement hat if the family squabble involves a felony, if a misdemeanor is committed in the officer's presence, or in self-defense. In attempting to disperse an unruly crowd or in escorting a mentally deranged person to the hospital, the order maintenance character of police action is blurred because the possibility of danger automatically invokes the shield of crime control. These difficult-to-categorize examples illustrate that the complexity and full dimensions of policework cannot be adequately captured in such useful abstractions as the law enforcement and order maintenance roles.

Some persons have suggested that the police be divested of certain order maintenance responsibilities that contribute to role conflict, divert them from patrol, are properly civilian activities, or detract from professionalizing the police field.[3] However, there are serious obstacles to transferring important police services to other public or private agencies: the police have a monopoly on the use of force, the ability to thrust citizens into the criminal justice system via arrest, and an around-the-clock availability to all callers. Also, other agencies and personnel are reluctant to do the "dirty work" performed so well by the police.[4]

Predominance of the law enforcement role

Research has revealed that between 40 and 80 percent of police assignments and/or time involve order maintenance tasks (see Table 3.1).[5] Nonetheless, their law enforcement role will probably continue to be the defining badge of the police subculture and the police profession for several reasons. First, responding to domestic disturbances is one of the

Table 3.1 Distribution of 700,000 Calls Received by the Baltimore Police Department, 1970

Type of Call	Percent of Total
Index crimes	10.7
Other crimes	8.4
Service calls (includes sick persons, dog bites, sanitation complaints, family disputes)	63.0
Accidents	5.0
Duplicate calls (more than one person reporting same incident)	6.8
Unfounded calls (false fire alarm, false crime report)	6.1

Source: Franklin G. Ashburn, "Changing the Rhetoric of 'Professionalism,'" *Innovations in Law Enforcement,* paper presented at the Fourth Symposium on Law Enforcement Science and Technology, May 1–3, 1972. *Criminal Justice Monograph,* U.S. Department of Justice, LEAA, National Institute of Law Enforcement and Criminal Justice, June 1973, p. 6.

most dreaded and dangerous tasks performed by the police and the second most common source of death in the line of duty. It is impossible to know in advance whether a family quarrel will result in a police injury, escalate to a more serious incident, or lead to arrest. The police must therefore approach all domestic disputes wearing both hats. Second, the police themselves view crime control as "real" policework, are ambiguous or indifferent to their community service role, and are disdainful of anything that smacks of social work. Third, despite its generous reliance upon the social services provided by the police, the public's valuation of and respect for the authority of the police is rooted in their crime control role rather than in the order maintenance role. Fourth, the entire police incentive and reward system is oriented toward law enforcement role activities. It is difficult for an officer to receive credit for good human relations work because departmental records reflect only crime control statistics. Fifth, at any given time, about one-third of the available police personnel are committed to dealing with crime and offenders, a far heavier investment than that made in any individual order maintenance activity.[6] Sixth, and most important, the ability of the police to perform order maintenance activities is in large measure dependent upon their policing authority rather than peacekeeping intentions.[7] The police respond to virtually every order maintenance situation with the knowledge, shared by the citizens involved, that they might have to make an arrest if things get out of hand. Until such time as these factors change, the importance of the law enforcement role of the police cannot be minimized.

A minority of police commentators note that the diverse, uneven scope of police matters is not a new phenomenon, but rather a renewed perspective of an old, basically unchanged, unchanging, and unchangeable role.

"The police of yesterday performed a variety of health, welfare, and other social service functions. These duties were considered commonplace and essential. There is no indication that there was a problem with what today's social scientists call 'role conflict'. . . . The police officer's dual function of performing law enforcement duties and peacekeeping community services has apparently been present as long as there have been municipal police departments."[8]

THE WORKING PERSONALITY OF THE POLICE

Danger

Three features of an officer's work environment account for the "working personality" of the police: danger, authority, and isolation* from the public.[9] Bureaucratic pressures for efficiency form the background of these dimensions of the police officer's working personality. From the time new recruits enter the training academy to their emergence as autonomous sworn patrol officers, they are alerted to the prospect of danger—the occupational hallmark of the police profession.[10] To protect themselves against potentially dangerous situations and persons who cannot be precisely identified in advance, patrol officers come to view everyone with suspicion.[11] The public in general and members of high-crime prone minority groups in particular are treated as "symbolic" assailants; no matter how apparently innocuous, any encounter with a citizen could jeopardize an officer's safety. Some symbolic assailants are more likely than others to become real assailants and to confront the authority of the police. Patrol officers learn through painful personal experience, the experiences of fellow officers, and crime statistics that they have the most to fear from young male minority group members in the ghetto. Hence, the seeds are planted for strained relations between police and community (minority) groups, the development of racial prejudice and authoritarianism, isolation of the police from society, and problems pertaining to police authority.

Authority and isolation

The police are viewed and view themselves as authority figures. As such, their contacts with citizens involve giving orders, exercising control in law enforcement and order maintenance situations, placing restraints upon freedom of action, enforcing traffic regulations and other unpopular laws, making searches and arrests, and using force to maintain their authority.[12] The public's response to the difficulties, inconveniences, and threats posed by police authority is to isolate themselves from the police, accord them low status, and withhold respect and deference to their authority.[13] In the very process of performing their duties and protecting the

* I have chosen to emphasize the "social isolation" of the police from the public rather than (as did the author of the working personality theory) "efficiency" as the third variable.

community, the police find themselves unappreciated, alienated, and rejected by those whose lives, property, civil rights, and well-being they are committed to safeguard.

The police develop an intensive solidarity among their peers in order to cope with the frustrations and the conflicting demands of their job and to survive without the respect of the community. The police can then derive professional worth and acceptance, respect for their authority, and appreciation of the danger in policework—all the things denied them by the public—from their own kind. All sworn personnel go through the same extended apprenticeship as patrol officers, acquire the same experiences, and are confronted with the same working personality problems.[14] Therefore they share critical common occupational values, experiences, problems, and responses to the problems of danger, authority, and isolation. This collective occupational solidarity of experience, attitudes, norms, and reaction is referred to as the police subculture.

The police subculture

The police subculture is characterized by "toughness," clannishness, aloofness from outsiders, a code of secrecy concerning internal operating procedures and job-coping techniques, a reflexive willingness to come to the aid of fellow officers, and a distrust of everyone except their own kind.[15] The subculture is transmitted to each new member of the police occupation through the socialization process of applying to the force, academy training, and being on patrol—and thereby experiencing the patterned, unavoidable dilemmas of the police officer's working personality. An apprentice in any trade or profession learns and adopts the working personality that characterizes the respective field and is the core of that occupational subculture. The distinctive quality of the working personality of the police and the police subculture is derived from, perpetuated by, and revolves around danger, authority, and social isolation.

Police Prejudice and Authoritarianism

Two aspects of an individual's personality are especially relevant, controversial, and problematic to the police, the police department, and the community: prejudice and authoritarianism.* For many years it was assumed that persons selected as candidates for policework possessed marked authoritarian and prejudiced personalities *before* they entered the police academy or became sworn personnel and a part of the police subculture.[17] The undocumented belief was that the status symbols of authority and power that belong to policework specifically attracted au-

* Authoritarianism is a complex personality trait that includes an inability to perceive differences between groups, inflexibility, superstition, a need for order and routine, "toughness" and aggressiveness, cynicism, a preoccupation with sex, an exaggerated concern for authority, punitiveness, conventionalism, and rigid adherence to middle class values and morality.[16]

thoritarian types, whose performance on the job created problems in the community and dilemmas for department administrators.

However, research has revealed that before being socialized into the police subculture and developing a working personality, police recruits are no more authoritarian than the general population.[18] They are basically no more aggressive than social workers,[19] handle aggressive feelings better than most people,[20] and accept the so-called status symbols of policework as the trappings of the trade or as necessary evils. Research also shows that white police officers are no more racially prejudiced than whites in the general population or Americans in similar socioeconomic circumstances.[21] Of course, this does not mean that the police department or the community can afford to accept persons having "only" average prejudice. It does show, however, that the police do not start out as racial bigots, nor do they end up that way after joining the force.

Origins of authoritarianism

In the process of becoming socialized into the police subculture and adopting its working personality, the patrol officer becomes more authoritarian, prejudiced, closed-minded (dogmatic), and conservative than he or she was as an individual before joining the force.*[23] Authoritarianism and prejudice are largely independent of an individual's personality traits prior to joining the force, are related to the nature of policing and policework, and may be unavoidable.[24] Attempts to explain observed police prejudice and authoritarianism principally in terms of individual personality traits and the recruiting of already highly biased persons were false approaches to the solution of the problem. The major causes of police prejudice and authoritarianism are to be found not in the backgrounds of police recruits but in the forefront of policework, the working personality that goes with the job, and the police subculture. When a professor of criminology with a Ph.D. left the campus to become a sworn police officer, he became punitive, cynical, racist, authoritarian, suspicious of others, antirehabilitation, skeptical of the constitutional rights of offenders, a supporter of capital punishment, and frustrated over court leniency.[25] What happened to the criminologist-turned-cop was simply that he became a part of the police subculture and took on the standard working personality of the police.

THE EXERCISE OF DISCRETION

The police are decision makers, and most of the decisions they make involve discretion. The police exercise discretion whenever they must use

* For example, at the beginning of recruit training only 32 percent of the trainees agreed with the statement, "Respect for the police in a tough neighborhood depends on the willingness of patrolmen to use force frequently and effectively." The proportion increased to 51 percent after one year of field assignments.[22]

their own judgment and personal experience in deciding what to do and how to handle the law enforcement and order maintenance situations that they encounter in the performance of their duty. An officer who observes a husband assault his wife may exercise discretion by deciding that the best way to handle the matter is by a warning or a referral to a social service agency rather than by making an arrest. Upon observing a moving traffic violation, an officer may decide to warn the driver, to issue a summons, to make a full custody arrest, or to ignore it. (The decision to do nothing is highly discretionary.) In making an arrest where resistance is encountered, an officer may decide to use reasonable force or to try to talk the suspect into submitting to authority. In pursuing a fleeing felon, an officer may decide to fire at the suspect or to let the person escape.

Full Enforcement of the Law Versus Selective Enforcement

The vast amount of discretion exercised by the police and its importance and impact upon the entire criminal justice system have been recognized by the American Bar Association,[26] both crime commissions,[27] and everyone who has studied the police.[28] Reliance upon discretion permeates both order maintenance and law enforcement situations. The fact of the matter is that the police do not enforce all the laws all the time against all law violators. There are several reasons for the absence of full, strict, or total law enforcement.

Broadness and Inflexibility of the Criminal Statutes. The codification of the law does not recognize exceptions to its enforcement. Nor does it make criminal statutes selectively applicable depending upon the circumstances surrounding the offense, the characteristics of the offender, or the quality of police-citizen interaction. Instead, the language of the laws is so broad that they "sweep together identical acts with their markedly different actors and infinitely variable circumstances."[29] Thus the task of fitting broad policy expressed in inflexible statutes to the individual case is left to the police officer's discretion. The police are expected to make in action the necessary classifications and subtle distinctions that the legislature is unable or unwilling to authorize in writing.

Ambiguity and Vagueness of the Law. The language of some criminal statutes is ambiguous, unclear, or vague. In much the same way as the terms used in the amendments to the Constitution require interpretation by the court, the written law must often be interpreted by the individual police officer to become the "living" law. What, after all, is disorderly conduct, pornography, an aggravated assault, criminal intent, or an obscene phone call? And when are "fighting words" likely to provoke a breach of the peace?

Obsolete and Outmoded Laws. Some laws are obsolete and irrelevant to society's needs for social control. Consequently, enforcement of such laws is routinely disregarded. Although never formally repealed, they are treated as dead-letter laws by everyone concerned, including the legislature. Among the obsolete and unenforced statutes in some states are laws against kite flying, swearing in public, entertaining on Sunday, and kissing or spitting in public.

Overcriminalization of the Criminal Law. "Overcriminalization" refers to the belief that there are too many laws* regulating too many activities that are purely personal matters, have no relevance to the public interest, and should therefore be beyond the reach of the law. The statutory offenses that best illustrate the principle of overcriminalization are the so-called victimless crimes: marijuana use, drunkenness, prostitution, gambling, homosexuality, abortion. Victimless crimes receive low enforcement priority and are particularly susceptible to selective police action.

Financial Constraints. Neither the police department, the criminal justice system, nor the public can afford a policy of strict (total) law enforcement. Although police departments receive the lion's share of the annual $9 billion criminal justice budget, it is inadequate to meet the demands for services placed upon them.[31] Police departments compete fiercely with other city agencies for limited public funds and remain severely understaffed. Thus they have no alternative to establishing law enforcement priorities as part of an overall efficient allocation of scarce resources.

The Need to Individualize the Law in Action. In the courtroom, justice is supposed to be blind. But the blind enforcement of the law in the streets is considered unreasonable, incompatible with a free society, and wholly unintended by the legislators who drafted the criminal statutes and the public from whom they derive their mandate. There is a need to temper the harshness of the written law, to comply with its "spirit," to tailor formal justice with mercy and common sense—with discretion in action. In practice, the public interest often demands that the law be applied selectively, or be routinely unenforced, on the theory that all offenders who commit the same crime are not alike. For example, the police may take organized gambling and commercialized vice more seriously than church bingo players and self-employed prostitutes. The elderly and the young who commit larceny may be given a break, while

* The average officer must be prepared to uphold about 30,000 federal, state, and local enactments.[30]

adult shoplifters are arrested and prosecuted because they should have known better.[32]

Variations in Community Composition, Needs, and Expectations. Equal enforcement of the law would make most sense if the communities where it is enforced were equal. They are not. Distinctive patterns of social behavior and norms are associated with different ethnic groups residing in particular communities. Police in the ghetto may routinely overlook open cohabitation, bigamy, disorderly conduct, the carrying of dangerous weapons, drug violations, certain sex offenses, and even felonious assault by one minority group member upon another.[33] By contrast, the police response to such conduct in middle class or suburban neighborhoods, especially if the violations are interracial, is likely to be much more law enforcement-oriented. This double standard of police law enforcement stems from political pressures upon the police to be sensitive to cultural differences, community expectations, and police perceptions that certain neighborhoods require a highly individualized administration of the law.

Factors That Influence the Decision to Arrest

The most important discretionary decision made by the police is whether to make an arrest when they have a legal basis for doing so. Albert J. Reiss found that when citizens called the police, in 43 percent of all felonies and 52 percent of all misdemeanor situations the police decided not to arrest although they had probable cause to do so.[34] For many years, sociologists believed that the police exercised their discretionary arrest power in an arbitrary, personalized, and racially discriminatory manner. In part, this perception of the police was traceable to William A. Westley's famous study, "Violence and the Police," which appeared in 1953. In an unidentified municipal police department near Chicago, Westley asked 73 policemen, "When do you think a policeman is justified in roughing a man up?"[35] Thirty-seven percent of the police legitimized using violence for showing "disrespect for police." Altogether, 69 percent were sympathetic to using force for clearly illegal ends.

Arrest for "disrespect"

More recent research confirms that police use their discretionary power to arrest when "disrespect" is shown them.[36] The police appear especially prone to punish "disrespect" with arrest in their contacts with juveniles.[37] On the other hand, in discretionary situations the police reward those who are deferential by not taking juveniles into custody and not arresting adults. It is therefore well established that selective law enforcement is in part a response to the subject's attitude and demeanor toward the police. In contrast, the extent to which arrests are based upon racial prejudice and discrimination is negligible. It is true that police invoke the criminal sanction more often against blacks. But they do so because minority members more often show "disrespect" to the police and because of the offender's previous record, family background, and the offense committed.[38]

Seriousness of the offense

The most significant factor influencing the police decision to arrest is the offense committed, supplemented by other information bearing on the severity of the offense and how serious an offender the police are dealing with. This supplemental information includes the person's mental state, whether weapons were involved, the availability of a complainant,[39] and the previous record.[40] Virtually every credible study has revealed that legal factors, combined with other socially relevant considerations, are the main determinants of the decision to arrest. Even when police arrests appear arbitrary or racially motivated, closer inspection generally discloses a more legalistic, socially acceptable, and reasonable basis for action.

Visibility of the decision to arrest

A third major determinant of police discretion to invoke the criminal process is the "visibility" of the decision itself. To a large extent, patrol officers are able to make low-visibility discretionary decisions because they operate in unsupervised field settings, where their actions are beyond the scrutiny of administrators and concealed from the rest of the community.[41] Visibility in the exercise of police discretion is heightened depending upon the time and place of the offense, whether others observe the officer's actions, and the presence of a complainant.[42] The visibility of the arrest decision is related to the officer's self-protection against public criticism, mistakes, departmental investigation, and charges of excessive force and selective law enforcement. Making arrests involves personal and professional risks on the part of the police. Injuries may be sustained by officer, suspect, or innocent bystander. Arresting without probable cause may expose an officer to a false arrest suit or charges of police brutality. There may be organized community protests over the incident. "Safe" arrests are those that involve individuals without the resources, social position, or power to cause trouble for the police officer: the poor, students, radicals, minorities. Thus the police do express prejudice and discrimination in their exercise of discretion. However, the basis of such police discrimination is the suspect's social class and status rather than race or ethnic group.

The Control of Discretion

Almost all authorities agree that police discretion is too unregulated, undirected, and unbridled and that it needs to be controlled.[43] The main problems with uncontrolled discretion are that it lacks uniformity, it may be discriminatory, it fosters police corruption in victimless crime, and it converts the law into a personal instrument of social control through "curbside justice." The patrol officer should not be granted virtually unlimited choice in deciding when, where, why, and against whom to enforce the law. To prevent and minimize the misuse and abuse of discretionary authority, discretion must be controlled.

Policy and guidelines

The most commonly endorsed method for controlling unrestrained police discretion is through department policy established by high-ranking administrators in the department.[44] Law enforcement policy should consist of clear, realistic, and useful operational guidelines that patrol officers can rely on in deciding what action to take in the field, guidelines that control without eliminating the use of discretion, as recommended by the Standards and Goals Commission.[45] In particular, policy statements should identify the factors and circumstances that justify or require invoking the criminal sanction, as opposed to those where selective law enforcement is more appropriate. Discretionary areas that should be subjected to policy control include domestic disturbances, "stop and frisk," the use of force to overcome resistance, the use of firearms to apprehend fleeing felons, crowd control during civil disorders, and making mass arrests. At present, too few police departments have meaningful policies, standards, and criteria for controlling field discretion. Police chiefs who issue policies controlling arrests for possessing small amounts of marijuana or the use of firearms are unfortunately in a slim minority.[46]

Guidelines would facilitate police decision making under difficult circumstances and reduce role conflict by shedding light on the grey areas. They would protect the officer from community criticism and invalid claims of abusive or discriminatory law enforcement. The chief virtue of well-developed, comprehensive departmental policy is that it would assure consistent—and therefore fair—law enforcement in an agency where selective law enforcement is inevitable. The process involved in developing, communicating, and implementing policy would make a low-visibility function more subject to departmental review and make both patrol officer and police department more accountable and responsive to the public. Of course, even with policy or direct orders as a guideline to decision making and action, there will always be situations in which common sense is the only rule never violated.[47]

Objections to policy formulation

Some police officers and officials are skeptical or threatened by the implications of controlling discretion through policy formulation. Police officials are reluctant to formally acknowledge patrol officer discretion and to develop policies controlling it, for several reasons: (1) Its acknowledgment would require police administrators to assume responsibility for formulating written guidelines, monitoring their implementation, and punishing offending officers, a time-consuming and difficult task that is not without its risks. (2) By in effect endorsing selective law enforcement, the police department might relinquish its desired image and statutory mandate of impartiality. (3) Some state statutes or police department regulations, like those in the Atlanta Police Department, may prohibit authorizing incomplete law enforcement.[48] (4) Such policies might be incompatible and actionable under the Fourteenth Amendment's guarantee of equal protection under law. (5) Explicit approval of selective law enforcement might foster police corruption, unless victimless crimes were decriminalized or repealed.[49]

Overcoming administrative opposition to policy development often boils down to outside reformers convincing police officials that if they wait passively for the courts to do the job for them, it will be *their* discretion that will be on the line. The possibility must also be candidly recognized that "in the last instance there is no effective means of controlling a police officer acting alone on the streets. Nor is there a better judge of the vagaries of the law enforcement encounter than the police."[50]

CRIME CONTROL AND THE POLICE

The major resources of municipal police departments are directed toward providing crime control services. This function is carried out within budgetary constraints emphasizing efficient and effective law enforcement efforts. The public also views the police as the first and last resort against crime and the fear of crime. And, whether justified or not, the field officer's working personality and self-concept revolve around crime control.

Traditionally, police departments have organized their delivery of crime control services around *general preventive patrol:* random motorized cruising by patrol officers when they are not responding to radio-dispatched calls. Considered the backbone of the police force, preventive patrol is intended to deter crime through the visibility of the police and their opportunity to apprehend offenders in the act or fleeing from the crime scene. Against the backdrop of the patrol function as the principal means of crime control, three critical questions arise. Do the police actually deter crime? Aside from general patrol, what other tactics, techniques, and technology of crime control are employed? Do the police make too many arrests?

Do the Police Deter Crime?

Operation 25 and the Rand study

One of the first attempts to test the belief that police visibility prevents crime was carried out in the New York City Police Department beginning in September 1954. Operation 25 involved doubling the police strength in the 25th Precinct in Manhattan.[51] Before Operation 25 began, as many as two-thirds of the foot beats in the areas were unstaffed, but none were left unattended during the four-month experiment. Operation 25 seemed to curtail serious crime, especially street crime, that is, offenses occurring in public places or involving street entries to private places. Nonetheless, certain problems in the way the study was conducted raised doubts about its findings and significance. For example, Operation 25 may not in fact have curtailed crime but merely displaced it to adjoining precincts. And

Operation 25 involved an enormous (100 percent) increase in police strength.

What effect would a smaller patrol increase have on crime? The New York City Rand Institute studied the effect of a 40 percent increase in the patrol force assigned to the 20th Precinct, starting in October 1966.[52] The crime rate in the 20th Precinct was compared with that in two nearby control precincts that maintained a normal level of police coverage and were similar in composition to the 20th. Over an eight-month period in the 20th Precinct, the incidence of street robberies, auto theft, and grand larceny observable from the street dropped substantially. And there was no indication of crime displacement.

Crime in the subways

The problem in deterrence studies of the failure to report crimes to the police was overcome in an examination of the impact of police increases upon subway robberies in New York City. There, most of the victims are transit employees who must report a crime, and efforts were made to facilitate other victims' notifying the authorities. Police patrols in the subways were increased from the regular level of 1,200 persons to over 3,100 for eight years starting in April 1965. During this period, the number of subway felonies occurring at night fell in 1965 and remained low. Although the increased police presence had a decided deterrent effect, the cost of such crime prevention was high: $35,000 per deterred felony.[53] Municipal police departments obviously cannot afford to put a cop on every corner, subway, or bus.*

The Kansas City Experiment

The most comprehensive and most significant effort to determine the deterrent effect of routine preventive patrol was conducted in Kansas City between October 1972 and September 1973, under a $145,000 grant from the Police Foundation.† It had long been assumed that routine preventive patrol—having officers drive or walk through their beats when their time was not committed to answering specific calls—was the best approach to crime prevention. The Kansas City Experiment was designed to determine the effect of routine preventive patrol on the inci-

* In response to a surge in violent subway crime in New York City in the first quarter of 1979, Mayor Koch instituted a $7.5 million program that increased the number of uniformed Transit police from 500 to 900, so that officers would be on all 600 trains between 6 P.M. and 2 A.M. The initial results of the program were encouraging, although there was apparently some crime displacement to the 2 A.M. to 7 A.M. period when the beefed-up patrols were not in effect.

† The Police Foundation was launched in the summer of 1970 under a five-year grant of $30 million from the Ford Foundation. To bring about constructive change in law enforcement, the Police Foundation sponsors various projects and programs designed to aid police agencies in developing their full potential. Besides the Kansas City Experiment described above, the Police Foundation has sponsored projects examining the role of women in policework and the value of team policing. Under its auspices the Dayton (Ohio) Police Department is formulating policy guidelines to govern police activity in areas too often left to officers' unsupervised discretion.[54]

ꞌeatly increased police patrols
om 1965 to 1973 reduced crime
the New York City subways

dence of crime and the public's fear of crime. This was accomplished by implementing three different levels of routine preventive patrol in 15 police beats, which were divided into five groups of three computer-matched beats each.[55] One beat in each group of three, chosen at random, was patrolled in the normal way by a single patrol car that cruised the streets when not responding to calls; this was the control patrol strategy. The second beat in each group had two to three times the number of cruising patrol cars. This strategy, implementing a greatly increased level of preventive patrol and police visibility, was designated "proactive patrol."* Preventive patrol was eliminated altogether in the third beat: a police car would enter these areas only in response to specific requests for service, based on a "reactive patrol" strategy. Thus the Kansas City Experiment varied police visibility from minimal (reactive) to normal (control) to intensified (proactive).

At the conclusion of the one-year undertaking, the Kansas City Experiment produced unexpected, sobering, and highly controversial results.[57] There were no significant differences among the three areas in the amount of crime officially reported to the police or according to victim surveys, in observed criminal activity, in the citizen's fear of crime,[58] or in the degree of citizen satisfaction with the police.[59] In effect, changes in the level or the strategy of general preventive patrol made no difference in crime control in Kansas City. Motorized police presence, as implemented in the experiment, did not further deter crime! The implications of the

* In a proactive role, the police generate their own information and mobilize themselves to take action aimed at preventing crime or nipping it in the bud. "Stop and frisk" is an example of proactive police conduct.[56] In a reactive role, the police respond to information received from sources outside the department, such as citizen calls for assistance, which the officer is dispatched to handle.

Kansas City Experiment raised serious doubts about the value of a crime control strategy that has been the prevailing standard in policework for 150 years.

The Rand detective study

If uniformed officers on patrol are unable to prevent crime from happening, a Rand study suggests that detectives are not very successful in solving crimes that do occur. Under a $500,000 LEAA grant, a two-year Rand study of 153 police jurisdictions concluded that detectives rarely solve major crimes on their own, that they spend as much time shuffling papers as cracking cases, and that most detective forces could be cut in half without any loss in their crime-fighting effectiveness.[60] Unless a suspect is caught in the act, apprehended as a result of community cooperation with the police, or identified by the victim, the crime is probably insoluble. One detective captain in Portland, Oregon, candidly acknowledged that his personnel are unable to investigate more than 10 percent of the reported burglaries and that the typical homeowner who notifies the police of one "might just as well be writing a letter to Santa Claus."[61] The relationship between size of police force, expenditures for law enforcement, the patrol function, and crime control is unsettled and complex.[62]

Special Approaches to Crime Control

Special Weapons and Tactics squads

An emerging and controversial law enforcement tool is the use of tactical squads: elite police teams that rely on an aggressive, overtly military approach to handling exceptionally dangerous situations. Such commando-style police units are carefully chosen and receive special training, weapons, and uniforms in preparation for their responding to the holding of hostages, airplane hijackings, prison riots.[63] The best-known examples of tactical "guerilla" units are SWAT police.[64] The Philadelphia Police Department's 100-man Special Weapons and Tactics (SWAT) squad, the first SWAT unit in the nation, was formed in February 1964 in response to a rash of bank robberies.[65] Probably the most highly publicized SWAT unit is the Los Angeles Police Department's 60-man team that was formed at the time of the 1967 Watts riot.[66] As of 1976, there were an estimated 500 to 3,000 SWAT-like squads in police departments throughout the country, in teams with as few as 2 or as many as 160 members.[67] Despite the accent on weaponry and toughness, SWAT leaders insist that exercising sound discretion is the keystone of their operation and that their personnel know not only how to shoot but when not to fire.[68] A survey conducted by the *New York Times* reported that SWAT-like tactical units have, overall, acted with commendable restraint and discipline.[69]

Police decoys

Another unconventional and proactive crime control tactic is the use of police decoys. In order to attract and apprehend street criminals in the act, nonuniformed police officers pose as potential victims of crime:

essed as a woman, the police-
n at left captured a rape sus-
ct in the San Fernando Valley

drunks, nurses, businesspeople, tourists, prostitutes, blind persons, isolated subway riders, the defenseless elderly. Closely related to decoy tactics is the technique of blending. Blending involves having police assume nonvictim roles as ordinary citizens—construction workers, shoppers, joggers, bicyclists, physically disabled persons—placing them close enough to observe and intervene should criminal incidents involving other persons occur in their presence.

One of the most highly developed and effective decoy-and-blending operations is the New York Street Crime Unit, designated an "exemplary project" by the LEAA. New York City's decoy anticrime measures were launched in 1970 in response to an outbreak of assaults and robberies against taxi and truck drivers. To contain these violent crimes, the Taxi-Truck Surveillance Unit was organized around selected members of the patrol and detective bureaus, who were given the equipment and played the role of truck and taxicab drivers. From 1970 to 1975, this decoy-and-blending approach to crime control reduced taxi robberies 40 to 50 percent.[70] All anticrime decoy strategies focus on reducing serious and violent street crime, apprehending perpetrators in the act, making quality arrests, and maintaining a high conviction record. In achieving successful prosecutions, decoy operations overcome the problem of witnesses and victims who are reluctant to cooperate with the authorities because of fear, apathy, or interminable court delays.[71]

Undercover operations

The police employ a variety of elaborate, low-visibility crime control tactics that involve bona fide undercover work, operations, and agents. The undercover aspects of law enforcement range from paying an informant for information needed to solve a murder case or to make a major drug bust, and infiltrating organized gambling and narcotic trafficking, to officers' posing as decoy prostitutes. Participation in genuine undercover operations always includes an element of impersonation and duplicity, but it is qualitatively different from the narrower decoy role discussed above, in which the officer's mere availability as a potential victim of street crime was the focus. In genuine undercover work the police (or their informants) play a much more active, expansive, sustained, and complex part in inducing, planning, and participating in crime commission. All undercover procedures are used to probe crimes that are immune from ordinary law enforcement methods or are beyond the reach of other special tactics. The principal application of undercover police agents and police informants is to deal with drug trafficking and other "consensual" crimes that might otherwise be insoluble.

Entrapment

In arrests and prosecutions on the basis of evidence secured through proactive undercover police methods, the issue of entrapment arises. *Entrapment* occurs if and when law enforcement officers "cause" an individual to commit a crime that the individual did not contemplate, was not predisposed to commit, and presumably would not have committed except for the enticement, participation, and collusive efforts of the police. Entrapment is a defense recognized in all states except Tennessee, accepted by most courts, and legislatively codified in a few states, such as Illinois.[72] In a series of cases between 1932 and 1976, the Supreme Court has consistently isolated the "predisposition" of the defendant to violate the law in deciding entrapment defense cases (see Close-up 3.1). The defendant's mental state, inclination, or criminal intent to commit the offense, regardless of the police role, is the critical legal element on which the entrapment defense hinges. In 1958, in *Sherman* v. *United States,* Chief Justice Earl Warren announced the then prevailing standard, which revolved around the accused's state of mind and criminal intent (*mens*

Close-up 3.1 SUPREME COURT DECISIONS ON ENTRAPMENT

In 1932, in *Sorrells* v. *United States,* the Supreme Court emphasized that it was the duty of a police officer to prevent crimes rather than to instigate them.[a] The case involved an undercover prohibition agent who induced the defendant to sell him a jug of moonshine. Following the defendant's repeated refusals to do so, the agent concocted stories about their having served in the same division during World War I. No evidence was presented at trial to suggest that the defendant was "predisposed" to commit the offense.

In 1958, in *Sherman* v. *United States,* the government used an informant to induce a known addict to secure heroin for him.[b] However, there was no evidence that the defendant was predisposed to make the sale to the informant, and the circumstances of the case were considered "shocking" by the Court. Accordingly, Sherman's conviction was reversed. In *Sherman* the Supreme Court drew the elusive line "between the trap for the unwary innocent and the trap for the wary criminal."

In 1973, in *United States* v. *Russell,* a federal narcotics agent infiltrated a laboratory suspected of manufacturing "speed" by offering to supply the defendant with a component used in its production.[c] The Court ruled that the entrapment defense is not a constitutionally protected right, that the law enforcement conduct involved was not shocking or unfair, and that a predisposition to commit crime invalidates the defense of entrapment.

In 1976, in *Hampton* v. *United States,* the Supreme Court held that it was constitutional to convict an individual for selling drugs even though undercover government agents or informants supplied the seller with the drugs and the purchasers were narcotics agents.[d] Containing two majority opinions, the *Hampton* decision was a complex one whose meaning provoked debate among legal scholars.[e] One reason for the Supreme Court's reluctance to draw hard lines in entrapment cases has been the "lack of a clear-cut handle in the Constitution"—as there is in the Fourth Amendment's ban on unreasonable searches and seizures.[f] The Court has often noted that the Constitution does not protect one individual from misplaced trust in another.

[a] *Sorrells* v. *United States,* 287 U.S. 435 (1932).
[b] *Sherman* v. *United States,* 356 U.S. 369 (1958).
[c] *United States* v. *Russell,* 93 S.Ct. 1637 (1973).
[d] *Hampton* v. *United States,* 425 U.S. 484 (1976).
[e] J. Alexander Tanford, "Entrapment: Guidelines for Counsel and the Courts," *C.L.B.* (January–Febrary 1977): 5–29; *Sunday New York Times,* July 18, 1976, section 4, p. 7.
[f] *New York Times,* April 24, 1975, p. 22.

rea): Had the police prepared a trap for the "unwary innocent" or for the "wary criminal"? If it can be proven that the person who violated the alcoholic, drug, or sex laws involved was not "predisposed" to break the law and did so because of police instigation, then dismissal or acquittal should follow.

The two most recent entrapment decisions by the Burger court, *United States* v. *Russell* and *Hampton* v. *United States,* have strengthened the hand of law enforcement by putting a lid on the entrapment defense. Both decisions involved federal law enforcement agents working undercover on narcotics cases. In *Russell,* the Court noted that "the gathering of evidence of past unlawful conduct frequently proves to be an all but impossible task" and that infiltrating drug rings was not only a recognized and permissible means of investigation but one of the only practical ways to detect drug-related offenses. In its *Hampton* decision, the Court in effect rejected the "police conduct" test and instead focused exclusively on the defendant's "predisposition" to commit the crime in question. Regardless of the inducement or involvement of government agents in the criminal act, if predisposition exists the *Hampton* decision makes it practically impossible for the defendant to successfully raise the entrapment defense. Thus the Court broadened the permissible extent of police participation in setting up an illegal act for the purpose of making an arrest or securing conviction.

Increasingly, the police are turning to undercover methods to control large-scale professional theft by posing as fences, or purchasers of stolen goods. One of the most successful and highly publicized such undertakings was the Sting, an undercover fencing operation in Washington, D.C., run by men from the Metropolitan Police Force, an FBI agent, and a Treasury man. All masqueraded as members of the "New York mafia." For five months beginning in October 1975, the police used a warehouse as a site for the purchase of $2.4 million in stolen merchandise (for $67,000). To show their appreciation to their patrons, the stingpolice threw a party for the sellers of stolen goods, which ended in a mass arrest. Although many of the 180 arrested customers invoked the entrapment defense, it resulted in freeing just one defendant.[73] The lone defendant was released because the circumstances of the case clearly showed that he was not predisposed to have committed the crime involved and that the police had gone too far in inducing him to do so. In the Return of the Sting operation four months later, the Washington police collared 150 more customers. The Sting model has since been successfully adopted in cities throughout the country.[74]

The Sting

Abscam

Abscam (Arab scam) was an elaborate FBI undercover investigation in which, over a two-year period ending in February 1980, federal agents posing as Arab sheiks and their American representatives implicated several congressmen in corruption, bribery, and illegal conflict of interest. In exchange for large sums of money offered to the legislators, they alleg-

ator Harrison Williams, enter-
Federal Court for his Abscam
l, was convicted of bribery and
spiracy, which led to efforts to
t him from the Senate

edly agreed to use their positions to do various favors for the Arab businessmen, such as obtaining a casino permit in Atlantic City (N.J.) and influencing government contracts in which the sheiks had an interest.[75] Although all of the congressmen were convicted, the issue of entrapment applied to white-collar crime and the legality of the Abscam tactics themselves is almost certain to reach the Supreme Court on appeal. Whether the FBI simply provided already corrupt (predisposed) legislators the opportunity for crime or improperly lured the unwary innocent into crime depends, in part, on whether the politicians were selected at random for investigation rather than—as the FBI contends*—on the basis of reasonable suspicion or probable cause.[76]

* The FBI claimed that they were led to the politicians by middlemen involved in the government's investigation of stolen paintings and securities in New York, which was the origin of Abscam. Nonetheless, the "new" rules on FBI undercover investigations issued in January 1981 allow the Director of the agency to authorize bribery payments even when there is no indication that the subject had previously engaged in illegal conduct.

In the first major statement by the federal judiciary on the subject, U.S. District Judge John P. Fullam overturned the Abscam conviction of two Philadelphia councilmen on the grounds of both entrapment and governmental overreaching. Fullam noted that the state had not offered sufficient proof of predisposition, the subjective test and narrow view of the entrapment doctrine consistently endorsed by the Supreme Court. At the same time, and in what may become the appellate focal point of the opinion, Fullam ruled that regardless of the defendants' predisposition, the government had violated their constitutional rights to due process by resorting to such extreme tactics as Abscam to ensnare them: "It is neither necessary nor appropriate to the task of ferreting out crime for the undercover agents to initiate bribe offers, provide extremely generous financial inducements, and add further incentives amounting to an appeal to civic duty."[77] Representing a de facto exclusionary rule* applied to Abscam investigative methods, this position is based upon the objective police test† exception to the predisposition standard, which was originally enunciated in 1973 by Justice William H. Rehnquist.[78]

> Some day [we may] be presented with a situation in which the conduct of law enforcement agents is so outrageous that due process principles would absolutely bar the government from invoking judicial process to obtain a conviction.

Should Judge Fullam's due process objections to undercover practices be upheld on appeal, it could seriously jeopardize all Abscam cases, thereby insulating corrupt elected officials from detection and conviction. Abscam was, after all, hardly the typical sting operation. And the Supreme Court has never decided a case dealing with entrapment issues in which contraband wasn't involved. For these and other reasons, Abscam should provide the Supreme Court with a unique opportunity to clarify the murky and elusive parameters of the entrapment defense.

Computer systems and 911 calls

The centerpiece of crime control technology is the computer and its related data processing systems. Computer technology has been utilized in patrol car and police deployment, for compiling and transmitting information on criminal suspects, and as the backbone of the nationwide 911 emergency police dial system.[79] The Kansas City Police Department's Automated Law Enforcement Response Team (ALERT) is one of the largest and most advanced computerized intelligence-gathering systems in the country. It became operational in 1968, the same year that Congress passed the Safe Streets Act. The ALERT system provides instantaneous information retrieval on outstanding arrest warrants, stolen cars, danger-

* The exclusionary rule is discussed in Chapter 6.

† The objective test of entrapment focuses on the conduct of the government agents (rather than the defendant's predisposition) and would dismiss cases where such actions were likely to cause a person of reasonably firm moral fortitude to succumb to crime.

e Sting, an undercover police
ncing operation in Washington,
C., resulted in 180 arrests in 1976

ous persons who pose a threat to police safety, conviction records, and so on. The LEAA made money available to other cities to establish their own local computer data banks, and 17 had done so by mid-1973.[80]

Emergency access to police services is available in over 200 cities by dialing 911.[81] Incoming emergency calls are taken by operators who solicit details about the incident and punch the data into a computer terminal. In turn, the computer transmits the information to a police radio dispatcher who determines the call's priority in relation to others and to available patrol resources, and dispatches the cop on the beat to respond. The computerized 911 system is geared to reduce police response time in emergency situations and to assure the most efficient and effective use of limited resources.* In theory, a police car should arrive at the scene of the reported emergency two minutes after a 911 dispatcher has acted. But the volume of 911 calls in some cities interferes with that goal, as does the misuse of the system by citizens who consider getting their cats down from trees a police emergency and the number of other invalid complaints received on the 911 hotline.[82]

* Response time is the time it takes for a radio car to reach the scene of a reported crime or emergency.

VICTIMLESS CRIME AND DECRIMINALIZATION

The relationship of "overenforcement" of the law to crime control and the criminal justice system revolves around the issue of *victimless crime.* Victimless crime by definition causes no direct harm, injury, loss, or threat to anyone; there is no "victim" in the ordinary sense, as there is in index offenses. In victimless crime the individual victim and the offender are one and the same, since the former is a willing participant in the illegal conduct. More than half of the persons arrested by the police have not laid an unwanted hand on anyone or stolen anything. Should victimless crime be treated the same as or different from other offenses? Should persons who violate victimless crime laws be subject to arrest and prison penalties? The answers depend upon the particular victimless crime in question, the relevant pros and cons, and one's personal political ideology concerning crime, the criminal justice system, and the criminal sanction.

Forms of decriminalization

Some people advocate that specified victimless crime laws be repealed, thereby legalizing the conduct. More practically, and as an interim step in that direction, they have proposed that victimless crime be *decriminalized.* Decriminalization involves (1) providing greatly reduced criminal penalties for victimless crime, (2) abolishing long prison terms for them, (3) punishing victimless crime with fines whenever possible, and (4) legalizing some forms of victimless "crime" while (5) continuing to prohibit other, related forms in the same victimless crime category. For example, stringent marijuana laws are said to be decriminalized if they are changed to provide for (1 and 2) a 30-day jail term for simple possession of more than 1 ounce, (3) a $5 fine for possessing less than 1 ounce in a public place, (4) no punishment whatever for puffing a joint in private, and (5) prison terms for selling any amount of marijuana. Thus decriminalization does not completely repeal the laws regulating victimless crime; that is, it does not legalize the conduct. Instead, decriminalization provides substantial moderation in the penalties attached to the violations.

Those who favor substantial decriminalization of victimless crimes take the position that the conduct behind the label is "none of the law's business."[83] Others argue that there is no such thing as a truly victimless crime. In fact, the umbrella concept of victimless crime covers and conceals a complex continuum of illegal acts and activities having varying degrees of perceived victimlessness. Some of the behavior considered victimless crime may be closer to being real crime—with victims. Some may be sins that do not merit legal immunity.[84] Other victimless crime conduct may be perfectly normal (if not healthy) behavior that is genuinely none of the state's business. In part, the degree of social approval granted specified victimless crimes determines whether the victimless crime label is warranted and the prospects for decriminalization and eventual legalization of the conduct.

Rationale for decriminalization

The principal factors sparking and sustaining the trend toward decriminalization are the economics of crime control and the high cost of operating the underfinanced criminal justice system. It is maintained that the resources spent on detecting, arresting, and prosecuting offenders should be restricted to combating serious crimes with their victims and their perpetrators; that these resources should not be used for enforcing questionable popular notions of morality or for protecting victimless crime violators from themselves. In addition to the arguments for efficiency, numerous other factors have contributed to the momentum of the movement for decriminalization.

1. There is extensive participation by the general public, especially the suburban middle class, in certain forms of victimless crime.
2. Attempts to deter victimless crime have not been very successful.[85]
3. The idea of decriminalizing certain offenses has become respectable. It is supported by many prominent political figures, professional groups, both crime commissions, and private citizens. Consequently, it has become politically unpopular to enforce these laws across the board and fiscally impossible to prosecute all the violators.
4. Law enforcement and prosecution of victimless crime is highly selective and discriminatory against certain groups. And it is practically impossible to design consistent, useful policy guidelines for enforcing victimless crime laws.[86]
5. The offenders' problems associated with victimless crime are not ameliorated by arrest, prosecution, and the imposition of criminal penalties.
6. Enforcement action against victimless crime violators may encourage the commission of more serious crime. For example, addicts may commit burglary or robbery to support their habits because the illegality of drug use makes the cost of drugs so high.
7. Victimless crime laws are an invitation to police corruption, harrassment, and abuse of discretion.[87]
8. Among the states, the amount of unwarranted variation in penalties for the same victimless crimes is especially pronounced.
9. Where there are convictions, the courts are reluctant to impose sentences geared to deterrence. And the criminal justice machinery has virtually no effective treatment resources for victimless crime violators.
10. The negative effects of making too many arrests for victimless crime are evident throughout the criminal justice system in overcrowded correctional institutions, delays before arraignment, unmanageable probation and parole caseloads, revolving-door justice, and conflict between criminal justice agencies over policies and priorities governing victimless crime laws.[88]
11. The legal status of victimless crime statutes and their selective enforcement raise gnawing constitutional questions. How can all citi-

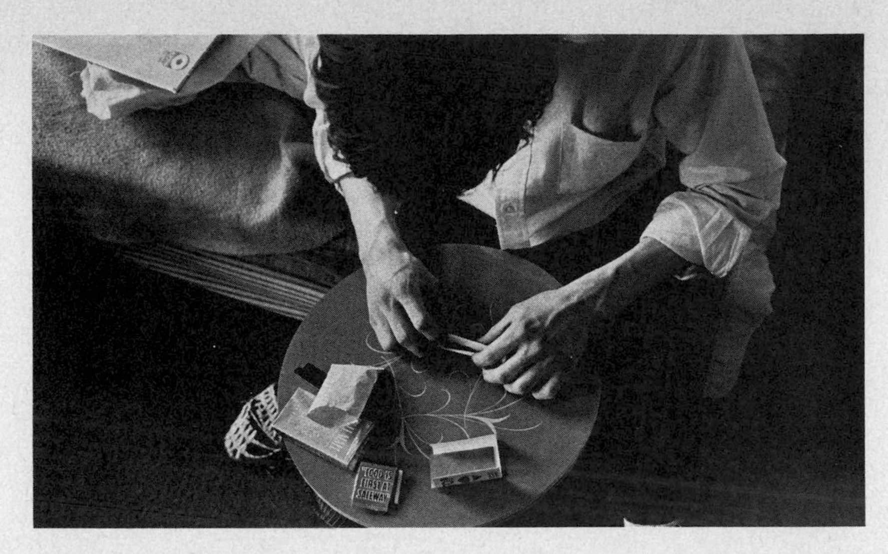

By 1977 eight states had decriminalized the possession of small amounts of marijuana

zens be guaranteed equal protection of the law, for example, if female prostitutes are arrested and their male clients are not?[89]

So far, efforts to decriminalize victimless crime have focused on marijuana use, drunkenness, gambling, and prostitution. Individually and collectively, these offenses constitute the lion's share of the victimless crime that drains the resources of law enforcement and overloads the entire criminal justice system.

SUMMARY

The police role revolves around law enforcement and order maintenance functions and the use of discretion in the selective enforcement of the law. The latter raises the spectre of police prejudice and authoritarianism, which are much more a product of the subculture of policework itself—the working personality of the police—than of the social background and personal traits of police recruits. Even then, the factors that influence the decision to arrest are the offense committed, the visibility of the decision itself, and the offender's social class and demeanor rather than racial discrimination per se. Nonetheless, for a variety of reasons police discretion needs to be more adequately controlled through standards, policies, and guidelines. The question of whether the police deter crime through standard crime control methods was discussed in light of social science research, particularly the Kansas City Experiment study of the impact of general preventive patrol. Special tactics and innovative approaches that appear to be particularly effective in crime control include SWAT, police decoys, the police posing as fences of stolen property, and the use of computer systems. In recognition of the unique problems involved in enforcing drug laws, the Supreme Court has made it much more difficult for offenders to avoid conviction by raising the defense of police entrapment. The discussion of the police role, selective enforcement of the law, discretion, and deterrence was completed with a consideration of victimless crime and decriminalization.

DISCUSSION QUESTIONS

1. What is the relationship between the law enforcement and order maintenance roles of the police?
2. What could or should be done to resolve the problems created by the police wearing too many hats?
3. What is the working personality of the police?
4. How can police discretion be most effectively controlled?
5. What factors in deciding to arrest illustrate discretion as well as the abuse of discretion?
6. What implications do the results of the Kansas City Experiment have for the way police departments should be operated?
7. Police pose as university students in order to become friendly with a group of student war resisters and to collect evidence of their illegal conduct. Is this a case of police entrapment? Why?

HESS

Chapter 4

THE POLICE AND THE COMMUNITY

"Police Brutality"

The Reiss study of police-citizen encounters / Philadelphia police brutality suit

Deadly Force

The fleeing felon rule / Deadly force and racial discrimination

Close-up 4.1: The Fyfe Study of Deadly Force

Controlling deadly force / Deadly force restrictions and police safety

Civilian Review Boards

Internal review of complaints / Philadelphia's Police Advisory Board / New York's Civilian Complaint Review Board / Police opposition to the CCRB

Suing the Police

Departmental efforts to control police misconduct / Section 1983, Civil Rights Act of 1871 / Police misconduct litigation / The good faith defense / The demise of sovereign immunity

Police-Community Relations

Origins of police-community relations / The police-community relations concept / Goals of police-community relations / Community Service Officers

Domestic Crisis Intervention

Incidence of domestic disturbances / Dangers in domestic intervention / The system's "do nothing" policy

Close-up 4.2: Thomas Promised

Police responsibility for handling domestic disputes / New

York's Family Crisis Intervention Unit / Effects of the FCIU
Community Crime Prevention
Neighborhood Crime Watches
National Neighborhood Watch Program
Citizen Patrols

Close-up 4.3: The Guardian Angels

Citizens as Police Auxiliaries
Citizens in uniform
Technology, Private Security Personnel, and Students
Target hardening and private police / Crime in the schools
Citizen Court Watchers
Policing the courts
Summary

"POLICE BRUTALITY"

Police misconduct takes many forms. Few of them are more disturbing than the use of deadly force (discussed in the next section) and physical brutality. Physical brutality is the excessive or unreasonable use of force in dealing with citizens, suspects, and offenders. Basically, the police may use whatever means and amount of force is reasonable in effecting an arrest, in self-defense, in the face of resistance, and in apprehending a fleeing felon. Using more force than is necessary to achieve these ends or using force for any other purpose* is automatically excessive or unreasonable force, is therefore illegal, and constitutes *police brutality.*

The Reiss study of police-citizen encounters

One major source of objective data about "police brutality" is a study of police-citizen encounters conducted by Albert Reiss. For seven weeks during the summer of 1966, 36 observers (college students with backgrounds in law, police administration, and social science) rode in patrol cars assigned to high-crime areas in Boston, Chicago, and Washington, D.C. During this time, the observers recorded and reported the outcomes of 5,360 "mobilizations" of the police. These were instances of police officers' going into action by responding to citizen phone calls to the department, being contacted in the field by citizens, or acting on their own initiative through on-sight observation.[1] The true purpose of the study,

* For example: in retaliation, to coerce respect, for verbal defiance of authority, in preferring to kill rather than capture.

concealed from the patrol officers involved, was to examine the quality, the determinants, and the outcome of police-citizen encounters.

Reiss found that police "verbal abuse" toward citizens was far more common than the use of excessive force. Police behavior was observed to be "uncivil" toward 13 percent of all citizens contacted. Thus the standard police complaint against the public—"They don't show me any respect"—is also a common complaint made by many citizens against the police. In contrast, during the seven-week period the observers found "only" 37 cases in which the police used force improperly.* Findings similar to these emerged from the questioning of citizens in 15 cities about police misconduct for the National Advisory Commission on Civil Disorders. In one sense, then, police uncivility (verbal disrespect) rather than police brutality (physical abuse) is the salient issue in the public's criticism of the police.

Although three-fourths of the white police officers in the Reiss study were observed to make prejudicial statements about blacks, they did not actually treat blacks any more uncivilly than they treated white citizens. Nor was there any evidence of racial discrimination against blacks in cases where the police unnecessarily assaulted citizens.[2] Reasons for the unnecessary use of force by the police were found in the citizens' social class and especially in whether offenders taken into custody deferred to or defied the authority of the police: about half of the cases of unnecessary force involved open defiance of police authority.[3] The police are more likely to use excessive force against suspects and citizens when they consider it necessary to clarify "who's in charge" and when harassing drunks, homosexuals, and narcotics users.[4] Significantly, the police code of silence is nowhere more vividly demonstrated than in police brutality situations. In more than half of the instances of excessive force, officers who were present but not party to the violence did not restrain or report their fellow officers.[5]

Philadelphia police brutality suit

In recent years the federal Justice Department has been increasingly active in taking legal action against police brutality in cities throughout the country, for example, in Mobile, Memphis, and Houston.[6] But nowhere has their drive against brutality been as ambitious and bold as in Philadelphia. Persistent charges of rampant police brutality in the City of Brotherly Love, a record number of annual complaints of police abuse (over 1,000), and television coverage of a confrontation between the Philadelphia police and a black radical group showing officers kicking protesters focused federal attention on the police situation in Philadelphia.

In August 1979, after an eight-month investigation, the Justice Department filed an unprecedented civil rights suit charging Mayor Frank Rizzo

* Reiss used a very rigorous definition of "improper or unnecessary" force that was the legal equivalent of "excessive or unreasonable" force.

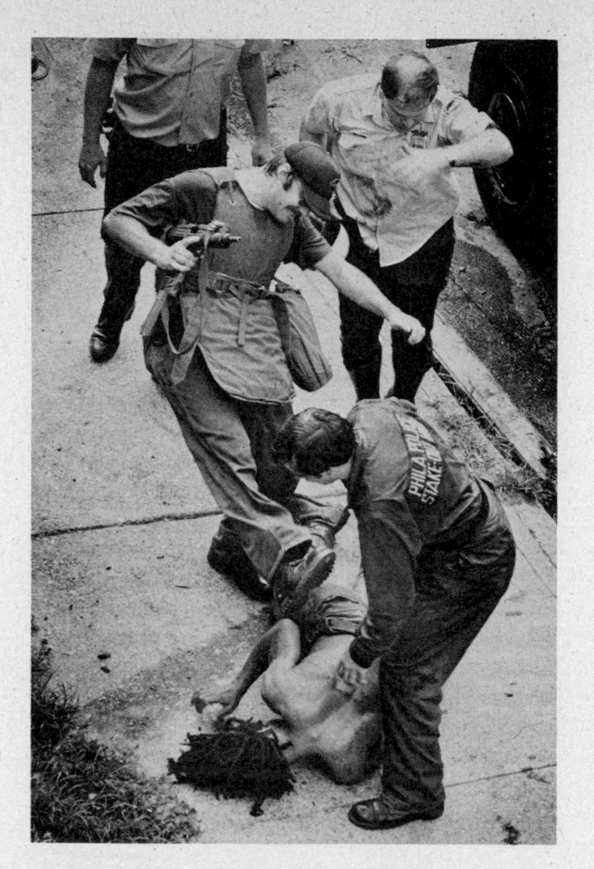

In an unprecedented case, the Justice Department filed a suit charging the entire Philadelphia Police Department with police brutality

and the city's entire 8,000-officer Police Department with pervasive and systematic police brutality—conduct which purportedly violated the 1964 Civil Rights Act, federal laws, and the Constitution. It was the first time that the federal government had charged an entire police force with indiscriminate brutality, rather than proceeding against specific officers. "The conditions we're addressing seem institutionalized, and putting away individual officers doesn't solve the problem."[7]

The suit asserted that the Philadelphia Police Department follows "procedures which result in widespread, arbitrary, and unreasonable physical abuse or abuse which shocks the conscience." In general, the government described a pattern of uncontrolled police violence in which excessive force against suspects, prisoners and citizens were routinely encouraged and concealed. In particular, the department was accused of shooting nonviolent and unarmed suspects who could be apprehended without deadly force; beating handcuffed prisoners; stopping pedestrians and motorists without probable cause and physically abusing those who protested; failing to investigate complaints of police brutality and pressuring citizens to withdraw their complaints; conducting illegal searches; and "inflicting disproportionate abuse upon black persons and persons of Hispanic origin."[8]

The suit asked the court to issue an order prohibiting the police from continuing to engage in these practices and to cut off all federal funds from Philadelphia until the necessary reforms were made. In October 1979, a federal district court dismissed the case on the jurisdictional grounds that the government lacked the authority to bring such an all-encompassing action, a decision that was upheld on appeal.[9] Nonetheless, most of the changes sought by the Justice Department have been instituted by Philadelphia's new mayor and new Police Commissioner.[10]

In practical terms, the outcome of the Justice Department's suit was similar to the million-dollar suit filed earlier by Alvestus Goode, a black service station owner who was allegedly beaten by several Philadelphia officers when he asked one of them to move the squad car blocking his station's driveway. After the incident, Goode received almost three hours of treatment in a hospital emergency room. The police charged Goode with assault and resisting arrest, charges that were later dropped.[11] In the Goode case, a federal district court ordered the Philadelphia Police Department to draft a comprehensive plan for handling citizen complaints against the police, in accordance with guidelines supplied by the court. But on appeal the Supreme Court reversed the decision, severely rebuking the lower court for "an unwarranted intrusion by the federal judiciary into the discretionary authority" of city and police officials performing their lawful duties.[12]

DEADLY FORCE

From the standpoint of the community, the police department, and the law, the police use of deadly force is a matter of the utmost concern and poses one of the greatest obstacles to police-community relations. Deadly force encompasses any police action which creates a high risk of death or serious injury, whether or not the incident actually results in death or injury.[13] Each year about 600 civilians are slain by police—6 times the annual number of police killed by suspects—and the number of civilians killed by police intervention has increased in recent years.[14]

The fleeing felon rule

According to common law, as a last resort the police could use deadly force to stop an escaping ("fleeing") felon.* Dating back to fifteenth-century England, the common law rule was derived from a time when all

* Such killings by police are justifiable or excusable homicide.[15]

Table 4.1 Types of State Laws on Deadly Force[a]

Deadly Force Provision	Number of Jurisdictions
1. *Common Law.* This, the least restrictive policy, authorizes the use of deadly force to arrest any felony suspect.	24
2. *Forcible Felony Rule.* The state specifies the kinds of felonies in which deadly force may be employed; or they provide that only "forcible felonies" justify the use of deadly force.	7
3. *Model Penal Code.* Ignoring the legal classification of the crime, the MPC firearms policies are based on the need to apprehend suspects, concern for the safety of the arresting officer, and the value of human life. Representing the most restrictive policy, the MPC does not permit police to use deadly force in felony arrests unless the force employed "creates no substantial risk of injury to innocent persons" and the officer believed that (a) the crime involved the use or threatened use of deadly force; or (b) there was a substantial risk the offender would cause serious bodily harm if apprehension is delayed.[b]	7
4. *No statutes limiting officer's use of deadly force.*	12

[a] *Source:* National Consultation on Safety and Force, *An Opportunity for Police-Minority Community Cooperation, Summary Report* (Washington, D.C.: Government Printing Office, 1980), p. v.
[b] Model Penal Code, section 3.07, 1962 draft.

felonies* were punishable by death so that "the killing of a felon resulted in no greater consequences than those authorized for the punishment of the offense."[17] In the United States, all felonies were punishable by death until 1800. As of 1976, half of the states followed the common law fleeing felon doctrine, permitting police to shoot to kill any felony suspect who cannot otherwise be captured (see Table 4.1). Virtually all of the states permit police officers to use whatever force is necessary, just short of killing, to arrest resisting felons and misdemeanants and in self-defense. Too few states and police departments have clearly operationalized, written policies, or any guidelines concerning the police use of force.[18]

Pursuant to the law of deadly force, police officers would be justified in shooting a person resisting arrest, an interfering bystander who attacked them with a weapon, or anyone who otherwise attempted to inflict great bodily harm or imperiled the officer's life. However, many courts have ruled that the slain person must have actually possessed or had immediate access to a weapon capable of causing great bodily harm. And the officer must generally believe that the use of deadly force was necessary to avert the danger of serious injury. For example, it would not be reasonable to immediately resort to deadly force where a subject's resistance

* The common law felonies included murder, rape, manslaughter, robbery, sodomy, mayhem, burglary, arson, escape from prison, and larceny.[16]

to arrest did not seriously jeopardize the officer's safety. Under these conditions, the police should employ whatever amount of greater force is reasonable to overcome the resistance to arrest or to protect themselves.

When applied to contemporary American criminal statutes, the fleeing felon rationale is weakened because many states have abolished capital punishment, and have added many relatively innocuous felonies which were never capital offenses. It is further weakened because of the de facto relinquishment of the death penalty as a punishment for crime. In effect, the fleeing felon rule subjects suspected offenders to far more severe penalties before adjudication than they would undoubtedly receive if convicted. These considerations have led some states, police departments, the President's Crime Commission, and the Model Penal Code to recommend confining the use of deadly force by police officers.[19] They recommend restricting deadly force to situations involving "serious, dangerous, forcible, or capital" crimes,[20] instances where a fleeing felon who cannot otherwise be captured presents a serious danger to others, in self-defense or to overcome resistance only if "the officer believes his life or the life of another is in imminent danger."[21] Even if authorized by statute, if the killing of a fleeing felon is unreasonable on the merits of the case, the courts may hold the officer civilly or criminally liable, or both. In practice, the legality of the use of deadly force depends upon whether the totality of the circumstances makes the officer's act reasonable or unreasonable. Even an officer who kills a nonresisting fleeing misdemeanant would not necessarily be at fault if the facts established that the officer reasonably, though erroneously, believed the escaping offender was a felon.[22]

Deadly force and racial discrimination

Virtually every study on the subject has revealed that blacks are disproportionately the victims of police shootings and killings. In a seminal investigation, Robin found that 87 percent of the civilians killed by Philadelphia police from 1950 to 1960 were black; blacks constituted only 22 percent of the city's population.[23] The Police Foundation study of police shootings in seven cities in 1973 and 1974 disclosed a similarly high proportion of black victims.[24] And of 584 suspects shot at by Los Angeles police between 1974 and 1978, 55 percent were black compared with a black city population of only 18 percent.[25] Nationwide, between 1960 and 1968, the police killed 1188 black males compared with 1253 white males, when the population was only 10 percent black.[26]

There are two different schools of thought concerning such racial disproportionality.[27] On the one hand, critics of the police attribute high rates of deadly force against minorities to police discrimination in one form or another, or variations thereof: To racism, genocide, the "rotten apple" theory (a few "trigger-happy" cops), differential enforcement of the law, violence-prone personality types being attracted to the occupation, and to the conviction that "police have one trigger finger for whites and another for blacks."[28] Basically, proponents of this school of thought contend that racial disproportionality is legally and morally indefensible, that police misconduct is a major factor accounting for the phenomenon, and that excessive police violence against minorities is traceable to prejudice and related police stereotypes that may be reinforced and perpetuated by the police subculture.

By contrast, the alternative school of thought relates deadly force racial disproportionality to overrepresentation of minorities in homicide arrests, arrests for serious and violent crimes,[29] and to community characteristics that reflect bona fide police safety concerns and police response to stress, threats, and danger—rather than to police prejudice and police pathology.[30] According to this view, racial disproportionality enters the deadly force picture because minority group members actually commit more violent crime than do whites, thereby precipitating more incidents leading to police discharge of weapons. If this is indeed the case, then in resorting to deadly force "the police officer is reacting to the community as he perceives it, a perception which is usually correct."[31]

A critical assumption behind this position is that official crime statistics, such as arrest rates, are valid measures of participation in crime. Police detractors, though, maintain that disproportionate minority arrest rates result from differential police deployment in minority areas and selective enforcement of the law *because* of police prejudice. Most commentators, however, disagree with these assertions. And victim survey results also confirm the disproportionate involvement of minorities in violent crime and indicate that "differential policing" of minorities is probably a responsible attempt to provide adequate police protection in areas where it is needed most.[32] Hayden's recent study of information used by police in making deadly force decisions also casts doubt on the police discrimination theory, disclosing instead the relevance of situational factors—and that officers who previously used deadly force were apparently no different from those who hadn't.[33] Perhaps the best available data bearing on the racial element in deadly force comes from a study conducted by Dr. James J. Fyfe, discussed in Close-up 4.1.

On balance, it appears that present evidence does not support the hypothesis that racial disproportionality in police shootings is the result of systematic police hostility toward blacks. Nonetheless, the preceding discussion of the role of police discrimination in deadly force is not the final word on the matter. Deadly force research is still scanty, some of the findings are contradictory, and any conclusions must be regarded as tentative. A comprehensive $800,000 study funded by the National Institute of Justice should be completed by the end of 1982.

Another problem at the heart of the public controversy surrounding deadly force is the fleeing felon rule permitting officers to kill escaping property offenders and, to a lesser degree, to kill other felons who pose no immediate threat to the victim's or officer's life or imminent danger to the community. (This issue is related to that of racial discrimination,

Close-up 4.1 THE FYFE STUDY OF DEADLY FORCE

Based on nearly 3,000 police shooting incidents in New York City from January 1971 to December 1975, Fyfe examined the relationship between police shootings and levels of violent crime in 20 police command zones ("neighborhoods"). His analysis revealed a significant correlation between a neighborhood's violent crime arrest rate and the frequency of police shootings. In particular, there was a very high correlation (+.78) between the overall homicide rate of an area and the rate of police shootings, a correlation which was even more pronounced (+.89) when the analysis was restricted to on-duty uniformed officers.

However, even in areas characterized by high violent crime rates (as black neighborhoods are), there is still the possibility that police use of deadly force might be racially motivated. For example, white officers assigned to high-crime black neighborhoods might use the prevailing high violent crime rates as a pretext for "shooting first and asking questions later." Fyfe investigated this possibility by analyzing the data by the race of the victim *and* the race of the officer. The result: black as well as Hispanic officers were each about twice as likely to kill civilians of their own race than white officers were.

Finally, Fyfe tabulated the police shootings according to the area of the city the officer was assigned to. Special attention was paid to officers on duty in the most hazardous precincts, where the highest incidence of police shootings was to be expected. Once again, there was no evidence of discriminatory employment of deadly force; the rate at which black, Hispanic, and white officers assigned to the most dangerous areas shot at civilians was virtually identical.[b]

[a] James J. Fyfe, "Geographic Correlates of Police Shootings: A Microanalysis," *Journal of Research in Crime and Delinquency,* January 1980, pp. 108–109.
[b] Fyfe, "Officer Race and Police Shooting," paper presented for the annual meeting of the American Society of Criminology, November 1979, cited in James Q. Wilson, "Police Use of Deadly Force," *FBI Law Enforcement Bulletin,* August 1980, pp. 18–19.

since it is in the fleeing felon context that the police decision to resort to or refrain from using deadly force is most discretionary.) If the threat of death or serious injury is used as the criterion for employing deadly force, than a sizeable proportion of all police killings are unjustified and unnecessary.[34]

Racial disturbances following questionable, bizarre or patently irresponsible police killings—often involving a fleeing unarmed minority

Using a video simulator in training, Seattle police are confronted with hypothetical deadly force situations and then given a split second to decide whether to shoot

group property offender or a juvenile—and growing dissatisfaction with the fleeing felon rule as a historical anachronism are the main reasons that police departments have begun to adopt stricter policies concerning deadly force. There is, fortunately, a clear trend within police departments to hold officers more accountable for employing deadly force on fleeing felons and suspects in custody.[35] Most of the new departmental firearms policies restrict deadly force to apprehending felons whom the police reasonably believe have committed violent crimes,[36] thereby overcoming the most common criticism of the common law fleeing felon doctrine.

Controlling deadly force

Some departments, however, have imposed more stringent controls on deadly force. The new policy in Prince Georges County, Maryland, prohibits deadly force unless the officer "knows" (rather than "suspects" or "reasonably believes") that the alleged felon might cause further injury or death unless apprehended. It also prohibits the firing of warning shots, as well as firing at or from moving vehicles,[37] provisions that are often incorporated into revised departmental firearms guidelines.[38] The 1979 Memphis Police Department regulations limit deadly force to stopping dangerous felonies in progress, to apprehending a suspect fleeing from a dangerous felony the officer has witnessed or "knows" was committed by the suspect, and prohibits deadly force against juveniles except in self-defense.[39] The New York City Police Department's 1972 guidelines narrowed officer shooting discretion considerably, emphasizing the "value of life" and that the police revolver is a weapon "for personal protection against persons feloniously attacking an officer or others at close range."[40] In 1977, the Los Angeles Police Department revised its liberal fleeing felon policy to confine deadly force only "to apprehending a fleeing felon for a crime involving serious bodily injury or use of deadly force where there is substantial risk that the person whose arrest is sought will cause death or serious bodily injury to others if apprehension is delayed."[41] The Philadelphia Police Department's 1980 directive forbids the use of firearms unless an officer is in serious danger or knows that a suspect has a deadly weapon or has committed a forcible felony.[42]

Going even further than the Model Penal Code proposal, the most restrictive firearms policy would limit deadly force to situations involving the defense of life, the rule followed by the Federal Bureau of Investigation.[43] Such defense-of-life-only policies have been adopted in Wayne County (Mich.),[44] the Atlanta Police Department in 1976,[45] the Houston Police Department in 1977,[46] and the San Jose Police Department in 1975. The San Jose directive stated that firearms are never to be used "solely for the purpose of apprehension." The directive was subsequently withdrawn by the police chief, however, when the police union asked the court to enjoin enforcing the firearms order. The union contended that the new policy involved a condition of employment on which they had not been consulted and that it would subject the police to greater danger from armed and dangerous criminals.[47]

Deadly force restrictions and police safety

The available evidence on the impact of departmental restrictions on deadly force indicates that such policies are remarkably effective in reducing police shootings and do not jeopardize police safety in the process. The best data on this point come from the Fyfe study in New York City, discussed above in another context. Prior to the department's new, more restrictive directive on deadly force, 18.4 officers fired their guns each week, a figure which dropped to 12.9 (a 30 percent decrease) after the new policy went into effect; and this occurred during a period when reported homicides and arrests for violent felonies were on the increase. Particularly striking and significant was the finding that shootings to prevent or stop crimes—which are usually fleeing felon cases—decreased by 75 percent under the new directive.[48] At the same time, the new directive had relatively little impact on police shootings in defense of life, regarded as the most justifiable incidents of deadly force. In 1971, the year before the new policy, New York City police killed 93 civilians. Only 28 were killed in 1979, a 70 percent reduction.[49] "The figures present rather compelling evidence that civilian injuries and deaths can be reduced if police administrators let their field personnel 'know what they want.'"[50]

Furthermore, there was no indication that the department's more restrictive deadly force guidelines made the officer's job more dangerous. On the contrary, the number of officer injuries and deaths in the line of duty actually *decreased* markedly after the new shooting policy was established: before the guidelines, 4.4 officers a week were seriously injured in violent confrontations compared to only 2.5 a week after the more restrictive policy; and one officer was killed in the line of duty every five weeks before the new directive, compared to every ten weeks afterwards.[51] In Los Angeles the number of civilians killed by police dropped by almost 50 percent after a new shooting policy took effect in late 1977.[52] And Atlanta's defense-of-life-only firearms policy resulted in a two-thirds reduction in the number of civilians killed or wounded with no appreciable effect on police safety.[53]

CIVILIAN REVIEW BOARDS

Civilian review boards were civilian-dominated committees, independent of the regular police bureaucracy, that were established in 1958–1966 for the sole purpose of facilitating, investigating, and hearing complaints from citizens against police officers. All power to discipline offending officers, however, remained within the province of the police department. In practice, civilian review boards concentrated upon or were restricted to accepting four types of complaints: (1) brutality, the unnecessary or excessive use of force; (2) abusive language or discourtesy; (3) abuses of authority, such as depriving suspects of their civil rights; and (4) discrimination, by deed or word, on the basis of race, religion, creed, or national origin.

Efforts to establish civilian review boards were spearheaded by the American Civil Liberties Union (ACLU), endorsed by other civil rights groups, and supported by liberal political leaders and coalitions. These citizens believed that police brutality and other forms of citizen mistreatment were commonly directed toward minority groups, and that ameliorating such police-citizen antagonisms was essential for improved police-minority relations. The community hostility that was generated by abrasive police conduct was considered responsible for the public's dissatisfaction, distrust, and disrespect toward law enforcement representatives. In theory, the existence of civilian review boards would make certain that the police were not immune from answering for their mistakes and malpractices and that police departments were fully accountable to the community. The usual departmental methods for responding to citizen grievances through internal, police-controlled review of complaints appeared to be wholly inadequate, inappropriate, and ineffective.

Internal review of complaints

There are several alleged deficiencies of the department-run internal review boards.

By virtue of their all-police personnel composition and the consequent conflict of interest, they cannot be impartial in judging fellow officers, which makes it impossible for complainants to get a fair hearing.

The procedures used for filing complaints are cumbersome, discourage citizens from reporting, and lend themselves to further abuse by the police.[54]

Police review boards make no genuine effort to solicit complaints or to inform the community of its existence or their rights.

Internal review mechanisms insulate the police department and its officers from public accountability.

Since cases heard by police-controlled review committees are invariably settled in favor of the offending officers, who are never disciplined, departmental review of citizen complaints against the police is perceived by the black community as a whitewash effort.

Having no faith in the police complaint boards, minority members are reluctant to register grievances with them.[55]

Internal review sometimes left something to be desired where the charged police officer was concerned, such as lack of notice of the formal charges or the evidence against the officer prior to the disciplinary trial.

Philadelphia's Police Advisory Board

The two most prominent civilian review boards were those operated in New York and Philadelphia. Against a background of strong ACLU support, the newly installed liberal mayor of Philadelphia created the Police Advisory Board (PAB) on October 1, 1958, the first civilian review board in the country.[56] A serious limitation of the five-person Police Advisory Board was that it had no investigating staff of its own. Consequently, it was forced to rely upon the police department's Community Relations Unit to investigate complaints, and this compromised the board's independence and the objectivity of the reports it received. Nonetheless, the PAB's position was external to the police department and not subject to procedures promulgated by the police commissioner. Upon completion of the investigations, the Police Advisory Board decided whether a public hearing into the matter was warranted. Based upon the hearings, the PAB made specific recommendations to the police commissioner that were strictly advisory but were usually followed: reprimand, suspension, dismissal, or commendation of the officer.

In resolving 868 complaints in 1958–1967, the PAB recommended disciplining the police officer in only 6 percent of the cases.[57] The most common disposition occurred without holding official hearings: 20 percent of the cases were settled through conciliation, an apology, or an explanation to the citizen. The board's 1965 annual report to the mayor recommended that the police rectify patterns of physical mistreatment of arrested persons at station houses and discourtesy toward civilian inquiries.[58] However, the board faced diminishing community response; the number of complaints filed annually were few, exceeding 100 only in 1964. From its inception, the Police Advisory Board had strenuous opposition from the Fraternal Order of Police, which on two occasions filed suit to enjoin the operation of the board. In December 1969 a new and less liberal mayor, influenced by the police commissioner, announced the termination of the Police Advisory Board.[59]

To fulfill a campaign pledge to change the department's methods of handling citizen complaints, New York City Mayor John V. Lindsay

New York's Civilian Complaint Review Board

created the Civilian Complaint Review Board (CCRB) by executive order in July 1966. The seven-member board consisted of four carefully chosen, salaried civilians and three police officials, two of whom had never been policemen and were appointed "deputy commissioners" merely to serve on the board. Thus the CCRB was civilian dominated. While there was no official policy, the practice was to seek representation of ethnic minority groups on the board. Like the PAB, if the CCRB could not settle a dispute informally, a closed hearing was held that would result in exonerating the officer or recommending to the police commissioner that charges be brought against the officer at a departmental trial.

During its four months in operation, the CCRB received 442 complaints, many of which originated from the officer's order maintenance role in domestic family disturbances. The number of cases processed by the board in this brief period was more than twice the number previously reported annually to the department's internal review board.[60] A bare majority (51 percent) of the complainants were nonwhite, and the most common allegation was the use of unnecessary force. Of the 170 cases disposed of before its demise, 55 were settled through conciliation, 110 complaints were found not substantiated and were dismissed, and 5 were forwarded to the police commissioner for action.

Police opposition to the CCRB

From the outset, New York's finest, the Patrolmen's Benevolent Association, and the incumbent police commissioner were adamantly opposed to the Civilian Complaint Review Board and determined to abolish it.[61] Accordingly, the Patrolmen's Benevolent Association brought the CCRB issue to a head in a public referendum on November 8, 1966. In a blistering campaign against the CCRB that had racial overtones and exploited the public's fear of crime, the police urged its elimination.

The most serious complaint against the civilian review board concept was its debilitating effect on police morale and its possibly divisive impact on police-community relations. Even the reform-oriented President's

Citizens protest New York's short-lived Civilian Complaint Review Board in 1966

Crime Commission went on record against "the establishment of civilian review boards in jurisdictions where they do not exist, solely to review police conduct."[62] An underlying current against the Civilian Complaint Review Board was that the police viewed it as a mechanism for appeasing irresponsible, radical, and even criminal elements in the minority community and for purchasing peace in the ghetto when the rest of the country was engulfed in riots. The depth of police hostility toward such boards and their persistent, single-minded determination to abolish them were no match for the fragmented constituencies and waning liberal sentiment that supported the civilian review board. Having emerged as a unique political creature through mayoral fiat, New York's Civilian Complaint Review Board was terminated through the political process. In the referendum on November 8, 1966, just four months after the board began operation, the public voted to abolish the CCRB by an overwhelming 2-to-1 margin.

SUING THE POLICE

Departmental efforts to control police misconduct

In seeking more positive approaches to controlling police misconduct, some police departments are making special efforts to involve the community in developing departmental policy concerning complaint review procedures.[63] Others are going even further to prevent police misconduct from occurring or reoccurring. Under a Police Foundation grant, the Dallas Police Department's Psychological Services Unit hopes to identify the stresses and pressures in policework that may lead to acts that could bring formal complaints. Officers are referred to the unit for evaluation and counseling by the internal affairs division on the basis of a pattern of complaints lodged against the officer, by supervisors who spot the behavioral trouble signs of misconduct, or through self-referral.[64] The Kansas City (Missouri) Police Department's Peer Review Panel consists of experienced officials within each departmental area who are trained to identify job stresses and officers with personality problems and psychological disorders. Officers also come to the attention of the panel through self-referral, through referral by other police officers, and by having accrued three negative incidents within 12 months.[65]

When all other means to prevent, curtail, or punish police misconduct through administrative procedures fail, the aggrieved citizen may decide there is only one thing left to do: Sue the cops!

In the fall of 1972, a 37-year-old laborer got drunk and led Charlotte, North Carolina, police on a 100-mile-an-hour automobile chase. Officers caught him only after he had smashed his car through two police-car roadblocks. The laborer, Richard Hinson, was found guilty of four different offenses and served eight months in jail. Recently, Hinson was back in court to sue the officers who had arrested him.[66] Hinson claimed that the Charlotte police had used unreasonable force in dragging him out of his car and breaking his jaw and two ribs. At the civil trial, Hinson admitted to his drunken escapade and the police denied using excessive force. The federal court ordered each of the five officers to pay Hinson $200 in damages. Hinson's suit against the police was brought under a federal statute used increasingly by citizens charging brutality and other violations of their civil rights: Section 1983 of the Civil Rights Act of 1871, which protects citizens from constitutional violations of their civil rights by state and federal law enforcement officers.

Section 1983, Civil Rights Act of 1871

Although not originally designed to control police misconduct, the Civil Rights Act was first used to do so by the Supreme Court in 1961. In 1971 the Supreme Court strengthened the act's hold over the police by in effect creating a federal cause of action based on Fourth Amendment violations.* The Civil Rights Act, for example, was the basis upon which a District of Columbia jury awarded $12 million to the 1200 persons illegally arrested during a May Day peace demonstration in Washington in 1971, for violating the demonstrators' First Amendment right to free speech and assembly.[68] Civil rights advocates hail the use of civil litigation against the police as the only direct, truly deterrent method for cracking down on police who are racist, brutal, unstable, or grossly irresponsible. On the other hand, the law enforcement community views the trend in police misconduct suits as harassment of the police and a problem only somewhat less alarming than crime itself. Claims against Denver's 1375-member police department, for example, quadrupled between 1973 and 1976.[69]

Police misconduct litigation

According to a survey conducted by the International Association of Chiefs of Police (IACP) on behalf of Americans for Effective Law Enforcement, the number of civil suits brought against police throughout the United States more than doubled between 1967 and 1971, totaling a projected 13,000 lawsuits for the five-year period (see Table 4.2).[70] About 20 percent of the suits were filed in the federal courts, primarily under the Civil Rights Act, and that figure reached 25 percent in 1971. Two-thirds of the suits alleged either false arrest or brutality. Legally, excessive force suits are allegations of civil assault and civil battery that typically occur in the course of making an arrest. Of the total number of suits initiated against the police in 1967–1971, only 3.8 percent were "lost" by the police defendants. But in roughly one out of four cases tried in court, 18.5 percent of the judgments were against the police defendants, who on the average were ordered to pay the plaintiffs

* The scope of police misconduct covered by Section 1983 of the Civil Rights Act of 1871, under which citizens may bring the police into court, is enormous. It encompasses almost everything except the police failing to inform the plaintiff of his or her Miranda rights upon arrest![67]

Table 4.2 Types of Civil Suits Filed Against Police, 1967–1971

Type of Principal Claim	Survey Sample	Projected National Total	Percent of Total
False arrest, imprisonment	2,393	5,242	40.6
Brutality, assault, battery	1,602	3,509	27.2
Misuse of firearms	364	797	6.2
Libel, slander, defamation	53	116	0.9
Illegal search or seizure	163	357	2.8
Allegations of harassment	90	197	1.5
Poor jail conditions	56	123	1.0
Injunctive relief	350	767	5.9
Miscellaneous claims	667	1,461	11.3
Unknown diverse allegations	155	339	2.6
Total	5,893	12,908	100.0

As might be expected, the largest group of suits involved brutality and false arrest claims, constituting 67.8 percent of the total number of suits brought.

Source: Survey of Police Misconduct Litigation 1967–1971, Americans for Effective Law Enforcement, 1974. Prepared by Wayne W. Schmidt.

$3,000 per case.* Huge damages may be awarded in cases where the police committed wrongful killings (homicides), inflicted grievous bodily injuries that were unreasonable under the circumstances, or acted in a grossly irresponsible manner.[71] Since municipalities, police departments, and police officials are ordinarily not liable for the misconduct of their employees and subordinates,† the financial burden falls directly upon the officers charged.

The gist of most suits against the police is that the arresting officer lacked probable cause to make the arrest. This possibility raises a colorable claim that the restraint necessarily involved in the arrest constituted unnecessary force. The arrestee's continued detention for purposes of transportation to the police station, booking, and arraignment may then legally expose the arresting officer to the civil charge of false imprisonment. In such situations, the arrested "criminal" becomes the plaintiff pressing civil charges against the police, who become the defendants in a lawsuit. Because it is a civil rather than a criminal proceeding, the plaintiff need only prove the case against the police by a "preponderance of the evidence" rather than "beyond a reasonable doubt." If the judge or jury find that the preponderance of the evidence test is met, they may impose financial "compensatory" damages on the officer, intended to compen-

* A large number of the tort actions against the police were dropped by the plaintiffs, settled informally, or still pending.

† If the officers can show that they were simply complying with the department's policy or administrative directives or orders, the police agency or official may be liable.

sate the plaintiff for actual losses incurred through improper police conduct, as well as "punitive" damages, intended to teach the officer a lesson.

The good faith defense

In seeking exoneration, the police may point out that criminal charges of resisting arrest and assault and battery of an officer were placed against the plaintiff at the time of arrest. Or they may invoke the *good faith* defense in cases taken against them under Section 1983 of the Civil Rights Act.[72] In 1967 the Supreme Court ruled that even if the arrest was made without probable cause, and was thus illegal, a good faith defense could shield the police from civil liability. The good faith defense does not hinge upon whether the officer had, in the constitutional sense, probable cause to arrest. Rather, the principle of reasonableness is pushed to its limits by using it to determine whether it was reasonable for the officer to have acted unlawfully, that is, to *believe* he or she had probable cause to arrest even though probable cause was lacking as a matter of law. The good faith defense to charges of police misconduct liability is being accepted increasingly by the federal courts. Nonetheless, it seems inevitable that the police will have to add "being sued" to the occupational hazards of being injured or killed on duty, being brought before internal and external review boards, being the target of verbal abuse from citizens, and being unappreciated by the community.[73]

The demise of sovereign immunity

For the last two decades, civil rights police misconduct cases were, by necessity, brought against individual officers rather than the police department itself. This was because of the Supreme Court's ruling in *Monroe* v. *Pape* in 1961. In this case, the Court refused to hold the Chicago Police Department liable for a warrantless search and ransacking of a family's home and the illegal detention of the head of the household.[74] The Court stated that the proper avenue of citizen redress was against individual police officers rather than the police department because municipalities were categorically immune from liability. This doctrine of sovereign immunity had its roots in the common law precept that "the King can do no wrong."[75]

In a landmark decision in 1978, *Monell* v. *Department of Social Services of New York City,* the Supreme Court broke with *Pape* by ruling that local governments have no absolute immunity from damage suits for civil rights violations under section 1983.[76] The decision opened the door for suing police departments and other municipal agencies. Basically, in *Monell* the court defined cities as "persons" within the meaning and scope of section 1983 of the Civil Rights Act. Under *Monell,* however, local governments can be sued only if the alleged unconstitutional action is the result of official policy or governmental "custom," even if such custom has not received formal approval through authorized decision-making channels. The purpose of this limitation was to insulate governing bodies against vicarious liability solely on the basis of *respondeat superior:* The doctrine that the master (employer) is automatically responsible for the torts of his servants (employees) which are job-related.[77] By refusing to apply *respondeat superior* to municipalities, the Court sought to confine *Monell* to the systematic denial of civil rights by governmental entity.[78]

The important question of whether local government is entitled to the same qualified good faith immunity that is granted to most individual employees (such as patrol officers) sued under section 1983 was left open in *Monell.* Two years later, in *Owen* v. *City of Independence* in 1980, the Supreme Court emphatically declared that the good faith defense was not available to municipalities charged with civil rights violations.[79]

> How "uniquely amiss" it would be, therefore, if the government itself were permitted to disavow liability for the injury it has begotten. A damages remedy against the offending party is a vital component of any scheme for vindicating cherished constitutional guarantees. . . . Yet owing to the qualified immunity enjoyed by most government officials, many victims of municipal malfeasance would be left remediless if the city were also allowed to assert a good-faith defense.

The combined effect of *Monell* and *Owen* will make it easier to bring and win civil rights suits against police departments and other units of local government. The decisions may also encourage citizens, whenever feasible, to sue the police department rather than individual patrol officers or police administrators because of the "deep pocket" incentive for doing so: the prospect of obtaining much larger monetary damages from the city than from its employees, whose financial resources are meager by comparison. Finally, the thrust of *Monell, Owen,* and related Supreme Court decisions on executive liability[80] may prompt police departments to establish legally defensible written policies covering a wide range of ministerial and discretionary patrol practices, fearing that failure to specify appropriate standards of performance may make them more vulnerable to successful civil rights suits and claims of vicarious liability.

POLICE-COMMUNITY RELATIONS

Police departments began engaging in public relations as early as 1930. These gestures were thinly veiled propaganda attempts aimed at image building, selling the police and the department to the public, and appeasing the critics. They included programs such as Philadelphia's Operation Handshake in the streets and Officer Friendly in the schools,[81] and one in Fort Worth (St. Louis) where police officers welcomed conventioneers with information packets describing their city.[82] The 1950s saw the limited introduction of formal community relations units in police departments that were still principally concerned with winning public popu-

A police officer visits a Washington, D.C., schoolroom in the Officer Friendly program

larity contests, advertising the virtues of the law enforcement profession, and achieving superficial image enhancement without making accompanying changes in the police role or departmental operations.

Origins of police-community relations

The contemporary police-community relations (PCR) idea, ideal, and movement grew out of the civil disorders and riots of the 1960s. It was reinforced by the President's Crime Commission's focus on upgrading the police and their concern that "police relations with minority groups had sunk to explosively low levels."[83] The role of the police—specifically, white officers on routine patrol in the ghettos—in precipitating the disorders in black communities was pinpointed by the 1968 National Advisory Commission on Civil Disorders: "Abrasive relationships between police and Negroes and other minority groups have been a major source of grievance, tension and, ultimately, disorder."[84] The way in which the police officer handled the initial incident and police-citizen encounter determined whether it remained a minor event or developed into a major disturbance. Thus police management of their discretionary authority suddenly became a prominent issue of public policy.[85]

The Kerner "riot commission" acknowledged that minority group relations were not exclusively a police problem, though the police invariably bear the brunt of displaced black animosity. However, the commission emphasized that the police bore a major responsibility for effecting changes to reduce black rage, minority group hostility toward prejudiced police and a white racist society, and the likelihood of future civil insurrections. Central to the Kerner commission's criticism of the police were the charges that as a group the police are prejudiced toward minorities, are insensitive to the tensions that exist in ghetto areas, and have little understanding, appreciation of, or training in essential human relations and social service aspects of policework.* The President's Crime Commission noted that "few police officers today have a proper background in psychology, sociology, or the culture of the poor, minority groups, or juveniles. . . . He must acquire information and understanding concerning human relations."[86] Finally, police administrators also find community relations a bothersome and stressful aspect of their jobs.[87]

The police-community relations concept

The mold for contemporary police-community relations had been cast. Its objectives centered around police-initiated social services as part of the human relations dimension of the police role, facilitating meaningful two-way communication between the police and the policed, and heightened police sensitivity to minority group members and their problems. In actuality, police-community relations is a loose-knit, emerging, sometimes controversial set of facts, ideas, values, and assumptions about how the police should and do relate to minority groups in particular and the public in general in their daily encounters with citizens. The three interrelated hallmarks of the police-community relations equation are: (1) The police are prejudiced against minorities, thereby creating gnawing real and imagined law enforcement and social problems. (2) Stemming in part from police prejudice, the affected minority communities become alienated, hostile, and resentful toward the police; this reaction causes innumerable problems for the police, the police department, and the rest of society. (3) The resulting unsatisfactory relations between the two groups and their prejudices toward each other can be improved through police-community relations (PCR) efforts—a process the police must lead and assume major responsibility for.

The Police Are Ethnically Prejudiced and Do Not Provide Adequate Protection or Fair Law Enforcement in Minority Communities. There is little evidence that police are recruited from among segments of the population where prejudice is high. But there is ample evidence that while on the force police officers become biased against minority group members and treat them as less than first-class citizens. In testifying before the National Advisory Commission on Civil Disorders, Albert Reiss noted that three out of four white policemen in primarily black precincts in certain northern cities had prejudiced attitudes toward blacks. His own studies in Boston, Chicago, and the District of Columbia revealed that "close to half of all the police officers in predominantly Negro high crime rate areas showed extreme prejudice against Negroes."[88]

While the claims of physical police brutality are probably exaggerated,

* The Kerner commission was unconcerned with the etiology of police prejudice or the possibility that its level might not be much greater than that in the general population.

their symbolic impact upon the community compensates for their relative infrequency. The more common practices of mistreating ghetto residents through verbal abuse, harassment, inadequate protection, and selective law enforcement appear too prevalent to be justified under any circumstances. Such practices cause irreparable damage to public trust and confidence in law enforcement. On balance, the studies of police prejudice and their implications for the police working personality are encouraging and disturbing at the same time. They reveal that the police are "only" somewhat more or less racially prejudiced than the rest of the white society.[89] However, this revelation is considered cause for alarm rather than relief because of the powerful public role of the police and the minority community's demands for equal treatment and respect from their public servants.

The Minority Community Is Hostile to the Police and Dissatisfied with Their Performance. Studies of minority opinions, perceptions, and experiences with the police disclose that nonwhites are hostile to the police, dissatisfied with their performance, made to feel like prisoners in their own communities, fear the police, and are even more suspicious of the police as aggressors than the police are of them as offenders and potential assailants. A nationwide survey conducted by the National Opinion Research Corporation (NORC) for the President's Crime Commission found that twice as many nonwhites (16 percent) as whites (7 percent) thought that the police were doing a "poor job" and that twice as many nonwhites (63 percent) as whites (30 percent) questioned their honesty.[90] The profile of minority perceptions of the police that emerges from numerous research studies is one of deep distrust, resentment, animosity, and dissatisfaction with the police.[91]

Police-Community Relations Units, Programs, and Efforts. While the negative effects of police prejudice and ghetto hostility are more conspicuous and heartfelt among minority group members than among police officers, their implications for law enforcement are nonetheless real and consequential. Professionalism requires that the police and the police department be responsive to their critics and make reasonable attempts to enhance their reputation and credibility in the community. Citizens who have little respect for the police may be reluctant to report crimes, provide information leading to arrests, serve as witnesses, and assist officers in distress.[92] Conversely, the attitudes and behavior of alienated minorities add to the role conflicts inherent in policework, are an impetus to police assaults, and increase the risk of civil disorders.

When the riots erupted in the 1960s, government leaders and police officials recognized the immediate need to quell the disorders and to reestablish law and order. The 1968 Safe Streets Act made sure that state and local police departments would have the necessary equipment and riot-trained personnel to do so. But they were equally aware that, in the long run, a brute force response to the symptoms of minority frustration was an unacceptable, unmanageable, and ineffective technique of social control in a free society. Accordingly, the President's Crime Commission endorsed, and the LEAA funded, police-community relations programs, projects, and efforts under a variety of auspices, arrangements, and systems of delivery.[93] By far the most common machinery for providing these yet-to-be defined services were Community Service Units or PCR Units within police departments, or similar programs operated by the city.[94] Staffed by minority group members, the PCR Units were given the task of developing police-community relations programs, projects, and efforts.

Goals of police-community relations

In principle, the two main goals of PCR are to eliminate police prejudice toward minorities (blacks, youths, students) and to reduce the minority community's hostility toward the police. The process for doing so involves neutralizing mutually held negative perceptions; it is intended to result in supportive, cooperative, friendly, functional PCR through which enduring problems can be worked out on a nonadversary basis. While PCR is loosely considered a two-way street, the major responsibility is placed upon the police for taking the first step, sustaining the pace of improved relations, and reaching out to their suspicious benefactors. Three types of PCR programs, projects, and efforts may be identified, although in practice there is considerable overlap among them.

The first type are those which seek to establish a meaningful dialogue between the police and the community as a means of getting to know, accept, and respect one another. Such efforts encompass neighborhood meetings, citizens' advisory groups, community education in crime prevention, ride-alongs with the police, and school visit programs.

The second type are those which provide services to the community, thereby improving the police image and the reputation of the department among groups that hold them in low esteem. PCR in this area include helping ghetto youngsters get jobs, arranging for child care when parents become incapacitated, providing faster response time to service calls, increasing foot patrols, opening storefronts in the community, operating recreation programs, and becoming advocates for the legal and social rights of the poor.[95]

Community Service Officers

Within this second category, one of the most important PCR ideas was the President's Crime Commission recommendation that a new level of police personnel be established for the specific purpose of improving communication between the police and the community and engaging in community relations work: the Community Service Officer (CSO). Visualized as police apprentices who could work their way up to become regular sworn police officers, the CSOs would preferably be young minority group members assigned to perform PCR work in disadvantaged high-crime areas. The commission proposed that CSOs not have full law enforcement powers or carry arms. But it was equally concerned that minority youths with minor criminal records and without a high school education not be barred from joining the force in this specialized entry level position and that CSOs not be saddled with clerical duties. Under funds from the Model Cities Program, and following the Commission's recommendations to the letter, the New York City Police Department appointed its first group of 25 CSOs to the police academy in January 1970.[96]

The third type of PCR programs are those experimenting with new learning approaches or environments aimed at expanding and changing the police role. A variety of techniques have been used to increase the officer's ability to respond to incidents, exercise discretion appropriately, demonstrate sensitivity to minority members and their problems, confront police prejudice and racial stereotyping, and demilitarize the police image. PCR in this category include sensitivity training,[97] role playing and participant observation, race relations,* human relations training laboratories, continuing education for inservice personnel, developing special skills and techniques to manage conflict situations and social crises,[99] demilitarizing the police image by wearing blazers instead of regular patrol uniforms,[100] and creating more PCR Units in police departments. Police Community Relations Units are the visible symbols of the department's commitment to the minority community and the organizational base for many of the efforts which cut across the three categories of PCR. In the long run, though, the changes occurring in the professionalization of the police (to be discussed in the next chapter) may be more important determinants of PCR than those reviewed above.

DOMESTIC CRISIS INTERVENTION

One of the most common, dangerous, and disliked assignments—and one for which police are given little training—is responding to domestic disturbances. *Domestics* are family situations that involve disputes, misunderstandings, quarrels, or fights between husbands and wives, common law spouses, or lovers. Occasionally other family members, a landlord and tenants, or neighbors are the disputants. These family crises and conflicts are the patrolperson's single most prevalent call for service; they well exceed the total annual number of index offenses. During one month in 1966, of the 135,000 calls for service to the Chicago Police Depart-

Incidence of domestic disturbances

* The National Center for the study of Police Community Relations at Michigan State University concluded that the primary purpose of the community relations programs it surveyed was improved race relations. In its bid to gain greater credibility and widespread acceptance, the PCR movement is trying to evolve beyond the race-relations classification stage.[98]

sponding to a domestic disturnce call is a common—and potially dangerous—police asnment

ment, 23,000 were for "criminal incidents" while 33,000 were for "domestic disturbances." In Los Angeles, a substantial number of the 1,500 cases a month handled at the main office by the prosecutor's staff in informal hearings involve intrafamily violence. The number of wife-assault cases reported to the police is increasing so rapidly that some cities have created courts with exclusive jurisdiction in family violence matters.[101] About half of the cases on the docket of Chicago's Court of Domestic Relations involve domestic disputes.[102]

ngers in domestic intervention

No less significant than the prevalence of domestics are their relationship to police safety and their implications for police-community relations. On a national basis annually, 20 to 25 percent of the police officers killed in the line of duty meet their deaths while responding to domestic disturbances. Family crisis intervention is, therefore, the consistent leading or runner-up cause of police killings over the years. And about 40 percent of police injuries are incurred in handling domestic disturbances.[103] In addition, the manner in which officers respond to domestics may influence the quality of police-community relations.[104] It may determine whether a minor squabble will escalate into serious injury or death to citizens or police, lead to charges of police brutality, criminal homicide, civil suits against the officers, or even trigger a riot.[105]

The standard methods of police intervention in domestic crisis situations, prosecutorial responses, and judicial disposition of such cases have been costly, inadequate, and ineffective. The result is a high rate of domestic-call recidivism, police injuries and fatalities, a profile of homicides rooted in private crises between family members, and the seeds of alienation between the police and the community.[106] In keeping with the IACP position that in "dealing with family disputes the power of arrest should

The system's "do nothing" policy

be exercised as a last resort," the police have in effect adopted a nonarrest policy in domestics, for several reasons.[107]

After suffering 13 years of beatings, Jennifer Patri killed her husband in self-defense and was convicted of manslaughter

1. The victim, who is typically a battered wife, does not want her husband-offender arrested. The estimated one million battered women a year come from poverty households, have large families of underage children to care for, and have minimal marketable skills.[108] Thus they cannot afford to have their husbands, men friends, and common law spouses arrested. The abused women also often fear that their mates will retaliate against them and the children after being arrested. Sometimes the police officer considers the wife-beating episode normal for the culture of the couple and not seriously objectionable to the victim.[109] Under ordinary circumstances, the victim in a family disturbance calls the police to scare her mate into behaving himself, to get her husband out of the house temporarily, or to have them take her to the hospital for treatment. As for battered wives who do want the police to take official action against their spouses, the New York City Police Department reversed its long-standing nonarrest policy in a 1978 consent judgment which requires police to arrest husbands who assault or threaten their wives. This may be the first such mandatory arrest agreement of its kind in the country.
2. Even when victims say that they want the offender arrested, they often change their mind after cooling off, do not seek arrest warrants, fail to appear in court as complainants, or ask the court to drop the matter before trial. In over half the cases before Chicago's Court of Domestic Relations, the wives and mistresses of the defendants either requested dismissal of the charges or did not show up when the case was called.[110] In one district in Maryland, 95 percent of the charges against the arrested offenders were dropped.[111]
3. Having more serious cases that require their attention, and having limited resources, prosecutors do not want to be bothered with "nuisance" domestic disturbance cases, and they turn their back on them whenever possible.[112] In some jurisdictions in California, such as Berkeley, prosecutors hold informal citation hearings (which are not authorized by statute) to warn potential defendants that they will be arrested the next time.[113] Whenever possible, prosecutors prefer to avoid taking domestic cases through standard criminal justice system channels and instead rely upon special "diversion" methods and projects to dispose of the offenders.
4. In the case of domestic offenders who are arrested and prosecuted, the action taken by the court is totally ineffectual. Convicted defendants are given a slap on the wrist: a lecture, a small fine, unsupervised probation, or treatment that is ineffective because it is nominal, too late, or unwanted.[114] The prevalent police complaint of

> court leniency may well be borne out in judicial dispositions of domestic disturbance offenders, as Close-up 4.2 illustrates. Institutional sentences are so rare that it seems that the courts consider wife beating a victimless crime (violence between consenting adults?) that should not carry the criminal penalty of incarceration—or that such petty family squabbles must escalate to mayhem before anything should be done about them. Ironically and tragically, some battered wives have begun to protect themselves and to retaliate by killing their husbands.*

Domestic disturbance cases, then, involve judicial ineffectiveness and insensitivity to victims, prosecutorial mishandling of battered women, police reluctance or inability to make arrests, and victims who are ambivalent and vulnerable to the official action taken and its outcome. These factors make reliance upon arrest and the criminal justice system particularly inappropriate in coping with domestic disturbances The courts, prosecutors, and social agencies, more so than the police, have failed to recognize the serious problems present in and represented by apparently minor violent and nonviolent domestic disturbances. But practical factors combine to place the major responsibility for improved handling of domestics upon the police doorstep. Domestic disputes occur primarily on weekends and between 6 P.M. and 3 A.M., when most prosecutors, judges, and social agencies do not have office hours—which leaves the police to handle the situation.[115] Most important, domestic disturbances are always fraught with the possibility of physical danger for citizens. Since the police have a legal monopoly on using force, they are the only social agents equipped to handle a situation at its boiling point, and therefore they have initial exclusive jurisdiction over domestic disturbance cases.

Police responsibility for handling domestic disputes

Traditionally, the police received virtually no formal training for intervening in domestic crises. Thus, through word or deed, they sometimes unintentionally caused injury to citizens or to themselves, escalated a domestic argument, were cornered into making an arrest, and perhaps damaged police-community relations in the process. Their typical choice in responding to domestic disturbances lay between doing nothing and making an arrest. Occasionally, the two possible responses were interspersed with erratic, intuitive, and untested makeshift dispositions. The police frequently pleaded in exasperation that they were not marriage counselors or social workers and therefore could not help the couple resolve their problems. But whether it be classified as social work or not, reacting to domestic disturbances is work that law enforcement officers

* Increasingly, women tried for murdering assaultive husbands are pleading self-defense and are acquitted, found not guilty by reason of temporary insanity, given light sentences for murder, or convicted of reduced charges.

Close-up 4.2 THOMAS PROMISED

One evening in 1973, Thomas S. severely beat his common law wife Loretta G. He slashed her face and ear so badly with a kitchen knife that 23 stitches were required to save the ear. Loretta filed charges and the police arrested her husband. Upon arraignment the criminal court judge promptly released Thomas on his promise to stay away from Loretta. Thomas promised.

One morning in April 1974, Thomas savagely assaulted Loretta as she was on her way to work. In court for the second time, Thomas was released by the judge on his promise not to bother Loretta again. Thomas promised.

In June 1974, Thomas broke into Loretta's apartment and beat her so badly with his fists that she was hospitalized. From bedside, she filed charges. Thomas was arrested and then released by the court on condition that he not disturb Loretta in the future. Thomas promised.

In November 1974, Thomas again broke into her apartment. Using a broken broom handle this time, he beat Loretta so badly about the face and head that she had to have her right eye removed. Back in court, Thomas promised and was released for the fourth time in one year. It took Loretta longer to get fitted with a glass eye and released from the clinic than it did for Thomas to be back on the streets.

One evening in February 1975, just after new furniture had been delivered to her apartment, Loretta was jolted from her sleep by the sound of splintering wood and heavy pounding. She hurriedly dialed 911. It was you-know-who making his periodic housecall. After destroying the new furniture and punching her repeatedly in the stomach, Thomas left Loretta semiconscious on the floor.

Thomas was arrested and arraigned for the fifth time. The magistrate sitting in night court was informed by the police and the assistant district attorney about the previous assaults, dispositions, broken promises, and the need to do something this time. Peering at the judge through her one good eye and listening for the sentence through her stitched-back ear, Loretta waited patiently to see justice done.

Thomas was released with the stern stipulation that he leave Loretta alone! For the fifth time, Thomas promised, smiled to himself, and left the courtroom a free man. The assistant district attorney grimaced. The arresting officer swallowed hard to keep from shouting or crying. Loretta cried. The judge called the next case.

Sometimes it seems that justice really is blind.

Source: Adolph W. Hart, "Thomas Promised That He Would," *New York Times,* June 10, 1975, p. 39.

cannot avoid in the foreseeable future, especially when they are the first to contact citizens in the throes of a family crisis, where arrest is generally not feasible.

New York's Family Crisis Intervention Unit

A more appropriate, positive, and systematic approach to responding to domestic disturbances awaited Morton Bard's Family Crisis Intervention Unit (FCIU) and training for police officers in the New York City Police Department on May 1, 1967. In the preparatory phase of Dr. Bard's action research project, 18 handpicked volunteer patrolmen were selected from West Harlem's 30th Precinct to be given special training in the management of domestic disturbances and to constitute the Family Crisis Intervention Unit.[116] For their participation, the nine black and nine white volunteers received three college credits with City University's John Jay College of Criminal Justice. The experimental group of volunteer uniformed patrolmen, the Family Crisis Intervention Unit, was dispatched to handle all family disturbances in the 30th Precinct, in addition to performing their normal general patrol functions. The FCIU's effectiveness in terms of crime control and police safety was measured against that in the 24th Precinct, the control area, where regular untrained patrol officers responded to domestics as usual.

The first month of the training project was set aside for 160 hours of full-time, on-campus classroom training for the 18 officers. The officers were sensitized to how psychological cues, nonverbal gestures, the choice of words, communication and interpersonal skills, and an understanding of family dynamics, conflict resolution, and crisis intervention techniques could be used to alleviate a tense domestic confrontation. The final week of training was directed at developing a police referral capability to the city's social service agencies. After mediating, containing, and making a preliminary diagnosis of a family problem, the intervention specialist officers were to act as mental health paraprofessional casefinders, referring troubled disputants to the appropriate social agency.

a crisis intervention workshop Maui, Hawaii, police learn how handle domestic disturbances

The FCIU's training did not stop after the first month. Throughout the project's duration, team members appeared on campus weekly for individual consultation with doctoral students in clinical psychology and for group discussions led by professional project staff. This periodic inservice training was considered essential in reinforcing the earlier, intensive learning experience and in constantly upgrading the officer's crisis intervention skills.

Effects of the FCIU

The FCIU was in operation in the 30th Precinct demonstration area from July 1, 1967 to May 30, 1969. The primary goals of the FCIU undertaking were to reduce the volume of domestic complaints and the number of injuries to citizens and police in the 30th Precinct (as compared with the 24th Precinct). The FCIU was judged a success.

1. The number of assaults on family members in the 30th Precinct (368) was less than that in the control precinct (506).
2. No injuries were sustained by members of the FCIU compared to three noncrisis-trained patrolmen injured in the control area.
3. Arrests for assault in family disturbances were slightly lower in the 30th Precinct.
4. The FCIU made referrals to social agencies in 75 percent of the interventions, compared with 55 percent in the control precinct. And about 20 percent of the referred cases actually applied for assistance from the recommended agencies. Thus domestic crisis training prompted many families who would not otherwise have done so to seek professional treatment for their problems.
5. The feasibility of a police generalist-specialist role was established. The specially trained FCIU members continued to perform their general patrol duties, which were not impaired by their special assignment status. The team members preserved their identities as police officers without becoming marriage counselors or social workers.
6. There were indications that the FCIU contributed to improved police-community relations.[117]
7. Police professionalism was enhanced by expanding the officers' repertoire to include the ability to handle domestic confrontations and by shaping their behavior into a less authoritarian mold.

The FCIU project was more significant for what it illustrated and led to than for its less well substantiated findings and conclusions.[118] As the first and most ambitious program of its kind, it was the impetus for similar crisis intervention programs in police departments throughout the country. At least nine police departments have modeled their family crisis training entirely on the New York experiment, and all departmental crisis intervention efforts trace their origin to Morton Bard's pioneer FCIU work.[119] The FCIU was responsible for widespread formal recognition of

ighborhood crime watches en-
irage citizens to report suspi-
us persons and activities to the
ice

the need for human relations training for police officers, including endorsement by the "riot commission" and the IACP. It illustrated the feasibility of utilizing the police as early casefinders, mental health aides, and links to social service agency treatment. It established the principle that improved intervention strategies and skills have a potential for crime prevention, police safety, PCR, community mental health efforts, and innovative collaboration between the police department and the mental health system as a diversionary resource. It proved that within the context of responding to intrafamily violence, police work and social work are not such strange bedfellows.

COMMUNITY CRIME PREVENTION

As never before, private citizens acting on an individual or a collective basis are taking direct, concrete steps to prevent crime, assist in its solution, and reduce recidivism. These practical community crime prevention efforts consist of five kinds of programs.

Neighborhood Crime Watches

Of the various community efforts to curb crime, the most widely used is citizen surveillance of one's own block or neighborhood: neighborhood crime watches.[120] The primary goals of neighborhood crime watch programs are to prevent burglaries, to increase crime reporting, and to utilize citizens as the eyes and ears of the police. While it is not possible to put a cop on every corner, it is possible to have a citizen police every block. The idea of neighborhood watches originated with the Los Angeles Police Department's encouraging citizens to "look out for one another."

National Neighborhood Watch Program

The model for many state and local crime watch efforts is the LEAA's National Neighborhood Watch Program, operated by the National Sheriffs' Association.[121] Under the neighborhood watch program, citizens are organized and trained to be alert to potential burglaries, to watch each other's homes, and to report suspicious persons, cars, and activities to the police. Block captains and neighborhood committees work closely with authorities in 2,000 police and sheriffs' departments. Jacksonville, Florida, for example, has 29 neighborhood watch programs operating under LEAA auspices. At a time when UCR burglary rates for the nation were increasing, communities participating in the National Neighborhood Watch Program or operating their own crime watches reported reductions in burglaries of 12 to 50 percent as well as sharp drops in vandalism.[122] In one form or another, neighborhood crime watches are found in cities throughout the country.

Citizen patrols scout on foot or in cars and report illegal activity to the police

Citizen Patrols

Citizens participate more directly and more actively in community crime prevention through citizen patrols: unpaid groups of citizens who, under the auspices of the police department, patrol their blocks, neighborhoods, or buildings on foot or in private cars to deter crime and report illegal activity to the authorities. Lacking bona fide law enforcement powers, the citizen patrollers are instructed not to act as vigilantes, and they do not carry weapons, engage in car chases, investigate cases, or detain suspects. Begun in 1972 when Camden, New Jersey, had the second highest nonviolent crime rate in the country, its citizen patrol is credited for the 41 percent drop in property crime in two years.[123] Similar car and foot patrol programs are found in Hartford, Connecticut; Onawa, Iowa; Pontiac, Michigan; Chicago; and New York City.[124]

One of the commonest forms of citizen patrols are tenant patrols: those involving residents who patrol their own buildings, apartment complexes, or housing development projects. A $175,000 LEAA grant was made to Detroit for the purpose of establishing an 80-person citizen patrol to decrease crime and vandalism in two public housing projects.[125] New York's Housing Authority program involves over 12,000 tenant volunteers who are equipped with walkie-talkies for direct access to the police. They maintain surveillance over 650 buildings by screening visitors, inspecting stairs and hallways, and checking on the infirm and el-

Close-up 4.3 THE GUARDIAN ANGELS[a]

Perhaps the most unique and controversial citizen patrol anti-crime effort is the Guardian Angels, created in 1979 by Curtis Sliwa to make the New York City subways safer for passengers. Ranging in age from 15 years to the mid-20s and wearing red berets and white insignia t-shirts, this multiracial band of amateur crime fighters patrol the subways one to a car. Each Angel goes on at least two four-hour patrols a week, paying their own fare as a symbolic gesture of their nonestablishment status.

The Guardian Angels are different from traditional citizen patrol groups in several respects. They are an independent, self-appointed force who operate without any formal ties to the police or city authorities. The New York City Transit Authority offered the Guardian Angels auxiliary status in return for agreeing to take orders from the city police; but Sliwa refused to be coopted into the official law enforcement structure because doing so would destroy the distinctive value of the program. Although unarmed while on patrol, the Angels are a paramilitary organization whose up-to-three month training program stresses the martial arts, self-defense against armed attack, and mental and physical toughness. Most important, they routinely make citizen arrests on their own initiative, come to the aid of subway victims at the point of crisis, and are prepared to use whatever force is necessary to stop crimes in progress and apprehend the offender.

A study by Fordham University found that the Guardian Angels are adored by the public and resented by the police. The police accuse them of fomenting violent encounters, acting as vigilantes, lacking experience in law enforcement, and being troublemakers not above breaking the law themselves. "We are the representatives of law enforcement for the society, not a bunch of rag-tag kids with sneakers on who have absolutely no concept of what law enforcement is." It is true that most of the Guardian Angels come from high-crime, low-income neighborhoods, and that some were once committing rather than preventing crimes. But Sliwa emphasizes that the Angels' backgrounds make them a more effective deterrent to violent subway crime, that the Angels (unlike vigilantes) do not punish suspects but simply turn them over to the police, and that they serve as positive role models for many youths who would otherwise identify with the worst criminal elements in society.

Undaunted by criticism, the Guardian Angels have grown from 13 members in New York City to over 1,000 participants nationwide, operating or having been invited to form new chapters in

Philadelphia, Atlanta, Los Angeles (where they ride the buses), Boston, Providence, and several cities in Connecticut. They have also expanded the scope of their activities to include patrolling Central Park, the suburban streets of Long Island, and high-crime housing projects in New Jersey—where they are welcomed with open arms by the elderly tenants. UCLS sociologist Maurice Zeitlin believes that "the Guardian Angels may have touched the conscience of the nation's youth and may just become their movement of the eighties." Public assessment of the Guardian Angels may be less visionary but no less optimistic concerning the group's future: "I would trust a street kid to know how to handle other street kids more than I'd trust a cop. I think the Guardian Angels deserve recognition and respect."

[a] *Source:* Transcript of *ABC Newsmagazine 20/20,* broadcast April 16, 1981.

Founded by Curtis Sliwa, the Guardian Angels are considered vigilantes by many police, but an adoring public views them as fearless crusaders against crime

e volunteer police auxiliary is an
ıarmed citizen, trained by the
ılice, who patrols in uniform

derly.[126] As with all citizen patrol and crime watch groups, their role and authority is restricted to that of providing eyes and ears for the police, a role that precludes any attempt to abort criminal activity—except for the Guardian Angels (see Close-up 4.3). About 850 citizen patrols were active in urban areas in the United States as of 1976.[127]

Citizens as Police Auxiliaries

Citizens in uniform

The most direct and most dangerous form of citizen participation in community crime prevention consists of joining the police department as a volunteer police auxiliary or reserve. Citizens on patrol as police auxiliaries are given formal training by the police department before receiving assignments, come under the direct supervision of the police, are deployed in areas where they are needed most, and wear uniforms almost identical to those of sworn officers. Young citizens often join the police reserve as a stepping stone to a career in policework. Although uniformed and bearing a badge, police auxiliaries are not armed and have no more law enforcement powers than do ordinary citizens. This limits their participation to a role as eyes and ears of the police, rather than authorizing them to take direct action against suspects. Los Angeles has about 500 members (including 95 women) in its police reserve corps, with 400 others awaiting the required five-and-one-half-month training program; another 1,900 citizens are in the Los Angeles sheriffs' reserves. Police reserves in Kansas City, Missouri, undergo extensive training prior to assuming their once a month 24-hour tour of duty.[128] New York City has 5,400 police auxiliaries, 100 of whom patrol Central Park on horseback in the evenings and on weekends, after taking a ten-week training program.[129]

Technology, Private Security Personnel, and Students

Target hardening and private police

The business community is a high-risk victim of serious crime. In self-defense, businesspersons (and private citizens) are relying increasingly upon two major weapons to prevent theft: technology and private police. Improved locks, doors, windows, building design, other target hardening devices,* lighting, communications and alarm systems, and property identification have become the order of the day. The LEAA-sponsored Operation Identification is a nationwide program to encourage citizens to mark personal valuables with an electric etching pencil and to file the property's identification number with the police.[130] The nationwide Op-

* *Target hardening* approaches are aimed at reducing the opportunities for successful crime commission. For example, cashiers and gasoline station attendants do business behind bulletproof collectors' booths; bus drivers do not give change or carry money; and department stores use new kinds of theft-resistant packaging.

eration Whistlestop program encourages citizens to carry with them at all times a specially developed small "horn" or whistle that emits a shrill distress signal as an emergency call to the police that a crime is in progress.

The business community's most dependable and most preferred crime deterrent is the same as that of the ordinary citizen: the "police." As of 1977, employers were using a half million private security officers (private police)—more than the number of nationwide public police—to protect themselves, their property, and their employees from internal and external victimization.[131] These private police, or contract guards, whose cost is usually less than that of sworn officers, now outnumber regular police officers in most areas. California, for example, has 50,000 "rent-a-cops" compared with 45,000 sworn officers.[132] So far the use of private police has been restricted to the business sector, but this picture may be changing. Residents in some cities have formed block associations to hire private street guards to patrol their neighborhoods, offer escort service, and check unoccupied residences.

Crime in the schools

Between 1970 and 1975, school vandalism, violence and property offenses skyrocketed, costing taxpayers $600 million a year.[133] As a result, school administrators and city officials began experimenting with new methods to control school crime. In some schools in Los Angeles, teachers began to wear small radio transmitters that when pressed sent an alarm signal to security agents at a central location. The Detroit school system spends $230,000 a year on alarm protection designed to reduce its $1 million a year vandalism bill. Electronic scanners are used in a South Boston high school to detect concealed weapons on students, a task that other schools handle by security pat-down and student identification procedures. Besides technology, school security forces are being beefed up through expansion, the addition of students as volunteers or paid part-timers, and assistance by the police department.

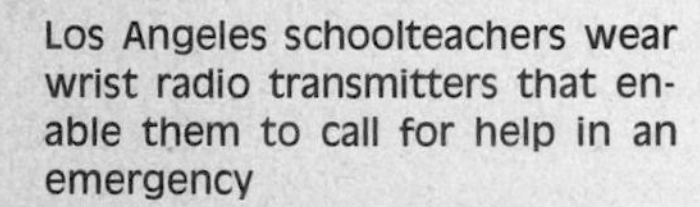

Los Angeles schoolteachers wear wrist radio transmitters that enable them to call for help in an emergency

To protect the more than four million women on their campuses, colleges have installed expensive new security systems, established escort services for females going out at night, offered free courses in self-defense, and utilized volunteers to free professional campus security for patrol. Northwestern University in Evanston, Illinois, spent $140,000 to light up dark areas of its suburban Chicago campus and, like the University of Wisconsin at Madison, began operating a free taxi service for women students. The campus security force at Duke University is using policewomen as decoys to apprehend potential rapists and molesters. The Wayne State University campus in Detroit is dotted with blue lights that identify access to hotline phones; as soon as the receiver is removed, the university police have the trouble scene pinpointed. At the home of the University of Michigan, where the incidence of reported rapes increased sharply in 1974, the Ann Arbor city council voted a $50,000 expenditure to develop a comprehensive community crime prevention program.[134]

me colleges have escort ser-
ces for women and use student
lunteers as additional security
rsonnel

Perhaps the most important factors in turning the tide against college crime in 1976 were the students' changed attitudes toward "law and order" and their participation in maintaining campus security. In 1976 at the University of California at Berkeley, the birthplace of the campus protest movement of the 1960s, student volunteers rode in police cars to help locate individuals suspected of crime. As part of a citizen ride-along project at Michigan State University in East Lansing, students and local merchants accompanied police officers on patrol. Twenty student aides at Cornell University in Ithaca, New York, work 15 hours a week patrolling buildings and isolated footpaths and assisting in crowd control and traffic enforcement.[135] After a woman student was raped and murdered at San Diego State University, 70 students volunteered to participate in an escort service and others began working at campus police headquarters to release regular security officers for patrol.[136]

Citizen Court Watchers

Many private citizens believe that the first step in curbing crime is the imposition of tougher sentences by the courts. Those who volunteer to do something about it on an organized basis, by attending criminal trials and observing and recording the sentencing behavior of judges, are called court watchers.* By monitoring judicial dispositions and the reasons for them in individual cases over time, these unpaid court watchers (house-

* Other types of court-watching groups are concerned with protecting the rights of defendants, court modernization, and administrative reform.

tizen court watchers enter a
urthouse in Boston, where they
ll monitor the performance of
dges

wives, students, the retired) can determine which judges are too lenient toward offenders and unresponsive to the rights of victims. Appropriate strategies are then developed by the court-watching group or organization to correct the situation, perhaps by pressuring judges to impose stricter sentences. Court watchers may publish the court's sentencing "batting average" or publicize the disposition of individual cases, oppose the offending judge at reelection or attempt to remove the judge from office or the criminal bench. The court-watching organization in Oakland, California, Citizens for Law and Order, claims 2500 members in 197 cities.[137] Similar citizen court-watchers programs exist in New Orleans, Miami, Boston, and Chicago.[138] The one in Chicago watches local judges for punctuality, a full day's work, and courtroom demeanor.[139] Has the time come for the courts to stop "policing the police" in defense of individual civil rights and for citizens to begin "policing the courts" in the name of community crime prevention?

Policing the courts

SUMMARY

"Police brutality" is rooted in the use of excessive force by the police, but the concept has been expanded to include the much more common form of police misconduct involving verbal abuse toward citizens. Civilian review boards were established to control these and other types of police misconduct of greatest concern to the community, to hold errant police officers accountable for violating their public trust, and to increase the police department's credibility with the minority community. Owing largely to intense opposition from the police themselves, however, the civilian review boards were short-lived. They have been superseded by two contemporary approaches aimed at achieving the same goals in different ways. On the one hand, citizens aggrieved by police misconduct are increasingly resorting to suing the police (for false arrest, violating civil rights, police brutality). On the other hand, the police-community relations movement seeks to reduce the minority community's hostility and dissatisfaction with the police through greater mutual understanding, communication, and enlightened changes in the police role. One of the most frequent yet dangerous assignments performed by the police is responding to domestic disturbances. Depending upon how they are handled, domestics may result in unnecessary injuries to citizens and police, lead to charges of police brutality, trigger a riot, or—conversely—become an opportunity for effective conflict management of interpersonal problems and contribute to improved police-community relations. Domestic (family) crisis intervention training for police has become the pragmatic cutting edge for emphasizing and developing the human relations and conflict management (social worker?) roles of the police in modern society. In the final analysis, the police cannot be effective in either their order maintenance or their law enforcement role without the cooperation of the public, which is increasingly becoming an active partner in crime control under the auspices of community crime prevention.

DISCUSSION QUESTIONS

1. What could groups (other than the police) within and outside the criminal justice system do to relieve the problem of domestic disturbances?
2. Should citizens be able to sue the police for mistakes made by the police in the line of duty? Why?
3. Are you in favor of or opposed to civilian review boards? Why?
4. A police car is dispatched to handle a domestic disturbance at an apartment building. As they climb the stairs, the officers hear the screams of an hysterical woman, punctuated by a man's cursing. "Police," they announce. The door is opened cautiously by a large man with fresh scratchmarks on his face. Behind him stands his wife, holding a towel to her puffed and swollen eye, who says, "Get him out of here. I want him arrested." Before the officers can reply, the husband tells them, "You ain't got no business here. This is my home, and unless you got a warrant, you ain't coming in." What would you do if you were the police officer? Why?
5. Is the public's concern over "police brutality" justified or exaggerated? Explain.

Chapter 5

THE PROFESSION-ALIZATION OF THE POLICE

College Education

Educational requirements for three personnel levels / Lateral entry / LEEP grants for higher education / Proposals of the Standards and Goals Commission / Benefits of college education for police / The Sherman Report

Training

Content of police training programs / College instructors and legal advisors / State training commissions / Project STAR / The Accreditation Commission

Ethnic Minorities in Police Departments

Title VII, Civil Rights Act of 1964 / Job-related tests / *Griggs* v. *Duke Power Co.* (1971) / Equal Employment Opportunities Act / Affirmative action / Court-imposed racial quotas / Efforts to attract minority recruits / The problem of reverse discrimination / *Bakke* v. *University of California* (1978) / *United Steelworkers* v. *Weber* (1979) / *Fullilove* v. *Klutznick* (1980)

Policewomen on Patrol

The Metropolitan Police Department study / Women perform patrol work adequately / Sex discrimination suits / Increasing numbers of women in policework

Close-up 5.1: Homosexuals as Police Officers

Operating Police Departments More Efficiently

The Consolidation of Police Services

Advantages of consolidation / Consolidation in practice

Civilians in Police Departments

One-Person Patrol Cars

New Arraignment Procedures for Police
New York's Appearance Control Project
Neighborhood Team Policing
Paramilitary police organization / An alternative patrol strategy / Team leader and patrol officers / Personal involvement and responsibility / Effects of team policing
Summary

Police departments today are faced with unprecedented demands and pressures for greater efficiency, effectiveness, and improved human relations with citizens. The central dilemma created for police administration is how to meet its legal, social, and institutional responsibilities to the public, to public policy, and to the police themselves, given operating budgets that will never keep pace with the need for services. The police department's search for the solution to the interrelated problems of improved productivity, efficiency, and human relations is increasingly focusing upon (1) professionalizing the police through college education, supplemented by training standards and expanded training programs, (2) opening police department doors to ethnic minorities and women, (3) adopting operational measures designed to reduce costs without sacrificing the quality or scope of police services, and (4) experimenting with a less paramilitary model of police management and organization, to be implemented through team policing.

The professionalization of the police is spearheaded by the drive for higher education. But all of the issues discussed in this chapter bear on police professionalism; even efficiency is a characteristic of professionalism. Indeed, the three styles of policing described by James Q. Wilson—watchman, legalistic, and service—are rapidly being superceded by one common police style and standard: professionalism.[1] Collectively, the innovations reviewed in this chapter have the potential for revolutionizing the administration of police personnel and services and for meeting the challenge of successfully managing police departments in a free society.

COLLEGE EDUCATION

As it is for every group of workers in America, higher education is the route to professionalization for the police, the route to developing a professional occupational identity, to gaining social acceptance as professionals, and to the transition of policework from a craft to a profession.*

* James Q. Wilson maintains that policework is a "craft." As such, the police field allegedly is not capable of codifying its values, experience, principles, and knowledge in ways that can be systematically transmitted through higher education, which is necessary for it to become a "profession."[2]

Advanced academic learning for police can be traced to August Vollmer and the development of two-year associate degree programs at junior colleges in California in the 1920s and 1930s. By 1957, of the 56 educational institutions offering college degrees in the criminal justice area, 26 were located in California, many of whose police departments have established minimum college education requirements on their own.[3] Despite the progressive strides made by California and a few other states by 1963, the idea of college-educated police was highly localized and had little generalized social approval or national political support.

Three major interrelated developments were responsible for putting college education for police on the national map. Round one in the call for more-educated police forces was opened by the President's Crime Commission, which recommended in 1967 that "the ultimate aim of all police departments should be that all personnel with general law enforcement powers have baccalaureate degrees."[4] At that time, about half of the nation's 450,000 law enforcement officers had not finished high school; while 70 percent of the nation's 40,000 police agencies required a high school diploma as a condition of employment, almost 12,000 did not, and accepted high school nongraduates as police officers.[5] The commission's long-range goal called for four-year college degrees for all sworn officers. However, its more immediate plans and specific recommendations linked educational requirements to a proposal to establish three entry-level police personnel categories in large and medium-size police departments.

Educational requirements for three personnel levels

Police Agent. Police agents were to be the most knowledgeable and most responsible police officers, who would be given the most difficult assignments, permitted the greatest discretion in performing them, receive the highest status and compensation, and be required to have the most education: at least two years of college and preferably a baccalaureate degree in the liberal arts or social sciences.

Police Officer. The police officer is the equivalent of the traditional and contemporary patrol officer. The police officer would enforce the laws and investigate crimes that might be solved without extended follow-up investigation, perform routine preventive patrol, render emergency services, respond to minor domestic disturbances, and work in concert with police agents in solving major crime and PCR problems. A high school education would be required for joining the force in this capacity.

n Diego began using Commun- Service Officers in 1978. The y's 45 CSOs are assigned to trol duties and a crime preven- on task force.

Community Service Officer. Serving basically as police apprentices, community service officers would be youths between 17 and 21 years of age, preferably from minority groups, who would have no general law enforcement powers and would not carry a weapon or make arrests. Unlike many police cadets who are used in civilian capacities in police departments, the CSO would not perform clerical duties. Because of their social background and greater understanding of ghetto problems, CSOs would in effect be police-community relations representatives. They would work with juveniles to prevent delinquency, try to improve communication between the police department and the community, refer citizen complaints to appropriate agencies, investigate minor thefts, perform selected emergency services for the disabled, and provide continuous community assistance to families encountering domestic problems.

In order to pave the way for recruiting blacks and other minorities into the police field as CSOs, the commission specified that "a high school diploma should not be a rigid prerequisite for serving as a CSO."[6] Similarly, because up to 60 percent of black youths growing up in the slums acquire arrest records, the commission recommended that a minor previous criminal record should not bar minority group members from being CSOs. The commission's relaxation of educational standards for CSOs represented a sociopolitical compromise and a strategy for introducing blacks into departments previously closed to them. As CSOs they would presumably be motivated to remedy academic deficiencies and go on to higher education in order to advance within the department.

A frequent criticism of higher education requirements for police is that college graduates will not be attracted to a field that requires all new members to start at the same bottom rung, freezes employees into entrance positions for a lengthy period, provides little incentive for the individual to pursue preferred career paths, and restricts interdepartmental mobility by precluding the transfer of "credits" from one police agency to another. In contrast to this traditional profile of police personnel management, the commission endorsed "lateral entry." Lateral entry is the opportunity to enter the police department at an advanced rank—that is, without starting at the bottom of the ladder—and to be given credit for prior service, experience, and achievement when applying for appointments in other agencies. The commission would allow more educated and experienced individuals to enter police departments in staff positions (or remain in patrol work if they preferred).[7] In effect, the tri-level entry plan constituted a form of intradepartmental lateral entry whereby a college recruit would be allowed to advance to police agent after an adequate but not interminable internship as a patrol police officer. At present, however, lateral entry is virtually unknown in the police field. And judging by the responses of police administrators, it will be a long time coming.*

Lateral entry

* Fifty-three of 72 police administrators interviewed in 1970–1971 were unwilling to alter conventional entry and promotion procedures to attract college graduates.[8] However, 46 percent of the 54 police departments in Missouri indicated they would be willing to implement a lateral entry policy. The chiefs who endorsed lateral entry were much more committed to higher education for patrol officers than were those who were unsympathetic to lateral entry.[9] Under the auspices of the Commission on Peace Officer Standards and Training (POST), lateral entry has probably made the greatest strides in California, where 145 police agencies had accepted it as of 1972.[10]

The second round in the nationwide professionalization of the police, which brought the commission's educational recommendations a giant step closer to realization, was LEAA's Law Enforcement Education Program. Between mid-1969 and 1974, more than 190,000 criminal justice practitioners and preservice students received LEEP grants at a total federal cost of $111 million. In 1974 alone, there were almost 100,000 LEEP recipients attending 1,036 participating educational institutions, at a government-subsidized cost of $45 million.[11] As of 1966, there were only 134 degree programs available to the law enforcement community, a plurality of which were in junior colleges in California.[12] Spurred by the infusion of massive LEEP funds, the number of known programs increased eightfold in five years. Nonetheless, between 1967 and 1973, the majority of state, county, and municipal law enforcement agencies had taken no steps toward mandating college education as necessary preparation for policework and employment.[13] During this time, 32 police agencies in California and those in nine states required education beyond high school.

EEP grants for higher education

The third and most recent round in the call for college-educated police began with the reports of the Standards and Goals Commission, released in 1973. By that time, about 10 percent of the police possessed four-year college degrees, while fully 50 percent had never attended college.[14] The Standards and Goals Commission boldly recommended that within specified time periods police departments make higher education a condition of employment—and that by 1982 police agencies hire only applicants with four-year college degrees. Instead of following its predecessor's advice to establish three entry-level personnel points, the Standards and Goals Commission reinforced the existing single career path by recommending the creation of multiple paygrades within the basic rank of patrol officer-investigator. The pay level and personnel classification plan would be predicated upon the educational standards, duties, and responsibilities involved in the jobs performed. Significantly, this arrangement allows advancement within the basic patrol rank, permits equity between patrol officers and investigators, provides for efficiency pay for personnel in specific field activities, and offers financial and status incentives for progressing within the basic rank along a nonmanagerial career path if that is the employee's choice.[15]

Proposals of the andards and Goals Commission

Making a high school diploma the standard prerequisite for joining the force occurred at a time when a relatively small proportion of the general population finished or went beyond high school. Hence, adopting the high school standard served initially to maintain the high calibre of police recruits and officers. The picture changed, however, as progressively larger proportions and absolute numbers of the general population became high school graduates and continued their education.[16] Meanwhile, police departments stubbornly resisted upgrading their educational entrance requirements, with the result that police candidates were being drawn from the bottom of the educational barrel. This *de facto* progressive lowering of recruitment standards led to a decline in the average quality of police officers.

Benefits of college education for police

The main case for college-educated police is the belief that higher education produces better police, police service, and police departments. It is assumed that college education will make those who become (and those who already are) police officers less cynical, prejudiced, punitive, authoritarian, hostile, and ready to resort to force, and that it will result in superior field performance as measured by fewer civilian complaints, higher supervisors' ratings, fewer injuries to self and citizens, and fewer instances of police misconduct. The research evidence regarding the effects of college education on police, policework, and the police occupation is a mixed bag (see Table 5.1).

Both crime commissions spoke in idealistic generalities about the need, the value, and the benefits of college education. Yet in the opinion of one researcher, "the hard evidence based upon research which would support these conclusions continue to range from slim to none."[17] In particular, the predicted impact of college education on reducing prejudice and authoritarianism has so far found little solid support. The most frequently cited research that concludes that college reduces authoritarianism[18] has been criticized on methodological grounds.[19] Many writers have concluded that whatever value, potential, or effects college exposure has in reducing prejudice and authoritarianism is negated by the overwhelming

The main route to professionalization of the police is through higher education

ble 5.1 The Effects of College Education on Police, Policework, and the Police Occupation

POSITIVE RESULTS	NEGATIVE RESULTS
llege education is associated with fewer civilian mplaints against police, superior performance, and higher pervisor ratings.	College education is associated with a high rate of job turnover, need for dominance, and heightened perception of danger related to daily assignments.
lice administrators believe that college education entifies the best candidates for employment.	More "professional" police departments stress aggressive patrol and high arrest rates.
ore educated officers were less likely to condone the use of ce in dealing with citizens.	Exposure to college does not make police students less authoritarian or less prejudiced.
posure to college results in improved self-esteem and less nitive attitudes toward others.	College education makes police officers more cynical than their less-educated peers.
lice who graduate from college are less authoritarian than lice who do not attend college.	In exercising discretion, officers in more "professional" police departments opt for arrest and strict enforcement of the law more often than officers in less "professional" agencies.
lice department college education requirements are sponsible for a lower crime rate, lower agency turnover, gh morale, a reduction in disciplinary problems, the sence of citizen complaints, and a police department t can operate both efficiently and effectively.	Education makes no difference in police officer responsiveness to the community.
lice recruits with some college exposure respond to scretionary situations by avoiding arrest more often than recruits with only a high school background.	Many uneducated police administrators are ambivalent, threatened by, or hostile toward higher education for their subordinates. They may actively discourage lower echelon police personnel from pursuing college education and fail to reward those who do.
re educated police officers are more likely to reject a et tough" approach as the solution to the crime problem; more likely to believe that probable cause requirements search and seizure do not reduce police effectiveness— t is, they are more protective of civil liberties; are more eptive to Supreme Court decisions and appreciative of constitutional form of government; and are more willing olerate social protest and dissent.	
re highly educated police officers make more arrests.	

impact of the daily negative experiences and pressures of policework.[20] When a professor of criminology at Florida State University left the campus to become a full-time working policeman, he admitted, "I found that when I put on that blue suit, I can't be a scientist." As discussed at length in Chapter 14, Philip Zimbardo found that when college students were placed in the shoes of prison guards, their liberal attitudes toward humanity, equality, and impartiality did not accompany them into the prison.

The relevance of higher education to policing rests largely upon an article of faith rather than proof beyond a reasonable doubt, as is true for many other fields that have attained professional stature. Perhaps many of the benefits of higher education to policing cannot be verified empirically, but they are nonetheless real. The relevance of knowledge of the social and behavioral sciences to a police occupation concerned increasingly with social services and human relations cannot be minimized. Even the skeptics of college education recognize that it broadens one's horizons and exposes individuals to new ideas, information, and values, thereby counterbalancing police insulation to diverse community needs.[21] In an ever-changing and dynamic environment, the infusion of college graduates who are more cosmopolitan and oriented to change is bound to make police departments more sensitive to the larger society and the multiple communities of which it is an integral part. College education can be expected to develop a more professional set of police attitudes that reflect the complexity, responsibility, and gravity of problems inherent in the police function.[22]

The Sherman Report

If the value of college education for police has not yet lived up to all expectations, part of the reason may be the quality of the educational programs themselves. Based upon data available from existing national surveys of police education programs, the National Advisory Commission on Higher Education for Police Officers (the Sherman Report) concluded that basic changes in program objectives, curriculum content and faculty employment practices were needed for the promise and potential of college-educated police to be realized. The Sherman Report posited as a goal the educating of police for institutional change. The Report was sharply critical of the narrow academic focus of many police education programs, the absence of attention to value choices and ethical dilemmas of policework, programs that emphasize vocational training courses (police science or technology approaches) similar to those taught in police academies, and various faculty characteristics found predominantly in community college police programs. The following are some of the commission's far-reaching and often highly controversial specific recommendations.[23]

The required number of specialized courses in police and criminal justice in any police eduation program should not exceed one-fourth of the total course work for a degree.

Police education programs that offer vocational training courses (courses that train students to perform specific police tasks) should replace those courses with more analytical and conceptual courses on related issues.

Police education programs at the undergraduate level should give greater emphasis to the major issues in doing police work and less emphasis to issues of police management and supervision.

Police education programs using a "criminal justice system" framework for their required curriculum should also include comprehensive treatment of the most commonly performed police work, which falls outside of the criminal justice system.

Colleges should rely on a core of full-time faculty to staff their police education programs and should rely much less on part-time faculty.

Colleges should grant no academic credit for attendance at police agency training programs.
Community colleges should phase out their terminal two-year degree programs in police education.
Faculty members in police education programs at any level should be required to have completed at least two full years of postgraduate education.
Police education programs should actively seek out Ph.D.s in the arts and sciences to serve as faculty members.
Educational background, teaching ability, research, and commitment—rather than prior employment in a criminal justice agency—should be the most important criteria of faculty selection in police education programs.
Part-time faculty appointments in police education programs should be limited to people with unique practical expertise.

Predictably, the Sherman Report spurred active debate in the academic and law enforcement communities concerning the proper nature of higher education for future police officers, and that debate may be a fortunate and healthy development.[24] For in the final analysis, the issues involved in upgrading the educational standards of policy may be inseparable from that of improving the quality of higher education delivery systems to which preservice and inservice students are exposed.

TRAINING

The amount, the type, and the features of training received by police recruits leave much to be desired. A 1967 study by the IACP revealed that the average police officer received less than 200 hours of formal training; in contrast, embalmers received 5,000 hours, barbers 4,000 hours, and beauticians 1,200 hours of training for their trades. In cities of less than 250,000 population, police departments provided on the average three weeks of training.[25] And recruits in many police agencies received no academy training at all. To remedy these deficiencies, the President's Crime Commission recommended that an "absolute minimum of 400 classroom hours" be established for basic police training in all departments.[26]

Content of police training programs

Just as important as the length of training is its content. A 1972 IACP survey of the 50 states found that the training curriculum concentrated on criminal investigation, evidence and criminal law, firearms, traffic and patrol duties, and physical fitness. In most states less than 10 percent of training time was spent on "people" subjects such as police-community relations, psychology, sociology, human relations, and family crisis intervention. Of 165 police departments surveyed in cities of more than 100,000 population, on the average only 11 hours were devoted to human relations training.[27] Thus training programs are lopsidedly geared to the law enforcement aspects of policework while neglecting the order maintenance, social services, and conflict management dimensions of the police role—which consume the lion's share of policing.[28] "Current training programs, for the most part, prepare an officer to perform police work mechanically, but do not prepare him to understand his community, the police role, or the imperfections of the criminal justice system."[29]

College instructors and legal advisors

A final feature of police training that requires improvement is the tendency to have programs operated entirely by sworn police personnel on police academy grounds. This procedure lends itself to insularity, the loss of instructional expertise by nonpolice, and an overemphasis on law enforcement. One response to this problem has been to have the training performed by university professors either at campus locations or at the police academy, which provides an opportunity to introduce more social science and human relations material into the training curriculum. A second approach is to delegate more of the training responsibility to police department legal advisors. In general, police legal advisors serve as in-house training and legal resources in matters of the law such as search and seizure developments, the preparation of warrants, confessions, line-ups, the right to counsel, and the defense of officers or officials facing lawsuits stemming from alleged misconduct.[30] By late 1974, some 275 major law enforcement agencies had in-house counsel.[31]

State training commissions

The major impetus to increasing the length and quality of police training programs has come from state training commissions. These are professional organizations authorized to require or recommend minimum training levels and curriculum content for the state's law enforcement agencies and to offer certification to officers who successfully complete the requirements. The first state training commissions were created in 1959, when New York established its Municipal Police Training Council, and in 1960, when California[32] established a Commission on Peace Officer Standards and Training (POST).[33] The expansion of state training commissions was spurred by financial support from the LEAA and its predecessor agency in 1965. Eighty-five percent of the 39 State Law Enforcement Training Commissions have come into existence since 1965.[34] By the end of 1974, 45 states had mandatory minimum standards for police that, on the average, required 240 hours of training.[35]

In cooperation with the American Justice Institute and funded partially by the LEAA, in 1975 the POST commission completed a multimillion-dollar, three-and-one-half-year project based on research conducted among 1,500 criminal justice agencies in California, Michigan, New Jersey, and Texas. Designated Project STAR,* it was a comprehensive effort

Project STAR

* STAR is an acronym for Systems and Training Analysis of Requirements for Criminal Justice Participants.

to define criminal justice roles and functions, identify job requirements and performance objectives, determine knowledge and skill requirements, and formulate education and training recommendations responsive to the personnel needs of the entire criminal justice system.[36] In late 1974, the LEAA awarded a $3.2 million contract to the National Planning Association to conduct a nationwide two-year survey of the type of criminal justice training and educational requirements most urgently needed by practitioners, and to devise strategies for meeting them in the future.[37] And in 1975 the LEAA awarded a grant of $451,284 to the Los Angeles Police Department to develop national standards for police executive recruitment and job performance.[38]

The Accreditation Commission

The most recent and ambitious development in, but going substantially beyond, improved police training is the Commission on Accreditation for Law Enforcement Agencies, initiated in September 1979 under a $1.5 million LEAA grant. The Accreditation Commission is designed to accredit law enforcement agencies based on their attainment and compliance with national administrative and operational standards adopted by the commission.[39] Functioning in a staff capacity, four major police organizations had the task of drafting realistic, concrete, and measurable standards, to be used for evaluating police departments. While building upon previous police reform efforts, the standards of the Accreditation Commission are different in that they are strictly applicational and intended for agency consumption. Each standard refers to a specific facet of law enforcement, is accompanied by an explanatory comment, and can be answered "yes" and "no" by the police department. Among the topical areas included in the commission's program are standards for recruitment, selection, and promotion of officers; characteristics of patrol and investigations; job classification and pay scales; deployment of patrol officers; the use of force; the operation of specialized units such as juvenile bureaus, detectives, vice and narcotic squads; and standards governing riot control, labor relations, and maintaining internal discipline.[40]

The basic goal of the Accreditation Commission is to increase the efficiency and effectiveness of the delivery of police services by promulgating a comprehensive set of standards that can be uniformly applied to police agencies throughout the country. At the same time, accreditation is expected to encourage and institutionalize change and innovation in a positive atmosphere, because the yardsticks for measuring police agency performance have been developed by practitioners and knowledgeable citizens responsive to the problems of law enforcement. As envisaged, police agencies will apply for accreditation, be sent a self-assessment form to complete, and be awarded accreditation status after an evaluation ("audit") team has made a site visit to the agency and confirmed its compliance with the standards.[41] Police department involvement in accreditation is entirely voluntary. But it is assumed that the program's appeal to agency prestige and the practical value of being accredited—increased public confidence, attracting qualified recruits, and added political clout at budget time—will offer strong incentives for participation. Moreover, as accreditation gains acceptance and momentum, there may be pressure for municipal and police officials to obtain the commission's stamp of approval, lest the community have reason to believe it is receiving second-class police services.

The third and final phase of the commission's work, a 15-month stage begun in January 1981, involved developing a methodology for objectively assessing an agency's performance against the standards, field-testing the accreditation process, refining and modifying the standards as indicated, and full-scale implementation of the accreditation program.[42] If the Accreditation Commission is successful in its landmark attempt to standardize and overhaul law enforcement policies and practices nationwide, it will be a major contribution toward professionalizing the occupation and is bound to have a dramatic effect on "police training" in the broadest and most profound sense of the concept.

ETHNIC MINORITIES IN POLICE DEPARTMENTS

The national call and modus operandi for opening police departments to ethnic minorities—principally blacks and Hispanics—was signaled by the President's Crime Commission's plea that "written examinations should be analyzed to ensure no cultural or other bias against minority groups exist."[43] As a corollary, the commission endorsed the revision of certain traditional selection standards that "may have the unintended effect of arbitrarily barring large numbers of minority group applicants who could adequately perform police work."[44] The commission proposed that some rigid physical entrance requirements be reduced (for example, minimum height, weight, eyesight, and physical agility standards). In effect, it advocated lowering educational requirements for community service officers in order to increase the representation of ethnic minorities in police agencies. A survey of 28 police agencies conducted by the National Advisory Commission on Civil Disorders found that the median percentage of black sworn personnel was 6 percent, whereas the median percentage of blacks in the general population was 24 percent.[45] In every city, county, and state where statistics were available, substantial underrepresentation of minority group members is the rule rather than the exception, as Table 5.2 shows.

Title VII, Civil Rights Act of 1964

The body of emerging federal law used to pry open police department doors to qualified minority applicants began with the Civil Rights Act of 1964, which also established the Equal Employment Opportunity Commission (EEOC) to enforce Title VII of the act: "It shall be an unlawful employment practice for an employer to fail or refuse to hire or to discharge any individual, or otherwise to discriminate against any individual with respect to his compensation, terms, conditions, or privileges of employment, because of such individual's race, color, religion, sex, or national origin." Originally directed at the private sector, the objectives of Title VII were to achieve equality of employment opportunity and to remove artificial discriminatory barriers, past and present, that favored white employees over other groups.[46] The Civil Rights Act of 1964 prohibited not only overt and intentional discrimination by large private employers but also practices that, while apparently fair in form, in practice had the result of systematically discriminating against identifiable classes of persons.

Job-related tests

Traditionally, police departments used various intelligence, mental ability, aptitude, and psychological tests as qualifying entrance requirements for employment. These tests were often alleged to be culturally bi-

e Civil Rights Act of 1964 helped
en police department doors to
nority applicants

Table 5.2 Percentage of Nonwhite Population and Percentage of Nonwhite Police Officers in Selected Cities

City	Percent of Nonwhites in Total Population	Percent of Nonwhites Among Police Officers
Atlanta	38	10
Baltimore	41	7
Boston	11	2
Buffalo	18	3
Chicago	27	17
Cincinnati	28	6
Cleveland	34	7
Dayton	26	4
Detroit	39	5
Hartford	20	11
Kansas City	20	6
Louisville	21	6
Memphis	38	5
New Haven	19	7
New Orleans	41	4
New York	16	5
Newark	40	10
Oakland	31	4
Oklahoma City	15	4
Philadelphia	29	20
Phoenix	8	1
Pittsburgh	19	7
St. Louis	37	11
San Francisco	14	6
Tampa	17	3
Washington, D.C.	63	

Source: Robert Michael Regoli and Donnell E. Jerome, "The Recruitment and Promotion of a Minority Group into an Established Institution: The Police," *Journal of Police Science & Administration,* December 1975, p. 412. Reprinted by permission of Northwestern University.

ased in favor of the middle class white majority, thereby barring blacks and other minorities from the police field. It was assumed (but never proven) that performance on the written entrance tests was significantly related to actual performance on the job, that is, that the tests were *job-related.*[47] Thus blacks who were rejected for employment because of their lower test scores but who could perform equally well on the job were being denied equal employment opportunity.

Griggs v. *Duke Power Co.* (1971)

The issue of the legality of employer tests that have the effect of preventing blacks from being hired (or promoted) was settled by the Supreme Court in March 1971 in *Griggs* v. *Duke Power Co.*[48] Black employees of the Duke Power Company, a private employer, brought a class action suit under Title VII of the Civil Rights Act of 1964, challenging the firm's requirement that a standardized general intelligence test be passed as a condition of employment or for transfer to a higher position. In *Griggs* the Supreme Court prohibited the use of the company's entrance and promotional tests because "neither was directed or intended to measure the ability to learn to perform a particular job or category of jobs. . . . If an employment practice which operates to exclude Negroes cannot be shown to be *related* to *job* performance, the practice is prohibited." Basically, the *Griggs* decision represented an endorsement of the EEOC policies against employment discrimination and an acceptance of emerging lower federal court decisions on the matter.[49]

Equal Employment Opportunities Act

Two later developments brought the matter of written entrance examinations used by police departments under the firm control of the Civil Rights Act of 1964, the EEOC, its affirmative action guidelines, and the related principles of racial quotas and preferential hiring. Passed in March 1972, the Equal Employment Opportunities Act extended the provisions of the Civil Rights Act of 1964 to cover the employment practices of state and local government agencies, and it empowered the EEOC to sue public employers it deemed guilty of discrimination. This 1972 amendment to the Civil Rights Act brought the personnel selection procedures of police departments under the jurisdiction of the EEOC and made *Griggs* applicable to law enforcement employers. Prior to that time, the role of the EEOC was restricted to the private employment sector and was only an advisory role, one limited to conducting studies, developing guidelines, and making recommendations to private corporations and labor unions.

Affirmative action

The EEOC's hand was strengthened further with the signing of the Affirmative Action Amendment by President Nixon in March 1973. *Affirmative action* denotes the special endeavors by police departments (or other employers) to recruit, hire, retain, and promote minority group members and to eliminate the sources and effects of past and present employment discrimination.[50] The EEOC insisted that law enforcement agencies adhere to their affirmative action guidelines in hiring and promotion, and it strictly prohibited using any tests that adversely affect minority group employment.[51] In order to use entrance exams, other hiring requirements (such as character investigations or height, weight, and physical agility standards), and screening devices that "favor" white applicants, police agencies must be able to establish that their selection procedures are associated with improved performance—that is, that they are job-related. Otherwise, the EEOC and the courts may step in to correct the discriminatory departmental personnel practices.

Ethnic minorities have been gaining ground in police departments under the collective impetus of the law as formulated in the Civil Rights Act of 1964, enunciated by the Supreme Court in *Griggs,* and implemented through compliance with EEOC's affirmative action guidelines. While affirmative action includes any and all steps taken to correct past and present discrimination, the most forceful, effective, and controversial affirmative action efforts are those based on *racial quotas.* Judges throughout the country have resorted to racial quotas to correct employment discrimination in police departments.[52]

Court-imposed racial quotas

In 1973 the Department of Justice filed suit against the Chicago Police Department to enforce the Civil Rights Act of 1964 and the LEAA's equal employment opportunity regulations. The suit charged that the department discriminated against blacks and Spanish-surnamed persons, who respectively constituted 16 percent and 1 percent of the department's 13,500 police personnel. At the same time, Chicago's population was 33 percent black and 7 percent Hispanic.[53] In November 1974 the court found that the written examination used by the Chicago Police Department had "disproportionate (disparate) impact" upon minority groups and that the tests had not been validated as job-related, and it prohibited their further use.* In January 1976 a federal court imposed a sweeping quota system on the Chicago Police Department: of the next 400 to 600 officers hired, 50 percent had to be black or Hispanic males, 16.5 percent women, and 33.5 percent white males. Until the department complied with the order, the judge withheld $95 million in revenue-sharing funds earmarked to pay police salaries.[54]

In a suit initiated by the nonprofit law firm Public Advocates Inc., a federal district court in 1973 prohibited the San Francisco Police Department from using their old written tests for hiring and promotion. The court ordered the SFPD to hire 3 minority persons for every 2 majority patrol recruits until minorities comprised 30 percent of the force.[55] It also ordered the department to appoint them to the rank of sergeant on a one-to-one basis until 30 percent of the sergeants were minority members.[56]

The Southern Poverty Law Center filed suit to desegregate the all-white

* The court also found that the department's background check (character investigation) contained items not shown to be job-related, and the court enjoined its use.

Alabama State Troopers. In February 1972 a federal court ordered the Alabama Department of Public Safety to begin immediately to hire qualified black troopers in equal numbers as white, until 25 percent of its 644-person force was black (the same proportion as blacks in the state's population). The Alabama Highway Patrol had not hired a single black person as a trooper or in a support capacity in 37 years.[57] After three years under the federal court hiring plan injunction, Alabama had the nation's largest percentage of blacks (4.5 percent) among uniformed state police officers.

By the late 1970s, virtually all police departments sensitive to the problem of job discrimination had taken measures to comply with the government's affirmative action policy in order to avoid losing LEAA funds, to forestall further court intervention in police department matters, and out of a genuine belief in the propriety and benefits of having a more ethnically representative police agency. Aggressive recruitment became the order of the day; minority candidates were sought at military bases, at predominantly black colleges, in the South, through police storefronts in the ghetto, and with recruitmobiles. Efforts were intensified to develop police department programs involving cadets, reserve officers, auxiliaries, Community Service Officers, and similar positions primarily reserved for young minority members who might go on to a career in law enforcement.[58]

Efforts to attract minority recruits

The results were impressive. Culture-free, job-related, criterion-based tests began to replace the older, unvalidated, and discriminatory entrance examinations used by police departments.* Height and weight tests were revised to accommodate Puerto Rican and Mexican-American applicants.[60] City ordinances were passed that allowed candidates with lower test scores to be selected for appointment over those with higher scores.[61] Innovative approaches were aimed at overcoming minority group skepticism toward police department efforts on their behalf, tokenism, and the fear of rejection.† Operating since September 1971 under $521,000 in LEAA grants, the center for criminal justice minority employment at Marquette University has mapped out minority recruitment programs for 35 law enforcement jurisdictions. Their recruitment plan designed for the California Highway Patrol is an outstanding example of vigorous efforts to recruit minorities.[63] Of the 89,065 police officers employed in the na-

* The EEOC guidelines recommend criterion-related entrance examinations—tests that are not culturally biased and that correlate well with external, objective measures of police performance on the job (such as supervisor ratings, departmental commendations, civilian complaints). Yet even these job-related entrance tests have been attacked by the EEOC for discriminating against minorities when they did not advance the agency's commitment to social equality.[59]

† In Dallas, for example, minority applicants are given training in how to take and pass the entrance tests.[62]

tion's 50 largest cities, the proportion of blacks rose to 9 percent, according to a survey released in 1974 by the Race Relations Information Center. Atlanta led the country with a 20 percent black municipal police force.[64]

The problem of reverse discrimination

The social and legal complexities involved in bringing ethnic minorities into police departments are monumental. The issue of racial quotas and preferential hiring reaches far beyond the confines of police agencies. It confronts all occupations, employees, and the constitutionality of "reverse discrimination" itself. The dilemma separates blacks from whites, skeptics from idealists, men from women, liberals from conservatives, and the EEOC from everyone who believes in a strict "merit" principle for employment and advancement. University professors and union members who lose jobs, promotion opportunities, and security benefits are among the growing numbers of majority member workers who are starting to complain bitterly about their own civil rights being abridged —and filing reverse discrimination suits in court.

The lay person's or majority position towards minorities in policework is summarized by the concern that "for every deserving minority group member who is provided a job or promotion through preferential quotas, there is also a deserving non-minority person who is thereby deprived of a job or promotion."[65] In particular, official recognition of a color-bound double educational standard for employment seems to run counter to the emphasis on higher education as the *sine qua non* for entrance to the police field and for advancement within it. As for the EEOC, it is adamant about increasing minorities in policework, even if it means eliminating certain educational incentives for police. In 1975, for example, the EEOC challenged the practice of giving pay increases for college credit on the ground that since whites are more likely to attend college than blacks, white officers were receiving preferential treatment.[66] Privately, some administrators concede that there are contradictions between securing the best qualified candidates and racial quotas that require changes in educational and physical requirements to accommodate blacks and Hispanics.[67]

Bakke the Supreme Court ap-
oved of affirmative action but
approved of racial quotas for
hieving it

The courts themselves are deeply divided over the propriety and constitutionality of the reverse discrimination that is implicit in minority quotas and double standards. Some courts have held that certain standardized intelligence tests used for police department employment were job-related, only to be overruled by appellate courts that said they were not.[68] Some judges have endorsed racial quotas and stated that "members of the white race may not seek relief for racial discrimination under Title VII."[69] Other courts have overturned racial quotas, finding them "repugnant to the basic concepts of a democratic society"[70]—in effect agreeing with Chief Justice Burger's position that racial quotas are a case of "robbing Peter to pay Paul."[71]

Bakke v. *University of California* (1978)

The Supreme Court's 1978 decision in *Bakke* v. *Regents of the Univer-*

sity of California did little to clarify the constitutional status of employment quotas.[72] It was the policy of the medical school at Davis to set aside 16 places in an entering class of 100 students for minority applicants, who were accepted even if they had substantially lower scores than those of rejected white applicants such as Allan Bakke. In *Bakke* the Court ruled that (a) universities could not use such a rigid racial quota because it violated Title VI of the Civil Rights Act of 1964, and (b) it was permissible to take race into consideration as one—but not the only—factor in a university's admission policy. Thus the Supreme Court approved the principle of affirmative action but disapproved the quota method for implementing affirmative action in the circumstances of the case at hand. The opinion allowed that quotas might be permissible if it were demonstrated that they were essential for promoting a "compelling state interest." But the medical school, which had no history of discriminating against minorities, failed to prove that its quota system was justified by the need to achieve an ethnically diverse group of students. It remains to be seen whether the Supreme Court would condone racial (or sex) quotas in police departments—where the case for ethnic community representation, the need to overcome long-standing discrimination, or other state interests may be far more compelling and demonstrable.

United Steelworkers v. *Weber* (1979)

The Supreme Court's decision in *United Steelworkers of America* v. *Weber* in 1979 has far greater implications for racial quotas in police departments than *Bakke.* Brian Weber, an unskilled white employee, applied for admission to Kaiser's training program for skilled craft positions in Gramercy, Louisiana. In voluntarily establishing the training program in 1974, Kaiser sought to increase the small number of blacks in skilled craft jobs at the Gramercy plant and, toward that end, set aside half of the training program slots for minority employees. When Weber was turned down but two black employees with less seniority were accepted into the training program, Weber filed a class-action suit charging that the company's policy constituted an illegal quota under Title VII of the Civil Rights Act. In a strong and clear endorsement of affirmative action, the Court upheld the company's racial preference policy. The court emphasized, however, that the only issue ruled upon was whether private employers can voluntarily give special preference to blacks to eliminate "manifest racial imbalance" without violating Title VII of the Civil Rights Act.[73] In stating that they can, the Court left unresolved whether public employers can be ordered by courts to adopt racial hiring quotas without violating the equal protection clause of the Constitution. The immediate effects of *Bakke* and *Weber* may be an unprecedented amount of litigation over reverse discrimination in employment areas ranging from policing to teaching.*

Brian Weber brought a "reverse discrimination" suit against Kaiser Aluminum, which reserved half of its job training slots for minority employees

* It may be significant that three months after *Bakke* the Supreme Court denied certiorari and thus left standing a district court decision that imposed a sex hiring quota on the Philadelphia Police Department.[74]

Fullilove v. *Klutznick* (1980)

The Supreme Court's strongest endorsement of racial quotas in employment occurred in *Fullilove* v. *Klutznick* in 1980, a decision whose relevance to affirmative action may ultimately overshadow the more celebrated *Bakke* and *Weber* cases.[75] In *Fullilove,* the Court upheld a 1977 congressional law which provided that out of $4 billion allocated by the federal government to the states for public works, at least 10 percent had to be awarded to minority business enterprises. In doing so, the Court clarified a fundamental constitutional question left open in *Weber:* The equal protection clause of the Fourteenth Amendment does not flatly prohibit affirmative action programs. The essential rationale underlying *Fullilove,* which may or may not be validly extended to police departments, was that (1) under certain circumstances, racial employment quotas may be used to compensate for past discrimination, and (2) even though white employees who suffer under racial quotas are not themselves guilty of any discrimination, a "sharing of the burden" by such innocent parties is sometimes permissible as part of a carefully devised plan to remedy the present effects of previous racial bigotry. The Court also had no intrinsic objection to awarding federal contracts to minority businesses who are not the lowest bidder—a practice whose counterpart in some police departments is hiring minority applicants whose entrance test scores are lower than rejected white applicants. The *Fullilove* Court emphasized, however, that its decision was anchored in the broad remedial powers Congress possesses to assure compliance with federal antidiscrimination laws, that the remedy must be narrowly tailored to avoid giving minorities blatant or unreasonable preference, that the 10 percent set-aside was not inflexible but could be waived for cause in individual cases, and that its opinion did not deal with the issue of judicially-mandated racial quotas. Thus, at least nominally, the Court in *Fullilove* offered no indication of how it might view racial quotas for the public employment sector imposed by state agencies or the courts.

POLICEWOMEN ON PATROL

The most recent minority group to demand access to police departments as working patrol officers are women. Traditionally, the employment of women in police agencies has been restricted to behind the scenes, nonpatrol activities: clerical or matron duties, light work investigation, and assignment to the women's bureau, youth bureau, juvenile division, and PCR unit. Unlike the basis of discrimination against ethnic minorities, the exclusion of women from patrol positions was based on the belief that they were incapable of performing adequately in that capacity.

The Metropolitan Police Department study

A Police Foundation-sponsored study laid to rest this long-held but erroneous assumption. Conducted in the Metropolitan Police Department of Washington, D.C. in 1972, the study evaluated the performance of 86 new female recruits during their first year as policewomen on patrol with that of a matched group of 86 new male officers. It was the first time that any police department had integrated a substantial number of women officers into the backbone of the force. (At the time, there were only about 250 women serving as sworn patrol officers in the entire country.[76]) The research project thus made it possible to assess the ability of women to perform patrol work successfully, their impact on the operations of an urban police department, and their reception by the community. The conclusion: "In sum, the study shows that sex is not a bona fide occupational qualification for doing police patrol work" (see Table 5.3).[77]

The major reservations about female patrol personnel expressed by their male partners, police officials, and the community at large stem from the traditional concern for their limitations in taking aggressive action when appropriate: in making arrests, handling verbal threats, physical resistance, and assault, and providing protective aid to fellow officers. The counterargument is that by acting less aggressively, patrolwomen

Table 5.3 Findings of Policewomen on Patrol Study, Metropolitan Police Department, Washington, D.C.

SIMILARITIES IN THE PERFORMANCE OF POLICEWOMEN AND POLICEMEN	NOTABLE DIFFERENCES IN THE PERFORMANCE OF POLICEWOMEN AND POLICEMEN
They responded to similar types of calls while on patrol and saw similar proportions of citizens who were dangerous, angry, upset, drunk, or violent.	Patrolwomen made fewer felony and misdemeanor arrests and issued fewer traffic citations than the men. (Making more arrests is not necessarily a sign of superior police performance.)
They obtained similar results in handling angry or violent citizens.	Policewomen received lower anonymous supervisory ratings on their ability to handle various types of violent encounters and on general competence to perform street patrol (handling disorderly males, public fights, protecting partners from assault).
Policewomen made arrests that were just as likely to result in convictions (28%) as those made by the new patrolmen (26%).	Citizens were more skeptical about the women's ability to deal with violence.
They worked well together in two-person patrol cars.	Injured policewomen were more likely to be placed on light duty than injured patrolmen, but their injuries did not cause them to be absent from work more often than the men.
They received the same amount of backup assistance from other police units.	Patrolmen were charged more often than patrolwomen with serious conduct unbecoming an officer.
They were shown equal respect and acceptance by the community.	Policewomen were better than male recruits at performing certain crime-related tasks (such as questioning rape victims).
They had about the same number of sick days, injuries sustained, and days lost to injuries.	Policewomen received a greater degree of cooperation from the community than did male recruits, that is, they were better at PCR.
Women were no more likely to resign from the force within 16 months after appointment than were men.	

Source: Peter Bloch and Deborah Anderson, *Policewomen on Patrol: Final Report,* Washington, D.C.: Police Foundation, May 1974, pp. 1–7.

may be less likely to incite aggression. They can use their unique minority group skills to defuse potentially dangerous situations without resorting to arrest or force (and thereby improving PCR in the process). The less aggressive behavior of policewomen may have a beneficial spillover effect toward "humanizing" policemen.[78] And they may be especially effective in mediating domestic disturbances. The small proportion of patrol work that involves law enforcement and crime control, as compared with their order maintenance and human relations duties, further offsets the women's lower performance in aggressive activities.

Women perform patrol work adequately

Some aspects of the policewoman on patrol experiment and its findings have been legitimately criticized.[79] Nevertheless, the major substantiated conclusion of the Washington study—subsequently bolstered by a Police Foundation study in New York City[80] and departmental experience in Boston, Miami, and Dayton[81]—is that, as a class of persons, women can perform patrol duties adequately. Therefore sex is not a bona fide barrier to patrol work, and being male is not a job-related requirement for "real" policework. Unless police agencies can prove that sex *is* a bona fide qualification for active policework, women may force police departments to accept them as patrol members by taking their job discrimination cases to federal court under the Civil Rights Act of 1964.

Sex discrimination suits

A lawsuit against the San Francisco Police Department in 1973 resulted in a federal court order requiring that an experimental quota of 60 women be hired as patrol officers at a rate of 15 per 60-member academy class. The order also revised the height and weight requirements that had artificially barred women from patrol jobs.[82] Twenty-seven women had been appointed as patrol officers by July 1975, the first women since 1916 to be employed by the SFPD in other than clerical or custodial positions.[83]

With the threat of a lawsuit in the offing, by the spring of 1972 the New York City Police Department had ended its height requirements, "unfrozen" its list of women applicants, and increased its policewomen on patrol to 400 in a brief period of time.[84]

In response to a lawsuit filed by the Department of Justice, Maryland agreed to recruit more female state police officers. Similarly, in October 1975 the New Jersey State Police agreed to establish within one year "hiring goals" for women in both classified and unclassified positions.[85] As of mid 1974, similar suits were pending in Buffalo and Philadelphia.[86]

In 1973 a rejected female applicant filed suit against the California Highway Patrol, charging that its male-only restriction unlawfully discriminated against women under Title VII of the Civil Rights Act of 1964. Following the favorable results of a two-year feasibility study of employing women as state traffic officers, a judgment was made in the plaintiff's favor. In June 1976 the California Highway Patrol officially

dies have shown that women
rol officers do their jobs as
as male officers

began accepting qualified women for state trooper positions, terminating a 46-year tradition of men only in the driver's seat.[87]

In September 1973 the court enjoined the Cleveland Police Department from imposing its minimum 5′8″ height and 150-pound weight requirements on women, on the ground that these criteria were not job-related and were therefore discriminatory under the Civil Rights Act. Since then, police departments across the country have lowered their height requirements or abolished them altogether.[88]

Increasing numbers of women in policework

The barriers that discriminate against women in policing are gradually fading, and policewomen on patrol are becoming visible in cities and states throughout the nation. In the United States their number has risen from less than 12 in 1971 to 1,050 by mid 1974.[89] Atlanta leads the nation—over 7 percent of its 1,535 sworn officers are patrolwomen—followed by the District of Columbia with 6 percent and New York with 2 percent.[90] Women are being deployed in all types of policework, and they are beginning to assume command and supervisory positions.[91] The principle of sexual equality in policing may even have been stretched to its limits in Okeechobee, Florida, where a 5′1″, 80-year-old grandmother was named sheriff![92]

Women in policing have undoubtedly come a long way, but they have a still longer way to go. A 1973 nationwide survey (by the Police Foundation and the IACP) of all police departments with 50 or more sworn personnel disclosed that women filled less than 2 percent of the sworn positions. One-third of the responding police agencies did not employ any sworn policewomen; and promotion practices and procedures were stacked against females.[93] As a rule, even the most progressive departments do not have more than 3 policewomen to every 100 policemen.[94] Yet, even the most conservative policemen may come to view female patrol officers favorably when compared with the next minority group seeking unrestricted employment in police departments: homosexuals (see Close-up 5.1).

OPERATING POLICE DEPARTMENTS MORE EFFICIENTLY

Despite the fact that nationwide police department expenditures increased from $3 billion (with 339,000 officers) in 1967 to $8.6 billion (with 445,000 officers) in 1974,[95] police departments in some cities are so strapped economically that they have placed a freeze on hiring, they cannot handle the flood of 911 calls, and they cannot afford the services of high-priced informants. Some have adopted informal policies of not dispatching patrol personnel to take reports of burglaries and larcenies under $50 in value,[96] not having detectives investigate burglaries under $5,000 in value,[97] and discouraging arrests that would entail overtime

Close-up 5.1 HOMOSEXUALS AS POLICE OFFICERS[a]

One of the most volatile current issues in police personnel policy is the employment of homosexual officers. So far, the San Francisco Police Department is the only one in the country that has actively recruited gay police applicants. Several problems surround the hiring of gay police officers. Straight police are hostile to homosexuals in general, and especially hostile to the prospect of their employment in a male-dominated occupation that values masculinity and middle class morality. Opponents allege gay police would reduce the community's respect for the force, be detrimental to department morale, be incompatible with the unique features of policing and the police subculture, could not be counted on to come to the aid of fellow officers, and might force their sexual attentions on other officers. Hiring gay officers also raises certain legal difficulties, since homosexual acts are still against the law in 30 states.

On the other hand, proponents contend that homosexuality does not affect job performance, that gay police are not noticeably effeminate, that if they prove their worth as officers gay recruits will gradually be accepted by their peers (just as women patrol officers have been), and that a police force should reflect the composition of a community that, in most major urban areas, contains a significant element of homosexuals. Although the Civil Rights Act may not specifically prohibit discrimination based on sexual identity, if gender is not a bona fida job-related requirement for police department employment, then it is all the more untenable to maintain that sexual preference is. In any case, it is likely that homosexuals are already a statistical reality in most larger police agencies but simply conceal the fact in order to avoid ostracism by colleagues and loss of their jobs, as indicated by the following comment from a closet gay officer in New York City.

> I started out as a rookie cop in Bed-Stuy in Brooklyn over 20 years ago and worked my way up through the ranks. Now I've gone beyond the maximum civil service position of captain. I was a member of the Patrolmen's Benevolent Association for years and I have several major citations, one involving a shootout. My record is clean and I've never been subjected to any disciplinary action. Despite this record, I constantly feel that it can be wiped out in a moment if the department discovers I'm a homosexual.[b]

[a] *Source:* Randy Shilts, "Gay Police," *Police Magazine,* January 1980, pp. 32–33.
[b] Samuel DeMila, "Homosexuals as Police Officers?" *New York Times,* February 10, 1978, p. 25

pay. As the second most costly item (after education[98]) in the budgets of local government—a single round-the-clock officer costs $80,000 a year—police departments are struggling to find economical new ways of providing the public with improved law enforcement, order maintenance, PCR, and social services. The economic plight of urban police departments has led to a search for more efficient ways of operating police agencies and providing police services. Recent major efforts to reduce costs without decreasing effectiveness center around the consolidation of police services, the civilianization of police departments, the use of one-person patrol cars, and new procedures for police at arraignment.

The Consolidation of Police Services

Many of the nation's 40,000 law enforcement agencies have less than ten full-time sworn officers; and 33,000 of them are small law enforcement agencies.[99] Within a single area, there may be a needless proliferation of police agencies providing overlapping, fragmented, and duplicated services. Narrowly drawn jurisdiction boundaries hamper crime control efforts by giving the highly mobile criminal sanctuary from the short arm of the law. Small police departments lack the supportive staff, facilities and equipment, specialization and expertise, and officer training necessary for modern, professional law enforcement operations.

Advantages of consolidation

The solutions to some of these problems may involve (a) the consolidation or coordination of police services, in which two or more jurisdictions agree to perform certain services jointly; (b) police department mergers, where two or more smaller police departments pool or merge to create one larger, unified, centralized law enforcement unit; and (c) the contracting of services, in which smaller police departments may purchase specific services from the private sector or from larger police agencies. All three forms of streamlining police department operations are geared to provide less fragmented and more coordinated police services, to eliminate duplication of effort, and to increase the crime control and social service capacity of police agencies. They are intended to make specialization and expertise more readily available, to create an opportunity for experimentation and innovation, and to perform the police function and role more efficiently and effectively.

The President's Crime Commission strongly endorsed the principle of consolidation of police services, with the particular form to be determined by individual circumstances. The Standards and Goals Commission recommended that "police agencies that employ fewer than 10 sworn employees should consolidate for improved efficiency and effectiveness."[100] Coordination is generally more feasible than outright merger of police departments, which is "the ultimate form of jurisdictional consolidation."[101] For mergers involve legal barriers, political obstacles, and intense interagency hostility to the prospect of relinquishing some autonomy for the heightened efficiency and effectiveness that usually accompany more large-scale, centralized operations. Regardless of how consolidation of police services is achieved—through voluntary coordination, formal merger, or purchase of services through contracts—the President's Crime Commission considered it applicable to a wide range of police department activities and needs.[102] Various jurisdictions and police departments have adopted consolidation in one form or another.

Consolidation in practice

In Florida, the Jacksonville Police Department (391 officers) and Duval County Sheriff's Office (225 officers) merged in 1968. The integration of the two previously separate communications centers, investigation units, and identification records and the development of a central index "has increased our crime solution rate substantially."[103]

California utilizes the contracting of police services on a widespread basis. Under the Lakewood Plan, the Los Angeles County Sheriff's Department provides complete police coverage to 29 cities on a contract arrangement.[104] The Los Angeles Police Department contracts one of its computer systems out to several cities.[105] Contracting allows each locality to decide the type and amount of police services it wants and can afford to purchase.

In August 1972 the Erie County Department of Central Police Services was created. This new countywide police agency made available to the 27 police agencies in the Buffalo, New York, area a coordinated communications system, computerized criminal history records, a forensic science laboratory, and a centralized training facility for police officers.[106]

The principle of consolidation has recently been extended to the partial merging of units within oversized police departments, where some of the problems of duplication, inefficiency, questionable effectiveness, and absence of performance accountability are the same.[107] It is not yet clear, however, whether consolidation of police services has all the benefits—including that of economy—that its advocates claim.[108]

Civilians in Police Departments

"Civilianization" is the replacement of sworn police personnel with civilian employees in police department jobs that do not require the training and experience of a bona fide police officer: clerical duties, research and planning, traffic control, operation of communications systems, photography, fingerprinting, community relations. The principal advantage of using civilians in police agencies is an economic one. A survey conducted by the Urban Institute in 13 cities found that the average starting salary for policemen was $10,872, compared to $8,348 for civilians employed in police agencies.[109] And the start-up costs for police officers, including training and fringe benefits, are much higher than those for civilians. Moreover, the utilization of civilians frees police officers for street patrol duty, where they are desperately needed, while assuring that essential police department work is carried out efficiently by persons trained specifically for the tasks involved.[110] Civilians may also bring an unbiased perspective to certain job-related problems and have a humanizing effect on the force. For these reasons, the proportion of civilians in police departments* increased from 7 percent in 1950 to 16.6 percent in November 1975, with continued growth expected.[113]

The trend toward civilianization, however, is not without its problems. Along with their perennial distrust of outsiders, sworn officers are concerned about the threat that civilianization poses to job security, particularly the light duty jobs filled by officers who are disabled, in poor health, or nearing retirement.[114] And the prospect of filling middle and upper level administrative positions with civilians might remove the incentive for police officers to obtain a college education in order to pursue a career path leading to executive responsibility.

One-Person Patrol Cars

One-person patrol cars have been adopted by some police departments for reasons of economy and efficiency

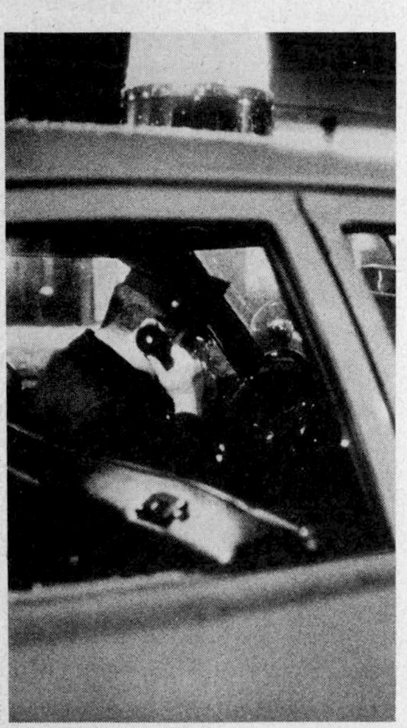

Demands for more police visibility, more crime control services, and shorter response time from a public unwilling to pay more for them are the factors behind the trend toward one-person rather than two-person patrol cars: the second person in the cruiser may cost $80,000 to $100,000 a year.[115] By switching to one-person cars during daylight hours in low-crime area, the New York City Police Department hopes to save $5 million a year.[116] The chief objection to one-person cars is that they are "an absolutely unacceptable hazard" to police safety.[117] However, one-person cars may actually be less dangerous than two-person cars because a solo officer is more careful and attentive to duty, is not easily distracted in idle talk with a partner, and is more likely to call for needed assistance sooner than when accompanied by a fellow officer.[118] Nearly half of the nation's police departments use one-person cars exclusively,[119] and very few rely entirely on two-person cars.[120] Many departments have opted for a balanced deployment of one- and two-person patrol cars, depending on tour of duty, location, type of assignment, and the experience of the individual officer.

* The New York City Police Department is a primary exponent of civilianization. A command decision was made in the fall of 1972 to hire 3,200 civilians by June 1974 and to civilianize every possible non-law enforcement job.[111] At a cost of one-half that of sworn officers, the anticipated savings of its civilianization program would be close to $20 million per year.[112] By early 1975 there were 6,447 civilians among the department's 37,000 employees, and the possibility of extending civilianization to administrative and staff positions was in the offing.

New Arraignment Procedures for Police

A substantial amount of police time is spent in appearances at arraignment court. Often officers are there only to watch an attorney obtain a continuance, to see the case dismissed, to learn that the defendant has jumped bail, or to find that their testimony is not then needed. Accompanying their prisoner-defendants to the initial court appearance and waiting idly to have the case called are costly and divert police officers from street patrol. In New York City some $10 million a year is spent for police overtime for court arraignment appearances.[121] Any weekday in the arraignment courts of New York City, more officers are "patrolling" the court corridors than are on the streets of the Bronx.[122]

New York's Appearance Control Project

In an experimental effort to improve the administration of police appearances at arraignment, the Appearance Control Project was initiated in January 1970 in the New York City Criminal Court. Police officers eligible for the project were telephoned on the morning their arrestees were to be arraigned and told whether their presence was required that day or at a later time. Originally this "alert" procedure was applied to misdemeanor cases where the defendant was not in jail. In the pilot period, from August 1970 to June 1972, 3,500 police officers were placed on alert status. However, only 20 percent of them were activated and thus required to appear in arraignment court within an hour of notification; the remaining 2,800 police officers were spared the needless inconvenience of appearing. The public benefited from the officers' continued performance of street patrol duties, and the revised arraignment procedure was responsible for projected annual savings of $4 million.[123] Many police officials have long asserted that the arresting officer is normally not needed during the initial arraignment, especially in felony cases, where nothing substantive occurs at this stage. Because of its success, the system was expanded in June 1972 to include felonies and misdemeanant detainees.

NEIGHBORHOOD TEAM POLICING

Paramilitary police organization

Police departments in the United States are organized along the lines of paramilitary organizations. The essential characteristics of the military model are rigid bureaucracy, specialization of function, centralized administration, a hierarchical chain of command principle, unquestioned obedience to authority, and strict regulation of patrol operations. Personnel and services are allocated on the basis of a specialized division of labor, to be performed according to standardized operating procedures. In departments with separate detective units, specialization requires that patrol officers who take the initial crime complaint immediately turn the matter over to specialist investigators. Thus the backbone of the force rarely participates in the development of cases or in the decisions concerning their resolution.

In the paramilitary model, all significant decision making and the management of tactical operations are centralized at supervisory and administrative levels. Middle and upper echelon personnel unilaterally establish policy and transmit it downward through an autocratic system of superior and subordinate relationships. Status, authority, and autonomy are directly related to position and rank in the police organization. The performance and operational activities of patrol officers are highly circumscribed, regimented, and mechanized. Career routes are rigidly and narrowly prescribed, with promotion dependent upon impersonal evaluations by supervisors and administrators who lack firsthand knowledge of the subordinate's performance. The entire system is closed, resistant to change and innovation, rejective of civilian input, and insulated from public accountability.

At one time, this monocratic and routinized model of organization was a rational and viable mechanism for operating police agencies efficiently and controlling police corruption. Today the quasi-military basis and philosophy of administering police agencies is becoming an obsolete mold for responding to the contemporary needs of police professionalism, the exercise of discretion, shared decision making, participatory management, community responsiveness, and the increased complexity of the police role and patrol function. According to the American Bar Association, "the semimilitary model that is the dominant form of organization in police agencies . . . is in fact a serious impediment to effective fulfillment of the overall police function."[124]

An alternative patrol strategy

Changing views on what constitutes sound administration of the backbone of the force point to *team policing* as an innovative managerial, organizational, and tactical patrol alternative to the traditional patrol strategy and its accompanying paramilitary features. As a new patrol structure and philosophy of the patrol function, team policing revolves around a team of officers who are given fixed, continuous, and expanded responsibilities for providing all police services to a well-defined geographical area (neighborhood).[125] The team (from 7 to 10 officers in small departments; 14 to 50 in larger agencies[126]) is unified under the supervision of a team leader who facilitates democratic participation in policy formation, decentralized decision making, and participatory management of the group's efforts.

Team leader and patrol officers

The team leader assumes round-the-clock responsibility for protecting the community and providing services to the neighborhood's citizens. Supervision is direct, informal, flexible, professional, and collegial. The team leader acts as a resource and guides and monitors the situational leadership exercised by all team members. Under team policing, the patrol officer functions both as generalist and specialist. To their usual duties of routine preventive patrol are added those of investigation: con-

am policing is a flexible, demo-
ıtic model for delivering police
rvices

ducting the preliminary follow-up criminal investigation and carrying the case through to completion whenever feasible. If specialist detectives are assigned to the team, they are a supportive element who will contribute to developing investigative knowledge and skills in patrol personnel. In teams without detectives, patrol-investigators are expected to draw upon their individual and collective group resources and to call in outside specialist personnel only when absolutely necessary. They handle situations and resolve problems on their own, and they assume continuity of responsibility for case management and outcome.

Personal involvement and responsibility

The premises underlying team policing are that the individual field officer is in the best position to know the varied and changing needs of the community, to devise appropriate crime control and social service approaches for meeting them, and should be given maximum freedom of action and responsibility. The stability of work location permits patrolpersons to become even more thoroughly enmeshed in, familiar with, and concerned about "their" neighborhoods. Continuity of responsibility and expanded role requirements develop a healthy competitive spirit among team members, who become committed to the successful outcomes of "their" cases. Team policing emphasizes a full human service model in which community relations, interpersonal skills, and contacts with citizens are an integral part of the generalist police role.

Team policing is designed to build community trust and confidence in the police, reduce alienation between the two groups, underscore their common interests and goals, and heighten community cooperation and participation in crime control. Team members are required to maximize contacts with community members under a wide variety of conditions. This heightened police sensitivity and involvement with the community is expected to increase the flow of crime-related information from the neighborhood to the police. It should also minimize dependence on the kind of aggressive crime control methods that exacerbate police-community relations. Based upon ratings from the team leader, it becomes possible to reward police officers for social services, human relations, and police-community relations contributions to "law and order."

Effects of team policing

After its introduction in Syracuse and Detroit,[127] team policing had spread to 70 law enforcement agencies in mid-1976.[128] It has received strong recommendation by the President's Crime Commission,[129] more limited endorsement by the Standards and Goals Commission,[130] and was the LEAA's major police technology transfer project in fiscal 1975.[131] A proposed extension of the team policing idea would utilize the police as part of community human service teams composed of health officers, nurses, public assistance experts, lawyers, and family counselors.[132] Dayton's community-oriented team policing project was a step in this direction; a police team member who responded to a domestic disturbance could call in a mental health specialist who was available 24 hours a day to provide immediate family crisis counseling.[133]

The results of team policing to date have been impressive. Current evidence suggests that team policing can

reduce the crime rate[134] and increase crime clearances;[135]
increase the community's participation in crime control;[136]
reduce the public's fear of crime;[137]
improve police-community relations;[138]
increase police morale and their level of job satisfaction;[139]
facilitate career development;
reduce police overtime costs, duplication of effort, and mismanagement of limited resources.

Notwithstanding associated problems, it may cautiously be concluded that team policing has increased the overall efficiency, effectiveness, and productivity of police services. It is especially appropriate, and perhaps inevitable, that a democratic forum for providing police services should emerge in response to the challenge of crime, order maintenance, and community relations in a free society.

SUMMARY

The need to professionalize the police and the management of police departments was never greater. The centerpiece of police professionalization is the movement toward college-educated police, which grew out of the civil disorders of the 1960s, recommendations by the President's Crime Commission, and their implementation by the LEAA. Considerable progress has been made in improving the training received by police officers, under the auspices of state training commissions and supplemental input from police legal advisors, the university community, and research into personnel needs. At the department level, professionalization is expressed in new attitudes and policies toward hiring minority group members and women, innovative approaches to achieving greater efficiency without decreasing the quality of police service, and experimenting with team policing as an alternative to the traditional paramilitary form of police organization. The number of black and women patrol officers has increased dramatically under the aegis of Title VII of the Civil Rights Act of 1964, the EEOC, affirmative action and racial quotas, and the Supreme Court decision that police department hiring criteria must be job-related and cannot have a "disproportionate impact" on excluding minorities from the force. Steps taken to operate police agencies more efficiently include the consolidation of police services, civilianization, the use of one-person patrol cars, and new arraignment procedures that keep patrol officers on the streets rather than in the courtrooms. In team policing, patrol officers perform as both generalists and specialists, their decision-making authority is enhanced, and police-community relations is central rather than peripheral to the police role in contemporary society.

DISCUSSION QUESTIONS

1. How important is a college education to policework?
2. How could the training of police recruits be made more relevant to actual policework and be used to identify those applicants who are not suitable for the occupation?
3. Are you in favor of or opposed to the policy of affirmative action and the racial quotas that accompany it? Why?
4. What do you think of the President's Crime Commission proposal for Community Service Officers?
5. Are you in favor of opening up police departments to women as patrol officers? Why?
6. What is the relationship between team policing and any major concepts bearing on the police that were discussed in previous chapters?
7. What are the most important reasons for the use of one-person patrol cars? Does their use have any serious disadvantages for police personnel?

Chapter 6

THE POLICE AND THE CONSTITUTION

The Exclusionary Rule

Search warrants / Exceptions to the warrant requirement

Mapp v. *Ohio* (1961)

The Court's decision / Reaction to the decision

Viability of the Exclusionary Rule

The rule as deterrent / The rule's inflexibility / Alternatives to the rule

Close-up 6.1: The Dropsy Defense

Custodial Interrogation and Confessions

Voluntary and involuntary confessions / *Brown* v. *Mississippi* (1936)

The Prompt Arraignment Rule

McNabb v. *United States* (1943) / *Mallory* v. *United States* (1957)

Escobedo v. *Illinois* (1964)

The conditions that led to reversal / The questions raised by *Escobedo*

Miranda v. *Arizona* (1966)

The coerciveness of custodial interrogation / The *Miranda* safeguards / Consequences of *Miranda* / When *Miranda* warnings are not required / *Miranda* and juveniles / *Miranda*'s effect on confessions and convictions

Stop and Frisk: Street Interrogation

Stops and arrests

Terry v. *Ohio* (1968)

Reasonableness of a stop and frisk action / Five conditions for a stop and frisk action

Decisions of the Supreme Court under Burger

The Retreat from the Exclusionary Rule

United States v. *Calandra* (1974) / Restricting habeas corpus / Third party searches / Automatic standing / *United States* v. *Salvucci* (1980)

The Erosion of *Miranda*

Harris v. *New York* (1971) / *Michigan* v. *Tucker* (1974) / *Michigan* v. *Mosley* (1975) / *Oregon* v. *Mathiason* (1977) / *Brewer* v. *Williams* (1977) / *Rhode Island* v. *Innis* (1980)

The Expansion of Stop and Frisk

Adams v. *Williams* (1972) / *United States* v. *Robinson* (1973)

Close-up 6.2: Reasonable Suspicion and the Drug Courier Profile

Other Decisions Compatible with Police Interests

Kirby v. *Illinois* (1972) / Miscellaneous decisions

Summary

The boundaries of the police role in a free society are found in the amendments to the United States Constitution and their interpretation by the Supreme Court. The trend of Supreme Court decisions under Chief Justice Earl Warren in the 1960s was toward recognizing the legal rights of suspects and the accused. Federal constitutional safeguards were imposed upon the states through the Fourteenth Amendment. The number and scope of guarantees available to citizens in the custodial arms of the law were expanded. Critics of the Warren court charged it with being "soft" on crime and criminals, with "legislating" new law and social progress, and "handcuffing the police" in the performance of their duties. According to this view, the Court had tipped the scales too far in favor of civil liberties, the individual, the accused, and criminals through its "liberal" interpretation of the Constitution. On the other hand, supporters of the Warren court contended that its decisions were necessary to safeguard the rights of all citizens and to preserve the foundations of ordered freedom and liberty. According to this view, the Court's actions were correct, constitutional, and necessary to assure equal justice for all regardless of race, social class, background, or financial position.

THE EXCLUSIONARY RULE

> The right of the people to be secure in their persons, houses, papers, and effects, against unreasonable searches and seizures, shall not be violated. . . . (Fourth Amendment)

During the period of the "due process revolution" the Warren court invoked the Fourth, Fifth, and Sixth amendments in order to provide guidelines for the police so that they might abide by and enforce the Constitution while enforcing the substantive criminal law. The two monumental Supreme Court decisions of the 1960s were *Mapp* v. *Ohio* in 1961 and *Miranda* v. *Arizona* in 1966. In order to enforce the Fourth Amendment's prohibition against unreasonable search and seizure, the *Mapp* decision imposed the exclusionary rule upon the states.

The *exclusionary rule* provides that evidence obtained by unreasonable search and seizure—a violation of the Fourth Amendment—is inadmissible in court. Any such physical, tangible, or "real" evidence of crime commission can be *excluded* from being used by the prosecutor in attempting to prove the defendant's guilt at trial. Thus probative evidence obtained by illegal police methods cannot be used to convict the accused in formal court proceedings. The primary purpose of the exclusionary rule is to enforce the Fourth Amendment's prohibition against unreasonable searches by attempting to police the police.[1] The exclusionary rule is a legal remedy designed by the courts to protect the right to privacy im-

e Supreme Court in 1957. Earl rren (seated, center) was chief tice from 1953 to 1969 plicit in the Fourth Amendment from unconstitutional police invasion of one's person, home, premises, or other effects.

The Fourth Amendment mandates that, whenever possible, searches are to be authorized by warrants issued by neutral magistrates based upon a showing of probable cause. The process involved in obtaining search warrants from the judiciary requires police officers to present their reasons for seeking permission to search. By having the police convince an impartial court officer that there is probable cause to search, the right to privacy embedded in the Fourth Amendment is protected from arbitrary and capricious police intrusions. Hence searches authorized by warrants assure that the attendant invasions of privacy are not unreasonable —even when the place searched is a newspaper office and the innocent third party has not first had an opportunity to respond to a subpoena.[2] Search warrants place further restraints upon capricious police conduct by limiting the search to the person, items, and area described in the warrant.

Search warrants

For all practical purposes the problem of unreasonable searches arises when the police conduct warrantless searches, that is, when they do not first establish probable cause before a magistrate and obtain a warrant "particularly describing the place to be searched, and the persons or things to be seized." For this reason, the Supreme Court has consistently emphasized that whenever possible searches should be made pursuant to valid warrants that are properly executed.[3] Except in an emergency, even the scene of a murder cannot be searched without first obtaining a warrant.[4] In practice, a valid search warrant that is properly served by the police makes the search reasonable. By expressing a strong preference that police officers obtain valid search warrants before compromising a citizen's privacy, the Fourth Amendment sought to reduce police discretion and the arbitrary invasion of privacy to a minimum.

Exceptions to the warrant requirement

There are, of course, exceptional circumstances under which warrantless police searches are entirely reasonable and thus constitutional: (1) searching a suspect immediately after making the arrest, that is, searches "incident to arrest," (2) searching the immediate area within which a suspect could reach a weapon,[5] (3) searching a car stopped in "hot pursuit" from the scene of a crime, and (4) searching a car stopped for a routine violation after inadvertently observing contraband "in plain view" on the back seat.[6] Whether or not a warrantless search violates the Fourth Amendment (is unreasonable) or is a recognized exception to the warrant requirement (is reasonable) will depend upon judicial analysis of the totality of the circumstances of the search. There is a considerable body of complex and often confusing law that seeks to define "unreasonable" searches and to identify exceptions to the warrant priority.

Before the twentieth century, the Supreme Court neither adopted the exclusionary rule in federal cases nor imposed it on the states.[7] Until then, American courts were free to follow the common law doctrine that authorized the use of illegally obtained evidence at trial so long as it was reliable and trustworthy. Then in a series of decisions, the Supreme Court (a) made the exclusionary rule binding in all federal criminal cases in *Weeks* v. *United States* in 1914,[8] (b) refused to extend the exclusionary rule to the states in *Wolf* v. *Colorado* in 1949,[9] and (c) reversed its *Wolf* decision and, in *Mapp* v. *Ohio* in 1961, imposed the exclusionary rule on the state courts through the due process clause of the Fourteenth Amendment.[10] *Mapp* v. *Ohio* marked the beginning of the "due process revolution" of the Warren court and became the landmark Supreme Court decision on unreasonable searches and the Fourteenth Amendment.

Mapp v. *Ohio* (1961)

On May 23, 1957, three Cleveland police officers arrived at the residence of Dolree Mapp, acting on a tip that a bombing suspect was hiding there and that gambling apparatus was concealed in the house. The officers demanded entrance, but after telephoning her attorney Ms. Mapp refused to admit them without a warrant. The police returned three hours later with additional officers, and when Dolree Mapp did not immediately come to the door, the police entered forcibly. Ms. Mapp insisted on seeing a search warrant, whereupon one of the officers held up a paper that was claimed to be a warrant. She grabbed the "warrant" and placed it in her bosom. In the ensuing struggle, the officers removed the piece of paper and handcuffed Ms. Mapp. The police then proceeded to search the entire apartment. Obscene materials were discovered in the course of this widespread search. Dolree Mapp was subsequently convicted of possessing obscene matter and sentenced to prison. At her trial, no search warrant was produced by the prosecutor.

The Court's decision

In reversing the conviction, the Supreme Court emphasized that the Fourth Amendment was binding on the states through the due process clause of the Fourteenth Amendment. The Court indicated that the defendant's Fourth Amendment right to privacy had been violated by the unreasonable search and that the exclusionary rule is an essential part of that right. "We hold that all evidence obtained by searches and seizures in violation of the Constitution is, by that same authority, inadmissible in a state court." In support of its decision to impose the exclusionary rule on the states, the Supreme Court made several points: (a) since the Court's *Wolf* decision in 1949, a majority of the states considering the issue had adopted the exclusionary rule in whole or in part; (b) the influential California Supreme Court had reluctantly switched to the exclusionary rule in 1955; (c) the exclusionary rule was the only effective means available for deterring police from violating the Fourth Amendment; and (d) the need to maintain "judicial integrity" sometimes re-

Police authority to conduct searches derives from the Fourth Amendment as interpreted by the Supreme Court

quires that a criminal go free rather than have the government become a partner in law violation.

Reaction to the decision

The *Mapp* decision fell like a bombshell on the 26 states that until then had rejected the exclusionary rule in toto.[11] The police complained bitterly that *Mapp* was an unreasonable invasion of their already strained efforts to control crime and convict the guilty, as well as a usurpation of legislative authority and state sovereignty. To the veteran, street-wise patrol officer struggling to contain crime in the streets, the *Mapp* decision symbolized the elevation of the rights of criminals over the public's right not to be invaded by crime. From such a vantage point, *Mapp* appeared to be a lopsided balancing of the scales of justice in favor of the obviously guilty.[12] In contrast, other groups approved of the *Mapp* decision and described it as a long overdue measure to insure that the nation's police forces observe the Constitution and protect the individual's right to privacy guaranteed in the Fourth Amendment—something the police should have been doing regularly long before *Mapp* was decided.

Viability of the Exclusionary Rule

Three questions concerning the exclusionary rule go to its very foundation and ask whether it will survive, in its present form or at all, the test of future Supreme Court examination.

The rule as deterrent

1. Does the exclusionary rule actually deter police from violating the Fourth Amendment? (Deterrence has become the sole purpose of

the exclusionary rule;[13] *Mapp* was not made retroactive because no deterrent function would have been served by doing so.[14])

According to its critics, the exclusionary rule is not capable of achieving its goal of deterrence because the supposed punishment to the police —the prospect of not convicting the guilty—is so indirect as to be meaningless.* Much police search activity is undertaken without the intent to make a formal arrest that would lead to prosecution. For example, illegal searches where prosecution is not contemplated are used by the police to take weapons and drugs out of circulation or to harass petty criminals into becoming informants.[16] And the operation of the exclusionary rule encourages false testimony tailored to meet the requirements of evidence admissibility, such as the "dropsy" justification for the search (see Close-up 6.1). According to the rule's supporters, however, the police are not insensitive to the need to secure convictions, to cooperate with the prosecutor, and to observe the law of the land.[17] And while the exclusionary rule may not always or directly deter police from illegal searches, pressures from the community and the prosecutor—stemming from the rule's "freeing criminals"—will compel police departments to supervise patrol officers and detectives more closely and to discipline offending officers.

2. Should the exclusionary rule's inflexibility be modified so that under certain circumstances evidence obtained illegally by the police could be admissible at trial?

The rule's inflexibility

The inflexibility of the exclusionary rule treats all violations of the Fourth Amendment the same, which the police consider unreasonable. Evidence illegally obtained through oversight or honest errors in police judgment is subject to the same sanction as deliberate, flagrant, and shocking abuses of the Fourth Amendment, as occurred in *Mapp*. Since the exclusionary rule is a drastic method for enforcing the Fourth Amendment, some groups contend that its application should be restricted to serious, substantial, or flagrantly illegal violations of the Constitution.[18] A balancing test and the totality of the circumstances could be employed by the court or a jury to determine the reasonableness of the search and whether the rule should be invoked. According to its supporters, however, the inflexibility of the exclusionary rule is an integral part of the rule itself and its deterrent strength rather than a defect: where the Constitution is concerned, there can be no selective or discretionary observance of the law by the police. Across-the-board application of the rule is viewed as the only way to deter persistent and flagrant violations of the Fourth Amendment and to prevent "isolated" mistakes from escalating to a pattern of more serious abuses.

* Research on the deterrent impact of the exclusionary rule reveals that it has had a negligible effect on changing police practices in conducting searches.[15]

Close-up 6.1 THE DROPSY DEFENSE[a]

The Supreme Court's *Mapp* decision in 1961 was intended to discourage unreasonable warrantless searches by the police, as frequently occur in the case of narcotics possession. However, the law of search and seizure still permitted the police to conduct searches, leading to arrests, if they inadvertently observed the contraband "in plain view."[b] This would occur if the addicts intentionally dropped the narcotics on the ground when approached by the police, rather than be caught with the goods on their person.

To determine police compliance with *Mapp,* the arrests made by Manhattan police in narcotics possession cases for a six-month period before and after the *Mapp* decision were analyzed. Plainclothesmen arrested 5.1 percent more addicts after *Mapp* than before, compared with uniformed officers whose post-*Mapp* arrests increased by 22.6 percent. The post-*Mapp* cases in which the uniformed officers claimed the suspects dropped the evidence within plain view increased by 79.6 percent and by 71.8 percent for the plainclothesmen. Even the Special Narcotics Squad, whose arrests for narcotic possession fell after *Mapp,* reported a 45.3 percent increase in their dropsy explanation for conducting searches after *Mapp.*

[a] *Source:* Sarah Barlow, "Patterns of Arrest for Misdemeanor Narcotics Possession: Manhattan Police Practices 1960–1962," *Criminal Law Bulletin,* December 1968, pp. 549–582.
[b] *Harris* v. *United States,* 390 U.S. 234 (1968).

3. Are there other means for enforcing the Fourth Amendment besides the exclusionary rule? (If there were, the rule could be made more flexible—thereby meeting the major objections to it—or eliminated.)

Alternatives to the rule

Its critics maintain that there are alternatives to the exclusionary rule that, in principle, would be equally if not more effective in deterring unlawful police behavior and redressing citizen grievances. For example, court injunctions may be issued against police departments whose search and seizure policies violate the Constitution. Offending police officers may be directly sanctioned through criminal prosecutions and civil suits in state courts, or by a tort action under the federal Civil Rights Act. Individual officers may also be disciplined as a result of complaints filed against them and investigated by internal police review, civilian review boards, or state commissions. Other groups, however, contend that the exclusionary rule as enunciated in *Mapp* is required because the proposed alternatives are totally ineffectual. In *People* v. *Cahan,* California Supreme Court Justice Traynor observed, "Experience has demonstrated . . . that neither administrative nor civil remedies are effective in suppressing lawless searches and seizures."[19] Indeed, the Supreme Court implied in *Mapp* that the exclusionary rule was the only deterrent available to contain lawless police conduct.

The exclusionary rule has certain virtues not found elsewhere. The rule goes into operation automatically upon the defendant's going to trial. In such cases, no special effort or expense is required of the abused citizen to prevent the government's benefiting from official lawlessness. The exclusionary rule provides a minimum threshold of enforcement for the Fourth Amendment. The police themselves concede that it has made them more careful in conducting searches and seizures.[20] The rule has been responsible for the enormous increase in search warrants obtained by police departments, a practice that was almost nonexistent before *Mapp.*[21] When the final vote is taken, even the most severe critics of the exclusionary rule opt for retaining it until viable alternatives are developed.[22]

CUSTODIAL INTERROGATION AND CONFESSIONS

> No person . . . shall be compelled in any criminal case to be a witness against himself. . . . (Fifth Amendment)
> In all criminal prosecutions the accused shall enjoy the right . . . to have the assistance of counsel for his defense. (Sixth Amendment)

A *confession* is an oral and/or signed statement in which an individual admits having committed and being guilty of a crime or crimes. Ordinarily, confessions are obtained through police interrogation of suspects that takes place at the police station shortly after arrest. Such in-custody (custodial) interrogation by the police occurs in the interval between arrest and first arraignment before a magistrate. Securing confessions through interrogation is thought to be essential to solving crime, obtaining convictions, and promoting deterrence and effective law enforcement.

Voluntary and involuntary confessions

Traditionally, the standard test used by American courts for determining the admissibility of confessions at trial was whether the confession was voluntary or involuntary. Voluntary confessions are incriminating statements that are given to the police freely—without compulsion or fear, without inducements or promises, without trickery or deceit, without physical, mental, or psychological coercion. Voluntary confessions are admissible in court because, by definition, they are trustworthy and reliable; that is, they are unquestionably truthful expressions of guilt. Involuntary (coerced) confessions are inadmissible at trial because they are untrustworthy and unreliable: they carry the stigma of falsity and the seeds for convicting the innocent. Hence involuntary confessions can be excluded from court proceedings upon a motion to suppress.

Before *Miranda* v. *Arizona* in 1966, the Supreme Court decided on a cumbersome case-by-case basis whether a confession was voluntary or involuntary, and therefore legally or illegally obtained. In determining whether a confession was voluntary or not, the Court took into consideration the totality of the circumstances[23] and, in particular, the length[24] of police detention and interrogation of the suspect.[25] These were the yardsticks used by the Court to determine whether confessions were made freely or had been coerced. The constitutional protections upon which the Supreme Court subsequently came to anchor its confession decisions were the due process clause of the Fourteenth Amendment, the right to counsel provision of the Sixth Amendment, and the protection against self-incrimination contained in the Fifth Amendment.

Brown v. *Mississippi* (1936)

In *Brown* v. *Mississippi* in 1936, the Supreme Court for the first time excluded confessions obtained through physical brutality from admission as evidence in state trials, on the constitutional grounds that such action violated the defendant's due process rights under the Fourteenth Amendment.[26] The case involved three black men who were arrested for murdering a white man, convicted at trial, and sentenced to death solely on the basis of involuntary confessions extracted through physical brutality. (The defendants had been whipped and told that the whippings would continue until they confessed.) At trial the defendants testified that their confessions were false, and the deputy sheriff proudly admitted his part in the beatings. All of the officials connected with the case were aware of the circumstances surrounding the confessions.

In reversing the convictions, the Supreme Court emphasized that the use of involuntary confessions obtained through barbaric tactics deprived the defendants of the essential elements of due process to which they were entitled by the Fourteenth Amendment. The Court found that by accepting confessions thus secured into evidence at trial, the state had offended a "principle of justice so rooted in the traditions of our people as to be ranked as fundamental"—and therefore subject to constitutional protection afforded by the Fourteenth Amendment's due process clause. The due process clause requires "that state action, whether through one agency or another, shall be consistent with the fundamental principles of liberty and justice which lie at the base of all our civil and political institutions." In the *Brown* decision the Supreme Court invoked for the first time the Constitution as a barrier to the use of involuntary, coerced confessions secured by state officials; the facts of the case had left no doubt that such coerced confessions were potentially untrustworthy and unreliable.

The Prompt Arraignment Rule

McNabb v. *United States*[27] in 1943 and *Mallory* v. *United States*[28] in 1957 were cases that involved confessions obtained as a result of delays in "prompt arraignment" of the defendants before a federal magistrate. Whether the confessions were voluntary or involuntary was not addressed by the Court. The issues in both cases were how soon after arrest federal officers were required to take suspects before a committing magistrate and whether evidence (confessions) obtained during the interval was admissible in federal courts.

Rule 5(a) of the Federal Rules of Criminal Procedure provides that: "An officer making an arrest under a warrant issued upon a complaint or any person making an arrest without a warrant shall take the arrested person without unnecessary delay before the nearest available commissioner. . . ." Rule 5(a) was intended to prevent federal police from using postarrest detention to extract confessions through interrogation. It was also intended to prevent federal police from justifying illegal arrests (arrests made without probable cause) with confessions subsequently obtained through prolonged interrogation. Prompt arraignment would allow a neutral magistrate to determine whether there was probable cause for continued detention and prosecution. The period of detention and interrogation, therefore, was to be strictly limited to the time consumed in booking, in performing administrative tasks related to arraignment, or in awaiting the availability of a magistrate. The period between arrest and arraignment was not to be reserved for interrogation and eliciting confessions.

***McNabb* v. *United States* (1943)**

The McNabbs were a clan of five Tennessee mountaineers living off illicit moonshine operations near Chattanooga.[29] During a raid on their operations made by federal agents, one police officer was killed. Two McNabbs were convicted on the strength of their confessions and were sentenced to 45 years imprisonment for second-degree murder. None of the five McNabbs had been promptly arraigned upon arrest, that is, presented without unnecessary or unreasonable delay before a United States commissioner, as required by congressional statute. Instead, three McNabbs were detained initially in a barren cell for 14 hours and were then subjected to continuous interrogation over the next two days, during which time two confessed.

***Mallory* v. *United States* (1957)**

In *Mallory* v. *United States* in 1957, the Supreme Court underscored the prompt arraignment mandate laid down in *McNabb*. The defendant, a 19-year-old of limited intelligence, was convicted of rape in the District of Columbia and sentenced to death. The youth had been arrested the day after the crime, taken to the police station, and questioned intermittently over a ten-hour period; he finally confessed under steady interrogation by the polygraph operator police officer. Despite the availability of magistrates, the police made no attempt to arraign the youth until after securing his confession. The delay in arraignment was a clear violation of Rule 5(a).

In both cases, the Supreme Court sidestepped the issue of whether the confessions were voluntary or involuntary. Instead the Court decided the cases on the basis of its authority to formulate rules of criminal procedure for federal courts and on Rule 5(a). In reversing the convictions, the Court in effect ruled that violation of the congressional prompt arraignment statute meant that the incriminating evidence obtained during the delay was acquired unlawfully. Therefore the confessions were inadmissible in federal courts, regardless of whether they were voluntary or had been coerced under constitutional due process standards. Even voluntary confessions could be excluded by virtue of the time element alone, if obtained under conditions of delayed arraignment.* The *McNabb-Mallory* Prompt arraignment rule was binding only in federal crimes, but it was hoped that the policy of federal courts in excluding confessions secured during prolonged interrogation in violation of prompt arraignment would set an example for the states to follow. This would have made it unnecessary for the Supreme Court to intervene directly in state and local police operations concerning interrogation and confessions. It did not.[30]

Escobedo **v.** *Illinois* **(1964)**

On the evening of January 19, 1960, Danny Escobedo's brother-in-law was fatally shot. Danny, a 22-year-old of Mexican extraction, was arrested early the next morning, interrogated intermittently, and released in the afternoon when his lawyer obtained a writ of habeas corpus. He made no statements to the police during this detention. Based upon information linking him to the crime, Escobedo was arrested ten days later and taken to police headquarters. On route to the stationhouse he was handcuffed, interrogated, and urged to admit his guilt. He refused to answer the questions of the detectives: "I am sorry but I would like to have advice from my lawyer."

Shortly after Escobedo reached police headquarters and interrogation began, his lawyer arrived and sought to confer with him. Every attempt by Escobedo's counsel to gain access to his client was rebuffed by the police. Similarly, every request by Escobedo during interrogation to speak with his lawyer was denied by the police. During interrogation, Escobedo eventually admitted guilt in the slaying and signed a confession. At trial, his defense counsel made an unsuccessful motion to suppress the con-

* Similarly, in *Dunaway* v. *New York* in 1979 the Supreme Court ruled that even when a confession follows a valid waiver of *Miranda* rights, the confession is inadmissible if it resulted from an illegal arrest.

fession on the grounds that Escobedo had been denied counsel at the time.

The conditions that led to reversal

On June 22, 1964, the Supreme Court reversed Escobedo's conviction because, *under the conditions that characterized the case,* the defendant's Sixth Amendment right to the assistance of counsel, made obligatory upon the states through the Fourteenth Amendment, had been violated:[31]

1. The investigation was no longer a general inquiry into an unsolved crime but had begun to focus on a particular suspect.
2. The suspect had been taken into police custody.
3. The police had carried out a process of interrogation that lends itself to eliciting incriminating statements.
4. The suspect had requested and been denied an opportunity to consult with his lawyer.
5. The police had not effectively warned the suspect of his absolute constitutional right to remain silent.

The significance of the *Escobedo* decision lay in the factors that prompted the Supreme Court once again to "police the police" and to invoke the Sixth Amendment as the means for doing so. Prior to *Escobedo,* the Court had been saddled with a stream of confession cases, cases that were characterized by conflicting testimony over the voluntariness of the confessions. The Court had used the traditional but unwieldy "totality of the circumstances" test in determining voluntariness, and invariably the defendants involved had been without counsel at the time of interrogation.[32] Under these conditions, the Supreme Court had great difficulty in deciding, on the individual merits of each case, whether the confession was truly voluntary or involuntary. By requiring the police to comply with the requests of suspects to see their lawyers, *Escobedo* gave the Court the opportunity to avoid or resolve the thorny problems arising in confession cases—because "any lawyer worth his salt will tell the suspect in no uncertain terms to make no statement to police under any circumstances."[33] As for defendants who agree to police interrogation after consulting with counsel, any forthcoming confessions could be assumed to be unquestionably and genuinely voluntary.

The questions raised by *Escobedo*

As written, however, the *Escobedo* decision raised more questions concerning proper police procedures and treatment of suspects than it answered. Did the decision mean that all five conditions had to exist in order to make a confession inadmissible? How were the police to identify the point at which an investigation begins to "focus" on a particular suspect? Were police required to warn suspects of their right to remain silent? If a suspect had not requested a lawyer, could the police proceed with interrogations? What happens when the suspect requests a lawyer but, unlike Escobedo, does not have retained counsel available at the interrogation site? The *Escobedo* opinion offered a vague and confusing sketch for local and state police to follow upon making arrests and con-

Ernesto Miranda's conviction based on his confession led to the Court's prescribing the *Miranda* warnings as protection against self-incrimination

ducting interrogation. Consequently, the ruling had no impact on the problems associated with confession cases and the police procedures that gave rise to them.[34]

Miranda v. *Arizona* (1966)

The Supreme Court's due process revolution reached its climax in *Miranda* v. *Arizona* in 1966.[35] Henceforth, there would be no confusion concerning proper police procedure in conducting interrogations, the character of voluntary or involuntary confessions, or their admissibility in state trials.

On March 13, 1963, Ernesto Miranda, a 23-year-old Mexican, was arrested at home, taken to a Phoenix police station, placed in a lineup, and identified by a woman as the man who had kidnapped and raped her. Miranda was then taken to Interrogation Room No. 2, where he was questioned by two police officers. After two hours, the officers left the room with Miranda's signed confession. On the strength of that confession, introduced at trial over defense objection, Miranda was found guilty of kidnapping and rape and was sentenced to concurrent prison terms of 20–30 years on each count. The Supreme Court reversed the conviction in 1966.

The Court's decision in *Miranda* hinged upon its view of the relationship between custodial interrogation, genuinely voluntary confessions, and the constitutional rights of suspects in the arms of the law. At the outset, the Court admitted that Miranda's confession might not be involuntary as traditionally defined and understood: there was no evidence of physical force, deception, or deliberate mental duress. But the Court was resolved to break with tradition in *Miranda* in order to insure that any statements obtained from suspects during custodial interrogation "were truly the product of free choice." The major portion of the *Miranda* opinion is devoted to making and substantiating a single, critical point: regardless of the circumstances under which it occurs, regardless of who the examiners are, and regardless of who the suspects are, custodial interrogation is inherently coercive—psychologically, if in no other way. Custodial interrogation makes *any* statements obtained from suspects during this period "compelled" and thus not "voluntary" beyond a reasonable doubt.

The coerciveness of custodial interrogation

Consequently, the practice of interrogation is at odds with the Fifth Amendment, which guarantees that in criminal cases no person shall be compelled to be a witness against himself. The Fifth Amendment also applies to suspects in the arms of the law during the investigative phase of a criminal case. An individual's privilege against self-incrimination is jeopardized when he or she is taken into custody, otherwise deprived of freedom of action in any significant way, and subjected to custodial interrogation. To give such suspects the opportunity to exercise their constitutional privilege against self-incrimination, certain safeguards must be observed.*

The *Miranda* safeguards

1. Prior to any questioning, suspects must be warned, in clear and unmistakable terms, that they have the right to remain silent.
2. Prior to any questioning, suspects must be informed that anything they say can and will be used against them in a court of law.
3. To protect the Fifth Amendment privilege, prior to questioning, suspects must be clearly informed that they have the right to consult with counsel and to have counsel with them during interrogation.
4. Prior to questioning, suspects must be told that if they cannot afford counsel, counsel will be appointed for them if they so desire.

The suspect's right to remain silent and to have counsel present remains unfettered throughout the interrogation process. Prior to or at any time during interrogation, then, if the suspect in any way indicates a wish to remain silent or to have an attorney, the interrogation must stop. If interrogation begins and continues without counsel present, the government must be prepared to demonstrate at trial that the suspect was given the proper warnings and validly waived the privilege against self-incrimination and the right to counsel. The fourfold *Miranda* warning and a valid waiver are prerequisites to the admissibility of any statement made by the suspect in state criminal trials. In effect, the Court proposed the use of its *Miranda* warnings as an effective way to counteract the inherent compulsion of custodial interrogation, to permit suspects to exercise their right to remain silent, and to guarantee the voluntariness of police-solicited confessions.

Consequences of *Miranda*

Even its supporters were surprised by the far-reaching action taken by the Supreme Court in the *Miranda* opinion. Without much warning of its own, the Supreme Court had resolved once and for all to dispose of the clouded and increasing problems posed by confession cases and the Court's case-by-case approach to them. In *Miranda,* the Court (a) fashioned a blanket rule that prescribed an operational code of police procedure to be used whenever the possibility of custodial interrogation existed, (b) apparently adopted a new test for the admissibility of confessions, one that abandoned voluntariness per se, (c) extended the Fifth Amendment protection against self-incrimination to the arrest stage, and (d) effectuated the Fifth Amendment by means of the Sixth Amendment in assuring all suspects—indigent or not—the right to counsel before and during interrogation.

The *Miranda* warnings must be given whenever an individual (a) has been "taken into custody" or "otherwise deprived of his freedom of action in any significant way" *and* (b) is about to be asked police-initiated questions designed to elicit incriminating statements that will be used in

* Or others equally effective in informing suspects of their right to remain silent.

court. Thus there are a number of situations in which the *Miranda* warnings are not required.

When *Miranda* warnings are not required

1. *Miranda* warnings are not required when the statements to be obtained during custodial interrogation are not intended for use in court or needed to convict (for example, when conviction can be secured on the basis of external independent evidence, eyewitnesses, or firsthand testimony—as when a demonstrator assaults an officer).
2. *Miranda* warnings are not required when a person makes a completely unsolicited and uninvited—a spontaneously *volunteered,* not voluntary—statement to the police (for example, when a person rushes into a police station and blurts out a confession to the desk sergeant). The Supreme Court specifically exempted such spontaneously volunteered declarations from the *Miranda* warnings because they are not the result of custodial interrogation.
3. *Miranda* warnings are not required in general on-the-scene questioning concerned with discovering the facts surrounding a crime or other exploratory questioning of citizens as part of the investigative fact-finding process. Of course, the persons questioned under these general on-the-scene conditions must not have been placed under arrest, be in custody, or be subjected to custodial interrogation. (Any of these circumstances would require the *Miranda* warnings.)
4. As the Supreme Court made clear in *Beckwith* v. *United States,* the focus-test per se does not trigger the *Miranda* safeguards.[36]
5. *Miranda* warnings are not required in street encounters (including the stop and frisk procedure) in which questioning does not constitute custodial interrogation.
6. *Miranda* warnings are not required in situations where the police must ask standard questions of an administrative nature in connection with completing routine accident and incident reports.
7. *Miranda* warnings are not applicable to nontestimonial evidence secured involuntarily from a suspect in custody. The Fifth Amendment prohibition against self-incrimination pertains to testimonial evidence secured from the suspect's verbal admissions of guilt during interrogation, that is, from the subject's own mouth. Thus *Miranda* does not cover compelling suspects to give evidence against themselves through taking blood samples, fingerprinting, being photographed, displayed in a lineup, being forced to speak and write for voiceprint, voice, and handwriting identification, and certain physical intrusions into their bodies.*

* In *Schmerber* v. *California* in 1966, the Supreme Court found no Fourth or Fifth Amendment violation when the police instructed a physician to take a blood sample from a person arrested for driving while intoxicated.[37] But in *Rochin* v. *California* in 1952, a case in which

Miranda and juveniles

If the intent is to introduce statements obtained from juveniles into juvenile court hearings, then *Miranda* applies to juveniles upon being taken into custody and subjected to interrogation, just as it does with adults. In fact, because of the special problems involving "valid waivers" and the ability of juveniles to "consent" to be interrogated without counsel, some states insist upon granting juveniles more due process rights than the Supreme Court required in *Miranda*. California, for example, requires that before questioning juveniles, the police must inform them of their right to the presence of their parents or guardian.[39]

Miranda's effect on confessions and convictions

The most persistent, impassioned, and significant criticism of the *Miranda* warnings was that they deprived the police of a critical law enforcement tool, thereby making their jobs that much more difficult. The upshot of *Miranda* was expected to be fewer confessions and convictions and more work with less payoff. The Supreme Court's supporters countered that this could be avoided by more skillful investigation, that the decision did not abolish interrogation but only unconstitutionally obtained confessions, and that only about 10 percent of all criminal cases involved confessions.[40]

The major criticism on which the attack against *Miranda* was based—that it handcuffed the police and the prosecutor in the effective performance of their crime control functions—was put to rest by social science research. In studies conducted in several cities,[41] particularly in New Haven,[42] the unanimous decision of the research investigators was that *Miranda* and the alleged need for interrogation had no significant impact on obtaining confessions or convictions. The New Haven researchers found in their observation of 119 interrogations that 58 of them resulted in confessions—50 of which were volunteered after the *Miranda* warnings were given. "The *Miranda* rules, when followed, seem to affect interrogations but slightly. The police continue to question suspects, and succeed despite the new constraints."[43]

STOP AND FRISK: STREET INTERROGATION

It is common practice, especially in high-crime areas, for police to stop on the street persons whose behavior is suspicious, detain them briefly by questioning them for identification purposes, and frisk (pat down the outer clothing of) those whose answers or conduct arouse further suspicion of criminal involvement or threaten police safety. The purpose of the stop and frisk is to nip crime in the bud by aggressively investigating

---

the police pumped a suspect's stomach to retrieve narcotics he had swallowed, the Supreme Court reversed the conviction because the police conduct "shocks the conscience" and was a violation of the Fourteenth Amendment.[38]

crimes that may have just occurred, are occurring, or may be about to occur.

Stops and arrests

Routine field interrogation or investigative detention may or may not be followed by a frisk of the suspicious person, depending on the outcome of the officer's questioning. In the majority of field interrogations, the stopped suspects properly identify themselves within a few minutes[44] or give a satisfactory explanation of their suspicious conduct, and they are allowed to go on their way without being frisked.[45] The initial stop, which is based only on the *suspicion* of crime, does not legally amount to an arrest because probable cause is absent at this point. However, probable cause may be established as the result of a frisk, at which point the officer can arrest (see Table 6.1 and Figure 6.1).

Before the Supreme Court clarified the legal status of stop and frisk in 1968, the authority for stop and frisk came from departmental directives, police discretion, state judicial policy,[46] or statutes such as New York's stop and frisk law.[47]

> *Temporary questioning of persons in public places; Search for weapons.* A police officer may stop any person abroad in a public place whom he reasonably suspects is committing, has committed or is about to commit

Table 6.1 Legal Differences Among Stops, Frisks, and Arrests

	Stop	Frisk	Arrest
Justification	Reasonable suspicion that subject has just committed, is committing, or is about to commit a crime	Reasonable suspicion that subject is armed and dangerous and that safety of officer and others is jeopardized	Probable cause to believe that subject has committed a felony
Purpose	To prevent and detect crime	Self-protection and the safety of others; if no weapon is discovered through pat-down, frisk must terminate and subject is free to go	To take into full custody with intent to enter formal charges
Authority to Search	None; only investigative questioning is permitted	Pat-down of outer clothing to discover objects that feel like or could be used as weapons and whose discovery would then constitute probable cause to arrest; if no weapon is discovered subject should be released	Full body search permissible

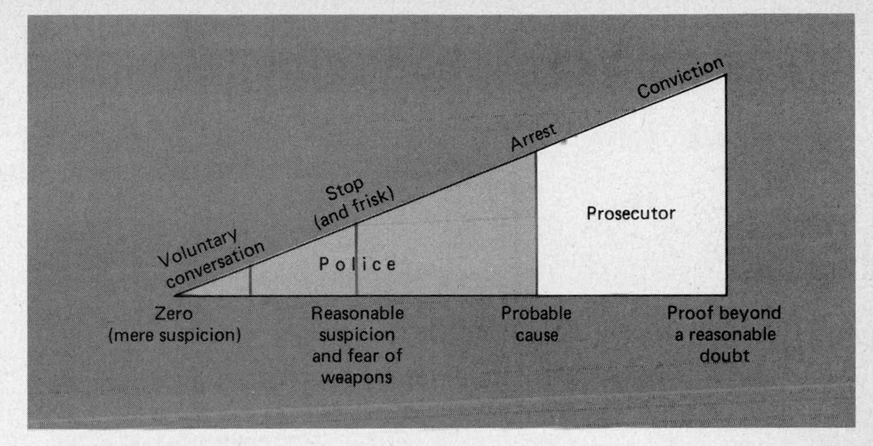

GURE 6.1 Amount of informa-n needed for a stop and frisk, rest, and conviction. *Source:* hn Dennis Miller, "Investigative tention," *FBI Law Enforcement lletin,* January 1975, p. 29. Re-nted with permission.

> a felony or any of the crimes specified in section five . . . and may demand of him, his name, address and an explanation of his actions.
>
> When an officer has stopped a person for questioning pursuant to this section and reasonably suspects that he is in danger of life and limb, he may search such person for a dangerous weapon. If the police officer finds such a weapon or any other thing the possession of which may constitute a crime, he may take and keep it until the completion of the questioning, at which time he shall either return it, if lawfully possessed, or arrest such person.

Partially in response to controversy surrounding New York's law and other factors, pressures were developing for the Supreme Court to clarify the legal status of stop and frisk. The Court took its first step in that direction in *Terry* v. *Ohio* in 1968.[48]

Terry v. *Ohio* (1968)

Plainclothes Officer McFadden became suspicious of two men standing on a street corner in Cleveland's downtown shopping district at about 2:30 P.M. One of the suspects peered into a store, walked on, returned to look at the same store, and then joined a companion. The companion went through the same sequence of suspicious behavior. Between the two of them, they paused to stare in the same store window 24 times. The pair then met with a third man, whom they followed up the street ten minutes after he left them. Officer McFadden suspected the men were casing a store for a stickup and thought they might be armed. McFadden walked up to the three men, identified himself as an officer, and asked

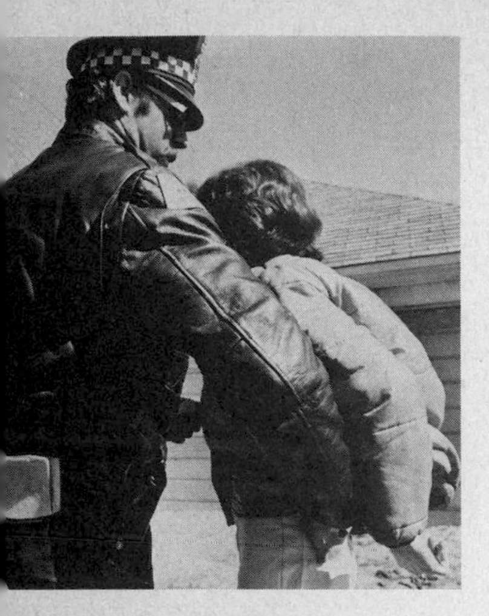

A stop and frisk is not an arrest, though it could lead to one

their names. When the men gave a mumbled reply to his question, the policeman spun Terry around, patted down (frisked) the outside of his clothing, and felt a gun, which he then seized. A frisk of Terry's companion uncovered another pistol; the frisk of the third man turned up nothing.

Terry was then arrested and charged with carrying a concealed weapon. Terry made a motion to suppress the introduction of the weapon as evidence against him at trial. He claimed the gun was inadmissible because Officer McFadden had violated his Fourth Amendment rights by seizing the weapon without a warrant. The motion was denied by the trial judge, who upheld the officer's action on a stop and frisk theory. Terry was convicted of carrying a concealed weapon and appealed his conviction to the Supreme Court. In a consolidated opinion involving three other stop and frisk cases, the Supreme Court issued its decision on June 10, 1968.

The Court focused on the frisk portion of the stop and frisk sequence: the grabbing of Terry and the pat-down (frisk) of his outer clothing. At the outset, the Court acknowledged that Terry was surrounded by the Fourth Amendment as he walked down the Cleveland street that afternoon. But while the Fourth Amendment contains a strong preference for arrest and search warrants, the legal criterion of an officer's conduct is *reasonableness* rather than the warrant: "would the facts available to the officer at the moment of the seizure or the search 'warrant a man of reasonable caution in the belief' that the action was appropriate?" Thus the Court narrowed its consideration to the specific issue of whether the frisk (limited search) of Terry was reasonable or unreasonable under the circumstances.

Reasonableness of a stop and frisk action

The Court concluded that even when probable cause does not exist to make a full custody arrest, there are circumstances that may justify temporarily restraining a suspect and conducting a limited search (frisk). These conditions obtain when the officer's "stop" action is reasonable and when the subsequent "frisk" action is reasonable. McFadden was "able to point to specific and articulable facts which, taken together with rational inferences from those facts, reasonably warrant that intrusion" (the frisk). Since the sole justification of the search was the protection of the police officer and others nearby, it must initially be limited in scope to learning whether the suspect is armed: to a pat-down (limited search) of the outer clothing for the purpose of discovering guns, knives, clubs, or other hidden instruments that might be used to assault the officer or others.

Five conditions for a stop and frisk action

The Court insisted that only when five conditions exist does an officer have the right to frisk. When these five conditions are present, the limited search (pat-down or frisk) conducted in *Terry* is a reasonable search under the Fourth Amendment, and any weapons seized in the pat-down may be introduced as evidence against the defendant at trial.

We merely hold today that
1. where a police officer observes unusual conduct which leads him reasonably to conclude in light of his experience that criminal activity may be afoot [*McFadden reasonably suspected that Terry and his companions were casing a store for a stickup*];
2. and that the person with whom he is dealing may be armed and dangerous [*McFadden suspected the men were planning to rob the store, and robbers are frequently armed*];
3. where in the course of investigating this behavior he identifies himself as a policeman [*McFadden notified the suspects that he was a police officer*];
4. and makes reasonable inquiry [*McFadden asked the men their names, which is reasonable inquiry*];
5. and where nothing in the initial stages of the encounter serves to dispel his reasonable fear for his own or other's safety [*the muddled response to McFadden's question did not reduce his fear for his own safety and that of others*],

he is entitled for the protection of himself and others in the area to conduct a carefully limited search of the outer clothing of such persons in an attempt to discover weapons which might be used to assault him. Such search is a reasonable search under the Fourth Amendment, and any weapons seized may properly be introduced in evidence against the person from whom they were taken.

Like *Escobedo,* the *Terry* decision did not resolve all of the questions and problems that it raised. For example, the *Terry* opinion did not indicate whether *Miranda* warnings are required in stop and frisk situations. The consensus of expert opinion is that the warnings are not required because stops are not arrests and a brief street detention is not the type of custodial interrogation in which suspects are restrained in a significant way that was contemplated in *Miranda.* But if the stop is made at gunpoint or the police forcibly detain a suspect during street interrogation or the pat-down, then the *Miranda* warnings are required because genuine custodial interrogation obtains.[49] Similarly, the *Terry* decision did not indicate how long the police could take in conducting a stop and frisk before deciding to arrest or release the suspect. The American Law Institute has recommended a maximum of 20 minutes;[50] that standard is endorsed by the Model Rules on Stop and Frisk sponsored by the Police Foundation.[51] The Uniform Arrest Act would permit up to two hours.[52]

DECISIONS OF THE SUPREME COURT UNDER BURGER

Chief Justice Earl Warren retired in October 1969, and President Nixon sought to appoint to the Supreme Court justices who would be opposed to expanding the rights of criminal defendants. The new, more conservative Supreme Court came to center on Chief Justice Warren Burger.[53] The decisions of the Burger Court in the area of criminal procedure and the Constitution have resulted in (1) a retreat from the exclusionary rule as enunciated in *Mapp,* (2) the erosion of *Miranda,* (3) an expansion of stop and frisk, and (4) omnibus decisions compatible with police needs and interests.

The Retreat from the Exclusionary Rule

United States v. *Calandra* (1974)

In *United States* v. *Calandra* in 1974, the Court declared that the exclusionary rule was not applicable to the presentation of illegally obtained evidence at grand jury proceedings.[54] Federal agents armed with a search warrant authorizing them to seize gambling equipment in Calandra's machine-tool plant had instead seized evidence of Calandra's involvement in loansharking activities. Calandra was subsequently subpoenaed to testify before the grand jury concerning his loansharking dealings. He refused on the grounds that the evidence against him had been obtained illegally—that the search warrant had not authorized looking for and confiscating evidence of loansharking activities. Hence, he argued, the evidence should be suppressed under the exclusionary rule. The Court majority, which included Nixon's four appointees, took a different view. In allowing the evidence to stand, the Court said that suppressing the illegally obtained evidence would needlessly interfere with the effective and efficient discharge of grand jury duties and would not significantly deter police from conducting unlawful searches.

Restricting habeas corpus

Under the historic common law principle of habeas corpus, state prisoners who had allegedly been convicted and incarcerated on the basis of

The Court in 1982, *from left to right:* Harry Blackmun, Thurgood Marshall, William Brennan, Chief Justice Warren Burger, President Ronald Reagan, Sandra Day O'Connor, Byron White, Lewis Powell, William Rehnquist, and John Paul Stevens

illegally obtained evidence could appeal to the federal courts for relief. Federal judges have traditionally been more willing than state courts to protect the constitutional rights of criminal defendants. Thus, by filing a habeas corpus petition with the federal courts, state prisoners convicted and imprisoned on illegally obtained evidence could have their state convictions set aside and be released from prison. In *Stone* v. *Powell* in 1976 the Supreme Court, retreating further from the exclusionary rule, announced that such prisoners may no longer pursue their constitutional rights through the use of habeas corpus.[55]

The decision hinged upon a case from Omaha, Nebraska, in which a Black Panther named Rice was convicted of murder after a police officer was killed by a booby-trap bomb. By means of an illegal search conducted with a faulty warrant, the police found 14 pounds of dynamite and other bomb ingredients in Rice's home, and this evidence was admitted at his trial. Rice filed a federal habeas corpus petition with a United States district court, which then reversed the conviction under the exclusionary rule. The prosecutor appealed the reversal decision to the Supreme Court, which reinstated Rice's conviction.

In doing so and ruling that federal habeas corpus review need not be granted, the Court practically closed the federal courtroom doors to state prisoners convicted by means of illegal searches.* The Court noted that the exclusionary rule was not aimed at freeing guilty defendants but at deterring police from making illegal searches, a matter that could be entrusted to the state courts. And in 1980 in *Allen* v. *McCurry,* the Court ruled that defendants whose Fourth Amendment claims are adequately reviewed by state courts can not relitigate the illegal search issue in federal court by suing the police under section 1983 of the Civil Rights Act.[56] By his own admission, Chief Justice Burger had been waiting for the "right case" in which to rule that trial courts may use any evidence seized by police officers who are performing their duties "reasonably" and "in good faith" under the totality of the circumstances.[57]

Third party searches

In recent years, the Burger Court has severely curtailed the availability of the exclusionary rule in the context of third party searches,† contrary to the more liberal position taken by the Warren Court in this area. In 1960 in *Jones* v. *United States,* the Warren Court held that a defendant charged with possessory crimes was *automatically* entitled to challenge the legality of the search leading to the criminal evidence used against the accused.[58] In that case, federal agents executing a search warrant found

* The court conditioned its withdrawal of habeas corpus to apply to cases where "the state has provided an opportunity for full and fair litigation of a Fourth Amendment claim" in its own state trial and appeal process.

† Third party searches refer to searches of premises or things that the defendant does not own, have possession of, or have an appropriate legal interest in.

narcotics and narcotic paraphernalia in a friend's apartment where Jones was living at the time, evidence that was subsequently used to convict him. Jones attempted to suppress the evidence from being introduced at trial, claiming that the search warrant had been issued without a showing of probable cause. The Court dismissed his motion to suppress on the grounds that Jones lacked "standing"—the necessary status or qualifications—to challenge the legality of the search. By denying defendants the right to a suppression hearing by virtue of standing, the accused is deprived of the major vehicle for invoking and exercising the exclusionary rule. Hence, the conditions under which standing obtains is a pivotal Fourth Amendment matter.

In order to establish standing prior to *Jones,* appellate courts generally required defendants to claim that they owned or possessed the seized items, or that they had a substantial possessory interest in the premises searched. The effect of complying with these traditional standing requirements, however, was self-incrimination, since admitting to possession or ownership of the contraband was a material element used to convict the defendant on the same charges. To avoid placing defendants in such an untenable position and chilling their constitutional rights, the Warren Court in *Jones* adopted what is known as the Fourth Amendment *automatic standing* doctrine: anyone "legitimately on premises where a search occurs" may challenge its legality by a motion to suppress, without first passing judgment on their possessory or property rights to the things taken. The *Jones* decision was based on the premise (or "target theory") that any defendant at whom a search was directed is covered by the Fourth Amendment and should therefore be granted standing to assert these rights through the exclusionary rule.

Automatic standing

United States v. *Salvucci* (1980)

In 1980 in *United States* v. *Salvucci,*[59] the Burger Court abandoned the automatic standing doctrine and, in doing so, markedly restricted the scope of the exclusionary rule in third party searches. The evidence (12 checks) used to indict Salvucci and Zackular of possession of stolen mail was discovered during police execution of a warrant to search the apartment of Zackular's mother. The defendants claimed that the grounds for issuing the search warrant did not meet probable cause and the court, relying on *Jones,* granted their motion to suppress the checks. In *Salvucci,* however, the Burger Court concluded that the principal rationale for recognizing automatic standing in *Jones* was no longer valid because of the Court's *Simmons*[60] decision in 1968. *Simmons* prohibits the prosecution from using at trial a defendant's self-incriminating testimony made in connection with a suppression hearing. In *Salvucci* the Burger Court also rejected the yardstick of "legitimately on the premises" as too broad a gauge for measuring Fourth Amendment rights and one that results in a needless loss of probative evidence. Instead of focusing on the concept of standing as a separate threshold inquiry, the Burger Court opted for a more circumscribed and stringent approach for resolving Fourth Amendment questions in third party searches: did the defendant have a "legitimate expectation of privacy"[61] in the premises, place or area searched, an issue that is to be determined on the individual merits of each case.

Basically, the Burger Court's decision in *Salvucci,* and in a series of important related opinions,[62] sought to codify the uniquely personal nature of Fourth Amendment rights, to preclude their vicarious assertion, and to confine the exclusionary rule to situations where the defendant's *own* rights have been infringed. Building upon *Rakas* v. *Illinois* in 1978, this line of cases established the principle that standing and access to the Fourth Amendment no longer depend upon property interests but instead derive from privacy interests.[63] Accordingly, ownership or possession do not, in themselves, trigger the Fourth Amendment. Rather, they are now to be viewed as but one factor to be considered—along with other competing factors—in determining whether the defendant had a legitimate expectation of privacy in the area searched. The bottom line of the Burger Court's analysis of third party searches is that many defendants will be denied an opportunity to suppress the fruits of illegal searches, individuals who, under the Warren Court, could have relied upon the exclusionary rule to vindicate their Fourth Amendment claims.

The Erosion of *Miranda*

Harris v. *New York* (1971)

The Court's retreat from the *Miranda* decision and doctrine began with *Harris* v. *New York* in 1971.[64] Harris was arrested for selling heroin to an undercover New York police officer on two occasions. Prior to custodial interrogation, however, his *Miranda* rights were violated: Harris was not informed that he had a right to appointed counsel. During questioning, Harris confessed in writing that he sold narcotics to the undercover officer on the two occasions in question. At his trial before a jury, Harris admitted during direct examination that the first sale was heroin but claimed that the second was only baking powder. To impeach Harris' credibility, the prosecutor on cross-examination referred to Harris' signed police confession, which in part contradicted his testimony in court. The trial judge instructed the jury that the statements allegedly made by Harris during custodial interrogation could be considered only in passing on his credibility and not as evidence of his guilt. Considering the appeal of Harris' conviction, the Supreme Court held that statements made in violation of the *Miranda* warnings are admissible at trial if: they are trustworthy; the accused's testimony contradicts his prior statements to police; and the statements are used not to show guilt but to impeach the defendant's credibility as a witness in his own behalf.[65]

Michigan v. *Tucker* (1974)

The *Miranda* decision was cut back further in *Michigan* v. *Tucker* in 1974.[66] The police arrested Tucker for rape but failed to give him the full *Miranda* warnings at the police station: he was not advised of his right to free counsel as an indigent. After agreeing to be questioned without a lawyer, Tucker gave the police the name of a witness to his activities on the night of the rape. When contacted by the police, however, the "alibi's" statements seriously incriminated Tucker. Tucker appealed his conviction, claiming that he had been deprived of his Fifth Amendment rights because of the defective *Miranda* warnings. The Court, however, ruled that the Fifth Amendment does not require that derivative evidence (the incriminating "alibi's" statements) be excluded, even if it is obtained through interrogation made without the full *Miranda* warnings. Thus the third-party evidence discovered through a violation of *Miranda* is admissible at trial.* In its opinion, the Court once again referred to the police as having acted in good faith and to the trustworthiness of the "alibi" evidence. Notably, it also defined the scope of the Fifth Amendment as encompassing only "genuinely compelled" statements, which the Court found lacking in Tucker's confession.

The rationale of the *Miranda* decision was severly undermined in *Michigan* v. *Tucker*. In *Miranda* the Court had declared that custodial interrogation was so inherently coercive that unless *all* the *Miranda* warnings were given, anything said to the police automatically violated the Fifth Amendment right against self-incrimination; the tenor of the *Tucker* decision signaled a return to the voluntariness test and the totality of the circumstances in determining the admissibility of confessions.[67] *Tucker* was thus another significant retreat from the *Miranda* doctrine.

Michigan v. *Mosley* (1975)

The Court's next encounter with *Miranda* came on December 9, 1975, in *Michigan* v. *Mosley*.[68] The *Mosley* decision upheld the renewed questioning of a suspect who had previously been given the *Miranda* warnings and had refused to answer any questions. Mosley was arrested in Detroit in connection with two robberies. The arresting officer gave Mosley the *Miranda* warnings and promptly terminated questioning when Mosley indicated that he wanted to remain silent. Two hours later, a homicide detective gave Mosley the *Miranda* warnings before questioning him about a murder. This time Mosley did not object to being interrogated, and he made incriminating statements that were used to convict him of murder.

The Michigan Court of Appeals reversed the conviction on the grounds that the homicide detective's interrogation was an automatic violation of the *Miranda* doctrine that once a suspect has refused to speak—as Mosley had done in connection with the robberies—any statement taken thereafter is "compelled" and thus in violation of the Fifth Amendment. The prosecution appealed the appellate court's decision, and the Supreme Court reversed the appellate court on the grounds that the critical safeguard offered by *Miranda* was the suspect's "right to cut

* In *Tucker*, the defendant was interrogated before the *Miranda* decision was handed down, but he went to trial after the decision was issued. Thus the *Tucker* decision is restricted to cases that fall into this category. Its symbolic significance, however, is far greater than the small number of defendants actually affected by it.

off questioning" and that this safeguard had been scrupulously honored by the police with Mosley. The Court commented that "permanent immunity" from interrogation for a criminal suspect would "transform *Miranda* safeguards into wholly irrational obstacles" for the police.[69]

Oregon v. *Mathiason* (1977)

An Oregon state police officer investigating a burglary focused on Carl Mathiason, a parolee, as suspect. Unable to contact Mathiason, the officer left a note at the suspect's apartment, asking Mathiason to call him because "I'd like to discuss something with you." Mathiason telephoned the next day and made arrangements to meet at the state patrol office. The officer told Mathiason that he was not under arrest. The officer then informed Mathiason that he was a suspect in the burglary, falsely stated that his fingerprints were found at the scene of the crime, and told Mathiason that his truthfulness in the matter would possibly be considered by the district attorney or the judge. At that point Mathiason admitted committing the burglary. The officer then gave Mathiason the *Miranda* warnings and took a taped confession. On the evidence of his confession, Mathiason was convicted at a bench trial of first-degree burglary.

On appeal, the Supreme Court of Oregon reversed the conviction because "the interrogation took place in a 'coercive environment'" even though Mathiason had not been formally arrested or detained. The State of Oregon then appealed to the Supreme Court, which reversed the Oregon Supreme Court's decision, thereby reinstating the conviction. In *Oregon* v. *Mathiason* in 1977, the Supreme Court found that Mathiason's Fifth Amendment and *Miranda* rights were not violated because he was not in custody or "otherwise deprived of his freedom in any significant way." In other words, the circumstances under which Mathiason originally made incriminating statements to the police officer did not constitute custodial interrogations.[70]

Brewer v. *Williams* (1977)

The most serious—but unsuccessful—challenge to the *Miranda* ruling came in *Brewer* v. *Williams,* decided by the Court on March 23, 1977.[71] On Christmas Eve 1968 in Des Moines, Iowa, a 10-year-old girl was abducted, sexually molested, and strangled to death. Two days later Robert Williams, who had recently escaped from a mental institution, surrendered to the police in Davenport on the advice of his lawyer, McKnight. At McKnight's insistence, the Des Moines detective dispatched to pick up Williams in Davenport agreed not to interrogate him on the 160-mile return trip. However, during the trip Detective Leaming engaged Williams in conversation for the purpose of soliciting incriminating statements and information about the crime. Addressing Williams as "Reverend," the detective began the discussion with statements—rather than questions—about the importance of finding the child's body so that she would have a proper Christian burial. "I do not want you to answer. I don't want to discuss it further. Just think about it as we're riding down the road." Shortly after Leaming's "Christian burial speech," Williams directed the officer to the child's frozen body.

Williams was convicted of murder by the trial court, over counsel's ob-

In arguing that Williams' murder conviction should not be reversed, the prosecutor urged the Supreme Court to abandon the *Miranda* doctrine

jections to the admission of evidence resulting from Williams' incriminating statements made during the trip. The Iowa Supreme Court affirmed the conviction on the basis that Williams had waived his right to counsel during the ride from Davenport to Des Moines. When Williams appealed to the Supreme Court, Iowa's attorney general asked the Court to overrule *Miranda:* "Let's take the handcuffs off the police." Twenty-two states, the National District Attorneys Association, and Americans for Effective Law Enforcement joined in requesting that the Court abandon the rationale of *Miranda* in favor of more flexible police interrogation standards by returning to the pre-*Miranda* voluntariness test.[72]

On March 23, 1977, by a 5-to-4 vote, the Supreme Court overturned Williams' conviction on the grounds that Williams had not waived his right to counsel. Therefore the evidence used to convict him was obtained in violation of the Sixth Amendment's right to counsel and should have been barred from trial use under the exclusionary rule. While not disposing of the case on Fifth Amendment grounds, the Court left little doubt that the detective's "Christian burial speech" constituted "custodial interrogation." In *Williams* the Supreme Court declined the opportunity to abandon the *Miranda* rule, and Chief Justice Burger castigated his more liberal colleagues in open court and issued a strong dissent from the majority opinion: "The result reached by the Court in this case ought to be intolerable in any society which purports to call itself an organized society."

Rhode Island v. *Innis* (1980)

In *Rhode Island* v. *Innis* in 1980 the Supreme Court, for the first time, addressed the issue of what constitutes "interrogation" under *Miranda.*[73] Providence police arrested Thomas Innis on the street in connection with the sawed-off shotgun murder of a cab driver and robbery of another cab driver with the same weapon. Innis was advised of his *Miranda* rights by a police captain and replied that he wanted to consult with a lawyer. The captain instructed the three officers assigned to drive Innis to the police station not to question or intimidate him in any way during the trip. While en route, two of the officers had a conversation between themselves concerning the missing shotgun. One of them stated that there were "a lot of handicapped children running around in this area" and "God forbid one of them might find a weapon with shells and they might hurt themselves." Innis then interrupted the conversation and told the officers to turn the car around so he could show them where the gun was hidden. The trial court allowed the weapon and testimony related to its discovery to be introduced at trial, and the jury found Innis guilty of robbery and murder.

That Innis had been fully informed of his *Miranda* rights, had invoked his right to counsel, and was in custody while being driven to the police station were uncontested matters. The only issue considered by the Supreme Court, therefore, was whether the officer's remarks amounted to interrogation, in which case Innis' right to silence under *Miranda* would

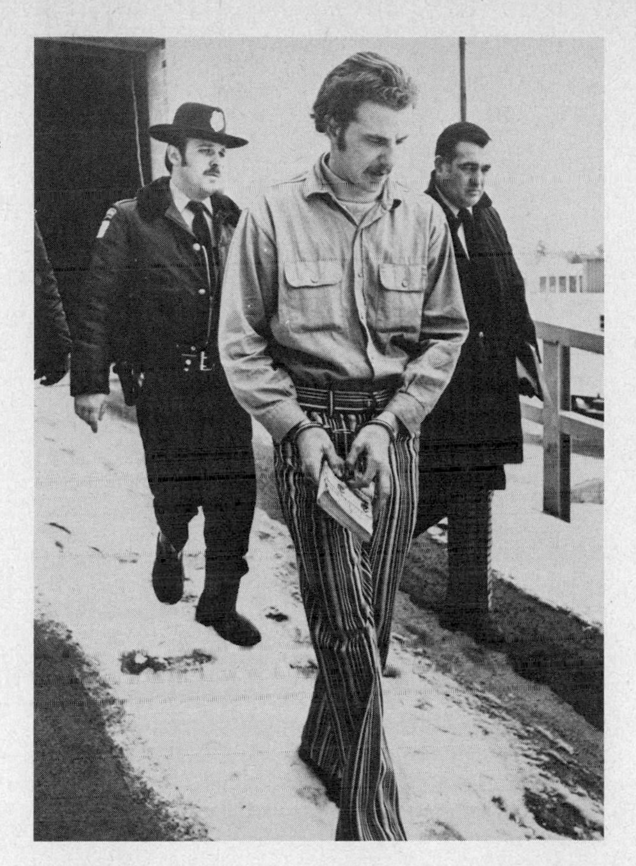

Rhode Island v. *Innis,* the Court ated that interrogation consists express questioning or its unctional equivalent" and sus- ined the murder conviction of e defendant (pictured here)

have been violated. In *Innis* the Court established a two-pronged definition of interrogation, concluding that the *Miranda* safeguards come into play whenever a person is subjected to either "express questioning" or to its "functional equivalent." The nature of the police conversation clearly did not constitute interrogation according to the express questioning yardstick.

The core of the *Innis* decision was the Court's enunciation of a functional-equivalent test of interrogation. This measure of interrogation refers to any words or action by the police that "they *should have known* were reasonably likely to elicit an incriminating response" from the suspect. On this basis, the Court ruled that Innis had not been subjected to the functional equivalent of interrogation, thereby sustaining the conviction. Conspicuously absent from the *Innis* decision was any attempt to indicate the circumstances under which the police can reasonably anticipate ("should have known") the self-incriminating impact of their words and actions. Presumably, the functional-equivalent test would cover situations like *Brewer*, where the purpose of police "conversation" is intended to elicit an incriminating response by appealing to the suspect's known vulnerabilities.

The *Innis* decision may be read as both an expansion of and severe retreat from the *Miranda* doctrine. Theoretically, *Innis* strengthens *Miranda* by recognizing that interrogation comes in more than one form. In principle, *Innis* establishes that, under certain circumstances, psychological ploys against suspects involving conversations between police are prohibited by the *Miranda* safeguards. In practice, however, the difficulties in meeting the "police should have known" requirement give the police ample room and incentive to utilize various conversational scenarios covertly designed to elicit incriminating statements and evidence. Rather than clarifying the boundaries of interrogation, *Innis* may have added new elements of uncertainty that, on balance, are more compatible with the interests of law enforcement than with protecting suspects against induced self-incrimination.

The Expansion of Stop and Frisk

Adams v. *Williams* (1972)

In *Adams* v. *Williams*[74] in 1972, the Court extended stop and frisk authority to a situation in which the officer's reasonable suspicion of criminal activity and a dangerous suspect were based upon information received[75] rather than upon personal observation (as in *Terry* v. *Ohio*). Thus *Adams* v. *Williams* lowered the threshold of reliability needed to justify a stop and frisk action and extended the concept to purely possessory crimes.

On patrol in a high-crime area at 2 A.M., an officer was informed that a man seated in a nearby car possessed narcotics and had a gun in his waistband. Approaching the car, the officer asked its occupant, Williams, to open the door. Williams opened the window instead. To protect himself, the officer reached into the car and removed a concealed revolver from Williams' waistband. Williams was arrested and booked on a charge of illegal possession of a weapon. At a later hearing, Williams contended that the officer's search and seizure was unreasonable under the stop and frisk standards set in *Terry*. In rejecting these contentions, the Court increased the authority of the police to stop and frisk.

United States v. *Robinson* (1973)

One of the Burger court's most controversial and significant decisions was *United States* v. *Robinson* in 1973.[76] An officer had reason to stop Robinson and to arrest him for driving on a revoked licence in the District of Columbia. Incident to the arrest, the officer proceeded to pat down the suspect. He felt a soft object in the coat pocket and removed it. The object was a crumpled cigarette package that contained heroin, for the possession of which Williams was convicted and sentenced to prison.

A lower federal court reversed the conviction on the grounds that in making a traffic violation arrest, the officer was "substantially safe" and was thus restricted to conducting a brief pat-down for weapons. The prosecution appealed the reversal to the Supreme Court.

In *Robinson* the Supreme Court held that upon custodial arrest of a traffic violator, the arresting officer may immediately conduct a full search of both the clothing and the person—even though the officer has no reason to believe the suspect is armed, is not concerned for his safety, has time to obtain a search warrant, and the discovered evidence would not have been destroyed in the interval. The Court flatly declared that a lawful arrest automatically justifies a full search of the person.

> It is the fact of the lawful arrest which establishes the authority to search, and we hold that in the case of a lawful custodial arrest a full search of the person is not only an exception to the warrant requirement of the Fourth Amendment, but is also a "reasonable" search under that Amendment.

Retreating from the philosophy of the Warren Court, the Burger Court had reordered the priorities by making reasonableness* of police action rather than warrants the new standard.[78] In doing so, the Burger Court has had occasion to comment on reasonable suspicion in a number of new contexts (see Close-up 6.2).[79]

Other Decisions Compatible with Police Interests

Kirby v. *Illinois* (1972)

In *Kirby* v. *Illinois* in 1972, the Court gave police lineups a new lease on life by holding that counsel was required only at lineups that take place *after* indictment or other "adversary criminal proceedings" such as arraignment or the preliminary hearing.[80] Most police lineups occur *before* indictment and the initial court appearance; they are used to obtain evidence on which to confirm probable cause at the preliminary hearing and to seek indictment. Thus *Kirby* v. *Illinois* preserved an important law enforcement tool that had been threatened in *Wade* v. *United States* in 1967, a decision that gave defendants the right to the presence of counsel at lineups held after indictment.[81]

* In *Delaware* v. *Prouse* in 1979 the Supreme Court ruled that spontaneous, wholly discretionary random stops of motorists to check their license or registration are a violation of the Fourth Amendment. The police officer involved admitted that he had *no reason* to suspect or believe that the stopped motorist had or was about to break the law: "I saw the car in the area and was not answering any complaints so I decided to pull it off." The *Prouse* decision, however, does not preclude states from devising methods for making spot checks of drivers' credentials that do not involve the unconstrained exercise of police discretion, such as roadblock inspections.[77]

Close-up 6.2 REASONABLE SUSPICION AND THE DRUG COURIER PROFILE

Since 1974, agents of the Drug Enforcement Administration have been using various Drug Courier Profiles (DCP) to identify, stop and question airline passengers suspected of trafficking in drugs. Now operational in 25 airports,[a] each drug courier profile consists of a set of factors believed to be indicative of persons transporting narcotics. Typical factors in the DCP used at different airports around the country include traveling between drug "source" and "use" cities (import and distribution points), the absence of luggage or carrying of an empty suitcase, nervousness, possessing an unusually large amount of cash, using an alias, and being of Hispanic descent. *Reid* v. *Georgia* was the first time that the Court directly addressed[b] the legal status of the drug courier profile as grounds for establishing reasonable suspicion to stop passengers.[c]

Upon arriving at the Atlanta airport, Reid and a companion were stopped by federal agents, who asked for identification and to see their tickets. Both travelers fit the drug courier profile: they (1) flew in from Fort Lauderdale, a principal source city for cocaine, (2) arrived early in the morning, when law enforcement activity is diminished, (3) apparently tried to conceal the fact that they were traveling together, and (4) had no luggage except for shoulder bags. Cocaine was found in Reid's bag following the stop. The Court ruled that Reid had been illegally detained because the agent, relying on the drug courier profile, did not have reasonable suspicion to believe that criminal activity was afoot. Indeed, the Court noted that three of the profile factors did not relate to specific conduct and were applicable to a large category of presumably innocent travelers. And the fourth factor, attempting to conceal their traveling together, was deemed little more than a hunch that is "too slender a reed to support the seizure in this case."

The *Reid* decision is not a blanket constitutional rejection of the drug courier profile per se. Other profiles may meet the reasonable suspicion standard if they contain a mix of valid factors that more accurately differentiate drug-smuggling passengers from law-abiding passengers, in much the same way that some employment tests are legally acceptable if they can be shown to be job related.[d] The common thread in *Reid* and a series of Burger court decisions dealing with the same issue is the Court's abhorrence of random stops,[e] which can only be stopped by strict adherence to the indicia of reasonable suspicion.

[a] Andrew D. Gilman, "Police and the Law," *Police Magazine*, September 1980, p. 62.
[b] *United States* v. *Mendenhall*, decided one month before *Reid*, involved a drug courier profile stop of a passenger arriving at the Detroit Metropolitan Airport. But the majority opinion sidestepped the stop issue by concluding that Mendenhall had voluntarily consented to the strip search that disclosed heroin on her person. *U.S.* v. *Mendenhall*, 100 S.Ct. 1870 (1980).
[c] *Reid* v. *Georgia*, No. 79-448. Decided June 30, 1980.
[d] Some analysts view the matter differently. They contend that *Reid* is consistent with lower court holdings that drug courier profiles, standing alone, cannot satisfy reasonable suspicion criteria and that the courts can not be bound by a profile developed by those whose actions are being reviewed. Brook Hart and Lila B. LeDuc, "Airport Searches by Drug Enforcement Agents," *Search And Seizure Law Report*, June 1981, pp. 104–105.
[e] Jeffrey A. Carter, "Airport Searches and Seizures: Where Will the Court Land?" *Journal of Criminal Law and Criminology*, Winter 1980, p. 516.

In a wide assortment of other cases and contexts, the Supreme Court in the 1970s handed down opinions that weighted the scales of justice toward the police, the state, and society rather than toward the individual, suspects, and defendants.

Miscellaneous decisions

In *United States* v. *Russell* in 1973 and *Hampton* v. *United States* in 1976, the Court narrowed the entrapment defense (see Chapter 3).

The Court upheld taking fingernail scrapings from a defendant over his protests and without a warrant.[82]

The Court held that the police may circulate to local merchants a list of "active shoplifters" that contains the name and picture of a person who was once arrested for shoplifting but was never prosecuted, the charges having been dismissed.[83] The court noted that one's reputation is not encompassed by the Fourteenth Amendment's protection of life, liberty, or property.

In a serious blow to citizens concerned with "police brutality," the Court held that evidence presented to document police abuse in Philadelphia was insufficient to justify intrusion by the federal judiciary into the authority of local officials and police administrators. A federal district judge had ordered city officials to devise a comprehensive plan for dealing with citizen complaints of police misconduct. The Supreme Court overturned the lower federal court's decision in *Rizzo* v. *Goode* in 1976.[84]

The Court held that the right to counsel did not apply to postindictment photographic identification where the defendant was not present. Thus, after indictment, police may show photographs of suspects to witnesses in the absence of suspect's counsel.[85]

In a case involving the Washington, D.C., police department, the Court handed down a decision making it harder to challenge allegedly biased personnel tests and set higher requirements for proving racial discrimination.[86]

In a highly significant decision, the Court ruled that the Fourth Amendment does not require police to obtain warrants—even if there is time to do so—before making arrests in public places. The Supreme Court had never previously addressed directly the validity of arrests without warrants; now it declared that so long as the officer has probable cause to believe that the arrested person committed a felony, warrantless arrests in public are permissible. "Law enforcement officers may find it wise to seek arrest warrants when practicable to do so . . . but we decline to transform this judicial preference into a constitutional rule."[87]

SUMMARY

In a sense, the boundaries of the police role are shaped by the United States Constitution as interpreted by the Supreme Court. The legal rights of the accused were expanded by the Court under Chief Justice Earl Warren, during its "due process revolution." The constitutional road taken for "policing the police" began with the Court's decision in *Mapp* v. *Ohio* in 1961, which imposed the exclusionary rule on the states as a means for inducing the police to observe the Fourth Amendment. The severest restrictions on the police came with the Court's decision in *Miranda* v. *Arizona* in 1966, which required that *Miranda* warnings be given prior to custodial interrogation—in order to protect the defendant's Fifth Amendment right against self-incrimination and to insure that any forthcoming confession is genuinely voluntary. However, the *Miranda* warnings do not apply to stop and frisk police actions, whose constitutionality was approved in *Terry* v. *Ohio* in 1968. The decisions of the Court under Chief Justice Warren Burger in the 1970s signaled a retreat from the exclusionary rule, an erosion of the *Miranda* doctrine, an expansion of stop and frisk authority, and a more conservative attitude toward the civil liberties of unconvicted offenders.

DISCUSSION QUESTIONS

1. Are you in favor of retaining the exclusionary rule in its present form, modifying it, or abolishing it altogether? Explain your answer.
2. If you were a Supreme Court justice reviewing the case of Williams, who sexually assaulted and murdered a ten-year-old girl, would you uphold the use of the defendant's response to the detective's "Christian burial speech" as evidence at trial? Why?
3. If the police proceed to a suspect's home and ask him incriminating questions, are they required to give the *Miranda* warnings? Explain the reasoning behind your answer.

4. If a police officer stops a suspicious person on the street and proceeds to search her for drugs, is the officer's action legally proper or improper? Why?
5. If, during a frisk for drugs, an officer finds a weapon instead, can the suspect be convicted for illegal possession of a weapon on the strength of the seized evidence? Why?
6. If an officer makes a frisk for a weapon and finds burglar tools instead, can the suspect be convicted for illegal possession of burglar tools on the strength of the seized evidence? Why?

Chapter 7

THE COURTS

The State Court System
Lower Courts
Nonjury trial / Overload in urban courts / Inadequate legal training in rural courts
Trial (Felony) Courts
Trial *de novo* / Jury trial
Appellate Courts
Reviewing the record for errors of law / Basis for appeal

Close-up 7.1: Two Successful Appeals

The right to appeal / Appeal of sentence / Reverse and remand / Instructing the trial court / Purposes of appellate rulings

The Federal Court System
U.S. commissioners and U.S. magistrates / Increased workloads in the courts / Exhausting state remedies
The Supreme Court
Original and appellate jurisdiction / Discretionary review / Writ of certiorari / Reverse and remand / Balancing the scales of justice

Close-up 7.2: Women on Juries

Court Reform
Judicial Discipline Commissions
California's Commission on Judicial Performance
Merit Selection of Judges
The Missouri Plan / Continuing judicial education programs
Court Administrators and Court Unification
Functions of court executives / The need for court reorganization
Summary

In the criminal justice system the court is the final arbiter, the front-line defender of democracy, personal freedom, human dignity, and public protection. It is the only institution capable of identifying and maintaining the proper balance between the competing rights of the individual and those of the state and society. It has the responsibility of enforcing the criminal law against defendants who commit crimes and at the same time protecting the same defendants from the violation of their rights by criminal justice agents. It is to the courts that everyone turns to see that justice is done.

The United States has a dual court system: one system of separate *state courts* to prosecute and try crimes defined by the state legislatures, and another system of essentially nonoverlapping *federal courts* whose jurisdiction is restricted to the federal crimes defined by the acts of Congress.

THE STATE COURT SYSTEM

Because each state is a sovereign government, there are in effect 50 separate court systems. The consequent variation among the states in court organization and personnel makes the state court system the least coordinated and most disorganized component in the criminal justice apparatus; it is impossible to identify the different types (levels or tiers) of state courts by their names alone. The role of the individual state courts within each state's judicial system can best be understood by describing their functions, which depend upon the court's *jurisdiction:* the court's legal authority to preside over, handle, and take action (decide issues) in certain kinds of cases. There are three levels, categories, or tiers of state courts. Each has a separate and distinct jurisdiction.

1. The courts of *limited* jurisdiction are the lower, inferior, misdemeanor, or minor courts, or the courts of first instance.
2. The courts of *general* jurisdiction are the trial or felony courts.
3. The courts of *appellate* jurisdiction are the highest rung in the state judicial ladder.

The structure and jurisdiction of the state courts is illustrated in Figure 7.1.

Lower Courts

The 13,221 courts of limited jurisdiction that are distributed throughout the country are the judicial system's entry point for all defendants. Following their arrest, defendants are brought before the inferior courts for arraignment. These are the courts that conduct the first arraignment

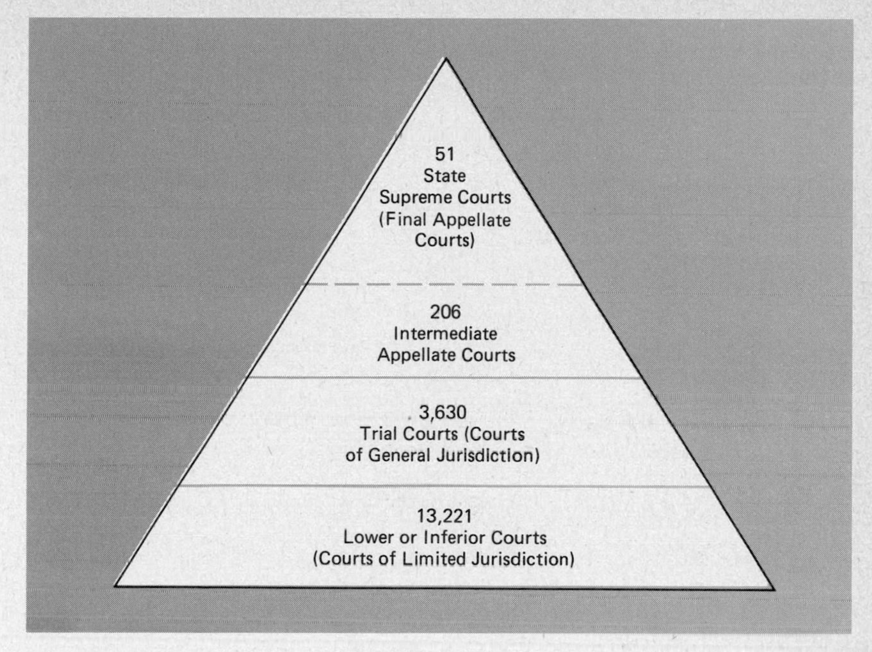

GURE 7.1 The state court sys-m. *Source: LEAA Newsletter,* pril 1974, p. 6.

(presentment) in felony cases, and they generally preside over the preliminary hearing. In the cities, the lower courts are generally referred to as magistrate courts. In rural areas, they are generally called justice of the peace (J.P.) courts. Magistrate and J.P. courts perform identical functions, although each lower court division has a somewhat different mix of problems associated with its caseload, facilities, and personnel. In some jurisdictions, lower court judges are not required to be lawyers. The United States Constitution says nothing about judges being members of the bar or lawyers. In *North* v. *Russell* in 1976, the Supreme Court refused to require lower court judges to be lawyers or have a legal background.[1]

The lower tier of the state court system has *limited* jurisdiction because its authority to try and to sentence defendants is restricted to petty offenses and lesser misdemeanors that ordinarily carry a maximum one-year jail term. Ninety percent of all criminal cases are disposed of in these inferior courts. The inferior court has the authority and responsibility to try and to sentence this group of defendants, thereby fully disposing of their cases. The lower courts are not uniformly proceedings *of record;* that is, transcripts of the proceedings are not always made, unless the defendant pays for them. This may reduce the chances of indigent defendants having their convictions reviewed and reversed by a higher (appellate) court, which relies on transcripts to detect and correct lower court errors.

Nonjury trial

The request for a jury trial in limited jurisdiction cases is rare; some states provide that when a misdemeanant requests a trial by jury, the case must be handled by a court of general jurisdiction. However, the lower courts have no jurisdiction over felony cases. In felony cases, the lower court simply processes them to the next stage (the preliminary hearing) on route to their being heard and disposed of by a court of general jurisdiction, the trial court.

The major problem faced by the urban lower courts (magistrate courts) is case overload

With a few exceptions, defendants who are charged with misdemeanors and whose cases are handled completely by the lower courts are entitled to the same constitutional and procedural safeguards as are felony defendants. All defendants at their initial appearance before the lower courts are supposed to be informed of the charges against them and advised of their rights to remain silent, to retain their own attorney or have state-supplied defense counsel if indigent, and to have reasonable bail set. The rules of evidence and the constitutional guidelines are supposed to be observed in every adversary court proceeding—every judicial inquiry where guilt may be determined and conviction and criminal penalties are at stake. Upon pleading guilty, the several million defendants before the lower courts face the possibility of up to one year's incarceration and/or a fine.

The sheer volume of cases terminated at this court level makes the inferior courts the most visible symbols and providers of justice. The public's image, experience with, and respect for the courts and the judiciary is heavily influenced by the quality and qualifications of lower court judges, their effective performance of their duties, and their fairhanded and lawful dispensation of justice.

Overload in urban courts

The major problems of the urban lower courts today are traceable to *overload*. In a single year, three judges in Atlanta disposed of a total of more than 70,000 cases.[2] Many local judges handle as many as 30,000 cases annually.[3] Given these numbers, "clearing the dockets" in the urban inferior courts becomes the primary objective of all concerned. At times the continuous pressure of overload may result in a disregard for the rights of the accused, five-minute trials, and hasty sentencing decisions made in public without benefit of presentence reports, which are usually required only in felony cases.[4] In addition, urban lower courts have been criticized for operating in an atmosphere of great legal informality and, occasionally, complete disorganization.

Inadequate legal training in rural courts

In small towns, villages, and rural areas, justice of the peace courts are the counterpart to the urban lower courts. The questionable quality of justice in the justice of the peace courts is related to the background and legal qualifications of the justices rather than to case volume.[5] Frequently, justices of the peace have no legal training whatever and may

lany J.P. courts in rural areas ave no legal background and ttle education

not even be high school graduates. In some states, such as South Carolina, up to 85 percent of the criminal defendants are tried by inferior courts whose legal knowledge is sketchy at best and whose courtroom is the kitchen, the barn, or the porch. Only a handful of South Carolina's J.P.s are lawyers; some have never opened a law book, despite the fact that each justice hears 90 cases a month. The average J.P. there has a high school education, but many have not gone beyond the tenth grade. Only half their time is spent on judicial duties; the remainder may be devoted to pumping gas or selling insurance, for being a judge is often a sideline to their main work as gas station attendants, storekeepers, insurance salespersons, or truck drivers.[6]

Another unprofessional feature of the lower rural courts is the fee system. In 32 of the 35 states that have the J.P., the judge's income or fee depends on the number of cases handled, their outcome, or a percentage of the fines collected. In three states, the J.P.s were paid only if they convicted and were able to collect their fees from the defendants. This illegal practice continued despite a Supreme Court ruling in 1927 making it unconstitutional.[7]

Trial (Felony) Courts

About 10 percent of the defendants brought before the lower courts are charged with felonies and misdemeanors that carry penalties of more than one year in prison. These defendants are candidates for trial by the courts of *general jurisdiction,* the felony or trial courts. Between their initial appearance in the inferior courts and their arraignment in the trial courts, some of these defendants will be screened out at the preliminary hearing or by the grand jury.

For those accused of felonies and high misdemeanors, the initial presentment before the lower courts is not a trial or hearing. It is the earliest opportunity following arrest for a court of law to inform defendants of their constitutional rights, to make arrangements for state-supplied defense counsel, and to set bail. Setting bail is an important function of the lower courts because several months may elapse before the case is scheduled for trial. Those charged with more serious offenses are thus technically not arraigned in the lower courts; the inferior court does not have the jurisdiction to try felony defendants—only the trial courts of general jurisdiction do. The charges entered at the initial court appearance in felony cases are tentative and subject to grand jury action, whose indictment contains the finalized formal charges to which felony defendants plead at arraignment before a court of general jurisdiction. Pleas of not guilty may be entered by felony defendants at the initial court appearance, but this is merely for the record, an administrative device for moving the case along to the trial courts.

Trial courts have *original* and *exclusive* jurisdiction over felonies. In principle, their jurisdiction begins where that of the lower courts ends. For example, if a lower court can try misdemeanors whose penalty does not exceed a fine of $200, a defendant charged with a misdemeanor that carries a $500 fine or a jail term would have to be tried in the felony courts. The trial courts are also "higher" than the inferior courts in another respect: They usually have the power to set aside a lower court's decision in a petty case and to retry the defendant a second time anew (trial *de novo*). The second trial may be conducted without regard for the lower court's judgment or sentence.

Trial *de novo*

These are the major features of trial and the trial courts of general jurisdiction:

Judges are necessarily lawyers and members of the bar because of the complex legal issues involved in felony cases.

Almost all trial judges are full-time criminal justice practitioners; the fee system does not exist.

The judge accepts a guilty plea only after establishing that it is voluntary and informed.

Trials are public events that can be attended by the press and the community, for openness encourages justice, fairness, and accurate fact-finding.

Trial proceedings involve due process, rules of evidence, and other procedural safeguards which are known in advance and by which the opposing attorneys must abide.

The adversary, court-supervised adjudication of guilt or innocence is cloaked in due process to guarantee the accused fundamental fairness and justice.

The formalities of procedural criminal law and the effective assistance of counsel at trial equalize the resources available to both sides. Thus the result reflects the defendant's actual innocence or guilt. Neither side is allowed to win at any cost but only within the carefully defined rules of the contest. These procedural restrictions make for equal protection under the law.

There is full compliance with the procedural criminal law and the constitutional rights of the accused; this may involve pretrial motions and motions at trial to suppress evidence illegally obtained by the police.

Formal adjudication of guilt under judicial supervision protects the defendant against the use of force or coercion by criminal justice agents.

Jury trial

There is a constitutional right to trial by jury in felonies, and jury trials are common in these cases. The traditional requirement of a unanimous verdict is a protection against convicting an innocent defendant.

Trial judges take the issue of criminal penalties (and criminal responsibility) seriously, and this process maintains the public's respect for the law and the entire criminal justice system.

Felony courts are courts of record; a transcript is made of the entire proceeding, and that record is essential in appealing convictions.

Appellate Courts

Every state has at least one appellate court. The highest appellate court in most states is called the State Supreme Court. Each state's highest tribunal is a single judicial body composed of from three to nine judges. The justices are either elected or appointed to terms of from six to ten years in most states, but the length of their terms can vary between two years and life.[8] In some states, appellate courts "sit" in one permanent location. In others, the court travels throughout its circuit, sitting for a few months at each location and then moving on to the next circuit point. (In large states, several intermediate appellate courts each serve a particular area and the trial courts within it.) Appellate judges may decide issues while sitting as a group (*en banc*) or as a panel of two or three members. Or they may individually review the record (transcript), meet to discuss the issues, and either concur with or dissent from the judge assigned to write the majority decision. The view of the majority is binding.

Appellate courts do not have the power to try or retry cases. Their function is to determine whether there were *errors of law* associated with the defendant's conviction or sentence, and they do this by reviewing the record of the trial court proceedings. Legal mistakes, judicial irregularities, and errors occurring at the trial court level may involve:

Reviewing the record for errors of law

depriving defendants of their constitutional rights;
violating the rules of evidence governing trial procedures;
accepting a guilty plea that was not voluntary and intelligent;
admitting into evidence an illegally obtained confession;
charging a jury improperly;
permitting a racially biased jury to be empanelled;
failing to make clear the possible consequences of a guilty plea, despite any sentencing "promises" made by the prosecutor to the defendant;
passing an unlawful sentence.

Appellate court functions are restricted to reviewing *procedural* criminal law issues surrounding conviction and sentence: *How* was the incriminating evidence obtained? *How* did the trial court charge the jury? *How* was the jury selected? *How* did the trial judge determine the guilty plea was voluntary? *How* were the defendants given all their constitutional rights? *How* was the sentence decided upon?

The appellate court determines whether errors of law occurred at trial court that may have affected the defendant's conviction and sentence by (1) inspecting the record of the trial court, including pretrial papers and the transcript and testimony of trial proceedings, (2) considering defense counsel's written *brief* stating why the conviction or sentence should be reversed (overturned)—and the prosecutor's brief stating why the conviction or sentence should be affirmed (upheld), and (3) listening to short oral arguments by the opposing attorneys. The brief oral presentation gives the appellate court a chance to obtain clarification on points in the written briefs. However, no new evidence or arguments can be considered by the appellate court, and no witnesses can be called. There is no jury because the appellate court does not retry the facts of the case.[9]

Basis for appeal

Almost anything that could have reasonably prevented the defendant from receiving a fair hearing and sentence may become the basis of an appeal: police entrapment; unfavorable pretrial publicity; holding the trial where the entire community is openly hostile to the defendant; racial composition of the jury; failure to give indigents state-supplied counsel; sentencing the defendant without a presentence report; not permitting the trial to be held in a different county from where the crime occurred (failure to order a change of *venue*); unethical or illegal conduct by the prosecutor; having a defendant appear in court for trial while still wearing jail clothing, and so on (see Close-up 7.1).

Close-up 7.1 TWO SUCCESSFUL APPEALS

Conviction for Distributing Marijuana: Overturned

Otis Johnson, a black militant leader, was arrested for passing one marijuana cigarette to an undercover police officer who had infiltrated the communal house where Johnson lived in order to develop a personal relationship with him. Johnson was tried by an all-white jury, and two of the jurors admitted knowing of the defendant's reputation as a militant radical. Despite this, a motion for change of venue was denied. The prosecutor demanded a 20-year sentence. After deliberating for half an hour, the jury sentenced Johnson to 30 years.

Johnson appealed his conviction to the state appellate court and lost (his conviction and sentence were affirmed). He continued his appeal efforts, and in January 1972 a federal appellate court overturned the conviction. The court ordered that Johnson be retried or set free: "Outside influences affecting the community's climate of opinion were so inherently suspect as to create a resulting probability of unfairness."[a]

Sentence for Possessing Heroin: Overturned

Janice W. was convicted of possessing one pound of heroin. The crime carried a prison term of from 5 to 20 years, to be determined at the discretion of the court. Before reading the presentence report, the trial judge stated that he was going to impose the minimum sentence of 5 years. After reading the report, the court sentenced the defendant to the maximum 20-year term. She appealed.

The appellate court found that the sentence had been increased fourfold on the basis of unsworn evidence and unverified statements in the presentence report. The charges made by narcotic agents in the presentence report had flimsy support. The appellate court ordered the trial judge to resentence the defendant without considering the damaging statements in the presentence report unless there was more convincing proof to support them.[b]

[a] *Time,* March 13, 1972, p. 50.
[b] *Time,* November 8, 1971, p. 80.

The appellate court cannot on its own initiative review the action of a trial court; it can only consider cases brought to it on appeal by the defendant. Ordinarily, the prosecutor cannot appeal an acquittal in criminal cases because of the constitutional protection against *double jeopardy:* "nor shall any person be subject for the same offense to be twice put in jeopardy of life or limb."

The right to appeal

The defendant has no federal constitutional right to appeal. However, all states have appellate machinery that, in effect, provides the defendant with at least one chance to appeal, and many state constitutions or statutes provide a right to appeal. Because of the ease of appealing convictions and the large number of appeals taken, 23 states have established intermediate appellate courts; they are ordinarily called simply courts of appeal. Where there are intermediate appellate courts, the defendant's right to appeal directly to the state's highest tribunal is usually at the high court's discretion.[10]

For two reasons, it is typically the conviction rather than the sentence that is appealed. First, defendants who are found guilty at trial are more interested in having a second chance at acquittal than in receiving a less severe sentence. Second, appeals are based on alleged errors in procedural criminal law for which the trial court is responsible. Until the early 1970s, procedural law was concerned almost entirely with the defendant's right to a fair trial in order to avoid unlawful conviction. Before then, little attention was given to guaranteeing the convicted defendant a fair (lawful) sentence.

Appeal of sentence

While sentencing is a separate stage, it is still within the trial courts' jurisdiction. A sentence can be appealed whenever the method used by the judge in selecting penalties violates the Fourteenth Amendment's provisions for due process or equal protection of the law. The intent of due process is to provide fundamental fairness to the offender at every critical stage in the criminal justice system. A *critical stage* is any processing step in the criminal justice system at which the offender can suffer serious personal loss as a result of decisions (such as sentencing) made by those in charge. The specific type and enforcement of due process varies with the circumstances of each case and the critical stage involved. However, all due process violations involve decisions affecting the offender that are illegal, unreasonable, or unconstitutional.

In practice, very few sentences are appealed, compared to the number of convictions appealed. This is because there are few procedures that the court is required to follow at sentencing, while a mountain of rules applies to the trial (conviction) stage. Because the sentencing function is so discretionary and invisible, it is extremely difficult to establish a violation of due process at this critical stage. The appellate court is also reluctant to criticize its judicial colleagues in such a sensitive area as sentencing discretion.

Reverse and remand

In the vast majority of cases, the appellate court finds that the trial court's conviction or sentence was proper. When it finds that the trial court acted improperly, however, the appellate court reverses and remands the case to the trial judge. A *remand* is the sending of a lawsuit back to the court where it originated, for retrial or other action; it includes instructions on how the trial court should correct the mistakes it made.[11] Appellate courts will not remand cases where the trial court's error was harmless. *Harmless errors* are mistakes of law occurring at trial that could not have made a difference in the conviction or the sentence.

The appellate court never changes a conviction to an acquittal or resentences the defendant. These functions are a part of trying defendants, and trial is not within the jurisdiction of the appellate courts. Even when the appellate court reverses and remands, it cannot be known in advance whether there will be any difference in the outcome. When errors of law that *could* have affected the conviction or the sentence are corrected, the result is usually the same, rather than an acquittal or a reduced sentence. For example, when the Supreme Court reversed Miranda's conviction and remanded the case to trial court for retrial without using his confession, Miranda was again convicted and sentenced to 20–30 years. Of course, the effect of an appellate court's "remanding with instructions" based on its ruling can only be known after the trial judge has complied with the order.

Instructing the trial court

The instructions given to the trial court will vary with the specific errors of law committed in each case. They may order:

resentencing the offender without using unsupported or inaccurate information contained in the presentence report;
a retrial that excludes illegally obtained evidence;
the court-supervised selection of a more racially balanced jury;
the dismissal of the defendant in cases involving gross abuse of the law.

A successful appeal is an opportunity for the defendant to start over from the beginning—or from the point at which the legal error occurred. Appellate reversal of a verdict or a sentence is not an automatic "victory" that turns conviction into acquittal or reduces the penalty. Principles of law and criminal procedure established by the state's highest appellate court are legally binding on all state courts. In future cases in which the facts are basically the same, the inferior and trial judges must apply the law as settled by the appellate court. This rule of precedent (*stare decisis*) requires that all state courts in similar cases abide by the legal principles established by the state's highest tribunal.

Purposes of appellate rulings

Appellate court rulings have two major purposes. The first is to implement the Bill of Rights of the United States Constitution; appellate reversal is one of the few means available to enforce constitutional rights. The second is to deter criminal justice personnel from violating a citizen's constitutional rights. Reversals are intended to deter police and other officials from violating procedural criminal law by making it more difficult for illegally obtained convictions and illegal sentences to stick. Many convictions, for example, are appealed on the basis of police violations of the Fourth and Fifth amendments (as discussed in the preceding chapter).

Appellate reversals and rulings also have an educational function. They inform personnel in all agencies of the correct procedures of criminal justice administration. Appellate rulings are a source of recognized legal authority that can be cited in similar cases in the future. Their reference value helps police, prosecutor, correction agents, and the lower and trial courts themselves to avoid repeating a mistake. When mistakes are about to be repeated by trial courts, defense counsel can prevent them by citing appellate precedent. When the trial court repeats its mistakes, defense counsel can correct them by citing precedent to the appellate court.

All three purposes of appellate court rulings—implementation of the Constitution, deterrence, and education—are related in practice. The Constitution is implemented by deterring criminal justice agents from violating its provisions. And in order to avoid using incorrect procedures in administering the criminal justice system and in doing their jobs, the practitioners must learn which procedures are illegal.

THE FEDERAL COURT SYSTEM

As Figure 7.2 shows, the federal government has a three-tier court system: (1) The 97 district courts, the only trial courts in the federal judiciary, are staffed by about 450 judges. (2) The 11 Courts of Appeals, comprising the intermediate appellate court level, are staffed by 97 justices. Each Court of Appeals serves a particular circuit—a group of states and territories—the eleventh being designated for the District of Columbia. (3) The United States Supreme Court, with nine justices, is the highest federal appellate court. The appellate courts review the records of cases sent to them on appeal from the district trial courts. All judges in the federal system hold office for life during good behavior, and their salaries cannot be reduced.[12]

The volume and types of federal offenses differ sharply from those of state crimes. Excluding traffic violations, 85 to 95 percent of the criminal cases in the United States are handled by the states, which clearly makes crime a local rather than a national problem. The relatively small number of federal crimes includes very little street crime and a great deal of white collar crime. Almost all crimes of violence are state offenses. Federal crimes include mail theft, theft from interstate commerce, taking a stolen auto across state lines, counterfeiting, destroying federally owned property, income tax violation, violation of federal drug laws, and robbery of a national or federally insured bank.

GURE 7.2 The federal court stem.

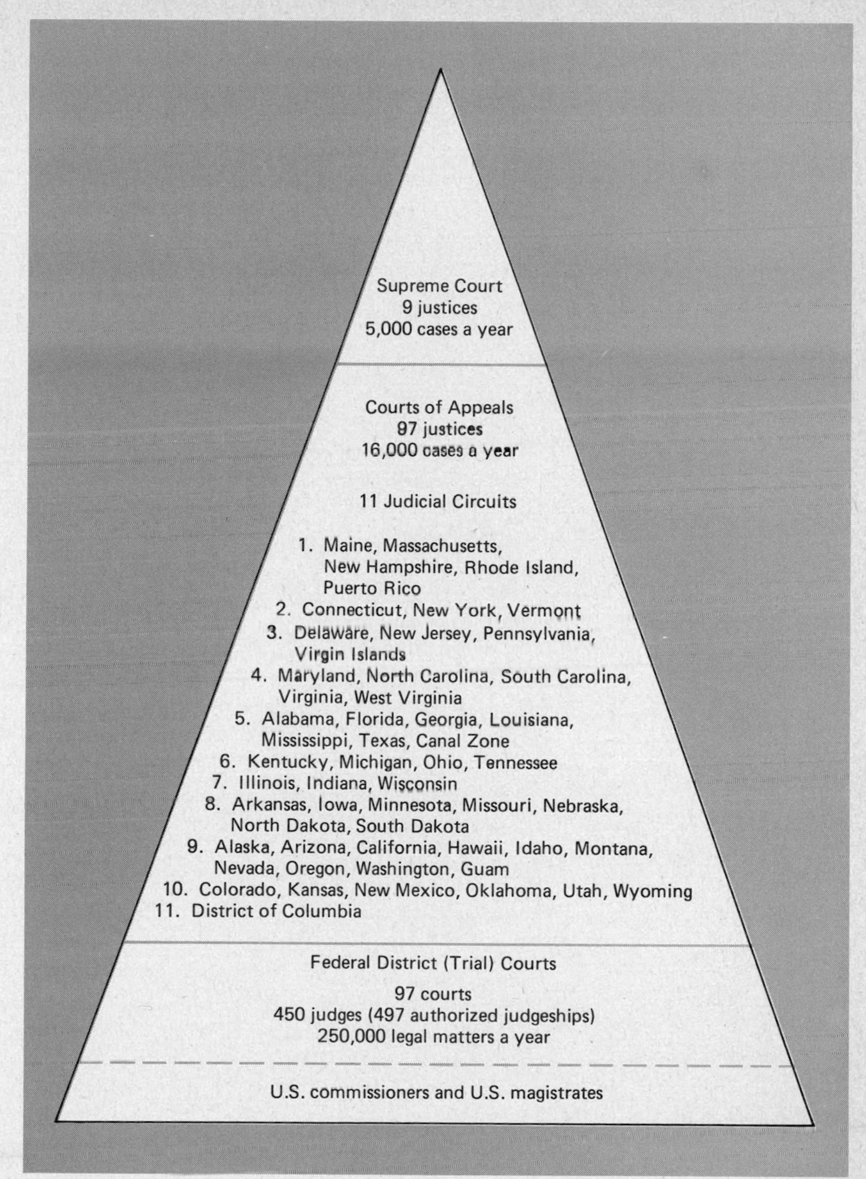

U.S. commissioners and U.S. magistrates

Until 1968, the front-line judiciary in the federal court system were the U.S. commissioners. In some ways, these judicial officers were similar to the J.P.s in the state court system: many were nonlawyers who worked part time, were compensated on a fee basis, and did not operate as courts of record. Then the Federal Magistrates Act, passed by Congress in 1968, provided for a three-year phasing out of the office of U.S. commissioner. Their functions are now performed by U.S. magistrates, lawyers who try lesser misdemeanors, set bail in more serious cases (which they bind over to the district trial courts), and assist the district courts in legal matters.[13] The magistrates' primary function is to reduce the ever-increasing workload of the district courts: in 1972 the district courts handled more than a quarter of a million transactions.[14]

Increased workloads in the courts

Starting in the 1950s, new rights of citizens were established by the legislatures, Congress, and court rulings in a wide variety of areas. The expanded rights of citizens in trouble with the law then contributed to vast increases in district court caseloads. Between 1950 and 1970, and paralleling the situation in the state trial courts, case filings in the district courts doubled—to reach an all-time high of 143,284 in fiscal 1974.[15] There has been a 38 percent increase from 1968 to 1973 alone. The federal backlog of 69,000 cases in 1960 had become 125,000 in 1972. In turn, this situation affects the workload and problems of the Courts of Appeals. The Courts of Appeals receive a substantial amount of their business from appeals taken from the district trial courts. In 1960 only 21 percent of those convicted appealed—compared with 55 percent in 1970. The number of cases filed with the Courts of Appeals in fiscal 1974 set a new record of 16,436.[16] Appellate overload has caused some Courts of Appeals to stop writing opinions for their decisions and to forgo hearing oral arguments by the attorneys.

The response to the Supreme Court's first overload crisis in 1891 was to create an entirely new layer of federal courts in the form of the 11 Courts of Appeals, in order to reduce the amount of litigation reaching the high tribunal. By 1925 the Supreme Court's caseload had again become unmanageable, and Congress responded by giving the Supreme Court broad discretion to reject cases coming before it for review. (Until 1925, the Supreme Court had to hear every petition within its jurisdiction.)[17]

Much of the federal courts' growing caseload has come from an increased number of habeas corpus petitions filed by state and federal prisoners. The right of habeas corpus is guaranteed by the U.S. Constitution as well as by state constitutions. A writ of habeas corpus is used to test whether a prisoner is being confined illegally; it orders the official restraining the inmate to establish before an appropriate court of law that the detention is legal. The writ is ordinarily served on the jail superintendent, prison warden, or corrections commissioner.[18] A habeas corpus petition that originates in the states can be carried forward in the federal court system only after the state prisoner has unsuccessfully appealed his or her detention to the highest state court. The law requires that convicted state defendants first appeal their grievances throughout the state court system before they will be considered by a federal court. This is called *exhausting state remedies*. When that has been accomplished, the appeal process can be continued in the federal courts if a violation of constitutional rights is involved. Only after exhausting state remedies will a federal court review action taken by a state court (see Figure 7.3).

Exhausting state remedies

The Supreme Court

Original and appellate jurisdiction

The Supreme Court has two kinds of jurisdiction over cases: original and appellate. *Original* jurisdiction means that cases may be taken directly to the Supreme Court for a decision and the Court is required to accept them. Original cases usually involve suits between two states or issues that test the constitutionality of a state law or rule. In its *appellate* jurisdiction, the Supreme Court for the most part has the discretion to resolve conflicts of law that raise a "substantial federal question." Almost without exception, the substantial federal question deals with an

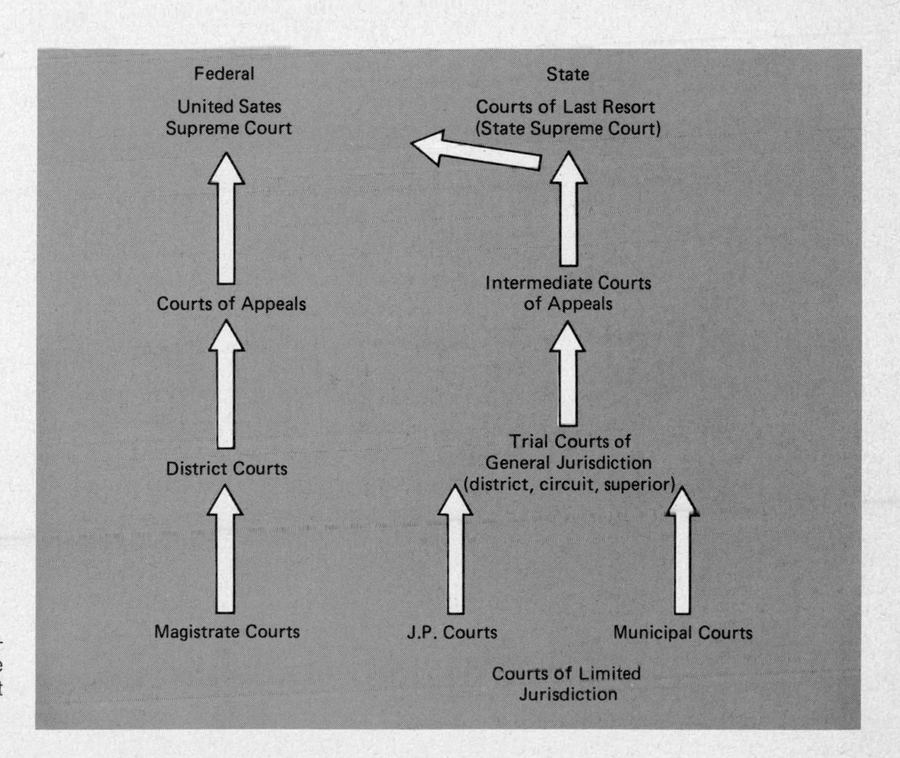

URE 7.3 Before a case origi-
ng in the states can reach the
reme Court, it must "exhaust
e remedies."

interpretation of the Constitution or the constitutionality of state statutes and court decisions.

There are three appellate situations in which the Supreme Court *must* hear the case and decide the issue: (1) when the highest state court has ruled that a federal statute is unconstitutional, (2) when the highest state court has upheld a state law or a provision in the state constitution whose federal constitutionality was challenged, and (3) when a three-judge Court of Appeals has declared that a state law or constitutional provision is contrary to federal law or the U.S. Constitution, and the state has appealed this decision. Appeals falling into these three categories and original cases are the only cases that the Supreme Court is required to review. Altogether, they are rare events in the Supreme Court's workload, and they have negligible impact on the administration of criminal justice.

Discretionary review

The principal business of the Supreme Court is the review *at its discretion* of appeals by defendants and prisoners who have been convicted, sentenced, and incarcerated by state courts and the lower federal courts. Almost two-thirds of its cases come from the lower federal courts and one-third from state courts.[19] In 97 percent of the Supreme Court's workload, it considers the substantial federal issues involved in how the defendant was convicted, how the defendant was sentenced, the legality of incarceration, and the legality of the conditions of imprisonment.[20] The Supreme Court is not required to review or to issue decisions in any of these cases; here the Court has absolute discretion to accept or reject cases that it has been petitioned to decide. It will not even screen cases of convicted state criminals unless the defendant has exhausted state remedies in appealing the outcome of trial or the sentence.

The Supreme Court will accept for review only cases in which its decision could make a difference to the appellant. It does not render advisory opinions. Until the Supreme Court rules on the constitutionality of an issue or a practice, the lower federal courts and state courts may continue to enforce different interpretations of the Constitution within their jurisdictions. The unique power of the Supreme Court is that its interpretation of the law is the last word. Under the supremacy clause of the Constitution, the Supreme Court has final and absolute jurisdiction over all federal and state courts, which are legally bound to abide by the High Court's decisions. In this way, the word of the Supreme Court becomes the law of the land and establishes the mandate for uniform implementation of the principles and procedures of justice.

Writ of certiorari

A convicted defendant who wishes to have his or her case reviewed by the Supreme Court files a *writ of certiorari* with the Court. This is a formal petition that requests the Court to review the case from the record and to render a decision. The Supreme Court quickly screens all certiorari petitions to determine which ones it will accept for deliberation. Certiorari applies only to cases where a federal statute or the defendant's constitutional rights may have been violated, thereby raising a substantial federal issue. If the appeal issue does not involve a significant constitutional question, it will be decided by a state appellate court or the Court of Appeals. The number of petitions filed annually with the Supreme Court has increased from 1,000 in 1935 to 5,000 in 1978.[21] The Court hears just 2 percent of the cases in which certiorari petitions are filed.

Reverse and remand

In reversing an appellant's conviction or sentence, the Supreme Court remands the case to the court of original jurisdiction with instructions on how to proceed. When it overturns a conviction or a sentence, the Court does not free the defendant or impose a lighter penalty; the Supreme Court is an appellate body, and no appellate court can try or sentence defendants. Upon reversing and remanding, the Court may:

order a new trial before a different judge;
exclude the defendant's confession from consideration by the jury in reaching a verdict;
order a change of venue because of prejudicial pretrial publicity or because community hostility interfered with an impartial hearing;
order institutional authorities to remedy the unconstitutional conditions of incarceration.

In cases where the Supreme Court reverses a conviction or a sentence, the defendants may be released temporarily from confinement on bail until they are retried, resentenced, or reinstitutionalized according to procedures that do not violate their rights and are consistent with the Court's ruling in the case. The Supreme Court's majority decision becomes the law of the land. Yet even when the Court accepts a case for review and reverses the conviction or sentence, most new trials result in reconviction and reimprisonment.

Balancing the scales of justice

The Supreme Court's clearest responsibility is to uphold and enforce the Constitution. The main act of the Court is to balance the scales of criminal justice between the rights and interests of the individual and

Supreme Court seeks to re-
e substantial federal ques-
s involving the interpretation
he Constitution

those of the state and society. Individual and social rights are always subject to change because no law or interpretation of the Constitution is immutable. Legal rights are "given" to individuals and groups by the legislatures, Congress, state and federal constitutions, and court decisions; and they can be taken away by the same processes.

The Supreme Court is not required to follow its own precedent. In response to changing social and political conditions or expectations, the Supreme Court may break sharply from an earlier ruling—as it did, for example, in its position toward women on juries (see Close-up 7.2).

Close-up 7.2 WOMEN ON JURIES

In 1961 the Supreme Court ruled that discriminating against women in jury selection did not violate a defendant's constitutional right to an impartial jury and a fair trial. But the Court broke with its own precedent in 1975 in *Taylor* v. *Louisiana.*[a] The New Orleans case involved a defendant convicted of rape by an all-male jury and sentenced to death. Louisiana state law barred women from serving on juries unless they specifically requested to do so in writing. The defendant claimed that he was, thus, denied his right to a fair trial. In agreeing, the Supreme Court reversed his conviction and gave the defendant a chance to be retried: "If it was ever the case that women were unqualified to sit on juries or were so situated that none of them should be required to perform jury service, that time has long since passed."

The Supreme Court's most recent decision concerning women on juries was in 1979 in *Duren* v. *Missouri.*[b] Missouri (and Tennessee) permitted any woman requesting it an automatic exemption from jury service. Duren, convicted of murder and robbery by an all-male jury, claimed that Missouri's automatic exemption statute violated his Sixth Amendment right to be tried by a jury representing a fair cross section of the community. In support of his appeal, Duren established that while 54 percent of the adults in the community were women, usually only 15 percent of the citizens available for jury service were women. In reversing the conviction on the grounds alleged by Duren, the Court noted that the role women have in home and family life does not justify their disproportionate exclusion from jury service as a result of the state's automatic exemption provision.

[a] *Taylor* v. *Louisiana,* 419 U.S. 522 (1975).
[b] *Duren* v. *Missouri,* 99 S.Ct. 664 (1979).

The provisions contained in the Bill of Rights—the first ten amendments to the Constitution—set the *minimum* protections that are guaranteed to state citizens, suspects, defendants, and prisoners through the Fourteenth Amendment. The states can, at any time on their own, provide *more* due process to their citizens than that outlined in the Constitution. California, for example, places greater restrictions upon the police in questioning suspects than the Constitution requires, gives the defendant's counsel the right to inspect the presentence report, and requires that lawyer-judges preside over trials punishable by a jail sentence.[22] The significance of the Supreme Court under Chief Justice Earl Warren was that from 1960 to 1969, through the Fourteenth Amendment's due process clause, its decisions extended and imposed upon the states almost all of the Bill of Rights provisions dealing with criminal justice administration.*

COURT REFORM

Current efforts to control abusive practices and incompetence on the part of individual judges, to upgrade the caliber of the judiciary, and to improve the organization of the court system and judicial administration fall into three categories, respectively: establishment of judicial discipline commissions, appointment of judges through merit selection, and unification of the courts and the use of court administrators.

Judicial Discipline Commissions

"The fundamental problem is this: a judge exercises more power with less accountability than any other official in our society."[23] Until recently, it was virtually impossible to do anything about judges who were incompetent, disabled, senile, corrupt, unethical, racist, abusive, who shirked their duties, or who conducted courtroom proceedings without decorum and the appearance of justice. State and federal law usually provided for the removal of judges only through impeachment—a cumbersome procedure tainted with politics and an ineffective device for responding to the range of problems associated with judicial shortcomings.[24] Less extreme sanctions such as censure, public reprimand, suspension, and reassignment generally did not exist.[25] Thus, in many cases, "judicial independence had become a cloak for a brand of judicial absolutism."[26]

* The three exceptions were the Second Amendment right to bear arms; the Fifth Amendment requirement of a grand jury indictment for all capital or infamous crimes; and the Eighth Amendment prohibition against excessive bail.

The current nationwide approach to the control of judicial misconduct and incompetence had its origin in California, which pioneered the idea of a permanent commission to investigate charges against judges and to recommend punishment where warranted. Established in 1960, California's nine-member Commission on Judicial Performance consists of citizens, lawyers, and judges; it has the authority to investigate complaints against judges, to demand explanations from them regarding their alleged misconduct, and to recommend formal disciplinary measures to the California Supreme Court, which generally follows the commission's proposals.* The broad jurisdiction of the California commission encompasses "conduct prejudicial to the administration of justice that brings the judicial office into disrepute." And pursuant to its constitutional authority, the commission may recommend admonishing judges for having any case pending 90 days after it was first submitted to the court for a decision.

California's Commission on Judicial Performance

The results of California's court-watching operation have been striking. It has "induced" retirements and resignations from 39 judges at all court levels.† It has been responsible for the censure of six judges and the suspension of others for "eccentricities" that denigrated the appearance of justice.‡ And it has established precedents for removing judges for senility and "conduct unbecoming a judicial officer" (such as vulgar and abusive behavior in the courtroom).[28] The mere prospect of being investigated by the judicial review board was often enough to deter or correct questionable or improper court conduct. Previously, there had been no mechanism to make judges accountable for abusing their discretion or failing to perform their duties adequately.

By 1978, 35 states had established judicial discipline commissions modeled directly on California's,[29] and only three states were without some type of special panel for investigating errant judges.§ The New York State Commission on Judicial Conduct, for example, dismissed a city judge for repeatedly failing to hold trials promptly and letting cases pile up for months,[30] removed another judge who had a street vendor brought to his chambers in handcuffs for serving "terrible coffee,"[31] and reprimanded another for treating witnesses and lawyers disrespectfully.[32]

* An allegation of judicial incompetence may be based on any number of factors, including grossly inadequate legal training. Whether such complaints are accepted by a commission depends on its jurisdiction and its policy toward various kinds of complaints. Generally, commissions will not pursue complaints that take issue with a judge's ruling or a sentence in a specific case.

† Most were associated with physical disabilities.

‡ The judge in question dispensed justice while holding her Chihuahua on her lap, had her chambers painted pink, and carried a .38 pistol conspicuously displayed on her person.[27]

§ They were Maine, Mississippi, and Washington.

Judicial discipline commissions have made it possible to take appropriate action against judges who forget that they are accountable to society, that they are only one part of the criminal justice system, that they are not above the law, and judges who are unwilling to retire gracefully when unable to keep up with the workload. Perhaps as important as the correction of individual abuses of judicial power is the commissions' role in bolstering the sagging public confidence in the courts.

In 1978 legislation was pending in Congress that would establish a commission to discipline those unfit judges who have lifetime tenure and —short of impeachment—cannot effectively be sanctioned for improprieties in office.* Besides the official judicial commissions, there are a large number of professional and private groups, including the community court watchers (see Chapter 4), who have become involved in judging the judges.[34] Despite the value of and the need for the judicial discipline commissions, their ability to remove unfit judges is limited. This problem—and many others addressed by such commissions after the fact —could be avoided altogether if better qualified judges were appointed to the bench in the first place.

Merit Selection of Judges

Traditionally, the selection of judges has been influenced by political considerations—a matter of who the applicants knew rather than a strict choice of the best person for the job. This applied to the selection of both federal judges, who are appointed by the president with the consent of the Senate, and state judges, who are usually elected officials.† The result was many of the problems discussed above.

The Missouri Plan

The model for upgrading the quality of judges and removing politics from office holding is the Missouri Plan, a procedure in which judges are screened and in effect selected by a blue-ribbon, nonpartisan judicial nominating commission. Representatives from the judiciary, the general public, and the legal profession make up a seven-member commission that submits to the governor a list of candidates when a vacancy occurs. If the governor fails to fill the vacancy within 30 days, the commission makes the appointment. After a two-year probationary period, the new judge faces the voters in an uncontested "retention" election, seeking a full term on the bench.

The principle of strict merit selection by a diversified judicial nom-

* No federal judge has been impeached in more than 40 years.[33]

† In 33 states some or all judges are elected. And in 15 of these states the candidates appear on a party ticket.[35]

Joseph Hatchett became a justice of the Florida Supreme Court on recommendation of the state judicial nominating commission

inating commission appointed by the governor,* and a probationary period after which the new judge stands unopposed at election, had been adopted in one form or another by 28 states as of 1978.[37] Colorado has a nine-member nominating panel that submits the names of three candidates to the governor when a vacancy occurs. If the governor does not appoint one of the three within 15 days, the chief justice of the state's highest court picks the new judge from the list.[38] Under the California Plan, the governor and mayor select judges at each level, subject to confirmation by a nineteen-member commission consisting of representatives of the judiciary, the public, and the legal community.[39] New York's governor, who created a judicial nominating committee in 1975, agreed not to appoint judges unless they were rated "very qualified" under the new system.[40]

In 1977, for the first time in history, President Carter adopted merit selection in filling vacancies in the U.S. Courts of Appeals,[41] a particularly significant step in view of the anticipated increase in circuit court (appellate) judgeships from 97 to 132.[42] The selection of federal district court (trial) judges by merit is slower in coming because of senatorial reluctance to relinquish control over these positions for patronage purposes.† However, a few states are moving in the direction of merit selection of the lower federal courts on their own. Florida's Federal Judicial Nominating Commission, for example, seeks qualified applicants when vacancies occur in the U.S. District Court of Florida. It also has an intensive screening process that is similar in its thoroughness to the police department's "character background" investigation of police recruits.[44]

Continuing judicial education programs

Finally, while theoretically a matter separate from merit selection, even the best qualified judges can become "stale" if they do not keep up with the latest developments in the field. Accordingly, 15 states have begun comprehensive continuing judicial education programs, following the lead of Wisconsin, which in 1975 adopted a mandatory 60-credit education program for its trial judges.[45] But the best intentions behind merit selection, continuing education, and judicial discipline commissions may be of little avail if the basic structure of the courts is not reorganized and if improved techniques for judicial administration are not forthcoming.

Court Administrators and Court Unification

Judges are not noted for possessing administrative skills; and usually have little interest in these skills and little opportunity to acquire them. Yet the daily operation of the courts, their relationship to other criminal

* Many of the nominating commissions are dominated by lawyers, though some plans require or strive for a nonlawyer majority on the panel.[36]

† Traditionally, the president fills vacancies on the federal trial court level from "recommendations" by the senators in whose state the vacancies occur.[43]

justice agencies, and the quality of justice depends on the performance of tasks that are often more administrative than judicial in nature: personnel management, budgeting, docket control, monitoring productivity and backlog, jury and witness arrangements and supervision, public information, and public relations.[46] The operation of the courts is a complex business that requires the expertise of a professional manager to handle the nonjudicial aspects of courtwork efficiently and effectively, thereby conserving scarce judicial resources for duties that cannot appropriately be delegated to others. Until recently, however, judges themselves have halfheartedly attended to or neglected this important dimension of the court system. The result has been a "waste of judicial power"—using a surgeon to do a nurse's work—and mismanaged or unmanaged courts.[47]

Functions of court executives

The emerging response to these problems is the retention of *court executives* or *administrators* to assume responsibility for nonjudicial functions associated with pretrial motions, bail setting, hearings, trials, juries, and appeals. Their professional and social detachment from the bench facilitates their monitoring judges' productivity, work schedules, backlog, granting of continuances, and other areas in which presiding judges are loathe to perform out of collegial courtesy. As a result of their studies, court administrators are in a position to recommend setting standards and policies, establishing more rational and fairer judicial practices, introducing computers and other office procedure technology, and actions to avoid the abuse of discretion and the prospect of being disciplined. The main objectives of court administrators are to ensure judicial productivity, accountability to society, and the appearance and reality of justice. In essence, court executives are employed for the purpose of making sound modern business principles and management philosophy standard operating procedure in running the courts—in the same way that civilianization and consolidation are being used to achieve better managed police departments.

In 1958, the Los Angeles Superior Court was the first and largest (then 134 judges) trial court in the country to delegate administrative functions to a professional court executive.[48] The Supreme Court hired its first staff administrator in 1971. By 1976, 43 states were utilizing court executives to relieve judges of purely administrative matters. Many of the nation's court administrators were trained at the National Center for State Courts in Denver, which was established in 1971 to address the entire range of problems facing—and generated by—the courts and their administration.[49] The future of the courts, judges, and justice may eventually be determined by decisions made in the executive suite rather than in chambers.

The need for court reorganization

Perhaps the major problem with the court system is the multiplicity of decentralized courts that are autonomous, may have overlapping jurisdiction, and are subject to no "unity of command." The result is fragmentation of services, wasteful allocation of judicial resources, varying standards of justice, lack of accountability, and resistance to innovation. The main approach to rectifying this situation is through unification of the courts: the consolidation and centralization of the courts within and/or between jurisdictional levels. The advantages of unification are the avoidance of duplication and judicial anarchy, uniform jurisdiction, flexibility in deploying personnel and transferring cases, standardized rules and policies, and prompt disposition of cases. All of these are made possible by a clearly recognized source of judicial leadership to whom the consolidated courts are accountable.[50]

In practice, unification might eliminate J.P. courts altogether, place magistrate courts under the direct supervision of the trial courts, provide for a single statewide trial and appellate court structure, or unify all of the state's courts under the administrative authority of the State Supreme Court. Unification would also facilitate merit selection, methods for disciplining judges, and the hiring of court executives, who will be needed to handle the greater administrative burdens associated with unification. The political obstacles to unification are formidable, however, because unassimilated judges fear that in the process they may lose their status, their discretion, their independence, or their jobs. Nonetheless, many states have taken steps and are moving in this direction.

SUMMARY

The key to understanding the court system is jurisdiction, which differentiates the lower courts, the trial courts, and the appellate courts. In the states, the major problems in the lower courts are case overload (backlog) and the questionable legal qualifications of many incumbents, especially in the J.P. courts. Another major problem of the trial or felony courts is that a substantial proportion of convictions are taken to the appellate courts for reversal. Appellate courts do not retry cases; they correct errors of law associated with the conviction or sentence by reversing and remanding the case to the trial courts. In the federal court system, the Federal Magistrates Act of 1968 addressed the problems of lower courts, but the due process revolution was partially responsible for increasing the proportion of state trial and U.S. district court cases that are appealed to the Courts of Appeals and to the Supreme Court. By exercising its discretion, the Supreme Court accepts only a small number of the writs of certiorari and habeas corpus petitions, those which raise a substantial federal issue concerning the Constitution that involves the Court in balancing the scales of justice. Contemporary efforts to reform the courts include judicial discipline commissions, merit selection of judges, the use of court administrators, and unification of the courts.

DISCUSSION QUESTIONS

1. What danger is there in the trend toward judicial discipline commissions with broad jurisdiction over the types of complaints they accept and act on?
2. Why is it more difficult to appeal successfully a sentence than a conviction? What could be done to rectify this situation?
3. Why does the Supreme Court require that appellants exhaust state remedies before it will decide whether or not to grant certiorari?

Chapter 8

THE BAIL SYSTEM

The Right to Bail
Stack v. *Boyle* (1951)
The Administration of Bail Before the 1960s
Criticisms of the bail system / Preventive detention / The bondsperson
Pretrial Detention
Direct economic costs / Social and human costs / Counting detention time when sentencing / Detention as punishment / The legal consequences
The Manhattan Bail Project
Release on recognizance

Close-up 8.1: The Manhattan Bail Project in Action

Results of the project / Significance of the project
Ten Percent Cash Bail
Conditional Release
Release With Services
The Bail Reform Act of 1966
Conditions of release / Inadequate resources of the D.C. Bail Agency / Failings in the conditions of release / Omission of preventive detention provisions / The 1970 preventive detention statute
Bail: A Current Perspective
Preventive detention and bail reform
Summary

Excessive bail shall not be required. . . .
(Eighth Amendment)

In the United States the bail system is used to determine whether persons accused of crime will be released or detained in jail during the interval between arrest and the trial stage, an interval that may be many months or even years long. Bail is a procedure and an opportunity for releasing arrested defendants on financial or other conditions in order to insure that they appear for their second arraignment and trial. The lower courts set bail at the initial court appearance in all felony cases and in misdemeanor cases that are not disposed of immediately. Bail requires that money, property, or other surety be deposited with the court to guarantee the defendant's presence at trial. The prospect of forfeiting monetary bail to the state is supposed to deter released (bailed) defendants from failing to appear at trial. The only legally recognized function of bail is to make the accused available for trial purposes: to enter formal pleas to the final criminal charges at arraignment, to stand trial when the plea is not guilty, and to be sentenced when a guilty plea has been entered.

THE RIGHT TO BAIL

Stack v. *Boyle* (1951)

The Eighth Amendment to the Constitution specifies that "excessive bail shall not be required." However, it has never been resolved whether this terminology establishes an absolute constitutional right to have bail set in all criminal cases other than capital offenses, or whether the states and courts have the right to make certain noncapital crimes nonbailable. Despite extensive debate, scholars continue to be divided on the interpretation of the Eighth Amendment's excessive bail clause as it relates to the "right" to bail.[1] In its principal bail case ruling, *Stack* v. *Boyle* in 1951, the Supreme Court left unsettled the constitutional status of the right to bail.[2] However, the Court did define "excessive" bail as more than that which is required to guarantee the defendant's presence at trial. Under the circumstances in *Stack,* the Supreme Court approved the absolute right to pretrial bail in noncapital cases in order to preserve the presumption of innocence, to avoid punishment in the form of pretrial detention, and to enable the accused to prepare a defense.*

It is generally agreed that the Constitution does not specifically grant a

In 1972, New York Judge Bruce Wright, known for strict adherence to the constitutional prohibition against excessive bail, released on $500 bail a man accused of killing a police officer

* In *Mastrian* v. *Hedman* in 1964, the Supreme Court explicitly declined to extend a constitutional right in state criminal proceedings: "Neither the Eighth Amendment nor the Fourteenth Amendment requires that everyone charged with a State offense must be given his liberty on bail pending trial."[3]

right to bail, although it does grant a specific right not to have excessive bail imposed.[4] To some extent, the constitutional status of the right to bail is moot because of federal bail policy and the manner in which the states have chosen to handle the matter. The statutory right of federal defendants to have bail set in all but capital cases was established by the Judiciary Act of 1789, which provided that "upon all arrests in criminal cases, bail shall be admitted, except where the punishment may be death. . . ." (The issue of bail in death penalty cases was left to the discretion of the courts.) This eighteenth-century right to bail doctrine has been incorporated into the Federal Rules of Criminal Procedure and included in the constitutions or penal codes of the states.[5] Only six states do not provide for an absolute right to bail in noncapital cases.[6]

THE ADMINISTRATION OF BAIL BEFORE THE 1960s

Prior to the early 1960s, the lower courts relied almost exclusively on cash bail as the condition and means for authorizing pretrial release. The courts decided the amount of cash bail strictly according to the seriousness of the criminal charges and the defendant's prior record.* Each court, acting on its own, established standard bail amounts for different crimes or offense categories. Under these circumstances, the bail system created problems and gave rise to many criticisms.

Criticisms of the bail system

1. The amount of cash bail required was too high for a substantial number of defendants to meet.[8] The effect of this high-bail policy needlessly detained many defendants who were good risks for appearing at trial and who would not have recidivated if released. At the same time, wealthier defendants charged with the same offenses were able to purchase their pretrial freedom. In practice, therefore, bail became a form of economic bondage that punished indigent defendants for being poor.

2. The courts showed little concern with whether the amount of bail set violated the Eighth Amendment prohibition against excessive bail.

3. Little consideration was given to the routine use of nonmonetary conditions or forms of release. There was no policy of releasing defendants whenever possible without cash bail or collateral, that is, freeing defendants on their verbal promise to appear for trial, on their own recognizance, or under other nonfinancial conditions. There was no preference or means for protecting and preserving the liberty of pretrial defendants. Instead, there was an exaggerated concern that defendants released on low bail or noncash bail would fail to appear at trial or would commit serious felonies in the meantime. This attitude, combined with the courts' reluctance to sacrifice their discretion in setting bail, perpetuated the

* Ordinarily, the lower court's bail decision will not be overturned unless flagrant abuse of discretion can be established.[7]

overreliance on monetary bail and high-bail policy. The actual risks of defendants' fleeing or recidivating while on bail (which were low) were not considered, accepted, or acted upon.

4. Defense counsel was thought to be less effective in representing its clients' interest in securing low bail than the prosecution was in pressing for and obtaining high bail, for two reasons.[9] First, the overall quality of legal services provided by state-supplied attorneys is considered to be inferior to that of private counsel. Attorneys for the poor are often poor attorneys. Second, the relationship between court and prosecutor is closer, more personalized, and more "cooperative" than that between the court and defense counsel.

5. Bail determination ordinarily occurs at the initial court appearance, within a matter of hours after arrest. The court therefore had little time or opportunity to acquire adequate information upon which to make an informed bail decision. In particular, the courts lacked essential information about the defendant's social background, character, and ties to the community. Knowledge of this type of relevant, comprehensive biographical data might warrant nonmonetary release under the own recognizance (OR) programs that marked the beginning of the bail reform movement of the 1960s. Lacking such information, the courts relied entirely on the criminal charges and the defendant's previous record for setting bail, and these were not valid indicators of the defendant's likelihood of appearing at trial—the only legal purpose of bail.[10]

Preventive detention

6. The courts sometimes utilized the high-bail policy for the purpose of *preventive detention:* jailing defendants the court believed would commit serious new crimes (especially dangerous or violent offenses) during the pretrial period if released on bail. In order to prevent serious pretrial recidivism by defendants considered an imminent danger to the community, the courts intentionally set excessively high bail that could not be raised. Preventive detention has been criticized on several grounds.

The constitutional status of the practice is questionable. Since the only proper function of bail is to guarantee presence at trial, it is contended that using the cash bail system for crime prevention is unjustifiable, unconstitutional, and an abuse of judicial discretion. However, the constitutionality of preventive detention has never been reviewed by the Supreme Court.

The courts are unable to identify or predict accurately which defendants will commit serious or dangerous new crimes while awaiting trial in the community. Research suggests that the proportion of released defendants who are rearrested for crimes against the person in the pretrial period is about 5 percent and that the proportion who commit property offenses is low.[11] Consequently, the effect of preventive detention is to incarcerate a large number of detainees who pose no substantial threat to the public, who would not recidivate while awaiting trial in the community, and who could be safely released on bail instead of being detained.

The courts rely on preventive detention to avoid being criticized by the press, the public, the police, and prosecutors whenever bailed defendants commit serious crimes that become publicized. To protect itself against the charges and the consequences of "turning dangerous criminals loose" before trial, the court plays it safe by misusing the bail system for the purpose of preventive detention.

Indigent defendants are invariably the victims of preventive detention. Yet a defendant's ability to afford bail has little relationship to recidivism before trial.

The bondsperson

7. The primary purpose of monetary bail—to guarantee the defendant's appearance at trial—is severely hampered by the role of the *bondsperson* in the bail system. Few indigent defendants are able, without help, to raise the funds required by the court for release on cash bail. When this occurs, the defendant may try to secure release by purchasing the services of a commercial bondsagent. In exchange for a fee from the defendant, the professional bondsagent deposits with the court the cash bail required or its equivalent, a bail bond in that amount.

There are various administrative arrangements by which the bondsperson assumes fiscal responsibility for the defendant's cash bail, that is, "goes bail" for the accused. They all amount to an agreement by the bondsagent, or the company he or she represents, to forfeit to the court the amount of cash bail set if the defendant fails to appear for trial. In return for posting bond and assuming the risk of forfeiture to the state, the bondsperson charges defendants nonrefundable fees of between 5 percent and 10 percent of the cash bail set in their cases.[12] Whether or not the defendant appears for trial, no part of the bondsperson's fee is returned to the accused. In the majority of cases where bail is provided to the court, it is furnished through transactions with the bondsperson.[13] The bondsperson can always refuse to write a bail bond; any such decision to withhold services need not be justified and is not subject to review.

The bondsperson's role in the administration of the bail system has been severely criticized.

The basic assumption that underlies the cash bail system is the threat of the defendant's forfeiting his or her own funds or collateral for not appearing at trial. However, this assumption is undermined by a bail system that in practice transfers the financial risks of forfeiture to the bondsperson, exacts no penalty from defendants who do not appear for trial, and offers no financial incentive to those who will show up for trial.

The fact that no portion of the bondsagent's fee is returnable to defendants who appear for trial may reduce the incentive to appear at trial.

The commercial bail bond operation has been plagued with corruption, collusion, and unethical connections between bondspersons and court officials, police, lawyers, and organized crime.[14]

In principle, the court is responsible for deciding who it will release on bail and who it will detain. In effect, this decision often rests with the bondsperson by virtue of the agent's right to deny services, the size of the premium, and the requirement of collateral as a condition of going bail in some cases. Defendants who are considered good risks may be charged a lower fee or given special credit arrangements that are denied to other defendants, even though the court has set the same bail for both.[15] For these reasons, professional bondsagents are said to have the power to veto the bail decision of the court and to hold the keys to the jail.

The pretrial fate of legally innocent defendants is in the hands of outside businesspersons whose only interest in the criminal justice system is a profit-making interest.

The bondsperson's fee is the price and penalty exacted from many defendants for being poor. Thus the economic discrimination inherent in a cash bail system is exacerbated by the bondsperson's purely financial stake in bail administration.

The need to raise funds to pay the bondsagent's fee may lead some defendants to commit crime while out on bail.[16]

Methods occasionally used by bondspersons to insure that their clients appear at trial have been unsavory, unethical, or illegal—such as threats, the use of violence, and unauthorized arrests. In locating and taking into custody clients who have jumped bail, bondsagents may also abuse the special power and procedures sometimes granted them by law.

8. There was unwarranted variation in the amount of bail set by different judges for similar defendants arraigned on identical charges. The bail imposed in each case reflected the court's personal opinion of the seriousness of the alleged crimes; the court's informal bail "price list" of criminal charges; the judge's personality, philosophy of law, and attitude toward punishment and rehabilitation; the court's understanding of the legal purpose of bail and its willingness to comply with it; and the use and abuse of judicial discretion. The consequent disparity in bail-setting practices among judges eroded the perception and the actuality of justice at the bail-setting stage.

PRETRIAL DETENTION

The main problem in the bail scene was making release dependent on the defendant's financial resources. The consequence of relying on a high-cash bail system as traditionally administered was the unnecessary and inequitable pretrial detention of a large number of untried defendants. While the percentage of defendants who are unable to make bail varies widely from place to place, it is nonetheless substantial. In 1966 a nationwide study of 11,000 felony defendants in 190 sample counties revealed that, on the average, only 47 percent were released before trial in the larger counties, compared with just 39 percent in the smaller areas. As few as 7 percent of the felony defendants were released before trial in some counties.[17]

The social, economic, and legal burdens and hardships associated with pretrial detention are considerable.

Direct economic costs

1. The direct economic costs of jailing detainees are enormous. The most reliable figures come from New York City, whose annual pretrial detention bill of $10 million is half the amount of that of Los Angeles County.[18] The President's Crime Commission estimated that pretrial detention expenses exceeded $100 million for the nation as a whole.[19] Significant savings in custodial expenses could be achieved by greater reliance upon alternatives to the cash bail system.

2. Pretrial detention interferes with the preparation of an adequate defense. Detained defendants are unable to participate as fully or as effectively in their defense as bailed defendants. Detainees are not available to assist in locating witnesses and evidence; they are less available to provide counsel with important factual details on which to base pretrial motions and to plea bargain; they have less opportunity to seek the services of private counsel. Incarceration may also restrict the defendant's access to counsel in jails where contacts with attorneys are limited to the hours set for visitors.

Social and human costs

3. The personal and social toll exacted by pretrial detention involves the disruption of family life, lost jobs and opportunities for employment, and the consequences of being stigmatized as a criminal.[20] By preventing normal contacts and relations with families, pretrial detention encourages separation, divorce, and parental abandonment. By making it difficult to support themselves and their families, pretrial detention forces many defendants and their dependents onto the welfare rolls; it results in lost tax revenues; and it makes it more likely that the community will have to incur the expense of providing state-supplied defense counsel.

4. Pretrial detainees are treated like (if not worse than) convicted offenders who have been sentenced to jail as a punishment for crime.

5. Pretrial incarceration and its associated hardships can coerce defendants into pleading guilty in order to get out of jail or to settle the matter quickly. Thus guilty pleas may be entered that are not truly voluntary, and innocent defendants may be convicted. These are possibilities to which bailed defendants are not exposed.

Counting detention time when sentencing

6. When detainees are subsequently convicted and given a jail or a prison sentence, their time spent in pretrial confinement may or may not be counted in determining the sentence, at the court's discretion. Courts

that take pretrial detention time into consideration at sentencing may deduct the time already spent in jail from the sentence that would otherwise be imposed; they may impose a sentence of probation rather than incarceration; or they may sentence to the time served in pretrial detention, which would result in the defendant's full discharge from custody. However, there is considerable variation in the degree to which the fact or length of pretrial detention is considered by the court in sentencing. Convicted defendants who are incarcerated or given probation without regard to their time served are exposed to an unfair double standard of justice that punishes them twice. Endorsing the provision in the Model Penal Code, the President's Crime Commission recommended that detainees who are subsequently convicted and sentenced to jail or prison should be given full credit for all time spent in pretrial detention.[21] Detainees who are subsequently acquitted might be reimbursed on a per diem rate.[22]

7. Pretrial detention erodes the prospects and the opportunity for rehabilitation in two ways. First, many correctional authorities believe that incarceration under any circumstances offers training for further crime rather than a deterrent to crime commission. This is especially significant where first-offender detainees are exposed to the influence and role models of more experienced, hardened criminals who are serving jail sentences. Second, pretrial detention deprives defendants of the opportunity to establish their reliability by voluntarily appearing for trial and staying out of trouble until then—performance that is likely to result in probation or a suspended sentence rather than institutional commitment.

Detention as punishment

8. Pretrial detention is sometimes used by the courts as a method of punishing defendants for having committed the crimes with which they are charged. This is a clear abuse of judicial discretion and a misuse of pretrial detention; punishment without conviction is *illegal.* When bail is set at the initial court appearance, there is nothing to punish defendants for. The misuse of pretrial detention expresses the reluctance of some judges (especially J.P.s) to follow the law, and it reflects their ignorance of the legal purpose of bail. When asked what the function of bail was, a justice of the peace in South Carolina replied, "It is for violation and a good reminder not to do it again."[23]

The legal consequences

9. Perhaps the most serious, disabling, and inequitable effects of pretrial detention are to be found in its legal consequences: detainees are more likely to be indicted, convicted, and sentenced more harshly than released defendants.[24] Research studies undertaken as part of the Manhattan Bail Project were instrumental in highlighting the prejudicial impact of pretrial detention on disposition and sentencing. (The findings have been effectively utilized as an urgent call for bail reform.) The first study, based on an analysis of 3,459 cases from the Court of General Sessions in 1960, showed that detainees were more often convicted and sen-

Table 8.1 Conviction Rates and Prison Sentences for Released and Detained Criminal Defendants, New York Court of General Sessions, 1960

Offense	CONVICTIONS		PRISON SENTENCES	
	Bailed Defendants	Jailed Defendants	Bailed Defendants	Jailed Defendants
Assault	23%	59%	58%	94%
Grand larceny	43	72	48	93
Robbery	51	58	78	97
Dangerous weapons	43	57	70	91
Narcotics	52	38	59	100
Sex crimes	10	14	—	—
Others	30%	78%	56%	88%

Source: Daniel J. Freed and Patricia M. Wald, *Bail in the United States* (Washington D.C.: U.S. Department of Justice and the Vera Foundation, 1964), p. 47.

tenced to prison than released defendants (see Table 8.1).[25] Another of the studies, based on a sample of 374 defendants arraigned in Manhattan's Magistrates Felony Court between October 16, 1961, and September 1, 1962, disclosed that (a) only 27 percent of the jailed defendants were not convicted, compared with 47 percent of those released on bail, and (b) 64 percent of the detainees were given prison sentences, compared with 17 percent of the bailed defendants.[26] Pretrial detention itself was found to increase the likelihood of conviction and commitment to prison.

The shortcomings, problems, and criticisms of the bail system and pretrial detention described above led to the bail reform movement, which began in the early 1960s.

THE MANHATTAN BAIL PROJECT

The modern bail reform movement and the "revolution" in bail began in 1961 with the Manhattan Bail Project, conducted by the Vera Foundation.* The premise of the Manhattan Bail Project was the need to seek alternative forms of pretrial release in lieu of the traditional cash bail. Its major hypothesis was that, while awaiting trial, many more persons could be safely and successfully released without requiring any cash bail or surety. This decision was to be based upon verified information concerning the defendant's character, social background, and ties to the

* The Vera Institute of Justice (formerly the Vera Foundation) is a private agency whose primary focus has been on the relationship of poverty to the administration of criminal justice. Vera has conducted extensive experimental research and operated various action programs designed to improve the criminal justice system.

Bail project interviews seek information about the defendant's social ties to the community

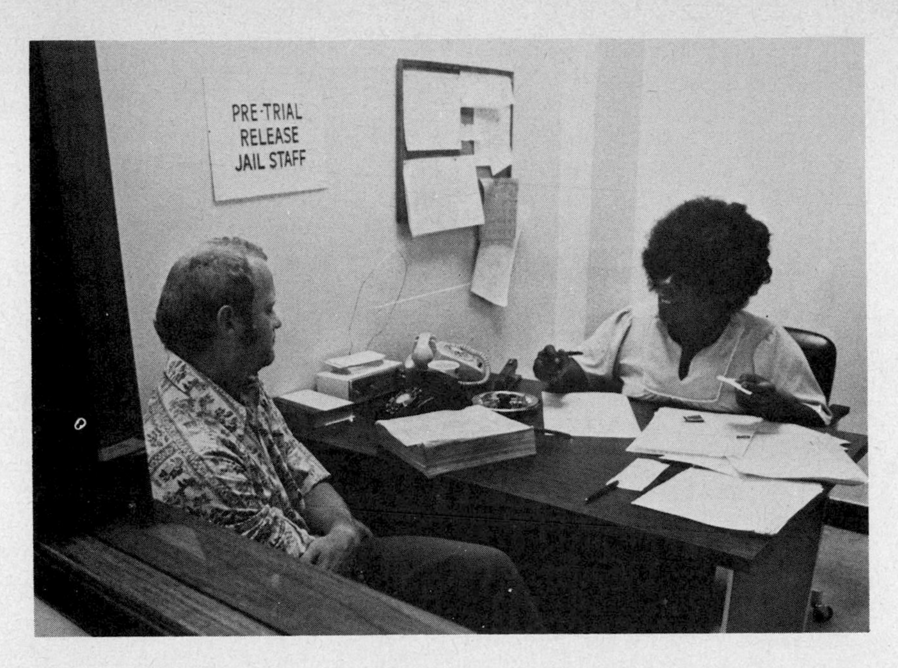

Release on recognizance

community, to be made available to the court at the time of bail determination in order to justify *release on recognizance* (ROR).

Using a short questionnaire administered to detainees, the project staff identified four key factors as a basis for evaluating whether a defendant would be a good risk for recommending ROR to the court: residential stability, employment history, family contacts in New York City, and prior criminal record. The first three factors comprised the defendant's "social ties to the community." Ties to the community were considered a more valid measure for deciding who should be released without cash bail than the instant criminal charges or previous record taken alone, or the discretion of the court. Each of the four factors was then scored according to a point system. If the defendant obtained at least five (verified) points, project staff made a formal recommendation to the court and the prosecutor for release on recognizance (see Close-up 8.1). The rationale that the Manhattan Bail Project sought to demonstrate through its action phase was that a defendant with social roots in the community was not likely to flee while awaiting trial—precisely because of those ties to job, family, and residence. If this is true, the opportunity for pretrial release should not depend on the defendant's ability to make cash bail or be based strictly on the criminal charges and prior record.

Close-up 8.1 The Manhattan Bail Project in Action

Walter L. has been arrested and booked for felonious assault and possessing a concealed weapon. While in the detention pen awaiting his first court appearance, he is interviewed by a law student who is a member of the project. The interviewer learns whether Walter has a job, has contact with and supports his family, receives welfare—that is, what his social ties to the community are.

Walter L. has a previous record of a felonious assault charge that was reduced to simple assault, and a misdemeanor for which he received a 30 day suspended sentence. Before that, in 1961, he received the same sentence for a drunk driving conviction; in 1957 he was convicted for driving while intoxicated and was fined $100. Walter has been living with his family at his present address for six months and has a verified previous residence of one year. He has worked as a counterman for the last three months; his verified prior employment lasted three years.

According to the Manhattan Bail Project's point system, Walter has five verified points, the minimum number needed for an ROR recommendation:

- −1 point for three misdemeanor convictions
- +2 points for a stable residence
- +2 points for family ties
- +2 points for good ratings on present and prior jobs

Accordingly, copies of Walter's project file will be forwarded to the prosecutor and court with a formal recommendation made to the court to release Walter without bail on ROR.

Source: National Conference on Bail and Criminal Justice, Interim Report, May 1964–April 1965 (Washington, D.C.: U.S. Department of Justice and the Vera Foundation, 1965), pp. 44–45.

Results of the project

The results of the Manhattan Bail Project established the feasibility and effectiveness of ROR programs and its underlying principles. Between October 16, 1961, and April 8, 1964, project staff interviewed 10,000 eligible defendants, and this resulted in 4,000 ROR recommendations to the court. Of the 2,195 cases in which the court accepted the project's recommendations and granted ROR, only 15 defendants—less than one percent—failed to appear at trial. During the three years that

Vera operated the program, 3,505 defendants were released on ROR and only 56 failed to return to court.[27] These ROR failure-to-appear (FTA) rates are less than those commonly reported for defendants released on bail.

Project results also showed that ROR recommendations made substantial differences in whether defendants were released or detained, in the disposition of cases, and in the penalties imposed. Fifty-nine percent of the ROR-recommended defendants were freed by the court pending trial, compared with only 16 percent of a control group of defendants not recommended.[28] Thus ROR recommendations were responsible for keeping four times as many defendants out of jail than would otherwise have been the case. Fifty-nine percent of the ROR-released experimental group avoided conviction, compared with 23 percent of the ROR-qualified but detained control group. Only 21 percent of convicted ROR-released defendants were sentenced to prison, compared with 96 percent of the detained defendants.[29]

Over the life of the Manhattan Bail Project, there was a significant increase in the proportion of defendants recommended for ROR by the staff and granted ROR by the courts, as well as in the types of cases considered eligible, apparently without any appreciable increase in FTA rates.[30] In many cases it was found that failure to appear was due to the defendant's illness, confusion about the legal process, family emergencies, and not knowing where to appear, rather than to actual flight from prosecution. To remedy these administrative causes of nonappearance for trial, the Manhattan Bail Project initiated a "notification" experiment that reminded ROR defendants to keep their arraignment appointments. After being run by Vera for three years, responsibility for operating the ROR program was transferred to the New York City Probation Department in September 1964. Under the department's auspices, the program was expanded to the criminal courts in the city's five boroughs, and this has resulted in the release on recognizance of 25,000 defendants.

Significance of the project

The Manhattan Bail Project set the stage, the pace, and the pattern for bail reform in the United States. It demonstrated that the most relevant deterrents to the failure to appear are ties to the community rather than financial risks, which for most indigent defendants are more apparent than real. It showed that ROR can safely be used with a substantial number of defendants who would otherwise be confined for long periods before disposition, treated like ordinary criminals in jail, and exposed to the hardships associated with pretrial detention, including the increased likelihood of being convicted and sentenced to prison. It documented that the failure to appear rates for ROR defendants are at least as low as those for bailed defendants, if not lower. It established the feasibility of investigating the defendant's background in the limited time available before the initial arraignment without disrupting law enforcement, prosecutorial, and judicial operations. It placed indigent defendants on an equal footing with those who could afford bail by individualizing pretrial release decision making and making it more reasonable, responsible, and informed. And the Manhattan Bail Project spurred the creation of similar pretrial release programs in over a hundred jurisdictions throughout the country.[31] Such Vera-type projects were responsible for 170,000 persons obtaining their pretrial freedom through ROR in 1973.[32]

TEN PERCENT CASH BAIL

Release on recognizance was designed for defendants who were "good risks," persons who could be trusted to return to court on their own, without having to purchase their release, without supervision in the interval, and without penalty for reneging on their promise to appear. Not all pretrial defendants fall into this category, however. In some cases, more than "own recognizance" requirements are necessary to justify release before trial. Defendants who are not such clear-cut risks for ROR may be safe to release under the second major reform alternative to conventional bail, the ten percent cash bail program.

Having originated in Illinois in January 1964, the ten percent cash bail system is a modified monetary bail program that makes bail affordable to indigents and gives them solid incentive to appear at trial. Under the program, the defendant is required to deposit with the court only ten percent of the amount of bail set, and 90 percent of that deposit is returned to the accused upon appearance for trial.[33] Thus a defendant whose bail is set at $1,000 would be released upon depositing $100 with the court; and upon appearing for trial, $90 of the bail deposit would be returned to the accused. The proportion of the ten percent cash deposit that is refunded will vary with the particular statutory guidelines, jurisdiction, and project refund policy. The Atlantic County, New Jersey, ten percent cash bail program, for example, returns the entire cash deposit upon appearance. Other projects may refund 98 percent of the deposit, and so on.[34] Similarly, some partial bond projects based on the Illinois model require a deposit of only five percent of the total bail imposed.

Despite these minor variations in the proportion of bail deposited and the proportion of deposit refunded, the basic rationale behind all percentage cash bail programs is the same: (a) to establish meaningful and affordable financial conditions as a deterrent to flight and (b) to use a maximum cash refund as an incentive for appearing at trial. Besides facilitating the pretrial liberty of indigent defendants who do not qualify for unconditional ROR, the Illinois ten percent cash bail system had the intended effect of eliminating the bondsperson in the administration of the state's bail operation. Thus, the ten percent cash bail system was another successful bail reform endeavor, another step away from the bondsagent-controlled, fully money-based, nonrefundable, high-cash bail system. Defendants released under it were no more likely to fail to appear, or to commit new crimes, than persons released under conventional bail requirements; their FTA rates hovered around the five percent level found in most ROR programs.[35]

CONDITIONAL RELEASE

ROR programs are geared to "good risk" defendants who can be released outright without attaching conditions to their pretrial freedom. The ten percent cash bail system, which handles a slightly higher risk group, requires a small deposit as a basis for release; but once released, the defendants have no conditions to observe, and there are no restrictions on their freedom. Defendants who pose the higher risk of flight, however, require more than unconditional release or the prospect of forfeiting a ten percent cash bail to assure their appearance in court. For such defendants, the ticket home may be *conditional release:* being under supervision in the community and/or observing conditions that place restrictions on their liberty, such as not moving out of the court's jurisdiction, not driving a car, enrolling in a drug treatment program, and receiving remedial education. In this respect, conditional release might be thought of as informal probation before conviction; it is subject to revocation if the conditions of that probation are violated.

Conditionally released defendants are often required to have periodic contact (to report in) with specified criminal justice agents, such as the police, courts, or probation officers, who in principle are responsible for their supervision and for enforcing the conditions of release. Defendants may also be conditionally released in the custody of a private person or an organization willing to supervise them and to assure their appearance at trial. Such third parties may be the defendant's lawyer, religious advisor, employer, landlord, friend, relative, civic group, or the victim. One advantage of this type of third-party conditional release is the involvement of individuals and groups outside the criminal justice system with the problems of crime, corrections, and processing offenders.[36]

Release With Services

The Release With Services (RWS) component of the Des Moines Project illustrates the best that conditional release has to offer. Under the Des Moines community-based treatment umbrella, persons who do not score five points are rejected for ROR but not forgotten. Instead, they are passed on to the project's second phase, where they are considered for release under the more stringent conditions involved in Release With Services. Described as a prep school for probation for subsequently convicted defendants, the RWS program focuses on the offender's problems and the need to begin resolving them before trial (which is three months away). RWS counselors work closely with defendants in trying to locate jobs. They also function as resource brokers by referring RWS clients to the community's 150 social agencies for employment preparation and drug counseling and to other services as required. Defendants must also take courses in remedial reading, drug abuse or alcoholism control, budgeting, and child care. Some receive psychiatric therapy. All clients have to report to their counselors daily. Despite the fact that almost one-third had drug or drinking problems and more than one-half had previous convictions, everyone turned over to RWS appeared for trial, and only five were arrested for new crimes in the interval.[37] Significantly, only 25 percent of the RWS clients who were convicted landed in jail; 60 percent of those rejected for RWS and detained instead were incarcerated after conviction.[38]

THE BAIL REFORM ACT OF 1966

In 1966 Congress enacted the Bail Reform Act, which applied to the federal courts and created the District of Columbia Bail Agency to provide District of Columbia courts with facts and recommendations concerning release. This was the first major overhaul of the federal bail law since the Judiciary Act of 1789, which established in principle the right to bail in noncapital cases (a right that was frequently disregarded in practice).[39] The Bail Reform Act emerged in response to bail issues and problems that were virtually identical to those of the state court system discussed above.

Two major related principles underlie and were reflected in the Bail Reform Act. (1) The accused shall be released pending trial, unless convincing reasons can be offered for believing that he or she will not appear. While the act did not disregard the risk of flight, it created a strong presumption in favor of release, and its provisions were intended to encourage judges to comply with its pro-release position. Instead of a traditional bail hearing that focused on the possibility of flight—which in practice led to detention—the act called for a judicial proceeding that focused on selecting the least restrictive conditions of release for each defendant, except in capital cases. Thus the usual decision-making context that fostered a presumption of detention was replaced with a presumption of release. (2) The defendant's appearance at trial, rather than his or her possible "danger to the community" during the pretrial period, was to be the only factor considered in setting bail conditions.[40]

Conditions of release

The Bail Reform Act specified a variety of conditions of release in the order of their importance and preferred imposition. (1) Unconditional release on personal recognizance or execution of an unsecured bond.* This was to be the standard pretrial disposition; the accused's social ties to the community were to be taken into account in authorizing unconditional release, but release on personal recognizance was more liberal than the stricter ROR requirements, which rejected persons who did not receive five points. If personal recognizance was not an adequate device to assure appearance, the more restrictive conditions of release were to be considered by the judicial officer. (2) Supervised custody. (3) Restrictions on travel, residence, and association. (4) Ten percent cash bail, fully refundable upon appearance. (5) Secured bail bond or deposit of cash with the court. (6) Any other condition reasonably necessary, including daytime release from detention.[42] The court was to rely on money bail only as a last resort, when no other condition or combination of conditions would assure appearance at trial. If the defendant was not released within 24 hours after the initial arraignment, the court was required to explain its failure to release, and the accused could appeal to a higher court.[43]

Inadequate resources of the D.C. Bail Agency

Three major deficiencies in the Bail Reform Act of 1966 seriously reduced its effectiveness. First, the District of Columbia Bail Agency was not given adequate resources with which to perform its designated functions. Thus the Bail Agency was severely hampered in supplying the courts with the appropriate verified information about the defendant's social background and ties to the community, in recommending conditions of release, and in making the results of its investigations available to the courts in time to be useful. Under these circumstances, federal prosecutors and judges were reluctant to release defendants on personal recognizance, and they had little to guide them in choosing the least restrictive alternative from the remaining conditions of release. Consequently, many federal courts continued to insist on money bail, to impose other conditions that defendants could not meet, or to violate the act by refusing to release under any combination of restrictive conditions.[44]

Failings in the conditions of release

Second, the least restrictive conditions of release were by and large unenforceable, only theoretically available, or lacked incentives for assuring appearance at trial. Release on personal recognizance, for example, meant simply the defendant's unsupported verbal promise to appear, without a rigorous screening procedure or an organization such as Vera to stand behind and prod defendants to make good on their promises. The severe penalties provided in the act for not appearing were rarely used, and therefore they were of doubtful value in fostering accountability or deterrence. Concerning secure custody dispositions, the act made no provision for how such third parties were to be secured, how they were to supervise defendants released in their custody, and how it would

* An unsecured appearance bond is basically a promissory note whereby the accused agrees to pay a sum of money if he or she does not comply with the promise to appear in court.[41]

be assured that they actually performed their duties. Similarly, a release with restrictions on travel, abode, and association was merely a verbal judicial directive that lacked any real mechanism for enforcement. Over and above these three major shortcomings in the Bail Reform Act, many judges were not sympathetic to the legislation's emphasis on nonfinancial conditions of release. And certain legal aspects of the bail hearing detracted from its value as a proceeding for identifying the least restrictive release conditions warranted in each case.

Omission of preventive detention provisions

Third, the Bail Reform Act did not authorize preventive detention. Since the only purpose of bail recognized in the act was to assure the defendant's appearance at trial, release could not be denied solely on the ground that pretrial defendants were considered an imminent danger to the community. Thus the legislation was intentionally conspicuous in failing to allow pretrial preventive detention of persons expected to commit serious or violent crimes while awaiting trial in the community. Implicitly, the act prohibited the courts' manipulating the conditions of release for the purpose of achieving preventive detention indirectly. For example, the courts were not allowed to impose release conditions that they knew could not be implemented, in order to assure the detention of defendants expected to commit crimes if released.

While preventive detention was unlawful in principle under the Bail Reform Act, it was unenforceable in practice. The act's failure to legalize preventive detention was a sore point among many judges, prosecutors, the police, and the voting victims of crime in the District of Columbia. Many addicts, for example, were arraigned on charges of larceny committed to support their $50-a-day habit. To release one of them was to virtually guarantee thefts amounting to $250 a week. Since addicts cannot leave their source of supply, however, the prospect of flight was almost nonexistent. Because they were such good risks for appearing at trial, the Bail Reform Act in effect required that addicts be released under personal bond at best. Yet this meant knowingly exposing the public to future burglaries, robberies, felony murders, larceny, and tampering offenses certain to be committed by them upon release.[45]

The courts were thus faced with the dilemma of either complying with the spirit of the Bail Reform Act by releasing defendants who posed an immediate threat to the community or paying only lip service to the act. Many judges opted for the latter course and continued to detain defendants they perceived as a danger to the community even though they were good risks for appearing at trial. Thus unconditional release and other less restrictive conditions of release were often bypassed for the purpose of achieving preventive detention.[46]

The Bail Reform Act of 1966 was a thorn in the side of many who objected to its lenient treatment of "criminals," its provisions for turning all defendants loose before trial, and especially its refusal to authorize preventive detention of the worst offenders. Accordingly, four years after its passage, the Bail Reform Act was amended in response to criticism from law enforcement officials and trial judges, concern over sharply rising crime rates in the nation's capital (allegedly caused by the act), and in order to fulfill President Nixon's "war on crime" campaign promises. The District of Columbia Court Reform and Criminal Procedure Act of 1970 authorized pretrial detention without bail (preventive detention) under carefully prescribed circumstances and well-defined procedures. Its statutory authorization of preventive detention was a significant departure from the Judiciary Act of 1789 and 181 years of federal bail policy that precluded preventive detention except in capital cases.[47] Persons eligible for preventive detention action were those charged with enumerated "dangerous crimes" and "crimes of violence." The statute permitted preventive detention without bail for 60 days on the basis of a judicial determination of dangerousness at an evidentiary hearing.[48]

The 1970 preventive detention statute

During the first ten months of the new law (February 1 to November 30, 1971), the preventive detention statute was invoked in just 20 out of 6,000 felony cases, and it resulted in 10 preventive detention orders.[49] Supporters of the statute faulted the courts for not using a vital crime control weapon that had finally become legally available. The law's critics, however, pointed to its nonuse as evidence that it was not needed or wanted. The court's infrequent use of the preventive detention law may have been due to (a) the ease with which the same objective could be accomplished by setting high money bail; (b) the judicial desire to avoid the added work and inconvenience associated with invoking the preventive detention law, and (c) the courts' desire to avoid hearings and challenges to their detention orders issued under the statute. These and other factors made it impossible to determine whether the preventive detention law facilitated the identification of defendants likely to commit predatory crimes if released and whether it made the community safer by their detention. The only safe conclusion was that most pretrial crime is committed more than 60 days after initial release—the same time at which detained defendants had to be released under the statute's provision for the expiration of detention.[50]

BAIL: A CURRENT PERSPECTIVE

Despite the accomplishments of the bail reform movement begun in the early 1960s, money bail is still the most frequent condition of release, the rates of pretrial detention are high, and prolonged detention is common. Despite the emergence of ROR programs that demonstrate that a defendant's ties to the community are critically related to appearance at trial, judges continue to set cash bail according to the current charges and the prior record.[51] Despite the questionable legal status of preventive detention in the absence of statutory authorization, courts persist in setting excessively high cash bail in order to detain dangerous defendants or as punishment without conviction.[52]

In part, the progress made by the bail projects was responsible for their declining success: as eligibility requirements were liberalized, the FTA rates increased. Thus the FTA rates of the Manhattan Bail Project went from 1.4 percent[53] in its early stage, when eligibility criteria filtered out defendants charged with the more serious crimes, to 15.4 percent when virtually all defendants were accepted for ROR except those charged with homicide and drug offenses.[54] More recently, "high" FTA rates were reported for defendants released on their own recognizance in counties of Massachusetts (15 percent)[55] and on five percent cash bail in central Los Angeles (25 percent).[56] Regardless of eligibility requirements, any significant increase in FTA rates becomes an obstacle to sustaining the interest in and the momentum of bail reform.

Preventive detention and bail reform

In part, bail reform has become a casualty of its inability to come to grips with the issue of preventive detention. By insisting that the probability of flight is the only factor to be considered in deciding whether to release, bail reform advocates have risked alienating taxpayers and politicians who are increasingly concerned about crimes of violence, dangerous offenders, and pretrial recidivism.[57] According to reliable findings from some studies, as much as 25 percent of the defendants released on recognizance again turned to crime upon returning to the community.[58] One of the most careful and comprehensive investigations found that in the District of Columbia in 1968, of those charged with "crimes of violence" and released, 17 percent were rearrested in the pretrial period; and of those charged with "dangerous crimes" and released, 25 percent were rearrested.[59] Aside from the proportion of released defendants who recidivate in the pretrial period, bail reform has had the effect of increasing the total number of known offenders in the community, thereby automatically increasing the crime rate. Even bail project directors and defense counsel believe that the increased use of preventive detention would reduce crime, and they would prefer that it be used more often.[60]

Compelling questions thus remain concerning the legitimate role and use of preventive detention. It may simply be unrealistic to try to dispose of preventive detention and its relation to the "fear of crime" on narrow legal grounds alone.* The real lesson to be learned from the experience with the preventive detention statute in the District of Columbia was that in setting bail, judges will not exclude consideration of the defendant's

* The Supreme Court has never determined the constitutionality of preventive detention, but it will have an opportunity to do so in its October 1981 term. Public defenders have asked the Court to review a Court of Appeals decision upholding the District of Columbia's 1970 Preventive Detention Act.

danger to the community or the likelihood of serious recidivism, even if it means breaking the law! Indeed, the New Jersey Supreme Court has articulated a standard, to be followed by the judiciary in determining the amount of bail, that in effect incorporates consideration of the defendant's danger to the community.[61] In his 1981 annual address to the American Bar Association, Chief Justice Burger urged that bail laws be revised to authorize preventive detention of dangerous persons, based upon their present changes and prior records.[62] And the Task Force on Violent Crime has recommended that courts be permitted to deny bail "to persons who are found by clear and convincing evidence to present a danger to particular persons or the community."[63] The problems in predicting dangerousness and recidivism are complex, but perhaps no more so than in predicting appearance at trial before the Manhattan Bail Project took the case.

Bail, pretrial detention, and bail reform raise doubts that any segment of the criminal justice system can be significantly improved until the entire system is overhauled. The sheer number of accused persons entering the system through arrest creates crushing overload that results in interminable delays before trial and final case disposition. For those released, the longer the pretrial period, the greater the opportunity for flight and committing new crimes. For those detained, the longer the pretrial period, the more hardships to be suffered in the conditions of jail and in being treated like prisoners. To alleviate the deprivations of detainees and to minimize the opportunity that released defendants have to flee, to commit new crimes, or to avoid conviction by "waiting it out," the pretrial period must be shortened for both groups. What is required is that all pretrial defendants, whether detained or released, be given a speedy trial. This will be discussed in Chapter 10.

SUMMARY

Judicial reliance on high cash bail for pretrial release, whether such a policy violated the Eighth Amendment prohibition against excessive bail or not, and problems associated with pretrial detention were responsible for the bail reform movement, which began in 1961 with the Manhattan Bail Project. The Manhattan Bail Project established that "good risk" defendants could be released on recognizance, based upon their social ties to the community, and that their failure-to-appear rate was as good as those released on regular cash bail. The ten percent cash bail program proved to be an equally effective reform for defendants who did not qualify for ROR, who posed a somewhat higher risk of flight, and who therefore required a greater incentive to appear at trial. Conditional release was used with defendants who required supervision while out on nonmonetary bail, with similarly encouraging results. In response to the same problems surrounding the administration of bail in the states, the federal Bail Reform Act of 1966 incorporated all of the bail reform measures adopted by the states—yet fell short of its objectives for various reasons. The act's intentional failure to authorize preventive detention was a sore spot for members of the law enforcement community, the voting victims of crime, and many judges. This omission was rectified in a 1970 amendment to the act that authorized preventive detention in the District of Columbia. But it was a victory for the amendment's supporters that turned out to be more symbolic than real, and it left the question of the effect of preventive detention on pretrial recidivism unresolved. Despite the progress in bail reform attributable to the Manhattan Bail Project and its progeny, extensive reliance on high cash bail and pretrial detention continue to characterize the current bail system, in part because the ROR model has become a victim of its own shortcomings.

DISCUSSION QUESTIONS

1. Are you in favor of or against preventive detention laws? Why?
2. Since the Eighth Amendment prohibits excessive bail, why is there not an absolute right to have bail set in all cases?
3. What practical problems might be associated with starting a program like the Manhattan Bail Project?

Chapter 9

THE PROSECUTOR AND DEFENSE COUNSEL

The Role of the Prosecutor

Deciding whether to prosecute / Legal strength of case / Terminating prosecution through a nolle / Prosecuting on reduced charges / Dropping multiple counts / Making sentencing recommendations

The Management of Prosecution

The certainty of punishment / Selective prosecution / Case-evaluation systems / The career criminal program

The Bronx Major Offense Bureau

PROMIS / Responsibility of the arresting officer / Utilizing numerical case evaluation / Cooperation of the courts / Results of the MOB project

Close-up 9.1: The Major Offense Bureau at Work

The Right to Counsel

Powell v. *Alabama* (1932) / *Gideon* v. *Wainwright* (1963) / *Argersinger* v. *Hamlin* (1972) / The right to effective counsel

Public Defenders and Court-Assigned Counsel

Eligibility for supplied counsel / Mixed criminal defense systems / Legal aid societies / Deficiencies of assigned counsel systems / Deficiencies in public defender programs / Availability of investigative resources / The effect of *Argersinger* / Circumventing *Argersinger* / Complying with *Argersinger* / Law students as defense counsel

Summary

THE ROLE OF THE PROSECUTOR

The prosecutor occupies a unique position in the criminal justice system. As the lawyer for the state, the prosecutor is automatically considered an officer of the court; at the same time, the prosecutor is formally a member of the executive branch of government and is thus independent from the judiciary. The enormous powers of discretion that prosecutors have place their actions and decisions beyond the control of the courts and make them answerable only to the legislature, the electorate, and the press.[1] Yet the prosecutor's ability to influence the determination of the sentence through plea bargaining transforms the prosecutorial function into a semijudicial one.

In principle, securing convictions is less important among the prosecutor's responsibilities than administering justice as an officer of the court, a duty that includes protecting the legal rights of the guilty as well as those of innocent defendants. But these priorities are sometimes reversed under the pressures and incentives for efficiency, in waging an effective battle against crime, in maintaining a respectable conviction "batting average," in the face of public criticism and considerations of personal career advancement, and in the need to cooperate with the courts in reducing backlog. Prosecution in criminal cases is taken on behalf of the People (the State v. the accused) rather than on behalf of an individual victim or complainant. Unfortunately, the "social contract" premise that underlies public prosecution, combined with practical administrative considerations, may result in sacrificing the human rights and needs of the victim in individual cases. More so than that of any other criminal justice practitioner, the role of the prosecutor spans the entire criminal justice system (see Table 9.1).

Whether the case is tried by a judge or a jury, in order to secure an in-court (adjudicated) conviction, the prosecutor carries the entire burden for proving the accused guilty beyond a reasonable doubt. When a defendant is convicted, the prosecutor attends the sentencing hearing usually held several weeks later, to allow time for a presentence report to be prepared by the probation officer and studied by the court and the prosecutor. At sentencing, the prosecutor may advocate harsh punishment or leniency, based on considerations of justice, the needs of society, and rehabilitation. The prosecutor's final routine responsibility is to make convictions stick when they are appealed. Through written briefs and in oral arguments, the prosecutor tries to convince the appellate court that no legal errors were committed at or before trial that would justify overturning the conviction. This problem is not encountered in convictions obtained through guilty pleas because those who plead guilty automatically relinquish the right to appeal. Although it is not usual, the prosecutor may also decide to oppose the early parole release of dangerous or unrehabilitated offenders.

Deciding whether to prosecute

The prosecutor has absolute, unrestricted discretion in the performance of duty. Prosecutorial discretion typically enters the picture immediately after arrest, when police reports are forwarded to the prosecutor for review. The prosecutor screens and evaluates the documents (and, time permitting, may talk to the arresting officer) in order to decide whether to accept or reject the case for prosecution.[2] The prosecutor who decides to accept a case issues a *complaint,* upon which the suspect is arraigned before a magistrate. The reasons for selective prosecution—the decision not to prosecute certain cases—are basically the same as those for selective nonenforcement of the law by the police: ambiguity in the penal code, the need to individualize justice, overcriminalization, and so on. In one case, for example, a Wisconsin prosecutor concluded that "This is a once-a-year gathering of lawyers in which one [poker] table got out of hand—

ble 9.1 The Role of the Prosecutor in the Criminal Justice System

vestigation	Arrest	First Court Appearance	Preliminary Hearing	Grand Jury
epares search and rest warrants	screens cases to decide whether to initiate prosecution; decides that some cases will not be prosecuted	sees that cases accepted for prosecution are arraigned in magistrate courts; "cooperates" with court in summary disposition of minor misdemeanors; requests high bail in felonies; may discontinue prosecution through a nolle	establishes probable cause before judge; may nolle a case	establishes probable cause before grand jury in seeking indictment on single criminal charge or multiple counts

raignment	Pretrial Motions	Trial	Sentencing	Appeal	Parole
aigns felony de- ndants, who ter formal plea charges in lictment or secutor's in- mation; may ow defendant to ead guilty to a luced charge to a single arge in a mul- e-count lictment	opposes motions to suppress illegally obtained evidence or to dismiss a case	must prove guilt beyond a reasonable doubt to obtain a conviction	recommends harsh or lenient disposition at sentence hearing	argues that conviction was obtained properly and should not be overturned	may oppose early parole release of dangerous offenders from prison

not a commercial type of game that occurs frequently. . . . If there is a repeat, there will be charges filed against the players."[3] For a variety of reasons, it is just as unrealistic to prosecute every person who is arrested as it is to arrest every person who breaks the law.

Legal strength of case

An especially important factor that influences the decision to charge a person with a crime is the legal strength of the case. This encompasses the prosecutor's judgment that the suspect is in fact guilty, the willingness or reluctance of witnesses to testify, and the likelihood that the prosecutor can legally prove the defendant's guilt beyond a reasonable doubt to a judge and jury. There is a wide gap between the probable cause that the police need to make a legal arrest and the "beyond a reasonable doubt" standard that the prosecutor must meet in order to convict at trial. Whenever the likelihood of obtaining a conviction seems slight, the prosecutor may decline prosecution. An LEAA study of felony arrests in Washington, D.C., Salt Lake City, Los Angeles, New Orleans, and Cobb County, Georgia, revealed that a majority of the felony arrests were rejected or nolled by the prosecutors because they would have been unable to prove guilt beyond a reasonable doubt.[4]

In some jurisdictions, the police, the complainant, or the court participate in the decision whether or not to prosecute. Sometimes the police alone will prepare the charges, usually as a practical response to prosecutorial overload. However, the common practice is that the prosecutor is the dominant, if not the sole decision maker in the charging process.[5] Even after prosecution has commenced (by virtue of the defendant's initial court appearance), the prosecutor may subsequently decide to drop all charges, discontinue prosecution, and seek a dismissal. The belated decision not to prosecute ordinarily occurs when the prosecutor becomes aware of factors that make prosecution inadvisable, when the prosecutor has not had the opportunity or the mechanism for screening cases prior to the first arraignment, or where the police routinely make the preliminary decision to file charges.

Terminating prosecution through a nolle

When formal prosecution has begun and is a matter of public record, the prosecutor may decide to terminate prosecution through the nolle (*nolle prosequi*). A *nolle* is a request made by the prosecutor to the court for approval to terminate further criminal prosecution. This request is a formality that courts routinely grant without question; ordinarily the prosecutor is not even required to give reasons for wanting to nolle a case. Technically, a suspect whose case is nolled has the charge suspended for a period of 12 months. This suspension of legal processing is intended to have a deterrent effect on the offender and to facilitate the resumption of prosecution if the suspect gets into trouble during the period. At the end of 12 months, the nolle status expires and automatically becomes a full dismissal of the charge. The prosecutor uses the nolle primarily to reduce case overload, court backlog, and delays in bringing defendants to trial. In some jurisdictions, the prosecutor nolles as many as one-half of the cases.[6]

Prosecuting on reduced charges

The most significant, prevalent, and controversial expression of prosecutorial discretion is the decision to mitigate the defendant's sentence through (a) reducing the charge, (b) dropping multiple counts to leave a single criminal charge standing, and (c) recommending leniency to the court at sentencing. As a matter of law and discretion, the prosecutor has the authority to prosecute the defendant for a less serious crime than the one that was committed, identified in the police report, contained in the indictment or prosecutor's information, or entered at arraignment. These less serious (and less severely punishable) crimes are referred to as reduced charges. The prosecutor may reduce the charge, for example, from armed to unarmed robbery; from forcible rape to assault; from burglary to petty theft. The charge may be reduced by the prosecutor at the screening stage, the initial court appearance, the preliminary hearing, or the arraignment; it may even be reduced after trial has begun if the defendant agrees to plead guilty to the reduced charge.

Dropping multiple counts

Many defendants are arrested for committing several different crimes during an uninterrupted sequence of illegal conduct. For example, forcible rape may be the primary intended crime in a series of criminal acts that includes illegal entry to an apartment (burglary), brutally beating the rape victim (assault and perhaps murder if death results), and theft of cash under threat (robbery). Each crime is a separate offense that carries its own penalties; a defendant who is prosecuted and convicted on the multiple counts of an indictment may be sentenced to a consecutive prison term.* Offenders may also be charged with multiple counts for committing the same crime over a period of time. For example, an embezzler may be charged with a 50-count or 100-count indictment, stemming from every separate occasion on which embezzlement occurred or records were falsified. A 12-count indictment may be filed against a forger for passing bad checks on 12 separate occasions or for passing 12 bad checks in one transaction. And persons arrested for committing several different crimes at different times and places may be charged with all of the offenses involved—multiple counts. The prosecutor has the discretion to drop the multiple criminal counts and to charge the defendant instead with a single crime, one which may or may not be the most serious crime (the top charge) involved. To assure a less severe sentence, the prosecutor will ordinarily drop all counts except the one to which the defendant agrees to plead guilty and be sentenced on.

* In a consecutive prison term, the penalties (years of imprisonment) imposed for separate crimes are added together in arriving at the total length of incarceration, which is the full sentence.

Making sentencing recommendations

Finally, the prosecutor may seek a conviction on multiple counts or on the original top charge alone and at the same time plan to recommend leniency in sentencing or the imposition of concurrent sentences.* The prosecutor's use of discretion to mitigate the sentence in any individual case may reflect a judgment of the proper disposition, rather than job pressures to dispose of a large number of cases through plea bargaining. Ordinarily, however, the implementation of prosecutorial discretion through reduced charges, the dropping of multiple counts, and a favorable sentencing recommendation is attributable to plea bargaining (which will be discussed in Chapter 10). Although prosecutorial discretion is rarely authorized by statute, it is a powerful unwritten law that has been recognized by the courts, accepted by the Supreme Court, and endorsed by both crime commissions. The only direct response to flagrant abuses of prosecutorial discretion is through indictment of the prosecutor for misconduct in office for gross failure to prosecute,[7] or by use of the Fourteenth Amendment's equal protection of the law clause to prove discrimination in being unjustly singled out for selective prosecution.[8]

THE MANAGEMENT OF PROSECUTION

The certainty of punishment

The most important factor in preventing and deterring crime is the certainty of punishment, the frequency with which those who commit crime are arrested, prosecuted, convicted, and punished. For recidivists, career criminals, and violent offenders—those who contribute excessively to the crime rate—crime does pay in that too often they avoid conviction and prison sentences. Since the certainty of punishment depends mainly on effective prosecution and appropriate sentencing, the first step in deterring these groups is the responsibility of the prosecutor. However, because of delays and other problems associated with prosecution, often these offenders are not convicted, or they beat the rap through plea bargaining, or they are placed on probation instead of being sentenced to prison. Long delays between arrest and final disposition reduce the likelihood of conviction on the original charges, increase the likelihood of dismissal or acquittal on all counts, and make it more likely that convicted defendants will avoid prison sentences. Delays in prosecution inevitably work to the advantage of offenders, reducing severely the actual and perceived likelihood of punishment.

In the early 1970s, efforts were made to improve the management of

* In a concurrent prison sentence, the separately imposed prison terms for each count are not added together but allowed to run at the same time. Thus the full sentence is the longest single prison term imposed, usually for the most serious count.

prosecution in order to increase the certainty of conviction and punishment for the most serious cases and the worst repeaters. This goal was approached through a procedure that quantified the prosecutor's policies and practices and formed the basis for selective and vigorous prosecution of serious offenders and career criminals. In selective prosecution, special attention is given to the uncompromising prosecution of recidivists, violent offenders, and those committing serious crimes.

Selective prosecution

> The correctness of the charging decision and the quality of trial preparation have a greater impact on the quality of justice than any other process within the prosecutor's control. Ideally, each offender [should] be charged at precisely the level that could be supported by all the evidence available, and each case would be prepared and presented by an experienced, well prepared, assistant prosecutor in a timely and expeditious manner. In reality, the prosecutor is faced with too many cases of widely varying degrees of seriousness, too few assistants, and too few or poorly allocated court resources.[9]

It is in response to these problems—and their effect on the certainty of punishment—that selective prosecution by case evaluation enters the picture. Prosecutorial case-evaluation systems quantify the chief prosecutor's "policy and priorities in terms of (1) the seriousness of the offense based primarily on the extent of personal injury and property or damage—rather than by an arbitrary legal definition of crime; (2) the seriousness of the defendant's record; (3) the subjective assessment of the evidentiary strength of the case in terms of the probability of conviction."[10] Cases that receive a high score (such as those of serious offenders, recidivists, and career criminals) are given top prosecution priority. They are prosecuted promptly, vigorously, with minimal plea bargaining, and with the objective of getting stiff prison sentences. In practice, selective prosecution by case evaluation should increase the certainty of punishment and deter criminality among the worst offenders, those most committed to crime and those who commit most of the crime.

Case-evaluation systems

At the Annual Conference of the International Association of Chiefs of Police on September 24, 1974, President Gerald Ford emphasized the need and announced his intentions to deal more effectively with "repeat offenders." Under the direction of Attorney General William Saxbe, the LEAA promptly launched a new $3 million "career criminal" program in which the improved management of prosecution was to guarantee swift, sure, and appropriate punishment to career criminals.[11] The selective case-evaluation system was to be the means for accomplishing this goal. *Career criminals* are recidivists, violent offenders, professional criminals, and other serious violators whose success in avoiding punishment is at least partially responsible for their careers in crime. According to official estimates, there were 500,000 career criminals in the United States in 1975.[12]

The career criminal program

The Bronx Major Offense Bureau

The president's call to wage war on repeat offenders through improved prosecution techniques represented an acceleration of and a new emphasis on the prosecutor's role in crime control that was begun by the LEAA in the early 1970s. To cope with growing caseloads and to increase the certainty of punishment for serious offenders, the Prosecutor's Management Information System (PROMIS) was developed under LEAA grants of $292,320 and initially utilized in the U.S. Attorney's office in the District of Columbia Superior Court in January 1971. PROMIS ranks pending cases by four factors: seriousness of offense, defendant's criminal record, legal strength of evidence, and age of case or number of continuances. The computerized* daily list of priority-sequenced cases generated by PROMIS assures that important matters are not overlooked and enables prosecutors to allocate their resources efficiently and effectively. As a result of PROMIS, the conviction rate for serious misdemeanors increased by 25 percent during a six-month period in the District of Columbia.

PROMIS

Spurred by the success of PROMIS and the expanded federal initiative against career criminals, a Major Offense Bureau was subsequently established within the jurisdiction and office of the District Attorney of the Bronx, New York, under a $453,239 LEAA grant. The Bronx Major Offense Bureau (MOB) was a specialized unit created to identify, prosecute vigorously, and concentrate intensively on recidivists, violent offenders, and career criminals through the use of a numerical case-evaluation system supported by highly qualified staff.[13] By minimizing delay and thereby maximizing the chances for conviction and prison sentences, such projects should increase the certainty of punishment and consequently deter crime. The Bronx Major Offense Bureau began operation on September 1, 1973. Its implementation and success are a tribute to what can be accomplished when police, prosecutors, and courts function as a coordinated team and as a system.

Responsibility of the arresting officer

The effectiveness of the MOB depended on the immediate and full cooperation of the arresting officer with the unit so that the case could receive instant prosecutorial attention. Because the police are the first link in the system, an immediate working relationship between police and prosecution allowed the prosecutor to become involved in the investigative process, to evaluate the legal strength of the case, to review the actions taken by the police while the facts were still fresh, and to make better informed decisions concerning the state's course of action in prosecution and plea bargaining. To accomplish this goal, arresting offi-

* In Wayne County, Michigan, the prosecutor's office is using a manual version of the PROMIS concept for ranking the priority of cases.

aff of the Bronx Major Offense reau, headed by District Attorey Mario Merola (center), in 1978

cers were directed to notify the Bronx District Attorney's Office immediately upon apprehending persons for committing serious crimes.

Traditionally, thousands of felony arrests have been processed each year in the complaint room of the Bronx District Attorney's Office. There inexperienced DAs who were new to the office and without trial practice were required to make, virtually on their own, complex and important decisions concerning prosecution. It was here that the numerical case-evaluation system was utilized as a tool for implementing efficiently, effectively, and consistently the policies and priorities of the chief prosecutor. The MOB Office Evaluation Form provided concrete guidelines for scoring each case reviewed by clerks and the assistant district attorney, who were on duty around the clock, seven days a week. In general, the higher the final score on the evaluation form, the more serious was the instant charge, the greater was the personal injury or property loss and damage, the more likely was the defendant to commit violent crimes, and the stronger was the case legally. The final ranking of the case determined the prosecutorial action to be taken and the prosecutor's management of the case.

Utilizing numerical case evaluation

Thus objective standards for decision making that could be implemented easily and uniformly by clerks and inexperienced DAs replaced a system of subjective evaluation. In the process, speed and efficiency overcame the customary delays that had lessened the certainty of punishment.

Indictments were not sought in cases that on the MOB Office Evaluation Form received low rankings or rankings below the cutoff score for prosecutorial action. The selective prosecution project reduced the number of indictments sought by 42 percent by the end of 1974. The Major Offense Bureau was thus a promising method for dealing with serious crime, improving the quality of prosecution, and increasing certainty of punishment; it also proved to be invaluable in reducing the backlog of cases flooding the Bronx courts. MOB cases that were prosecuted were usually submitted to the grand jury within 24 hours of arrest and presentment.

Cooperation of the courts

The effectiveness of the MOB project was dependent on its having the understanding and the cooperation of the courts. The question of bail was extremely important; because project cases involved the most serious crimes and criminals, the risk of their flight while out on bail was great. However, the courts were reluctant to set high bail because of constitutional requirements and the kinds of jail conditions to which legally innocent pretrial detainees would be subjected. Therefore it was necessary to convince the court to set a bail amount that the defendants could not meet in order to prevent pretrial release and the high risk of flight associated with it for MOB defendants. This was accomplished by explaining to the courts that the project's emphasis on speedy prosecution meant that defendants would not languish in jail awaiting trial and that the state had prepared strong legal cases (see Close-up 9.1). Because the prosecutor was prepared for trial at arraignment, the number of continuances requested by the state was reduced. In turn, the state's readiness to proceed with the case in court encouraged the judiciary to be more critical of requests for continuances and delaying tactics on the part of the defense.

Results of the MOB project

Since its inception, the MOB has taken action against 800 defendants in cases ranging from attempted murder of police officers to bribing a witness. So far more than 700 defendants have been convicted, most of them on the top count of the indictment. Under a restricted plea bargaining policy, the remainder were permitted to plead guilty to only one count below the highest charge. On the average, MOB cases were disposed of within 90 days and had an overall conviction rate of 96 percent. The conviction rate of defendants brought to trial by the MOB was over 90 percent, while that of a control group was only 50 percent. Ninety-three percent of the defendants prosecuted by the bureau have been incarcerated. An average minimum sentence of over three years was imposed in 70 percent of the cases. (A control group consisting of the same type of offenses received an average minimum sentence of less than six months.)[14] Finally, the MOB project increased the morale of police officers by guaranteeing that arrested recidivists and dangerous offenders were not returned to the streets before the police had returned to their beats. The impressive results of the Bronx MOB and of similar efforts underway elsewhere may be a significant step toward proving that crime does not pay.[15]

Close-up 9.1 THE MAJOR OFFENSE BUREAU AT WORK

On September 25, 1973, Edward Switzer walked into Mantel's Delicatessen in Bronx County, put a knife to the throat of the elderly owner, took $30 and checks from the cash register, and fled. He was arrested a short time later. Switzer's criminal record showed a score of prior conflicts with the law. In 1968 he committed a robbery, took a plea, and served 14 months in New York State Prison. In 1971 he committed a burglary and served a few months more. Switzer, now 29 years old, was confident that he could beat the system again.

At 9:00 P.M. on the night of the delicatessen robbery, an assistant district attorney from the Major Offense Bureau went to the 44th Precinct in Bronx County. After interviewing all witnesses and otherwise directing the investigation, he obtained a copy of the defendant's rap sheet and promptly accepted the case for prosecution by the bureau. The (assistant) prosecutor then drafted the complaint and handled the preliminary arraignment. During bail application, the prosecutor was able to demonstrate to the court that the defendant was a dangerous recidivist without substantial roots in the community. The defendant was held in lieu of $25,000 bail. The next morning the prosecutor again met with the witnesses and presented the entire case to the grand jury. The resulting indictment was immediately typed, signed, and filed with the court.

Before arraignment the assistant DA conferred with the chief of the MOB and a plea offer was established. If the offer were accepted, the defendant would plead guilty to the top count of the indictment and the prosecution would recommend that a sentence of no less than 12 years be imposed. On October 3 the defendant was arraigned, entered a plea of not guilty and was informed of the plea offer. Subsequently his lawyer and the prosecutor met to discuss the case, and the nature of the case against the defendant was candidly revealed. Switzer refused the offered plea and it was thereupon withdrawn. On November 15, just 50 days after the commission of the crime in Mantel's Delicatessen, a jury found Edward Switzer guilty of first-degree robbery and all other counts in the indictment. On December 19 Edward Switzer was sentenced to a maximum of 25 years in prison, with the stipulation that he be ineligible for parole until he had served 12½ years.

Source: The Prosecutor, vol. 11, no. 1, p. 12.

THE RIGHT TO COUNSEL

> In all criminal prosecutions the accused shall enjoy the right . . . to have the assistance of counsel for his defense. (Sixth Amendment)

Powell v. *Alabama* (1932)

The prosecutor's counterpart in the courtroom is *defense counsel,* the lawyer who represents the accused. Defense counsel representation is rooted in the constitutional right to counsel expressed in the Sixth

In 1932 the Supreme Court reversed the rape convictions of the "Scottsboro boys" because the state had failed to provide them with counsel

Amendment. The first Supreme Court case in which the right to counsel was a major issue was *Powell* v. *Alabama* in 1932.[16] Nine black youths rode in a freight car with seven white boys and two white girls on a train passing through Alabama. During a fight the white boys were thrown off the train, and a message was relayed ahead reporting the incident. When the train was stopped by a sheriff's posse in the town of Paint Rock, the two girls said they had been raped by the black youths, who were then taken into custody. To avoid the possibility of mob violence, they were transferred to a safer jail in Scottsboro under the protection of the National Guard.

1963 the Supreme Court over- rned the felony conviction of arence Gideon because his right counsel had been denied

From the time of their arrest to the day of the trial, the uneducated, illiterate, and unemployed defendants were without counsel. At the last minute, on the opening day of the trial, the presiding judge assigned as their counsel a reluctant local lawyer who had no time to prepare an adequate defense. The nine youths were tried in groups of three, each trial lasting but a day from the time of jury selection to the verdict. Medical and other evidence clearly established that the two white girls, who were alleged to be prostitutes, had not been raped.[17] Nonetheless, all nine "Scottsboro boys" were convicted and sentenced to death. The Supreme Court reversed the convictions on the ground that "the failure of the trial court to make an effective appointment of counsel was . . . a denial of due process within the meaning of the Fourteenth Amendment." The Supreme Court's recognition of the constitutional right to counsel in *Powell* applied only to cases involving the death penalty.

Gideon v. *Wainright* (1963)

The basic right to counsel established by the Supreme Court in *Powell* was extended to felony cases in *Gideon* v. *Wainwright* in 1963.[18] The charge against Gideon contained in the prosecutor's information was breaking and entering a poolroom with the intent to commit a crime, a felony offense under Florida statute. Appearing in court without funds or counsel, Gideon asked the court to appoint counsel to represent him. The court refused on the ground that Florida law authorized court-appointed counsel only for indigents charged with a capital offense. Gideon chose to represent himself before a jury, was convicted, and was sentenced to five years in prison. The Supreme Court reversed the uncounseled conviction on the basis that the Sixth Amendment right to counsel, imposed upon the states through the Fourteenth Amendment, had been violated. The Court emphasized that the appointment of counsel for an indigent defendant was "a fundamental right, essential to a fair trial." In doing so, the Supreme Court broke with its own precedent, established in *Betts* v. *Brady* in 1942, in which the Court had ruled that counsel was not essential to a fair trial in all felony cases.[19]

Argersinger v. *Hamlin* (1972)

In *Argersinger* v. *Hamlin* in 1972, the Supreme Court extended the Sixth Amendment right to counsel to misdemeanor defendants facing incarceration, regardless of how brief the period of deprivation of liberty.[20] The indigent, unrepresented defendant in this case was charged with the misdemeanor of carrying a concealed weapon. Not informed of his right to counsel, he pled guilty and was sentenced to 90 days in jail. The Supreme Court reversed the conviction. "We hold, therefore, that absent a knowing and intelligent waiver, no person may be imprisoned for any offense, whether classified as petty, misdemeanor, or felony, unless he was represented by counsel at his trial."

The right to counsel cited in the *Escobedo* and *Miranda* decisions was the right to counsel at the police or arrest stage (see Table 9.2). In *Escobedo,* it involved the right to be granted access to privately retained counsel who was already available and seeking to confer with his client; in *Miranda,* it was a matter of the suspect's being informed of the right to counsel before interrogation could begin, rather than an absolute right to have counsel supplied. The substantive right to counsel enunciated in *Powell, Gideon,* and *Argersinger* focused on the trial stage and the obligation to obtain a fair legal determination of the defendant's guilt or innocence. These three cases involved not merely being *informed* of the right to counsel but, more important, actually *having* counsel assigned before the trial can take place. (All competent defendants have the constitutional right to reject, or waive, professional legal representation and to conduct their own defense, that is, to act as their own lawyer.[21])

The right to effective counsel

In 1932 the *Powell* decision not only established the basic right to counsel but foreshadowed the right to *effective* counsel. In the mid 1970s, various groups began to grapple with the issue of improving the

Table 9.2 The Right to Counsel at the Police and Trial Stages

Arrest	Misdemeanors Tried Before Lower or Magistrate Courts (limited jurisdiction courts)	Felonies Tried Before Felony Courts (general jurisdiction courts)
1. the right to confer with on-the-spot private counsel before being questioned by police (*Escobedo* v. *Illinois,* 1964) 2. the right to be informed of the right to counsel, to avoid coerced confessions (*Miranda* v. *Arizona,* 1966)	1. the right to counsel for indigent defendants facing incarceration (*Argersinger* v. *Hamlin,* 1972) 2. the initial court appearance is usually the first opportunity to have counsel assigned 3. misdemeanor cases may be continued until counsel can confer with client and prepare adequate defense 4. lower courts are not authorized to accept guilty pleas in felony cases but may appoint counsel	1. the right to have counsel in capital cases to obtain a fair adjudication (*Powell* v. *Alabama,* 1932) 2. the right to have counsel in any felony case because counsel is essential to a fair legal determination of guilt or innocence (*Gideon* v. *Wainwright,* 1963) 3. counsel in felony cases may be assigned at the second arraignment or by the magistrate court at the initial court appearance
The purpose of the right to counsel at arrest is to prevent improper police practices that could result in involuntary confessions	The purpose of the right to counsel at trial is to guarantee a fair trial	

quality of legal services, especially to indigent criminal defendants. To weed out incompetent counsel and prosecutors, the American College of Trial Lawyers proposed that lawyers practicing in federal courts be required to demonstrate minimum qualifications by passing a required set of courses in evidence, advocacy, professional responsibility, and trial experience.[22] The plan has been enthusiastically endorsed by Chief Justice Burger.[23] To eliminate the "defective assistance of counsel," some states are moving toward adopting mandatory continuing education for lawyers. The first state to do so, under an order from the state supreme court, was Minnesota in April 1975.[24] That state requires all active lawyers and judges to take 45 hours of refresher courses every three years.[25] In eight states, including Washington and Wisconsin, lawyers can have their licenses suspended if they do not attend legal education courses for at least 15 hours a year. Lawyers who specialize in civil and criminal trials can now obtain certificates of competence from the prestigious National Board of Trial Advocacy, under a program launched in 1979. And in recent years law schools have taken steps to increase training in practical skills and courtroom tactics, especially through clinical course offerings.[26]

PUBLIC DEFENDERS AND COURT-ASSIGNED COUNSEL

Three types of legal representation are available to criminal defendants. (1) Defendants who can afford to do so may hire their own lawyers, that is, retain private counsel. Indigent defendants are given free state-supplied counsel in the form of (2) a public defender or (3) court-assigned counsel. Whether defendants in state courts are considered indigent[27] and therefore eligible for supplied counsel is usually left to the discretion of the court.[28]

Eligibility for supplied counsel

Defendants who are prosecuted for federal crimes have easier access to free counsel because indigency is not the sole criteria for eligibility. Under the Criminal Justice Act of 1964, any federal defendant who is "financially unable to obtain adequate representation" is entitled to have counsel supplied by the government.[29] This more liberal basis for determining eligibility makes it possible to supply counsel to marginally poor federal defendants whose counterparts in state courts might not be deemed indigent. Going beyond the Criminal Justice Act, the Standards and Goals Commission recommended that the state supply counsel when defense costs would cause "substantial hardship to the individual [defendant] or his family."[30] The significance of supplied counsel in the criminal justice system is indicated by a study conducted by the National Legal Aid and Defender Association. Its LEAA-financed National Defender Survey found that 65 percent of all felony defendants and 47 percent of all misdemeanor defendants could not afford to hire their own lawyers.[31] Such

In urban areas the majority of indigent defendants are represented by public defenders

individuals are dependent on public defenders and court-assigned counsel for legal services.

Public defenders are full-time or part-time state employees who earn a fixed salary and specialize in representing indigent criminal defendants. The size of the public defender system, organization, or office in any given jurisdiction may range from a single defender in rural counties with small criminal caseloads to several hundred public defenders in high-crime urban areas. Los Angeles leads the nation with 392 full-time and 51 part-time public defenders;[32] in Columbia, Missouri, a single public defender is responsible for a two-county area.[33] The majority of cities have between 5 and 15 full-time public defenders.[34] Whether public defenders are elected, as in Florida, or appointed by the governor or the state supreme court, as in most state-financed systems,[35] their operations are independent of the judiciary.

Court-assigned (appointed) counsel are lawyers in private practice who are selected and assigned by the court to represent indigent defendants on a case-by-case basis, and they are compensated accordingly. Unlike public defenders, court-assigned counsel are not ordinarily dependent on representing indigents for a livelihood. Their income from this source of employment depends on the fees approved by the court or established through legislation, the seriousness of the case, the length of the trial, the number of criminal justice stages at which their services are required, how often they are called upon, and their personal relations with the courts who appoint them. The hourly rate for assigned counsel is generally much less than they would earn in private practice and below the $20–$30 per hour rates authorized by the Criminal Justice Act for assigned counsel in federal cases. The courts select assigned counsel from among rotating lists of bar members who have expressed an interest in serving as attorneys for the poor,[36] courtroom "ambulance chasers,"[37] committee or commission recommendations of competent lawyers, and the court's personal knowledge of and preference for particular attorneys.

Mixed criminal defense systems

Public defender and assigned counsel systems are not always as distinct in practice as they are in principle. Many jurisdictions have "mixed" criminal defense systems for the poor. There are three types of mixed systems.

1. *The public defender and assigned counsel share responsibility for representing indigents.* New Jersey's statewide public defender system draws on a pool of assigned counsel, who represented 22 percent of the total indigent caseload in 1972. The Seattle-King County defense system in Washington allocates three cases to the public defender's office and every fourth case to assigned counsel.[38] There is a fifty-fifty division between public defenders and assigned counsel in San Diego.[39] A coordinated public defender/assigned counsel system has operated in the District of Columbia since 1970; its Public Defender Service is permitted by

statute to represent up to 60 percent of all indigent defendants.[40] The Standards and Goals Commission endorsed these types of mixed or coordinated systems as being preferable to either public defenders or assigned counsel alone.[41]

Legal aid societies

2. *Public defenders may work in a separate division within a legal aid society or association.* Financed by the state and/or private contributions, legal aid societies have a centralized organization staffed by lawyers who earn their living representing the poor. Unlike public defenders, however, legal aid attorneys concentrate on civil rather than criminal cases. In Detroit the public defender program, which handles 16 to 25 percent of the indigent criminal cases, is a branch of the legal aid society.[42] The criminal division section within the New York Legal Aid Society has 450 lawyers who are concerned exclusively with representing accused indigents.[43]

3. *Legal aid society lawyers may occasionally represent criminal defendants.* If public defenders are swamped with cases while the legal aid association has a light civil caseload, the latter may accept some criminal cases. Some legal aid societies may agree to assume permanent responsibility for a designated segment of the criminal caseload. For example, since February 1973 the Birmingham Legal Aid Society has been under contract to provide legal services in misdemeanor cases.[44] Marginally poor offenders who are technically not indigent and are thus ineligible for public defender services may be accepted by legal aid lawyers, whose eligibility criteria are more flexible. Legal aid society lawyers may represent criminal defendants whose cases would create a conflict of interest if handled by the public defender or assigned counsel. And criminal defense may fall to legal aid lawyers by default if there are no other practical alternatives for representing indigent offenders.

As public defenders are the principal source of legal services to the criminally accused in urban America, their characteristics are an important indicator of the quality of defense representation. When it comes to comparing the relative merits of assigned counsel and public defenders, the defenders appear to have the edge in a close contest that involves many trade-offs.[45] The superiority of public defenders stems from their organization and centralized delivery of defense services. This (1) makes public defenders relatively independent of the judiciary, (2) fosters professionalism, expertise in advocacy, and experience in criminal procedure and trial, (3) institutionalizes knowledge acquired on the job and standards of performance, and (4) allows for greater continuity of responsibility from the beginning of the case to its final disposition.

Deficiencies of assigned counsel systems

Assigned counsel, in contrast, may be selected by the court on the basis of favoritism, political patronage, or personal whim. Being dependent on the court's goodwill for the approval of fees, the number of cases received, and future appointments, assigned counsel may be concerned more with pleasing the court than with helping the client. Consequently, assigned counsel may avoid arguing for lower bail or ROR, filing a large number of pretrial motions, objecting to court rulings and utilizing other recognized defense tactics that, if they are not employed, work to the detriment of the defendant.

Deficiencies in public defender programs

Public defender operations also suffer from problems unique to their status as bureaucratic agencies within the criminal justice system. In jurisdictions where the courts appoint public defenders, the issues of favoritism, competence, divided allegiance, and adequate defense representation are essentially the same as those that characterize assigned counsel systems. Even where defenders are not indebted to the courts for their jobs, judicial threats[46] to remove "uncooperative" public defenders may result in the same questionable quality of defense services. "Uncooperative" defenders may be those who delay prompt and permanent disposition of cases by entering frequent not guilty pleas, filing regular pretrial motions, demanding jury trials, and appealing convictions.[47]

Many of the defender's institutional advantages in specialization, competence, and training may be offset by the cynicism bred by crushing caseloads and a clientele that is unappreciative or indifferent to the good faith efforts of public servants. Like many police officers who start their jobs with a deep and uncompromising dedication to alleviating social problems, public defenders may become frustrated and hardened through constant exposure to negative experiences, public complaints, lack of respect from clients, and other demoralizing aspects of the subculture of public defender work.[48] And being dependent on public and private funds, defender programs may face uncertain annual renewal, staff cutbacks, and large caseloads that make individualized justice the exception and assembly-line processing the norm.

Availability of investigative resources

The outcome of trial often depends as much on investigators who do the legwork behind the scenes as it does on the lawyers who argue the case in court. In this regard, the investigative capability of public defender organizations is greater than that of assigned counsel.[49] However, both groups of indigent defendants are at a disadvantage because of the superior investigative resources available to the prosecutor. In Chicago, for example, the state's attorney has 93 investigators compared with the public defender's 6.[50] The statewide Massachusetts Defenders Committee has only 10 investigators to assist the committee's 60 public defenders, each of whom carries an annual caseload of close to 400.[51] In addition to their own staff of investigators, prosecutors have at their disposal an army of "investigators" in the form of police, computer systems, centralized records, and information systems. The National Defender Survey found that 60 percent of the public defender systems had no full-time investigators and that two-thirds of assigned counsel had no funds available to hire an investigator to assist them.[52] Another recent survey of public defender programs in cities with populations of more than 50,000 found that the average number of investigators was 2.2 and that 20 percent of the programs had no investigative personnel. "In no city was the number of public defender investigators equal to the number of investigators found in the prosecutor's office.[53] As a result, "in the majority of jurisdictions the indigent accused goes into court at a decided disadvantage."[54] To meet the Standards and Goals Commission's recommendation for adequate supportive defense services,[55] it is estimated that an additional 3,000 full-time defense investigators would be required.[56]

The proliferation of public defender programs has come in response to the Supreme Court's *Gideon* decision, which established the right to counsel for indigents in felony cases. Just a few years before *Gideon*, defender systems existed in only 3 percent of the nation's counties, serving only one-fourth of the population. A decade later, defender systems were found in 28 percent of the counties, serving two-thirds of the population

GURE 9.1 The growth of orgazed defender systems in the ited States. *Sources:* Lawrence Benner, "Tokenism and the nerican Indigent," *American iminal Law Review*, Spring 75, p. 587.

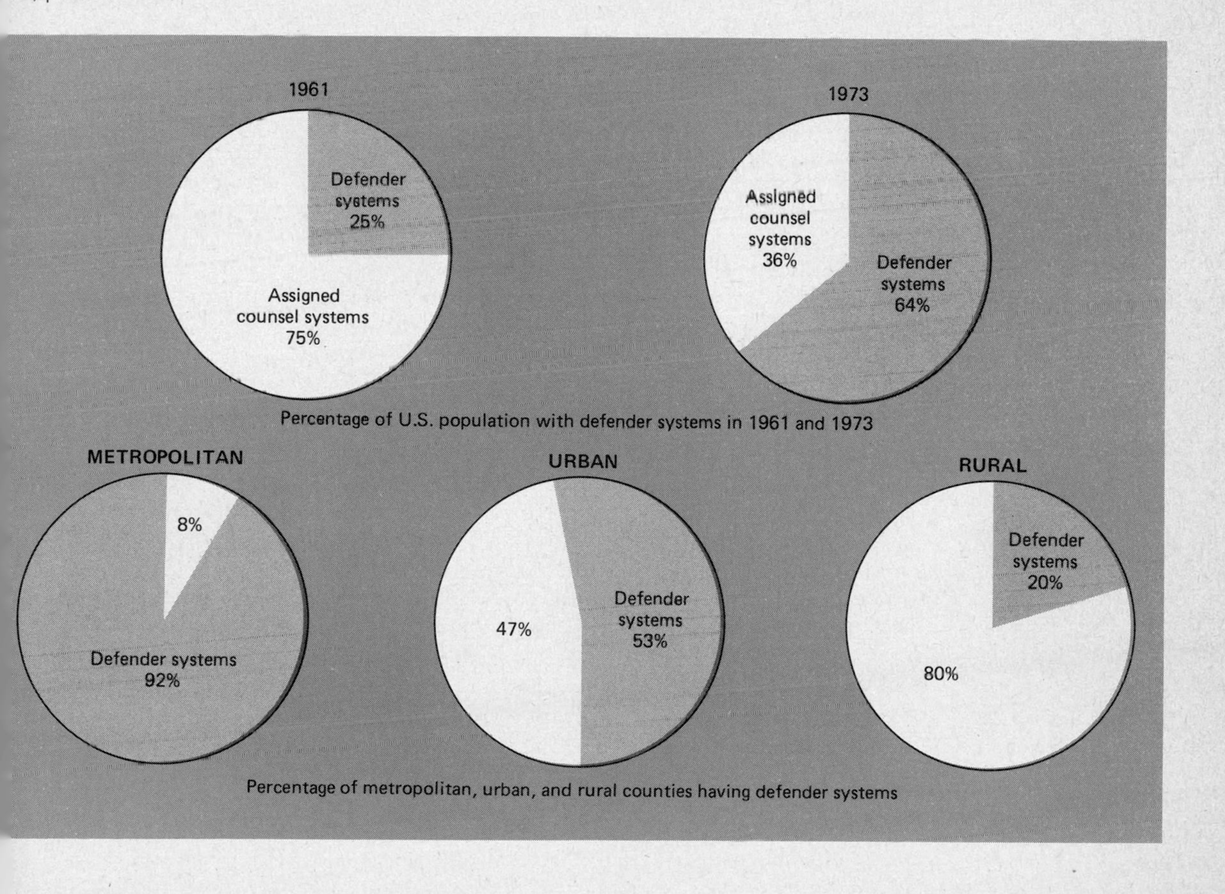

(see Figure 9.1). Seventy percent of the public defender programs came into existence after (and as a result of) *Gideon* v. *Wainwright*. As of 1975, the average public defender program had been in operation eight years, and one-half of them were less than six years old.[57]

The states had barely finished meeting the mandate of *Gideon* when they were abruptly faced with a second revolution in the right to counsel. This was signaled by the 1972 *Argersinger* decision, which said that no imprisonment may be imposed in misdemeanor cases unless the accused is represented by counsel. *Argersinger* placed unprecedented financial, administrative, and personnel demands upon the states by extending their obligation to provide counsel in 700,000 felony cases annually to an additional 3 million misdemeanor cases a year.[58] Before *Argersinger*, most states provided counsel only in selected misdemeanor offenses that entailed lengthy incarceration, and 11 states recognized no right to counsel in misdemeanor cases.[59]

The effect of *Argersinger*

The core of the dilemma in meeting the *Argersinger* mandate is the number of additional defenders and assigned counsel required, how they are to be obtained, the costs involved, and the actions to be taken by the states and courts in response to *Argersinger*. An estimated additional 14,400 full-time public defenders would be needed to implement *Argersinger* and *Gideon* faithfully, at a cost of between $391 million and $560 million (or more), a figure eight times the amount now spent each year for indigent legal representation.[60]

How have the states and courts reacted to the heavy fiscal, administrative, and personnel demands placed upon them by *Argersinger?* Some states and courts have sought to circumvent or to avoid complying with the constitutional mandate of *Argersinger*, through a variety of approaches.

Circumventing *Argersinger*

1. Proposing the decriminalization of misdemeanors currently punishable with a jail term.[61] By eliminating the possibility of incarceration in misdemeanor cases, it would be constitutionally unnecessary to provide counsel to indigents because *Argersinger* restricted the right to counsel to situations in which the defendant faced the possibility of imprisonment upon conviction.
2. Utilizing stringent definitions and procedures for determining indigency. This would make poverty-line misdemeanant defendants legally ineligible for supplied counsel. For example, to reduce the state's public defender caseload, in July 1975 the Arizona Supreme Court discarded the Standards and Goals Commission's "substantial hardship" test then in use in the state's misdemeanor and felony courts for determining indigency. The revised rules required that defendants demonstrate financial inability to hire their own lawyers before Arizona taxpayers would incur the costs of providing them with defenders or assigned counsel.[62]

3. Failing to advise indigent misdemeanants of their right to counsel or to obtain a proper waiver.* The National Defender Survey found that occasionally courts will accept a guilty plea from uncounseled defendants without first clearly informing them of their right to free counsel, inquiring whether they wanted to waive that right, obtaining a valid waiver, or explaining the possible sentence involved.[63,64] An 18-month study of compliance with *Argersinger* in nine cities conducted by Boston University's Center for Criminal Justice found "widespread misuse" of waiver by committing judges.[65]
4. Prejudging the defendant's guilt and sentence before the case is heard. The court may decide to provide counsel only to indigents who upon conviction would be sentenced to incarceration. This would require the court to make a prejudgment of the defendant's guilt and probable sentence before the case is tried, thereby in effect rejecting the legal presumption of innocence. Remarkably, the chief justice of the United States, in attempting to supply guidelines for the provision of counsel in petty and misdemeanor cases, has suggested that in jury cases the prosecutor should help the judge decide *in advance of trial* whether incarceration is "a significant likelihood."[66]
5. Disregarding *Argersinger*. Nearly 10 percent of the judges covered in the National Defender Survey were simply not implementing the Supreme Court's *Argersinger* decision.[67] Most of the courts that were ignoring *Argersinger* were located in the South.[68]

Complying with *Argersinger*

At the same time, positive efforts have been proposed or taken to comply with the spirit and letter of *Argersinger*. The most common approach by the courts is to provide counsel automatically to every indigent charged with a misdemeanor (other than traffic offenses) punishable with incarceration. Strictly speaking, the *Argersinger* decision did not require such action. It required only that in any individual misdemeanor case counsel must be provided if the sentence imposed—not the criminal statute itself—involves a deprivation of liberty; *Argersinger* did not specify that the right to counsel is automatically applicable to all misdemeanors punishable by incarceration.† As a practical matter, however, it is impossible for the court to know in advance whether it will impose a jail term on a convicted misdemeanant rather than a fine, probation, or a suspended sentence. In practice, therefore, the only consistent way for the court to observe scrupulously the right to counsel goal established in *Argersinger* is to provide counsel whenever the possibility of incarceration exists. And that possibility exists wherever the criminal statutes include

* Examples of judicial noncompliance with *Argersinger* presented here illustrate the *means* for doing so rather than the prevalence of such practices.

† In *Scott* v. *Illinois* (1979), the Supreme Court declined to extend the right to counsel to all cases in which incarceration is a possibility.

jail terms among the penalties in misdemeanor cases.[69] By providing counsel automatically to any such defendant, the court can then proceed to try the case impartially and impose sentence (which usually will not be a jail term).

Some courts may routinely forego incarcerating indigent misdemeanants because of an inability to provide them with counsel. Depriving misdemeanants of counsel when they have not waived their right to counsel in effect restricts the court to imposing probation, fine, or a suspended sentence.[70] Another effect of *Argersinger* was to accelerate the trend toward statewide public defender systems, which 16 states had in the mid 1970s and many more were considering.[71] And the proposal to draft the nation's 400,000 lawyers to volunteer their services periodically as assigned counsel or to make themselves available at reduced fees would go a long way toward making the promise of *Argersinger* a reality.[72] But it would first have to overcome the opposition of the organized bar.

Law students as defense counsel

One of the most promising methods for implementing *Argersinger* is the utilization of law students to assist in the defense of needy criminal defendants. Forty-one states and the District of Columbia permit some degree of law student practice within their jurisdiction. As part of clinical programs in the criminal area operated by law schools, students ordinarily receive course credit for participation and may be placed in public defender offices as legal interns. The New York City Legal Aid Society has one of the largest legal intern programs in the country. The law student program in Hennepin County (Minneapolis), Minnesota, includes 30 law students who represent misdemeanant defendants under the supervision of staff attorneys and their professors from the University of Minnesota Law School.[73] The pitfalls in having law students defend indigents are the criticisms that the defendants are being used as guinea pigs to develop the legal skills of aspiring lawyers and that they are being deprived of the *adequate* assistance of counsel, which only a member of the bar can provide. In the last analysis, it will be up to the private bar to decide how best to meet the challenge of criminal defense for the needy in a free society.

SUMMARY

The state's legal representative in criminal matters is the prosecutor, whose main responsibility is to convict offenders. In this regard, career criminal programs are proving effective in making the certainty of punishment a reality for recidivists and violent offenders. The prosecutor's enormous discretion is exercised in the decisions whether or not to prosecute, to nolle a case, to reduce the charges, to drop multiple counts, and to make recommendations at sentencing. The prosecutor's counterpart is defense counsel, whose responsibility is to have the case dismissed if possible, to obtain an acquittal at trial, or to get his client off with a lenient sentence. The right to counsel, rooted in the Sixth Amendment, has evolved in a series of Supreme Court decisions culminating with *Argersinger* v. *Hamlin* in 1972. The majority of defendants are indigent and therefore dependent on public defenders and court-assigned counsel for legal services. Each system of criminal defense for the poor is confronted with distinctive as well as overlapping problems. The *Argersinger* decision has placed unprecedented demands on the states to implement the right to counsel, and these demands are being met and avoided in a variety of ways.

DISCUSSION QUESTIONS

1. Who has more discretion, the police or the prosecutor? Why?
2. If you were the defendant, would you prefer to be represented by a public defender or court-assigned counsel? Why?
3. In the long run, what do you consider the most effective means for fulfilling the *Argersinger* mandate?

Chapter 10

PLEA BARGAINING AND SPEEDY TRIAL

Plea Bargaining

Discretionary authority of the prosecutor

The Prosecutor's Incentive to Plea Bargain

Efficiency / Legally weak cases / Effectiveness

Defense Counsel's Incentive to Plea Bargain

The interests of clients / Economic advantages / Caseload pressures

The Plea Bargaining Process

Operational considerations

Close-up 10.1: Plea Bargaining in Homicide Cases: Getting Away with Murder?

Santobello v. *New York* (1971) / *Blackledge* v. *Allison* (1977) / *Bordenkircher* v. *Hayes* (1978) / The courts' interest in plea bargaining

The Case for Plea Bargaining

The Case Against Plea Bargaining

Close-up 10.2: Assembly Line Justice

Restructuring the Plea Bargaining Process

Impracticality of abolishing plea bargaining

The Pretrial Conference

Presence of the defendant / Mutual disclosure / Participation of the court / Objections to the court's participation / The omnibus hearing

Restricting the Scope of Plea Bargaining

Prohibition of plea bargaining / Selective abolition of plea bargaining / Standards for sentencing recommendations / Guidelines for the reduction of charges / Invoking habitual offender statutes

Speedy Trial

Obstacles to speedy trial / *Barker* v. *Wingo* (1972)

The Speedy Trial Act of 1974

Allowance for necessary delays and continuances / Dismissal of the charges / The prospect of mass dismissals

Close-up 10.3: Should Murderers Go Free Because the Prosecutor Has Blundered?

Speedy trial rules and plea bargaining

Summary

The prosecutor may obtain a conviction in one of two ways. If the defendant pleads not guilty, the prosecutor must be able to prove at trial, before a judge sitting alone or to a jury, that the accused is guilty beyond a reasonable doubt. If the indictment contains multiple counts, each criminal charge that is proved beyond a reasonable doubt subjects the defendant to additional penalties. Because they involve trials and the highest standard of proof, in-court or adjudicated convictions are time-consuming and expensive, and their outcome is always uncertain.

However, defendants who plead guilty need not be *proved* guilty in a court of law. In felony cases, guilty pleas are usually entered at the second arraignment before a court of general trial jurisdiction, which is the plea-taking stage. But a guilty plea may be entered at virtually any time, even in the rare situation in which the defendant decides, after the trial has begun, to withdraw a not guilty plea and to plead guilty instead. Guilty pleas count as convictions; they immediately subject the defendant to the next step in the criminal justice process, the sentencing. Because guilty pleas do not involve trials, they are an efficient, convenient, and reliable way of disposing of cases, so far as the prosecutor and the courts are concerned.

PLEA BARGAINING

Ordinarily, whenever a sentence may entail lengthy incarceration, misdemeanor and especially felony defendants will not plead guilty unless they have something to gain by making a guilty plea. Since defendants naturally want to minimize their punishment, their motive for pleading guilty is the expectation of a lighter sentence than they would probably receive by pleading not guilty and being convicted at trial. The process of discussion or negotiation between defense counsel and prosecutor, aimed at reaching an agreement whereby the prosecutor uses discretion to obtain a lighter sentence in exchange for the defendant's entering a guilty plea, is *plea bargaining*. Nationally, an estimated 90 percent of convictions in state courts come from guilty pleas.[1] A substantial proportion of this number is the result of plea bargaining; that is, they are bartered guilty pleas.[2] In exceptional cases, plea bargaining may require more from the defendant than a guilty plea and may promise the accused more in return. For example, the agreement may make extraordinary leniency dependent on the defendant's returning stolen property, testifying against accomplices, or providing information or making admissions to the police that will clear other crimes.

Discretionary authority of the prosecutor

The prosecutor's ability to implement the plea bargaining agreement rests in the discretionary authority to (a) reduce the charge(s) at arraignment, (b) drop multiple counts and charge the defendant with a single offense, and (c) make recommendations to the court at sentencing. In any individual case the prosecutor may sweeten the deal for the defendant by trying to have the case come before a "soft" judge for sentencing or by agreeing not to prosecute the accused on related or unrelated charges that may be pending. The prosecutor may recommend that the judge sentence a young adult under the Youthful Offender Act, which allows defendants who might otherwise be incarcerated to return to the community. If the defendant has several prior felony convictions, the prosecutor may agree not to invoke any applicable "habitual offender" statute, which would automatically increase the potential punishment substantially.

The most common method of plea bargaining is to negotiate a guilty plea in exchange for a reduced charge. Often the charge to which the defendant is allowed to plead has been reduced from a felony to a misdemeanor. Or it may be reduced from a more serious (and thus more severely punishable) felony to a less serious one. Similarly, by dropping multiple counts and accepting a guilty plea to the remaining top count in the indictment, or to a reduced charge, the prosecutor can virtually guarantee a lighter penalty by precluding any possibility of consecutive sentences. When the plea bargain hinges on the prosecutor's recommendation to the court at sentencing without any concession being made in the charges themselves, the court usually follows the recommendation, though it is not legally bound to do so.

The Prosecutor's Incentive to Plea Bargain

Efficiency

The prosecutor relies on plea bargaining for three primary reasons. The chief advantage is efficiency. The overwhelming number of arrests made by police in urban areas gives the prosecutor too many cases to

Table 10.1 New York City Felony Arrests Reduced to Misdemeanors, 1973 and 1974

	1973			1974		
	Felony Arrests	Felonies Disposed of by the Lower Court*	Percent	Felony Arrests	Felonies Disposed of by the Lower Court	Percent
Manhattan	31,098	23,845	77%	32,830	26,752	81%
Brooklyn	24,907	17,858	72	27,744	22,924	80
Bronx	21,411	16,466	77	24,501	20,172	82
Queens	11,929	7,543	63	13,775	10,340	76
Staten Island	1,698	1,018	60	1,898	1,163	61
Total	91,043	66,710†	73%	101,748	81,351	80%

Source: New York Times, February 11, 1975, p. 78. © 1975 by the New York Times Company. Reprinted by permission.

* Disposition through plea and sentence bargaining to a misdemeanor, adjournment in contemplation of a dismissal, probation, conditional or unconditioned discharge.

† The remaining 24,333 cases were sent to grand jury and resulted in indictment, dismissal or return to the criminal court. A small percentage of the grand jury cases originate in District Attorney's bureaus and not the criminal courts. Figures were not available for these cases.

handle in relation to staff resources and facilities. In Manhattan there are 200 assistant district attorneys to handle the 100,000 annual felony arrests made by the police, of which 15 percent typically result in felony convictions and 5 percent in prison sentences.[3,4] To convict a single killer through trial proceedings can easily involve 20 percent of available staff time for more than four months. That is one reason why only 74 of 685 persons formally charged with homicide in 1973 went to trial.[5] In all of New York City, there are just 680 assistant district attorneys to handle a quarter million annual arrests and only 116 trial judges to hear these cases.[6] (Table 10.1 and Figure 10.1 provide further data on the disposition of cases through plea bargaining.)

While the prosecutor's resources are superior to those of defense counsel, they are nonetheless scarce and must be deployed frugally. Continuing case overload therefore makes it impossible for prosecutors to dispose of their workload through the adversary method of trial determination of guilt except in a very small proportion of cases (3 to 10 percent). Even an apparently small increase in the number of cases going to trial—especially those that will be heard by juries—may place an intolerable burden upon the prosecutor's ability to try them.[7] The penal code offers the prosecutor no guidelines on how to handle the problems associated with case overload in prosecuting offenders.[8] By pleading guilty, the defendant automatically waives the right to trial and to appeal.

Legally weak cases

A second major advantage of plea bargaining is found when the legal strength of the case is weak, making it impossible or unlikely that the prosecutor will be able to prove guilt beyond a reasonable doubt at trial.[9]

GURE 10.1 Method of disposition for convicted defendants in United States District Courts the fiscal years 1964–1971 excluding the District of Columbia and territories). *Source:* Federal Offenders in United States District Courts, 1971 (Washington, D.C.: Administrative Office of U.S. Courts, 1972), p. 5.

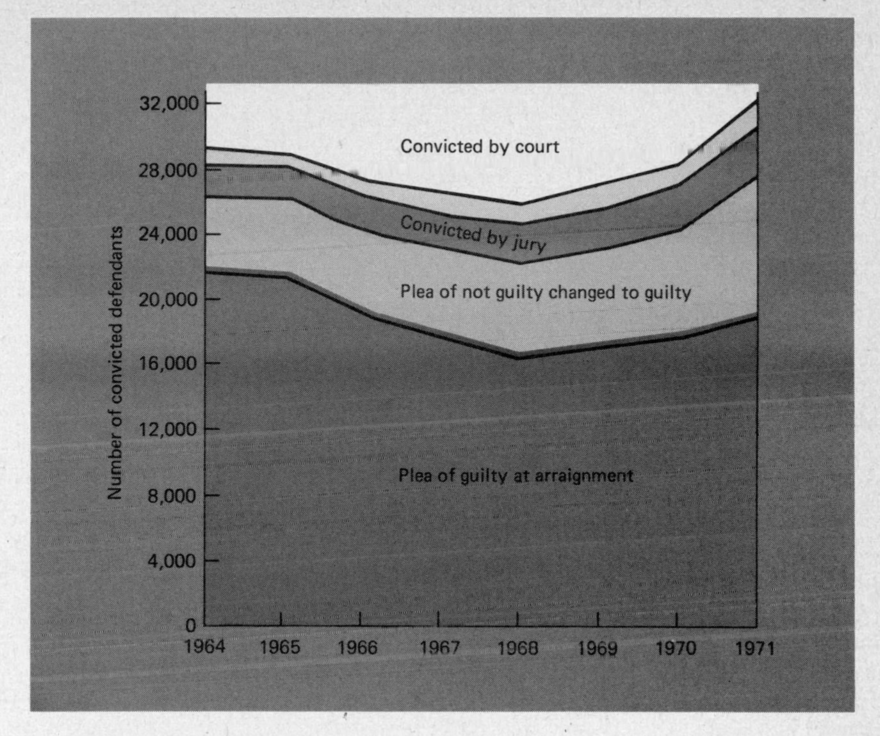

Thus there is always the possibility of losing the case and the conviction if the defendant insists on pleading not guilty and the matter must be settled at trial. Any factors that weaken the prosecutor's ability to prove guilt beyond a reasonable doubt will strengthen the defense attorney's plea bargaining hand. When this happens, the prosecutor is forced to plea bargain to avoid losing the case completely through dismissal or acquittal: "When we have a weak case for any reason, we'll reduce to almost anything rather than lose."[10] The passage of time invariably weakens the prosecutor's case at trial. "Evidence goes stale; witnesses disappear or lose interest; cases pile up; prosecutors are tempted to plea bargain."[11] Prosecutors frequently plea bargain domestic disturbances because of the difficulty in proving that an illegal act was committed, the absence of tangible evidence, and the victim's "precipitation" to the alleged offense.[12]

A principal (and perhaps unavoidable) factor responsible for the prosecutor's need to plea bargain is that police arrests are based on probable cause, a much lower standard of proof than that required for conviction in court.[13] Critics of the police sometimes call this source of plea bargaining "bad arrests." Anticipating legal difficulties in achieving a trial conviction because of such arrests, prosecutors may "overcharge" the defendant to strengthen their hands during plea bargaining by creating legally weak or repetitive charges that they can offer to drop.[14] Other factors that may contribute to legally weak cases include illegal arrests, illegally obtained evidence, problems in arranging for citizens to make identifications and appear at trial, defense-requested continuances, the reluctance of witnesses and victims to cooperate with the prosecutor and to testify, and the failure of a jury to believe a witness.

Effectiveness

Finally, plea bargaining gives the prosecutor the incentive to achieve an easy victory, and it is a sign of prosecutorial effectiveness: bartered guilty pleas count as convictions and expose the accused to certain criminal penalties, no matter how mild. In the long run, and as a stepping-stone to higher political office, prosecutors must maintain a respectable conviction "batting average" in order to maintain their reputation, job, and career options. Convictions are what prosecutors expect from themselves, what the community requires of the office, and what society demands from the criminal justice system. Together, these factors make it necessary for the prosecutor to rely on plea bargaining as standard operating procedure.

Defense Counsel's Incentive to Plea Bargain

The interests of clients

The incentives for defense counsel to plea bargain and to advise clients to accept a deal involve professional responsibilities, economic considerations, and efficiency. Defense counsel have a professional duty to protect the interests of their clients, even those who are in fact guilty. If it is possible to have their clients acquitted or dismissed legally, they are obligated to try to do so. However, in more than 80 percent of the cases the defendants are in fact legally guilty of the crimes charged. Defense counsel recognizes that going to trial would ordinarily serve no useful purpose for the client and would probably result only in a harsher sentence.[15] Given the legal strength of the prosecutor's case and the fruitlessness of trial as a standard defense procedure, there is usually nothing to be gained by insisting on settling the matter in court. In the typical case, then, it is the defendant's sentence rather than guilt or innocence that is the major issue to be resolved. This professional concern was enunciated by Martin Erdmann, who in a 25-year career with the New York City Legal Aid Society was involved in defending thousands of indigents. Erdmann admitted freely that 98 percent of his clients were guilty but emphasized that his duty was to get them acquitted or to obtain the lightest sentence possible through plea bargaining.[16]

Economic advantages

Defense counsel must also take into account economic considerations. Professionalism notwithstanding, assigned counsel and privately hired lawyers earn their living by representing criminal clients. In a profession in which time is money, the less time an attorney spends on a case, the more profitable it will be. Since cases in which there is a guilty plea require a minimum investment of defense resources, assigned counsel and private attorneys can at the same time maximize their fees and satisfy their clients by advising them to plead guilty in exchange for the lighter sentence. By staying out of courtrooms, private attorneys stay in business. "I can't make any money if I spend my time in a courtroom. I make mine on the telephone or in the prosecutor's office" (plea bargaining).[17]

Caseload pressures

Finally, public defenders in urban areas have large caseloads that make them as sensitive to administrative efficiency as the prosecutor is. To retain their jobs and to advance in the organization may depend on their ability to plea bargain successfully a substantial portion of their caseload. The operation of many public defender programs is geared to plea bargaining quotas that, if not met, could cause chaos in the agency. While plea bargaining may begin at any time, in felony cases it often gets under way following indictment, when the defendant has been arraigned and has pled not guilty and the case has been scheduled for trial within a few months. By that time, both sides are aware of the legal strength of the state's case and, with the prospect of a trial hanging over their heads, have the greatest incentive to negotiate a guilty plea.

The Plea Bargaining Process

Operational considerations

In plea bargaining, prosecutor and defense counsel consider several questions: To what lesser charge (carrying lighter punishment) can this offense be reduced in order to arrange for a guilty plea? How many of the multiple counts will be dropped and which ones? What disposition will the prosecutor recommend at sentencing? The plea bargaining process, then, focuses on the sentencing deal the prosecutor will be willing to make in return for a guilty plea. Ordinarily, the prosecutor seeks to charge the defendant formally with the most serious offense below the top count. At the same time, defense counsel seeks to obtain the least serious criminal charge and the most favorable sentencing recommendation, without being so demanding that the prosecutor will refuse to plea bargain.[18]

A proposed reduced charge will usually be rejected by the prosecutor if it grossly minimizes the severity of the actual crime, violates the criminal law in principle, or is demoralizing to the professional administration of criminal justice. For example, a murder charge would not be reduced to battery because homicide is punishable by life in prison while battery carries a sentence of just six months in jail. However, the prosecutor may be prepared to reduce murder to manslaughter or even to assault with a deadly weapon as part of the plea bargain (see Close-up 10.1). Burglary, which normally carries a penalty of no more than two years in a state prison, may be routinely reduced to petty theft, whose sentence usually ranges from 6 to 12 months in the county jail. The major consideration in

Close-up 10.1 PLEA BARGAINING IN HOMICIDE CASES: GETTING AWAY WITH MURDER?[a]

Huge court backlogs, delays in providing speedy trial, insufficient personnel, the unpredictability of juries and legally weak cases in New York's criminal court system are responsible for the prosecution routinely plea bargaining murder charges into lesser offenses and more lenient sentences: eight out of every ten defendants accused of the top homicide count who plead guilty to a reduced charge are placed on probation to receive a prison term of under ten years.

The two main reasons that district attorneys plea bargain with killers are volume of cases and fear of acquittal if the defendants go to trial on the original indictment. There are over 1,600 killings a year in New York City. To convict a single killer through trial proceedings can easily involve 20 percent of available staff for more than four months. Even with a substantial commitment of resources, the prospect of killers being acquitted is all too real. The most rigorous evidence is required to secure a conviction, evidence which may be ruled inadmissible at trial. Such cases often depend upon eyewitness testimony within a context of fast-moving and highly emotional events. Juries are not skilled in evaluating testimony or applying the rules of evidence in complex homicide cases. And they are reluctant to make decisions that could result in life imprisonment or death sentences.

The prosecutor's willingness to accept a changed plea of not guilty to murder in exchange for a guilty plea to manslaughter is also related to the jury's consideration of "victim precipitation." Seventy percent of the suspects arrested for murder in 1973 in New York City were related to the victim or knew each other. Juries usually look beyond the letter of the written law and technical evidence to the prior relationship between victim and defendant. Given a prior personal relationship, the jury may acquit or convict on the reduced crime of manslaughter, the same offense to which most original murder charges are plea bargained. "The DA's are not stupid and when they get an offer of a plea that is similar to what they would probably get if they go to trial, then they'll take the plea."[b]

The preceding factors account for the fact that out of 1,600 homicides committed in New York City in 1973, only 74 defendants went to trial, and that a ten-year sentence for cold blooded murder —with possible release on parole in three years—is an optimistic state goal that is considered a "bargain" for public safety.

[a] Robert Daley, "How Killers Get Away With Murder," *New York* magazine, July 22, 1974, pp. 35–40.
[b] *New York Times,* January 27, 1975, p. 1.

plea bargaining is the difference in sentence outcome between the original and the reduced charges, and the reasonableness of that difference.[19]

In *Brady* v. *United States* in 1970 the Supreme Court telegraphed its approval of plea bargaining: "We cannot hold that it is unconstitutional for the State to extend a benefit to a defendant who in turn extends a substantial benefit [the guilty plea] to the state."[20] A year later the Court squarely confronted and placed its stamp of legitimacy on the practice of plea bargaining in *Santobello* v. *New York*.[21] Santobello, indicted on two felony counts, initially pleaded not guilty to both. In plea negotiations with Santobello's lawyer, the assistant DA agreed to accept a guilty plea to a reduced charge that was punishable by a maximum one-year prison term and to abstain from making any sentencing recommendation to the court. The defendant accordingly changed his plea to guilty to the reduced charge—with the understanding that the prosecution would keep its promise to make no specific sentencing recommendation.

Santobello v. *New York* (1971)

By the time the sentencing hearing was held, however, a different prosecutor had taken over the case, and he was unaware of the promise made by his predecessor to remain silent at sentencing. The new prosecutor urged the court to impose the maximum one-year term, which the court did. The Supreme Court agreed with the defendant that he was the victim of "broken promises" by the state. "When a [guilty] plea rests in any significant degree on a promise or agreement of the prosecutor, so that it can be said to be part of the inducement or consideration, such promise must be fulfilled." Accordingly, the Supreme Court directed the state court either to have Santobello resentenced by a different judge, without a recommendation from the prosecution, or to allow the guilty plea to be withdrawn.

Blackledge v. *Allison* (1977)

The Supreme Court confirmed its disapproval of broken promises in *Blackledge* v. *Allison* in 1977.[22] Allison was informed that his case had been "discussed" with the prosecutor and the judge and that his sentence would not exceed ten years in return for his pleading guilty. Accordingly, the prosecutor dropped the multiple counts and Allison pleaded guilty to attempted safe robbery, which carried a sentence of ten years to life. In keeping with the procedure used in North Carolina to determine that guilty pleas are voluntary, the trial court at arraignment asked Allison if anyone "made any promises or threat to you to influence you to plead guilty in this case?" Although the court was apparently aware of the plea bargain, it accepted Allison's answer of no and his guilty plea—and sentenced him to 17 to 21 years. In reviewing the case, the Supreme Court found that Allison's guilty plea had been induced by an unkept promise to limit his punishment to ten years in prison. In view of the state's failure to live up to its side of the plea bargain, the Supreme Court ruled that Allison was entitled to be resentenced or to withdraw his guilty plea.

The Supreme Court rulings on broken promises do not deprive the courts of their role as final arbiter in sentencing, nor do they bind judges

nas Palermo, sentenced to up 5 years for a $4 million jewel bery, was released after one because of "broken prom-' related to his bargained y plea

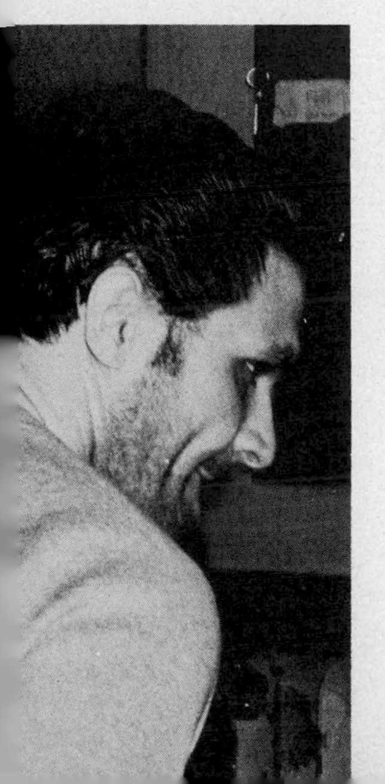

to compliance with the prosecutor's recommendations. So long as the prosecutor does not *guarantee* the defendant a particular outcome, the court continues to exercise a free hand at sentencing. So long as prosecutors comply with their agreement to *recommend* leniency or to take other action on a defendant's behalf, the court may disregard such recommendations and rely entirely on its own discretion at sentencing. Under these conditions, the imposition of a harsher sentence than that anticipated by the defendant would be entirely proper because the prosecution acted in good faith, did not misrepresent its authority, and fulfilled its side of the plea bargain—there were no broken promises.

Bordenkircher v. *Hayes* (1978)

In *Bordenkircher* v. *Hayes* in 1978, the Supreme Court strengthened the state's plea bargaining hand by allowing prosecutors to threaten defendants with reindictment on a more serious charge if they refuse to plead guilty to the initial charge and demand a trial.[23] Hayes was indicted by a Kentucky grand jury for forgery, which carried a ten-year maximum term, and the prosecutor offered to recommend a five-year sentence if Hayes pled guilty. The prosecutor also warned Hayes (who had two prior felony convictions) that if he insisted on a trial, the prosecutor would seek a second indictment against him as a habitual offender, which would subject Hayes to a mandatory life sentence. When Hayes refused to plea bargain to the original charge, the prosecutor carried out his threat, and Hayes was given a life term. A federal Court of Appeals concluded that the sentence violated Hayes' rights because defendants are protected from the type of prosecutorial vindictiveness directed against him, but the Supreme Court held otherwise. In a decision that turned on the free-market character of plea bargaining and the breadth of prosecutorial discretion, the Supreme Court found no Fourteenth Amendment due process violation in implementing the threat of reindictment under the circumstances present in *Hayes*. An essential aspect of the plea bargaining negotiations in *Hayes* was the fact that the prosecutor had explicitly notified Hayes of the consequences of not pleading guilty to forgery: there was no hidden agenda, subterfuge, or broken promises on the part of the state. While recognizing that it is illegal to punish a person for exercising a constitutional right, the Court declared that in the give-and-take of plea bargaining "there is no such element of punishment or retaliation so long as the accused is free to accept or reject the prosecutor's offer."

The courts' interest in plea bargaining

Plea bargaining allows state misdemeanor and felony courts to control overcrowded dockets, to reduce court backlog, to provide speedy justice, to avoid having their decisions questioned through appeals, and to save the taxpayers some of the high costs of judicial administration.[24] Judges are administratively overburdened, under pressure to dispose of large numbers of cases efficiently, and must cooperate with correctional authorities in relieving overcrowded jails and prisons. The "due process revolution" has diverted a major share of judicial resources to pretrial motions and posttrial proceedings.[25] The number of judicial personnel has not kept pace with the burgeoning workload caused by the explosion of new criminal laws. The result of these factors is that "there is today an administrative crisis of major proportions in our criminal courts."[26]

The Case for Plea Bargaining

Plea bargaining holds a number of distinct advantages for the criminal justice system.

1. Without extensive reliance on plea bargaining to dispose of cases, the entire administration of criminal justice would collapse. The funds, facilities, and personnel required to handle even a modest increase in trial dispositions will not be forthcoming in the foreseeable future.[27]
2. Plea bargaining preserves the unique value of trial by screening out cases in which there is no substantial issue of the defendant's guilt. The presumption of innocence at trial is meaningful so long as trial is the exceptional means of disposing of cases.
3. The adversary system is not restricted to the trial stage. There is a considerable adversary character—challenge, conflict, argument, and assertion of opposing positions and interests—to the pretrial plea bargaining process.[28] It is only when this less formal adversary forum cannot resolve the matter that the more formal adversary procedure of public trial need be invoked.
4. Plea bargaining allows the state to secure convictions in "bad arrest" and other legally weak cases, where offenders would otherwise be freed.
5. Plea bargaining is a necessary discretionary tool for tempering the letter of the law with individualized justice, responding to statutory overcriminalization, and mitigating the stigma associated with such conviction labels as sex offender and drug addict.[29] At one time in Michigan, the charge of breaking and entering at night carried a mandatory 15-year prison term while daytime entry had a 5-year maximum.[30] Should the prosecutor allow the difference of a few hours in when the crime occurred to make a difference of ten years to the offender?
6. The prosecution acts on behalf of the people rather than on behalf of the victim. While in any individual case the victim may feel aggrieved by it, plea bargaining in the overall picture acts in the best interests of society by facilitating convictions and taking serious offenders off the streets.
7. In some cases, such as rape, plea bargaining makes it unnecessary for the victim to suffer the humiliation and trauma associated with testifying at a public trial.

8. Unlike trial convictions, which are frequently appealed, convictions that result from guilty pleas automatically relinquish the right to appeal. Plea bargaining thus makes for finality in the disposition of criminal cases—and thereby increases deterrence.

The Case Against Plea Bargaining

Plea bargaining also has certain disadvantages in its role in the criminal justice system.

1. Research has shown that plea bargaining is demoralizing to the police and a source of friction with the prosecutor, who relies on the police as an investigative arm in cases that go to trial.[31]
2. Because of plea bargaining, defendants who should be confined longer are not, and defendants who should be released are incarcerated.[32] Offenders are disposed of undeterred, untreated, and with minimal regard for public safety.
3. Plea bargaining undermines the basic premise of "crime and punishment" that is the foundation of the criminal law and the criminal justice system.
4. Plea bargaining is an infringement on the court's responsibility and discretion in sentencing.
5. Plea bargaining makes the preparation of presentence reports by probation officers a wasted effort because the sentence has already been negotiated. When presentence reports are ignored, sentences have minimal correctional or punitive value. Indeed, the information disclosed in the presentence report may cast doubt on the wisdom of the plea bargain (which the state must nevertheless exercise in good faith to avoid the accusation of broken promises).
6. Bargain-basement justice is always more of a bargain for the defendant than it is for the state and the public. If the defendant does not consider a plea bargain offer generous enough, he or she can simply hold out for trial, knowing that the legal strength of the state's case will be weakened further by time.
7. Plea bargaining provides the opportunity for defense counsel (and prosecutors) to place their own economic and occupational needs ahead of the fundamental interests of their clients.[33]
8. Plea bargaining may result in convicting the innocent by virtue of the prosecutor's making an offer that the defendant cannot refuse, such as the chance to avoid the death penalty or life imprisonment.[34] In *Alford* v. *North Carolina* in 1969, the Supreme Court approved the principle that even innocent defendants could plead guilty to obtain a lighter sentence.[35]
9. Unfair sentences can be imposed on defendants who plead not guilty

and are convicted at trial. The sentence may reflect a punishment for not having entered a bartered guilty plea, thereby penalizing the defendant for exercising the constitutional right to trial.[36]

10. Plea bargaining is dominated entirely by practical considerations that should be irrelevant to the disposition of criminal cases. Such factors neglect justice, penological considerations, the plight of the victim, and the needs of society.[37,38]
11. By sidestepping formal court proceedings and due process, plea bargaining allows unconstitutional police practices to go unchecked and even to contribute to successful prosecution.[39]
12. Unwarranted variation in prison terms attributable to plea bargaining is a source of inmate riots. "No sentence should [ever] be imposed simply because it may result in less expensive, faster resolution of the case."[40] Bartered guilty pleas are not evidence of genuine repentence for crime, the acceptance of the legitimacy of punishment, or the potential for rehabilitation.
13. Plea bargaining is destructive of the adversary method of justice, which is the cornerstone of the criminal justice system in a free society. The adversary system breaks down in plea bargaining because the prosecutor and defense counsel (and the judge) act in their own best interests rather than on behalf of the people, the defendant, and justice.
14. Defendants do not have equal opportunity to negotiate guilty pleas or to refuse offers. The confinement of detainees places inherent pressures on indigent defendants to plea bargain in the hope of receiving probation, a sentence to time served, or a sentence to a better institution.
15. Plea bargaining may be responsible for the practice of prosecutorial overcharging: charging defendants with multiple counts that are virtually indistinguishable from one another and that would probably be dismissed or result in concurrent sentences, and charging defendants with crimes impossible to prove in court.
16. Defendants themselves are dissatisfied with the way they are treated by the system under plea bargaining as Close-up 10.2 indicates.

The core of plea bargaining criticism is that there seems to be something in it for everyone—defendant, prosecutor, defense counsel, courts, jail and prison administrators—except the victim, society, and the police. There is something deeply disturbing about a criminal justice system in which lawyers avoid the due process model like the plague,[41] in which the outcome of cases depends on the personal interests and administrative convenience of the practitioners, and in which sentences are unrelated to the crimes committed or to the defendant's genuine correctional needs. Even the plea bargainers are dissatisfied with the situation, recite its shortcomings, and acknowledge the need to overhaul the practice.

Close-up 10.2 ASSEMBLY LINE JUSTICE[a]

In the conveyor belt known as "assembly line justice," the end product is the mass production of guilty pleas. The conveyor belt begins when the indigent accused is given a public defender or assigned counsel suspected of being inferior to privately retained attorneys. It is also moved along by hired lawyers who thrive on guilty pleas at the expense of their clients. Assembly line justice ends with consummated plea bargains perceived by defendants as having been forced down their throats by public defenders who sell-out to the prosecution. Casper's study in Connecticut revealed that defendants represented by public defenders felt they had been treated as cases or files in an assembly line geared to grinding a guilty plea out of them.

The defendants Casper interviewed felt betrayed by the public defenders, whom they did not view as "their" lawyers. The defenders spent very little time with their clients and were thought to have nothing to gain by fighting hard for them since "he gets his money either way." The first thing the public defenders said to the dedefendants was, "I can get you . . . if you plead guilty." The defenders were viewed as agents working for the government because of their amicable relations with the prosecutor and their status as state employees. As a public defender in Chicago candidly observed, "It's our court. It's like a family. Me, the prosecutors, the judges, we're all friends. I drink with the prosecutors. I give the judge a Christmas present, he gives me a Christmas present."[b] The proximity of the defender's office to the prosecutor's further reinforced the perceived "double agent" role of public defenders,[c] many of whom aspire to become prosecutors.

Casper's defendants felt they were told what to do by the defender and forced to plea bargain without being consulted, involved in the negotiations, or advised of the consequences and alternatives to pleading guilty—defense tactics which are frowned upon by the American Bar Association. In the haste to generate bartered guilty pleas and to keep the assembly line moving, the defendants were treated as objects, lost in the shuffle, and left out of the very process which sealed their fate. Such treatment made them skeptical of their lawyers' desire and ability to give them their undivided allegiance and do a first-class job on their behalf. Casper believes that the defendants' perception of "rough justice" has a deleterious effect on the rehabilitation of offenders. Defendants who lose faith in the ideal of justice, feel manipulated, and become alienated through their encounters with criminal justice representatives purportedly cannot learn to respect and observe the law.

[a] *Source:* Jonathan D. Casper, "Did You Have a Lawyer When You Went to Court?" *Yale Review of Law and Social Action,* Spring 1971, pp. 4–9; Casper, "Criminal Justice from the Bottom," *Intellect,* February 1975, p. 317
[b] "Justice on Trial," *Newsweek,* March 8, 1971, p. 17.
[c] Abraham S. Blumberg, "The Practice of Law as Confidence Game: Organizational Cooptation of a Profession," *Law and Society Review,* June 1967, pp. 15–39; Blumberg, "Lawyers with Convictions," *Transaction,* July-August 1967, pp. 18–24.

RESTRUCTURING THE PLEA BARGAINING PROCESS

Plea bargaining in the states is typically an informal, off-the-record process controlled by the prosecutor and defense counsel, without direct participation by the court or the accused. There are no formal rules to guide the lawyers in arriving at a plea bargain that is mutually satisfactory, fair to the defendant, acceptable to the court, and in the best interests of the public. Neither lawyer has much knowledge of the legal strength of the other's case, and thus both must bargain in the dark. The plea bargain is negotiated without the presentence reports that are essential to informed sentencing and the protection of society. Plea bargaining occurs almost at random, whenever and wherever opposing counsel happen to talk to each other; discussions may begin as early as the arrest itself and continue after the trial has begun. No record is kept of the concessions or promises made by the prosecutor, the conditions that may have been attached to the state's offer, the defendant's acceptance of the deal, or the court's willingness to abide by the prosecutor's recommendation. Plea bargaining today is invisible, without procedural regularity, needlessly prolonged, inefficiently administered, and unjust.

Impracticality of abolishing plea bargaining

The President's Crime Commission, the American Bar Association, and other organizations, aware of the defects in plea bargaining as it is currently and commonly administered, have urged the restructuring of the plea bargaining process. And in one of its most controversial and extreme recommendations, the Standards and Goals Commission urged the complete abolition of plea bargaining by 1978.[42] Few others have taken such an uncompromising position, recognizing instead that "so long as it remains impossible for our criminal system to permit every defendant his right to a jury trial, some inducements for the surrender of that right will be necessary. At the moment, plea bargaining is our only vehicle for granting such inducements."[43] Total abolition of plea bargaining in jurisdictions with a substantial criminal caseload would seem to be impractical. However, restructuring the plea bargaining process to control prosecutorial discretion and its abuses, to eliminate the major defects of plea bargaining, and to make plea bargaining fairer are realistic immediate goals. The principal approaches to reforming plea bargaining are (1) the pretrial conference and (2) various methods for limiting the scope of the sentence reductions that the prosecutor may offer.

The Pretrial Conference

Some jurisdictions have introduced the *pretrial conference,* a formal, one-stop plea bargaining session. The mechanics of the pretrial conference vary from one jurisdiction to another, but the model has certain characteristic features.

The pretrial conference is an administrative procedure that allows plea bargaining discussions to take place and to be concluded at a single formal, on-the-record conference that is held as early as possible (ordinarily, soon after indictment or arraignment). While the prosecutor and defense counsel may have discussed the case beforehand, the intensive, final, and binding plea bargaining negotiations are reserved for the conference.

Presence of the defendant

In addition to the two attorneys, the defendant and a judge may be present at the pretrial conference. Defendants are present so that they will have a sense of participation and control over their fate, though the actual negotiations are left to their lawyer. The defendant's availability also avoids delays in communicating the prosecutor's offer, waiting for it to be accepted, and returning to prolonged haggling if it is not. Presumably, the defendant's own observation of the negotiations and defense counsel's efforts on his or her behalf will dispel any skepticism concerning assembly-line justice and the propriety of the sentence.

Mutual disclosure

The pretrial conference can serve as a forum in which prosecutor and defense counsel voluntarily reveal the legal strength of their respective cases. The assumption behind the full mutual disclosure of information is that the sooner each side knows the other's cards, the sooner they can proceed to negotiate a plea bargain in good faith—or realize that the case will have to be settled at trial and dispense with plea bargaining efforts. By leveling with each other at the pretrial conference, the lawyers resolve any uncertainty surrounding the need to prepare for trial. The filing of time-consuming motions and continuances is avoided. Nothing disclosed at the conference is likely to affect the outcome of cases that subsequently go to trial. And, being aware of the legal strength of the state's case, the defendant may be less demanding about the sentence reduction for pleading guilty.

Participation of the court

The critical and most controversial feature of the pretrial conference is the court's participation. The judge assumes a prominent role at the conference because the fact that plea bargaining is a veritable sentencing procedure requires that it be supervised by the court. Participating judges would order presentence reports in advance of the conference, and these would be given to the prosecutor and defense counsel. The presentence report would serve as a focal point and provide guidelines for the plea discussions. The information and sentencing recommendation contained in the presentence report would allow the court to decide whether to accept the prosecutor's recommendation for leniency or to accept a guilty plea to reduced charges carrying nominal punishment.

Reliance on the presentence report would assure that the negotiated sentence was related to the offender's actual criminal conduct, penological considerations, and public safety. Information about the defendant not otherwise known to the prosecutor would become available on a regular basis, thereby strengthening the state's position in the conference. The participating judge would also protect the legal rights of the defendant by refusing to permit illegally obtained evidence to influence plea negotiations, discouraging "overcharging" by the prosecutor, not allowing the attorneys to tempt defendants who maintain their innocence into pleading guilty, and informing the accused of the sentencing alternatives that would exist under a bartered plea and following a conviction at trial.

By virtue of judicial involvement in formal plea bargaining at the pretrial conference, guilty pleas would be voluntary and informed and would have a factual basis, broken promises would be avoided, and abuses of prosecutorial discretion would be curtailed. The presence of the judge and the presentence report would in part compensate for the superior investigative resources of the prosecutor, whose personal relationship with defense counsel would no longer enter into the plea bargain. The pretrial conference, with its special emphasis on the presentence report and the court's role, is expected to make plea bargaining more rigorous, consistent, principled, swifter, and more oriented to society's needs.

Objections to the court's participation

The chief objections to the participation of the court in the pretrial conference involve the improprieties of any form of direct judicial intervention in plea discussions and the determination of guilt and sentence before conviction. In effect, the judge's role at the conference is to act alternately as an advocate and as an adversary of the defendant. These aspects of the judge's involvement in the pretrial conference may tarnish the impartiality, integrity, and image of the court. The judge's mere presence and personal contact with the defendant at the conference (ordinarily held in the court's chambers) may be inherently coercive: it may induce innocent defendants to plead guilty, it may render any guilty plea involuntary, and it may raise doubts about the fairness even of a trial that is held before a different judge. "No matter how well motivated the judge may be, the accused is subjected to a subtle but powerful influence."[44]

For these reasons, the American Bar Association and the President's Crime Commission strongly opposed any judicial participation in plea discussions and opted for the method used in the federal system, the om-

The omnibus hearing

nibus hearing.[45,46] The *omnibus hearing* in federal cases is a formal, one-stop plea bargaining conference that is restricted to the participation of the prosecutor and defense counsel, incorporates full mutual disclosure, and bars the court from direct participation in formulating the plea bargain.[47] The plea bargain agreement reached by the attorneys at the omnibus hearing is submitted to the court for tentative ratification or rejection, pending the court's inspection of a presentence report that is prepared at that time. At the state level, there is considerable variation in whether judges participate in the pretrial conference and in their willingness to take on-the-record responsibility for the proposed plea bargain. In courts such as those in Brooklyn and Chicago, judges participate actively in the pretrial conference negotiations.[48] In New Haven, judges follow the omnibus procedure of accepting (ratifying) or rejecting the agreement that emerges from the pretrial conference.[49]

Alaska Attorney General Gross banned plea bargaining in 1975. The result was stiffer sentences and only a slight increase in the proportion of defendants requesting jury trials

Finally, there is the question of the impact that judicial participation in pretrial conferences will have on the "price" and the number of guilty pleas. Like the prosecutors, the courts have many administrative pressures that encourage them to go all out to secure guilty pleas. Might they not, then, offer sentencing deals that are even more generous than those suggested by the prosecutor when confronted by aggressive defendants? Could participating judges afford to protect the public interest in plea bargaining if it meant adding to court backlog and jury trials? There is conflicting evidence on whether the pretrial conference and the court's participation in it can expedite the disposition of criminal cases, conserve judicial resources, and increase the number of guilty pleas.[50,51,52]

Restricting the Scope of Plea Bargaining

The only direct, reliable method for protecting more adequately the public's interest in crime control and justice is to limit sentence concessions and restrict the scope of plea bargaining. Various approaches have been taken and proposed for putting a lid on plea bargaining.

Prohibition of plea bargaining

In rare instances, district attorneys may impose a ban on plea bargaining in their jurisdiction. The district attorney of Ulster County, New York, began a no plea bargaining policy on January 1, 1975, the only one to do so among the state's 61 chief prosecutors.[53] The New Jersey Supreme Court prohibited plea bargaining in misdemeanor cases, a step that other states may have to take to contain the plea bargaining explosion caused by the *Argersinger* decision.[54] In August 1975, Alaska became the first and so far the only state to abolish plea bargaining entirely, in an effort to overcome "too lenient sentences . . . often handed out as a result of judges being bound by arrangements between attorneys."[55] In contrast, there is the development of uniform charging standards, to be voluntarily adopted by prosecutors and to serve as a guide for more responsible plea bargaining—the approach taken in California.[56]

In some jurisdictions, plea bargaining has been virtually eliminated in cases of serious violators, repeat offenders, career criminals, and professionals. When the district attorney adopted this policy in 1974, the use of plea bargaining in Orleans Parish, Louisiana, dropped from 75 percent to 9 percent.[57] Plea bargaining may be eliminated for selected offenses, such as rape, kidnapping, and certain types of homicide. In New York, plea bargaining has been abolished by statute in cases involving the killing of on-duty police officers and prison guards. The New York drug law barred plea bargaining for persons charged with possessing or selling the smallest amount of narcotics, thereby exposing them to a mandatory one-year prison term upon conviction. Similarly, Boston's mandatory one-year-term gun law also involved plea bargaining restrictions. And the district attorneys in Portland, Oregon, and Seattle, Washington, eliminated plea bargaining for certain major crimes.[58]

Selective abolition of plea bargaining

When plea bargaining hinges on the prosecutor's sentencing recommendation, such recommendations may be based on formulated standards that are oriented toward deterrence, adequate punishment, and uniform penalties. The Seattle County prosecutor developed sentencing recommendations that stressed the seriousness of the crime, the offender's previous criminal record, and consistency in application rather than "the perceived needs or character of the individual defendant," that is, individualized justice and treatment. His standardized sentencing recommendations are available to defense attorneys and the public, and any exceptions to them must be explained in writing and approved.[59]

Standards for sentencing recommendations

Limits may be placed on the extent of charge reductions permissible during plea bargaining. Manhattan's district attorney issued guidelines restricting charge reductions to one punishment level (from a Class A misdemeanor to a Class B misdemeanor, from a Class B felony to a Class C felony, from armed robbery to unarmed robbery). Exceptions to the one-level charge reduction have to be explained in writing and are permitted only if there are specified mitigating factors in the case: the defendant is a first offender, very young, or very old; the victim is forgiving; the defendant aids the authorities in solving other crimes. On the other hand, charge reductions can be prohibited if there are sufficient aggravating factors in the case: the crime has a severe impact on the community; the defendant is a total stranger to the victim; serious injuries were sustained; the victim was a defenseless elderly person who was assaulted or raped; a loaded gun was used in connection with the crime. The district attorney's guidelines also require that multiple counts be charged against defendants arrested for committing separate crimes at different times and places—thereby discontinuing the "sales special" of two crimes for the price of one![60]

Guidelines for the reduction of charges

More stringent plea bargains that result in stiff sentences can be achieved by the prosecutor's taking advantage of existing habitual offender statutes. Habitual offender statutes authorize the court to impose

Invoking habitual offender statutes

greatly increased prison sentences on defendants with prior convictions. For example, a burglary defendant in New Orleans having no previous felony conviction may be sentenced to 0–9 years in the penitentiary, at the court's discretion. But under Louisiana's Multiple Offender Act, the same burglar with one prior felony conviction may be sentenced to 3–18 years. And if the guilty plea to burglary is a fourth felony conviction, the defendant could receive 20 years to life.[61] Prosecutors have often ignored habitual offender statutes in order to give defendants a break at sentencing. But prosecutors like those in New Orleans, Manhattan, and Seattle, who are more intent on giving society a break, are beginning to file separate habitual offender charges whenever possible.

The success of any effort to restrict plea bargaining depends on the number of additional not guilty pleas that such reform measures will produce, and especially on the number of jury trials generated and the capacity of the system to meet the increased demands for trial disposition. If restricting plea bargaining were to reduce the current nationwide proportion of guilty pleas in serious crimes from 90 percent to "only" 80 percent, the trial load would double, require substantial increases in personnel and facilities, and perhaps necessitate court reorganization. Alaska was able to abolish plea bargaining only because the state had a relative abundance of judges, a unified court structure, and a statewide court administrator.[62]

In jurisdictions with a sizeable criminal caseload, restricting plea bargaining has led to fewer guilty pleas and consequently more trial dispositions.[63] In the small community of Kingston, New York, the elimination of plea bargaining resulted in an eightfold increase in cases disposed of through trial, and it meant that the prosecutor's staff worked around the clock.[64] Even in the well-financed federal system, which does not have the caseload problems of the states, a decrease in plea bargaining occasioned by the Criminal Justice Act resulted in an increase in trial dispositions.[65]

SPEEDY TRIAL

> In all criminal prosecutions, the accused shall enjoy the right to a speedy and public trial. . . . (Sixth Amendment)

The Sixth Amendment to the Constitution guarantees the right to a "speedy trial." Speedy trial is the defendant's right to have and the state's obligation to insure a prompt resolution of the criminal action taken against the accused: to move rapidly to dismiss or acquit legally innocent defendants, and to convict and sentence guilty offenders. Neither bailed nor detained defendants should be subjected to the stigma and the hardships associated with prosecution for a longer period of time than is absolutely necessary. To minimize the opportunity for governmental abuse, to avoid the consequences of having unresolved criminal charges hanging over accused citizens' heads indefinitely, and out of fundamental fairness to every defendant, the right to speedy trial permits all defendants to demand their day in court in order to obtain prompt disposition of their cases.

Obstacles to speedy trial

The major obstacles to achieving speedy trial are the unnecessary delays that occur within the pretrial period. This is the interval between arrest or initial court appearance and the plea-taking arraignment or the beginning of trial proper; it is the same period for which bail and pretrial detention are critical issues. Before the Supreme Court's principal ruling on speedy trial in 1972 and the passage of the Speedy Trial Act of 1974, however, implementation of the right to and recognition of the need for a speedy trial went largely unnoticed.

In practice, the time consumed in processing defendants up to the time of their trial comes closer to assuring a slow trial than it does a speedy trial. In New Orleans, many defendants waited as long as two years from accusation to trial.[66] The average time between arrest and trial for "major" cases in Philadelphia in 1971 was about six months.[67] For cases going to trial in Washington, D.C., the average time between arrest and final disposition is half a year.[68] As of late 1975, 15 percent of all felony indictments in New York State had been pending for over one year.[69] Similar pictures of delay are common in courts throughout the nation, and the average time before trial is on the upswing.[70] The model timetable of the President's Crime Commission recommended 45–55 days and would allow up to three months between arrest and trial for all but the most exceptional felony cases. However, the Standards and Goals Commission recommended a shorter interval between arrest and trial in felony cases (see Figure 10.2). The assembly-line intervals and speedy trial standards offered by the commissions provide a yardstick with which state and local practices can be compared and revised. (The problem of providing speedy trial was also discussed by the American Bar Association in its *Standards Relating to Speedy Trial,* published in May 1967.)

The Supreme Court addressed the issue of speedy trial in *Barker* v. *Wingo* in 1972.[71] Barker and an accomplice were each charged with murder. The accomplice was tried first, the state hoping he would implicate and later testify against Barker. The accomplice was tried five times before he was finally convicted. Meanwhile, Barker spent more than five years waiting to be brought to trial. The state requested and was granted 16 continuances of Barker's trial without opposition.

Barker v. *Wingo* (1972)

The Supreme Court found that Barker had not been denied the right to speedy trial. It held that a defendant's constitutional right to a speedy trial cannot be determined by an inflexible rule or measured in quantitative terms, that it can be determined only by an ad hoc balancing test in which the conduct of the prosecution and that of the defendant are weighed. The factors to be considered in this balancing process include: (1) the length of the delay, (2) the reasons for the delay, (3) whether a defendant "demands" the right to a speedy trial, and (4) how prejudicial to the defendant's case is his being denied a speedy trial. The Supreme Court refused to set hard and fast rules for implementing speedy trial or identifying its denial. It said that to do so would usurp the function of Congress.[72]

The Speedy Trial Act of 1974

Congress met the challenge two years later with the passage of the Speedy Trial Act of 1974. The Speedy Trial Act was the most significant and comprehensive legislative program for implementing speedy trial, for resolving the practical problems surrounding prompt justice, and for controlling crime and career criminals by means of swift punishment.[73] The federal law was largely the result of the efforts of Senator Sam Ervin, Jr., of North Carolina. Taking effect in July 1975, the Speedy Trial Act called for the gradual reduction, over the subsequent four-year period, of the time between arrest or service of a summons and trial. By July 1,

FIGURE 10.2 Recommendation of the Standards and Goals Commission for steps to achieve trial in a felony case within 60 days of arrest. *Source:* National Advisory Commission on Criminal Justice Standards and Goals, The Courts (Washington, D.C.: Government Printing Office, 1973).

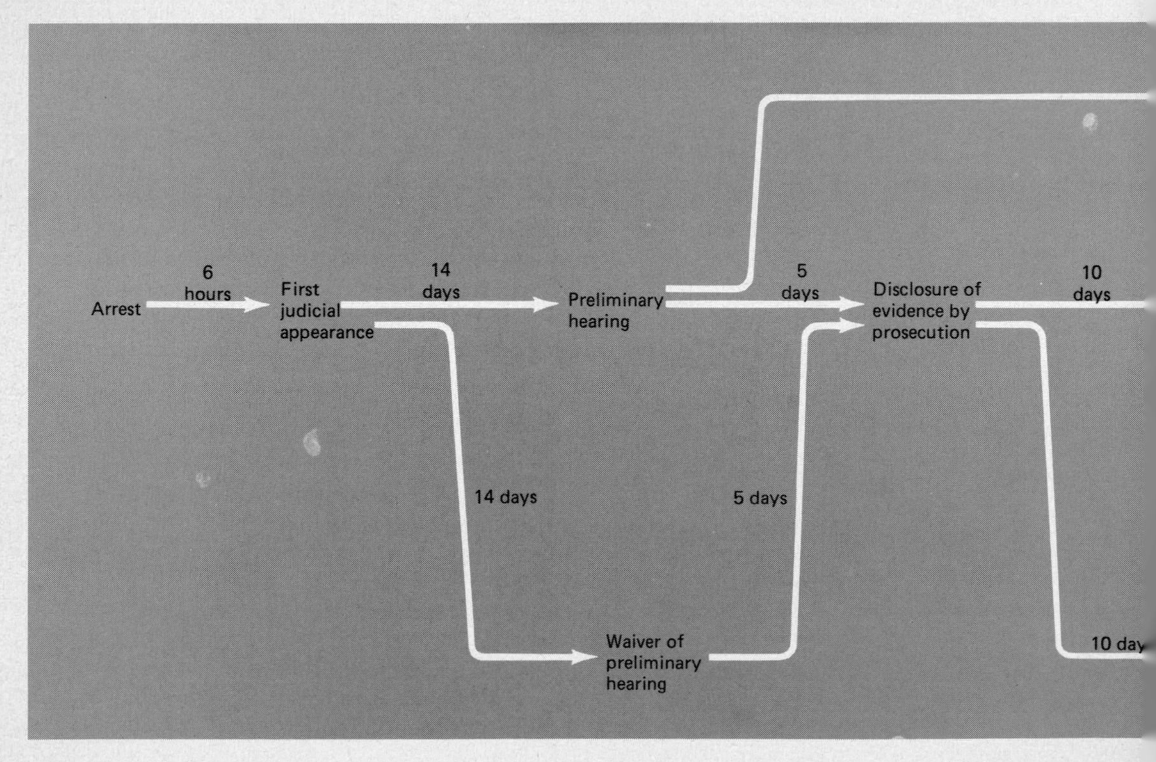

1979, all persons charged with a federal crime were supposed to be brought to trial within 100 days after being arrested or receiving a summons (see Table 10.2). If an indictment or an information is not filed within the required period after arrest or summons, the charges against the defendant are to be dismissed.

The Speedy Trial Act was based on an exhaustive three-year study of the problem. In drafting the legislation, Congress followed the lead of such states as Florida, California, and Arizona; at the same time, the act was an improvement over many state speedy trial provisions.[74] Although the number of federal prosecutions (39,000) is only 2 percent of all defendants prosecuted annually (1.5 million), the Speedy Trial Act also provided a model that the states could voluntarily adopt.[75] To reduce "intolerable delay" in disposing of court cases, for example, New York adopted standards to be achieved in stages beginning October 1, 1975, and ending January 1, 1979, by which time no felony case in New York could be pending for more than six months.

Allowance for necessary delays and continuances

The difficulties in implementing speedy trial involve distinguishing between necessary (reasonable) and unnecessary (unreasonable) pretrial delays and then eliminating the latter. Necessary, justifiable, or reason-

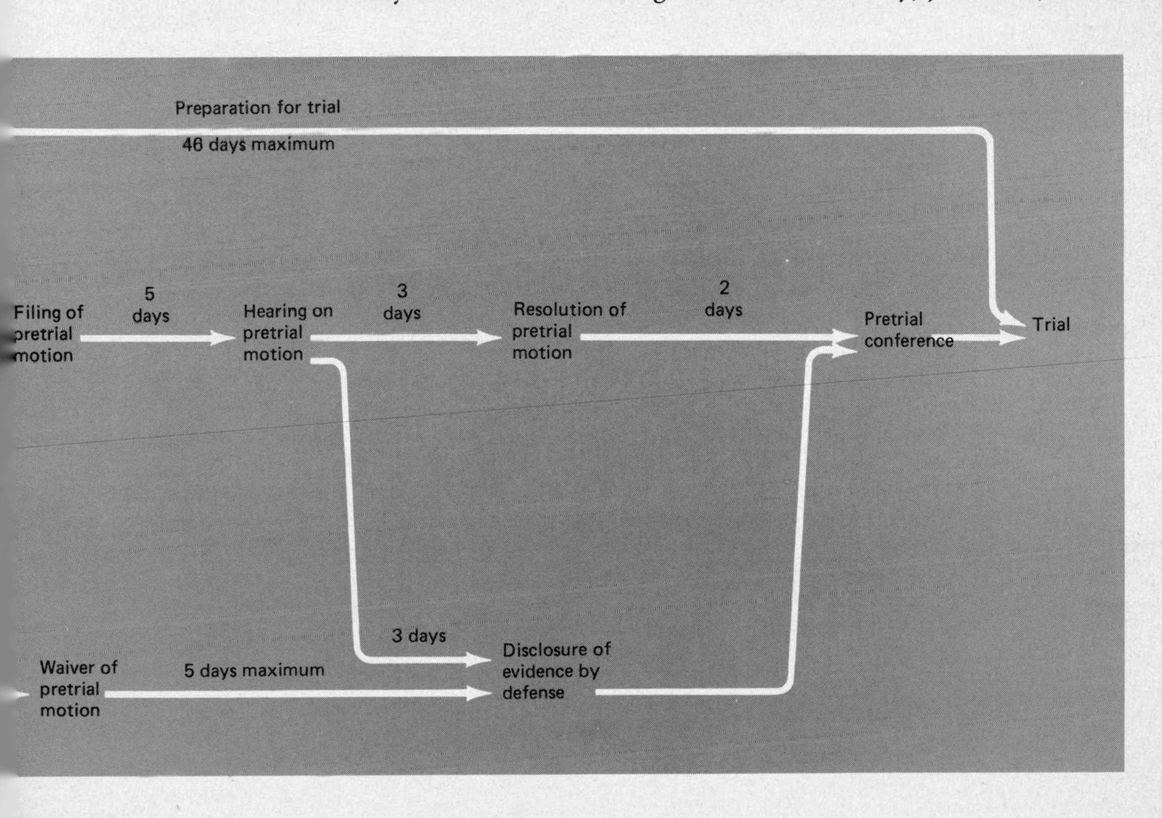

Senator Sam Ervin was largely responsible for the passage of the Speedy Trial Act of 1974

able pretrial delays are not counted as part of the specified interval between arrest and indictment or trial. In computing these intervals, the Speedy Trial Act excludes, for example, delays caused by mental competency hearings, appeals, pretrial discovery and hearing motions, proceedings related to other charges against the defendant, and the unavailability of essential witnesses. The first appellate court interpretation of the Speedy Trial Act was handed down on November 12, 1976; it concerned the time consumed in mental competency hearings and the psychological examination of Sara Jane Moore, who was accused of attempting to kill President Ford on September 22, 1975.[76]

The thrust of the Speedy Trial Act was no longer to allow court congestion (backlog and overload) and unnecessary continuances to interfere with achieving a speedy resolution of the defendant's guilt or innocence. Research has shown that excessive continuances granted by the court are a major cause of pretrial delay.[77] The number of continuances is also closely associated with the outcome of prosecution and trial. One major study of continuances found that the proportion of convictions decreased as the number of continuances increased.[78] To discourage unjustified requests for continuances, the act (1) identified criteria to be used by the court in granting continuances, (2) prohibited continuances due to "lack of diligent preparation or failure to obtain witnesses on the part of the attorney for the Government," (3) provided disciplinary measures against defense counsel who request continuances for the purpose of delaying trial, and (4) required judges to specify, either orally or in writing, their reasons for authorizing continuances.[79]

Dismissal of the charges

After excluding necessary pretrial delay time from the calculation of the period preceding speedy trial, the act provides that if the state does not indict and bring to trial within the specified phased intervals, the charges will be dismissed and the accused released. The penalty to the state and to society for not meeting the Speedy Trial Act standards is the discontinuation of prosecution, the release of probably guilty offenders, and the relinquishment of the automatic right to reinstate prosecution

Table 10.2 Speedy Trial Act Intervals Between Arrest and Trial, by Phases

Period	Arrest or Summons to Indictment	Indictment to Arraignment	Arraignment to Beginning of Trial
7/1/76 to 6/30/77	60 days	10 days	180 days
7/1/77 to 6/30/78	45 days	10 days	120 days
7/1/78 to 6/30/79	35 days	10 days	80 days
7/1/79*	30 days	10 days	60 days

Source: Robert F. Olmert, "The Speedy Trial Act of 1974," *Law Enforcement Bulletin* (November 1975), p. 29.

* The final phase of the act, requiring that defendants be tried within 100 days of arrest, was postponed until 7/1/80 to allow courts more time to reduce their backlog of cases.

later on the same charges. The penalty to the criminal justice system for not complying with the act was intentionally severe; Congress believed that the threat of dismissal was the only way to compel prosecutors, judges, and defense attorneys to come to grips with inefficiency and delaying tactics. For too long, continuances and overload were used by the state as excuses for not implementing speedy trial, for not discovering the real causes of pretrial delay, and for failing to take effective steps to end delay.[80] In *Strunk* v. *United States* in 1973, the Supreme Court ruled that dismissal was the only remedy for defendants deprived of speedy trial, regardless of the apparent guilt of the accused.[81]

Plans to be submitted by the courts were intended to specify the funds, additional personnel, and improvements in prosecutorial and judicial case management that were needed to reduce unnecessary delay. After that, if too many cases are dismissed for failure to provide speedy trial, presumably public reaction and political repercussion will force prosecutors and judges to find ways to comply with the Speedy Trial Act. "The dismissal sanction has the effect of compelling judges and prosecutors to choose between speedy trial or no prosecution whatsoever." Given that choice, the court and its officers will have to become more accountable in their public roles and responsibilities, for their inefficiency and mismanagement. With these prospects in store, the criminal justice system might be receptive to experimenting with new forms of judicial administration or prosecutorial case management in order to comply with speedy trial requirements. Such improvements might include the use of court administrators and selective prosecution case-evaluation systems such as the Major Offense Bureau.

It remains to be seen whether the Speedy Trial Act will accomplish its goals and provide an effective model for the states. The specialized types of criminal cases and the relative absence of severe court backlog and plea bargaining in the federal system increase its chances of success there. The same factors, however, may interfere with the ability of the states to implement speedy trial provisions as rigorous as those of the federal government. Yet California has had a speedy trial statute that incorporates the dismissal sanction for over 100 years, without having to resort to frequent case dismissals. Of 17,000 annual criminal filings in San Diego, a mere three or four are dismissed for lack of speedy trial.[82] The New York State Supreme Court based its recent speedy trial program on the federal model, specifying a six-month goal to be reached in a series of stages to be completed by January 1, 1979.[83]

The prospect of mass dismissals

The most controversial and problematic aspect of the federal and applicable state speedy trial provisions is the possibility of mass dismissals of guilty defendants simply because they were not brought to trial in time. Should that occur, the dismissal sanction would have the unintended effects of penalizing society and reducing the certainty of punishment. Scattered reports from various states illustrate the problems asso-

Close-up 10.3 SHOULD MURDERERS GO FREE BECAUSE THE PROSECUTOR HAS BLUNDERED?[a]

In February 1970 Colette MacDonald and her two daughters, ages 5 and 2, were brutally stabbed to death in their Fort Bragg (N.C.) home. Her husband, Green Beret Dr. Jeffrey MacDonald, claimed that four drug-crazed intruders committed the heinous crime, one of whom allegedly carried a candle while chanting "Acid is groovy. Kill the pigs." Although skeptical of his explanation, the Army declined to prosecute Dr. MacDonald, apparently because of a bungled investigation that resulted in the loss of key evidence. The Justice Department took the case in 1972. But it was not until 1975 that MacDonald was indicted by a federal grand jury and his trial did not begin until July 1979. MacDonald was convicted of the stabbing deaths of his family and sentenced to three consecutive life terms.

In August 1980, however, a federal appellate court reversed MacDonald's conviction on the grounds that he was denied his right to a speedy trial. The court noted that bureaucratic indifference in empanelling a grand jury and the Justice Department's "calloused and lackadaisical attitude" was responsible for at least two years of unnecessary delay. It further emphasized that a nine-year interval between the crime and trial hampered the recollection of defense witnesses, thereby making a fair trial impossible. On learning of the court's decision to dismiss the indictment against the doctor, Mrs. MacDonald's stepfather (who was instrumental in having the case reopened) angrily echoed the controversy surrounding speedy trial: "Are we to let a triple murderer go loose just because he wasn't tried fast enough?"

[a] *Sources: Newsweek,* August 11, 1980, p. 32; *Time,* August 11, 1980, p. 58, *New York Times,* July 31, 1980, pp. 1, 12.

ciated with the dismissal sanction. In early 1971, the Florida Supreme Court directed that persons charged with felonies had to be tried within 180 days, those charged with lesser offenses had to be tried within 90 days, and any defendant who formally requested prompt disposition had to be tried within 60 days—or be set free! Because of large court backlogs in Dade County (Miami), in the first eight months of the ruling more than 100 defendants were released because the state was unable to try them within the speedy trial time limit. In response to criticism from the public as well as the bench concerning the prospect of continued mass dismissals, the Florida speedy trial standards were modified to give the

MacDonald's conviction of ırdering his pregnant wife and o children was overturned on eedy trial grounds. Should so- ty be penalized for the sys- n's inertia?

authorities more time to bring cases to trial.[84] The district attorney of Suffolk County, Massachusetts, expressed concern that if the federal speedy trial provisions were adopted in that state's judicial system, accused killers might have to be returned to the streets untried (see Closeup 10.3). Either that or "in order to prevent the wholesale discharge of alleged criminals the time may be coming when we'll have to confine ourselves to prosecuting only crimes of violence. . . ."[85] And to avoid the prospect of having to dismiss 17 percent (over 5,000 defendants) of the federal cases filed annually, the attorney general asked Congress to increase the time limits in phase four of the Speedy Trial Act.

Speedy trial rules and plea bargaining

Potentially the most disruptive aspect of rigorous speedy trial rules is their effect on the plea bargaining process. Even a slight increase in the percentage of defendants who plead not guilty and demand a jury trial could have paralyzing consequences for the entire criminal justice system. Some informed students and critics of speedy trial requirements believe that it will remove the incentive for defendants to plea bargain at all, and in any event it will strengthen their plea bargaining position. Why should guilty defendants be ready to enter a bartered guilty plea and receive a lighter punishment when by simply waiting it out they have a feasible chance of being dismissed and receiving no punishment at all? And in those cases where the state can meet the speedy trial time standards, what reason is there for defendants to plead guilty rather than demand a jury trial?

Answers to questions such as these and to the impact of speedy trial on plea bargaining and on jury trials will ultimately depend on the psychology of plea bargaining and speculation on how speedy trial regulations might alter that psychology. Evidence that speedy trial rules will not reduce the number of guilty pleas in the federal system has limited relevance for what state prosecutors and courts may expect.[86] Indeed, the prosecutors and judges in Dade County authorized extremely generous plea bargains so that the 5,000 defendants whose speedy trial time was expiring would not be dismissed outright and would not put the state to the time and expense of jury trials.[87]

The architects of the Speedy Trial Act of 1974 anticipated that it might result in fewer bargained guilty pleas and more cases going to trial. To meet these problems, the Act provided for a gradual phasing in of speedy trial requirements, during which time the courts could prepare plans describing the additional resources needed to cope with an increased workload and other changes in operation associated with the act. Liberals and conservatives alike may often oppose the cry for *more* as the solution to the problems besetting the criminal justice system; in the case of speedy trial, however, it is difficult to see how the need for more can be dismissed. More prosecutors, more judges, more courtrooms, more juries, more innovative management techniques such as court executives—more of everything—will be needed in order to avoid taking more instead of less time to dispose of criminal cases.

SUMMARY

Convictions are typically obtained through plea bargaining rather than at trial. The prosecutor's tools for plea bargaining are reducing the charges, dropping multiple counts, and making recommendations at sentencing. There are powerful incentives for the prosecutor, defense counsel, and the courts to rely on plea bargaining, a practice that the Supreme Court explicitly approved, with its condemnation of broken promises, in *Santobello* v. *New York* in 1971. The advantages of plea bargaining are outweighed by its disadvantages—so much so that everyone recognizes the need to do something about the situation. The Standards and Goals Commission proposal to abolish plea bargaining entirely is probably impractical for most jurisdictions. A feasible alternative may be to restructure the plea bargaining process through the pretrial conference, the omnibus hearing, and restrictions on the scope of the plea bargain. In the future, plea bargaining may depend increasingly on developments surrounding the constitutional right to a speedy trial, which itself has significant implications for deterrence and for bail. The Speedy Trial Act of 1974 is a model for implementing speedy trial; however, the effect of the act's dismissal sanction on bringing defendants to trial quickly, on deterrence, and on plea bargaining is problematic.

DISCUSSION QUESTIONS

1. Who stands to gain more through plea bargaining, the prosecutor or defense counsel?
2. What effect could speedy trial rules have on bail, bail reform, and pretrial detention?
3. Do you agree with the Standards and Goals Commission recommendation that plea bargaining should be abolished? Why?
4. What is the policy toward plea bargaining and how is it used in jurisdictions in your state?

Chapter 11

TRIAL

The Adversary Method of Justice

Duncan v. *Louisiana* (1968)

Public Access to Trial

Gannett v. *DePasquale* (1979) / *Richmond* v. *Virginia* (1980)

Selection of the Jury

Exemption from jury service / Sources of the venire
Shortened jury duty / Discrimination by exclusion

Close-up 11.1: Pretrial Publicity, Freedom of the Press, and Gag Orders

Change of venue / Challenges for cause / Peremptory challenges

Scientific Jury Selection: The Joan Little Case

The Beaufort County survey / The Wake County survey / The voir dire / Outcome of the trial / Evaluating scientific jury selection

Six-person Juries

Williams v. *Florida* (1970) / The case for six-person juries / The case against six-person juries / The need for further research

Nonunanimous Verdicts

Johnson v. *Louisiana* (1972) / *Apodaca* v. *Oregon* (1972) / The case against nonunanimous verdicts / The case for nonunanimous verdicts

Videotaped Trials

Taping the testimony of witnesses / Advantages of taped testimony / Taping and editing entire trials / Advantages of videotaped trials / Disadvantages of videotaped trials

Close-up 11.2: Supreme Court Gives Go-Ahead to Televising of Trials

Charging the Jury

Summary

> In all criminal prosecutions the accused shall enjoy the right to a speedy and public trial, by an impartial jury of the State and district wherein the crime shall have been committed. . . . (Sixth Amendment)

The hallmark of the criminal justice system is the jury trial. In some circumstances defendants may choose to have their case tried by a judge sitting alone; that is, they may request a bench trial. But where serious felonies are involved, defendants often stand a better chance of being acquitted or dismissed by exercising their constitutional right to a trial by jury. To what types of cases does the constitutional right to a jury trial apply? How are jurors selected? Would the interests of justice be equally well served by juries of less than 12 persons and by nonunanimous verdicts? Can videotaped trials be introduced without jeopardizing the defendant's right to a fair trial? And do the public and press have a right to attend trials? These are some of the questions to be discussed in this chapter.

THE ADVERSARY METHOD OF JUSTICE

The American system of justice is based on the legal presumption of innocence until proven guilty beyond a reasonable doubt in a court of law. This court contest is founded on the recognition of conflicting interests on the part of the defendant and on the part of society and the state. It is to the obvious advantage of the defendant, even when guilty, to avoid conviction and its consequences. When the defendant is guilty, it is equally necessary that the state secure a conviction. In this sense, the defendant and the state have an antagonistic, opposing, or adversary relationship. The adversary method of justice is based on the belief that the best way to get at the truth while providing fundamental fairness to the defendant is through a legal contest between two competent lawyers in a court of law presided over by a judge who sees that the rules of evidence and the defendant's constitutional rights are observed. The pinnacle of legal formalities in the criminal justice system is the trial, which is grounded in due process, procedural criminal law, and the legal rules of evidence.

Unlike the police and the prosecution, judge and jury have no personal or occupational stake in the outcome of the battle. They act as fair and neutral observers who listen to the arguments and the evidence presented by the prosecutor (speaking for conviction) and by the defense counsel (speaking for acquittal or dismissal). The job of judge and jury is one of fact-finding: to determine, within the guidelines of the law, whether the facts would cause a reasonable person to conclude that the defendant was guilty of the criminal charges. This involves weighing the evidence and deciding whether it meets the standard of proof beyond a reasonable doubt.

In the adjudication of guilt or innocence, the opposing attorneys present the most convincing arguments and evidence to support their respective positions, hoping that the neutral trier of fact (judge or jury) will find in their favor. The opposing attorneys cannot try to win the battle at *any* cost; they must observe the preestablished legal rules of trial. This trial arrangement is considered the most effective way for determining guilt or innocence and assuring justice in the individual case. Defendants in felony cases have the right to trial by jury, the right to counsel, and other protections guaranteed by the Constitution, but defendants can waive their right to counsel and represent themselves (proceed *pro se*).

Trials are rare in misdemeanor cases because of the high proportion of guilty pleas submitted. Rarer still are jury trials in misdemeanor cases. Because of the limited penalties involved, misdemeanants are more often willing to take their chances with a bench trial rather than request a trial by jury. And, in *Duncan* v. *Louisiana* in 1968, the Supreme Court ruled that the constitutional right to jury trial applies only to crimes punishable by incarceration of six months or more.[1] In so deciding, the Court reserved the scarce resources of juries and the protracted proceedings involved in jury trials for serious crimes that justified such an administrative burden on the criminal justice system.

Duncan v. *Louisiana* (1968)

PUBLIC ACCESS TO TRIAL

In many quarters, it had long been assumed that the Sixth Amendment gave the public and press the right to attend criminal trials; but that assumption was shattered by the Supreme Court's 5 to 4 decision in *Gannett* v. *DePasquale* in 1979.[2] The murder case involved a *pre*trial suppression hearing at which defense counsel, concerned about the effect of adverse publicity on a jury, asked the court to exclude the press and public from the proceedings.* The prosecutor did not oppose the request and the judge cleared the courtroom. A reporter covering the case for newspapers published by the Gannett Company later objected to being excluded from the pretrial hearing. The trial judge, however, insisted that the defendant's right to a fair trial outweighed the interest of the press and public to an open hearing, which would pose a "reasonable probability of prejudice to these defendants."

* Defense counsel argued that even if the court ruled the confession and murder weapon inadmissible at trial, prospective jurors would still learn about the incriminating evidence from newspaper accounts if the reporters were allowed to attend the hearing.

Gannett v. *DePasquale* (1979)

In *Gannett,* the Supreme Court ruled that judges can indeed close pretrial hearings to press and public if all of the participants in the litigation agree to do so. Taking as its point of departure the need to minimize prejudicial pretrial publicity, the Court rested its decision on two main observations. (1) The Sixth Amendment guarantee of a public trial is for the exclusive benefit of the defendant alone; that is, the right to a "public" trial does not belong to the public or press but solely to the accused. Accordingly, with the acquiescence of the prosecution and court, a defendant may forego the public aspect of trial without waiving the basic right *to* trial. (2) There is nothing in the Constitution which gives the public or press a separately enforceable, independent right to attend pretrial hearings or trials. Although the historical context of the Sixth Amendment permitted and may have even favored open trials, there is no evidence that the common law *required* pretrial proceedings to be public in nature.

The *Gannett* decision was initially more significant for the confusion it created than for the specific issue it addressed and resolved. The issue was that the public and press had no right under the Sixth Amendment to attend *pre*trial hearings. But the sweeping language in the majority opinion was replete with references to "trials" and seemed to suggest that they too could be closed to the public. In the aftermath of *Gannett,* trial judges throughout the country reacted to its conflicting signals by closing over 200 proceedings—including 30 trials—as well as some sentencing hearings.[3] Shedding their vows of silence, five of the Justices took advantage of speeches and interviews in an attempt to explain the meaning of Gannett, to little avail.[4] Concerned over the possible misreading and unauthorized expansion of *Gannett,* the Supreme Court acted with unusual speed in accepting a case for review that would allow them to clarify the limits of *Gannett* and squarely address the public's right to attend criminal trials.

In response to an unopposed motion by defense counsel, Judge Richard Taylor closed a Hanover County (Va.) murder trial to the public and press, which included two reporters from Richmond Newspapers, Inc. Although there was no demonstrable need for taking such drastic action, Taylor's closure order was upheld by the Virginia Supreme Court, which cited *Gannett* as its authority for finding no reversible error. But in a 7-to-1 decision, *Richmond* v. *Virginia* in 1980,[5] the Supreme Court ruled that the public and press have a strong constitutional right of access to trials derived from the First Amendment, a right that cannot be abridged through closed trials unless there is a compelling reason ("overriding interest") for doing so. After quickly noting that *Gannett* applied only to pretrial hearings and was disposed of on Sixth Amendment grounds, the Court proceeded to elaborate on its rationale for open trials, basing its decision on two major premises. (1) The history of criminal trials in Anglo-American justice and the benefits stemming from unimpeded public attendance support the presumption of open trials. Openness is not

Richmond v. *Virginia* (1980)

dge Taylor (pictured here) osed a murder trial to the public d reporters without compelling use to do so. In *Richmond* v. *Virnia* the Court declared that ese groups have a strong First nendment right to attend trials.

merely an appendage of the adversary system but an integral and indispensable part of the trial process.* (2) The First Amendment, an area not considered in *Gannett*, implicitly prohibits the government from summarily closing criminal trials. Freedom of speech, the press, and assembly —the key provisions of the First Amendment—"can be read as protecting the right of everyone to attend trials so as to give meaning to those explicit guarantees." If citizens were denied access to trial whenever it suited the litigants to do so, then vital aspects of free speech and press could be eviscerated. To be sure, the language of the First Amendment does not spell out the public's right to attend trials. But it is, nonetheless, an unarticulated constitutional safeguard embedded in the amalgam of First Amendment guarantees, just as the right to privacy and the presumption of innocence are unarticulated rights. The First Amendment rights of the public and press are not absolute, of course; but every feasible option to closure should be explored before abridging them.

Richmond did not reverse the *Gannett* decision—pretrial hearings can still be closed without a showing of strict necessity. But it was a clear and gratifying victory for the news media, all the more so because for the first time the Supreme Court had constitutionally protected their right to *gather* information. Up to then, the Court had only recognized the First Amendment right of the press to *disseminate* information already law-

* This position was somewhat of a retreat from their historical assessment of trials in *Gannett*.

fully in its possession, by placing severe restrictions on "gag orders" (discussed later). In effect, the *Richmond* decision proclaimed that closed criminal trials were incompatible with the principles of a democratic society, in which the press is a representative of the people and the nation's watchdog over bureaucratic corruption and complacency. The overtones of *Richmond* may also have the effect of moderating the unfortunate and unexpected consequences of *Gannett:* the courts' readiness to close pretrial hearings when there is no sound reason to conclude that openness would jeopardize the defendant's right to a fair trial. In this regard, the 1980 press guidelines issued by the Judicial Conference of the United States provide that pretrial hearings should take place in open court, unless there are no reasonable alternatives to closure for protecting the defendant's Sixth Amendment rights.[6] Although *Richmond* is only applicable to trials, its broader First Amendment implications may pave the way for gaining access to prisons, police department activities, and confidential records that have traditionally been off-limits to the fourth estate.

SELECTION OF THE JURY

In principle, all of the steps and activities involved in selecting a jury are intended to assure the defendant a fair and impartial trial, as guaranteed by the Constitution. In practice, this is accomplished by empaneling a jury that is representative of the community where the crime occurred and whose members are not prejudiced for or against the defendant. Most important, the jury is supposed to be chosen by a process that does not systematically exclude any legally recognized (cognizable) groups of citizens on the basis of race, sex, or ethnic origin. Three steps in the process of jury selection are critical in obtaining a fair trial.

The Venire. It is the responsibility of the designated official or agency to maintain and provide lists of the names of citizens from which jurors will ultimately be chosen. The master list, which constitutes the population of potential jurors, is the *venire*. Eligibility requirements for jury service usually include citizenship, the ability to read and write English, not having been convicted of a serious felony, and age restrictions.

Exemption from jury service

Certain groups are automatically exempted from jury service because of their occupation: dentists, doctors, nurses, police officers, lawyers, pharmacists, legislators, the clergy, firepeople, some members of the press, educators. In an effort to make venires as representative of the community as possible, Florida and other states have reduced the number of exempted occupations to lawyers, dentists, and morticians. The American Bar Association Commission on Standards of Judicial Administration has recommended that no citizen should be automatically exempted from jury service without having to show cause.* The ABA group also urged that persons convicted of crime who had served their sentences should be eligible for jury duty.[7] Individuals may be granted exemptions if jury service would place an undue hardship on them (the disabled or aged, mothers with young children, those who might lose their job). Until the practice was declared unconstitutional by the Supreme Court in 1975, Louisiana barred women from serving on juries unless they specifically requested, in writing, to do so.

Sources of the venire

Any source that is authorized by statute may be used to compile the master list of eligible jurors, including telephone directories, lists of utility customers, tax rolls, and motor vehicle registration records. The most commonly used venire source are voter registration lists. Obtaining a fair trial may depend on whether the venire contains a representative cross section of the community's citizens. Thus the best venire sources would be social security records, census files, and income tax returns, but these are generally not available because of legal restrictions. Voter registration lists are readily available, offer the widest convenient selection of names, and do not systematically exclude recognized social groups per se. It is also assumed that unregistered voters are not interested in participating in government or recognizing their civic duty to be available for jury service. For these reasons, voter registration lists remain the standard venire source in the states and are used by all federal courts.[8] When properly utilized, voter registration lists are adequate to the constitutional task of providing the citizens for an impartial jury.

The Jury Pool. A random selection of names from the venire is made to identify those citizens who will actually be summoned to begin their tour of jury service, which may last two to four weeks or more. The summoned juror candidates constitute the *jury pool.* They may be sent questionnaires and/or be interviewed to confirm their eligibility, to consider their individual requests for exemptions, and to determine their availability for the length of service involved. Because jury service often requires up to 30 days of a citizen's time (and may drag out to several months in complex or controversial trials), the summoned candidates may seek to be excused from jury duty. Nationwide the average juror fee is $10 per day, but it may be as little as $3 in some states, and it usually does not match the federal juror fee of $20 per day. While the statutes of most states prohibit the firing of employees who are absent due to jury service, few employers are required to pay employees for the time lost. Thus jury service may entail financial sacrifices in some cases.[9]

Shortened jury duty

Some areas are experimenting with ways to reduce the obstacles to jury

* As discussed in Close-up 7.2, the Supreme Court adopted this position in *Duren* v. *Missouri* in 1979 with regard to women serving on juries.

duty in the hope of making juries more representative. In 1975, Wayne County (Detroit), Michigan, replaced its minimum 30-day jury tour period with a "one day, one trial" jury system. Under the program, prospective jurors were required to appear for only one day in the jury pool. If they were not chosen for jury duty that day, they were dismissed. If they were chosen, they were required to serve for the duration of a single trial (an average of three days). The new system increased the number of citizens accepted for jury duty, allowed more trials to be held, and saved the county $72,835 in six months.[10] In 1975, Monroe County (Rochester), New York, began using a telephone-alert program that left persons summoned for jury duty free to continue their normal activities, provided they could be reached by phone and could arrive at the courthouse within 30 minutes.[11] For each day that the jury pool member was not called, the county saved the $12 juror fee and transportation expenses, and this amounted to a $64,800 saving for the year.

The size of the jury pool depends on the estimated trial needs of the courts, the size of the jurisdiction, the ability to gauge accurately juror utilization, and other practical considerations. The jury commissioner in Erie County, New York, maintains a jury pool of 115,000, which is about 10 percent of the county's population.[12] Because of poor planning, jury pools are often much larger than the number of jurors actually needed, with the result that some members may spend most of their time in the courthouse jury assembly room waiting to be called for a trial.[13]

Discrimination by exclusion

The manner of establishing the jury pool is a potential source of bias in obtaining a representative jury and a fair trial. In March 1977, a New York City judge dismissed bribery charges against a policeman because "the underrepresentation of women in the venire and in the master pool is the result of systematic and purposeful discrimination against women."[14] In New Haven, the lawyer for three members of the Black Liberation Army charged with a bank holdup and a shootout with the police tried to stop the upcoming trial because the 455 jury pool questionnaires disclosed only nine black citizens and four Spanish-speaking citizens.[15] The conviction of two black men for rape was overturned by the Arkansas Supreme Court on the grounds that the county in which they were tried systematically excluded blacks from juries.[16] The bribery conviction of an alleged Mafia figure in New Jersey was overturned because the jury selection process excluded residents of the community where the crime occurred.[17]

It is permissible to completely exclude community residents from juries only when their inclusion would violate the defendant's constitutional right to an impartial jury and a fair trial. This situation typically occurs when extensive pretrial publicity has been given to a case in the community where the crime was committed, or when virtually all members of the community are obviously hostile to the defendant. Under these conditions, defense counsel may request a *change of venue,* the holding of the

Change of venue

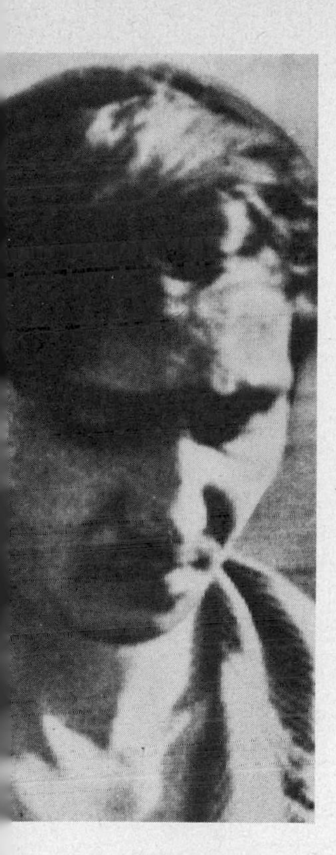

:onnection with the mass-mur- trial of Erwin Simants (pic- ed), the Supreme Court ruled t the court's gag order vio- d the First Amendment guar- ee of free speech

Close-up 11.1 PRETRIAL PUBLICITY, FREEDOM OF THE PRESS, AND GAG ORDERS

Erwin Simants, an unemployed handyman with an IQ of 75, was arrested on October 19, 1975, for murdering six persons in Sutherland, Nebraska (population 840). One of the murder victims, a 10-year-old girl, was raped before being killed. Three days later, both the prosecution and defense counsel asked the county court to restrict press coverage and the dissemination of information about the case. The court did so by issuing a "gag order" that prohibited the publication of any evidence incriminating the defendant. The court's concern was that such publicity might impinge on the defendant's right to a fair trial.

In taking this action, the judge may have been influenced by the famous pretrial publicity case of Dr. Sam Sheppard, who was convicted of murdering his wife in 1954. In 1966, Sheppard's lawyer convinced the Supreme Court that the amount and the nature of the publicity before and during the trial had prejudiced the jury, and the conviction was reversed. Gag orders were virtually unknown prior to the outcome of the Sheppard case.[a]

In the clash between the First Amendment guarantee of free speech and the Sixth Amendment right to a fair trial in the Simants case, the Supreme Court decided, in *Nebraska Press Association* v. *Stuart* in 1976, that the First Amendment came first and that the gag order was improper.[b] The Nebraska court had only speculated that the publicity might jeopardize Simants' right to a fair trial. Even if it would have, gag orders are an inappropriate remedy because they are "essentially unworkable." Before resorting to a gag order and chilling the First Amendment, other less drastic measures should have been employed to curtail the possibly harmful effects of pretrial publicity—such as change of venue, rigorous questioning of prospective jurors, and sequestering the jury.[c]

[a] "Conflict Over Gags," *Time,* May 3, 1976, p. 44.
[b] *Nebraska Press Association* v. *Stuart,* No. 75-817.
[c] "Pretrial Publicity: *Nebraska Press Association* v. *Stuart,*" *Journal of Criminal Law and Criminology,* (December 1976), pp. 430–436; Fred W. Friendly, "A Crime and Its Aftershock," *New York Times Magazine,* March 21, 1976, pp. 16ff.

trial in a different jurisdiction, where there has been less pretrial publicity or the residents are not prejudiced against the defendant. It is difficult to eliminate entirely the effects of pretrial publicity on jurors because freedom of the press is a revered constitutional right that the Supreme Court has protected (see Close-up 11.1).

The Voir Dire. The final step in the jury composition procedure and the one by which candidates from the jury pool become actual trial jurors is the *voir dire* examination: the questioning of individual prospective jurors by the prosecutor, the defense attorney, and sometimes the judge, in order to determine their fitness to serve as jurors in the trial in question. Pool members waiting in the jury room are called at random when it is time to empanel a jury for a specific trial (see Figure 11.1). Although no more than 12 persons will be needed to reach a verdict, as many as 30 names of prospective jurors—the panel—may be chosen from a revolving drum in order that 12 to 14 jurors who are acceptable to the state and to defense counsel may be chosen.[18] In some states, 14 jurors are empaneled instead of 12; the extra two serve as alternate jurors who sit through the trial and are available to take the place of regular jury members who may become ill, have to withdraw, or are disqualified while the trial is in process. In principle, the voir dire ("to speak the truth") is concerned solely with eliminating jurors who are not impartial or are otherwise unable to give the defendant a fair trial. This is the strictly constitutional purpose of voir dire; however, it is also used by the opposing attorneys as an opportunity to choose jurors who would be most favorable to their own side.

Challenges for cause

The tools used by the prosecutor and defense counsel to remove unacceptable jurors from the jury are *challenges for cause* and *peremptory challenges*. In challenging for cause, the lawyers must explain to the court their reasons for wanting a juror excused. Typically, challenges for cause

Selection of the members of a jury is made during the voir dire examination of potential jurors

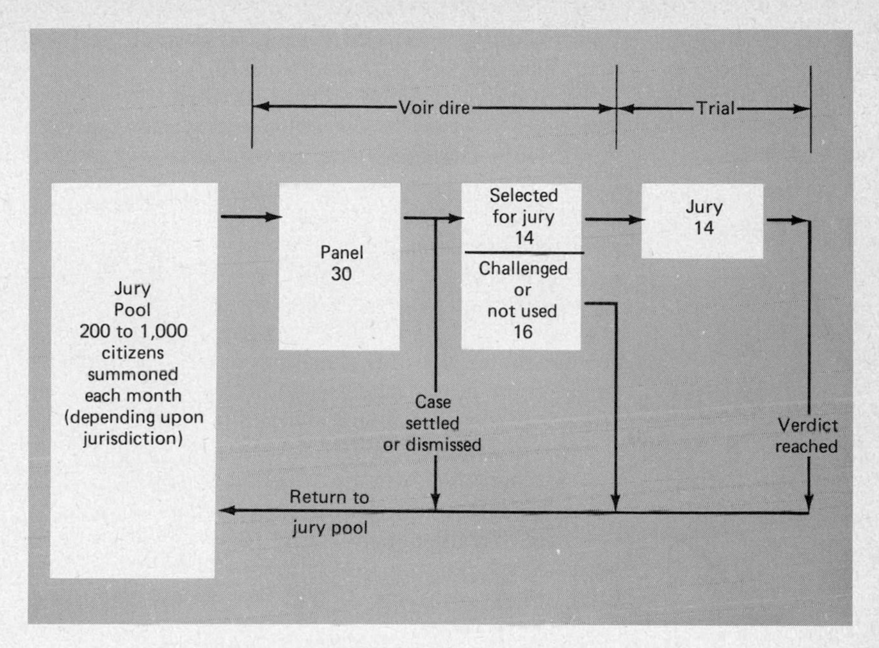

GURE 11.1 Selecting the mbers of a jury from the jury ol.

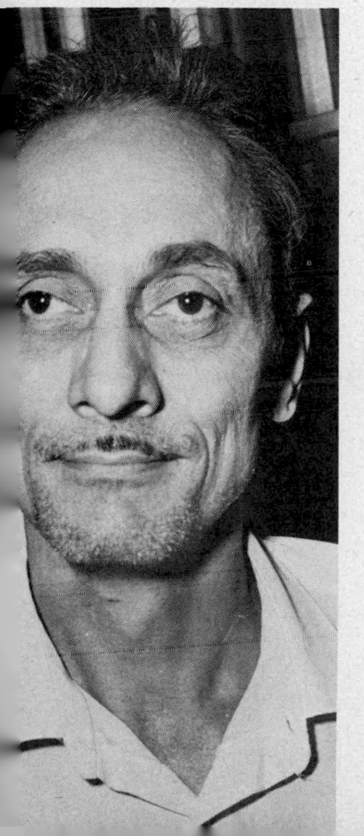

death sentence imposed on iam Witherspoon was reversed 968 because persons with con- ntious or religious scruples inst capital punishment had n automatically excluded from jury

allege that prospective jurors have prejudged the case, would be prejudiced against a minority group defendant, would not accept the presumption of innocence doctrine, could not reach an objective verdict in a death penalty case because of personal opposition to capital punishment, would infer guilt by the defendant's refusal to take the stand, and so on. Virtually any reason for a juror's not being impartial in judging the defendant is a basis for challenging for cause.

The decision whether or not to remove jurors for the reasons stated in the challenge is vested in the court. Judges ordinarily accommodate the lawyers' challenges for cause, unless it appears that they are being used to delay the trial or they are without foundation. Because there is usually no limit to the number of challenges for cause that both lawyers can make, in complex and controversial cases (especially "political" trials) the voir dire may take several days or even weeks. For example, 76 prospective jurors were questioned over nine days in order to select a 12-person jury in the trial of William and Emily Harris, members of the self-styled Symbionese Liberation Army, who were accused, along with Patricia Hearst, of assault, robbery, and kidnapping.[19] In the longest jury selection in California history, it took 17 weeks to pick a jury in the trial of the San Quentin Six: some 1,800 jurors were questioned during voir dire.[20] Challenges for cause that are overruled by the trial judge may be used as a basis for appealing a conviction. The problems of prolonged voir dire and overruled challenges in the state courts are largely eliminated in the federal courts, where most judges conduct the entire voir dire examination themselves.[21]

Peremptory challenges

Peremptory challenges differ from challenges for cause in that no reason need be given to the court for requesting the dismissal of a juror. Peremptory challenges are automatically granted by the court, but the number of peremptory challenges available to both sides is limited by statute or court rule. The defense is usually given a larger number of peremptory challenges than the prosecution.[22] Commonly, defense counsel may have the right to eight to ten peremptory challenges, and the prosecutor six to eight.[23] Peremptory challenges are used when either lawyer may have a hunch that a juror is biased but cannot offer the court convincing reasons for that hunch, or when either lawyer simply wishes to eliminate jurors who are not as sympathetic to the defendant or to the state as they would like. Jurors who are challenged and excused return to the jury pool room, where they wait to be called for service on another trial—when they will go through the voir dire examination again. In exceptional circumstances, defense counsel may take advantage of the voir dire to challenge the entire jury pool and the process by which juries are selected, claiming constitutional violation of a "body truly representative of the community" on the basis of sex, race, or age composition.[24,25]

Scientific Jury Selection: The Joan Little Case

On August 27, 1974, Joan Little, a 20-year-old black woman inmate in the Beaufort County Jail in North Carolina, killed the 62-year-old white night jailor by stabbing him 11 times with an icepick, and fled. Ms. Little had been in the Beaufort County Jail for 81 days while awaiting appeal of her conviction on a burglary charge. (On January 15, 1974, she and her younger brother were arrested for stealing $850 from two mobile homes. The brother got a suspended sentence through plea bargaining; she received a 7–10 year prison term. Unable to post the $15,000 bond for release on bail, she was detained in the Beaufort County Jail.[26])

Joan Little was acquitted of murder after scientific jury selection methods were used to find unbiased jurors

Eight nights after the killing and her escape, Ms. Little surrendered to the state law enforcement authorities. She maintained that the jailor had forced her to have oral sex with him while threatening her with an icepick. When the jailor allegedly dropped the weapon in the heat of passion, she used it to kill him in self-defense and then fled for her life. There was evidence to support her account of the incident: the jailor's shoes had been found outside the cell door, he was naked from the waist down when his body was discovered, and there was semen on his leg. And a week before the homicide, Joan had complained to her mother about "harassment" by the jailors.

Nevertheless, Joan Little was indicted for first-degree murder, a crime that carried a mandatory death penalty in a state that led the nation in sentencing convicts to death. If convicted of murder one, Ms. Little would join 83 other persons awaiting execution on death row.[27] At trial, Joan Little's defense against the charge of first-degree murder would be self-defense against rape. The prosecutor would contend that Joan used sex to lure the jailor into her cell in the middle of the night in order to escape from jail. The crucial question was whether it was possible to select an impartial jury from among the residents of the small, tightly knit, conservative rural Southern community of Beaufort County. Defense counsel used "scientific" jury selection methods to establish that it was not to obtain a change of venue, and to select a jury in another jurisdiction.

The Beaufort County survey

A Ph.D. candidate in psychology at North Carolina State University, aided by Dr. Richard Christie, a social psychologist at Columbia University, conducted a $39,000 public opinion survey among residents in 24 counties in the Beaufort area. Seventy interviewers asked residents about their attitudes toward race and justice, in a scientific effort to uncover racial prejudice.[28] They found that prejudice was especially high in the Beaufort community and that most people had already decided that Joan Little was guilty. In checking the venire lists, the researchers also discovered that blacks, women, and young persons were greatly underrepresented in the jury pool. As a result of these findings and expert testimony on the harmful effects of pretrial publicity on the defendant, the court granted a change of venue, moving the trial to Wake County. In the state capital of Raleigh, 100 miles from the scene of the "crime," it would presumably be possible to select an impartial jury, and Ms. Little's lawyers would have another opportunity to employ scientific jury selection methods in her defense.

The Wake County survey

A $12,500 survey of the Wake County population was made to determine whether the 300-member jury pool (selected from the voter registration lists) to be used in the Little trial was representative of the entire community, and to construct a psychological profile of jurors who would be sympathetic to the defendant. Twenty interviewers asked 954 residents about their income, occupation, political affiliation, reading habits, and attitudes toward capital punishment, law enforcement officers, blacks, and rape victims. The results disclosed that the race, sex, and income composition of the jury pool was a true cross section of the community. Meanwhile, Dr. Christie used a computer to correlate the demographic characteristics of the survey sample with trial-related attitudes, in order to come up with a picture of the "friendly" juror, that is, jurors who would be impartial or favorable for defense purposes.

The voir dire

By putting the same survey questions to prospective jurors at voir dire, defense counsel hoped to remove jurors who were prejudiced and to retain jurors who were sympathetic to Ms. Little.[29] "Do you think male jailors take advantage of female prisoners? Do you agree that most women who are raped may have encouraged the attack? Do you think that Richard Nixon was treated unfairly during Watergate? What magazines do you subscribe to?"[30] During the ten days of voir dire, the defense attorneys examined almost 150 prospective jurors with questions such as these, in order to detect anything that might affect a juror's vote and impartiality in the case. The prosecution successfully challenged for cause several jurors who said their opposition to the death penalty would prevent them from returning a first-degree murder conviction regardless of the evidence. The first six jurors who were accepted expressed reservations about capital punishment, but they were not flatly opposed to it, and they said they would not let the punishment affect their judgment of the evidence.[31]

The prosecutor began by trying to disqualify for cause all prospective black jurors. Midway through voir dire, he changed his strategy to one of excluding young black jurors, citizens who might easily identify with Joan Little and be determined to find her not guilty no matter how incriminating the evidence. Using the community survey, the defense tried to restrict on the jury the number of elderly white men with large families, those who might be inclined to convict because of their demographic resemblance to the victim. By the time a jury was finally empaneled, the prosecutor had used eight of the allotted nine peremptory challenges to excuse black jurors.[32] The empaneled jury consisted of six blacks and six whites, most of whom were middle-aged or elderly and were registered Democrats.

Outcome of the trial

At the conclusion of the five-week trial and just before the jury retired to reach a verdict, the judge reduced the charge from first-degree murder to second-degree murder and manslaughter, because the state had failed to establish premeditation to kill. The reduced charge removed the threat of the death penalty, but conviction for second-degree murder carried a sentence of 30 years to life. On August 15, 1975, after deliberating for 78 minutes, the "scientifically" selected jury acquitted Joan Little because the circumstantial evidence in the case was inadequate to prove guilt beyond a reasonable doubt. Chief defense counsel maintained that the scientific methods used to obtain a change of venue from Beaufort, to confirm the representativeness of the jury pool in Raleigh, and to choose individual jurors during voir dire were responsible for the acquittal. However, the price of justice was steep: $325,000, much of it contributed by the Southern Poverty Law Center to pay for an eight-member defense team, social science experts, and field surveys.

Evaluating scientific jury selection

The critics of scientific jury selection charge that it represents sophisticated jury tampering, seeks to identify jurors who are not simply impartial but partial to the defendant, replaces trial by jury with "trial by social scientists," and discriminates against the ordinary criminal defendant who cannot even afford the cost of a lawyer, let alone that of consultants and surveys. The advocates of scientific jury selection emphasize that it is only a tool for making more informed decisions about who is fit to be a juror, for detecting prejudice that would not come out in the normal course of voir dire questioning, and for implementing the constitutional guarantee of a fair trial by an impartial jury. Scientific jury selection matters most in cases where the personalities and attitudes of the jurors are more likely to determine the outcome of the defendant's fate than is the evidence presented at trial. "If the evidence against the defendant is very strong or very weak, it isn't going to matter who is on the jury. If the evidence is close, then scientific jury selection could make the difference."[33] Whenever there are sound reasons to believe that a defendant would be denied a fair trial by virtue of its locale, pretrial publicity, the method of drawing the jury pool, or the identity of the individual jurors, then scientific jury selection is an appropriate tool for responding to the challenge of guaranteeing fair trials in a free society.

SIX-PERSON JURIES

The Constitution makes no mention of the size of the jury or whether unanimous verdicts are necessary for conviction. At common law, jury size came to be fixed at 12, but this is believed to have been more a matter of historical accident than anything else. In a dramatic break with tradition, the Supreme Court, in *Williams* v. *Florida* in 1970, took a step that many liberals feared might ultimately lead to the abolition of the jury in criminal cases:[34] it approved the principle of six-person juries.* Williams had been convicted of robbery by a six-person jury (as provided by Florida law in all but capital cases) and sentenced to life imprisonment. The Supreme Court tersely disposed of the issue of whether a 12-person jury is an indispensable feature of the Sixth Amendment. "The question in this case then is whether the constitutional guarantee of a trial by 'jury' necessarily requires trial by exactly 12 persons, rather than some lesser number—in this case six. We hold that the 12-man panel is not a necessary ingredient of 'trial by jury' and that [the state's] refusal to impanel more than the six members provided for by Florida law did not violate petitioner's Sixth Amendment rights as applied to the States through the Fourteenth."

Williams v. *Florida* (1970)

At the time of the decision, some states had authorized six-person juries in misdemeanor cases or for petty offenses that carried penalties of less than one year. But only four states, in addition to Florida, used juries of less than 12 persons for felonies punishable by more than one year of incarceration.[36] In Virginia, for example, the courts had long operated under a system that required 12 persons for a felony trial but only five persons in misdemeanor cases. Similarly, New York required a jury of

* In *Ballew* v. *Georgia* in 1978, the Supreme Court ruled that six is the minimum number of jurors required in criminal trials.[35]

only six persons in misdemeanor cases carrying a maximum one-year sentence.[37]

The Court's decision in *Williams* v. *Florida* sparked a trend toward smaller juries: by the mid 1970s, 31 states allowed smaller than 12-person juries in at least some criminal cases.[38] Oregon amended its constitution in 1972 to provide for six-person juries in all criminal cases except capital crimes;[39] Connecticut introduced six-person juries in all but death penalty cases in 1973.[40]

The case for six-person juries

Proponents of six-person juries contend that they will save time by making it easier to select a jury, to try the case, to obtain convictions, and to avoid hung juries. According to this position, efficiency would be realized through the summoning of smaller jury pools, expedited trials, shorter voir dires, less time-consuming deliberations, savings in juror fees, and better juror utilization. Using six-person juries in New York, for example, would save the state 40 percent of the $5 million a year it spends on juries.[41]

A special advantage of six-person juries is that they should reduce the number of hung juries,[42] the situations in which a single juror or a few jurors holding out for acquittal (or conviction) can deadlock a jury, rendering it powerless to reach a unanimous verdict and requiring retrial, or perhaps resulting in the defendant's release if the prosecution decides to drop the charges. Six-person juries can be expected to result in fewer hung juries because the smaller the jury size, the less likely it will contain jurors who disagree with the majority.[43]

Six-person juries will also result in more convictions, for two reasons. First, so long as a unanimous vote is necessary to convict, it is obviously easier for the prosecutor to convince six persons than 12 that the defendant is guilty. Second, since most 12-person hung juries favor conviction[44] and six-person juries contain fewer dissenters, more convictions will result from smaller juries.

The case against six-person juries

Liberals strongly criticized the Supreme Court's endorsement of six-person juries on the grounds that "minijuries" offered a false promise of economy and that they would result in less representative juries and unfair trials and would fundamentally change the way that jurors function during deliberations, to the detriment of the defendant and the search for the truth. The most serious objection to six-person juries is that they reduce the opportunity for minority group representation, and in so doing weaken the very foundation of the jury system. The essential purpose of the jury—to interpose the collective conscience of the entire community between the defendant and the power of the state—is thwarted by six-person juries. Even a jury of 12 is too small to reflect all community views and segments of society, but "the smaller the size of the jury, the less frequently it even approaches community representation."[45] It has been demonstrated statistically, for example, that out of every 100 twelve-member juries, 72 will have at least one minority group juror. But out of every 100 six-person juries, only 47 will include minority representation.[46] The presence of a single minority juror may be needed to inhibit overtly prejudicial statements during deliberations, as the Harrisburg Seven defense team recognized in their desire to empanel at least one Catholic in the trial of Father Philip Berrigan and his codefendants. Judging matters of intent, consent, and victim precipitation may require a knowledge of different cultures and alternate lifestyles that minority-member jurors are more likely to possess.

Critics of the six-person jury also point out that traditional reliance on 12-person juries may have been less rooted in historical accident than is supposed. There is reason to believe that 12 persons is the optimal group size for achieving broadly based community representation and effective decision making.[47] The decisions of 12-person juries are better informed, fairer, less prejudiced, and closer to the truth than the decisions of six-person juries. Smaller juries are more easily swayed by the radical, irresponsible, or biased position of a single aggressive juror bent on imposing his or her own judgment on the group. Because six-person juries are more homogeneous and substantially smaller, the amount of actual deliberation—discussion, sharing of different viewpoints, constructive give-and-take—is greatly curtailed.[48] The proper manner of reaching a verdict of guilt beyond a reasonable doubt involves genuine communication during deliberation. By suppressing juror interaction and exploration of the defendant's guilt or innocence, however, six-person juries make it more likely that the juror's personality or prejudice, the pretrial publicity, and events occurring at trial that should be disregarded will influence the verdict. In using the yardstick of the reasonable person, the collective judgment of 12 people should be more reasonable than that of six.[49]

Six-person juries, critics maintain, make it easier for the prosecutor to convict by weakening the standard of proof beyond a reasonable doubt. What is considered proof beyond a reasonable doubt will vary with each juror.[50] With a 12-person jury, the prosecutor must get the vote of every member, including the juror who has the most stringent perception of proof beyond a reasonable doubt. Such individuals are more likely to be absent from six-member juries, making it more possible for the prosecutor to get by with a case that is legally weak.

There are two final objections to six-person juries: Research has shown that the alleged savings in time and cost attributable to six-person juries are modest at best.[51] And decreasing the jury size is a step toward closing the courtroom door to direct citizen participation in the criminal justice system.

The need for further research

Many of the arguments for and against six-person juries in criminal cases are necessarily speculative at this stage. More research is needed to shed light on the behavior of juries in criminal cases. (So far most of the research has been restricted to civil cases.) Many of the purported advantages and disadvantages of six-person juries are based on different assumptions and unresolved questions concerning how individual jurors function in the context of juries of different size. About all that can be said with confidence is that, as far as the defendant is concerned, there is safety in number.[52] The fairest summation of the status of six-person juries may come from a psychologist specializing in research on group decision making: "The six-member jury suggests neither a clear superiority meriting its immediate adoption, nor a marked inferiority, eliminating further consideration. A clear recommendation to adopt the smaller jury for all cases may be premature, but optimism concerning its feasibility is justified."[53]

NONUNANIMOUS VERDICTS

Johnson v. *Louisiana* (1972)

What some individuals consider the most serious blow to the jury system came two years after the Supreme Court declared that six-person juries were permissible. In *Johnson* v. *Louisiana* in 1972, the Court approved the principle of nonunanimous jury verdicts: the reaching of a verdict of conviction or acquittal on the basis of a split vote.[54] Louisiana's constitution provided that in criminal cases punishable by hard labor, a vote of nine jurors out of 12 was sufficient to return a verdict of guilty or not guilty. The robbery defendant claimed that in being convicted on the basis of a majority vote rather than a unanimous vote, he was deprived of the right to be found guilty beyond a reasonable doubt under the Fourteenth Amendment's due process clause.

In *Johnson* the Court stated that the constitutional requirement of proof beyond a reasonable doubt did not require a unanimous verdict in 12-person juries. "In our view disagreement of three jurors does not alone establish reasonable doubt, particularly when such a heavy majority of the jury, after having considered the dissenters' views, remains convinced of guilt. That rational men disagree is not in itself equivalent to a failure by the State, nor does it indicate infidelity to the reasonable-doubt standard." If nonunanimous verdicts were the equivalent of failing to prove guilt beyond a reasonable doubt, then hung juries would result in acquittal rather than in retrial.

Apodaca v. *Oregon* (1972)

In *Apodaca* v. *Oregon* in the same year, another nonunanimous verdict case from a 12-person jury, the Supreme Court ruled that the Sixth Amendment right to trial by jury does not include a unanimous verdict.[55] (Since 1958, Oregon's constitution has permitted juries to reach verdicts upon agreement of ten of the 12 jurors, except in capital cases, where unanimity is required.) Thus the Supreme Court settled and severed, for the moment, any relationship between a unanimous jury verdict and the standard of proof for conviction in criminal cases.* Prior to these de-

* In *Burch* v. *Louisiana* in April 1979, the Supreme Court ruled that conviction by a six-person jury in nonpetty offenses must be based on a unanimous verdict. Without addressing the standard of proof issue, the Court declared that allowing a defendant to be

cisions, some states had authorized nonunanimous verdicts, depending on the penalties that the crime carried. In nonfelony cases, for example, Montana and Missouri provided for verdicts based on a two-thirds vote, Oklahoma on a three-fourths vote, and Idaho on a five-sixths vote.[56,57] However, few jurisdictions had permitted nonunanimous verdicts in felony cases. With the Supreme Court's removal of any constitutional barrier to majority-rule jury verdicts, the door was wide open for states to experiment with nonunanimous verdicts in the name of efficiency and in the pursuit of law and order. Predictably, nonunanimous verdicts would lead to an increase in the number of convictions.[58] Indeed, when Oregon permitted felony verdicts to be reached by ten of 12 jurors, one-fourth of the verdicts were nonunanimous ones.[59]

The case against nonunanimous verdicts

The most serious criticism of nonunanimous verdicts is that they allow the majority to ignore the minority viewpoint and arrive at a hasty judgment without proper or responsible deliberation—especially when the dissenting opinion is held by a minority group individual. Once the majority needed for conviction has been obtained, deliberation may be terminated or may amount to nothing more than the formalities of polite conversation rather than a collective, earnest piecing together of the truth.[60] In this manner, discrimination against minorities in the jury system may be moved from the front burner of jury selection—where something can be done about it at voir dire or by scientific jury selection—to the jury deliberation room, where it is beyond the reach of the law. Indeed, the incentives that dissenters may have for sticking to their guns and trying to change the minds of others are diminished in the sweep of majority rule. And the prosecutor automatically benefits from the conviction bias in nonunanimous verdicts, through fewer hung juries and by no longer having to prove to *every* juror that the defendant is guilty.

The case for nonunanimous verdicts

The argument in favor of nonunanimous verdicts rests on four points.

Nonunanimous verdicts are expected to achieve efficiency in the administration of criminal justice in much the same way that six-person juries are supposed to achieve efficiency: less time need be taken in voir dire because both attorneys know that they need only nine votes to win, and there should be fewer hung juries, shorter trials, and less deliberation time.

The obstinate juror who insists on holding out for acquittal in the face of overwhelming evidence of guilt is no longer a stumbling block to justice. A case in point was the prosecution of Pennsylvania Congressman Daniel Flood in 1979 for taking $60,000 in bribes. Despite what was considered overwhelming evidence of guilt by other jurors, a lone holdout juror allegedly told his colleagues that he would never vote to convict because Flood, who was 75, was too old to be sent to jail.

---

confined for six months or longer on the vote of five out of six jurors, as Louisiana did, violated the substance of the right to jury trial guaranteed by the Sixth Amendment.

The bribery trial of Congressman Daniel Flood (Pa.) ended in a hung jury. The holdout juror refused to convict, allegedly because he felt that Flood, at 75, was too old to be sent to jail.

The problem of bribing a jury is resolved, for a solitary corrupt juror can no longer cast the deciding vote, and the likelihood of three or four jurors' being bribed is remote.

It is unreasonable to demand unanimous jury verdicts in a free society that operates on the principle of majority rule in all other important political realms.[61] The *Johnson* decision itself was a nonunanimous (5 to 4) Supreme Court vote! Even the Constitution and its amendments can be changed by a two-thirds vote of the Senate, ratified by three-fourths of the states.

Conservatives welcomed the six-person jury and nonunanimous verdict decisions as practical, contemporary, businesslike, no-nonsense approaches to administering trials and controlling crime. Liberals were concerned that, as the new constitutional features of the adversary system, minijuries and majority rule would replace the substance and the venerated procedural safeguards of the jury system with only the illusion of justice, fair trial, and community representation.

VIDEOTAPED TRIALS

A more recent innovation in trial procedures and one that perpetuates the controversy surrounding the jury system is the videotaped trial. Two major interrelated applications of videotapes in connection with trials are in the experimental stage and in the offing.

Taping the testimony of witnesses

One use of videotapes involves the testimony of witnesses who, for personal or professional reasons, would be unable to appear or would be seriously inconvenienced by having to appear in court, and whose testimony can be videotaped instead. The taped testimony would then be viewed by the judge or the jury at trial. The Midwest Research Institute, for example, has recommended using closed-circuit television to allow specialists who serve the Kansas City Police Department as expert witnesses to testify in court without leaving the laboratory. In a marijuana possession case selected as a legal test of the procedure, videotaped expert testimony was presented in a nonjury trial on March 6, 1973. Upon conviction and appeal, the Missouri Supreme Court affirmed the use of closed-circuit television for the receipt of evidence in trial proceedings.[62]

In the first extensive use of prerecorded videotape, on November 18, 1971, a judge in Sandusky, Ohio, conducted an entire trial by videotape, which was replayed to a civil jury in an automobile accident case, *McCall v. Clemens*. The testimony of the four witnesses, including that of a police officer, was prerecorded at mutually agreed upon locations two weeks before trial. Although no judge was present at the taping, opposing counsel raised objections to each other's line of questioning, as they would in a regular trial. Later in chambers, the judge reviewed the original tape with the attorneys, ruled on their objections, and prepared an edited tape for presentation to the jury. The original, unedited tape was retained for appeal purposes. Only the voir dire and counsels' opening and closing statements to the jury were made in person.[63] A trial that ordinarily would have taken five days was reduced to two and one-half hours of playing time and settled in one day of court time.[64]

In November 1971 the Ingham County courthouse in Mason, Michigan, became the scene of the first videotaping of criminal trial proceedings in the nation.[65] Within two years, prerecorded videotaped testimony had spread to the criminal courts in Erie County, Ohio, and been introduced in the criminal courts in Franklin County (Columbus), Ohio, under a $110,000 LEAA grant.[66,67] And the National Center for State Courts has initiated videotape testing in 25 courts in eight states.[68]

Advantages of taped testimony

The potential uses of prerecorded testimony are almost limitless. Elderly witnesses could have their statements taped immediately after a crime has occurred and while the events are still fresh in their minds, thereby guarding against evidence loss or deterioration in the pretrial period. The victims of sex crimes could be spared the hardships associated with a public trial by taping their testimony for the judge or jury. Instead of spending time in court waiting for trials to begin and for witnesses to appear, police officers could tape their testimony in a control room at headquarters or in police cars equipped for the purpose. Trials would not be hampered by witnesses who are terminally ill or who later change their mind about cooperating with the prosecutor. Videotape would permit jurors to see crime scenes and to view cumbersome physical exhibits that would otherwise have to be left to their imagination. Judges and juries could be transported to the scene of a crime without their ever leaving the courtroom.

ideotapes may be used to pre-
nt the testimony of witnesses
d even trials in their entirety

Lineup evidence and confessions could also be videotaped, thereby removing any doubt about their admissibility at trial. The St. Louis County Police Department began videotaping confessions in 1970 to establish that incriminating statements were not coerced.[69] The district attorney in the Bronx, New York City, has been using videotape since December 1975 for recording confessions, crime scenes, lineups, drunk driving charges, and the *Miranda* warnings.[70] In one of these cases, a defendant scheduled to go to trial entered a bartered guilty plea to manslaughter after viewing his confession on a videotape replay. The trial would have lasted two weeks, at a cost of $10,000 a day.

Taping and editing entire trials

Instead of recording testimony out of court, the testimony of witnesses can be videotaped in court in the absence of the jury. The trial-taped testimony would then be edited (as described above) for presentation to the jury; the unedited tape would be retained as a record for appeal purposes. The editing would delete prejudicial remarks, illegally obtained evidence, and other improprieties to which the jury should not be ex-

Close-up 11.2. SUPREME COURT GIVES GO-AHEAD TO TELEVISING OF TRIALS

In *Chandler* v. *Florida* in 1981, the Supreme Court unanimously declared that states can permit the televising of criminal trials.[a] Even if the defendant objects to the presence of cameras in the courtroom, television coverage does not automatically violate the defendant's right to a fair trial. The *Chandler* decision centered around a ruling by the Florida Supreme Court which authorized electronic and still photography coverage of all judicial proceedings, without regard to the consent of the parties involved. Two former Miami Beach police officers convicted of burglary at a televised jury trial challenged the Florida rule. They contended that the televising of criminal trials was an inherent denial of due process under the Fourteenth Amendment and cited the Supreme Court's 1965 decision in *Estes* v. *Texas*[b] in support of their position. There, a 5 to 4 Court reversed the fraud conviction of Billy Sol Estes because factors associated with his televised trial deprived him of a fair hearing. In *Chandler,* the Supreme Court clarified that the *Estes* decision was limited to the particulars of that case and did not establish an absolute constitutional ban against television (and photographic) coverage of trials under all circumstances.

The Court noted approvingly that Florida's program contained strict guidelines for the use of equipment and other special safeguards for protecting the rights of defendants. Moreover, since

States can televise criminal trials, even over the defendants' objections, without violating their constitutional rights

Estes was tried in 1962 television technology has improved vastly, making the presence of cameras in court less disruptive and intrusive. Above all, the *Chandler* court could find no justification for prohibiting televised trials across-the-board simply because they may have an adverse effect on juries in some cases.[c] The proper safeguard against this contingency is not the wholesale condemnation of televised trials, but rather the defendant's right to assert and show that media coverage was detrimental to a fair trial in his particular case—which the Florida defendants did not do.

In some ways, *Chandler* is as relevant for what it does not say as for what it does. It does not give the broadcast media the right to televise trials. It emphatically does not preclude having convictions reversed on the grounds that television coverage compromised the defendant's rights. It does not affect the situation in the ten states currently allowing cameras at trial only with the defendant's consent.[d] And it subtly does not foreclose the possibility of reaching an opposite conclusion in the future, *if* empirical data can prove that televised trials are invariably harmful to the interests of defendants. *Chandler* did little more than ratify a state's right to govern its own court system, fortified by the Court's refusal to stifle responsible social experimentation. Despite these qualifications, reporters hailed *Chandler* as a legal breakthrough for the broadcasting industry and a historic decision that will lift the curtain surrounding the judicial system.

[a] *Chandler* v. *Florida,* No. 79-1260. Decided January 26, 1981.
[b] *Estes* v. *Texas,* 381 U.S. 532 (1965).
[c] The advocates of televised trials believe that they have an educational value to the public, that citizens have a right to know what goes on in court, and that media exposure may improve the quality of trials by keeping the participants on their toes. Its detractors believe that televised trials will make witnesses nervous and apt to forget testimony, will divert attention from the issues at hand, might pressure judges and jurors to render decisions pleasing to the viewers, might damage the reputation of defendants acquitted of certain charges (like rape), and will transform a serious event into an entertainment spectacle by focusing on the dramatic content.
[d] Jonathan Friendly, "Some Doors Open for Television," *New York Times,* February 1, 1981, p. 9.

posed. It would no longer be necessary for the judge to instruct the jury to "disregard that statement" (and *hope* that they do). Pretrial publicity that creeps into taped testimony could be edited out before reaching the jury. The judge would have more time to make informed responses to counsel objections and motions, instead of being pressed to make hurried rulings in order to avoid delaying the trial. Judicial compliance with the rules of evidence and with constitutional safeguards might be improved in light of the knowledge that an unedited master record has been retained.

Many other advantages are associated with videotaped trials.

Advantages of videotaped trials

When defendants decline to testify in their own behalf, jurors would have less chance to be influenced by a defendant's race, appearance, clothing, and other nonverbal cues.

Not having daily personal contact with the defendant sitting in the courtroom, the jury would be less likely to hold a decision not to take the stand against the defendant.

The jury could view all of the testimony and the exhibits without interruption or distraction, and in the proper order of presentation, thereby enabling them to better understand and weigh the evidence.[71]

Because videotape improves the scheduling of trials, it becomes unnecessary for jurors to make daily trips to the courthouse, to experience prolonged stays in antiquated facilities, to face delays caused by continuances, and to appear at trial only to learn that the case has been disposed of through plea bargaining.

There would be less need for jury members to be sequestered, that is, not allowed to return home until the end of the trial, separated from fellow jurors in the evening, and perhaps confined to their rooms in order to insure that they do not discuss the case prior to deliberations and that they are not exposed to media coverage of the proceedings.

The amount of time and the hardships associated with jury duty would be reduced and individual and occupational exemptions could be largely eliminated, thereby contributing to jury composition that is more representative of the community.

Fatigue and loss of concentration that comes with sitting through long, complicated trials and listening to repetitious and conflicting testimony could be minimized by simply turning the video unit off and allowing the jurors to rest.

Are videotaped trials a shortcut to or a shortcircuiting of justice?

Videotape testimony could be replayed during jury deliberations to clarify factual points that jurors must now rely on recollection or the cumbersome rereading in the courtroom of trial testimony to settle.

The jury's deliberations could also be videotaped and be used to determine whether prejudice influenced the verdict.

If a juror has to be excused during deliberations, or in the event of a hung jury, new jurors can view the same trial (the videotape), thereby avoiding a costly retrial.

Judges can attend to other matters while the jury is attending to the tapes. Judges could also conduct trial business out of court. In one case involving alleged racial discrimination by the Akron police in 1975, the judge screened 50 hours of taped testimony at home and in chambers, without interrupting his regular work schedule.[72]

Disadvantages of videotaped trials

Videotaped trials, however, are not without their drawbacks, and critics see a number of disadvantages in them.

The alleged economy of videotape (time supposedly saved by juries and judges, reduction in court congestion, reduced costs) is greatly exaggerated.

There is some danger in permitting the judge to determine in advance of trial, through the editing of the tapes, what testimony will be heard by the jury.

The credibility of witnesses is communicated to jurors by body language as well as by what is said, and that information can only be captured fully through in-person testimony.

There is no way for jurors to request clarification from a witness under a trialvision format.[73]

The technological media by which jurors receive testimony might affect their verdicts; that is, the media rather than the testimony may become the message.[74]

The witness may "act" for the camera.

The critical, unanswered constitutional questions about videotaped trials are whether they deprive defendants of the Sixth Amendment rights to a public trial, to be confronted with the witnesses against them, and to the effective assistance of counsel.[75]

Videotaped trials remove the "human element" from jury trials, thereby further emasculating the jury system and the quality of justice.[76]

The application of videotape to criminal trials is still in its infancy. Nonetheless, it represents the first substantive change in trial procedure in over a century.[77] At least for the present, there are no insurmountable barriers to videotaping or to *televising* trials (see Close-up 11.2). It remains to be seen whether videotape will take its place alongside six-person juries and nonunanimous verdicts as a permanent feature in the criminal trial process.

CHARGING THE JURY

With or without videotape, the judge has the last word at trial. Just before the jury retires to deliberate, the court instructs or *charges* the jury, explaining the law as it applies to the issues in the instant case and as it should be followed by the jury in reaching a verdict. Depending on the complexity of the case, the charge may take only a few minutes or require several hours. In the trial of three men charged with murdering a lobbyist for the National Rifle Association, the court read 70 pages of instructions to the jury.[78] Jury charges may be especially long and technical in criminal cases in which the defendant's state of mind at the time of the crime is the central issue, as in cases that involve defenses of "insanity," of having been forced (under duress) to commit a crime, and of killing motivated by survival. In the charge to the jury, the judge may caution the jurors against prejudice, define legal terms, remind the jury that the defendant's refusal to testify cannot enter into its judgment, emphasize that the presumption of innocence requires the state to prove guilt beyond a reasonable doubt, indicate any reduced charges on which the jury may convict if it decides to acquit the defendant of the top count in the indictment, and sometimes even comment on the evidence in order to place it in proper legal perspective for the jury's consideration. In the Joan Little case, for example, the judge in his charge had to explain the meanings of second-degree murder and self-defense and that Ms. Little's incarceration at the time of the homicide could not be held against her.

Any impropriety in the court's charge to the jury may become the basis for appealing a conviction. Misstating the law, implying that the defendant is guilty, and making remarks that could prejudice the jury toward conviction are examples of such improprieties. A New York appellate court reversed the conviction of four men found guilty of killing a police officer during a robbery because the trial court's instructions to the jury were "very much imbalanced" and endorsed the prosecutor's cases.[79] Because the court's instructions may be highly legalistic and thus confusing[80] to layperson jurors, some jurisdictions are experimenting with simplified charges, written instructions to be distributed to the jury, and videotaped charges that jurors can replay during their deliberations.

The jury's duty during its deliberations is to weigh the evidence, judge the credibility of witnesses, and assess the facts within the applicable legal framework contained in the charge to them, that is, according to the law. In principle, the jury does not have the right to disregard the law governing the case out of sympathy or bias, personal disagreement with the law, or reluctance to impose a particular sentence. In practice, however, there is little way of preventing the jury from doing so.

When the jury has completed its deliberations and reached a verdict, it returns to the courtroom. There the foreperson delivers the verdict to the judge. To assure themselves that the verdict is valid and has been stated accurately to the court, and particularly in capital punishment cases, either lawyer may request that the jury be polled, that each juror state his or her vote for the record. On being informed of the jury's guilty verdict, or on entering a guilty judgment in a bench trial, the court has but one final task in connection with the convicted defendant: sentencing.

SUMMARY

Cases in which defendants plead not guilty are disposed of at trial, a process that is predicated on the adversary method of justice. In *Duncan* v. *Louisiana* in 1968, the Supreme Court restricted the right to a jury trial to crimes punishable by at least six months incarceration. The main requirements in jury selection are not to exclude systematically any significant (cognizable) social group from serving, to empanel a jury that is a representative cross section of the community, and to remove prospective jurors who would not be impartial. Jury selection entails choosing a sample of prospective jurors from the venire (ordinarily compiled from voter registration lists), empaneling a number of candidates for a specific jury, and conducting the voir dire examination, which is also used by the lawyers to select jurors who appear to be sympathetic to their respective cases. The potential of scientific jury selection in the empaneling of an impartial jury was demonstrated in the Joan Little case. Equally (if not more) controversial jury innovations include the Supreme Court's approval of six-person juries in *Williams* v. *Florida* in 1970 and that of nonunanimous verdicts in *Johnson* v. *Louisiana* in 1972. The most recent, and in many ways the most dramatic change in the trial process is the introduction of videotaped trials, whose impact on criminal juries has yet to be determined. Before the jury retires to deliberate and reach a verdict, the court charges the jury.

DISCUSSION QUESTIONS

1. Why is there ordinarily no limit to the allowed number of challenges for cause?
2. Are you in favor of or against scientific jury selection? Why?
3. Instead of using the methods of jury selection described in the text, would it be better to rely on a rotating group of social scientists and other highly educated persons to serve on juries?
4. In what ways might the systematic exclusion of persons 18 to 21 years old on juries deprive the accused of a fair trial?

   Are you in favor of or against six-person juries, nonunanimous verdicts, and videotaped trials? In what types of cases?

Chapter 12

SENTENCING

The Objectives of Sentencing

Retribution

Incapacitation

Deterrence

Rehabilitation

Punishment versus rehabilitation

The Presentence Report

Uses of the report / The recommendation / Disclosure / Fundamental fairness / *Gardner* v. *Florida* (1977)

Disparity in Sentencing

Evidence of disparity / Negative consequences of disparity / Disparity and individualized justice / The problems surrounding disparity

Sentencing Institutes, Councils, and Guidelines

Sentencing Institutes

Sentencing Councils

Sentencing Guidelines

Appellate Review of Sentences

Sentencing accountability / Structures for appellate review / Obstacles to appellate review

Close-up 12.1: Connecticut's Sentence Review Board

The Model Penal Code and the Model Sentencing Act

The Model Penal Code

The Model Sentencing Act

Alternatives to the Indeterminate Sentence

Rationale of the indeterminate sentence / Determinate sentences / Mandatory sentences / The U.S. Sentencing Commission bill

The Death Sentence

Furman v. *Georgia* (1972)

Cruel and unusual punishment / The states' reactions to *Furman* / Resumption of capital sentences

Gregg v. *Georgia* (1976)

Guided-discretion death penalty statutes are constitutional / Reasons Court retained capital punishment / Mandatory death penalty statutes are unconstitutional / Reaction to the Gregg decision

Close-up 12.2: The Course of Capital Punishment in California

Close-up 12.3: Have Judges Made the Death Penalty an Idle Threat?

Further restrictions on capital punishment

Summary

Some of the most complex, controversial, and unresolved problems in the administration of justice surface in the sentencing decision. Competing philosophies of corrections permeate the choice of sentence; the most prominent are the ideological conflict between punishment and treatment and the age-old issue of whether deterrence works. The judge's personality, attitudes toward criminals and particular crimes, and other nonlegal factors bear heavily on sentence selection. Enormous statutory variation among jurisdictions in penalties for the same crime, irrationally constructed penal codes, and different recommendations from probation officers evaluating similar presentence reports are additional sources of sentencing disparity.

More so than any other practice, the sentencing of offenders epitomizes the genuinely systemlike nature of the criminal justice organization. It reveals dramatically that the problems in any one segment of the system are in part caused by, passed on to, and soluble only through related changes in the other criminal justice agencies. In any individual case, for example, the sentence imposed may be determined by the plea bargain struck, the attitude of the victim, the place where the crime occurred, the position of the police, the persuasiveness of defense counsel at the sentencing hearing, the constraints imposed by scarce and inappropriate institutional facilities, or even what the judge had for breakfast.

The thrust of the "revolution" in sentencing is that the procedures and the decision-making process involved in arriving at a disposition be made more fair, rational, humane, open to inspection, subject to accountability, and—however measured—more effective. As perhaps never before, judges, criminal penalties, and sentencing are themselves on trial in a case with so many angles that a mistrial might be predicted even before the jury is empaneled.

There is an especially thin line between sentencing and corrections. The sentencing function is interwoven with and invokes all of the substantive issues confronting and comprising corrections (to be discussed in Chapters 13–16). Indeed, it is scarcely possible to conceptualize sentencing adequately without at the same time considering its correctional framework and its consequences for the offender and for society.

THE OBJECTIVES OF SENTENCING

There are four valid objectives of sentencing, that is, socially and legally acceptable reasons for imposing criminal penalties on convicted defendants. In one way or another, the objectives of sentencing are fundamental to all of the topics in this chapter and underscore the correctional foundation of sentencing.

Retribution

Retribution is concerned exclusively with making the punishment fit the crime, exacting an eye for an eye, and seeing that offenders get what they deserve. From the layperson's point of view, retribution is simply the desire for revenge, vengeance, getting even, or making the offender pay. From society's perspective, retribution is an expression of social condem-

-ibution as a major objective of
-tencing is gaining new popular
scientific support

nation that reinforces the values and norms that the defendant transgressed. The demand for retribution is that the sentence imposed should punish the offender strictly in accordance with the severity of the crimes committed. The emphasis on punishment (especially incarceration) in retribution is unrelated to any possible effect punishment may have in deterring the offender or others from committing crime in the future. After having long been held in disfavor by correctional authorities and professional students of crime, retribution is currently receiving renewed attention and acceptance as a proper objective of sentencing.

Incapacitation

The incapacitation goal of sentencing is to remove offenders from society through incarceration, so that they will be physically restrained from committing crime as long as they remain a threat to society. Strictly speaking, the incapacitative function of imprisonment is concerned solely with controlling the offender's criminal tendencies by eliminating the opportunity for victimizing the public, rather than with exacting retribution or trying to change the inmate's propensity to crime. Aside from the death penalty, incarceration is the only guaranteed crime prevention program, while it lasts. Thus an essential component of incapacitative sentencing is the prediction of the defendant's future criminality. In fulfillment of this sentencing objective, the length of incarceration would reflect the judge's estimate of when the offender will be a "good risk" for not recidivating.

Deterrence

Deterrence is the threat, or the actual imposition, of punishment. The function of deterrence is to prevent law-abiding citizens from turning to crime and to discourage punished offenders from returning to crime. There are thus two types of deterrence, depending on the group to which crime control is directed. Specific or special deterrence applies to offenders who have been convicted and sentenced. It is assumed that the punishment actually imposed on this group will prevent (deter) them from breaking the law again—or at least postpone their return to crime. At the same time, the specific punishment imposed on convicted offenders is designed to decrease the probability that others will succumb to temptation; this is the second type, general deterrence. General deterrence is directed to the public at large, the law-abiding who have never been convicted and punished, the nonoffender population. The constant and diffused threat of punishment that hangs over the heads of conforming members of society is an important social control mechanism for deterring them from crime. From the standpoint of crime control, the primary issues of deterrence are the specific deterrent effect that imprisonment has on ex-prisoners and its general deterrent impact on the law-abiding public.

Rehabilitation

Rehabilitation denotes the efforts to change an offender from a law-breaker to a law-abider and a useful member of society through treatment. The treatment process attempts to make the offender's attitudes, values, personality, and coping skills more compatible with legal norms and the expectations of society. All rehabilitation programs, whether carried out in prison or in the community, focus on the offender's personal problems, which presumably account for the criminal behavior, and respond to the defendant as a person in need of help who must be cured rather than as a criminal to be punished. Until recently, rehabilitation was widely endorsed as a laudable objective of prison sentences. Just as seriously ill persons must be hospitalized in order to be treated adequately, it was thought that some offenders afflicted with deep-seated psychological problems had to be incarcerated for an undetermined period until they were cured of (rather than merely deterred from) committing new crimes. However, rehabilitation is rapidly losing ground to retribution, incapacitation, and deterrence as proper reasons for incarcerating offenders.

In practice, every sentence illustrates and may contain all four sentencing goals. For example, a term of 5 to 15 years for armed robbery includes at least five years worth of retribution for the seriousness of the crime; it achieves incapacitation by taking the dangerous offender out of circulation for the foreseeable future; and being incarcerated for any substantial period of time automatically invokes both specific and general deterrence while opening the door to prolonged treatment leading to rehabilitation.

Punishment versus rehabilitation

Even the distinction between punishment and rehabilitation is somewhat misleading, for the two are not complete opposites. Retribution, incapacitation, and deterrence share a common inherent and explicit endorsement of punishment. But imprisonment under any circumstances, no matter how therapeutic it is intended to be, is punitive. The main difference is that the first three goals of sentencing accept the legitimacy of prisons as places for punishment and imprisonment as punishment, no more and no less. The rehabilitation orientation, however, conceives of prisons as places for treatment and imprisonment as a means for providing needed services; it relegates the punishment aspect of rehabilitation to the notation that pain often accompanies recovery. From the standpoint of an increasing number of criminal justice experts, it is time to abandon rehabilitation as a basis for incarceration. From the inside of a cell, prison and punishment are synonymous. From a scientific viewpoint, the opposite of punishment is reward, not rehabilitation—and the only reward associated with imprisonment is getting out.

THE PRESENTENCE REPORT

The presentence report is a document describing the defendant that is prepared by a probation officer in order to aid the court in reaching a sentencing decision. The presentence report will include: the offense; defendant's version of the offense; prior criminal record; family history; marital history; home and neighborhood environment; education; religion; interests, habits, and leisure activities; physical and mental health; employment record; military service; financial condition;* and—most important—the evaluation summary and recommended disposition.[1]

The presentence report is compiled from interviews conducted with the defendant, with others in a position to supply the necessary information, and with virtually anyone who can shed light on the defendant's personality, character, social background, behavior patterns, needs, reasons for engaging in crime, and prognosis for treatment. The probation officer also gathers information from various records that may contribute further to a complete picture and a condensed biography of the defendant. Because its contents are not limited by legal rules, the presentence report may inadvertently contain hearsay evidence that is inaccurate, unverified statements damaging (or favorable) to the defendant, and unsubstantiated facts.[2] Presentence reports are invariably prepared for state defendants following conviction, a practice that is endorsed by the American Bar Association.[3] About half of the federal probation officers, however, commence the presentence investigation prior to formal adjudication or upon learning that the defendant intends to plead guilty, a procedure that is endorsed by the Standards and Goals Commission.[4]

Uses of the report

The principal function of the presentence report is to serve as an indispensable sentencing tool for the court. Indeed, the presentence report is the only external sentencing aid that is practical, objective, readily available, and regularly used by the courts in disposing of offenders. The court has virtually no contact with the 90 percent of defendants who plead guilty. And the trial process provides minimal opportunity to learn enough about the defendant to provide a basis for sentencing, as the President's Crime Commission recognized.[5] Thus the presentence report fills a serious information gap and is essential in arriving at a sentence that is in the best interests of society and the defendant. The presentence report

* In a few states, such as Maryland and Indiana, the presentence report includes a "victim impact statement" describing the financial, physical, and psychological effects of the crime on the victim.

also contributes to correctional administration by (1) aiding the probation officer in treatment efforts and supervising probationers and parolees, (2) aiding the prison treatment staff in their diagnosis, classification, rehabilitation program, and plans for the inmate's release, and (3) furnishing the parole board with information pertinent to its decision to grant or deny parole.[6]

Statutes governing the use of presentence reports are of two basic types. One category of statutes makes presentence reports *mandatory* under specified conditions: most often in felony cases, for crimes punishable by a year or more in prison, where repeat offenders are involved, or as a prerequisite for imposing probation. The second type of statute makes the use of presentence reports *discretionary* on the part of the trial court, and this is the approach taken by the federal courts.[7] The major criminal justice reform groups are in basic agreement on the need for using presentence reports in all felony cases and with young offenders; they differ only over the priorities dictated by practical considerations.[8] Sentence is imposed on the defendant at a sentencing hearing, usually scheduled two to four weeks after conviction and is attended by the accused, the defense counsel, the prosecution, and possibly the probation officer.*

The recommendation

The probation officer's evaluation and recommendation is the gist of the presentence report.† Although the court is not bound to follow the recommendations, research has shown that judges place great store in them. Carter and Wilkins, for example, found that in each of seven years in 1959–1965, the California superior courts followed the probation officers' recommendations for probation in 96 percent of the cases, as did the courts in ten federal judicial circuits 94 percent of the time in 1964.[11] In the Northern District of California between September 1964 and February 1967, the courts followed recommendations for probation 91 percent of the time and the recommendation for imprisonment in 85 percent of the cases. In a related research project, Carter found that the two most important factors considered by probation officers in making their recommendations were the defendant's present offense and the prior criminal record. These were followed by a few other variables that reflected the offender's stability and attitude.[12] The reliance of probation officers on the instant offense and the prior record in making their recommendations illustrates the difficulty of separating completely the crime from the criminal or basing disposition on an isolated objective of sentencing.

Disclosure

The major controversy with regard to the presentence report concerns

* As a result of the Supreme Court's decision in *Mempha* v. *Rhay* in 1967, the defendant has the right to counsel at a sentencing hearing.[9]

† Depending on the policy of the court, the recommendation may specify the length of incarceration or the period and conditions of probation, or it may instead be expressed as a general choice between probation and confinement.[10]

whether its contents should be disclosed to the defendant and counsel or whether it should be kept confidential between the probation officer and the court. In the federal system and in most of the states, disclosure of the presentence report is discretionary with the court, which means that the judge can withhold presentence report information that may be responsible for the disposition. Ohio, for example, provides that the report "shall be confidential and need not be furnished to the defendant or his counsel or the prosecuting attorney unless the court, in its discretion, so orders."[13] Only a few states, such as Alabama, have mandatory disclosure of the presentence report to the defendant and counsel or, as in Virginia, permit the accused to cross-examine the presentence report investigator in open court on the report's contents and to present additional relevant information.[14,15] California goes so far as to make the presentence report a part of the court record, thereby opening it to public inspection.[16] The courts themselves are overwhelmingly opposed to mandatory disclosure.[17]

The chief argument against disclosure is that it would dry up confidential sources of information that the probation officer relies on in preparing the presentence report, as the President's Crime Commission acknowledged. Social agencies, physicians, school personnel, employers, and the wives of the defendants might be reluctant to supply information for a presentence report that will be made available to the defendants.[18] The foreclosing of the information sources of the presentence report would make the reports less complete, less accurate, and less useful to the court. In rebuttal, the advocates of disclosure contend that it is impossible for a probation officer to guarantee any informant that the information supplied will not be revealed to the defendant because the courts have the discretion to disclose the report, and many do so. About half of the courts in West Virginia, for example, usually disclose the presentence report to the defendant.[19] Twenty-five federal probation offices allow substantial disclosure of the report to the defendant or counsel.[20] The experience in those jurisdictions and in states such as California and Maryland where disclosure is mandatory do not suggest that vital sources of information will dry up under a policy of disclosure.[21]

Fundamental fairness

The principal arguments in favor of disclosure revolve around the theme of fundamental fairness to the defendant. Disclosure provides an opportunity for the defendant to detect and refute damaging information in the presentence report which is incorrect, misleading, exaggerated or distorted, biased, or unsubstantiated.[22] This is considered essential because the information contained in the report is completely unrestricted, it is not bound by the rules of evidence, its accuracy is not subject to other meaningful review, hearsay evidence may be relied on, overburdened probation officers may not always make a thorough investigation, and their recommendations are not infallible. Disclosure will thus lead to improved data-gathering techniques, make presentence reports more objective, less judgmental, less dependent on hearsay information, and more valuable to the court and to the correctional needs of the defendant.

The major criminal justice reform groups have endorsed the principle of disclosure, differing only on the identification of exemptions to full disclosure and on the manner of disclosure. The President's Crime Commission's recommendation captures the emerging progressive attitude and the trend toward disclosure: "In the absence of compelling reasons for non-disclosure of special information, the defendant and his counsel should be permitted to examine the entire presentence report."[23] Whenever feasible, the line between complete disclosure and strict confidentiality should be drawn on the side of the defendant, in the name of fundamental fairness.

The strongest proponents of disclosure maintain that disclosure is required on the basis of due process, the Supreme Court's language in *Kent* v. *United States* in 1966 (a juvenile delinquency case), and the Court's recognition of legal rights for convicted defendants in other areas. So far the Supreme Court has not confronted directly the issue of whether the defendant has a constitutional right to disclosure of the presentence report in routine felony cases involving lengthy prison terms.[24] The closest it has come here, in *United States* v. *Tucker* in 1972, was in ruling that where the trial judge sentences on the basis of erroneous information about prior convictions, the sentence fails to meet the requirements of due process.[25] In capital punishment cases, however, in *Gardner* v. *Florida* (1977) the Court declared that defendants *do* have a due process right to full disclosure of the presentence report; in addition, it must be made part of the official record so that the report is available for review on appeal.[26] In *Gardner* the trial court, based on information in an undisclosed presentence report, rejected the jury's recommendation of life imprisonment and sentenced the defendant to death instead. The Court's view in *Gardner* was that defendants facing death are entitled to rebut information in the presentence report relied upon to seal their fate—information that may be inaccurate, misconstrued, or given undue weight. Disclosure was also deemed necessary to ensure that the death sentence is administered in an even-handed manner, which requires that the factors prompting the decision be divulged. Significantly, the *Gardner* decision foreshadowed the Court's concern, expressed in subsequent decisions discussed later in this chapter, that in capital cases defendants should not be denied any opportunity to present mitigating circumstances that could make the difference between life and death.

Gardner v. Florida (1977)

DISPARITY IN SENTENCING

The major problem in the disposition process is unwarranted sentencing disparity: (1) the imposition of different sentences, for the same crimes or offenses of comparable severity, that cannot be justified by the offender's previous record, personality, or specific deterrence results, and (2) the imposition of different sentences, for different crimes and different offenders, that is nonetheless considered unfair, irrational, dysfunctional, or discriminatory under the circumstances.*

Evidence of disparity

There is ample evidence to support the claims and the concern over unwarranted disparity in sentencing (Figure 12.1). In *Criminal Sentences: Law Without Order,* Judge Marvin E. Frankel provides an insider's view of judges who double a prison sentence because the defendant was overheard cursing the court for the first sentence, who mechanically impose maximum sentences on all draft-card burners because of resentment against war resisters, and who retaliate against defendants who criticize the court at the sentencing hearing by increasing the prison term.[27] A landmark study demonstrated wide disparity in federal court sentences imposed on 645 defendants during a six-month period in 1972 in the Southern District of New York: with the exception of tax evasion, the proportion of black defendants given prison sentences was higher than whites for every crime.[28] An LEAA study completed in October 1972 found that for ten categories of crime, there was significant variation among the eleven circuits in type and length of sentence.[29] Other research has also revealed pronounced geographical disparity.[30]

One of the most comprehensive studies of disparity, conducted by the Federal Judicial Center in 1974, involved 50 New York, Connecticut, and Vermont judges in the Second Circuit. In the mock sentencing experiment, each judge was given 20 actual presentence reports drawn from probation offices within their jurisdiction and asked to render sentences.[31] The sentences imposed on identical cases indicated that "court sentences are as unpredictable as roulette."[32] For the defendant convicted of extortion, for example, the average sentence imposed by the judges was 10 years in prison and a $50,000 fine; but the most severe sentence was 20 years and a $65,000 fine, and the least severe sentence was 3 years imprisonment. And, as other studies have also found, the judges did not take a consistently "tough" or "soft" stand on crime; the judge who gave the strictest sentence in one case might have given the most lenient sentence in another case.[33]

Negative consequences of disparity

The attack on unwarranted sentencing disparity is based on a series of related premises and observations.†

* The narrow view of unwarranted sentencing disparity would exclude this second category, but the literature invariably discusses both forms as needless disparity in sentencing.

† In principle, the issue of disparity in sentencing is not concerned directly with whether individual sentences are "lenient" or "harsh."[34] Rather, the focus is on the court's decision-making process, unchecked judicial discretion, and wide open penal code provisions. These factors are responsible for nonuniform, irrational, personally motivated, unfair, and inadequate sentences—which in any given case may be too lenient *or* too harsh.

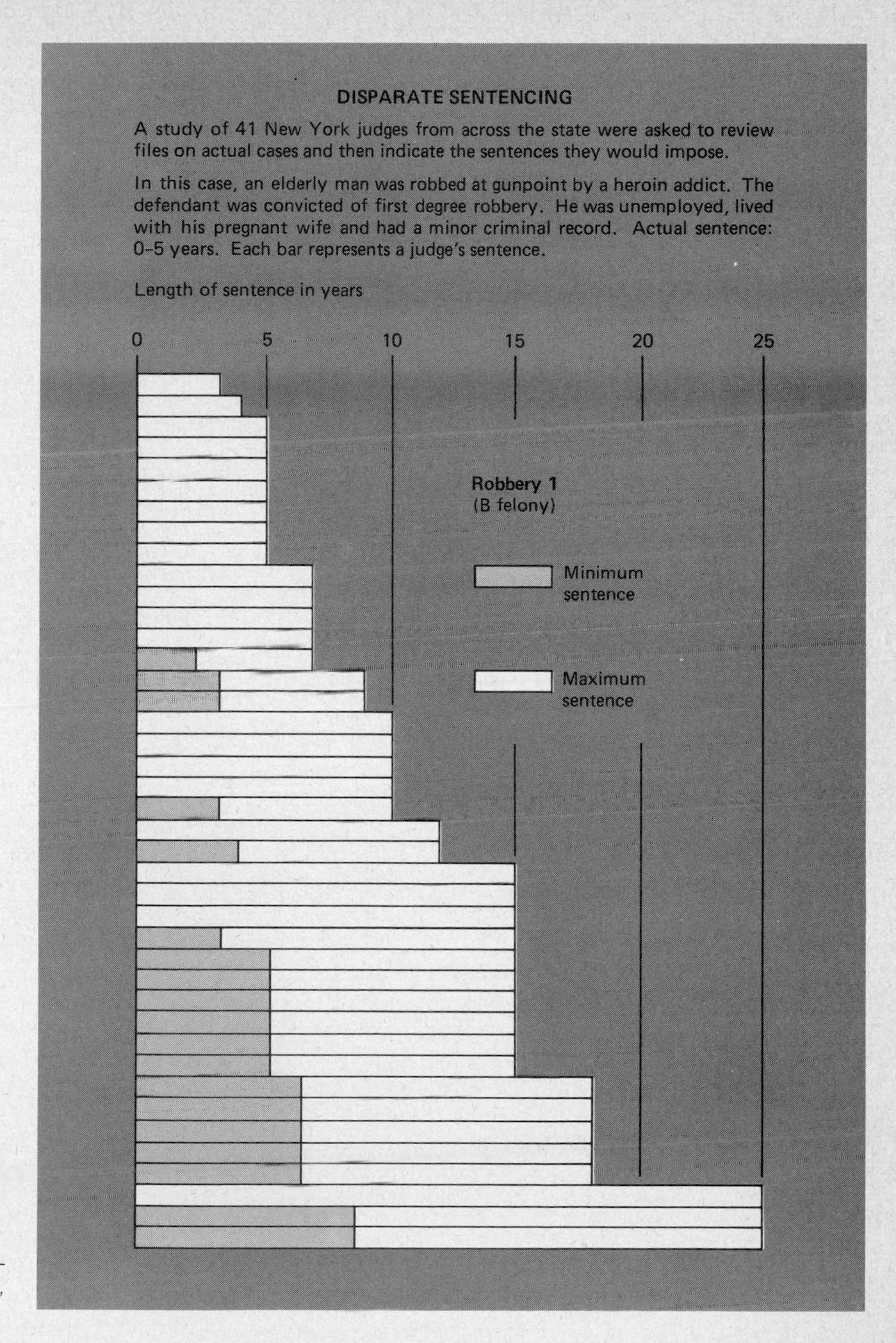

URE 12.1 Disparate sentenc- *Source: New York Times,* ch 30, 1979, p. B3.

Judge Archie Simonson of Wisconsin sentenced a 15-year-old rapist to one year of probation because the crime was a "normal" reaction to sexual permissiveness in the community

With rare exceptions, nonuniform penalties for the same or similar crimes are undesirable and should be avoided. Greater uniformity in sentencing should replace individualized justice.

In far too many cases the different sentences imposed for the same crimes depend on the identity of the judge, the locale of the crime, varying judicial ideologies concerning the objectives of sentencing, politics and political affiliation, disagreement over the seriousness of the offense, subjective perceptions of the offender, personal idiosyncrasies, social class and racial bias, and disparities in the background, legal training, and personalities of the judges.

Sentencing defendants who commit similar crimes to prison for different periods of time on the grounds of rehabilitation (a major justification for disparity) should be terminated. The priorities involved in the objectives of sentencing should be reordered, and much greater weight should be given to retribution, incapacitation, and deterrence.

Even when different sentences are meted out to unlike offenders who have committed different crimes, the disparate penalties must be based strictly on the comparative seriousness of the offenses, the prior criminal records of the offenders, and consideration of the reordered objectives of sentencing.

The two most important reasons for unwarranted sentencing disparity are that judges have unfettered discretion to impose penalties without explanation or review and that the penal codes of most states provide penalties ranging from probation to long-term incarceration for most felonies, with the specific sentence left to the discretion of the court. Both of these conditions must be changed.

The consequences of disparity lead defendants to try to beat the rap by judge shopping, deprive offenders of simple justice and fundamental fairness where it counts most, and are degrading to the public's sense of equality and fair play.

Disparity and individualized justice

In practice, the most glaring deficiencies of disparity pertain to similar offenders who commit similar crimes and who are given different (and therefore unjustifiably punitive) prison terms in the name of individualized justice. The critics of disparity have drawn a blanket indictment of institutional rehabilitation sentences—the touchstone of sentencing for several decades—on the grounds that they are inherently unfair to the offender, unjust to the victim, and unproductive for society. Sentencing disparity is eschewed because it results in sending convicted defendants to prison for the wrong reason: to be rehabilitated. There is growing awareness of the limitations on our ability to change people within captive settings, our ability to predict when inmates are ready for release, and the myth of rehabilitation. This recognition has added a new urgency to the call for more uniform penalties, shorter sentences, and the highly selective use of the imprisonment for restraining dangerous offenders, retribution for the most serious crimes, and possibly deterrence.

The problems surrounding disparity

The problems that surround disparity in sentencing are complicated by enormous difficulties.

1. Reaching consensus on what constitutes unwarranted, excessive, or unjustified disparity and what a fair and just sentence is in any individual case. The charges against disparity are not a blanket indictment of *all* variation in sentencing but of that which is "improper," something about which reasonable people may disagree.[35] The research on the determinants of sentencing has documented sufficient unwarranted disparity to be cause for doing something about it, but it has not indicated that the courts are completely erratic or irrational in sentence selection (the instant offense and the prior criminal record still account for the bulk of sentencing variation).[36]
2. Coming to terms with the role of rehabilitation as a factor in prison sentences. The opponents of disparity have identified individualized justice as the enemy; however, once the decision to incarcerate has been made on other grounds, most authorities and reform groups continue to leave room for taking the offender's rehabilitative needs into consideration in specifying the length of confinement.
3. All of the problems associated with plea bargaining.
4. Identifying the causes of disparity about which something can be done. For example, it is recognized that disparity in presentence report recommendations contributes to sentencing disparity.[37] Yet calls for "better recommendations" and "better judges" are euphemisms rather than realistic responses to the problem.
5. The persisting conflict between the social work approach to dealing with offenders, which stresses individuation of sentences geared to rehabilitation, and the punishment school of thought, which calls for retribution, deterrence, incapacitation, and "equal time for equal crime."
6. The critical questions of who should be sent to prison, for how long, what effects imprisonment should have, how release should be determined, and related correctional issues that are themselves in a state of turmoil.
7. Devising effective remedies to reduce unwarranted sentencing disparity. Judicial bias, geographical variation, and differing ideologies of crime control are able to come into play only because of the court's unbridled discretion to impose any sentence authorized by statute—without explanation, scientific guidelines for sentencing, special training for the task, consultation with other judges, or effective review of decisions. The remaining sections in this chapter discuss various approaches taken to reduce sentencing disparity.

SENTENCING INSTITUTES, COUNCILS, AND GUIDELINES

Sentencing Institutes

Congress passed a law in 1958 authorizing periodic *sentencing institutes* to bring together federal judges and others for the purpose of promoting "the interest of uniformity in sentencing procedures."[38] At these one-day or two-day seminars, the most frequent type of workshop session involves mock sentencing experiments based on actual presentence reports or hypothetical cases, followed by a discussion of the disparate sentences invariably observed.[39] The purpose of all such institute training approaches to controlling disparity is basically to sensitize trial judges to the issues of disparity and excessive sentence, their consequences, and the unconscious biases that affect disposition. For various reasons, however, sentencing institutes have not proven to be an effective approach to reducing disparity.[40]

Sentencing Councils

The *sentencing council,* or sentencing panel, originated in the U.S. District Court for the Eastern District of Michigan in November 1960.[41] The sentencing council consisted of a panel of three judges that was convened

regularly for the specific purpose of considering the sentences to be imposed in pending cases. The presentence reports of defendants awaiting disposition were distributed to panel members five days before the conference, as a basis for their preparing sentence recommendations. Since the council's recommendations were only advisory, the final sentencing decision remained within the discretion of the trial judge. As intended, the interplay between equals tended to suppress the imposition of excessively severe and unduly lenient sentences, thereby reducing disparity. A decade after the idea was introduced in Michigan, however, sentencing councils had been established in only two other federal districts and had not been adopted by the states.[42]

Sentencing Guidelines

The *sentencing guidelines* approach to controlling disparity is based on research on the actual sentencing behavior of judges, the major factors that account for variation in their dispositions, and the predicted likelihood of recidivism. Sentencing guideline tables represent the average sentences imposed by judges in a particular jurisdiction for various groups of offenders who have committed different crimes. The sentencing results are broken down according to (a) the seriousness of the present crime and (b) various characteristics of the offender that indicate the likelihood of recidivism. The findings are then statistically summarized in the form

-arity in sentencing often re-
s when penal codes allow the
-rts wide discretion in impos-
ndeterminate sentences

Table 12.1 Suggested sentencing guidelines for Felony 4 offenses, Denver, Colorado.

The Colorado Penal Code contains five levels of felonies (Felony 1 is the most serious) and three levels of misdemeanors; the Felony 4 category includes crimes such as manslaughter, robbery, and second-degree burglary. The legislated maximum sentence for a Felony 4 offense is ten years; no minimum period of confinement is to be set by the court. "Out" indicates a nonincarcerative sentence such as probation, deferred prosecution, or deferred judgment.

OFFENSE SCORE (Severity of Crime)†	OFFENDER SCORE (Likelihood of Recidivating)*				
	−1 −7	0 2	3 8	9 12	13+
10–12	Indet. min. 4–5 year max.	Indet. min. 8–10 year max.	Indet. min. 8–10 year max.	Indet. min. 8–10 year max.	Indet. min. 8–10 year max.
8–9	Out	3–5 month work project	Indet. min. 3–4 year max.	Indet. min. 8–10 year max.	Indet. min. 8–10 year max.
6–7	Out	Out	Indet. min. 3–4 year max.	Indet. min. 6–8 year max.	Indet. min. 8–10 year max.
3–5	Out	Out	Out	Indet. min. 4–5 year max.	Indet. min. 4–5 year max.
1–2	Out	Out	Out	Out	Indet. min. 3–4 year max.

*The higher the Offender Score, the higher the likelihood of recidivism.
†The higher the Offense Score, the more serious the crime.

Source: Jack M. Kress, Leslie T. Wilkins, and Don M. Gottfredson, "Is the End of Judicial Sentencing in Sight?" *Judicature,* December 1976, p. 221.

of a sentencing guideline table (see Table 12.1). Each cell in the table represents the average sentence imposed by judges on offenders convicted of certain types of crimes (offense score) and having certain background characteristics used to predict their likelihood of recidivating (offender score).

The availability of sentencing guidelines makes it possible for a judge who is about to impose sentence to know the typical sentences imposed by colleagues on similar offenders and to be guided accordingly. Judges who decide to impose a sentence that falls outside the recommended guidelines are requested to explain in writing their reasons for doing so, out of consideration to their colleagues and the defendant (and for possible use in the periodic revision of the guideline tables). The guideline approach attempts to curb disparity by structuring judicial discretion on the judges' own collective and common experience. It assumes that judicial discretion at sentencing is indispensable rather than dysfunctional, that a considerable amount of disparity is justified, that the courts have the ability and desire to control unwarranted disparity once they see the full picture and that the problem can be handled from within through voluntary self-improvement, without obliterating discretion or tampering with the penal code.[43]

One impetus to the courts' voluntary adoption of guideline tables may in fact be that it is viewed as the lesser of two potential evils that would reduce disparity and judicial discretion through more drastic means: appellate review of sentences and revision of the penal code.

APPELLATE REVIEW OF SENTENCES

The appellate courts have traditionally been used to correct procedural errors involved in conviction and (to a lesser extent) in sentences that were illegal because of *how* they were determined rather than because of *what* the sentences were. Four types of sentences have been subject to appellate review and reversal on largely constitutional grounds: (1) sentences not authorized by statute and therefore illegal in form, (2) sentences based on the defendant's race, sex, or financial position and therefore a violation of due process, (3) sentences bearing no rational relationship to the four objectives of criminal penalties, and (4) sentences so haphazardly determined or grossly disproportionate to the crime as to "shock the conscience," violate "evolving standards of decency," or constitute "cruel and unusual punishment."

Sentencing accountability

These isolated situations, however, leave untouched the core problem in sentencing disparity: legal but excessive sentences that represent run-of-the-mill rather than rare dispositions. "Sentencing has not been brought under the strict constitutional protections placed upon other pre-conviction proceedings and processes."[44] For all practical purposes, legal sentences in the federal system and in two-thirds of the states cannot be appealed.[45] In these jurisdictions, the appellate courts prefer whenever possible to relinquish the matter of sentencing to the "sound discretion" of trial judges, or to reverse the conviction for the covert purpose of correcting unwarranted sentences. In contrast with the United States, "every other major nation in the world has adopted sentence review by a higher court as a safeguard against disparity."[46]

Both the American Bar Association and the Standards and Goals Commission recommended that sentences be reviewable in every instance in which the conviction is reviewable.[47,48] The main argument in support of sentencing accountability is that the "lawless" nature of sentencing, which is responsible for disparity, can be overcome only by subjecting sentencing decisions to appellate review. Only in this manner can a systematic body of knowledge, precedents, and law of sentencing develop. In the course of reviewing allegedly excessive sentences, the appellate courts are expected to evolve rules, laws, and principles of sentencing for the lower courts to follow, just as they have in the trial and pretrial area, and just as the Supreme Court has been doing with respect to the death penalty.

Structures for appellate review

Review of the merits of a sentence is realistically available in all serious cases in about 15 states.[49] There are two methods by which sentence review may be accomplished. Seven states utilize special panels of trial judges that are convened for the sole purpose of reviewing the propriety of sentences and decreasing or increasing them.[50] Although staffed by trial judges, these sentence review panels function as appellate review courts for all intents and purposes. In other states where review is available, the regular appellate courts are authorized to review the sentence along with any other issue in the case. A reform related to the demand for appellate review of sentences is that trial judges be required to provide written explanations for the sentences they impose. Such a record is considered essential in order for the review group to determine whether the imposed sentence was proper, to reconstruct the aggravating or mitigating factors affecting disposition, and to assess the relative weights given to the four objectives of sentencing.[51]

Obstacles to appellate review

Obstacles to the goals and the effectiveness of appellate review of sentences are formidable. Trial judges are adamantly opposed to the double threat of sentence review and having to justify their discretion in writing.[52] The sentence review court may be reluctant to reverse sentences where it should, out of professional courtesy to colleagues in the lower court. Defendants legitimately aggrieved by excessive sentences may be deterred from appealing by the possibility of their sentences' being increased on review. The formulation of sentencing guidelines, principles, and criteria expected from the reviewing authority rarely occurs in practice. A minisurvey conducted by the American Judicature Society in five states with review panels disclosed that none of the panels' chief judges believed that their work helped to establish sentencing criteria.[53] Appellate review's potentially greatest contribution—reducing unwarranted disparity—is dependent on the *requirement* that trial judges state their reasons for each felony disposition. Yet as of 1975, only three states required judges to explain their sentences, a practice that has been adopted only by the more progressive courts in the federal system.[54,55] The Supreme Court has only once, and then under very limited circumstances, required a sentencing judge to explain the basis of the penalty imposed.[56]

While there is a strong climate of opinion that favors appellate review, appellate review itself may simply provide too little too late (see Close-up 12.1). It is intended to correct excessive sentences and to put a lid on disparity only after the fact; it does not prevent the courts from imposing

Close-up 12.1 CONNECTICUT'S SENTENCE REVIEW BOARD[a]

Consisting of three trial court judges, Connecticut's Sentence Review Division (Board) was empowered to increase or decrease imposed felony sentences. The board may require the sentencing judge to submit a statement of reasons for the sentence, but such written explanations are not mandated by legislation. As a substitute, the board can obtain a transcript of the sentencing hearing, a copy of the presentence report, and whatever other documents were available to the sentencing judge. To encourage the development of uniform sentencing criteria and their application throughout the state, the Board was required to hand down a written opinion in each case reviewed, stating *their* reasons for the action taken on appeal, which is then published for the legal community.

The Board meets about one day every two months to dispose of less than 25 appeals. Of the first 256 appeals heard, the Board reduced 15 sentences, increased 7, and affirmed the remaining 234. Because they can also increase sentences, most of the appeals have come from defendants who received close to the maximum penalty for their crimes and who thus have little to lose by appealing. Because of the Board's infrequent reduction of original sentences, inmates regard it as a sham. Prosecutors required to attend the sentence review meetings consider it a waste of their time. And the Board's work has raised little interest on the part of the public, bar, or bench.

The Board's most serious failure is in connection with its most important function: to write useful opinions on each appeal clearly describing the relationship between the factors in the case to the four objectives of sentencing. This was envisaged as a critical step in establishing criteria and providing a source of sentencing principles from which trial judges could benefit. With few exceptions, however, the Board's written explanations for their own sentencing decisions on appeals have not been enlightening. "It is extremely difficult if not impossible to deduce what aim or aims of the criminal law are being emphasized and, *a fortiori,* to abstract any sentencing principles." If special sentence review panels are unable to write meaningful opinions intended to reduce disparity, what is the value of appellate review and what is to be gained from trial courts providing written explanations of their sentences?

[a] *Source:* Note, "Appellate Review of Primary Sentencing Decision: A Connecticut Case Study," *Yale Law Journal,* July 1960, pp. 1453–1478.

improper or disparate sentences in the first place. All of the genuinely preventive approaches to disparity involve reducing the court's sentencing options through changes in the penal code.

THE MODEL PENAL CODE AND THE MODEL SENTENCING ACT

Unchecked judicial discretion, unwarranted disparity, and excessive sentences derive from the structure and content of the penal codes. State penal codes provide a broad range of penalties for most felonies, running the gamut from probation to lengthy imprisonment, with the choice in the individual case being left to the judge. There is enormous disparity across jurisdictions in the penalties authorized for the same or similar crimes. Vastly different penalties accompany a multitude of not so different crimes. In many instances, statutory penalties are inconsistent with the gravity of the offense. Colorado's penal code, for example, allows judges to impose a ten-year sentence for stealing a dog but only six months for killing one.[57] In California, a person could receive 15 years for breaking into a car to steal the contents of the glove compartment but only ten years for stealing the car itself.[58] The structure and content of American penal codes have minimal implications for the objectives of sentencing, and in fact they are contrary to much of our knowledge about how to control crime through punishment or treatment. Prior to 1962, the development of penal codes was haphazard, piecemeal, unsystematic, unplanned, and almost irrational.

The Model Penal Code

The resolution of these interrelated problems was the subject of ten years of intensive study by the American Law Institute (ALI), undertaken amid widespread prison riots during the 1950s.[59] The recommen-

Table 12.2 Model Penal Code Recommendations for Length of Prison Sentence in Felony Convictions

	Minimum Sentence	Maximum Sentence
First-degree felony	1–10 years	life
Second-degree felony	1–3 years	10 years
Third-degree felony	1–2 years	5 years

Source: Model Penal Code (Philadelphia: American Law Institute, 1962).

dations of the ALI to standardize penalties on the basis of meaningful classifications of crime seriousness, to make sentences fairer, and "to safeguard offenders against excessive, disproportionate, or arbitrary punishment" are presented in its publication, the *Model Penal Code.*[60]

The key to the Model Penal Code is its recommendation that all serious crimes be classified into one of three degrees of felony and its identification of the substantive crimes that constitute a first-, second-, or third-degree felony. Each degree of felony carries a penalty that is relatively standardized and generally more lenient than those specified by many state penal codes for the same crime (see Table 12.2). For example, forcible rape in which the victim is not otherwise physically injured is classified by the code as a second-degree felony, and carries a ten-year maximum sentence. For the identical offense, many states authorize sentences of 20–30 years in prison.

In this manner, the Model Penal Code would reduce the options that judges have in selecting from among an excessive range of prison sentences for a large number of crimes. The code does not *require* imprisonment in each and every felony; it allows the court to retain considerable discretion in deciding whether to place felons on probation instead. But once the court decides that incarceration is called for, the Model Penal Code places uniform limits on the length of prison sentences, based strictly on the objective seriousness of the crimes as designated by its felony category. By classifying all felonies into three categories or gradations of severity, the Model Penal Code intends to make sentences more purposeful, uniform, lenient, and rational. The Model Penal Code has been adopted by many states, and lawmakers are following its format closely.[61]

The Model Sentencing Act

The objectives of the Model Sentencing Act, a product of the National Council on Crime and Delinquency, are to stabilize sentencing in felonies, to eliminate disparity, to achieve rehabilitation, and to do away with long prison sentences except for dangerous offenders who commit crimes of violence.[62] The act's policy is that all defendants, including dangerous offenders, should be dealt with entirely according to their potential for rehabilitation. Accordingly, the Model Sentencing Act offers a statutory definition of "dangerous offender" and enunciates a strong preference for disposing of nondangerous felons (who now constitute the bulk of the prison population) through noninstitutional sentences. To reduce disparity, the Act recommends that statutes limit the maximum prison term for nondangerous felonies ("ordinary offenders") to five years, the period within which 80 percent of felony prisoners in state institutions are actually released. Dangerous offenders who cannot be safely returned to the community can be sentenced to extended prison terms of up to 30 years, but the Act emphasizes that such cases would be few. Life sentences are virtually eliminated except for first-degree murder. Because all prison commitments are to be rehabilitative, the Act rejects the use of minimum prison sentences for both groups of offenders and would eliminate habitual offender sentences.* As of 1976, Oregon was the only state to have adopted the Model Sentencing Act, in slightly modified form.[64]

ALTERNATIVES TO THE INDETERMINATE SENTENCE

The current prime suspect in the three-count indictment of excessive sentences, disparity, and uncontrolled judicial discretion is the indeterminate prison sentence for felonies that is found in most penal codes. An indeterminate sentence is one in which the defendant is sentenced to a range of years in prison, that is, 1–5 years, 4–8 years, 10–20 years, 6 months to 15 years, one year to life, and so on. At the time of sentencing, defendants who are given an indeterminate sentence do not know when they will probably be released; the decision is left to the discretion of the parole board, subject only to broad statutory regulation.

Rationale of the indeterminate sentence

The concept of the indeterminate sentence is based on the period of time that patients remain under the care of physicians or are hospitalized for physical ailments or mental problems, that is, the medical model.[65] In this model it is impossible and undesirable to set a fixed length of time for treatment; the patient who improves rapidly may be released in a few days, but if there is no sign of improvement, the hospitalization may be extended indefinitely. The same reasoning applies to the indeterminate sentence. Why incarcerate for a fixed, or flat, term of six months, two years, or five years an offender who has reformed before then? Why release at an arbitrary point in time an offender who has not reformed by then? The indeterminate sentence thus accepts crime as an illness and offenders as sick persons whose actual length of incarceration should depend on their progress toward rehabilitation, as decided ultimately by the parole board.

If this principle of individualized justice tailored to the needs of each offender is valid, then inmates should be confined until there is substan-

* In *Rummel* v. *Estelle* in 1980, the Supreme Court upheld the states' authority to enact habitual offender laws containing mandatory life imprisonment sentences, even in the case of petty property offenses.[63] In doing so, the Court rejected the argument that such recidivist statutes constitute cruel and unusual punishment, and pointedly refused to apply the Eighth Amendment beyond the context of the death penalty.

tial evidence of rehabilitation, and not a day longer. Since it is theoretically impossible to predict at the time of sentencing when any offender will become rehabilitated and therefore ready for release, the "pure" form of the indeterminate sentence is one day to life, a sentence that is rarely found in practice.[66] Instead, penal codes set a minimum (which may be as low as six months) and maximum (which may be as high as life), depending on the crime and the criminal involved.

Although the precise statutory provisions of indeterminate sentences vary by state and crime,* all indeterminate sentences have three elements in common: (a) the defendant is committed to a substantial range of time in prison, (b) the convict has little or no knowledge of when release will come; that is, there is uncertainty about the amount of time to be served, and (c) the rehabilitation of the offender is the ostensible goal. Because of the enormous variation among states in indeterminate sentences for the same crime and in the discretion allowed the courts in setting minimum and maximum terms, the indeterminate sentence is considered directly responsible for disparate, excessive, and unfair sentences. "At least this much seems clear: the wide range of sentencing provisions is a major reason for the gross disparity of sentences; and the more indeterminate the sentence, the more likely is this disparity to continue."[68]

Determinate sentences

The indeterminate sentence is rapidly losing its appeal in the scientific and political communities because of its direct link to sentencing disparity, the mounting evidence that rehabilitation does not work, the inability to predict postrelease adjustment from prison behavior, the concern over the manipulation of prisoners that occurs under the guise of rehabilitation, and the position that coercive treatment is none of the law's business.[69] In 1975 Maine became the first state in the nation to abolish the indeterminate sentence system, as well as parole, in favor of a "flat sentencing" law.[70] Indiana followed suit; in 1977 California ended the noble experiment in indeterminate sentences it had begun in 1917; other states such as Illinois and Oregon appeared on the verge of doing the same; and the movement toward more uniformity and more punishment in sentencing seems unmistakable. The proposal to eliminate parole is often attached to the abolition of the indeterminate sentence, for otherwise flat sentences would continue to have a considerable amount of indeterminacy by virtue of the parole board's discretion to determine release. For example, a flat sentence of 15 years in a jurisdiction where inmates are eligible for parole after serving one-third of their time is in effect an indeterminate sentence of 5–15 years.[71]

Strictly speaking, the presence of determinate (flat) sentences does not

* Forty-three states have indeterminate sentences that are applicable to ordinary offenders and common felonies.[67]

affect the court's discretion in choosing between probation and prison. Flat sentence statutes may provide that only *if* the court decides not to impose probation, a fine, or a suspended sentence, will the length of the prison sentence be taken out of the court's hands. In order for determinate sentences to end the disparity that results from the court's being able to choose between probation and prison, fixed sentence schemes would have to be mandatory. *Mandatory sentences* are penal code provisions that require the court to sentence persons convicted of specified crimes to a determinate (mandatory minimum) prison term. Mandatory sentences are intended to guarantee that career criminals, recidivists, and violent offenders will face the certainty of punishment.

Mandatory sentences

Maine's revised penal code incorporates a system of mandatory sentences of fixed length. Depending on the circumstances, murder carries mandatory life imprisonment or 20 years. There are mandatory four-year terms for crimes committed with firearms, mandatory incarceration for second-offense burglary, and so on.[72] In December 1975, the Massachusetts House of Representatives voted to impose mandatory sentences for auto theft. Adults would receive a 30-day jail term for "using a motor vehicle without authority" and a six-month term for damaging it; juveniles would have to spend ten consecutive weekends in a detention center for their first auto theft and six months for a second offense. The New York Assembly approved a bill that prescribed mandatory prison sentences and restricted plea bargaining for anyone over 16 years of age who victimizes the elderly or the physically disabled.[73]

Some states are turning to mandatory sentences to reduce disparity and increase the certainty of punishment

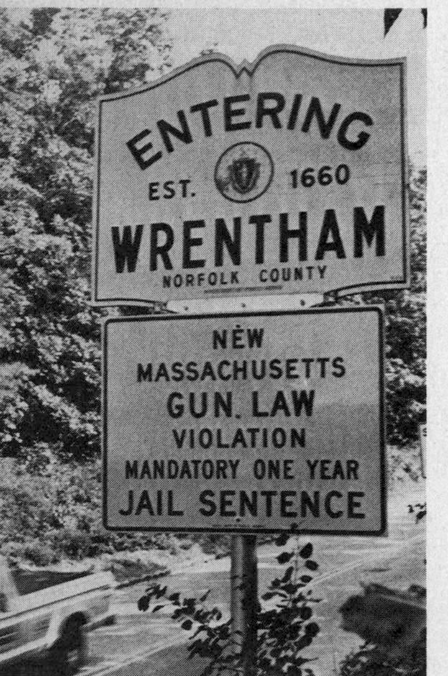

The Illinois Law Enforcement Commission has proposed determinate mandatory sentences for all crimes in order to achieve "fairness in sentencing and establish an atmosphere of certainty among prisoners." Under the proposed Illinois legislation, felonies such as rape or armed robbery would carry a flat mandatory sentence of eight years, and petty theft would draw two years. Courts could increase or decrease the prescribed mandatory sentence by up to 20 percent of sentence time, providing there were aggravating or mitigating circumstances in the case; but they would have to justify for the record any variation from the prescribed mandatory terms.[74]

By obliterating judicial discretion at sentencing, mandatory sentences tend to abolish all disparity—including that which is essential, justified, and fully warranted by the infinite variety of case circumstances that no statute can take into consideration. "Judges must maintain that quantum of discretion they need so that each sentence will be just and humane."[75] By threatening to throw out the baby with the bathwater, mandatory prison sentences create pressures that may simply shift the sentencing scales (and associated problems) from the judge to the prosecutor, who can counteract mandatory sentences by reducing the charge to one that does not carry a mandatory sentence. The history of mandatory sentences for drug violations consistently documents this avoidance pattern.

In the first four years of Detroit's mandatory sentence for selling narcotics, for example, of 476 persons originally charged with the offense, only 12 were convicted on that charge.[76]

The U.S. Sentencing Commission bill

Perhaps the most promising approach to achieving greater rationality, uniformity, and certainty in sentencing is Senator Edward Kennedy's bill to establish a United States Sentencing Commission, introduced in the 95th Congress as part of the federal Criminal Code Reform Act of 1977.[77] Consisting of a panel of judges supplemented by correctional officials and academic and police representatives, the proposed federal sentencing commission would be a vehicle for equalizing federal sentences nationwide and would be available as a model for the states to adopt. It incorporates in an integrated package the best features of sentence reform measures, such as fixed sentences in place of indeterminate sentences, a gradual phasing out of parole, the reasons for sentence selection, and appellate review of sentences. Under an initial three-year appointment, the sentencing commission would develop detailed guidelines to be followed by all federal courts at disposition, thereby assuming responsibility "for fixing the parameters of exactly what sentences should be imposed for what crimes in what situations."[78] Appellate review of sentence would be available to defendants who are sentenced to a term greater than the maximum allowed by the guidelines—as well as to the prosecutor in a case where the sentence falls below the minimum sentencing guidelines for the offense. The articulated philosophy behind the sentencing commission and its guidelines is rooted explicitly in punishment: retribution, specific and general deterrence, and keeping dangerous or habitual offenders off the streets (incapacitation). In the proposed legislation, rehabilitation is conspicuously absent as a legitimate purpose of imprisonment.

THE DEATH SENTENCE

> Excessive bail shall not be required, nor excessive fines imposed, nor cruel and unusual punishments inflicted. (Eighth Amendment)

The only sentence that has been subjected to intensive constitutional scrutiny and restraint is the death penalty. It is somewhat ironic that a penalty which is so infrequently imposed and rarely carried out has become the social, political, and constitutional focal point for the problems surrounding sentencing.

The number of executions in the United States reached a peak in 1933, dropped sharply in the 1950s, and became virtually nil after 1967.[79] The informal hiatus on capital punishment became official in 1972, when the Supreme Court, in *Furman* v. *Georgia,* ruled that the death penalty as then administered was cruel and unusual punishment, thereby presumptively invalidating all state death penalty statutes and staying the executions of all condemned prisoners. The moratorium was lifted by the Court's decision in *Gregg* v. *Georgia* in 1976, which held that the death penalty per se does not violate the Eighth Amendment's prohibition of cruel and unusual punishment. Six months later, on January 17, 1977, Gary Mark Gilmore was executed by a firing squad at the Utah State Prison, in a state that allows the condemned person to choose between the bullet and the gallows.

The movement to do away with the death penalty has been spearheaded by the NAACP Legal Defense Fund and the American Civil Liberties Union, two well-established, broadly based civil rights organizations whose long-range strategy is to turn the law and public sentiment against capital punishment.[80] At the same time, the Southern Poverty Law Center (SPLC), founded in 1971, focuses on defending guilty murderers and rapists who face the death penalty in Southern courts, attempting to get properly convicted persons off with life sentences by employing new trial tactics such as the scientific jury selection methods it used in the Joan Little case.[81]

Furman v. *Georgia* (1972)

The case that at first appeared to bring down the final curtain on the death penalty and to represent the culmination of abolition efforts by the Legal Defense Fund (which was then representing 450 of the 600 convicts on death row[82]) was *Furman* v. *Georgia,* decided by the Supreme Court on June 29, 1972.[83] In attempting to enter a household at night, Furman, a black man, killed the white occupant, was convicted of murder, and was sentenced to death. In *Furman,* for the first time in its history, the Court set aside death sentences on strictly constitutional grounds. However, in nine separate opinions written by the justices, the only point of agreement on which the cryptic 5 to 4 ruling rested was that "the imposition and carrying out of the death penalty in these cases constitutes cruel and unusual punishment in violation of the Eighth and Fourteenth Amendments."*

Cruel and unusual punishment

The decisive position in *Furman* was that the death penalty was cruel and unusual in practice because juries and judges had so much unlimited leeway in choosing between life and death: there were no standards to guide their discretion and no required procedural safeguards to protect

* Two earlier Supreme Court decisions in which the death penalty was not at issue provided some criteria for identifying "cruel and unusual" punishment. *Weems* v. *United States* in 1910 stood for the principle that punishment that is excessive for the crime may be cruel and unusual.[84] And in *Trop* v. *Dulles* in 1958, the Court stated that a punishment is cruel and unusual if it offends the "dignity of man" as measured by "the evolving standards of decency that mark the progress of a maturing society."[85]

defendants from death sentences that were discriminatory, excessive in relation to the crime and its circumstances, or otherwise unfair and unwarranted. The way in which the death penalty was meted out was haphazard, random, "freakish," capricious, an "invitation to discrimination," and a consequence of the unguided discretion of the jury or judge. Capital punishment sentences were cruel and unusual because, out of a much larger number of capital defendants who might have received them, the handful of offenders who did receive them was singled out in an arbitrary, unpredictable, and discriminatory manner, as the Legal Defense Fund had argued.[86] Justice Byron White observed that it could not be stated "with confidence that society's need for specific deterrence justifies death for so few when for so many [convicted of the same crime] life imprisonment or shorter terms are judged sufficient." The imposition of capital punishment was conducted like a lottery, one in which black and poor defendants were the invariable losers because the drawing was rigged against them. Thus it was the prevailing operation of the death penalty—rather than capital punishment in the abstract—that made the ultimate sanction unconstitutional.

The *Furman* decision was viewed by the abolitionists as a definitive victory that signaled the demise of capital punishment. However, the narrow victory of the majority ruling, the absence of even a plurality opinion, and the ambiguous implications of *Furman* raised more questions than it answered and left the status of the death penalty in limbo. Its immediate effect was to invalidate all existing state death penalty statutes and to stay the executions of 631 death row prisoners.[87]

The states' reaction to *Furman* was to revise their death penalty statutes in order to overcome the Court's objections to the cruel and unusual administration of the death sentence. The revised death penalty statutes fell into two categories.[88]

The states' reactions to *Furman*

Mandatory Death Penalty Statutes. Some states passed mandatory death penalty codes that *required* the imposition of death sentences upon conviction for designated crimes. Nevada's mandatory death penalty statute, for example, stated that "every person convicted of capital murder shall be punished by death."[89] And North Carolina made its previously optional death penalty for rape mandatory.[90] States taking this approach in order to comply with *Furman* assumed that mandatory death penalty provisions would eliminate the elements of chance and bias that had previously (and presumably) made the death decision arbitrary, random, and discriminatory.

Guided-Discretion Death Penalty Statutes. Toward the same end, and following the Model Penal Code's recommendation, other states enacted guided-discretion statutes that provided standards—a list of "mitigating" and/or "aggravating" circumstances—to be used by the jury or the judge in deciding whether to impose the death sentence.[91] Two other important safeguard procedures typically included in guided-discretion statutes were the appellate review of all death sentences and the provision for a "bifurcated" or two-stage trial proceeding that would separate the issue of guilt from that of punishment. In the first stage, the trial proper, the jury would be restricted to its traditional function of determining guilt or innocence. The jury would then proceed to impose punishment at a separate sentencing stage, at which aggravating or mitigating circumstances, the defendant's character, and other factors would be considered. Historically, the practice of lumping together guilt and punishment in reaching a verdict, along with the existence of mandatory death penalties, had led to jury nullification, a refusal or marked reluctance to convict in view of the consequences. This problem is mitigated by the bifurcated procedure.

Resumption of capital sentences

In the wake of *Furman,* 36 states and the federal government passed new mandatory or guided-discretion death penalty laws in order to hang on to capital punishment legally. The death row population, cut in half by the *Furman* decision, began to climb again under the revised statutes. In 1975 alone, 285 persons were sentenced to death, and by the nation's Bicentennial there were about 600 death row inmates, half of whom were black.[92] The imposition of capital punishment was once more alive and well in the United States, with the first execution awaiting only the go-ahead from the Supreme Court.

Gregg v. *Georgia* (1976)

The prayers of death penalty advocates were answered by the Court on July 2, 1976, when in five cases it handed down decisions that squarely addressed the two critical issues left open in *Furman:* (1) Does the death penalty inherently constitute cruel and unusual punishment; that is, are there any circumstances under which it would not violate the Eighth Amendment and would therefore be constitutional? (2) Could acceptable death penalty statutes be devised that would clear the way for the constitutional imposition of the death sentence and execution; that is, could laws provide for the making of death decisions in ways that are not arbitrary, freakish, erratic, or discriminatory?[93]

Guided-discretion death penalty statutes are constitutional

Death Penalty Statutes of Three States Upheld. In the major decision, *Gregg* v. *Georgia,* the Court found that Georgia's revised death penalty statute provided adequate standards in the form of aggravating circumstances to guide the jury in making its decision, allowed the jury to take into account the defendant's background and character, and contained other procedural safeguards to assure that individual death sentences were not unfair, excessive, or discriminatory. Gregg had been sentenced to death for murdering a motorist with whom he had hitchhiked a ride; murder and five other crimes were capital offenses. Under Georgia's bifurcated procedure, Gregg was first found guilty of armed robbery and murder.

Prior to the jury's deliberations at the penalty stage of the Georgia procedure, a presentence hearing is held at which evidence in mitigation and aggravation of punishment may be presented by the defendant, defendant's counsel, and the prosecutor; then the jury decides the sentence. Georgia's statute lists ten aggravating circumstances in connection with capital offenses. These are the standards intended to guide the jury's discretionary life-or-death judgment. Before a convicted defendant can be sentenced to death, the jury (or the judge in a bench trial) must find beyond a reasonable doubt that at least one of the ten aggravating circumstances is present and must identify the circumstance(s) in writing for the record. In *Gregg,* the trial court brought three of the ten aggravating circumstances to the jury's attention. The court emphasized that the jury was not authorized to impose the death sentence unless it found one of the three present beyond a reasonable doubt, and that they were free to consider any mitigating circumstances they knew of. The jury's sentencing verdict found that two of the aggravating circumstances were applicable.

Death sentences are reviewed automatically by the Georgia Supreme Court to insure that the decision is neither arbitrary nor influenced by prejudice, that it is supported by the statutory aggravating circumstances, and that it is not "excessive or disproportionate to the penalty imposed in similar cases, considering both the crime and the defendant." Under this kind of carefully designed guided-discretion death penalty statute that existed in Georgia, Florida, and Texas, the Supreme Court's essential ruling (which applied only to the crime of murder) was that "the punishment of death does not invariably violate the Constitution."

Reasons Court retained capital punishment

The Supreme Court refused to declare that the death penalty for murder is inherently cruel and unusual punishment, on two grounds.

1. Thirty-six states and the federal government had revised their capital punishment laws in response to Furman. Such widespread, concerted action was a clear democratic expression that society did not consider the death penalty an excessive punishment for murder under all circumstances, or categorically offensive to the "dignity of man" and "evolving standards of decency" on the eve of the country's 200th birthday. "In a democratic society legislatures, not courts, are constituted to respond to the will and consequently the moral values of the people."[94] That almost three-fourths of the states had taken bold steps to retain the death penalty was a "marked indication of society's endorsement of the death penalty for murder." Indeed, public opinion polls revealed a sharp increase in the proportion of adults who favored capital punishment. The March

1981 Gallup Poll found that 66 percent of the population wanted the death penalty, while only 28 percent opposed it.[95] This was the highest popular vote of confidence in capital punishment in 20 years; in 1966, "only" 42 percent of the people favored it.[96]

2. Retribution may justify the death penalty under certain circumstances, and capital punishment is not necessarily an excessive sentence for the crime of murder. Dismissing the deterrence argument as inconclusive, the Court in effect acknowledged the role of "just deserts" as cautiously expressed in the death penalty for murder: "The instinct for retribution is part of the nature of man, and channeling that instinct in the administration of criminal justice serves an important purpose in promoting the stability of a society governed by law."

Mandatory death penalty statutes are unconstitutional

Death Penalty Statutes of Two States Struck Down. Both North Carolina and Louisiana, which had a total of 155 persons under sentence of death, required death sentences upon conviction for first-degree murder.[97,98] These states and others that passed mandatory death penalty statutes in response to *Furman* had misread the Court's message in that ruling. It was not the mere presence of jury discretion that made the death penalty cruel and unusual in *Furman;* rather, it was the arbitrary, irrational, excessive, and discriminatory quality of its imposition. These vices would be intensified rather than overcome by mandatory death penalty laws like those of North Carolina and Louisiana. Resort to the extreme sanction should be undertaken with a sensitivity to aggravating and/or mitigating circumstances, the offender's background and character, the virtue of mercy, and the fundamental fairness of the death sentence as confirmed through appellate review. Mandatory sentences are a form of cruel and unusual punishment because they treat "all persons convicted of a designated offense not as uniquely individual human beings, but as members of a faceless, undifferentiated mass to be subjected to the blind infliction of the penalty of death." The immediate effect of the Supreme Court's two-part ruling in July 1976 was to lift the threat of execution from about half of the 611 death row inmates (those who were sentenced under mandatory statutes) and to pave the way for executions to resume in the states with guided-discretion statutes.[99]

Reaction to the *Gregg* decision

The death penalty's constitutionality came as a cruel and unusual blow to the Legal Defense Fund, which had won the battle in arguing the abolition case in *Furman* and then lost the war against capital punishment in *Gregg*. The new rulings were a bitter disappointment to those who believed that the "inevitability of mistake" in imposing death sentences and the deficiencies in the best-designed guided-discretion statutes would merely perpetuate the abuses they sought to eliminate.[100] Criminal justice purists maintained that the inequities associated with the death penalty were not solved by the decisions of July 1976 but were simply shifted to

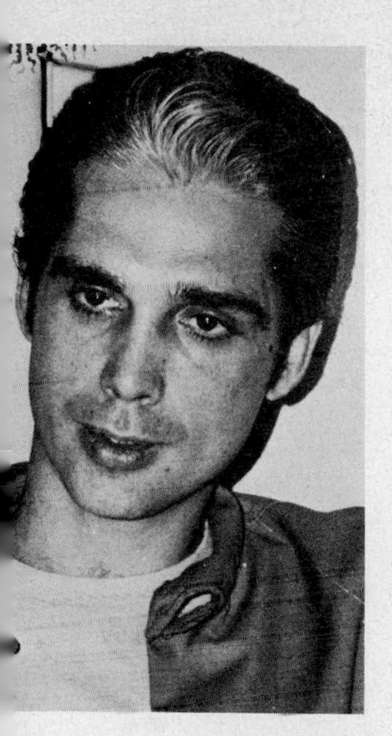

·hn Spenkelink was executed in
orida on May 25, 1979, the first
·rson involuntarily put to death
nce 1967

Close-up 12.2 THE COURSE OF CAPITAL PUNISHMENT IN CALIFORNIA

On February 18, 1972, just a few months before *Furman,* the California Supreme Court became the first court in the nation to declare that the death penalty was inherently "cruel and unusual" punishment and was therefore unconstitutional.[a] In doing so, the court spared the lives of 104 death row prisoners.[b] Then, in a referendum in November 1972, five months after *Furman,* California voters overwhelmingly approved an amendment to the state constitution that made the death penalty mandatory for train wrecking, perjury that resulted in the death of an innocent party, treason against the state, and deadly assault on a prison guard by a life-term convict.[c]

In December 1976 the California Supreme Court unanimously declared that the state's three-year-old mandatory death penalty was unconstitutional because the United States Supreme Court had struck down such "discretionless" laws in North Carolina and Louisiana in July 1976. In response, the California legislature simply drafted a guided-discretion death statute that included 15 kinds of murder for which the death penalty might be imposed. And the legislature then overrode the governor's veto of the bill. As of August 11, 1977, California—the first state to declare capital punishment unconstitutional—had the death penalty back on the books.[d]

[a] *People* v. *Anderson,* 6 Cal. 3d 628, 493 P.2d 880, 100 Cal. Rptr. 152 (1972), cited in Hugo Adam Bedau, "Reviews of Capital Punishment Literature," *Civil Liberties Review,* Summer 1975, p. 128.
[b] Sol Rubin, "Developments in Correctional Law," *Crime and Delinquency,* April 1973, p. 242.
[c] Susan Cohen, "Pot and the Death Penalty: Californians Choose," *Saturday Review of the Arts,* November 1972, pp. 12ff; Vaun Wilmott, "Capital Punishment Issue Stirred Anew by California Voters," *National Observer,* November 18, 1972, p. 2.
[d] Wallace Turner, "Cal. Legislature Overrides Veto of Death Penalty," *New York Times,* August 12, 1977, p. D14.

the pretrial stage, where prosecutors could exercise their own unguided charging and plea bargaining discretion to decide who shall live or die. Merely by enacting guided-discretion statutes, states with invalid mandatory ones, as well as abolition jurisdictions considering restoring capital punishment, now had a clear track to the electric chair, the gas chamber, the gallows, and the firing squad—or to introduce humane and unusual execution by drug injection, as Oklahoma* did in May 1977.[101]

The history of capital punishment in California embodies the struggle over the death penalty's constitutionality, traces one state's responses to *Furman* and *Gregg,* and symbolizes the American public's fear of crime, belief in retribution and deterrence, and infatuation with death (see Close-up 12.2).

Further restrictions on capital punishment

The bloodbath of executions that liberals feared might follow the constitutional retention of capital punishment did not materialize.[102] In the three years following the historic *Gregg* decision, Utah double-murderer Gary Gilmore, at his own insistence, and Florida murderer John Spenkelink were the only prisoners executed in the United States. (Utah had adopted a guided-discretion statute after *Furman.*) And the availability of the death penalty was further restricted by several important post-*Gregg* decisions.

In *Davis* v. *Georgia* in 1976, the Court ruled that even if one prospective juror with "scruples" about capital punishment is excluded during voir dire because of such beliefs, "any subsequently imposed death penalty cannot stand."[103] And in *Adams* v. *Texas*[104] in 1980, the Court held that prospective jurors cannot be excluded from jury service just because they are unwilling to take an oath that a mandatory death penalty would not affect their deliberations on any factual issues in the case. Excluding jurors who would be affected in any way by the prospect of a mandatory death sentence or their views about such a penalty would deprive defendants of the impartial jury to which they are entitled under the Sixth Amendment. These decisions brought the Court full circle from an earlier decision, *Witherspoon* v. *Illinois,* regarding the empaneling of a representative jury and juror qualms about the taking of life.[105]

Six months after the *Gregg* decision, Gary Gilmore was executed in Utah, which passed a guided-discretion death penalty statute in response to *Furman*

Following its ruling against mandatory death penalty statutes, the Supreme Court confirmed, in *Roberts* v. *Louisiana* in June 1977, that a mandatory death sentence for killing a police officer in the line of duty was not permissible.[106] The fact that the murder victim was an on-duty law enforcement officer may be regarded as an aggravating circumstance, "but it is incorrect to suppose that no mitigating circumstances can exist when the victim is a police officer."

In *Coker* v. *Georgia* in June 1977, the Court banned the death penalty for rape of an adult female, even where aggravating circumstances are present, because the death sentence is grossly disproportionate to the of-

* Oklahoma's decision may have been prompted as much by efficiency as humaneness. To repair the state's out-of-order electric chair would have cost $62,000 and building a gas chamber would cost $300,000. If the state hadn't switched from electricity to drugs, it might have found itself in the embarrassing position of needlessly prolonging the execution of death row prisoners for want of a chair or chamber—which could be considered "cruel and unusual punishment."

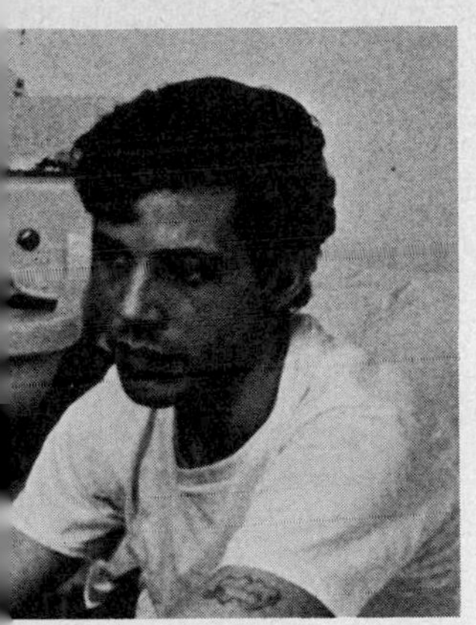

rry Selman, sentenced to death
rape, in Louisiana State prison
1974. The Supreme Court banned
at penalty for rape in 1977

fense: "the death penalty, which is unique in its severity and irrevocability, is an excessive penalty for the rapist who, as such, does not take human life."[107] Coker, who had three previous convictions for rape and the killing of one of his victims, had escaped from a Georgia prison where he was serving a life sentence, raped a 16-year-old mother, and abducted her as a hostage. The *Coker* ruling ended a long struggle by the Legal Defense Fund to eliminate the death penalty for rape.

In *Lockett* v. *Ohio* in July 1978, the Supreme Court ruled that death penalty statutes that prevent judges from considering *all* and *any* relevant mitigating factors in passing sentence violate the Eighth Amendment.[108] The Ohio death penalty statute allowed the judge to consider only three very specialized mitigating factors as grounds for mercy. By invalidating the statute, the *Lockett* decision spared the lives of 99 inmates on Ohio's death row.[109] Equally significant, *Lockett* established a legal basis for staying executions in other states with guided-discretion statutes that are unconstitutional because they do not permit judges to consider "as a mitigating factor, any aspect of a defendant's character or record and any of the circumstances of the offense that the defendant proffers as a basis for a sentence less than death."

In *Godfrey* v. *Georgia* in 1980, the Supreme Court turned its attention to the opposite side of the coin examined in *Lockett:* the aggravating circumstances used to justify imposition of the death sentence.[110] Georgia's capital punishment law required the jury to find the existence of at least one of 11 aggravating circumstances in murder cases before opting for death. The aggravating circumstances on the basis of which Godfrey was sentenced to death was that his offense was considered "outrageously or wantonly vile, horrible and inhuman." The Supreme Court, however, found nothing in this vague language, standing alone, to restrain juries from inflicting the death penalty arbitrarily and capriciously, or that provided guidance for distinguishing one murder from another. Godfrey had killed his wife and mother-in-law instantly with a shotgun, without physically abusing them beforehand. The *Godfrey* opinion strongly implied that in order for such an "outrageously-horrible" aggravating circumstance to meet constitutional requirements, there must be evidence that the murder involved torture, extreme suffering, or serious physical injury preceding death. Civil rights lawyers expected *Godfrey* to lead to a reprieve for dozens of Georgia's 97 condemned inmates who were sentenced under the same section of the state's law. By the same token, it could save an unknown number of prisoners awaiting execution throughout the country because most capital punishment laws have similar clauses concerning aggravating circumstances.[111]

In *Estelle* v. *Smith* in 1981, the Supreme Court ruled that before being questioned by a psychiatrist who might later testify against the accused at the penalty phase in a capital punishment case, the defendant must be informed of the right to remain silent and right to counsel.[112] After Smith

Close-up 12.3 HAVE JUDGES MADE THE DEATH PENALTY AN IDLE THREAT?

Although the Supreme Court upheld capital punishment in principle, its post-*Gregg* decisions and the actions of judges have made it possible for condemned defendants to indefinitely postpone the sentence from being carried out. There were nearly 800 inmates on death row in 1981. Despite this, judges have only allowed four men to be executed since 1967, thereby reducing the death penalty to an idle threat or ineffectual "sheathed sword."[a] In large part, this situation is attributable to the vast number of appeals available to condemned defendants, an issue which prompted Justice William Rehnquist in April 1981 to criticize his colleagues for tolerating seemingly endless procedural delays in capital punishment cases.

The occasion for Rehnquist's sharp rebuke was a routine appeal to the high court from Wayne Coleman, who was convicted by a jury in 1973 of murdering six family members, after torturing and raping some of them.[b] The Georgia capital punishment statute, under which Coleman was sentenced to death, had expressly been held constitutional in *Gregg*, and the Georgia Supreme Court affirmed the sentence. It was Coleman's second appeal to the Supreme Court, having exhausted state avenues of appeal. Rehnquist wanted the Supreme Court to accept the case for a full and final review, thereby forestalling further appeals. Because the Court denied *cert.*, Coleman is able and planned to start another round of appeals in the lower federal courts, which will probably take at least two years. After this he can petition the Supreme Court for a third time.

Rehnquist caustically noted that such delaying tactics, which are all too common in capital punishment cases, make a mockery of the criminal justice system and transform the death penalty into an illusion. The inevitable result of permitting innumerable delays in carrying out the death sentence is to reduce its deterrent effect, frustrate the purpose of retribution, and undermine the integrity of the sentencing process. "Even though we have upheld the constitutionality of capital punishment statutes, I fear that by our recent actions we have mistakenly sent a message to the lower state and federal courts that the actual imposition of the death sentence is to be avoided at all costs."

Rehnquist's position was enthusiastically endorsed by prosecutors across the country, who describe capital punishment as a "merry-go-round of litigation." In an attempt to do something about the problem, a new national association of prosecutors is examining ways to expedite the handling of death penalty cases.[c] The opponents of capital punishment, however, contend that the unique status of the death penalty justifies a cautionary go-slow approach, that time-consuming multiple routes of appeal are a safeguard against mistakes, and that the death penalty has little if any deterrent value. Efforts to change the ground rules governing death sentence appeals may or may not ultimately prove successful. But in the meantime, most death row inmates probably stand a better chance of dying of natural causes than of being executed by the state.

[a] *Newsweek,* May 11, 1981, p. 75.
[b] *Coleman* v. *Balkcom,* No. 80-5980. Decided April 27, 1981.
[c] *U.S. News & World Report,* May 11, 1981, p. 72.

was indicted for murder in Texas and while in jail, the court ordered a psychiatric examination to determine if he was competent to stand trial. Psychiatrist James Grigson indicated that he was, and Smith was tried by a jury and convicted of the charge. Texas law requires bifurcated proceedings in capital cases. At the penalty phase, if the jury affirmatively answers three questions that the state has to prove beyond a reasonable doubt, the judge must impose the death sentence. One of the questions is "whether there is a probability that the defendant would commit criminal acts of violence that would constitute a continuing threat to society." In testifying for the state at the penalty phase, Dr. Grigson based his opinion that Smith would continue to be dangerous on statements Smith made at the 90-minute pretrial psychiatric interview. The jury then resolved the issue of future dangerousness, and the other two questions, against Smith and he was sentenced to death. The Supreme Court, however, vacated the sentence in a decision which extended the *Miranda* doctrine beyond the confines of police interrogation and the determination of guilt. It did so on the grounds that the prosecution's use of disclosures by Smith at the psychiatric interview violated his privilege against self-incrimination, as well as his right to counsel, which attaches to the "critical stage" of such psychiatric interviews. The immediate effect of *Smith* was to invalidate the death sentences of at least 30 other Texas death row inmates against whom Grigson* had testified under similar circumstances.[113] The *Smith* decision casts doubt on the legality of capital pun-

* Nicknamed "Dr. Death" by defense counsel, Dr. Grigson has testified for the state on 70 occasions since 1967 concerning the defendant's future dangerousness. In every case but one the jury voted for the death sentence, which in Texas is administered by injection.

ishment laws in states such as Virginia and Oklahoma, which contain provisions like those in Texas.[114]

Finally, in 1981 the Supreme Court ruled that a defendant convicted of murder who is spared the death sentence under a bifurcated capital punishment structure cannot, upon retrial and conviction of the same charge, be sentenced to death.[115] In *Bullington* v. *Missouri,* the Court extended for the first time the Fifth Amendment protection against double jeopardy beyond the trial stage and specific issue of guilt to the sentence itself. (Ordinarily, criminal sentences can be increased on retrial without violating the double jeopardy clause.) It did so in *Bullington* by claiming that Missouri's penalty-determination phase in capital cases was like a trial because it required the state to "prove its case" beyond a reasonable doubt to a jury empowered to impose life imprisonment or the death sentence. It is well-established that the principle of double jeopardy ensures the finality of acquittal at trial. The Court reasoned that the same values underlying double jeopardy also bar the state from having more than one opportunity to prove that a defendant should receive the death penalty in the trial-like context of bifurcated proceedings.

These decisions, prolonged delays in carrying out the sentence (see Close-up 12.3), the ever-changing "evolving standards of decency," the shifts in the political composition of the Supreme Court, the fear of crime —all these factors augur that capital punishment is, and yet is far from being, a dead issue in the United States.

SUMMARY

The four objectives of sentencing set the stage for the choice of sentence by the court, but current efforts seek to downgrade the importance of rehabilitation and place greater emphasis on retribution, incapacitation, and deterrence. The presentence report is an invaluable aid to the court in reaching a sentencing decision, notwithstanding the controversy over whether the presentence report should be disclosed to the defendant. The core problem in sentencing is disparity. Sentencing disparity stems from the court's unguided and uncontrolled discretion, poorly constructed penal codes, inadequate appellate review of sentences, and (perhaps most important) the indeterminate sentence and its corollary, the rehabilitative ideal. Attempts to curtail disparity without changing the penal code have proved ineffective. The 1962 Model Penal Code was a significant step in the direction of more uniform and rational sentencing, but by retaining an indeterminate sentence structure for felonies, it did not go far enough to satisfy the contemporary critics of sentencing disparity. As rehabilitation loses ground to the "just deserts" model of sentencing, there is considerable support for abolishing the indeterminate sentence and replacing it with determinate or mandatory prison sentences. Senator Edward Kennedy's Sentencing Commission bill appears to incorporate the most promising features for reforming the sentencing decision, controlling disparity, and providing justice to the convicted defendant. The most awesome expression of disparity is reflected in the death penalty, whose existence was threatened by the Supreme Court's decision in *Furman* v. *Georgia* in 1972. However, in *Gregg* v. *Georgia* in 1976, the Court clarified the constitutional status of the death penalty by ruling that it was permissible under guided-discretion death penalty statutes. The message of *Gregg* was that, as applied to the unique sentence of death, informed discretion is the *sine qua non* for controlling unwarranted disparity, and that where the taking of life is concerned, it is unreasonable to relinquish all discretion in the name of uniformity (as mandatory death penalty statutes do).

DISCUSSION QUESTIONS

1. Why should the defendant have a right to disclosure of the presentence report?
2. Who has more discretion: the police, the prosecutor, or the courts? Explain.
3. What is the relationship between sentencing disparity and plea bargaining?
4. What is the most effective method for reducing sentencing disparity in the long run? Why?
5. Should mandatory death penalty statutes be permitted in certain types of cases? What types of cases, and why?

TWA's
Midweek Fare
To Los Angeles.

Chapter 13

JAILS

Corrections / Jails and prisons
The National Jail Survey
Jail populations and facilities / Jail personnel / Jail inmates
Contemporary Jail Problems
Dehumanization and degradation / Inadequate facilities
Local Administration of Jails
Attitudes and qualifications of jail personnel / Standards for jail operation
The Concern with Security

Close-up 13.1: The Federal Metropolitan Correctional Center

Custodial convenience / State-operated jails
The Manhattan House of Detention
Conditions in the Tombs in 1970 / The Tombs riot and its aftermath / The House of Detention on Rikers Island / The Rikers Island riot
Summary

Corrections

The term *corrections* has a special meaning in the criminal justice system. It is used to designate the various agencies and programs that assume legal responsibility for the custody, supervision, treatment, and punishment of convicted offenders, that is, for implementing the sentence and the objectives of sentencing. Corrections is an umbrella concept that encompasses every official decision bearing on convicted offenders as part of and pursuant to their sentence, in the course of paying their debt to society, and while they remain under the legal control of the state. The correctional phase of the criminal justice system begins as soon as the offender commences to fulfill his or her sentence; it ends when the offender —prisoner, probationer, or parolee—has fully satisfied the requirements of the sentence imposed and is legally discharged from state supervision and obligation, thereby regaining unconditional liberty and those rights of citizenship not lost permanently through a felony conviction. Each sentence, regardless of its content, sets the major course and context of corrections, whose goal is to prevent the convicted offender from recidivating. Even the death penalty is a form of corrections, for it is the way in which the convicted defendant legally "completes" the sentence.

There is another, less precise definition of corrections that is rooted more in ideology than in processing stages and that has, until recently, dominated the rhetoric associated with the tail end of the criminal justice system. The semantics of corrections has traditionally emphasized the rehabilitative or treatment value of whatever is done to, with, and for convicted defendants in the name of crime prevention. Stressing its personal and social benefits to the offender and to society, the ideology of corrections-as-rehabilitation was responsible for jails and prisons being called correctional institutions. However, emerging progressive principles of sentencing (discussed in Chapter 12) and the reality of the conditions of incarceration suggest that such facilities are principally *custodial* institutions.[1] Whatever genuine rehabilitation (corrections) may be achieved with convicted defendants, it apparently takes place in the community, whether it involves a direct sentence to the community or various release programs from jails and prisons. Indeed, for the foreseeable future, jail and prison personnel will have their hands and cells full simply trying to provide humane custody for the 363,000 daily inmates.

Jails and prisons

Jails are not prisons. Prisons contain only convicted defendants who are serving terms of more than one year, that is, adjudicated felons. Jails, on the other hand, contain two main groups: (1) detainees who are awaiting trial because they are unable to raise or were denied bail. For these individuals, accused of crime and presumed to be innocent, jails are temporary holding quarters to guarantee their presence at arraignment and trial. (2) Convicted defendants who are usually, but not always, serving terms of less than one year, that is, adjudicated misdemeanants. Both pretrial detainees and convicted petty offenders are referred to as jail inmates or prisoners by virtue of their incarceration, although for the former group custody is prompted by administrative necessity while for the latter it is a punishment for crime. Jails also house miscellaneous categories of persons that are rarely found in prisons: material witnesses, juvenile offenders, convicted felons awaiting appeal, probation violators awaiting revocation hearings, mental patients awaiting civil commitment, and others. Excluding stays of less than 48 hours, an estimated 3 to 5 million persons spend time in the nation's jails each year, and that is 10 to 15 times the number of inmates handled by all state and federal prisons annually.[2]

THE NATIONAL JAIL SURVEY*

The most comprehensive information on the nation's jails comes from the 1972 and 1978 National Jail Census and the companion Survey of Inmates of Local Jails for the same two years.[3,4] As of February 1978, there were 3,493 jails containing 158,394 inmates (an average of about 45 "prisoners" per jail).[5] When the first National Jail Census was taken on March 15, 1970, there were 4,037 jails containing 160,863 inmates. Thus the 1972 figures represent a 13 percent decrease in the number of jails and about a 1 percent drop in the number of inmates.

Jail populations and facilities

Of the 3,921 jails in 1972, 2,901 (about three out of every four institutions) had less than 21 inmates, 907 had 21–249 inmates, and 113 jails housed 250 or more inmates.[6] California's jails had the largest total number of inmates in both periods (about 25,500), accounting for one out of every six inmates in the country, followed by New York. When the jail populations of Texas, Florida, Pennsylvania, and Georgia are added to those of California and New York, the six states together account for half of the country's jail population. Sixty percent of all jails were located in police stations, courthouses, or the sheriff's office. A majority of the nation's jails had some multiple-occupancy cells and one-half had at least one dormitory. One-third of the jails were over 50 years old.[7] Virtually all of the jails that received juveniles (70 percent) separated them from adults, and nine out of ten jails segregated mental patients from the general inmate population. Significantly, three-fifths of all jails did not segregate detainees from the convicted, and three-fourths did not separate first offenders from repeaters. Forty percent of the jails had no recreation or entertainment facilities whatsoever for inmates; in the 60 percent that

* As of this writing, only a preliminary report was available on the 1978 National Jail Census. Therefore, much of the material in this section is based upon the 1972 census. In addition, in this chapter, many of the reference notes contain further commentary on the material in the text (rather than citations alone). The student should therefore consult the notes regularly; they begin on page 573.

did, the opportunities for diversion were quite limited. Only 16 percent of all jails, for example, had an exercise yard. Two-fifths of the jails had work release programs in which just 8 percent of all sentenced inmates participated; one-half of the institutions with work release had separate accommodations for inmates enrolled in the programs. Eighty-six percent of the jails had no medical facilities of any kind, and 90 percent had no educational facilities.[8]

Jail personnel

The nation's jails were operated by 44,298 employees, 89 percent of whom worked full time. Of the total labor force, 46 percent were custodial personnel (guards and jailors), 27 percent were administrative staff, 17 percent were clerical and maintenance staff, and 7 percent were in the professional category (see Table 13.1). In about half of the jails all custodial personnel are sworn police officers. Forty-five percent of the professional staff were part-time employees, as were 6 percent of the custodial and administrative workers. Only one-fifth of the nation's jails employed doctors, and no more than 5 percent of the jails employed any of the other professional staff listed in Table 13.1. The actual inmate-to-staff ratios for every position are much larger than those shown in the table, especially for the professional staff. This is because the number of personnel required to operate a jail facility 24 hours a day, 365 days a year, is much greater than the number of personnel on duty at a given hour. Thus there are about 1.6 full-time workers on duty per shift for every 36–40 prisoners.[9]

Table 13.1 Number of Jail Employees in the United States by Category and Inmate-to-Staff Ratios, 1972

Employee Positions	Number of Employees	Inmate-to Staff Ratio	Number of Jails (and percent of total number of jails) with One or More Professional Staff Employees
Professional Staff			
Academic teachers	367	385:1	136 (3%)
Vocational teachers	209	677:1	78 (2%)
Social workers	487	290:1	182 (5%)
Psychologists	137	1,033:1	95 (3%)
Psychiatrists	166	852:1	114 (3%)
Physicians	1,063	133:1	744 (19%)
Nurses	747	189:1	299 (6%)
Total	3,176	45:1	
Nonprofessional Staff			
Custodial officers	20,338	7:1	
Clerical and maintenance	7,530	19:1	
Administrative	12,107	12:1	
Other	1,147	—	
Total	41,122	4:1	
All Jail Personnel	44,298	3.2:1	

Source: The Nation's Jails: A Report on the Census of Jails from the 1972 Survey of Inmates of Local Jails (Washington, D.C.: Government Printing Office, May 1975), pp. 8–12.

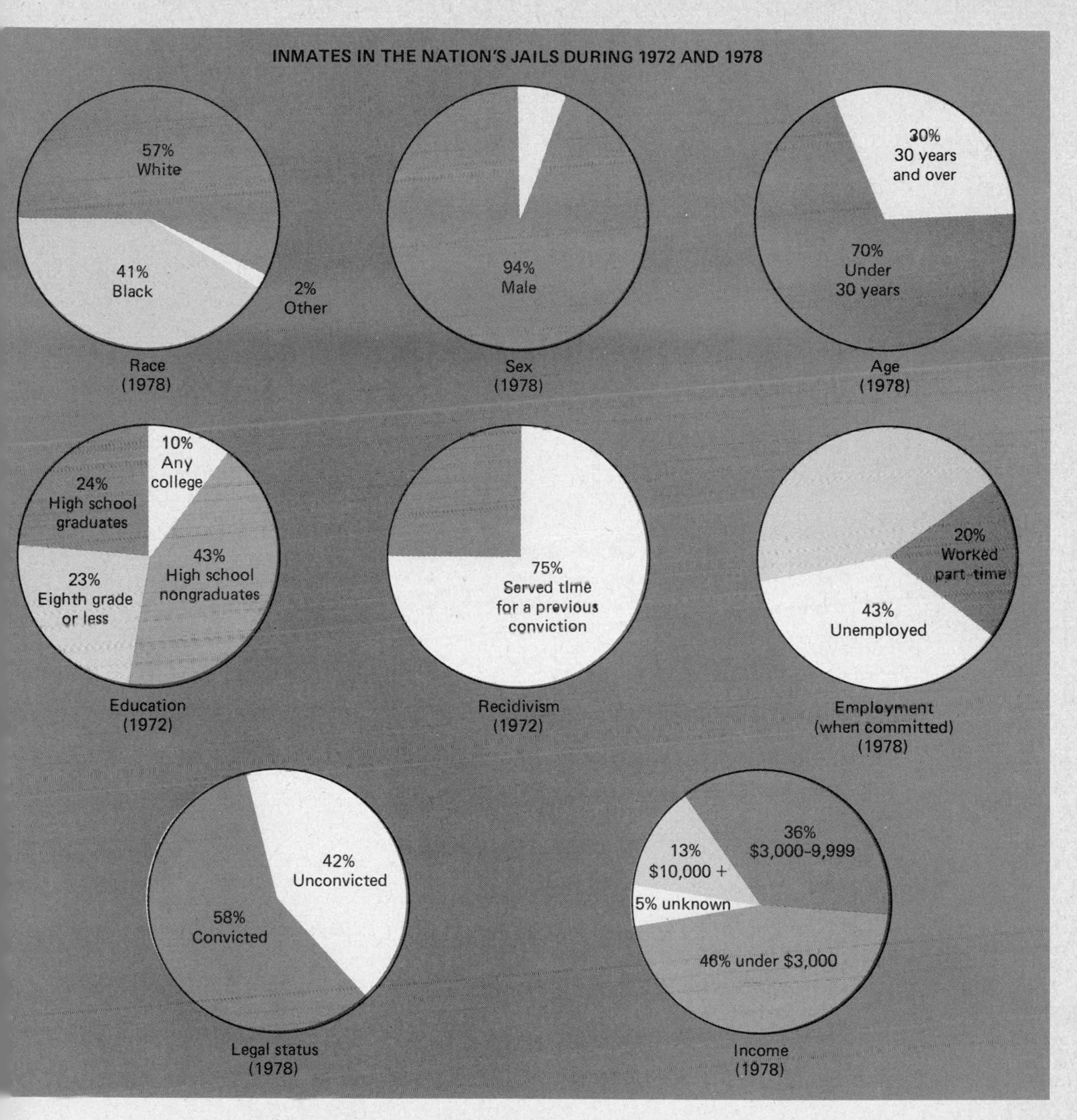

FIGURE 13.1 Characteristics of jail inmates in the United States, 1972, 1978. *Source:* Survey of Inmates of Local Jails 1972: Advance Report, Washington, D.C.: National Criminal Justice Information and Statistics Service, 1974, pp. 3–4; Census of Jails and Survey of Jail Inmates, 1978, Preliminary Report (Washington, D.C.: LEAA, February, 1979), no page number.

Jail inmates

The personal characteristics of inmates are shown in Figure 13.1. Although only 7,800 juveniles were detained in jail on any given day in 1972, some 100,000 juveniles spent time in jail during that year. (Many juvenile authorities condemn the jailing of juveniles despite their separation from adult prisoners.[10]) By 1978, however, there were only 1,600 juveniles in the daily jail population, reflecting a national policy toward segregating delinquents from adult criminals. The great majority of inmates were in their twenties, almost two-thirds had not completed high school, and 43 percent were unemployed prior to being jailed. One quarter of the inmates were regular or occasional heroin users. Of the total 1972 jail population of 141,600 inmates, 55 percent, or 78,000, had been convicted and 45 percent were unconvicted; in the 1970 National Jail Census, 52 percent of all inmates were unconvicted, compared with 42 percent in 1978.[11] Thus the jail is an institution in which the tried and the untried share roughly equal billing.

Perhaps the most unexpected findings of the 1972 National Jail Survey pertain to the crimes for which convicted inmates were sent to jail: *20,000 (one-third) of the 60,200 inmates serving sentences had committed index offenses.* Thus, according to the *UCR,* a sizeable minority of sentenced jail inmates had committed serious crimes and were felons.[12] In addition, some persons serving jail sentences for misdemeanors may originally have been charged with felonies that were reduced through plea bargaining. As for the 50,800 detainees awaiting trial, 30,600 (60 percent) were arrested for Part I offenses, 6,700 for drug violations, and only 3,700 for drunkenness, vagrancy, or traffic offenses.[13] Whether or not jails are populated by a smaller or larger number of petty offenders than is generally assumed, the aggregate contemporary problems represented by jails and the treatment of their inmates are far from being petty.

CONTEMPORARY JAIL PROBLEMS

With good reason, the country's jails have been described as the "ultimate ghetto," a "dumping grounds" for health and welfare cases,[14] "cesspools for crime," "festering sores in the criminal justice system,"[15] and "the most glaringly inadequate institution in the American correctional scene."[16] The dehumanization of inmates begins at intake, a "status degradation" ceremony in which both accused and convicted are stripped and frisked, given a one-minute "medical examination" (if any), categorized for security purposes, forced to relinquish their personal identity for numerical anonymity, and then left to learn the ropes of surviving in jail from "barn bosses," the stronger and more hardened criminals who are the self-styled leaders within the inmate social system.[17] Most of the time, inmates are confined in their cells, in the larger bullpen cages adjacent to the cells, or in open storage-bin dormitories that hold

Dehumanization and degradation

12–60 persons under conditions that foster assault, drug addiction, homosexual rape, racial strife, constant invasion of privacy, and the spread of communicable diseases.

The degrading impact of jails is perpetuated and exacerbated by the pervasive idleness and destructive boredom that characterize the jail experience everywhere. Meaningful jobs are virtually nonexistent, and what frequently passes for vocational training is a scarce supply of janitorial and maintenance tasks at which trusties get first crack.[18] The brevity of jail sentences, the inappropriateness of rehabilitating persons who commit victimless crimes and minor offenses, the legal restrictions against subjecting pretrial detainees to treatment or work, the logistical problems created by the presence of women and juvenile offenders under the same roof as adult men offenders, and the presence of miscellaneous groups awaiting further processing—all are formidable barriers to providing correctional programs in jail.

The larger jails, which contain a disproportionate number of the nation's inmates, are chronically and severely overcrowded, while the small rural facilities are constantly underutilized. This leads to the bizarre situation in which some jails have two and three inmates per cell and others, such as those in Vermont, have only one inmate per jail![19] Thus jail populations are either too small to justify expenditures for improved conditions, professional staff, and treatment programs, or too large to be operated efficiently, effectively, and humanely. The jail population is noted for its high incidence of infectious disease and sickness. Despite this, inmates are kept in antiquated, decrepit, poorly designed and equipped facilities that are notorious for their filth, their state of disrepair and neglect, health hazards, poor sanitation, inadequate heat and ventilation, and limited access to personal hygiene commodities.[20] Even such basic items as soap, towels, toothbrushes, showers, clean bedding, and toilet paper are often in short supply or await "dispensation" by an overworked, underpaid, and lethargic custodial staff. A handful of jails still rely on waste buckets rather than flush toilets![21]

Inadequate facilities

Most authorities on the subject have attributed the dehumanizing treatment of inmates and the deplorable jail conditions to (1) the local administration of the institutions by county sheriffs and city police chiefs, that is, management by law enforcement personnel, and (2) the obsessive concern with security that dominates the operation of jails.

Local Administration of Jails

The operation of county jails typically falls within the jurisdiction of the county sheriff, while city jails come under the authority of the chief of police. In either case, elected law enforcement officials steeped in local politics and patronage tend to view the jail as a sideline to their crime-fighting activities and as a temporary place for warehousing inmates. In some rural areas, the jailor's compensation is based on the fee system: the jailor retains any money saved from the allotment for inmate food and upkeep and pays for any excess out of his own pocket. Naturally, this arrangement encourages jail administrators to skimp on operating costs at the expense of the inmates, spending as little as $1.55 a day on food per prisoner, for example. Until the early 1970s, the Forrest County (Miss.) Jail sheriff's "salary" consisted of $4 for every arrest, $2 for each offender admitted to the jail, and $2 for each day the prisoner remained there. Because no public funds were available to feed and maintain the inmates, those costs came out of the sheriff's fees. Similar practices continue in hundreds of counties throughout the nation.[22]

Attitudes and qualifications of jail personnel

As for the custodial staff, most are sworn police officers who are often hostile to offenders and committed to putting and keeping them in jail, who are unsympathetic to inmate needs and grievances, and who occasionally misuse their discretion to achieve "justice without trial." Custodial officers are not usually subject to any form of civil service or merit system, and in-service training programs are few and far between. Consequently, jail workers possess minimal personal and educational qualifications for the trying tasks involved in managing jails and supervising inmates.[23] The low job requirements are reflected in employee salaries: in 1970 the average monthly earnings of full-time jail personnel was $617, and in some places it was as little as $350–$400 a month.[24] Sometimes new police recruits, who are at the bottom of the totem pole, will be assigned to jail duty, which is unpopular among experienced officers; regular officers may be "sent to jail" duty as punishment for inadequate performance in their police assignments.

The difficulties in attracting and retaining qualified guards appointed by the sheriff, and preserving on-the-job experience, are also complicated by the high turnover rates among officeholders who by statute cannot succeed themselves. The result is that for many guards (as with all inmates), jails are places they would rather not be, occupational choices of last resort. This attitude shows up in their performance. "The truth is that jail personnel are the most uneducated, untrained, and poorly paid of all personnel in the criminal justice system—and furthermore, there aren't enough of them."[25] In an effort to change this situation, in 1977 the National Institute of Correction announced the establishment of a National Jail Center in Boulder, Colorado, whose objectives include upgrading the country's jail personnel through training and technical assistance. A substantial portion of its $1.5 million first annual budget will be used to provide training programs and develop instructional material for jailors.[26]

Standards for jail operation

Besides the lack of professional qualifications for personnel, there is a dearth of effective state or county standards for maintaining and inspecting jails. Twenty-three states have no statutory provisions for the inspec-

Boulder, Colo., the National Jail nter is developing training pro- ams to improve the nation's jail rsonnel

tion, establishment, or enforcement of jail standards. Even states that have promulgated minimum standards for jail conditions and operation, such as California and Illinois, may lack the authority to compel local jurisdictions to comply with the standards. And where such authority does exist, it has rarely been invoked, possibly to avoid a confrontation in deciding between improving the jails or closing them down. In almost every state, the county grand jury has the primary responsibility for reporting on jail practices and providing decent jail conditions. In practice, however, this body has relinquished its role in jail reform under the prodding of prosecutors more interested in indicting criminals and putting them in jail rather than alleviating their brutalizing environment. The almost complete lack of explicit standards for the grand jury to enforce leaves the matter in the hands of local political officials and indifferent jail personnel, who are skeptical or hostile to "outside investigations" of their jails, their agencies, and their performance.[27]

Because there are no federal jails (see Close-up 13.1), the U.S. Bureau of Prisons carries out a rigorous program of local jail inspection, but it covers only 800 local institutions that are contracted to hold 3,500–4,000 unsentenced federal prisoners a day.[28] When federal inspectors consider a jail unfit for their detainees, their only alternative is to cancel the contract and transfer the detainees to other local facilities—which may be as bad or worse.[29] One encouraging sign on the institutional horizon is the emergence of standards for facility planning and construction. This effort has been spurred by the National Clearinghouse for Criminal Justice Planning and Architecture at the University of Illinois, set up in 1968 by the LEAA.[30]

Close-up 13.1 THE FEDERAL METROPOLITAN CORRECTIONAL CENTER

The federal system's first jail of its own was opened in December 1974, a $15 million, 22-story, high-rise "space age" jail located in downtown San Diego. (Two similar federal jail facilities have since been constructed in Chicago and New York City.) The west coast Federal Metropolitan Correctional Center, undertaken as an experiment in "dignity and humane concern," is designed to hold 500 inmates in tastefully furnished private rooms and small dormitories. The "residents" are free to wander about the air-conditioned floors, which contain community rooms with table tennis and billiard tables, color television, piped-in music, vending machines, and pay telephones; or they may decide to spend their time in the well-equipped recreation center atop the roof. Although these features give rise to the charge of "country club atmosphere," such humane conditions of incarceration are considered appropriate for persons who have only been accused of crime and are awaiting trial. "Imagine, being in stir and having a guard ask you politely if you find everything all right, just like you were a regular human being." Computerized alarms, television monitors, windows too narrow to squeeze through, unbreakable glass, and the absence of a room key are constant reminders, however, that the facility is no country club or Holiday Inn.[a] Very few state and local governments can afford the kind of jails they would like to have without federal aid. For example, the new $6.2 million air-conditioned Douglas County jail in Omaha, Nebraska, planned to open in 1978 and to hold 200 misdemeanants and detainees, was financed by the LEAA.[b]

[a] Everett R. Holles, "Dignity Stressed in New U.S. Jail," *New York Times,* December 8, 1974, p. 96.
[b] Rob Wilson, "Corrections on the Local Level," *Corrections,* December 1976, pp. 25–26.

The Concern with Security

Two related considerations dominate the daily operation of jails and control the lives of inmates and keepers alike: security and custodial convenience. The emphasis on security measures stems from the law enforcement orientation of jail personnel, facilities that were constructed as maximum-custody institutions for dangerous offenders, and the need to prevent escapes, riots, suicides, assaults, and the smuggling of contraband. These factors, along with the absence of any meaningful differential classification, are responsible for every accused person and convicted inmate's being treated as though each of them were Public Enemy Number One. The obsession with security is expressed in a steady routine of lock-ins, head counts, censored mail, visitation restrictions, frisks, cell inspections, shakedowns, opposition to programs, confiscation of personal property, punitive isolation, harassment, and incessant direct and technological surveillance.[31] The indignities and deprivations heaped upon inmates in the name of security are all-encompassing: lights too dim to read by during the day are left on at night so that prisoners may be observed, open commodes without partitions allow guards to monitor every inmate "movement," and strip searches are undertaken to discover contraband concealed in human cells.

Custodial convenience

However, the official focus on security is sometimes at odds with the natural tendency for jail personnel to take it easy and do as little as possible whenever possible. This might be called the principle of *custodial convenience.* The custodial function carries its own badge of boredom; constant security and responsive supervision are hard work, and thinly spread, underpaid, nonprofessional, and unmotivated guards resent "waiting on" criminals day and night. Accordingly, the inmates may be fed (as are cattle) twice instead of three times a day to suit the convenience of the staff. Sick inmates who request medical attention may be dismissed as malingerers or taken care of only when the guards get around to it. Supervision may consist of looking in on prisoners at night to make sure they are in their cells, have not died, and do not assault each other—or paying inmates 10 to 20 cents an hour to watch suicide-prone prisoners and to "call" if anything suspicious occurs.[32] The quality of jail conditions as measured by dehumanization, security, and custodial convenience is such that legally innocent defendants are worse off than sentenced offenders, and both groups are treated worse than felony offenders serving long terms in state prisons.

The plight and the problems of the jails are so extensive, deeply embedded, and stubbornly resistant to change that they seem to defy resolution. Anything that would reduce the size of the average daily inmate population would be a step in the right direction. Prospects include various bail reform measures (discussed in Chapter 8), speedy trial (discussed in Chapter 10), diversion (to be discussed in Chapter 16), having separate institutions for detainees and short-term sentenced offenders (as a few jurisdictions do now), and allowing the convicted to do their time on the installment plan through "weekend sentences."[33] A more visionary approach than that of simply taking some inmates out of the jails is the proposal to take the jails out of the correctional picture and replace them with a comprehensive system of community-based placement. The most frequently endorsed response to the major stumbling block to jail reform —local administration and the abuses that accompany autonomous and fragmented control of institutions—is state-operated jails.[34] The alleged

State-operated jails

virtues of state-operated jails include centralization of administration, merit hiring and professionalization, politics-free management, standardization of services, and upgrading of jail conditions. Adopted by the Standards and Goals Commission as a nationwide goal to be achieved by 1982, state-operated jails are currently found only in Connecticut, Vermont, Alaska, Rhode Island, and Delaware.[35]

Newly constructed and modern jail facilities, still thought to be the road to more civilized inmate treatment, have unfortunately not lived up to expectations. In a study of 19 modern jails—the best the system has to offer—made by The American Foundation for the LEAA, Nagel concluded that "the modern American jail, like its predecessor of the last century, is a cage and has changed only superficially. The concepts of repression and human degradation are remarkably intact."[36] "The trend in jail design is toward more extensive use of electronic equipment and steel bars. More and more staff functions are becoming mechanical in nature and the distance between inmates and staff is increasing. The result of these developments is an environment which is totally dehumanizing. The inmates are literally held in the system [as] mere items."[37]

In the long run, genuine and enduring jail reform may depend on the progress made by those prisoners serving felony sentences in 400 prisons throughout the United States who are demanding fairer treatment under the banner of prisoners' rights (to be discussed in Chapter 15). The story of the Manhattan House of Detention illustrates the problems found in the large urban facilities that hold one-half[38] of the nation's inmates; it demonstrates the explosive consequences of barbarous jail conditions, traces the legal avenues of reform which constitute the mainstay of the prisoners' rights movement, and testifies to the staggering obstacles to achieving lasting improvement in the lot of jail inmates—and the "evolving standards of *decadency*."

THE MANHATTAN HOUSE OF DETENTION

The Manhattan House of Detention for Men (the Tombs) is a 12-story fortress with 835 cells that was opened in June 1941. Built in the era of Ma Barker, Bonnie and Clyde, and John Dillinger, it reflected the American attitude that every criminal was a mad dog for whom the proper response was to "lock 'em up and throw the key away." In those days, crime rates were lower, trials were held quickly, the detention period was shorter, and overcrowding was not yet a problem.[39]

Conditions in the Tombs in 1970

The Tombs was constructed like a series of safe-deposit boxes: "You have to go through 8 doors to get to a cell, and every door but the last one requires a man on duty."[40] By 1970, the Tombs had become unfit for human habitation—but was apparently still fit for criminals. Food served to inmates contained hairs, glass, and waterbugs, and doctors were indifferent to requests for medical attention.[41] The men were locked in their cells continuously for long periods of time; when on lock-out, they wandered aimlessly in the corridors with nothing to do but play solitaire. Roaches, mice, and vermin were commonplace.[42] With a rated capacity of about 900, the institution usually held double that number of inmates. At times, three men were packed in a 4 foot by 9 foot cell—about as much space per man as each would get in a coffin. Security measures were oppressive, heating was inadequate, the jail reeked with foul-smelling air, and the clamorous noise level was itself a health hazard. A former New York City commissioner of correction admitted, "We shouldn't treat cattle the way we have to house our inmates." Through it all, the prisoners' chief complaints were about the "excessive" bail system that had put them there, the absence of speedy trial, and overcrowding.

he Tombs riot and its aftermath

On October 1, 1970, the Tombs held 1,416 persons, a population that was 57 percent above its rated capacity.[43] On that day, the inmates rioted and took 18 hostages, who were released four days later when Mayor John Lindsay agreed to discuss the prisoners' grievances with them. "I tried to explain [to the mayor] that our problem was not the corrections officers, but the system—the judicial system, the Legal Aid lawyers who tell us to plead guilty without asking if we *are* guilty, the bail system, the long wait for trials."[44] The rioters were assured there would be no reprisals, and the mayor promised to be responsive to their

›ting prisoners in the Tombs in ›tober 1970 hang a sign, "Justice ›w," from windows

demands for lower bail, speedier trial, and less crowding.[45] Conditions did change: they got *worse!* Thirteen months after the 1970 riot, the Tombs was 68 percent overcrowded, and the city had invested $2 million in 24 tons of steel on each floor to protect the staff from riotous inmates. Prisoners were sleeping in the receiving room of the Tombs to avoid being housed three to a cell.[46]

All was not lost. In the summer of 1970, the Legal Aid Society of New York began working to improve conditions at the Tombs through court action. The efforts paid off four years later, when U.S. District Court Judge Morris Lasker declared that conditions at the Tombs violated the constitutional rights of inmates and would "shock the conscience of any citizen who knew them."[47,48] Given the choice between complying with the court order to make the required changes and closing the Tombs, the city shut down the Manhattan House of Detention on December 20, 1974, and transferred its inmates to the House of Detention for Men (HDM) on Rikers Island.[49] Constitutionally unfit for prisoners, the Tombs was subsequently used as a site for training corrections officers.[50]

The House of Detention on Rikers Island

Rikers Island is the largest penal colony of its kind in the country. It consists of six facilities, each holding a different population of offenders; its total daily inmate count is 7,500, two-thirds of whom are awaiting trial.[51] When the Tombs was closed, 600 inmates were transferred to Rikers Island, and the HDM population ultimately swelled from 1,036 to 1,879, thereby replicating the conditions at the Tombs.[52] Almost 700 men were confined two to a cell.[53] Built in 1933, the detention facility was designed to house sentenced offenders, as could be seen in its prison-like eight cellblocks and tiers of cells within each. Several of the cell-blocks, which are the length of a football field, contained 300 detainees and were monitored by two or three guards.[54] On a clear day, the guards could not see what was happening at the far end of the field and were not anxious to mix with the inmates to find out, for a large number of the prisoners were accused of violent crimes, and there were Black Liberation Army members among them.[55]

In its report in June 1975, the Board of Corrections, a small watchdog agency that investigated inmate suicides, disturbances, and grievances, warned that the HDM on Rikers Island was dangerously overcrowded and understaffed.[56] There had been a 50 percent increase in jail population, budgetary cuts had reduced the number of officers to 340 from what should have been 500, prisoners had become more militant and rejective of authority, and there had been a 43 percent rise in inmate assaults on inmates and a 533 percent increase in assaults on officers![57] There were also the "cruel and *usual*" conditions of unsanitary surroundings, "hot" meals served cold, the absence of privacy, and daily food expenditures of $1.38 per inmate.[58]

The Rikers Island riot

The board's concern about the incendiary situation at the HDM was confirmed a few months later. In a riot that erupted on November 23,

e House of Detention for Men
Rikers Island, with nearly 8,000
isoners, is the largest penal
mplex in the country

1975, the inmates seized five guards as hostages and did $1 million in property damage to dramatize their dissatisfaction with overcrowding, trial delays, excessive bail, no-contact visits, inadequate medical care, and arbitrary discipline.[59] The 17-hour insurrection ended when the commissioner of correction and the Board of Correction head, meeting with inmate delegates, promised to be responsive to their grievances, and the district attorney offered the rioters amnesty in exchange for releasing the hostages unharmed. In the wake of the riot, some improvements in jail conditions were realized. The HDM population was reduced to 1,013 by transferring hundreds of detainees to the Bronx House of Detention—and to Sing-Sing prison![60] Some of the laid off corrections officers were rehired, and a contact visiting room was built.[61] Significantly, under an upcoming revision in the city charter, the Board of Correction would be authorized to establish minimum standards for the city's penal institutions and to subpoena witnesses.[62]

The inmates' victory was short-lived. Because the riot had destroyed two cellblocks containing space for 600 men, and because of increases in admissions, the HDM on Rikers Island was again headed for serious overcrowding and its associated disabilities. One month after the riot ended, several cellblocks had 325 inmates each, 85 over capacity.[63] By January 1976, 190 cells were being used for double occupancy.[64] To complicate the matter further, in February 1975 Judge Lasker ruled that jail conditions at the HDM on Rikers Island were unconstitutional.[65] The order called for improved visitation schedules, more adequate recreation periods, a classification system that would remove the vast majority of defendants from the cloak of maximum security, and an end to the practice of stacking two inmates in one cell.[66,67] Lacking the funds to comply with the court order, the city's only solution was to find new space and more suitable quarters for the Rikers Island detainees—which it did by petitioning Judge Lasker to *reopen the Tombs* so that 600 inmates could be transferred back to the facility that he had closed down the year before! Even Justice Jawn Sandifer agreed with the corrections commissioner that "the solution is to bring back the Tombs."[68]

Another judicial response to overcrowding is to release defendants who have been held the longest on the lowest bail. This course of action was threatened by Judge Orrin Judd if the Queens House of Detention could not otherwise comply with the federal court's "one man, one cell" order. The prospect of releasing criminals is highly controversial and legally complicated even within judicial circles. Reacting to such *federal* court orders, *state* judges allege that releasing prisoners would violate the orders of the *local* judges who sent the defendants to jail.[69] While the legal technicalities were being debated, the population of the HDM on Rikers Island, which becomes unmanageable over 1,000, soared to 1,740 in November 1977.[70]

SUMMARY

Jails are short-term correctional (custodial) facilities that house pretrial detainees and sentenced misdemeanants. The most recent and comprehensive information on jails, jail personnel, and jail inmates comes from the LEAA 1972 National Jail Survey. The principal contemporary jail problems are the dehumanizing effect on inmates, local administration of the facilities, an absence of standards for operating jails, and an exclusive orientation toward security. Developments at the Manhattan House of Detention (the Tombs) illustrate the deplorable conditions of incarceration in urban jails—which can lead to riots and judicial intervention in corrections.

DISCUSSION QUESTIONS

1. What are the main differences between jails and prisons?
2. What are the major problems surrounding the administration of jails?
3. What makes incarceration in jail cruel and unusual punishment?

Chapter 14

PRISONS

Types of Prisons

The Reception and Diagnostic Center

The Department of Corrections / Classification

The Overcrowded Prisons

Causes of the prison population increase

Close-up 14.1: Double Celling Passes Constitutional Muster

Administrative responses to overcrowding / New prison construction / Judicial response to overcrowding

Imprisonment as Cruel and Unusual Punishment

Holt v. *Sarver* (1970)

Close-up 14.2: The Tucker Prison Farm

James v. *Wallace* (1976)

The court's minimum constitutional standards / The court's timetable / Compliance with *James* / Appellate court restricts *James* decision

Ruiz v. *Estelle* (1980)

The Custodial Staff

Education and training / Racial imbalance / Women guards in men's prisons / *Dothard* v. *Rawlinson* (1977)

Restructuring the Role of Guards

Treatment teams / The guards' working conditions

Close-up 14.3: The Stanford Prison Experiment: College Students as Prisoners and Guards

Work, Education, and Treatment Programs

Vocational Training

Unemployment in prison / Slave wages and irrelevant training / State-use laws / Reforming prison industry / Reforming state-use laws / The private sector in prison industry / The Free Venture program
Education
Remedial and high school education / College-educated cons
Treatment

Close-up 14.4: The Therapeutic Community

Impediments to treatment / Conjugal visits
The Parole Decision
Parole eligibility / Goodtime credit laws / The membership of parole boards
Parole Board-Determined Release
The parole grant hearing / Absence of due process rights (*Greenholtz* v. *Inmates of Nebraska Penal Complex,* 1979) / Rehabilitation / The parole plan / Parole board procedures / The board's unrestricted discretion / The parole guidelines table / Criticisms of the guidelines table
Parole Contracts (Mutual Agreement Programming)
The need for parole contracts / MAP in Wisconsin / The virtues of MAP / The drawbacks of MAP
The Abolition of Parole
No-parole in California, Maine, and Indiana / The problems of no-parole
Mandatory Release and Discharge
Gate money
The Future of Imprisonment
Design and location of prisons / The Martinson study of rehabilitation / Coed prisons / Who belongs in prison?
Summary

TYPES OF PRISONS

Prisons are state and federal institutions that house felons who are serving terms of one year or more. The nation's 400 prisons range from the maximum- and medium-security facilities that are immediately recognizable as prisons to a few exceptional institutions in the minimum-security category that at first glance might be mistaken for hospitals, college campuses, rest homes, or country clubs.

The California prisons at San Quentin and Folsom exemplify the popular image of prisons as walled or fenced-in places that hold serious offenders in need of constant surveillance. The California State Prison at San Quentin has 3,000 inmates, 400 of whom at any one time are locked up in "segregation" units for having assaulted guards or other inmates or for their own protection. Folsom is a maximum-security prison that contains 2,000 hardened criminals who are considered incorrigible and beyond rehabilitation. They are men who have been in prison several times before, who are serving long terms for violent crimes or as habitual offenders, or who are considered serious escape risks.[1]

A sharp contrast to the traditional maximum- and medium-security prisons is the unusual minimum-security prison at the Fort Grant Training Center in Arizona. A $25 million complex nestled at the foot of Graham Mountain, Fort Grant has no secure perimeter. Its most prominent barrier to escape is a psychological one; a sign over the main gate proclaims, "A loser is made, not born." The physical boundaries for Fort Grant inmates are marked by a red line down the middle of a street that separates the residential area for offenders from the housing complex where most of the institution's 101 staff members live. The training center holds 300 young men who participate in running the prison through inmate councils (see Chapter 15) that confer regularly with the superintendent and who have keys to their own rooms rather than being locked up in cells. The inmates are being prepared for "making it" upon release through excellent vocational training programs offered by instructors from Northern Arizona University and college courses taught by professors who fly in weekly from Flagstaff.[2]

The Reception and Diagnostic Center

The Department of Corrections

Offenders sentenced to long-term confinement are usually turned over (committed) to the custody of the state's Department of Corrections, which is the administrative gateway to prison. The Department of Corrections is the agency responsible for operating all of the adult and juvenile facilities within the commonwealth, including the reception and diagnostic centers at admission.* The reception and diagnostic center may be located within the state's largest maximum-security prison, or it may be a completely separate facility. All prison-bound offenders are temporarily sent to the reception center for study, evaluation, and classification for the purpose of assignment to the institution in which they will serve out their sentence, the one that will most closely meet their correctional needs. Basically, the procedure serves to sort offenders into prisons of minimum, medium, and maximum security; it also provides diagnostic

* A few states, including California, have established a separate agency for the administration of juvenile institutions.

information that may be used by the receiving institution for internal classification, programming, and administrative purposes.

Classification

Because of its enormous prison population (22,000), its large number of adult institutions, and the size of the state, the California Department of Corrections has three regional reception centers (all autonomous parts of larger institutions) and the luxury of implementing more meaningful classification than most jurisdictions. Inmates remain at the California reception center for 30–90 days for testing, interviewing, and classification. In effect, California has separate institutions for emotionally disturbed and psychotic offenders, drug addicts, those who can benefit from vocational preparation, female violators, low security and escape risks, inmates who require tight security, and hardened criminals.[3] The Arizona Department of Corrections reception center is located within the state's main penal institution, the Arizona State Prison at Florence.[4] The reception center of the Kentucky Department of Correction, which administers seven penal facilities, is at the Kentucky State Reformatory at La-Grange, which holds about half of the state's 3,000 adult inmates.[5]

In principle, classification is the means for achieving the twin goals of security and rehabilitation. In practice, the custodial objective and the need to operate institutions in an orderly and efficient manner take precedence. The consequence is a maze of minimum-, medium-, and maximum-security facilities, units, sections, tiers, cells, cellblocks, quarters,

At the reception and diagnostic center, inmates are classified according to their correctional needs and security level

buildings, and grounds *within* designated minimum-, medium-, and maximum-security institutions.

THE OVERCROWDED PRISONS

Overcrowding is the overriding problem in prisons throughout the United States.[6] It contributes to all of the conditions of incarceration that have come under attack by the prisoners' rights movement, it adds to the mounting tensions that lead to riots, and it infects every facet of prison life. The total prison population in the United States reached an all-time high in 1981 with 320,583, which represented a 42 percent increase since January 1975 (see Figure 14.1).* The 1981 figure surpassed the previous year's record by 4 percent. Thirty-eight states had larger prison populations in 1981 than in 1980, and most of them reported overcrowded conditions of varying degrees. Texas had the largest numerical increase for the third year in a row, with 29,886 prisoners as of January 1, 1981—more inmates than are committed annually to the entire federal prison system. Nine states with prison populations of over 10,000 each accounted for fully half of the country's total inmates. Increases of 20 percent or more over the previous year were registered in Indiana, Maine, Mississippi, Rhode Island (which headed the list), South Dakota, Vermont, and Wyoming. At least a dozen states opened new prisons in 1980, but even they were unable to keep pace with the growth in prison population. Prison space was so scarce that almost 7,000 inmates were backed up in county jails awaiting openings. Alabama alone had 2,100 prison-bound inmates in a county jail holding pattern in July 1981.[7] As of January 1, 1977, there were 131 offenders in prison for every 100,000 citizens in the nation—the largest "prison rate" of any democratic country. Indeed, not only the absolute number but the rate of prisoners per 100,000 state population increased dramatically in almost every state from 1974 to 1975.[8]

Causes of the prison population increase

The turning-point in the prison count came in 1973, the end of a "decade of leniency" in which the prison population steadily declined while the crime rate soared. Several factors account for the unprecedented increase in the prison population. The most important one was the postwar baby boom, which swelled the number of 19–29 year olds in the general population. Persons of this age are disproportionately unemployed and prone to crime and therefore more likely to wind up in prison, where they constitute more than half of the institutional population. With the peak of the baby boom yet to come, burgeoning prison populations are

* Of the total number, 21,449 were in federal institutions. The prison population figures given here do not include inmates in jails or juvenile facilities, except for 6,889 prisoners backed up in county jails because of prison overcrowding.

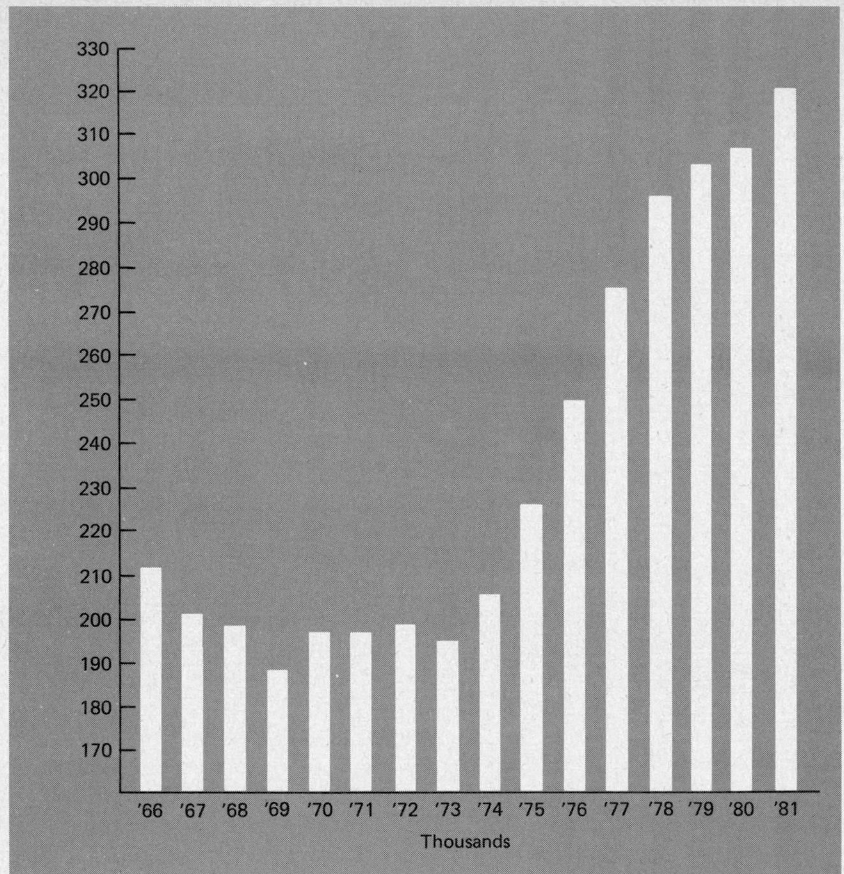

FIGURE 14.1 Total population of state and federal prisons in the United States, 1962–1977. The figures given are as of January 1 each year. *Source:* Based on *Corrections*, March 1976, p. 9; data from LEAA and *Corrections* surveys (not all states are included in the totals for 1969, 1970, and 1971).

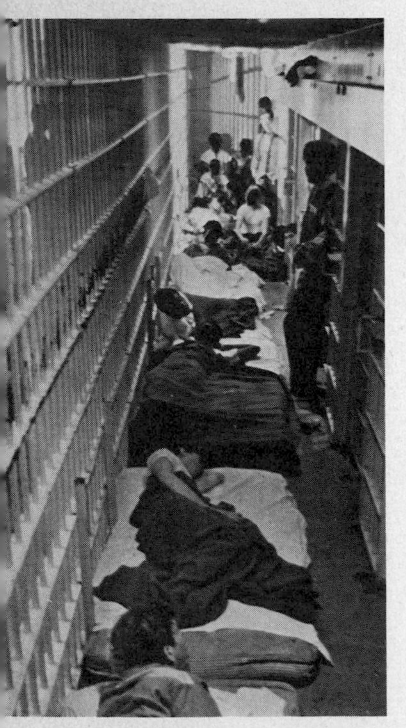

With prison populations at an all-time high, overcrowding is the major problem in United States prisons

expected at least until 1985, when there could be as many as 400,000 inmates in state facilitites.[9] Hardening public attitudes toward crime have placed pressures on the courts to get tough with criminals, on parole boards to cut back on granting early release, and on legislatures to pass mandatory minimum prison sentences. Of 27 states which have mandatory prison sentences for habitual offenders and those who use guns in committing crime, for example, two-thirds of the laws were passed between April 1979 and April 1980. The apparent failure of a "soft" approach to crime and increases in the proportion of violent offenses[10] have made unabated reliance on probation, nominal jail terms, and suspended sentences less viable options. In particular, the large number of inmates who fail probation repeatedly is causing some courts to turn directly to prison as a first rather than a last resort.* And prison administrators fear that the adoption of determinate sentences, though intended to reduce disparity, will become politicized and result in more and longer commitments to prison as they have in California and Indiana.[12] Finally, more effective law enforcement and better prosecution achieved through controlled plea bargaining, speedier trials, and career criminal programs have produced more convictions and stiffer sentences.

The result of these factors is that prisons in New Jersey, Arkansas, Mississippi, Georgia, Arizona, Indiana, Ohio, Illinois, Texas, and elsewhere have jammed two, three, and even four inmates into cells designed for one (see Close-up 14.2).[13] At Florida's Lake Butler prison, where 1,500 inmates were stuffed into an institution built for 700, "four men sleep in one-man cells no larger than small elevators. Inmates are forced to crawl over others sleeping on the floor and up against latrines."[14] Space is at such a premium that prisoners have had to sleep on the floor, on catwalks, in hallways and corridors, in storage closets, in basements, in 200-man dormitories that are veritable jungles which guards are afraid to enter at night, and even in shower stalls and on ledges above urinals![15] The situation is so bad that some prisons cannot afford the disciplinary luxury of solitary confinement, and when an inmate sexually assaults another inmate, "we may not be able to isolate him from that situation for two or three weeks until another bed becomes available."[16]

Administrative responses to overcrowding

With prisons in every part of the country bursting at their seams, harried prison officials have turned to emergency measures to relieve overcrowding (which is most severe in the South). To avoid putting four and five men in 6 foot by 9 foot cells, Florida converted a warehouse into a dormitory for 600 inmates, dismantled three quonset huts at Cape Kennedy that were annexed as a housing unit to the State Prison Diagnostic Center at Lake Butler, and in May 1975 erected 20 ten-man army tents in the prison yard at Starke—which were soon holding 14 men apiece! Other innovative administrators have converted hospitals, an air force base, and a radar site into prison facilities and, by advertising for space in newspapers, have put prisons on the "most wanted" list.[17,18] Inmates in Arkansas, Michigan, and New Jersey were temporarily moved into trailers obtained from the federal government.[19] To accommodate its rapidly growing female inmate population, Mississippi purchased a surplus Holiday Inn Jr., whose modular units were transported to the site of the Mississippi State Prison, where they provided 48 women prisoners with their own room, private bath, and air conditioner.[20] And Maryland and Louisiana came close to converting ships into floating prisons.[21]

* For example, only 60 percent of the convicted felons in Florida are now given probation, compared with 80 percent a few years ago. Florida parole boards have become stricter in granting release, with the parole rate dropping 30 percent in just one year.[11]

Close-up 14.1 DOUBLE CELLING PASSES CONSTITUTIONAL MUSTER

The Supreme Court addressed the issue of whether double celling constituted cruel and unusual punishment in *Rhodes* v. *Chapman* in 1981.[a] It was the first time the Court had dealt specifically with this issue. The suit was brought by two inmates in an Ohio maximum-security prison who were sharing a 63-square-foot cell. A federal District Court upheld their Eighth Amendment claim on the grounds that the prison housed 38 percent more inmates than it was designed for, several studies recommended that each inmate have at least 55 square feet of living quarters, and that double celling at the facility was not a temporary condition of incarceration.

In *Rhodes,* however, the Supreme Court found no justification for concluding that double celling at the Southern Ohio Correctional Facility amounted to cruel and unusual punishment. The Court emphasized that the Eighth Amendment prohibits punishment which involves the unnecessary and wanton infliction of pain, or is grossly disproportionate to the severity of the crime—neither of which applied to the prison in question, which was viewed as a first-class institution. Indeed, the double celling (which was prompted by overcrowding) did not result in any deprivations of essential services, intolerable conditions of confinement, or an increase in violence among inmates. That it may have had some marginal effect on the availability of rehabilitation aids does not come within the realm of the Eighth Amendment. To the extent that conditions of incarceration, such as double celling, "are restrictive and even harsh, they are part of the penalty that criminals pay for their offenses against society."

The *Rhodes* decision will undoubtedly have major significance for the nation's crowded prisons, where two-thirds of all inmates are confined in less space than the recommended 60-square-feet minimum.[b] The decision will have immediate impact in places like Maryland and Oregon, where double celling has been barred by federal courts.[c] On a long-term basis, *Rhodes* may have the ironic effect of both relieving and exacerbating the problem of prison overcrowding. For with the removal of any rigid constitutional barrier, prison administrators may be more inclined than ever to resort to double celling, thereby "reducing" overcrowding. But at the same time, *Rhodes* may encourage overcrowding by virtue of its tacitly allowing prisons to house more inmates than they were built to accommodate. These consequences aside, the *Rhodes* opinion left open the possibility that double celling might be unconstitu-

ny prisons, like this one in uth Carolina, are so antiquated at they cannot be renovated ec- omically

tional in prison settings less favorable than the one in Ohio, and it does not touch upon the legal status of placing more than two inmates in the same cell. *Rhodes* also has no direct bearing on court decisions which take a totality-of-circumstances approach in declaring that prison conditions violate the Eighth Amendment ban against cruel and unusual punishment.

[a] *Rhodes* v. *Chapman*, No. 80-332. Decided June 15, 1981.
[b] *New York Times*, June 16, 1981, p. 9.
[c] "Prison Rights," *Time*, June 29, 1981, p. 51.

A few states have taken drastic steps to reduce overcrowding. In October 1975, when 200 inmates were sleeping on prison floors, the Georgia Pardon and Parole Board issued an order for the immediate release of 1,000 inmates convicted of nonviolent offenses who had less than six months left to serve on sentences of two years or more.[22] It also trimmed one year from the sentences of 5,000 inmates, nonviolent offenders with less than a year left to serve, which resulted in the early release of 1,400 inmates over the following nine months.[23] In a similarly extraordinary move, Florida authorized accelerated parole to 1,055 prisoners who were completing the last two years of their sentences and who did "not represent any compromise to the safeguards of the community."[24] Michigan may be unique in having a law that prohibits placing more than one inmate in a cell.[25]

New prison construction

The most common (and most controversial) response to overcrowding is the pronounced trend toward the construction of more prisons. This number could increase substantially by virtue of the Task Force on Violent Crime, which has made the provision of federal subsidies to build state prisons a top priority.[26] An estimated 450 to 860 new penal facilities are under construction, on the drawing board, or in the proposal stage.[27] Abandoning its earlier decision to hold the line on adding more prisons, the Federal Bureau of Prisons, whose 43 institutions were 21 percent over capacity as of October 1976, added nine new facilities to the system, had four others under construction, and submitted a record-breaking $57 million appropriation request to Congress in 1977 that would buy 12,000 beds to accommodate its projected needs.[28] It is also planning to utilize, at a cost of $22 million, the facilities being built for the 1980 Winter Olympics at Lake Placid when they become available.[29] The ten-year federal prison construction plan carries a $510 million price tag, while the states are scheduled to spend at least $7 billion on new facilities. And still it is questionable that prison construction can keep pace with demand. Many facilities now under construction will have populations above capacity soon after they are completed. As has already occurred in Ohio, Pennsylvania, and the District of Columbia, some of the new buildings will replace, rather than supplement, presently antiquated institutions.[30] For half of the existing 113 maximum-security prisons were built in the nineteenth century and cannot be renovated economically.[31]

Judicial response to overcrowding

Under the momentum of the prisoners' rights movement (to be discussed in the following chapter), the court's response to overcrowding has been to order prison officials to reduce the inmate population to acceptable levels or face a judicial takeover, the closing of the offending institution, or an order to stop accepting new prisoners. Federal courts in Alabama, Mississippi, Florida, and Louisiana have found overcrowded prison conditions so horrendous as to constitute "cruel and unusual punishment."[32] A federal court gave Florida one year to reduce its state inmate population to "emergency" levels and six months more to reach "normal" levels.[33] In the first action of its kind, a federal judge in Montgomery ordered the release of 222 named Alabama prison inmates and asked the parole authorities to make 50 named inmates eligible for parole six months ahead of time.[34] Federal judges in Michigan and Texas subsequently issued similar orders to alleviate prison overcrowding.[35]

The strongest ruling yet issued against prison conditions came from U.S. District Court Judge Frank Johnson. As part of a comprehensive set of directives aimed at reforming the Alabama prison system, Johnson ordered a reduction in the state's inmate population from 4,000 to its rated capacity of 2,307, banned sending any more prisoners to the state system, and specified that each prisoner have 60 square feet of space per single cell and that only minimum-security inmates be housed in dormitories.[36] (Dormitories are considered highly conducive to violence, drug use, and sexual assaults.) Johnson noted that overcrowding had resulted in an "almost complete inability on the part of Alabama prison officials to control violence" within the institutions.[37] About half the states are under court order to ease overcrowding or face lawsuits claiming that such conditions are unconstitutional.[38]

IMPRISONMENT AS CRUEL AND UNUSUAL PUNISHMENT

Holt v. *Sarver* (1970)

In *Holt* v. *Sarver* in 1970, a United States district court broke new ground in declaring that by virtue of the overall deplorable conditions existing at the Cummins Farm Unit and the Tucker Reformatory, simply being incarcerated in the Arkansas penal system amounted to "cruel and unusual punishment." (See Close-up 14.2.)[39] It was the *combined* effect of several factors, rather than that of any one taken by itself, that made the operation of the state's prison system—and thus imprisonment in it—unconstitutional under the Eighth Amendment.* Armed inmate trusties were used extensively as guards, thereby placing inmates serving long or life terms in control of the institution. This situation led to wholesale corruption, extensive trafficking in drugs, proliferation of weapons in the prison population, physical abuse of inmates by trusties, and an abdication of official responsibility and proper supervision. All inmates resided in 100-man dormitories. Because there was no segregation by classification and no responsible security was provided, the open-barracks housing arrangement fostered rampant homosexual rape of the younger and weaker inmates. The facilities in general were dilapidated, unsanitary, and poorly ventilated and heated. Inmates being disciplined were placed in filthy, rodent-infested "solitary" confinement areas in which four men occupied an 8 foot by 10 foot segregation cell. Corporal punishment and unrestrained brutality by staff and trusties were commonplace.[42] There was also a lack of rehabilitation programs, medical care was virtually unavailable, and inmates working out of doors in severe weather were not outfitted properly. In the court's view, the totality of these conditions of incarceration added up to cruel and unusual punishment.[43]

Holt was the first time that the constitutionality of an entire prison system and imprisonment itself were successfully challenged. It was a landmark on the prisoners' rights road toward a decent and humane custodial environment. Other courts have since followed suit in invoking the Eighth Amendment to discredit an entire penal system or incarceration in a particular institution.[44] Yet none has gone so far as United States District Court Judge Frank Johnson did in *James* v. *Wallace* in 1976.

James **v.** *Wallace* **(1976)**

The court's minimum constitutional standards

In a consolidated ruling stemming from class action suits in *Pugh* v. *Locke* and *James* v. *Wallace* on January 13, 1976, Judge Johnson declared that "the living conditions in Alabama prisons constitute cruel and unusual punishment" under any current judicial definition of that concept.[45,46] Responding to a clear duty to alleviate the "massive constitutional infirmities" noted, Johnson ordered the state to comply with his minimum constitutional standards or risk a judicial takeover or the closing of the four institutions involved. As in *Holt,* it was a question of the *cumulative* effects, practices, and features of prison life that made confinement itself in the Alabama penal system unconstitutional. Unlike

* The first Cummins case, decided in 1965, involved complaints of whippings and other forms of corporal punishment arbitrarily administered by inmate trusties and guards. The court enjoined further whippings until proper rules were written to govern their imposition.[40] In the second Cummins case, *Jackson* v. *Bishop* in 1968, the use of the strap as a disciplinary measure was permanently banned on the grounds that it was cruel and unusual punishment.[41] This decision in effect put an end to corporal punishment in American prisons.

Close-up 14.2 THE TUCKER PRISON FARM

From February 1967 to March 1968 Thomas Murton was the superintendent of the Tucker Prison Farm, one of the Arkansas prisons that gained notoriety in *Holt* v. *Sarver*. Tucker inmates had to produce enough farm income to meet the entire costs of running the facility and were whipped for not doing their share of the work.

As part of his reforms, Murton ended corporal punishment, improved the quality of food, stopped discriminatory treatment of inmates, and allowed death row prisoners to intermingle with the general prison population. He is best known, however, for unearthing three skeletons at the Cummins prison that were alleged to be the bodies of murdered inmates. Murton claimed that the three men were among hundreds who had been killed by inmate guards and listed as escapees,[a] but his attempts to pursue the matter further were rebuked by the governor. He was threatened with arrest for "exhuming bodies without a permit" and three weeks later was fired for offending and embarrassing his political superior. Blackballed from the correctional field, Murton briefly headed a foundation set up to aid Arkansas parolees, and he subsequently became a criminal justice professor at the University of Minnesota.[b]

At hearings before a U.S. Senate subcommittee in March 1968, Murton testified on the abuses prevailing in the Arkansas penal system, which included the Tucker telephone, a torture device used to send an electrical shock to an inmate's testicles.[c] But it was the testimony of Commissioner Sarver, the head of the Arkansas Department of Corrections, that may have identified the most pressing problem facing inmates and staff alike. "When I read an exposé of homosexualities, bribings, escapes, [and] political corruption in prisons, I think most knowledgeable correction administrators think: 'So, what else is new?' "[d]

[a] Arkansas officials said that Murton had merely discovered a prison graveyard for indigent inmates, which years later was apparently found to be the case.
[b] Stephen Gettinger, "Brubaker: Making a Myth Out of a Mortal Man," *Corrections,* October 1980, pp. 42–44; *Kansas City Times,* September 7, 1974; Book review of Thomas Murton's *The Arkansas Prison Scandal, Crime and Delinquency,* October 1970, pp. 442–453.
[c] "Investigations: The Crime Hatcheries," *Newsweek,* March 17, 1969, p. 36.
[d] Book review of *The Arkansas Prison Scandal,* cited above, p. 451.

deral Judge Frank Johnson ed that the overall conditions incarceration in Alabama instiions amounted to "cruel and usual punishment"

Holt and its progeny, however, Judge Johnson's court order called for sweeping improvements that were more comprehensive, specific, and operational than had ever before been prescribed by the judiciary. The unprecedented order contained the first set of minimum constitutional standards to be imposed on a state's prisons. Johnson wrote 44 major guidelines covering every salient aspect of incarceration: the number of showers and toilets, the preparation of food, the number of guards (to be almost doubled), conditions of segregation, overcrowding (to be cut by almost half), inmate safety, medical services, mental health care, and other living conditions and physical facilities. In effect, the ruling promulgated a detailed code or prison manual that governed the daily operation of Alabama institutions and represented the most encompassing and most aggressive judicial intervention into a state correctional system to date.[47] In what was by far the most radical and controversial aspect of the ruling, Johnson recognized an affirmative "right to rehabilitative treatment" that had been negated in Alabama by basic deficiencies in the prison environment.

The court's timetable

Johnson refused to accept the contentions of correction officials that inadequate state funding made it impossible to alleviate prison defects that they admitted amounted to cruel and unusual punishment.[48] "[A] state is not at liberty to afford its citizens only those constitutional rights which fit comfortably within its budget." State officials were given until July 1976 to submit to the court a report describing the progress made in implementing each constitutional standard, the reasons for any delay, and a timetable for complying with the changes to be made within the one-year to two-year time limits set in the standards. Johnson also issued a stern warning that he was prepared to hold state officials (including Governor George Wallace) personally liable for monetary damages if his directives were not carried out fully. Failure to do so, he said, "will necessitate the closing of those several prison facilities herein found to be unfit for human confinement." The court order and admonition drew a sharp response from Governor Wallace, who accused Johnson of creating a vacation-resort "hotel atmosphere" for prisoners and of being insensitive to the problem of finding the $40–$100 million to pay for the reforms.

Lacking confidence in the ability of the prison administrators to bring about the required changes on their own, Johnson established a 39-member Human Rights Committee to monitor implementation of the order and to report its findings to the court. Johnson also authorized the University of Alabama's psychology department to devise a more effective system for classifying inmates, one that would reduce overcrowding, rape, and assault and enhance rehabilitation.

Compliance with *James*

The feared showdown between the judicial and executive branches of government in the event of noncompliance with Judge Johnson's order never materialized, for several reasons. The Alabama legislature formally enacted the court's minimum constitutional standards. Stirred by news accounts of the "standards of decadency" prevailing in the institutions, Alabama voters approved a $6 million bond issue for more prison facilities. The prison budget request was increased to $26 million, almost twice the previous level of appropriations.[49] By November 1976, 40 of the 44 standards had either been achieved or were approaching satisfactory completion. And many prison officials privately welcomed Johnson's unorthodox approach to penal reform because it accomplished in a short time what they had been unable to do by themselves in years of working through traditional channels.[50]

Appellate court restricts *James* decision

Significantly, in September 1977 a federal appeals court made substantial cutbacks in Johnson's comprehensive directives, while chiding the lower court for exceeding its judicial authority in several areas. "The Constitution does not require that prisoners, as individuals or as a group, be provided with any and every amenity which some person may think is needed to avoid mental, physical, and emotional detriment." In addition to withdrawing the right to treatment granted by Johnson, the appeals court set aside the requirement of 60 square feet of living space per prisoner, dissolved the Human Rights Committee, absolved Governor Wallace of any liability in the matter of compliance, and gave prison personnel a freer hand in searching visitors than Johnson did. The effect of the appeals court decision was to return a large measure of control to the prison authorities and to moderate one of the most ambitious constitutional bill of rights for prisoners yet imposed on a state penal system.[51]

Ruiz v. *Estelle* (1980)

In *Ruiz* v. *Estelle* in 1980, federal Judge William W. Justice criticized the Texas Department of Corrections (TDC) for permitting grossly deficient and unconstitutional prison conditions.[52] The opinion culminated one of the longest and most bitterly contested battles in the annals of prison lawsuits. In a 248-page opinion, Justice condemned what has now become a familiar litany of deplorable conditions of incarceration: brutality by guards, extreme overcrowding, inadequate medical care, a lack of staff training, disciplinary hearing improprieties, a trustie system that allegedly delegated security functions to inmates, and interference with inmates' access to the courts. Unlike *Holt* and *James,* the *Ruiz* decision did not technically rest on a finding that imprisonment in Texas penal facilities constituted cruel and unusual punishment by virtue of the existing aggregate conditions. Rather, the court invoked the appropriate constitutional safeguard—invariably the Eighth and Fourteenth Amendments—in examining various institutional practices, conditions, and features on an individual basis. The spirit and conclusion of the *Ruiz* opinion, however, places the decision in the same category as its famous predecessors: "no human being, regardless of how disfavored by society shall be subjected to cruel and unusual punishment or be deprived of the due process of the law."[53]

The *Ruiz* case took on added significance because of Texas' reputation as a leader in the corrections field, its enviable record in preventing escapes and promoting inmate safety, and the extraordinary scope of Judge Justice's implementing order issued on April 20, 1981. The order covered several areas that had not been addressed, or not addressed with such exacting criteria, in suits against other state prison systems. Among other things, for example, the order specified that:

All existing prisons must be reorganized and decentralized into "management units" of not more than 500 inmates.

New prisons cannot house more than 500 inmates and must be located within 50 miles of urban areas with a population over 200,000. In order to have this directive rescinded, prison officials must prove that they will be able to recruit enough professionals and paraprofessionals to staff a prison built in a more rural site.

The work release program must be expanded to include at least 2,500 inmates, and an additional 1,000 inmates must be enrolled in other types of community programs to be established by the Texas Department of Corrections.

There must be one guard for every six inmates. And for each dormitory in which an officer is posted, there must be a guard situated at some outside point to provide some type of direct and immediate communication.

Prison officials reacted sharply and swiftly to the action taken by Justice, contending that it went well beyond the constitutional issues and represented an unwarranted judicial intrusion into institutional operations.[54] There were even civil libertarians who conceded that some of the farthest-reaching provisions might be highly vulnerable to appellate attack. Bruce Jackson, the author of several books on TDC prisoners, probably echoed the sentiments of many correctional administrators in asserting that the tight discipline in Texas had been responsible for preventing violence rather than fomenting it. "The regimentation that comes out of that is hellish, but what is worse? In Texas they believed in keeping people from killing each other and [sexually assaulting] each other in the hallways, and they succeeded."[55] Texas state officials are currently in the process of appealing the Justice order, with a final decision in the matter not expected until 1983 or 1984.[56] It may be prophetic that, in the interval, the appellate court granted the state a stay in complying with some of the most controversial portions of the Justice order, citing "undue interference with the operation of the State's prison system" and the "administrative nightmare [TDC faces] in order to comply with the district court's quotas and deadlines."[57]

THE CUSTODIAL STAFF

Education and training

Since it is recognized that custodial institutions are faced with a new breed of prisoner, there is something to be said on behalf of the need for a new breed of correction officer—for guards with more formal education and training, for more minority group members and women in front-line positions, and for expanding the responsibilities of guards beyond a strictly custodial function. The lack of educational qualifications and adequate training for custodial personnel is more acute than in any other segment of the criminal justice system.[58] The Joint Commission on Correctional Manpower and Training reported in 1969 that 16 percent of corrections officers were not high school graduates and only 14 percent had received any in-service training.[59] In general the entry requirements for guards are minimal and vary considerably from state to state.[60]

As with the police, the route to higher education for guards has been paved with LEAA funds and limited financial or promotional incentives from the Department of Corrections. Between 1965 and 1974, for example, the Institute of Contemporary Corrections and Behavioral Science at Sam Houston University graduated 1,000 employees of the Texas Department of Corrections.[61] In Connecticut, recruits now receive four weeks of training at the Connecticut Justice Academy, which includes a simulated incarceration experience.[62] Georgia now requires recruits to undergo a four-week training course that includes two weeks at the state training academy at the University of Georgia, where the areas covered range from hand-to-hand combat to human relations.[63] Florida's new guards take 160 hours of classroom instruction at the Correctional Training Institute, created by the legislature in 1974 to establish minimum training standards for all state, county, and municipal corrections staff. The Arkansas Department of Corrections is developing a series of in-service training courses, in preparation for a full-scale preservice academy program.[64]

Racial imbalance

Possibly the most serious flaw in the composition of the corrections staff is the dearth of minority group guards and the consequent racial imbalance between the keepers and the kept. This source of racism is considered by prison administrators to be the most common underlying cause of riots.[65] Only 15 percent of the corrections staff at the Michigan Reformatory in Ionia, the rural center of the state, are nonwhite, compared with 60 percent of the youthful offender inmates, most of whom come from Detroit.[66] Similarly, two-thirds of the guards at the Louisiana State Penitentiary are rural whites, while 70 percent of the inmates are blacks, half of whom come from New Orleans.[67] In New York, at the time of the Attica riot (to be discussed in Chapter 15), there was not a single black guard in an institution in which 55 percent of the 2,000 inmates were black.[68] To a large extent, racial imbalance stems from the prisons' having been constructed in rural white areas and the difficulties in recruiting black employees from distant urban locations. Unfortunately, the tendency to build new institutions in isolated areas (where the available labor supply is nearly all white) shows no sign of declining.[69] The Federal Bureau of Prisons is feverishly attempting to recruit black staff in order to avoid a federal Attica, and the achievement of well-integrated staffs is becoming a top priority among responsible prison administrators throughout the states.[70] In California, for example, the proportion of minority correction officers rose from 6 percent in 1967 to 18 percent in 1976.[71] In this regard, two white male correctional officers employed by the California Department of Corrections challenged the agency's affirmative action program, which gave priority to hiring and promoting more minority and female workers; the officers filed suit after they were denied promotions because the positions involved were being kept open for affirmative action employees. In *Minnick* v. *Cal. Dept. of Corrections* in 1981, however, the Supreme Court refused to address the constitutional issues raised because of "significant ambiguities in the record concerning both the extent to which race or sex has been used as a factor in making promotions and the justification for such use."[72]

Women guards in men's prisons

The newest group to demand the right to be prison guards in male institutions are women. The two main objections to having women guard male inmates are the dangerousness of the job (which women allegedly cannot handle) and the invasion of sexual privacy that their presence would create. Feminist supporters, however, point out that the so-called dangerousness of custodial work is a smoke screen for guarding the prestige and the "macho" image coveted by male guards, that male inmates would be less likely to assault female guards, and that the standard response by male guards who are physically threatened is to call for reinforcements.[73] In California, where 55 women are being used as guards in all-male facilities in an experimental program, the shower areas have been screened and the women go about their business with an "eyes front" attitude.[74] Nevada has been employing women as guards in men's prisons for about three years, allowing them to work in maximum security housing areas as well as segregation units. Delaware recently ended a five-year experiment during which women guards could hold any position in the institution, even those involving routine strip searches. Despite these examples of progressive correctional policy, permitting women to perform the full range of duties expected from male guards is still not yet an idea whose time has come. While virtually all states as of 1979 utilized women guards in some capacity in men's prisons, they invariably were not permitted to work in housing areas or in posts that entail observing inmate showers or toilets—the very jobs that usually the stepping stone for obtaining promotions. Besides the objections to women guards noted above, male officers are also concerned that women guards will be hired and promoted *because* of their sex ("reverse discrimination") and that they cannot be counted on for back-up and support.[75]

In February 1977, the New York commissioner of corrections instituted a new policy aimed at giving women an equal shot at being guards in men's prisons—and permitted male guards to be assigned to female institutions. The immediate result was that 400 women inmates at Bedford Hills Correctional Facility filed a class action suit claiming invasion of privacy and violation of the religious rights of Muslims, whose faith prohibits exposing their bodies to anyone except their fathers or husbands.[76] Almost two years later, a federal district judge imposed restrictions on the use of male guards at the facility in order to avoid "impermissibly embarrassing" the women inmates and to protect their right of privacy. But in May 1980, a Court of Appeals decided there was no harm in assigning male officers to night duty in female housing areas, so long as the women inmates were provided with pajamas that completely covered their bodies![77] The legal battlelines used by blacks and women to break into prison professionally are the same ones they used to gain entrance to police departments: challenging job-related employment tests under the Civil Rights Acts and invoking the EEOC's affirmative action program.[78]

Dothard v. *Rawlinson* (1977)

In *Dothard* v. *Rawlinson* in 1977, the Supreme Court struck down Alabama's height and weight requirements for employment as a prison guard because they were not shown to be job related.[79] The requirements would have excluded 41 percent of the total female population from working as prison guards compared with less than 1 percent of the male population. But in the same opinion, the Court also ruled that the state could prohibit women from holding "contact jobs"—positions requiring close physical proximity to male inmates—in Alabama's maximum security male penitentiaries. This restriction was permissible because of the particular conditions characterizing these institutions, conditions which were declared unconstitutional in *James* the year before: rampant violence, a jungle atmosphere, conspicuous understaffing, large dormitory living quarters, prison industry that involved constant strip searches for contraband, a high proportion of sex offenders, and no attempt to classify or segregate inmates by type of offense or level of dangerousness. The essence of a correctional officer's duties in the present case was defined as maintaining prison security. Since the use of women guards in the instant situation would create a substantial security problem, the Court concluded that for prison contact posts sex was a bona fide occupational qualification which did not violate Title VII of the Civil Rights Act. This part of the *Dothard* decision was carefully limited to the especially violent conditions prevailing in Alabama prisons, which not only made contact positions too dangerous for women but notably reduced a woman's relative ability to preserve order and discipline in such facilities. The same reasoning would presumably not be applicable to the use of women guards in other types of men's prisons, where environments present no comparable barriers to equal employment.

Restructuring the Role of Guards

By virtue of their number, the amount of time that they too spend in prison, and their continuous direct contact with inmates, guards are potentially the most influential agents for change within the institution. Yet owing to an "old guard" philosophy concerned exclusively with custody and the failure of prison administrators to tap the resources of younger corrections officers, guards are "by and large, locked into a tradition of roles and role responses that are penologically counterproductive."[80] This limited view of the role of corrections officers is especially unfortunate because it prevents guards from participating in more diversified, more professional, and more prestigious activities that could enhance their status, advance their careers, and relieve the monotony and boredom of security work.

Treatment teams

Sporadic efforts are being made at various prisons to restructure the traditionally narrow role of guards by including them as part of treatment teams that have counseling and rehabilitation responsibilities. In the Missouri penal system, a correction-officer counselor is part of a treatment team that includes the institutional parole officer and the inmate's caseworker and work supervisor. The team's goals are to develop personalized inmate plans that map out a program for job skills training and acceptable behavior that will be related to preparation for release.[81] At Connecticut's minimum-security facility at Enfield guards are encouraged to volunteer for membership on treatment teams that act as a sounding board for inmate complaints, a means for counseling inmates, and a vehicle for making direct recommendations to the parole board.[82] In Pennsylvania, similar devices for closing the gap between custody and treatment are the support teams in which corrections officers make key decisions about the inmate's future while in prison.[83]

Few institutions have gone as far in expanding the role of corrections officers as the unusual Vienna Correctional Center in southern Illinois. At the coed, collegelike center, the guards wear green blazers, address the "residents" by name, get to know the residents well by eating with them and attending the same in-house college classes offered by Southern Illinois University, and are an integral part of the treatment team that reviews the resident's progress and makes disciplinary, work release, and furlough decisions. One reason for the eight applications for every custody job in 1975 was the increased job satisfaction and professionalism that went along with the position.[84] At the Draper Correctional Center in Elmore, Alabama, the Rehabilitation Research Foundation has been conducting manpower experiments in "correcting" the misconceptions and stereotypes of guards and teaching them behavior modification skills as a tool for rehabilitating inmates.[85] Whatever guard "brutality" exists in prison would presumably be counteracted by having more guards who are black, women, better trained, and more educated, who can relate to inmates on a flexible, personal basis and can assume treatment responsibilities.

Close-up 14.3 THE STANFORD PRISON EXPERIMENT: COLLEGE STUDENTS AS PRISONERS AND GUARDS

In 1971 Philip Zimbardo, a professor of psychology at Stanford University, conducted an unusual study of the behavioral and psychological effects of being a prisoner or a prison guard, using college students to play these roles. The students were recruited through an ad in the Palo Alto newspaper that solicited persons to participate in a simulated two-week prison experiment for $15 a day. The 24 selected as subjects were "an average group of healthy, intelligent, middle-class college males," who were randomly assigned to be "guards" or "prisoners." The basement of the psychology building at Stanford University was converted into a prison setting. The 12 student prisoners were arrested at their homes by the Palo Alto police, warned of their legal rights, searched, handcuffed, and transported blindfolded to the "Stanford County Jail."

Upon arrival, the prisoners were stripped naked, deloused, issued uniforms that were dresses, and had a chain bolted on one ankle. The purpose of the dress and the chain was to accelerate symbolically the process of degradation and oppressiveness that occurs in real prisons over a period of months and years. The guards wore khaki uniforms, carried police billy clubs, wore whistles around their necks and reflecting sunglasses that made eye contact impossible (in order to promote anonymity and social distance from the prisoners), and addressed the prisoners by number at all times.

On the second day, the prisoners staged an uprising by ripping off their clothing and barricading themselves inside their cells and began to taunt and curse the guards. The guards crushed the rebellion by spraying the prisoners with skin-chilling carbon dioxide, broke into the cells, stripped the prisoners, and placed the ringleaders in solitary confinement (a closet). The guards were angered by the riot, for it made them look bad and challenged their authority just when they were gaining a newfound sense of power and occupational solidarity.

The guards' working conditions

There is a great temptation to attribute the failures of prison to the guards. This attitude overlooks the fact that prisons are the final dumping grounds for all the problems and the failures that accumulate in the preceding stages of the criminal justice system. Corrections officers are

Over the next few days the guards stepped up their surveillance, control, and intimidation of the prisoners. The prisoners were not allowed to leave their cells to go to the toilet after 10 P.M. lockup, were not permitted to empty buckets in their cells filled with urine and feces, were ordered to do push-ups as a form of physical punishment, and were made to clean the toilet bowls with their bare hands.

By the fifth day, about one-third of the guards had become "extremely hostile, arbitrary, inventive in their forms of degradation and humiliation, and appeared to thoroughly enjoy the power they wielded."[a] Equally revealing was that the "good" guards never once interfered with an order by a cruel guard or did anything to rectify the situation, in effect condoning "guard brutality" by their silence. The scheduled two-week prison experiment had to be terminated after six days because both guards and prisoners had become lost in their roles—roles that had begun to destroy and brutalize both groups alike. By the fifth day, five of the prisoners were released because of extreme emotional depression.

"In less than a week, the experience of imprisonment undid (temporarily) a lifetime of learning; human values were suspended, self-concepts were challenged, and the ugliest, most base, pathological side of human nature surfaced."[b] Most of the guards were distressed by the decision to stop the experiment prematurely.[c]

[a] Philip Zimbardo et al., *The Stanford Prison Experiment: A Simulation Study of the Psychology of Imprisonment,* narrative text of slide presentation of the experiment, mimeo.

[b] Philip G. Zimbardo, "The Psychological Power and Pathology of Imprisonment," testimony prepared for the U.S. House of Representatives Committee on the Judiciary, October 25, 1971, mimeo, p. 3.

[c] Ali Banuazizi and Siamak Movahedi, "Interpersonal Dynamics in a Simulated Prison: A Methodological Analysis," *American Psychologist,* February 1975, pp. 152–159; Craig Haney, Curtis Banks, and Philip Zimbardo, "Interpersonal Dynamics in a Simulated Prison," *International Journal of Criminology and Penology,* February 1973, pp. 69–97.

no more the villains of the penal system than are the victims of crime, with whom they so genuinely empathize. The conditions of employment for guards are among the worst of any occupational group. Low salaries often force guards to turn to overtime, second jobs, and ultimately other occupations. The job is tedious, dangerous, and frustrating, and it offers little challenge, satisfaction, or opportunity for advancement. Guards are continually faced with contradictory demands in performing a largely thankless job, and they have limited means for controlling inmates. Thus guards too are prisoners of a sort, workers who pull time until they can escape through a retirement pension plan, themselves brutalized by the pernicious character of prison.[86] Dr. Philip Zimbardo's Stanford Prison Experiment indicates just how quickly college students who temporarily assumed the role of guards became hardened by the experience (see Close-up 14.3).

Guards are criticized for not letting their guard down in dealing with inmates and for their paranoid distrust of prisoners. Yet prisons do house a large proportion of dangerous offenders; prisons are populated with recidivists; inmate defiance of authority and assaults on staff are on the increase;[87] prisons do contain political radicals and extremist groups obsessed with revolution and violence;[88] and it is widely recognized that the institutions are racial powder kegs. As a group, incarcerated felons are not noted for having well-developed impulse control, tolerance for stress, or obedience to authority. Prisoners are manipulative, and they try constantly to con the staff. Given the anonymity within prisons, there is some truth to the notion that what the officers do not know about the prisoners might hurt them—unless they take necessary precautions. Attempts to get to know the inmates better are hampered by frequent assignment rotations, high inmate-to-staff ratios, and high officer turnover rates. Correction forces are dangerously understaffed, and the hazards of custodial work, even if statistically exaggerated, are nonetheless all too real in practice and over time: a handful of guards may be expected to supervise a cellblock of 100–500 inmates or to oversee 1,000 inmates roaming about mess halls and recreation yards, inmates whose individual and collective behavior is impossible to predict at any given time.[89]

WORK, EDUCATION, AND TREATMENT PROGRAMS

One of the most positive sides to the conditions of incarceration are various programs intended to occupy the inmates' time constructively by advancing their education, providing them with vocational training that may be useful upon release, and treating problems related to their criminality. Inmate needs with respect to work, education, and treatment are paramount considerations in their assignment to a particular institution by the reception and diagnostic center, and the process is continued at the placement facility by the classification counselor or committee. The most prominent institutional programs are those which attempt to prepare inmates for jobs on the outside, to teach them marketable skills and a trade, and to develop the responsible work habits that are fundamental to success in the occupational world. Under the rubric of prison industries and vocational training, inmates throughout the country are employed in a large number of jobs and fields that constitute an important part of the daily institutional routine.

Vocational Training

Unemployment in prison

Almost all of the problems associated with vocational training programs are financial in nature. Because of their high operating costs, they rarely reach more than a minority of the inmate population. Only 333 of

assignment of inmates to in-
tional maintenance jobs does
prepare them for meaningful
loyment upon release

the 1,800 inmates of Arizona State Prison at Florence are assigned to prison industry jobs, which pay between 10 cents and 33 cents an hour.[90] Only 250 of the 2,700 inmates at the Georgia State Prison at Reidsville have prison industry jobs, which carry no payment at all, and another 300 work on the prison's 10,000-acre farm. Of 2,645 inmates at Kentucky's three major prisons, about 350 have prison industry jobs, which pay 8 cents to 20 cents an hour.[91] Only 4,500 of Florida's 18,093 inmates have regular jobs. California industrial programs reach one in ten prisoners, and just 700 of the 5,700 inmates at the Southern Michigan Prison at Jackson can find work.[92] Even at the California Training Facility at Soledad, which was designed with an emphasis on vocational training, only 400 of the 3,000 inmates are enrolled in such training at any given time.[93] When budget cuts occur, prison industry programs are the first to go.[94]

Slave wages and irrelevant training

The low pay attached to prison jobs is of course a sore spot among inmates. States are legally able to pay inmates "slave wages" because the Thirteenth Amendment exempts prisoners from the prohibition against involuntary servitude: "Neither slavery nor involuntary servitude, except as a punishment for crime whereof the party shall have been duly convicted, shall exist within the United States or any place subject to their jurisdiction."

Next to their dissatisfaction with wages, inmates complain about the lack of relevance of prison industry jobs and vocational education programs to obtaining employment upon release. "I came in here a laborer and I will go out a laborer. They taught me to make [license] tags, but where else can I go to make tags? I got news for you, baby. In six months you'll have me back makin' those tags."[95] In response to such criticism, prison officials counter that the skills and habits developed in the work programs are needed in any job and are highly transferable. "In the license plate factory we use a fifty-ton press, and there are fifty-ton presses in use all over in industry" outside prison.[96] Inmates might consider themselves fortunate to have *any* bona fide prison industry job when the alternative is institutional maintenance work—degrading and meaningless work to which half of all inmates in the nation are assigned.[97]

State-use laws

That the leading prison industries are the manufacture of license plates and street signs is because of the state-use laws found in most jurisdictions.[98] The state-use laws protect the economic interests of the private sector from having to compete with cheap inmate labor by restricting the goods produced by prisoners to those used by the state and/or by otherwise limiting prisoner-made commodities that can be sold to the public. Furniture production, a common prison industry, is banned in North Carolina because the state's private employers are heavily involved in the furniture business.[99] California has agreed not to utilize inmate labor in jobs normally performed by union members.[100] Despite these problems,

e profits of prison industry
ow Texas to house its inmates
r $4.55 a day (compared with $15
more elsewhere)

there is no reason why the profits of prison industries that are self-supporting should not be used for more program materials and higher inmate wages (as happens at the New Mexico State Penitentiary at Cerrillos[101]) rather than go into the state treasury.

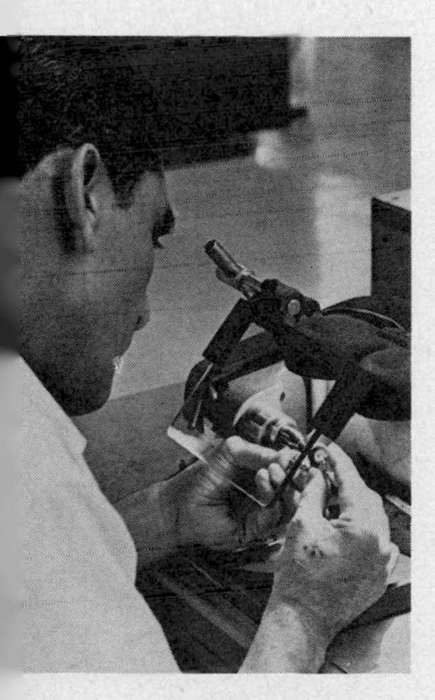

manufacture of false teeth is
of 21 jobs that replaced chain
ngs in Texas, where prison in-
stries earn $9 million a year

Factors other than the financial ones also enter the prison industry employment picture. Only 300 of San Quentin's 3,000 inmates choose to take advantage of the institution's 15 vocational training courses, and many of them sign up only to score points with the Adult Authority, which, like any other parole board, looks favorably on an inmate's efforts at "rehabilitation" when making its release decision.[102] Furthermore, the requirement that inmates have the equivalent of an eighth grade education to participate in vocational training programs automatically disqualifies thousands of California's 22,000 inmates, whose average reading level is at the sixth grade, and of whom 2,000 are illiterate. Given the severely limited employment background and skills of most inmates, it is probably realistic to recognize that "we're not going to make executives out of many people. . . . Our object is merely to make the man employable."[103]

The profile of vocational training in prison is not entirely bleak, and there are some encouraging signs of improved inmate working conditions. The list of institutions with well-financed industrial components is growing. The 600 inmates at the Yardville Correctional Center in New Jersey have access to an auto body repair shop containing $100,000 worth of sophisticated equipment. Here the main limitation is that few inmates are incarcerated long enough to become proficient in auto mechanics.[104] Florida's Union Correctional Institution at Raiford has its own inmate-operated slaughterhouse, cement block plant, and multimillion-dollar complex of greenhouses where prisoners learn horticulture and prepare shrubs for planting in state parks.[105] Although Florida inmates are not paid, such work experience can later be put to good use in the meat industry, construction trades, and florist markets. Connecticut's minimum-security facility at Enfield has an extensive vocational training program operated under the federal Manpower Development Training Act.[106] The modern vocational complex at the Fort Grant Training Center in Arizona is designed around highly marketable skills that are taught by instructors from Northern Arizona University. Those who successfully complete the welding program, for example, meet national certification requirements.[107] After conducting a study that revealed the need for qualified people in the field, the Arkansas Department of Corrections introduced a graphic communications training program at the Cummins prison, with modern equipment of the type used in 70 percent of all commercial printing plants and firms.[108]

Reforming prison industry

Reforming state-use laws

The key to solving the interrelated problems of low pay and motivation, vocational training of questionable value, and employment upon release lies in reforming the state-use laws, treating inmates more like commercial employees, and involving the private sector directly in prison industry development. The Michigan Department of Corrections took a modest step in this direction in April 1973, when it instituted a production incentive plan under which all profits realized in prison industry would be returned to the inmates.[109] The working conditions of Kentucky's inmates were vastly improved in 1972 when the pay scale was raised from 6–15 cents an hour to 8–20 cents an hour, bonuses were tied to production quotas, workers were permitted to spend their earnings as they chose, coffee breaks and other characteristics of commercial employment were allowed, and inmates received annual paid vacations —from the job, not from the prison.[110] Minnesota inmates at the Stillwater prison have a profit-sharing arrangement under which, in a good month, they can earn a bonus of up to $92 in addition to their regular wages.[111] Within the state-use framework, no American penal system has gone as far as Canada has in treating inmates as commercial employees. At the medium-security Joyceville institution near Kingston, 80 inmates are employed in an experimental program under which they receive the federal minimum wage, have income taxes deducted, work a seven-hour day Monday through Friday, have government holidays off, and can be fired for cause.[112,113]

The private sector in prison industry

Ultimately, the quality, viability, and relevance of prison industry may depend on the willingness of private employers to operate vocational training programs inside prisons, pay inmates the going rates for the same work on the outside, and hire satisfactory inmate workers upon release. Iowa cleared the way for such developments by revising its statutes governing prison industries. Under the new law, prison administrators can lease facilities on the institution's grounds to private corporations that will train inmates (at wages commensurate with similar jobs outside) and employ them upon release.[114]

One of the first institutions at which the role of the private sector in prison industries has gone beyond the talking stage is a women's prison. At the Bedford Hills Correctional Facility for Women in New York, a bank has installed equipment, is subsidizing the training of inmates in the clerical skills needed in banking, and has agreed to hire the program's graduates upon release.[115] Going one step further at the same institution, Sears & Roebuck provided $25,000 in equipment to be used to train a group of women inmates to become automobile mechanics, agreed to certify them on successful completion of the program, and said it would give priority to hiring them as regular mechanics for the company's auto center outlets.[116] Prior to these occupational breakthroughs, women offenders at Bedford Hills had little choice but to earn 8–28 cents an hour working in a garment factory whose sole product under the state-use policy was underwear for male prisoners.[117]

The Free Venture program

Perhaps the boldest and most promising approach to revitalizing prison industry is that represented by the Free Venture program, an experimental project in seven states* financed by the LEAA and administered by the American Institute of Criminal Justice in Philadelphia.[118,119] The broad goals of this model prison industry effort are "productive labor with outside world efficiency, outside world wages, and outside world relevance."[120] This dominant orientation, it is expected, will serve as the principal vehicle for making prison industries financially self-sufficient and for achieving reintegration of ex-offenders into society.

Basically, the Free Venture program is designed to emulate free world conditions of employment as closely as possible within the correctional setting. Its proposed realistic work environment includes a full workday, inmate wages based upon work output, productivity standards comparable to free world business, hiring and firing procedures, and transferable training and job skills. The concept also entails inmates' reimbursing the state for custody costs, making restitution to victims, job placement of inmates upon release, and operating prison industry at a profit. Free Venture is intended as an umbrella prison industry initiative, flexible enough to encompass a variety of business modes and operating procedures. Such business modes, for example, might involve state-run prison industry or privately managed prison shops, inmate-owned or inmate-operated enterprise under the supervision of state officials, and various

* Connecticut, Illinois, Minnesota, Iowa, Colorado, Washington, and South Carolina.

types of remuneration—including paid vacations! The aims and philosophy of Free Venture were enhanced by the passage of the "Percy Amendment" in 1980. Senator Charles Percy's bill will give federal funds to seven pilot states* to create new prison industries that will be allowed to sell their products in interstate commerce. By expanding marketing opportunities beyond state borders, private employers will hopefully be encouraged to subcontract work to prison industry shops.

One of the most successful and widely implemented applications of the Free Venture principle is found in Minnesota, which has a 1973 law permitting private companies to operate businesses within penal facilities. Stillwater Data Processing is the only private concern in America that operates entirely within a maximum-security prison. Sixteen of the firm's 19 employees are inmates who hold jobs as computer programmers. Interested inmates apply for Free Venture openings in much the same way any prospective employee does, the only stipulation being that they have at least one year left to serve. They are interviewed by a company manager who uses traditional selection criteria and, if hired, they start at the minimum wage of $3.35 an hour. Provided that job performance is satisfactory, inmates are granted regular raises to a top scale of $7 an hour. Their earnings are used to pay taxes and Social Security, support their families, make restitution, and save for the future. Free Venture inmates put in a 40-hour week, take coffee breaks, talk to clients on the phone, and accrue sick leave and vacation pay—all the things that outside employees do. And there are no guards in the prison shop area. Initially, Minnesota tried to collect room and board expenses from the inmates but eventually discarded the idea because of problems in administering the requirement equitably.

Another private company at the Stillwater facility runs the food service kitchens. It employs inmates as managers, cooks, and helpers, pays them real world wages, and offers many of them jobs in the chain upon release.[121] The Free Venture spirit is also much in evidence at Minnesota's medium-security Lino Lakes facility. Inmates there are engaged in private subcontracting for a dozen companies, including Western Electric and Toro, a manufacturer of lawn care and snow-removal equipment. The progress of Free Venture in Minnesota is partially credited to firms like Toro and Control Data, which make available financial support, expertise, and personnel to get the innovative program off the ground. The Free Venture agenda is by no means restricted to prison shops that are privately operated under subcontracted inmate labor. Free Venture funds have also been used to reorganize state-use industries to simulate private enterprise, and to expand existing vocational resources along free world lines. Regardless of the specific content, auspices, and logistics of individ-

* Only one of which overlaps with the seven Free Venture states.

ual Free Venture projects, they all share the common goal of treating inmates as bona fide employees rather than merely as sources of cheap labor to defray the costs of incarceration. The initial acceptance and results of the Free Venture ethic are encouraging. But time, politics, and fiscal considerations will ultimately determine whether Free Venture will become the impetus for radically altering the nature and definition of vocational training and prison industry.

Education

Remedial and high school education

Another program area of vital importance to prisoners is formal education, and with good reason: three-fourths of the nation's inmates have not completed high school, and one-half of all inmates are illiterate.[122,123] Most prisons offer remedial education and academic or vocational courses that lead to a high school diploma or its equivalent, the GED, which was first introduced into a penal institution by the Texas Department of Correction in 1956.[124] Some correctional systems rely on college instructors to teach these courses. In 1974, the Iowa State Penitentiary may have become the first state to turn over the administration of its entire inmate education program to an outside group, the Southeastern Community College.[125]

Inadequate resources, inmate disinterest, the attitudes of prison officials, the type of institution, and the competition from paying prison industries account for the variation in inmate participation in prison education programs. The result is that in some prisons only a fraction of the inmate population are enrolled in education programs; in others, especially in minimum-security and treatment-oriented facilities, the proportion is more substantial. For example, only 125 of 3,900 inmates at the Louisiana State Penitentiary at Angola are pursuing academic studies.[126] But 250 of 700 inmates at the Washington Corrections Center at Shelton are working for a high school diploma, and half of the inmates at Missouri's medium-security Training Center for Men at Moberly devote full time to schoolwork.[127,128]

College-educated cons

One of the most dramatic breakthroughs in prison education is the trend toward offering inmates credit courses that lead to a college degree without the inmate's ever leaving the institution—an innovation that is turning prisons into schools for criminals rather than schools for crime. The concept of college-educated cons got a boost from the federal government in 1967–1969, when the Office of Economic Opportunity funded college education projects at state prisons in Oregon, New Mexico, Minnesota, and Pennsylvania and the Federal Youth Center in Kentucky.[129] It was not long before community and four-year colleges throughout the country decided, on their own, to seize the opportunity to contribute to inmate rehabilitation (and at the same time bolster sagging

Inmates can take courses leading to a high school diploma in most prisons—and to a college degree in some

campus enrollments). Jackson State Prison in Michigan has 1,000 inmates enrolled in college courses, most of whom are in two-year degree programs offered by the Jackson Community College. In June 1976, the institution had its first graduating class of inmates who received bachelor's degrees after completing a four-year program taught by professors from Wayne State University.[130]

In Arizona, inmates at the Florence facility earn credits administered by Central Arizona College, and at the Fort Grant Training Center inmates take college courses ranging from literature to anthropology from six professors who fly in twice a week from Flagstaff.[131] The A.A. degrees offered to Iowa inmates by the Southeastern Community College are compatible with degree requirements at other area colleges, so inmates released before graduating can transfer their credits on the outside.[132] Washington State Prison's B.A. program is run by Washington State University, whose professors commute 100 miles from Pullman to meet their prison classes—which contain guards matriculating side by side with inmates.[133] Courses offered at Rikers Island by the John Jay College of Criminal Justice combine, in the same classroom, adults and adolescents, men and women, sentenced inmates and detainees, guards and prisoners.[134]

Treatment

Treatment programs make efforts to help inmates resolve personal problems related to the causes of their crimes, the conditions of incarceration, and preparation for release—those problems that are not already and more effectively addressed by the institution's vocational training and education programs. The core of most treatment programs is some form of individual counseling or group therapy provided by the professional staff; its goal is constructive personality and behavioral change that will turn offenders into law-abiding citizens.[135] The techniques for accomplishing this are variously identified as encounter groups, guided group interaction, reality therapy, behavior modification, marathon sessions, consciousness raising, self-help endeavors, psychotherapy, rap sessions, attack sessions modeled on California's Synanon drug treatment program, one-to-one casework, and the "therapeutic community." (See Close-up 14.4.) Because the concept of treatment is itself so nebulous, it may also encompass (a) outside volunteer groups who simply spend time talking to, empathizing with, entertaining, and educating inmates, or who perform other services that reduce inmate anxieties and frustrations, and (b) involuntary "behavior modification" programs that use deprivations of rights and privileges, drugs, and electroshock. In practice, the "treatment" of inmates is synonymous with "rehabilitation" as a consideration in sentencing and in granting parole.

Impediments to treatment

The success of treatment programs is hampered by several factors. The availability of professional "rehab" personnel, essential treatment programs, and facilities is grossly inadequate. Ratios of 1 counselor to 200 (or more) inmates are not uncommon.[136] Some prisons in which half of the inmates are drug abusers have no drug treatment program. The priority given to custody, the separation of the custodial and the treatment functions, and the antagonism between the two groups place severe limitations on realizing the potential of treatment. Many inmates who are resistant to being helped participate in treatment programs only in order to be able to present evidence of their "rehabilitation" to the parole board. It is an axiom of the helping professions that in order for treatment to be successful, it must be genuinely voluntary. Thus involuntary

Close-up 14.4 THE THERAPEUTIC COMMUNITY

The "therapeutic community" refers to special groups of inmates for whom treatment becomes a way of life while institutionalized and to which all other aspects of incarceration are subordinated. Such arrangements are only feasible where inmates have been committed to treatment-oriented institutions, committed under right-to-treatment statutes, or are segregated from the general inmate population in order to participate full-time in the rehabilitation program.

The principles underlying the therapeutic community include democratic decision making within limits, learning through the experience of other members, being accepted and respected by the institution's staff, avoiding regimentation, and inmates' playing an active role in their own treatment. The latter is accomplished through periodic group encounter sessions which bring together members as an informal family unit. The daily routine of therapeutic community residents revolves around gaining insight into their problems, assuming as much responsibility as they can handle, acquiring self-discipline and frustration tolerance, and observing the rules established by their group ("community") of peers. Basically, the therapeutic community is a device to resocialize inmates into conforming members of society through positive interactions with other members and staff. This entails learning new social skills necessary for survival on the outside, breaking all ties with the prison criminal subculture, and simulating the freedom of movement and choice in the free world.[a]

Federal defendants sentenced under the Narcotic Addict Rehabilitation Act[b] may be sent to any one of several federal institutions where the NARA treatment program is based on the therapeutic community.[c] In Florida, the Lantana Correctional Institution utilizes the therapeutic community approach to treat medium- and minimum-security youthful male offenders convicted of drug-related crimes.[d] At Connecticut's maximum-security Somers prison, program Empathy accepts 60 inmates with drug dependency problems, who live together in a special cellblock apart from the general inmate population.[e] In the same state's prison for women at Niantic, the therapeutic community is called the "just community" because it is based on the moral development theory of Lawrence Kohlberg. The 17 women in the just community live in a residential cottage separate from the other inmates.[f] The St. Albans facility in Vermont was originally designed as a therapeutic community where counsellors would provide intensive therapy to caseloads of less than 20 first offenders.[g] Finally, the "Bridge" at Washington State Penitentiary was a unique program that combined progressive vocational training and therapy within a self-governing group of inmates.[h]

[a] Bruno M. Cormier, *The Watcher and the Watched* (Montreal, Quebec, Canada, Tundra Books, 1975), pp. 41–48.
[b] The NARA law of 1966 allows federal courts to use indeterminate civil commitment in lieu of criminal prosecution for three classes of drug addicts. The criminal charges are dropped upon successful completion of the treatment.
[c] Gerald M. Farkas et al., "New Developments in the Federal Bureau of Prisons Addict Treatment Program," *Federal Probation,* December 1970, p. 52.
[d] "Group Encounter Program Works Well in Florida," *American Journal of Correction,* January–February 1977, p. 28.
[e] Roan Conrad, "Profile: Connecticut," *Corrections,* January/February 1975, pp. 67–68.
[f] Ibid., pp. 73–76; Lawrence Kohlberg, Peter Scharf, and Joseph Hickey, "The Justice Structure of the Prison," *Prison Journal,* Autumn–Winter 1971, pp. 3–14.
[g] Michael Kiernan, "Profile: Vermont," *Corrections,* September/October 1975, p. 39.
[h] R. V. Denenberg, "Profile: Washington State," *Corrections,* November/December 1974, pp. 45–52.

treatment or any type of coerced rehabilitation (including participation in vocational training and education programs) undertaken for the sole purpose of impressing the parole board may be doomed to failure. Even under the best of circumstances, the results of treatment (as measured by postinstitutional recidivism) have not lived up to promises or expectations. Whether the dubious efficacy of treatment is attributable to not knowing *how* to change offenders or instead to obstacles to proper implementation is one of the most complex questions facing the criminal justice system.

Conjugal visits

Conjugal (family) visits represent an unorthodox treatment program intended to alleviate the sexual and familial deprivations of incarceration: inmate and spouse are permitted to spend a day or two in private quarters on the prison grounds for the purpose of having sex, keeping the marriage intact, and preserving the family relationship. The presence of the inmate's children may also be an important part of conjugal visits. And unmarried prisoners are allowed to spend their family visits with close relatives where such programs exist. In the few jurisdictions that have these programs, prison administrators emphasize that they are primarily family visitation programs that, in the case of married inmates, also provide a sexual outlet.[137] In California's family visiting program, which began in 1968, medium-security inmates are eligible to spend 24–72 hours with their wives, children, and relatives in pleasantly furnished

Conjugal visit programs permit the inmate to spend time with family in homelike quarters on the prison grounds

trailers and apartments away from the main prison buildings but still within the walls. And minimum-security men have their family visits in apartments within two houses just outside the walls.[138]

As of 1978, few states allowed conjugal visits.* The usual barriers to instituting them were inadequate space and facilities, objections that inmates might find something pleasurable in incarceration, concern that outsiders eligible to participate in conjugal visits would ultimately include prostitutes (as they do in Mexico), and the "shocking" prospect of permitting women inmates the same heterosexual opportunities as male inmates.[139,140] So far, all attempts by inmates to establish a "right to sex" through litigation—by claiming that the denial of conjugal visits constitutes cruel and unusual punishment or aggravates homosexual tendencies—have been unsuccessful.

THE PAROLE DECISION

How soon inmates are released from prison depends on the parole board and the statutes that govern parole eligibility. The parole board has the responsibility and virtually unreviewable discretion for deciding whom

* New Jersey, Texas, and North Carolina are experimenting with conjugal visit programs.

to select for parole, when or if inmates should be paroled, and the conditions of parole and parole revocation. All adult paroling authorities are separate agencies that are administratively independent of institutional staff. In deciding whether to grant parole, the parole board functions as an unsupervised, autonomous, quasi-judicial body that is answerable neither to institutional authorities nor (yet) to the courts. For all practical purposes, parole board members can not be sued by victims for crimes committed by parolees.[141] About 75 percent of all prisoners ultimately return to society through parole, and this fact makes the parole board the most important gatekeeper in the custodial setting.[142]

Parole eligibility

The only constraint under which parole boards perform their main function are the statutes that govern *parole eligibility.** As a rule of thumb, inmates given an indeterminate sentence of the minimum-maximum variety are eligible for—but not automatically entitled to—parole after serving the minimum, for example, after doing 5 years of a 5–10 year sentence. State and federal inmates given fixed sentences or indefinite sentences of the type "not more than *x* years" generally become eligible for parole after serving one-third of their term: for example, after 5 years of a flat 15-year sentence or a sentence of "not more than 15 years." Statutes illustrating much less prevalent eligibility patterns make inmates eligible for parole (a) at any time, (b) after serving a designated proportion of the minimum in a minimum-maximum sentence, such as one-fourth, one-third, or one-half of the minimum, (c) according to an either-or-formula, such as one-fourth of the maximum sentence or a designated number of years, whichever is shorter.

Very few states make any group of inmates permanently ineligible for parole; those which do involve such low-frequency offenses as to be negligible in the prison population. Life imprisonment in 15 states commonly means parole eligibility after serving 10 or 15 years, and in two states it carries 7 years, so even lifers can look forward to the day they will meet the parole board.† Five states provide longer parole eligibility periods for persons convicted of violent crimes and for habitual offenders. In practice, then, virtually all inmates are eligible for parole well before the expiration of their maximum sentence.

Goodtime credit laws

In general, the parole board has more control over the length of time inmates will serve than the courts that sentenced them. The discretionary power of parole boards in determining length of incarceration is en-

* The statistics and patterns of parole eligibility discussed here were compiled by analyzing the raw "case" data presented in Vincent O'Leary's survey of state parole systems, the most recent comprehensive work on the subject.[143]

† Federal inmates sentenced to life imprisonment or more than 45 years are eligible for parole after serving 15 years.

hanced by *goodtime credit laws,* which can further shorten the parole eligibility period. There are three sources or types of goodtime credit.

1. Inmates may automatically receive statutory, regular, or *unearned* goodtime according to a fixed or sliding scale related to the length of sentence. The most common statutory goodtime pattern is a sliding scale that takes 2–5 days per month off the sentence for serving the first and second years and up to 10–15 days per month off the sentence after having served several years. Wisconsin takes one month off the sentence for the first year, deducts an additional month each year up to the sixth year, and gives six months goodtime credit for each succeeding year. In Massachusetts, the sliding scale runs from 2.5 days per month in the first year to 12.5 days per month in the fourth and succeeding years. Some states have a flat-rate statutory goodtime structure: 5 days per month in Maryland and Connecticut, 4 days in Iowa, 2 days in Louisiana, 10 days in New York and Wyoming.
2. *Industrial* goodtime, also called "work" or "extra" goodtime, is earned at specified rates for each month the inmate is employed in prison industry or a vocational training program. Vermont inmates, for example, can earn 5 days per month off their sentence for each month they work in prison industry.
3. *Meritorious* goodtime is awarded to inmates for exemplary behavior, at the discretion of prison officials.

The significance of the three types of goodtime (which can be added together in determining parole eligibility) is that almost half the states permit goodtime to reduce the standard eligibility criteria. Thus an Arkansas inmate given a 10–20 year sentence would be eligible for parole in about 8 years on the basis of statutory goodtime alone; and meritorious goodtime could take another 5 days a month off the minimum sentence. A Connecticut inmate serving 5–20 years can be eligible for parole in 3 years and 4 months with goodtime credit.[144] An Illinois inmate with a 20-year minimum sentence is eligible for parole after serving 11 years and 3 months with goodtime.[145] In Maryland, life imprisonment means parole eligibility in 15 years *minus* goodtime.

The membership of parole boards

According to the 1976 survey of all state parole systems conducted by O'Leary and Hanrahan, parole board members in 40 jurisdictions are appointed by the governor. Thus there is the possibility that the positions may be filled through political patronage, although a few states have moved toward merit selection of board members from recommendations made by other agencies or groups. Most parole board members are appointed for renewable terms of 4 to 6 years (16 and 17 states) to boards consisting of 3 or 5 persons (15 and 23 states). In 30 jurisdictions parole board members are full-time employees, in 18 they work part-time, and 4 jurisdictions have a mixture. Sixteen states have no statutory qualifications for appointment to the parole board, and 19 states have qualifications so vague as to be meaningless. Only 8 states require any of their parole board members to have college degrees, and 5 of these call for a licensed attorney to be on the board. Thus, in two-thirds of the states, "political contacts" may play a major role in an individual's becoming a parole board member. And part-time status further reduces the commitment, competence, and performance of parole board members to the varied and complex tasks at hand. A small but growing number of states are requiring the appointment of women and minority groups to parole boards.[146]

Parole Board-Determined Release

The parole grant hearing

The parole decision is made when the parole board makes its periodic visits to each prison in the state for the purpose of holding *parole grant hearings* at which eligible inmates are interviewed. Parole grant hearings are usually automatically docketed one to three months before the inmate's eligibility date. Only 20 states require that the entire parole board be present at the hearing, that is, that it meet *en banc*. For practical reasons, half of the jurisdictions permit panels of two or three members, representing the full board, to conduct the hearing and make the parole decision. In Michigan, for example, a two-member panel disposes of 5,000–6,000 cases a year; only 800 "special inmates" require the attention of the full five-member board.[147] In the majority of states, between 20 and 40 cases are heard per day in grant hearings. The amount of time devoted to one hearing is usually 10–20 minutes, and rarely does a hearing last more than half an hour.[148]

The interview with the inmate centers on three areas: the criminal record, the institutional performance, and the parole plan if the inmate were to be released. In response to their perceptions of parole board expectations at the hearing, inmates may "play the parole game" by appearing contrite and repentant for their crimes and their former lifestyles, but whether board members are often conned by the convicts is debatable.[149] In any given case, the board's decision could depend on the inmate's attitude and demeanor at the hearing, on whether the inmate appeared hostile or unrepentant, refused to admit guilt to the original or multiple counts that were dropped in plea bargaining, looked board members straight in the eye or gazed at the floor, shook their hands firmly, or slammed the door belligerently upon leaving.

Absence of due process rights (*Greenholtz* v. *Inmates of Nebraska Penal Complex*, 1979)

Inmates have no due process rights under the Fourteenth Amendment at the parole grant hearing, such as the right to counsel, to present evidence, or to cross-examine witnesses. The Supreme Court's decision in *Greenholtz* v. *Inmates of the Nebraska Penal and Correctional Com-*

plex[150] in 1979 was compatible with the view that early release is basically an act of "grace"* —a privilege that the parole board can bestow or withhold at will—rather than a constitutional right. "There is no set of facts which, if shown, mandate a decision favorable to the individual (inmate)." The implications of *Greenholtz* are that parole boards are free to adopt virtually any legal posture they choose at the parole grant hearing.

About three-fifths of the boards do not permit attorneys to attend the hearing, do not allow inmates to present witnesses on their behalf, and make no verbatim record of the proceedings. Since most inmates are indigent and only six states provide free counsel, inmates in almost all jurisdictions are largely on their own at the grant hearing. Half of the jurisdictions permit inmates to appeal the parole decision, which in many cases simply means that an inmate can formally request the board to review its action or to conduct another hearing. The lack of due process and the board's enormous discretion are facilitated by the broad statutory mandate under which the boards operate. Statutes typically authorize, but do not require, the parole board to grant release if "there is a reasonable probability that such prisoner will live and remain at liberty without violating the laws" and that "such release is not incompatible with the welfare of society."[151]

Rehabilitation

The parole grant hearing is simply the tip of the parole-decision iceberg that is anchored in the institutional reports that board members receive beforehand and in their personal assessment of the just deserts appropriate to the inmate's instant offenses. The institutional record is studied by the board in advance in order to determine whether the inmate is ready for release, that is, whether the inmate has been rehabilitated to the point of no return to crime. This is the major criterion for release in all enabling legislation from which parole boards derive their authority. The parole board predicts the likelihood of recidivism on parole from (1) evaluations of the prisoner's personality, problems, progress, and prognosis made by the institution's professional staff, (2) evidence of participation in prison industry, vocational training, education, and treatment programs, (3) the inmate's disciplinary record. Violation of prison regulations, especially committing major infractions and incurring serious penalties, carries considerable weight with parole boards, which assume that inmates who cannot behave themselves while confined cannot be trusted to conform to society's rules while under the nominal supervision of a parole officer.[152] Also considered are (4) the inmate's attitude, demeanor, and presentation

* The "grace" rationale originated in the now defunct view that incarceration strips a criminal of all civil and constitutional rights. The privilege-right distinction has traditionally been used to deny inmates any control over many conditions of incarceration, but that situation has changed drastically as a result of the prisoners' rights movement, discussed in Chapter 15.

of self at the parole grant hearing, and (5) the adequacy of the inmate's parole plan as reflected in the caseworker's report.[153]

The parole plan

The *parole plan* describes the inmate's employment status or prospects, living arrangements, and treatment needs upon release. Next to "going straight" (and related to it), the parole board's most common requirement in granting release is that the inmate have a job lined up.[154] Conversely, the most common reason for holding inmates beyond the date scheduled for their release is the unavailability of employment.[155] Having no guarantee of a job, however, is not an insurmountable barrier to release if the inmate has marketable skills and good prospects, is highly motivated to find work, and no useful purpose would be served by continued confinement. Underlying the parole board's concern with employment is the unanimous belief, reinforced by research findings, that work is rehabilitative and the only permanent antidote to crime and recidivism.[156]

At the same time, research has shown that regardless of favorable institutional performance, signs of rehabilitation, and the likelihood of not recidivating, parole boards are reluctant to release inmates before they have served the minimum amount of time "warranted" (in the board's opinion) by their offenses.[157] This is the resurrected and once again respectable viewpoint that serious offenders should get the punishment they deserve in addition to the rehabilitation they need. Finally, under certain circumstances, the parole decision may hinge on political factors more than on rehabilitation, recidivism, or notions of just deserts. To protect the board's reputation and to avoid criticism, inmates whose release would arouse strong community opposition might be denied parole even though the risk of recidivism is the lowest of any group of offenders —for example, murderers, sex offenders, and embezzlers.[158] Or the board may tighten up on parole grants in response to "law and order" campaigns on the part of police officials or a "hard line" taken by the district attorney.[159]

Parole board procedures

The parole hearing is closed to outsiders. However, the board may permit the attendance of the inmate's caseworker or other in-house officials who know the prisoner best, in order to supply valuable information, clarify the written record, and act as a decision-making resource.[160] Remarkably, guards and senior custodial staff members are rarely invited to make any direct contribution to the parole decision. In 35 jurisdictions, prison officials routinely make nonbinding parole recommendations to the board; in six states, they do so "in some cases." Virtually all parole boards now provide a written explanation for denying parole, though the "explanation" may be of dubious value to the inmate.[161] A negative decision at the hearing rarely disqualifies the inmate permanently for parole, unless it so specifies. Instead, the refused inmate receives a *set-off date,* the time of the next opportunity for parole consideration. The set-off date is determined by statute, board policy, or discretion; it may be left open or postponed until the inmate has a chance to improve in the areas responsible for the denial of parole.

Inmates who are granted parole continue to remain in the legal custody of the state and must "serve" the remainder of their unexpired maximum sentence (including the amount of goodtime by which parole eligibility was advanced) under the supervision of a parole officer, unless formally discharged before then. In addition to the standard conditions of parole that apply to all released inmates, the board may incorporate special requirements in the parole agreement that each inmate must sign before leaving the institution.

The board's unrestricted discretion

The major criticisms of parole boards center on their unchecked discretion, the impropriety of coerced participation in prison programs, and their inability to predict recidivism accurately. According to this view, it is impossible to identify the magic moment of rehabilitation (which of course is a myth), just deserts should be a major factor in the release formula, and poor crime forecasting keeps many inmates in prison who would not recidivate if released. Rehabilitation and recidivism are the main support of the argument for giving the board unrestricted discretion, and that discretion is responsible for a number of problems and inequities. Just as the sentence received may depend on the judge doing the sentencing, the release of inmates may depend on the parole board before which they appear.* Correction officials admit that the final decision is often based on "a lot of gut kinds of feelings about when a guy is ready. The critera are not well enunciated. . . ."[162] The basic problem (and the principal criticism) of parole boards is that they lack accountability, that they have too much uncontrolled discretion. Consequently, parole decision making is lawless, arbitrary, too heavily influenced by judgments of rehabilitation, unrelated to relevant objective criteria, and an invitation to unwarranted "release disparity."

The parole guidelines table

It was in response to just such criticism of its own operation that the United States Board of Parole sought to make the parole decision more equitable through the Parole Decision-Making Guidelines Project. The Board of Parole (the Parole Commission) is the nine-member board responsible for making the release decision in the cases of federal prisoners. The board also assumes related activities that involve its members in 18,000 decisions a year.[163] The Parole Decision-Making Guidelines Project was a research effort intended to provide a scientific, objective means for structuring discretion according to uniform standards instead of relying on subjective judgments, moral values, and unwritten rules that would result in "arbitrary and capricious" decisions. Starting in

* According to statistics culled from *Corrections* magazine, in eight states the proportion of inmates released by parole boards ranged from one-third in Arizona to 97 percent in Washington.

riticism of parole boards' use of scretion has led some boards to lopt the parole guidelines table

1970 under a $500,000 LEAA grant to the NCCD, researchers developed over a three-year period a parole guidelines table to be used by the examiners and the commission in making release decisions[164] (see Table 14.1).

To determine the release date for a particular parole applicant, the board member plots the "severity" of the crime and the "likelihood of recidivism" (salient factor score) on the guidelines matrix, or table. The statistical cell into which the inmate falls indicates the *customary time* to be served before release. For example, inmates incarcerated for marijuana possession (a low severity offense) who have a very high salient factor score (high probability of going straight) should customarily be released after 8–12 months, according to the guidelines. An inmate serving time for robbery or selling hard drugs (a very high severity offense) who has a poor prognosis for success should customarily serve 55–65 months before being released. The virtue of the guidelines table is that all inmates who are alike where it counts most are treated the same, articulated release criteria are provided, and board members are obligated to follow the specified release periods, unless they can justify in writing their reasons for not doing so. Significantly, 85 percent of federal inmates are being paroled within the customary time periods called for in the guidelines.[165]

The guidelines table is a device for structuring the parole board's discretion without eliminating it; clinical judgment can override the customary release periods whenever there are compelling reasons for not following the table. All of the recommended release intervals are based on the assumption that the inmate's institutional performance is satisfactory. Documentation of "outstanding institutional progress" or "poor institutional conduct" are the leading reasons for releasing inmates before or after the customary time.[166] The presence of mitigating or aggravating

Table 14.1 Parole Guidelines Table for Adult Inmates

Customary Time to be Served Before Release, by Severity of Offense Imprisoned for, and Likelihood of Recidivism

		PAROLE PROGNOSIS (Salient Factor Score)			
	Severity of Offense (examples)	Very Good (11–9)	Good (8–6)	Fair (5–4)	Poor (3–0)
Low	Immigration law violations Minor theft (under $1,000)	6–10 months	8–12 months	10–14 months	12–16 months
Low Moderate	Alcohol law violations Marijuana possession (under $500) Forgery, fraud (under $1,000) Income tax evasion (under $3,000) Theft from mail (under $1,000)	8–12 months	12–16 months	16–20 months	20–25 months
Moderate	Bribery of public official Possession of hard drugs by user (under $500) Possession of marijuana (over $500) Sale of marijuana (under $5,000) Embezzlement (under $20,000) Mailing threatening communications Receiving stolen property to resell (under $20,000) Motor vehicle theft	12–16 months	16–20 months	20–24 months	24–30 months
High	Burglary or larceny from bank or post office Sale of hard drugs to support habit Sale of marijuana (over $5,000) Possession of soft drugs (over $5,000) Embezzlement ($20,000–$100,000) Organized vehicle theft Receiving stolen property ($20,000–$100,000) Robbery (no weapon or injury) Theft, forgery, fraud ($20,000–$100,000)	16–20 months	20–26 months	26–32 months	32–38 months
Very High	Robbery (weapon) Possession of hard drugs by nondrug dependent user Sale of hard drugs for profit (no prior conviction for selling hard drugs) Sale of soft drugs (over $5,000) Extortion Mann Act (force) Sexual act (force)	26–36 months	36–45 months	45–55 months	55–65 months
Greatest	Aggravated felony (weapon fired or serious injury) Aircraft hijacking Sale of hard drugs for profit (prior conviction for same) Espionage Explosives (detonation) Kidnapping Willful homicide	Greater than above. However, specific ranges are not given due to the limited number of cases and the extreme variations in severity possible within the category.			

Source: Peter B. Hoffman and Lucille K. DeGostin, "Parole Decision-Making: Structuring Discretion," *Federal Probation,* December 1974, p. 12.

circumstances in the offense may also justify deviation from the guidelines. In the main, the guidelines act as a deterrent to postponing release because of the inmate's attitude during the hearing, the inmate's failure to participate in prison rehabilitation programs, the vague negative evaluations presented by treatment staff, and the personal whims, prejudices, and hunches of board members. By controlling discretion, the new ground rules make the parole decision more explicit, consistent, rational, and relevant to just deserts and public safety. And the guidelines abandon any attempt to make release dependent on rehabilitation.

Criticisms of the guidelines table

The most troublesome criticism of the guidelines is that, because inmates have no control over any of the factors which determine the customary time to be served, they are in effect prisoners of their past mistakes.* Moreover, the principle of individualized justice is apparently sacrificed, there is little incentive for inmates to improve themselves educationally and vocationally in prison, goodtime credit does not matter as much, and there is no longer the need to interview inmates in order to reach the parole decision.† The guidelines are offensive to judges, who do not understand them and believe that institutional progress (rather than "some statistician") should determine release.[167] And guidelines-based parole is unrelated to the sentence imposed. The major impetus for reforming parole release has come largely from those skeptical of incarceration who believe that parole board decision-making is erratic and detains too many prisoners who should be released earlier.

Despite the shortcomings of the guidelines, the table is now used routinely as an aid in federal parole selection decisions, and the guidelines have been adopted as a model for improved parole decision making by at least ten states.[168] California, for example, used the tables to establish firm release dates for its 20,000 inmates, who can be held longer than the customary time only because of involvement in a major disciplinary incident.[169]

Parole Contracts (Mutual Agreement Programming)

For better or worse, the guidelines' major innovative competition in the states seems destined to come from the emerging "right" to be released through *parole contracts.* Parole contracting, or Mutual Agreement Programming (MAP), is an arrangement under which an inmate agrees to fulfill specified goals in return for a definite parole date that is

* The only two items in the salient factor score that can be affected by the inmate's institutional performance are the parole plan and the obtaining of a high school diploma through the GED.

† However, goodtime credit may affect the determination of how soon the inmate gets out of prison on mandatory release (discussed below).

set shortly after the inmate's arrival at the institution.[170] The goals might include (for example) acquiring a job skill, undergoing counseling, making restitution, avoiding disciplinary problems, earning a GED. The inmate, assisted by a MAP coordinator or other institutional representative, negotiates the agreement directly with the parole board, and the agreement becomes a legally binding contract when it has been signed by the three parties. The institution's role in parole contracting is crucial because it controls the services, programs, and opportunities needed by the inmates to complete their contract. The inmate who fails to achieve the objectives stated in the contract, or who backs out of the agreement, simply reverts to being considered for release under the regular parole process, without prejudice. When inmates fulfill their part of the contract, the parole board must do likewise—hence the "right" to parole under Mutual Agreement Programming.

The need for parole contracts

Contract parole had its roots in the concern over the lack of communication between parole boards and institutional staff and its negative consequences.[171] This communication gap left inmates in the dark on how to earn release, and it was a hindrance to coordinating prison training programs with job placement upon release. For example, parole boards might require inmates to take prison programs that were not offered or were oversubscribed, might take action incompatible with the inmate's employability and labor market realities, or might give only lip service to the need for participating in rehabilitation programs. For its part, the institutions had little incentive or accountability for providing inmates with relevant prison programs or developing new ones; the selection of inmates to fill scarce slots was haphazard; and training cycles were not coordinated with possible release dates. Accordingly, in 1971 the Labor Department funded the $600,000 Parole-Corrections Project carried out by the American Correctional Association, which developed the MAP idea and implemented it in three different pilot projects in Wisconsin, Arizona, and California in 1972–1974.

MAP in Wisconsin

The programs in Arizona and California were not continued, but MAP worked so smoothly in Wisconsin that it was expanded under a $231,000 LEAA grant in October 1974 from the pilot facility to every adult institution.[172] All Wisconsin inmates with sentences of less than five years were immediately eligible for MAP, and 1,647 contracts were signed within two years. A typical parole contract covers counseling, vocational and academic training, discipline, and often work or study release. Contract objectives are made as detailed as possible (such as earning a particular grade in a course) in order to enhance their relevance and to facilitate determining whether the contract has been fulfilled, which is the responsibility of the MAP coordinator. About 80 percent of the contracts written, which average eight months in length, are successfully completed. Parole contracting is in operation in the District of Columbia and at least nine states, and it is on the drawing board in several others.

The virtues of MAP

The great attraction of MAP is that it offers something for everyone concerned with parole reform. It offers inmates a measure of self-determination, the promise of early parole, a clear "road MAP" out of prison that designates specific parole criteria, and the motivation to improve themselves. It offers the parole board direct and immediate input into the inmate's programming and eliminates the need for "academy award performances" at the hearing—which in turn becomes a business conference that determines whether the contract terms have been met. It reduces tensions within institutions and the complaints about parole that are commonly associated with riots. Parole contracting has a humanizing impact on corrections staff and makes their custodial function easier. MAP serves as a meaningful screening device for identifying poor parole risks (those who fail to complete their contract) and eliminates the reliance on guesswork. It encourages greater cooperation and coordination between the institution and the parole board. An important side effect of MAP is that it forces prison administrators to be accountable for the effectiveness and availability of prison programs, thereby moving a step closer to the "right to treatment." A further indication of its appeal is that MAP is being tried with juvenile offenders, in jails,* and in probation.[173] And states are adopting MAP despite research that shows that the recidivism rates, employment picture, and time served of released MAP inmates are the same as for inmates paroled without contracts!

The drawbacks of MAP

Most of the opposition to MAP comes from the parole boards themselves, who view contracting as a technique that formalizes the "game," erodes their discretionary powers, and releases unchanged criminals.[174] The most controversial and most serious criticism of parole contracting says that it is a throwback to the medical model and rehabilitation, which has been repudiated by everyone but those who make the parole decision. MAP supporters contend that parole contracts represent a step away from the rehabilitation model and toward responsibility, since inmates who fulfill their contract have shown themselves capable of abiding by rules and must be released even if they have not been rehabilitated. MAP makes parole release contingent on institutional performance; the guidelines table rules out institutional progress as a factor in parole. A third approach to improving the method of release would rule out both MAP and the guidelines: the abolition of parole.

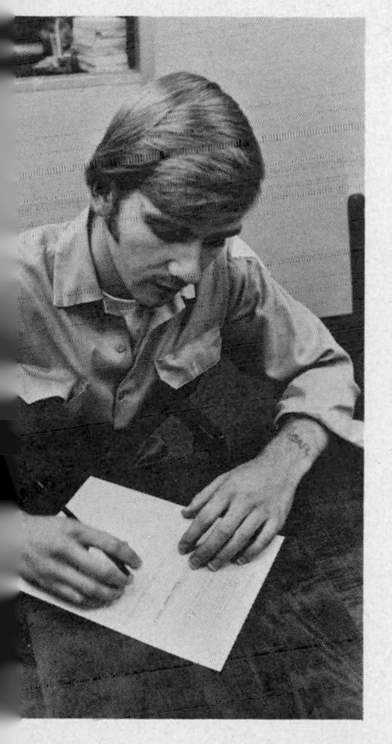

isconsin inmate signs a parole tract, a new procedure for aining early release from on

The Abolition of Parole

Extreme dissatisfaction with parole, disillusionment with its life-support system of indeterminate sentences,[175] and the belief that devices like

* For all practical purposes, parole has not yet broken into jail. A survey of local jails revealed that 62 percent had no parole mechanism at all; in those which did, only 8 percent of the inmates were released on parole.

MAP and the guidelines cannot reform parole decision making have led three states (California, Maine, and Indiana) to abolish parole, and others are following suit.* The position of the antiparole people is that parole board decision making is inherently arbitrary, oppressive, discriminatory, unethical, ineffective, wedded to rehabilitation, incapable of predicting recidivism, and unamenable to improvement no matter how much it is tinkered with. The three abolition states, and virtually all proposals to abolish parole release, recognize that the parole and sentencing processes are inseparable. Judges impose indeterminate sentences and lengthy fixed terms with rehabilitation in mind, and they expect incarcerated offenders to be released before serving their full sentence. Hence any drastic change in parole release requires changes in the structure of criminal penalties and sentencing discretion.

In its purest form, parole abolition entails adopting a system of relatively short fixed sentences and curtailing the court's discretion in deciding which flat term to impose (as California did, beginning in July 1977). In principle, inmates in no-parole states would be released automatically after serving their full fixed term and would not be subject to supervision upon release. In practice, however, the ties to parole release, its underlying concerns, parole boards, and supervision upon release are not easily severed.

No-parole in California, Maine, and Indiana

Except for first-degree murder and kidnapping for ransom, all crimes in California fall into one of four narrow sentence categories, each of which contains three fixed terms. The judge must impose the middle (base) term in the appropriate category unless mitigating or aggravating circumstances associated with the crime are proven. In that case, the judge can select the lower or upper term in the category, provided the court's decision is supported by a statement of the reasons for deviating from the prescribed base sentence.[177] The "enhancement" provisions in California's revised criminal code specify punishments in addition to the base term; they apply when the enhancement offenses are not legally a part of the main crime.† Under Maine's new criminal code, which abolished the indeterminate sentence and parole, judges select a flat term from within a range of years applicable to five classes of crime. Indiana's no-parole law and the Illinois proposal both contain fixed terms to be

* Illinois, Washington, Minnesota, Connecticut, Delaware, Alaska, and the federal government. Attempts by the New York Civil Liberties Union to abolish parole through the courts on constitutional grounds were unsuccessful.[176]

† For example, a man sentenced to four years for the crime of rape would receive an additional three years if great bodily injury was involved, three more years for having previously been convicted of a violent crime, another year for each consecutive count conviction, and so on. The court may forgo the enhancement punishment if there are sufficient mitigating circumstances.

selected from within a range established for different classes of crime, along with enhancement punishments.

The problems of no-parole

In essence, all parole abolition laws and proposals are based on the "just deserts" model of sentencing and the need to eliminate discretionary release. However, the no-parole schemes invariably entail substantial goodtime credit for reducing fixed sentences, but its availability may or may not depend on the discretion of prison officials! For example, Indiana inmates can have their flat sentence reduced by half, provided they do not receive a "high risk" security rating for violating prison regulations, and the rating is determined by prison officials. Through a combination of statutory and prison-programming goodtime, California inmates receive a four-month reduction for every eight months served, most of which depends on their not committing crimes while in prison.* Whether or not receiving goodtime credit under no-parole is as discretionary, unfettered, and unfairly administered as regular parole release is arguable. Yet parole board sympathizers claim that the goodtime provisions of no-parole statutes simply shift release discretion from the boards to the prison authorities, thereby retaining the indeterminacy of release —the major weakness that parole abolition and fixed sentences are supposed to correct.[178] Undoubtedly, the continued availability of goodtime under no-parole represents a consensus that inmates need an opportunity to obtain early release and an incentive for behaving themselves, no matter how short or fixed their sentences.

ɔarole officer interviews a paɛe. Under some no-parole ıemes, parole supervision ·uld be abolished.

Other features of existing no-parole legislation and their implications suggest that the coveted certainty of release may be as elusive as rehabilitation, and that no-parole does not necessarily mean the end of parole boards, supervision upon release, or revocation. In California, for example, most inmates released on no-parole will automatically be under supervision for one year. The new Community Release Board will conduct goodtime revocation hearings that could result in recommitment for up to six months, and it will conduct regular parole grant hearings in capital cases. Indiana's no-parole law also has an across-the-board one year supervision period, but revoked offenders can lose all of their goodtime and be recommitted to serve out their original presumptive sentence. Maine abolished both the parole board and supervision; but all imposed fixed sentences are tentative because the new law gave prison officials the discretion to ask the court to reduce the terms of any inmates who they believe deserve a shorter sentence! The parole plan in Connecticut calls for eliminating the parole board in stages, with parole supervision the first element to go. While the effectiveness of parole supervision in preventing recidivism is unsubstantiated, its complete elimination may cre-

* Of every eight months served, three months are reduced for not being involved in weapons offenses, escape, inciting to riot, drugs, destroying prison property.

ate more problems than it solves. "I think if I came out of prison today, I'd like to be sure there was at least one person who I knew cared about what happens to me tomorrow."[179]

Mandatory Release and Discharge

Being granted parole is not the only legal way of getting out of prison before the full sentence has been served. Inmates not paroled may leave through mandatory release or by being discharged from their sentence.

Mandatory release, or conditional release, means that inmates are automatically released from prison after serving their maximum term minus goodtime. This is required by statute rather than the result of a discretionary decision by the parole board. But because technically their full sentences have not expired, mandatory releasees are supervised as though they were on parole. And they can be returned to prison to serve out their goodtime deductions if they violate the conditions of mandatory release (which are the same as regular parole conditions). For purposes of supervision and revocation, therefore, mandatory releasees remain under the jurisdiction of the parole board. The theory of mandatory release is that offenders who return to society need a period of official supervision to help them make the transition from incarceration to freedom. (Most new crimes by ex-inmates occur in the first year of release.) Sixteen jurisdictions have mandatory release laws, although only 7,149 of the 120,000 inmates who left prison in 1975 got out through mandatory release.[180,181]

Discharged, or unconditionally released, inmates must by law be released after serving their maximum term minus goodtime, as in mandatory release. However, discharged inmates are released outright without supervision. No conditions are attached to their release, and their sentences are formally considered to have expired. Thus discharged inmates are fully free citizens, compared with those released on parole and mandatory release. Of the 120,000 inmates released from prison in 1975, about 27,000 left through discharge, that is, expiration of sentence. Thirty-six jurisdictions have discharge release rather than mandatory release. The chief benefit to the state in releasing inmates outright rather than on the conditional release are the costs saved on supervision. Only a negligible proportion of inmates "max out": are discharged after having served their full sentence in prison without goodtime reductions. (In New York 2.8 percent of the inmates max out, in Connecticut 2 percent.[182,183])

Gate money

Regardless of the release mechanism, virtually all states provide prisoners with "gate money" at the time of release, and a large majority also provide both transportation and clothing.[184] A typical departing inmate can count on a new suit of clothes, the cheapest method of transportation, and $20–$29 toward starting a new life, in addition to money earned in prison industry, medical experiments, and work release. An inmate leaving the federal penitentiary in Lewisburg, Pennsylvania, receives a new suit, a bus ticket, and $65.[185]

THE FUTURE OF IMPRISONMENT

It is likely that, in one form or another, prisons will remain a permanent and prominent component of the corrections system. The call to abolish prisons has gained little support outside limited professional circles. The strategy that would force prisons out of business by means of a moratorium on new prison construction (offenders would have to be retained in the community) has met with little success. In an almost self-defeating gesture, the antiprison people have turned to tabulating the number of new prisons being constructed and their high costs.[186] And by undertaking an assessment of new institutions, the nation's leading moratorium advocate implicitly recognized the legitimacy of incarceration itself.[187,188] New institutions must be built for humanitarian reasons alone: to accommodate increases in inmate populations and to replace ancient bastilles that make prison life abominable for staff and prisoners alike.

… new state prison at Leesburg, …w Jersey, has garden court…ds and one-person cells with …erable windows and outside …ws

The only grounds on which friends and foes of prison do not part company concern the design and location of new facilities.

Design and location of prisons

There is an informed consensus that new prisons, in order to provide humane custody, should not house more than 500 inmates, should not look like prisons, and should be located close to urban areas in order to attract an integrated and better educated staff, to take advantage of community resources, and to maintain visiting and family ties. Progress is being made toward realizing the 500-inmate goal: the average size of new major adult institutions surveyed by Nagel was 770, significantly below the 1,100 average of the pre-1960 period.[189] However, community resistance presents a serious obstacle to the construction of prisons in cosmopolitan centers whose economy is not dependent on the jobs and income generated by prison industry. But depressed rural areas may welcome such moves. Otisville, New York, where a new $19 million campuslike federal prison is being constructed for white collar criminals, has gained jobs for some of its 1,200 residents in building the prison and as guards.[190]

Wherever tomorrow's prisons may be located, their design and physical facilities promise to make prison life more habitable if not quite comfortable. Under the guiding hand of the National Clearinghouse for Correctional Planning and Architecture, new institutions are often achieving the look of campuses, shopping malls, and modern office buildings without sacrificing security.[191]

At the correctional institution in Fort Worth, Texas, inmate participation in rehabilitation programs cannot affect a release date

The role of rehabilitation in modern prisons is likely to be similar to that adopted at the $14 million medium-security federal prison opened in May 1976 at Butner, North Carolina. Guards wear blazers and slacks, inmates wear their own clothes or prison jumpsuits (available in four colors), there are two staff for every three inmates, and the prisoners have keys to their rooms.[192] At orientation, each inmate is given a definite release date and informed that nothing done in prison—including participation in available rehabilitation programs—can result in an earlier release.

The Martinson study of rehabilitation

The case against rehabilitation got a tremendous boost from the research findings of sociologist Robert Martinson, made public in 1974.[193] In order to study the effectiveness of rehabilitation, Martinson evaluated the outcomes of 231 prison programs identified in a survey of the literature from 1945 to 1967, the most comprehensive undertaking of its kind to date. His conclusion: "With few and isolated exceptions, the rehabilitative efforts that have been reported so far have had no appreciable effect on recidivism."[194] Criticism of Martinson's work, and the alternative conclusion that the evidence on rehabilitation is inconclusive, may temporarily keep alive the question, Is rehabilitation dead?[195,196] But the well-publicized Martinson report, spotlighted on television's *60 Minutes* and in *People* magazine, combined with the thrust of parole guidelines and contracts, suggest that old-time rehabilitation has had its heyday in prison.

Coed prisons

Pioneered by the Bureau of Prisons and carrying a special brand of rehabilitation, coed prisons may represent the ultimate in humane custody. The coed facility at the Federal Youth Center in Pleasanton, California, is among the newest of four federal "integrated" institutions (the others are in Fort Worth, Texas; Morgantown, West Virginia; and Lexington, Kentucky). The coed Massachusetts Correctional Institution in Framingham is operated by the state; Oregon, Idaho, Virginia, and Connecticut are considering the idea or planning to open coed institutions.[197] "An all-male or an all-female prison is an abnormal environment, so how can you learn to deal with normal society?"[198]

The inmate population at coed prisons is purposely kept as small as possible, first-rate prison and prison-release programs are generally available to the minimum-security residents, and some accoutrements of "country club living" may be present: casual dress, tennis courts, a swimming pool, movies, quadraphonic stereo, a poolroom, cottages nestled in the redwoods. Men and women inmates work, learn, eat, and play—but do not sleep—together; conjugal visiting is strictly prohibited and may result in the violator's transfer to a traditional prison. (Handholding is allowed.) There is less tension and markedly less homosexuality reported at coed institutions. Even in the most optimistic forecast, however, the prisons of the future are likely to remain unisex.

Ultimately, the future of prisons—their size, administration, prisoners' rights, effective programs, parole, staff-inmate relations—depends on the resolution of the interrelated questions, Who belongs in prison? and What is the deterrent effect of incarceration on the crime rate? The opponents of prison contend that only dangerous offenders should be incarcerated.[199] (They now constitute an estimated 5 to 20 percent of the entire prison population.[200]) According to this view, the substantial savings realized by decarcerating (emptying) prisons of nondangerous offenders could be used for building small institutions, providing humane and professional custody, and for improving community-based corrections. On the other hand, there is growing sentiment that recidivist property offenders and white collar criminals deserve to be imprisoned, that a policy of not incarcerating nondangerous offenders would render fines, probation, and suspended sentences impotent, and that the *certainty* of incarceration is the only effective deterrent to crime (and is especially useful in curtailing economic crime).[201] The controversy over who belongs in prison implicitly guarantees the future of prison and confirms the adage that so long as there is crime there will be prisons. "We know that confining criminals prevents them from harming society, and we have grounds for suspecting that some would-be criminals can be deterred by this confinement of others. . . . Wicked people exist. Nothing avails except to set them apart from innocent people."[202]

Who belongs in prison?

Coed prisons provide a more normal environment for preparing minimum-security inmates to return to society

SUMMARY

The problems associated with prisons make up an extensive agenda for reform and change. At the top of the list is prison overcrowding, a situation likely to worsen despite efforts by administrators to alleviate it and court orders to reduce population levels to design capacity. Overcrowding was one of the several factors cited in *James* v. *Wallace* in 1976 that, taken together, made the overall conditions of incarceration in Alabama prisons so bad that imprisonment there constituted cruel and unusual punishment and prompted Judge Johnson to require sweeping improvements in the administration of the facilities. Efforts to professionalize the custodial staff include changes in the education, training, role, and composition of correctional personnel, notwithstanding the burdens attached to the positions. Recent innovations concerning in-house prison programs include the reform of state-use laws, treating working inmates more like employees, college-educated cons, and conjugal visits. Nowhere have there been more controversial changes than in the methods used for determining release from prison, in a three-way race between the parole guidelines table, parole contracts, and no-parole release. While the prisons of the future may be quite different in terms of design, location, their deemphasis on rehabilitation, and living conditions, the future of imprisonment itself seems assured.

DISCUSSION QUESTIONS

1. Is it fair that prisoners may be able to get a free college education and a degree, while many regular citizens and criminal justice practitioners cannot afford to go to college themselves or to send their children to college? Explain.
2. What precautions could be taken to assure that dangerous prisoners who are not rehabilitated are not released too early by the parole board?
3. Is college education as important for prison guards as it is for police officers? Explain.
4. Discuss the major factors taken into consideration by parole board members at the parole grant hearing. Which are the most important? Which are the least important?

Chapter 15

PRISONERS' RIGHTS

The Conditions of Incarceration

The hands-off doctrine / Judicial activism

Close-up 15.1: Section 1983 of the Civil Rights Act

The Attica Riot of 1971

Prison conditions before the riot / The start of the riot / The demand for amnesty

Seeking Prisoners' Rights Through the Courts

Access to Courts and Counsel

Jailhouse lawyers / *Johnson* v. *Avery* (1969) / Legal correspondence / *Procunier* v. *Martinez* (1974)

Religion

Cruz v. *Beto* (1972)

Prisoners' Labor Unions

Jones v. *North Carolina Prisoners' Labor Union* (1977)

Medical Services

Estelle v. *Gamble* (1976)

The Right to Rehabilitative Treatment

Rouse v. *Cameron* (1966)

The Right Not to Be Treated

Informed consent / Electroshock programs / The START program

Discipline

Solitary confinement / Disciplinary hearings / Parole revocation: *Morrisey* v. *Brewer* (1972) / Probation revocation: *Gagnon* v. *Scarpelli* (1973) / Discipline: *Wolff* v. *McDonnell* (1974) / Transfer: *Meachum* v. *Fano* (1976) / Extant liberty interest

Inmate Safety

Escape to avoid rape: *People* v. *Lovercamp* (1974)

Close-up 15.2: Necessity as a Defense for Crime

United States v. *Bailey* (1980) / Judicial remedies
Legal Rights of Jail Inmates
Court responses to jail conditions / Rights of pretrial detainees / *Bell* v. *Wolfish* (1979)
Seeking Prisoners' Rights by Nonjudicial Means
Formal Grievance Procedures
Maryland's Inmate Grievance Commission / Wisconsin's grievance procedures / California's Ward Grievance Procedure
The Ombudsman
The ombudsman's employer / The ombudsman in Minnesota / Independence of the ombudsman
Inmate Councils
Washington's inmate council program / Who's running the prisons?

Close-up 15.3: Inmate Self-Government at Walpole Prison

The future of prisoners' rights
Summary

THE CONDITIONS OF INCARCERATION

Until the mid 1960s the prevailing position, supported by the courts, was that prisoners had no rights to speak of with regard to their conditions of incarceration. Sleeping facilities, access to library material, religious observances, correspondence and visitation, discipline, medical services, health and safety—all the conditions of incarceration and every facet of prison life were left entirely to the unregulated discretion of the administrative, custodial, and treatment personnel of the individual institution. It was assumed that the mere fact of confinement placed prisoners beyond the protection of the Constitution, which stopped at the prison gate. Prisoners had no recourse when faced with official decisions and prison conditions, however arbitrary, oppressive, abusive, inhumane, intolerable, or unfair. This point of view was enunciated by a nineteenth-century Virginia court that insisted that a convict not only forfeits liberty but "all his personal rights except those which the law in its humanity accords to him. He is for the time being the slave of the state."[1] Therefore, any concession made to inmates was a privilege granted as a matter of "grace" rather than a right, and it could be withdrawn without explanation. The court's refusal to involve itself in correctional matters by reviewing prisoner complaints of abuses and alleged constitutional deprivations was known as the "hands-off" doctrine.

The hands-off doctrine

The hands-off doctrine could not long remain oblivious to the need for prison reform, the force of the prisoners' rights movement, and the shock waves of riotous inmates in pursuit of simple justice.* Gradually, hands-off gave way to judicial activism, a newfound readiness to remedy correctional deficiencies, to accord prisoners legal rights, to compel changes in the conditions of incarceration, and to place limits on the operating authority of corrections personnel.

The shift from hands-off to hands-on was brought about by several factions that had common goals. Increasingly militant and volatile inmates, many of whom saw themselves as "political" prisoners, stubbornly insisted on having their day in court.[3] Civil rights lawyers, having established the legal rights of the accused, were ready to turn their attention to the legal rights of the confined. Judges, "shocked" by what they saw and learned about prison conditions, could no longer turn their backs on prisoner complaints. The alleged rehabilitative value of prison, which might have justified an unabated hands-off policy, was found wanting, and degrading prison conditions were seen to be antithetical to successful adjustment upon release. It was acknowledged that while prisoners may lose many rights, their citizenship and their constitutional rights remained inviolable. An enormously important tactical boost to the prisoners' rights battle was Section 1983 of the Civil Rights Act of 1965, which permitted any citizen deprived of constitutional rights "under the color of state law" to file a grievance directly with the federal court without first having to exhaust state remedies under habeas corpus,† which could take years (see Close-up 15.1).[4]

Judicial activism

The retreat from the hands-off doctrine and its replacement with judicial activism was foreshadowed in 1944 by a federal court's declaration that "a prisoner retains all the rights of an ordinary citizen except those expressly, or by necessary implication, taken from him by law."[5] This principle has become the cutting edge of the prisoners' rights movement. The last 15 years has been a period of unprecedented involvement of the courts (especially the federal bench) in overseeing custodial institutions. The progress made in achieving prison reform is nothing short of a civil

* The prisoners' rights movement is not significantly concerned with statutory "civil disabilities" that often attach to felony convictions and remain in effect after inmates are released from prison. For example, the rights to vote, to marry, to hold public office, to serve as a juror, to work in certain occupations, to enter into contracts, to obtain insurance and pension benefits, and many other civil disenfranchisements of inmates and ex-offenders are not high on the list of rights sought by prisoners while they are still incarcerated.[2]

† Habeas corpus, which is used primarily to contest the *legality* of incarceration, is not a suitable device for registering complaints about the *conditions* of incarceration.

rights revolution behind bars that may rival, if not overshadow, the due process revolution staged for the benefit of the accused during the Warren era. The constitutional linchpins of the prisoners' rights movement are the First Amendment guarantees of free speech, expression, and religion; the omnibus due process clause of the Fourteenth Amendment; and the Eighth Amendment prohibition against cruel and unusual punishment, each of which has been applied to essentially different conditions of incarceration. Yet the shift toward hands-on represents a trend, not a

Close-up 15.1 SECTION 1983 OF THE CIVIL RIGHTS ACT

The main weapon used by prisoners to challenge their conditions of incarceration is Section 1983 of the Civil Rights Act of 1965. Section 1983 was originally adopted by Congress as part of the Civil Rights Act of 1871 in order to provide civil relief against any state official who "subjects, or causes to be subjected, any citizen to the deprivations of any rights, privileges or immunities secured by the Constitution and laws" of the federal government. Intended originally to protect the newly freed slaves, Section 1983 remained on the statute books but was virtually ignored until the civil rights movement of the 1950s and 1960s, when it was revived as a means of forcing states to comply with federal desegregation orders and preventing groundless prosecutions for sit-ins and other demonstrations.

In a landmark decision, *Monroe* v. *Pape* in 1961, the Supreme Court held that Section 1983 enables federal courts to redress any deprivation of basic constitutional rights by the states, even when racial discrimination is not an issue. An especially attractive feature of Section 1983 for prisoners is that it may be invoked without first exhausting state remedies: inmate claims may be presented directly to the federal courts for review. In this there is more than a saving in time, for prisoners are reluctant to take their complaints to state courts where elected state judges may be unwilling to overrule state prison administrators with whom they have to work. Federal courts, in contrast, are more removed from, independent of, and unswayed by local politics. The type of relief possible under Section 1983 is monetary damages against the offending parties or, typically, a court order instructing prison officials to correct the specified defective conditions of incarceration.

Source: "Prisoners' Rights Under Section 1983," *Criminal Law Bulletin,* June 1970, pp. 237–266.

uniform judicial turnabout.[6] The rights of the confined are *emerging* rights; the prevailing mood in the state courts is still one of hands-off.[7] Federal district and appellate courts, which have taken the lead in reforming prison conditions, are far from reaching a unanimous verdict on their contribution to corrections. With each decision, the Supreme Court strikes a new balance between prisoners' rights and the hands-off philosophy.[8]

Beyond the Constitution and the role of the courts in enforcing it, there is another, more conspicuous side to prison reform: prison riots, which are invariably related to oppressive conditions of incarceration. Some people have identified the Attica riot of 1971 as the event most responsible for placing prisoners' rights on the corrections map and launching the movement. While the event's impact on the law is necessarily speculative, the spectre of Attica and the prospect of future Atticas has undoubtedly made corrections administrators more receptive to suggestions for improving the conditions of incarceration through all means available. Indeed, the National Prison Project of the ACLU, an organization in the forefront of the movement to expand prisoners' rights through litigation, was a direct outgrowth of the Attica riot. And practitioners commonly speak of Before Attica and After Attica—a grim reminder that history could repeat itself if prisoners are denied their rights. Attica, like any serious prison disturbance, offers the most pragmatic reasons for preferring writs over riots.

The Attica Riot of 1971

The Attica Correctional Facility in upstate New York at the beginning of the 1970s was a microcosm of every prison.[9] The conditions of incarceration existing at the time of the riot bore savage testimony to what was wrong with all prisons. And the riot that occurred at Attica on September 9–13, 1971, was a stark symbol of the enduring struggle for prisoners' rights.

Created as a traditional maximum-security prison in the era of the silence rule, for decades Attica remained virtually untouched by even token reform measures. The inmates, 85 percent of whom were blacks and Puerto Ricans from urban areas, were doled out privileges grudgingly by an all-white custodial staff from rural communities who were comfortable with inmates who knew their place.[10] In an atmosphere of "festering racism," custodial brutality was commonplace. At the time of the riot, there were 2,250 inmates in a facility that should not have contained more than 1,600.[11] Because there were few meaningful rehabilitation or education programs, "idleness was the principal occupation" for most inmates. The fortunate few who worked in the metal shop received paltry wages of 6–29 cents a day.

son conditions before the riot

In the summer months that preceded the riot, inmates were kept in their cells 15 hours a day, left to stagnate in boredom and to swelter in 100-degree heat; repeated requests for more "yard time" went unheeded. Inmates were allowed to shower and were given clean underwear once a week, and they had to make do with one roll of toilet paper every five weeks. The food ranged from inadequate to unedible. At best, medical care was dispensed in a callous manner by doctors who feared and despised their clientele. And many of the prison rules and regulations that set the pace for the daily operation of the institution were senseless and dehumanizing.

Against a background of constant regimentation, hopelessness, and degradation, emerging changes in the profile of the institution were, collectively and unwittingly, hastening the countdown. An influx of younger and more militant minority inmates who were racially and socially conscious resulted in increased tension and in confrontations with the custodial staff, who resented the undermining of their authority. A federal court decision, *Sostre* v. *Rockefeller* in May 1970, held that prison authorities could not censor an inmate's mail to lawyers and public officials, and that existing disciplinary procedures deprived inmates of due process.* And in January 1971, Russell Oswald, the newly appointed commissioner of correctional services, vowed "to give the whole system a new flavor." The mood of the correction officers, who criticized the courts and the commissioner for "coddling criminals," was increasingly one of helplessness in the face of recalcitrant inmates, diluted authority, understaffing, and dangerously lax security. In retrospect, the slowly emerging prisoners' rights at Attica appear to have been linked to the riot inasmuch as they contributed to rising expectations for reform which, when unfulfilled, added fuel to an already explosive situation.

The start of the riot

The spark that ignited the riot was reminiscent of the events that preceded the large-scale civil disorders of the 1960s. On September 8, 1971, an officer saw Leroy Dewer in a scuffle with another inmate in A Yard, where 500 men were taking their recreation. Dewer ignored a direct order by the guard to "come along quietly" and struck the officer in full view of the large crowd that had gathered. By the end of that memorable day, Dewer and another inmate who had stuck up for him had been placed in solitary confinement (the hole), and there was widespread belief among the inmates that the two had been brutally beaten on the way there. The riot that began the next day was an almost predictable "spontaneous burst of violent anger" that grew out of the Dewer incident.

On the morning of September 9, it was decided that 5 Company, to which one of the confined inmates belonged, would be sent to their cellblock after breakfast without being allowed the usual yard time. While

* On appeal, some of the lower court's requirements concerning mail inspection were reversed. Nonetheless, prison officials allowed the more liberal revised rules to remain in effect.

the company was being escorted from the mess hall, some men attacked the officer on duty, and in no time the inmates in A Block were on the rampage and in control of almost the entire prison. By afternoon, however, the state police summoned to Attica had regained control of most of the prison with minimum force and no loss of lives.

The demand for amnesty

There remained 1,281 rebel inmates assembled in D Yard and the 39 hostages they had taken. Unless 29 of their demands were met, the rebellious leaders promised to slit the throats of the hostages.* During four

* The demands were basically requests for improved conditions of incarceration that even some of the hostages considered fair and long overdue.[12]

ate police ended the riot at At-
:a prison in September 1971, kill-
g 19 inmates and 10 officer hos-
ges

days of negotiations, September 9 to 12, the state acceded to all the demands except that for total amnesty from prosecution, which the rebels refused to drop. In another extraordinary move, prison officials had permitted a group of outside civilian observers to meet with the riot leaders in order to work out a peaceful settlement, but their efforts were to no avail. As part of a last-ditch effort to buy time and prevent a bloodbath, the observers asked Governor Nelson Rockefeller to make an immediate personal appearance at Attica. He declined. With the situation at an impasse, the governor authorized Commissioner Oswald to quash the rebellion by force if necessary.

On the morning of September 13, a force of 200 state police led an assault that abruptly ended the Attica riot. Within 15 minutes the state troopers killed 29 inmates and 10 of the officer hostages and wounded 80 in "the bloodiest one-day encounter between Americans since the Civil War."

SEEKING PRISONERS' RIGHTS THROUGH THE COURTS

Access to Courts and Counsel

The preferred rights protected by the First Amendment include religion, communication, and the opportunity "to petition the government for a redress of grievances," that is, access to the courts. Access to the courts is the most important right that prisoners have, for without it they would be unable to contest the legality or the conditions of their incarceration. All of the other prisoners' rights—adequate medical care, safety, protection against overcrowding, fair disciplinary procedures, freedom from cruel and unusual punishment, racial equality, religious preference—depend on the inmate's having access to the courts in order to litigate the specific issues involved. In practice, access to the courts encompasses both access to counsel and legal assistance and access to legal materials.

Jailhouse lawyers

Since inmates who are indigent cannot afford to hire outside counsel to prepare and present their grievances to the court, *jailhouse lawyers* have emerged to fill the need for legal advice and assistance. They are prisoners without formal legal qualifications who become self-taught in the law and specialize in writing writs and filing petitions for themselves and for other inmates. Writ writers were long considered a nuisance, a threat to security, and an embarrassment to the prison administration. Accordingly, prison regulations often prohibited or placed restrictions on such activities and provided punishment for offenders.

Johnson v. *Avery* (1969)

The situation changed when the Supreme Court put its stamp of approval on practicing law without a fee behind bars, in *Johnson* v. *Avery* in 1969.[13] Johnson was a jailhouse lawyer serving a life sentence in the Tennessee State Prison who spent 11 months in solitary confinement for repeatedly violating the institution's rule against writ writing.[14] The Supreme Court emphasized that the access of prisoners to the courts must not be obstructed and that "if such prisoners cannot have the assistance of a 'jailhouse lawyer,' their possibly valid constitutional claims will never be heard in any court." The Court therefore declared that all such prison regulations are invalid *unless* the "State provides some reasonable alternatives to assist inmates in the preparation of petitions for post-conviction relief."

The right of inmates to assist one another would be of little value if prison libraries lacked the necessary law books and legal periodicals that jailhouse lawyers need to research their cases and prepare their petitions. Accordingly, in *Younger* v. *Gilmore* in 1971, the Supreme Court affirmed a California court decision that required the state to maintain an adequate list and number of law books in prison libraries, as an essential means for facilitating access to the courts.[15, 16] According to the decision, states must maintain adequately stocked prison law libraries when no other reasonable alternatives for legal assistance are provided.

Legal correspondence

The most direct route to court access is through correspondence with the courts and with lawyers and attorney visitations. Mail to and from lawyers, judges, and public officials is accorded the greatest First Amendment protection because of the trustworthiness of these groups, their "particularized interest" in communicating with inmates, and the lower security risks involved. Therefore, prison authorities may not intercept, delay, withhold, censor, or inspect correspondence with these groups—unless there are exceptional circumstances that threaten institutional order. A recent Supreme Court decision, for example, authorized prison officials to open and read mail from lawyers because the need to detect contraband outweighed the prisoner's First Amendment right to unmonitored communication with counsel.[17] In general, however, the trend is clearly toward unrestricted communication with courts, attorneys, and public officials.[18]

Procunier v. *Martinez* (1974)

After years of conflicting lower court decisions, the right of prison officials to censor nonlegal, general correspondence was clarified by the Supreme Court in *Procunier* v. *Martinez* in 1974.[19] The case dealt with regulations of the California Department of Corrections, applicable to everyone except lawyers and public officials, that authorized the censorship of inmates' letters which are "lewd, obscene or defamatory, contain foreign matter, or are otherwise inappropriate," or express "inflammatory political, racial, religious, or other views or beliefs." In *Procunier* the Supreme Court ruled that prison mail censorship is constitutional only when two criteria are met: (1) the regulation or practice must further a "substantial governmental interest," such as security, order, or rehabili-

In 1969 the Supreme Court approved of jailhouse lawyers as a means of furthering access to the courts

Cruz v. *Beto* (1972)

tation, and (2) the restrictions imposed must not be greater than necessary to satisfy the particular government interest involved. When measured against these standards, the Court found that California's censorship regulations were unjustifiable, and it invalidated them. So long as prison officials can establish that security, discipline, and rehabilitation factors—the "substantial government interest" in support of operating procedures—outweigh the competing constitutional considerations, almost any infringement on communications rights will probably be tolerated by the courts.

Religion

The First Amendment provides that "Congress shall make no law respecting an establishment of religion, or prohibiting the free exercise thereof." Following access to the courts, religious freedom was the next preferred right of prisoners to confront successfully the hands-off doctrine. The religious battlelines were drawn in the early 1960s in a series of lawsuits involving Black Muslim prisoners who were denied rights comparable to those accorded members of other faiths. In a seminal case, *Fulwood* v. *Clemmer* in 1962, the U.S. District of Columbia Court recognized the Muslim faith as a religion, enjoined institutional officials from continuing to prevent its followers from holding services, and ordered that Fulwood be released from the disciplinary unit and returned to the general prison population.[20] Significantly, the court did not accept the correction commissioner's "clear and present danger" explanation for the restrictions: that the Muslims teach racial hatred, which is inflammatory and likely to create disorder. In the only religion case to reach the Supreme Court, *Cruz* v. *Beto* in 1972, the Court declared that it would be "palpable discrimination" for a Buddhist prisoner to be denied "a reasonable opportunity for pursuing his faith comparable to the opportunity afforded fellow prisoners who adhere to conventional religious precepts."*

Because of its "fundamental" status and acknowledged rehabilitation value, religious exercise may be curtailed only if prison officials can establish a compelling need for doing so or can demonstrate that a "clear and present danger" would otherwise exist. Under these demanding standards, Muslims and members of other recognized religions have won the right to have special dietary considerations, to wear denominational ap-

* Cruz, a Buddhist, was not allowed to use the prison chapel, and for sharing his religious material with other inmates he was placed in solitary confinement. Cruz also claimed that prison authorities violated the establishment clause of the First Amendment by rewarding conventional religious participation with favorable job assignments and early parole.[21]

parel, to receive religious publications, to attend services, and to talk to ministers. Even inmates in segregation may not be entirely and arbitrarily deprived of such access to religion as a Bible or periodic visits from a minister. On the other hand, religious restrictions are legally permissible whenever they are necessitated by considerations of security, order, or rehabilitation. Thus inmates in segregation with a record of disrupting order or attempted escape were not allowed to attend Mass with the general prison population. And Muslim demands to have their meals after sundown were legally denied because of the security risks inherent in transporting a large number of inmates to the mess hall at night.[22] Nonetheless, the contemporary mood of the courts is increasingly one bent on stamping out all forms of religious discrimination among the confined.*

Prisoners' Labor Unions

The First Amendment secures the right of "assembly" or "association"; that is, it permits citizens to take group action through organizations—such as unions—for virtually any peaceful reason whatsoever. Since 1970, various types of prisoners' unions have been organized behind bars as a means for improving secular conditions of incarceration, and prisoner labor unions have been in the vanguard of this diffuse movement.[24] The formation of labor unions to press demands for better wages and working conditions is one of the First Amendment rights most coveted by inmates. But it is opposed by administrators and guards, who view such organizations as a breeding ground for trouble, an obstacle to efficient institutional management, and an infringement of their authority. The precise constitutional status of such forums of collective expression was unsettled until the Supreme Court handed down its decision in *Jones* v. *North Carolina Prisoners' Labor Union* in June 1977, a bitter and unexpected setback to advocates of prisoners' rights.[25]

Jones v. *North Carolina Prisoners' Labor Union* (1977)

The North Carolina Prisoners' Labor Union was incorporated in 1974 to seek improved working conditions through collective bargaining. It quickly attracted 2,000 members in 40 prison facilities throughout the state. Dismayed at these developments, the Department of Corrections issued regulations prohibiting inmates from soliciting others to join, barred the union from holding meetings, and refused to deliver incoming bulk mailings intended for union promotional purposes. The Prisoners' Labor Union claimed that prison authorities violated their First Amend-

* The Supreme Court put an end to racial segregation of prisoners in *Lee* v. *Washington* in 1968, over the claims of correction administrators that integration would lead to racial conflict and the breakdown of discipline, that is, that it would create a "clear and present danger" to security.[23]

ment rights as well as their equal protection rights, since other organizations (Boy Scouts, Jaycees, Alcoholics Anonymous) had been granted concessions denied them.

In an opinion permeated with the hands-off philosophy, the Supreme Court rejected all of the union's claims. There was no equal protection violation in permitting such groups as the Jaycees and AA to operate within prisons because there was a "rational basis" for distinguishing the union from such service organizations. The latter served a rehabilitative purpose, were compatible with administrative goals, and "had been determined not to pose any threat to the order or security of the institution." However, "the case of a prisoners' union, where the focus is on the presentation of grievances to, and encouragement of adversary relations with, institution officials surely would rank high on anyone's list of trouble spots"—high enough to curtail the First Amendment's associational rights.* "The restrictions imposed are reasonable, and are consistent with the inmates' status as prisoners and with the legitimate operational considerations of the institution." Therefore, First Amendment rights "must give way to the reasonable considerations of penal management."

Medical Services

In principle, prisoners as individuals and as a group have a right to "adequate" medical care.† The state is obligated to provide prisoners with a level of medical treatment comparable to that which is available to the general public outside the institutions.[26] Whenever feasible, however, the courts have followed the hands-off doctrine in assessing claims of negligent or inadequate treatment, especially in the case of individual inmates. At the same time, the courts have been much more willing to intervene when the entire delivery system of medical services (that is, for prisoners as a group) was flagrantly substandard or grossly violated the basic tenets of adequate health care. This included conditions of severe understaffing, of unsanitary medical facilities, and where "some inmates with serious contagious diseases are allowed to mingle with the general prison population."[27]

Most of the prisoners' rights cases in this area allege that denied or improper medical treatment constitutes cruel and unusual punishment or is a violation of the Fourteenth Amendment's due process and equal protection clauses. In order for inmates to get a medical hearing in court and

* Prison officials were apprehensive that a labor union would create friction between member and nonmember inmates, give union leaders an upper hand, and lead to work stoppages, riots, and constant security problems.

† The right is protected by Section 1983 of the Civil Rights Act of 1965, by the common law, and by state statutes.

obtain relief under Section 1983, they must be able to prove that the refusal or failure to provide treatment, or the inadequate treatment received, was "shocking, barbaric, willful," or involved deliberate indifference to a request for essential medical attention. Mere dissatisfaction with the quality of individual medical treatment is not considered cause for action under Section 1983. "Differences of opinion over matters of medical judgment" are considered mere negligence claims and are invariably dismissed because they do not raise constitutional issues and should be handled through normal state channels governing malpractice suits. In keeping with judicial deference to the prison physician's expertise, courts are beginning to forbid custodial and administrative staff from interfering with the inmate's access to medical attention and to require them to provide the care and treatment prescribed by medical personnel.

Estelle v. *Gamble* (1976)

The basic position that had been developing among the lower federal courts toward inmate medical grievances was adopted by the Supreme Court in *Estelle* v. *Gamble* in 1976.[28] Gamble, a Texas prisoner, brought a class action suit against two prison physicians and two correction officials for inadequate treatment of a back injury he incurred while unloading a truck. Gamble claimed that he was subjected to cruel and unusual punishment because he disagreed with the treatment prescribed, x-rays were not taken, and prison guards failed to comply with the prescribed treatment and impeded his access to medical attention. Noting that medical personnel had seen the inmate 17 times in three months and treated his injury continuously, the Supreme Court refused to consider the "adequacy" of treatment on its own merits, relegating such technical matters to malpractice claim status, to be pursued elsewhere. But the Court did identify a level of medical nonresponsiveness against which prisoners have a right to be protected. "We therefore conclude that *deliberate indifference* to serious medical needs of prisoners constitutes the 'unnecessary and wanton infliction of pain' proscribed by the Eighth Amendment. This is true whether the indifference is manifested by prison doctors in their response to the prisoner's needs or by prison guards in intentionally denying or delaying access to medical care or intentionally interfering with the treatment once prescribed." The Court remanded the case to the federal appeals court for a determination of whether the complaints against the guards amounted to "deliberate indifference," thereby violating the Eighth Amendment and making the claim actionable under Section 1983.

The Right to Rehabilitative Treatment

The proposal for recognizing a right to rehabilitative treatment for prisoners (hereafter the right to treatment) is based on the belief that prisons and society have an obligation to provide inmates with more than warehousing or humane custody.[29] According to this theory, prisoners have a right to be helped with their problems, to be afforded opportunities for responsibility and personal growth, and to be prepared for successful release through a variety of prison programs collectively designated as "treatment": vocational training, counseling, education, therapy, prerelease experiences, and so on.

Arguments for a prisoners' right to treatment are rooted in the medical model, the indeterminate sentence, the rehabilitative ideal, and legal developments in this area among other institutionalized groups. Morton Birnbaum coined the term *right to treatment* in a 1960 article in which he emphasized the need to treat a mentally ill person committed to a public institution "so he may regain his health, and therefore his liberty as soon as possible."[30] The right to treatment first received strong judicial recognition by federal court Judge David Bazelon in *Rouse* v. *Cameron* in 1966. Although *Rouse* was decided on statutory grounds, Bazelon's discussion of the related constitutional issues laid the foundation for later decisions that linked the right to treatment to due process, equal protection, and the cruel and unusual punishment concept. After the mentally ill, the second major group covered by the right to treatment are juvenile delinquents committed to training schools—on the theory (and on statutory grounds) that the sole purpose of their confinement is therapeutic.[31] The third group entitled to treatment are adult criminal defendants committed under special statutes designed with rehabilitation in mind; these include defective delinquents,* sexually dangerous persons, and federal defendants sentenced under the Narcotic Addiction and Rehabilitation Act (NARA).

Rouse v. *Cameron* (1966)

In the case of involuntarily committed mental patients, institutionalized delinquents, and designated categories of adult offenders, treatment is by statute the express and exclusive reason for deprivation of liberty—and institutionalization is the *modus operandi* for effectuating treatment. There are no contradictory objectives competing with treatment, and each group sacrifices some procedural safeguards in exchange for the promise of treatment. In contrast, prisoners have given up no procedural safeguard as a *quid pro quo* for treatment. The penal purposes of incarceration include a large dose of punishment. The medical model and rehabilitation motif of prisons, without which the right to treatment cannot survive, are on the wane. And the problems of defining and providing "adequate treatment" are formidable.[32] Even where the need for treatment is most obvious (as in mental illness), the Supreme Court refused to establish a constitutional right to treatment when it had the opportunity in *O'Connor* v. *Donaldson* in 1975.[33] For all these reasons, the sociological theory of a prisoner's right to treatment will probably not ripen into a constitutional guarantee in the foreseeable future.

* The term *delinquent* in this context does not refer to juveniles.

The Right Not To Be Treated

The reverse side of the right to treatment coin is the right not to be "treated," which concerns two kinds of highly controversial prison programs: (1) the use of prisoners as guinea pigs in medical experimentation, drug testing, and consumer product development, which have nothing to do with crime control, and (2) behavioral modification techniques imposed on inmates that, although ostensibly for rehabilitation and crime control purposes, are morally and legally objectionable. Physical abuses, purported economic exploitation, and other problems associated with using inmates as research subjects have lately received impassioned critical attention.[34] The main indictment of experimentation on prisoners hinges on the doctrine of *informed consent,* the legal requirement that the decision to participate in research experiments must be a voluntary one.[35] Opponents of such programs assert that prisoners are incapable of providing genuinely voluntary consent because of the pressures inherent in the prison environment. Their position is that the prison setting makes any such decision to volunteer involuntary, regardless of the precautions taken. States such as Pennsylvania, Massachusetts, and Illinois have banned the use of inmates as subjects, with the candid admission that "no man is a free agent in prison."[36] Based upon similar concerns, the Food and Drug Administration put a stop to "nontherapeutic" medical experimentation on prison inmates, effective June 1980. This regulation makes obsolete using prisoners (healthy subjects) to determine whether or not new drugs induce harmful side effects. It does not affect, however, giving already tested experimental drugs to inmates suffering from the ailment the drug is intended to treat.[37]

Informed consent

As the failure of standard "soft" rehabilitation programs became apparent in the 1960s, stronger treatment measures seemed to be called for in order to change certain inmates into law-abiding citizens and to make uncooperative inmates more receptive to therapy and to their roles as prisoners. Behavior modification programs and techniques held out the promises of reforming sex offenders through electroshock or psychosurgery and "helping" undisciplined prisoners learn the virtue of conformity through exposure to programs that involved rigorous sensory deprivation. One electroshock program for habitual child molesters was begun in 1973 at Connecticut's maximum-security prison at Sommers.[38] The programmer displays intermixed slides of children and adults, giving the inmate a mild shock whenever a picture of a naked child appears. The repetition of this "voluntary" treatment over a period of months is expected to repress completely the subject's ability to think of children as sex objects. Despite the program's apparent success, the ACLU filed a class action suit to ban it on the grounds that the expectation of favorable parole board action coerced inmates to participate, thereby invalidating the voluntary consent requirement.

Electroshock programs

The START program

The other major type of behavior modification program to come under fire in the early 1970s was the Special Treatment and Rehabilitative Training project (START) at the Federal Prison Medical Center in Springfield, Missouri. A group of "offenders who had demonstrated an inability to conform to institutional standards" (prisoners identified as troublemakers by the guards) were involuntarily transferred to the Springfield facility "to promote [their] behavioral and attitudinal change" through participation in START.[39] The intractable prisoners were placed in an "adjustment center" (solitary confinement), where they could earn points (awarded by the staff) for good behavior. The points were the basis for promotion to better living conditions, could be used to purchase goods and privileges, and functioned as incentives for rehabilitating the inmates to the degree that they could be safely returned to their home institutions. A suit filed by the ACLU, a congressional investigation into the subject, official denunciation of the inhumanity of such programs, and the spectre of thought control all combined to put a stop to START in 1974.[40,41]

The essential problems with electroshock, psychosurgery, START, and other behavior modification programs are their enormous potential for abuse, their tendency to legitimize too much in the name of therapy, the ease with which punishment can be disguised as treatment, and the questionable ethics of producing better-adjusted prisoners.[42] Because of the irresistible appeal of anything bearing the treatment label in prison, however, the courts have moved cautiously in prescribing a right not to be treated, leaving the matter largely to the courthouse of public opinion for the time being.

Discipline

The conditions of incarceration include prison rules and regulations whose violation may result in various types of disciplinary measures. Minor misconduct such as an inmate's kissing his wife during a no-contact visit may bring a simple reprimand or temporary withdrawal of visitation rights. Inmates who constantly report late to prison industry jobs may have their pay docked, may be fined, or may lose their jobs. Those who are persistently defiant, whose consensual homosexuality causes trouble, or who refuse to shave or to cut their hair may have their infractions brought to the attention of the parole board by means of an "incident report" placed in their prison file. They may also face a loss of their privileges to use the commissary, to look at television, to receive packages, or to make phone calls, and they may be padlocked.*

* *Padlocked* or *lockeeped.* Confinement of inmates to their cells for a larger proportion of each day than is usual.

Serious violations of prison rules—assaulting a guard or an inmate, participating in a riot, attempting escape, being incessantly disruptive, making forcible homosexual advances—may result in the most drastic form of discipline, solitary confinement (punitive segregation).[43] Solitary confinement is total separation from the general prison population in an isolation cell. It is often accompanied by the revocation of all privileges, the curtailment of one's constitutional rights, meager physical surroundings, and perhaps a restricted diet.

Solitary confinement

Like the death sentence, solitary confinement per se does not (yet) constitute cruel and unusual punishment under the Eighth Amendment. Depending on how it is administered in practice, instances of punitive segregation may amount to cruel and unusual punishment if the courts find them (a) shocking to the conscience, barbaric, or offensive to evolving standards of decency,* or (b) grossly disproportionate to the prison infractions for which they were imposed.[45] In reaching these issues, the courts have examined the duration of confinement, the special characteristics of confined inmates, and the extent of deprivations, particularly the conditions relating to medical attention, sanitation, hygiene, heat, physical abuse, and inmate health and safety. In a landmark case, *Jordan* v. *Fitzharris* in 1966, the federal district court ruled that the inmate's confinement in a "strip" cell at the California Correctional Training Facility at Soledad was cruel and unusual punishment.[46]

Regardless of its potential for cruel and unusual punishment in any individual case, the decision to impose solitary confinement—or any other severe sanction for violating prison regulations, such as the loss of good-time credit—is ordinarily made at a *disciplinary hearing*. For several years the federal courts took different positions on what specific procedural due process rights prisoners had at the disciplinary hearing. Some courts required that extensive procedural protections accompany the disciplinary committee hearings; others were satisfied with much less formality.[47] Before the Supreme Court settled the issue of prisoners' due process rights at disciplinary hearings in 1974, it issued two significant opinions on which some courts had relied in their rulings on disciplinary hearings, and which placed the Fourteenth Amendment rights of the convicted in perspective.

Disciplinary hearings

In *Morrisey* v. *Brewer* in 1972, the Court ruled that before parolees could have their parole revoked and be reincarcerated, they were entitled to a parole revocation hearing that incorporated certain due process procedures (see Table 15.1).[48] The Court deemed that these procedural safeguards were necessary at the parole revocation stage in the criminal justice system, in view of the "grievous loss" and substantial change in

Parole revocation: *Morrisey* v. *Brewer* (1972)

* The test established in *Trop* v. *Dulles* in 1958.[44] Virtually all of the cruel and unusual punishment litigation in solitary confinement cases has revolved around this "shock" test.

status attached to parole revocation—the loss of conditional liberty and the demotion from parolee to prisoner.

Probation revocation: ***Gagnon* v. *Scarpelli* (1973)**

In *Gagnon* v. *Scarpelli* in 1973, the Court held that probationers facing revocation were entitled to the same due process requirements at a probation revocation hearing as had been granted in *Morrisey*.[49] The "grievous loss" stemming from probation revocation is the same as in parole revocation: conditional liberty and a radical change in status from probationer to prisoner. Furthermore, *Gagnon* specified that indigent probationers and parolees had a limited right to appointed counsel at their revocation hearings (a right that was to be determined on a case-by-case basis) and that the grounds for refusing to grant a request for counsel should be stated in the record.

Table 15.1 Due Process Rights of Inmates at Various Hearing Stages, as Determined by the Supreme Court, 1972–1979

Parole Revocation Hearing (*Morrisey* v. *Brewer,* 1972)	Probation Revocation Hearing (*Gagnon* v. *Scarpelli,* 1973)	Prison Disciplinary Hearing Where Punishment is Loss of Goodtime Credit or Solitary Confinement (*Wolff* v. *McDonnell,* 1974)	Classification (Disciplinary) Hearing Where Inmate is Subject to Involuntary Transfer to a Less Desirable Institution (*Meachum* v. *Fano,* 1976)	Parole Grant Hearing (*Greenholtz* v. *Inmates of Nebraska Penal Complex,* 1979)
written notice of alleged violation of conditions of parole	written notice of alleged violations of conditions of probation	written notice of charge at least 24 hours before hearing	no rights under the due process clause; transfers do not jeopardize any vested "liberty interest" and are entirely within the discretionary realm of prison officials	Due Process Clause of Fourteenth Amendment does not cover inmates at the parole grant hearing stage. Specifically, inmates being considered for parole have no right to counsel, to present documentary evidence in their behalf, or to a statement of the "particular evidence" parole board relied on in denying parole.
hearing before a neutral and detached body, such as a parole board, whose members need not include lawyers	hearing before a neutral and detached body	hearing before an impartial tribunal or fact-finder		
no right to counsel	limited right for indigent probationers and parolees to appointed counsel, to be determined on a case-by-case basis; grounds for refusing to grant request for counsel to be stated in the record	no right to counsel; but in unusually complex cases and those involving illiterate inmates, the accused should be allowed to seek aid from a fellow inmate or be given assistance from the staff		
opportunity to be heard in person	opportunity to be heard in person	opportunity to be heard in person and to present defense		

Discipline: *Wolff* v. *McDonnell* (1974)

It was against this background of expanded due process rights for the convicted that the Supreme Court temporarily resolved the question of the Fourteenth Amendment rights of prisoners who faced the serious disciplinary measures of solitary confinement or the loss of goodtime credit, in *Wolff* v. *McDonnell* in 1974.[50] In a Section 1983 class action suit, inmates at the Nebraska Penal and Correctional Complex at Lincoln alleged that the institution's disciplinary proceedings violated their Fourteenth Amendment rights.* Prison regulations specified that major

* They were not given counsel, adequate notice of the charge, an opportunity to cross-examine their accusers and adverse witnesses, or a written statement of the evidence relied on and the reasons for the action taken.[51]

able 15.1 *(Continued)*

arole Revocation earing (*Morrisey* v. *rewer*, 1972)	Probation Revocation Hearing (*Gagnon* v. *Scarpelli*, 1973)	Prison Disciplinary Hearing Where Punishment is Loss of Goodtime Credit or Solitary Confinement (*Wolff* v. *McDonnell*, 1974)
mited "right" to con- ont and cross- kamine witnesses, nless hearing officer ds good cause for ot allowing cross- kamination; in effect, right to confronta- on and cross- amination	limited "right" to confront and cross-examine witnesses, unless hearing officer finds good cause for not allowing cross-examination; in effect, no right to confrontation and cross-examination	no right to confront and cross-examine witnesses
pportunity to present tnesses and docu- entary evidence	opportunity to present witnesses and documentary evidence	recommendation (no right) that inmate be allowed to call witnesses and to present documentary evidence when doing so would not be unduly hazardous to institutional safety or correctional goals, according to the discretion of the disciplinary committee
sclosure to parolee evidence used ainst him/her	disclosure to probationer of evidence used against him/her	
itten statement of idence relied on d reasons for voking parole	written statement of evidence relied on and reasons for revoking probation	written statement by fact-finder regarding evidence and reasons for disciplinary action; the statement need not be a full transcript of the hearing, and it may exclude evidence where necessary to maintain personal safety or institutional security

In 1974 the Supreme Court specified due process rights for disciplinary hearings that might result in solitary confinement and loss of goodtime credit

misconduct be reported formally to the Adjustment (Disciplinary) Committee, whose sanctions included solitary confinement and the forfeiture of goodtime credit.* The rudimentary due process rights spelled out by the Court in *Wolff* (see Table 15.1) represented a compromise between the full panoply of adversary resources sought by inmates and civil rights advocates and the Court's continued deference to the hands-off doctrine in a highly sensitive area. "The procedures we have now required in prison disciplinary proceedings represent a reasonable accommodation between the interests of the inmates and the needs of the institution."

In essence, the rationale of *Wolff* was that the "grievous loss" at stake in serious disciplinary cases (goodtime credit cancellation or solitary confinement) is less severe than the deprivations that accompany revocation of parole and probation and does not result in an immediate qualitative change in status. Hence disciplinary hearings do not require the same measure of due process as probation and parole revocation. At the same time, the Court left the door open for future Fourteenth Amendment maneuvers at disciplinary hearings by noting candidly that its decision not to require all of the *Morrisey* and *Gagnon* safeguards "is not graven in stone." Although the *Wolff* decision established minimum (rudimentary) due process for prisoners facing goodtime loss or solitary confinement,

* The status of inmates' rights with respect to minor misconduct and lesser penalties than goodtime credit revocation or solitary confinement were not dealt with in *Wolff*.

the ruling was a bitter disappointment to prisoners' rights advocates who hoped the Supreme Court would acknowledge an absolute right to counsel, to cross-examination, and to call witnesses, as some other court decisions had.[52,53]

The *Wolff* decision in 1974 was framed in terms of due process procedures applicable to the loss of goodtime credit. But in a footnote the Court left little doubt that the ruling also covered proceedings that govern the imposition of solitary confinement. Both types of serious sanctions fell into the category of grievous loss of liberty. Left completely unresolved in *Wolff,* however, were the constitutional procedures to be observed if lesser penalties were imposed, such as loss of privileges or transfer to a more secure institution.

ransfer: *Meachum* v. *Fano* (1976)

The Supreme Court settled these issues in a disciplinary transfer case, *Meachum* v. *Fano,* in June 1976.[54] Fano was one of several prisoners in the Massachusetts Correctional Institution at Norfolk charged with setting fires at the medium-security facility. The charges were substantiated in a classification (disciplinary) hearing that fell short of the due process procedures laid down in *Wolff,* and Fano was transferred to Walpole, a maximum-security prison. By definition, the conditions of incarceration at a more secure facility are harsher and usually result in a relative loss of privileges. In a strongly worded endorsement of the hands-off doctrine, the Court observed that the Constitution does not "guarantee that the convicted prisoner will be placed in any particular prison" and rejected "at the outset the notion that any grievous loss visited upon a person by the State is sufficient to invoke the procedural protections of the Due Process Clause." The essential holding in *Meachum* was that the Fourteenth Amendment comes into play behind bars only when a prisoner's *existing liberty interest* is threatened by official action. In *Wolff* there was an extant liberty interest involving goodtime credit derived from state statute.* But in *Meachum* Massachusetts law did not confer on its prisoners a right not to be transferred to a less desirable institution. This being the case, the punishment of transfers does not involve a vested liberty interest, which is necessary for invoking the cloak of the due process clause.

Extant liberty interest

The principle of extant liberty interest is that once an offender has been given something with a significant liberty value—probation, parole, accrued goodtime credit, placement in the general prison population—the state cannot summarily take away that vested liberty interest without the benefit of due process. In *Meachum,* however, there was no evidence that

* Presumably, penal codes that provide for sentencing convicted defendants to prison imply a liberty interest with respect to the inmate's remaining in the general prison population. Hence the disciplinary prospect of solitary confinement would jeopardize this liberty status and require *Wolff's* procedural safeguards. Convicted defendants are, after all, sentenced to prison, not to punitive segregation.

the state had ever officially recognized an inmate's right to remain in a particular institution or that the transfer decision was anything but a discretionary matter. Thus the Court declared that a transfer to a more secure prison does not infringe any liberty interest; the mere fact of lawful conviction "has sufficiently extinguished the defendant's liberty interest to empower the State to confine him in any of its prisons." The *Meachum* ruling was an unexpected setback to those who advocated the extension of due process to involuntary transfers and a wide range of other institutional practices.[55] The question of whether being considered for parole involves a liberty interest was answered by the Supreme Court in *Greenholtz* v. *Inmates of the Nebraska Penal and Correctional Complex* in 1979. Emphasizing the similarity of the determination of parole and the transfer decision, the Court in effect ruled that the due-process clause of the Fourteenth Amendment does not cover inmates at the parole grant hearing stage.

Inmate Safety

Inmates have the right to be kept in a safe environment, a right that is jeopardized by overcrowding, abusive custodial treatment, and assaults by other inmates. However, the judiciary is extremely reluctant to interfere with the custodial staff's treatment of inmates. It was not until 1968 that corporal punishment (whipping) as a disciplinary measure was effectively abolished by a federal appellate court decision dealing with the use of the strap in Arkansas penitentiaries.[56] Like the police, guards are authorized to use as much reasonable force as necessary and as may be warranted by the totality of the circumstances. In order to subdue an uncontrollably violent inmate, to place a prisoner in solitary confinement, or to respond to a riot, guards may be justified in using gas, mace, drugs, clubs, or other weapons, and even dogs. These actions are permissible if they are a reasonable response to the gravity of the problem, when there is a need to take immediate action and there are no less drastic alternatives available. The requirement of *reasonable* force is intended to prevent "the use of a cannon to stop a fly" and to restrain criminal justice workers from taking the law into their own hands in acts of racism or retaliation.

A prevalent and complex problem is the continual danger that prisoners face of being forcibly raped by other inmates. Homosexual rape, committed by an individual or a group, is commonplace in most prisons. The options available to inmate rape victims are wholly inadequate and often lead to heightened personal physical insecurity. For some, the only way out of their predicament is to escape from prison.

Escape to avoid rape: *People* v. *Lovercamp* (1974)

In *People* v. *Lovercamp* in 1974, the acknowledgement by a California court of appeals of a "right to escape" under certain circumstances involving rape was a remarkable departure from precedent, and it opened a ercrowded prison dormitories e a breeding ground for sexual saults

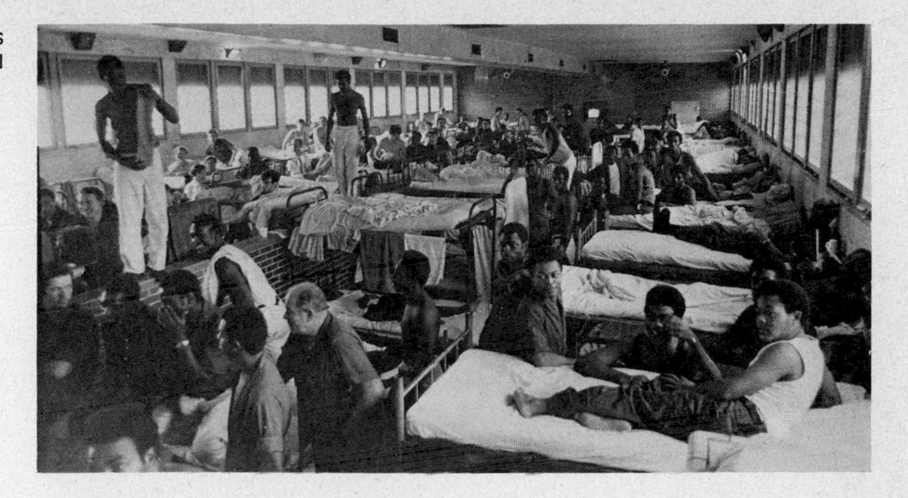

new door in the battle for prisoners' rights.[57] During the first months of their confinement, two women at a California rehabilitation center were continually threatened by a group of prisoners who demanded that the pair submit to their homosexual advances. The two inmates complained to the prison authorities on several occasions, to no avail. On the day of their escape, they were again threatened by a gang of 10 to 15 women, a fight broke out, and the lesbians promised to return later to beat the resisters into submission. Fearful of their own safety and seeing no alternative, the women escaped later that day but were caught immediately. Their conviction on the escape charge was reversed by the appeals court, which recognized "necessity" (see Close-up 15.2) as a valid defense to the crime of escape provided that five specific criteria were met.* In doing so, the appeals court in effect created a limited "right to escape" from prison for inmates who are the victims of rape and expanded the scope of prisoners' rights to the outermost boundaries.

United States v. *Bailey* (1980)

The Supreme Court had occasion to comment on those boundaries in *United States* v. *Bailey* in 1980.[58] Four men had escaped from the District of Columbia jail allegedly to avoid the coercive and intolerable conditions of confinement to which they were exposed: frequent fires that were

* The five conditions are: (1) the prisoner is faced with a specific threat of death, forcible sexual attack, or substantial bodily injury in the immediate future; (2) there is no time to make a complaint to the authorities or there exists a history of futile complaints that would make the expectation of any result from such complaints illusory; (3) there is no time or opportunity to resort to the courts; (4) there is no evidence of force or violence used toward prison personnel or other "innocent" persons in the escape; and (5) the prisoner immediately reports to the proper authorities upon attaining a position of safety from the immediate threat.

Close-up 15.2 NECESSITY AS A DEFENSE FOR CRIME[a]

The defense of *necessity* involves proving that the only reason the defendant committed the crime was because it was "necessitated" (compelled)—and therefore justified—by the exceptional circumstances with which the accused was confronted at the time. If violating the law is an inevitable, reasonable, and preferable response in a given situation, then there is no *mens rea* and the individual should be exempted from the consequences of criminal responsibility. Traditionally, the source of the danger which allegedly requires the commission of crime is found in natural disasters, catastrophes, and social threats of one sort or another, events over which the defendant has no control.[b]

The classic necessity case was *Regina* v. *Dudley* in 1844, in which three men and a 17-year-old cabin boy were shipwrecked and set adrift in a small boat. They were 1,600 miles from land, without food or water for 20 days, and on the verge of starving to death. The men killed the boy so that they could remain alive by eating his flesh and drinking his blood. In a similar case two years earlier, *United States* v. *Holmes,* members of a shipwrecked crew threw 14 passengers overboard in order to lighten the sinking life boat. And in *State* v. *Wooten,* a sheriff illegally deported 1,200 riotous strikers and their sympathizers from Arizona to New Mexico, to prevent widespread destruction of life and property that would have occurred otherwise.

The necessity defense in such cases is based upon the premise that under certain circumstances crime commission is the "lesser of two evils." The greater evil consists of the injury that would almost certainly be inflicted on innocent victims, if the defendant had not taken the law into his own hands. In essence, a valid necessity defense makes legal whatever action is considered reasonable under the circumstances. As was recognized by the National Commission on Reform of Federal Criminal Laws, "it makes no sense to punish persons who have acted to avoid great harm, even if they have broken a law to do so." The core problem in applying the doctrine of necessity, however, is that of resolving the choice-of-values question: when should avoiding a greater evil by committing a crime take precedence over obeying the law, and what constitutes "greater harm"? These threshold issues, on which the necessity defense depends, are all the more complex when the crime committed ("lesser evil") is escaping from jail or prison. This is because the defendant is a convicted and incarcerated criminal, the circumstances purportedly justifying escape do not fit the conventional mold of necessity, and identifying the greater evil in that context is an especially controversial and formidable task.

[a] *Source:* Edward B. Arnolds and Norman F. Garland, "The Defense of Necessity in Criminal Law: The Right to Choose the Lesser Evil," *Journal of Criminal Law and Criminology,* September 1974, pp. 289–301.
[b] Common law distinguished between the defenses of necessity and duress. In duress the peril responsible for crime commission is more direct, immediate, personal, and predictable than in necessity, as when A at gunpoint forces B to participate in a robbery.

not extinguished, inadequate medical care, beatings, and death threats from guards and the like. After this evidence was introduced at their trial on escape charges, the defendants requested the District Court to instruct the jury on the defense of duress (or "necessity") so that they could consider whether the deplorable jail conditions justified or mitigated the crime. In *Bailey,* however, the Supreme Court ruled that the defendants were not entitled to claim duress and be exonerated on those grounds because after escaping they had not made any effort to surrender to authorities. In essence, the Court concluded that their failure to turn themselves in or to satisfactorily explain their continued flight from custody discredited any affirmative defense to escape. At the same time, *Bailey* makes it clear that if escapees surrender immediately or make a genuine effort to do so, juries may receive instruction on the duress defense and indeed decide that such inmates had a "right" to escape under the circumstances.

Judicial remedies

As to the liability of prison administrators and custodial staff in deprivations of inmate safety, the reasonable person and the totality of the circumstances are the determinants. The courts will rarely award aggrieved prisoners monetary damages levied against their keepers unless prison authorities (a) willfully, maliciously, or deliberately contributed to the situation of inadequate inmate safety or (b) were grossly negligent in performing required duties that would have protected the inmate from injury.[59] Ordinarily, in lieu of monetary damages, the courts are inclined to issue group injunctive relief orders that are aimed at eliminating those ongoing practices that jeopardize inmate safety. In extreme situations, where no alternatives are available, the courts may order the release of prisoners to reduce overcrowding or to prevent the repeated rape of an inmate whom correctional officials admit they are powerless to protect; may be more inclined to accept "justification" as a defense for assaulting guards and escaping from prison; or may declare that imprisonment itself is cruel and unusual punishment.[60]

Legal Rights of Jail Inmates

The emerging prisoners' rights of those incarcerated in jails is taking a course remarkably similar to that in the prisons. Yet the conditions of incarceration in jail are worse than those in prison, and the deprivations to which all jail inmates are exposed are less justifiable for pretrial detainees by virtue of their legal status (they are presumed innocent), the inequities in the bail system, and the lack of speedy trial, which are responsible for their confinement. The achievement of legal rights for jail inmates has been hampered in part by the brevity of their stays: by the time lawsuits have been filed and relief granted, many inmates have already been released, sentenced to time served, or sent to prison. Class action suits, however, are proving an effective means for overcoming the impediments to correcting jail conditions through litigation. Short-term detention facilities are an integral part of the due process revolution in corrections, and special attention is being given to the legal rights of pretrial detainees.

Court responses to jail conditions

State and federal courts throughout the country have found that overcrowding in jails constitutes cruel and unusual punishment, and they have ordered the reduction of populations to design-capacity levels, the release of inmates, and the closing of jails.[61,62,63] By 1978, the conditions in more than 100 city and county jails had been found unconstitutional by federal courts.[64] In St. Louis, a federal judge imposed a limit of 228 inmates on the city's jail, ordered an expansion of recreational facilities, and required that two corrections officers be present on each jail floor 24 hours a day to assure inmate safety.[65] Finding that "severe and inhumane overcrowding" existed in the Harris County jail system in Houston, Texas, a federal district court in December 1975 ordered sweeping, specific relief similar to that given to Alabama prisons by Judge Johnson.[66] Some combination of overcrowding, unsanitary cells and physical facilities, grossly inadequate medical services, sexual assaults, and insufficient protection is usually enough to bring jails within the scope of the Eighth Amendment and to cause the courts to act accordingly. And just as with prison reform, the courts are becoming less willing to accept inadequate funding as a reason for tolerating the status quo in jails.[67]

Rights of pretrial detainees

The strongest case for the legal rights of jail inmates has been made on behalf of pretrial detainees. Ironically and tragically, their shield of innocence is a barrier to their participating in rehabilitation, education, vocational, and prerelease programs, which are restricted to the convicted population pursuant to the objectives of sentencing. Until recently, however, the presumption of innocence has not shielded them from being treated the same as (if not worse than) convicted criminals. Judicial recognition of the unique claims of pretrial detainees to legal rights began in 1971, under the auspices of the Eighth and Fourteenth amendments.[68] After the "evolving standards" test (the most common one), the excessiveness test and the "least restrictive means" criteria are especially applicable to pretrial detainees. It may be easier, for example, to conclude that conditions of incarceration that are acceptable for convicted jail inmates are "excessive" and therefore cruel and unusual punishment when applied to innocent defendants awaiting trial. In *Hamilton* v. *Love* in 1971, an Arkansas district court maintained that because detainees are not convicts or prisoners, they should not be subjected to any punishment.[69] Their conditions of incarceration, the court held, must meet the "least restrictive means" test: the only permissible deprivations are those that are essential to guarantee the detainee's presence at trial. Any deprivation or hardship imposed on detainees, beyond those necessary to insure their presence at trial, may be construed as *de facto* punishment applied without due process of law and a denial of equal protection (equal to that afforded persons who are free on bail while awaiting trial). The result of this heightened sensitivity to the legal rights of detainees has been a number of favorable court decisions providing generous relief, in which convicted inmates often reap substantial benefits. Thus *Rhem* v. *Malcolm* in 1974, a case brought by pretrial detainees, ultimately led to the closing of the Tombs in New York City.[70]

Designed primarily to hold detainees, and hailed as a model jail facility when it opened in August 1975, the federal Metropolitan Correctional Center in New York City was ripe for reform just 17 months later, when a federal judge issued an order affecting "intolerable crowding," mail, meals, searches, clothing, and length of incarceration.[71] In Jacksonville, Florida, Judge Charles Scott found that detainees in the Duval County jail were exposed to worse conditions than most convicts, thereby depriving them of due process and equal protection of the law and subjecting them to cruel and unusual punishment. Scott mandated comprehensive, detailed improvements that included reducing the population from 600 to 410, hiring more corrections officers and nurses, serving hot food, and constructing recreational facilities.[72] The judicial handwriting on the jailhouse wall could be seen in a U.S. court of appeals comment on overcrowding at city jails in Brooklyn and Queens: Inadequate funding "can never be an excuse for depriving detainees of their constitutional rights," detainees are entitled to "the presumption of innocence, a speedy trial, and all the rights of bailees," and the jails that hold detainees "must be more than mere depositories for human baggage."[73] The best way to achieve these objectives is to house detainees in modern institutions set aside exclusively for persons awaiting trial, institutions whose staffing and operation is geared to the special needs, status, and legal rights of detainees. Short of completely separate facilities, the same goal can be approached by classification that segregates detainees from convicted jail inmates and provides them with an environment befitting the presumption of innocence.

Bell v. *Wolfish* (1979)

In the future, the success of jail reform efforts may be jeopardized by the Supreme Court's decision in *Bell* v. *Wolfish* in 1979, a decision that represented a major setback to expanding the legal rights of pretrial detainees.[74] The Court reversed the federal court order (mentioned above) requiring improvements in the conditions of incarceration of detainees at the Metropolitan Correctional Center in New York City. The Supreme Court found no constitutional violations in housing two inmates in one room, body-cavity searches, prohibiting inmates from receiving packages of food and personal items from the outside, placing limitations on the books that inmates may receive, and not allowing inmates to be present during unannounced inspections ("shakedowns") of their sleeping quarters. In *Bell* the Court reiterated its endorsement of the hands-off doctrine as applied to becoming "enmeshed in the minutiae of prison operations," rejected any relationship between the presumption of innocence and the rights of pretrial detainees, and concluded that the need to maintain order and security in the center justifies the imposition of the aforementioned conditions and restrictions.

SEEKING PRISONERS' RIGHTS BY NONJUDICIAL MEANS

The relative success of prisoners at winning lawsuits and having them effectively implemented encourages inmates to take to the courts an ever-widening array of grievances whose resolution through constitutional principles is not always appropriate. The Supreme Court has observed that the courts are "ill-suited to act as the front-line agencies for the infinite variety of prisoner complaints" and that "the capacity of our criminal justice system to deal fairly and fully with legitimate claims will be impaired by a burgeoning increase of frivolous prisoner complaints."[75] The shortcomings of litigation and a distaste for outside intervention have prompted correctional officials to turn to internal administrative devices for ameliorating the conditions of incarceration.

Three major institutional devices have been designed to resolve prisoner concerns and complaints about the conditions of incarceration without their going to court. (1) Formal grievance procedures for investigating and settling individual prisoner complaints through an administrative appeals process within the correctional bureaucracy is the most prevalent device used by correctional institutions.[76] (2) The ombudsman's exclusive job is to investigate and make recommendations for disposing of individual prisoner complaints. In the grievance procedures, which are much more formal, the focus is on the procedures used, and the organizational structure for the delivery of services is varied and complex. In the case of the ombudsman, the emphasis is on discretionary authority, good-faith efforts, and the positive image of the position itself to settle complaints fairly, efficiently, independently, and with as little formality as possible. (3) Inmate Councils are elected or appointed groups of prisoners who meet with prison authorities on a regular basis to discuss general problems and institutional policy. Unlike the ombudsman and grievance procedure devices, inmate councils do not handle complaints of individual prisoners. Rather, the councils provide a forum and an opportunity for contributing to the basic decisions that affect the long-range management of the institution and, to that extent, give the inmates themselves a voice in running the prisons and shaping their conditions of incarceration. All three devices are safety valves that can relieve the patterned dissatisfactions, deprivations, and problems that occur in penal settings and that, if unheeded, might lead to litigation or to riots.

Formal Grievance Procedures

The formal grievance procedures enable inmates to submit their complaints in writing to an institutional representative or committee, to appeal negative decisions to a higher correctional official or level, and to receive replies to each of their actions within specified time periods. The strength and credibility of grievance mechanisms of this type lie in the openness, the formality, and the safeguards afforded by the procedures utilized in processing complaints. Because grievance procedure mechanisms are still in the developmental stage and are tailored to the needs of individual institutions or correctional systems, there are variations in their generic operational features: the number of appeals authorized, the involvement of "outside" nonjudicial review in the appeals process, the time intervals between steps, the composition of the grievance hearing bodies, the participation of inmates in decision making (not ordinarily allowed), and the auspices under which such programs function.

Almost all grievance mechanisms have come about through their voluntary adoption by individual prisons or through administrative action by the Department of Corrections.[77] One distinct exception to this rule is found in Maryland, whose legislature in 1971 established a five-member Inmate Grievance Commission to be appointed by the governor to handle inmate complaints.[78] Located within the Department of Public Safety (a superagency with jurisdiction over the Corrections Division), the Inmate Grievance Commission (IGC) can reverse disciplinary committee decisions concerning guilt and penalties, review classification decisions, order specific medical treatment for inmates, and may compensate inmates for personal property lost through the negligence of prison personnel.

Maryland's Inmate Grievance Commission

Of the 727 rulings issued by the Maryland commission from its inception in late 1971 to September 30, 1974, 483 were directed against the inmates and 211 substantiated their complaints. Of the 211, only 20 were later revised or modified by the department head. Since the commission's establishment, the number of prisoners taking their complaints to court has dropped conspicuously: inmate petitions to state judges decreased by two-thirds, and in fiscal 1974, the number of suits in federal courts declined by 26 percent from the previous year. Grievances that could have taken years to dispose of judicially were processed administratively in 11–24 weeks. Prisoner satisfaction with the grievance procedure was high; only 35 of the 483 decisions against them were pursued further in the courtroom. As a result of the IGC's uncovering and correcting poor institutional practices, prison staff began to keep better records "because they know . . . that they may have to explain their actions a few months later, which they never had to do before." And officials became more careful with the personal property of inmates, and they are "doubly careful now about assuring inmates adequate medical care."[79]

Wisconsin's grievance procedures

Since November 1972, Wisconsin has operated a nonstatutory (administratively adopted) inmate complaint review system that has handled over 4,500 formal grievances. The Wisconsin grievance procedure contains several levels of review. It begins when an inmate files a complaint with an institutional complaint investigator, whose report is then submitted to the warden for action. The warden's decision can be appealed to a state official, the corrections complaint examiner, whose decision may be appealed to the Department of Health and Social Services, the highest review level. The psychology of this elaborate multilevel administrative appeals hierarchy persuades inmates with gripes that they are being listened to, that their complaints are being taken seriously, and that the decisions affecting their cases are not being made arbitrarily or capriciously. Even so, the full grievance procedure is infrequently invoked: only 585 of the 4,591 complaints filed by September 1974 were appealed following the warden's decision. Most of the complaints dealt with institutional rules, lost property, medical care, and mail and visiting privileges. About 40 percent of all complaints are settled in favor of the inmates, a statistic that conceals the larger victory of winning through grievance techniques prisoners' rights that would often be lost or a long time in coming through judicial decree because of their "trivial" nature or their failure to raise substantial federal issues. The primary benefit to prison officials is that 80 percent of the cases handled through the grievance process would have otherwise gone to the courts. Thus the limited resources of the courts are conserved for more appropriate matters.

California's Ward Grievance Procedure

The most advanced application of formal grievance principles has been in the California Youth Authority, half of whose institutional population comes from the adult criminal courts, charged with an array of serious crimes similar to those of prisoners committed to the California Adult Authority.* The brainchild of Allan Breed, former director of the Cal-

* The name Youth Authority is somewhat misleading; YA inmates range in age from 13 to 25 and "are not that different from their adult counterparts."

ifornia Youth Authority, the Ward Grievance Procedure (WGP) incorporates three critical features that are generally absent from and are therefore the weak links in most other grievance mechanisms: (1) a major role for the wards (the inmates) themselves, who participate in an official decision-making capacity and on an equal footing with institutional personnel in responding to complaints; (2) a labor-management model of grievance resolution that strives for genuinely independent outside review by a neutral third party and a modified version of binding arbitration; and (3) formal training for institutional personnel in the art and science of grievance resolution techniques, provided by a professional group with expertise in the subject.

California's WGP was launched experimentally in a treatment unit in the Karl Holton School in Stockton in September 1973. The WGP selected by the inmates and staff was a labor model approach to dispute settlement that consisted of three steps. First, an inmate files a complaint with a grievance clerk, an inmate elected by peers, whose position is similar to that of a shop steward in an industrial setting. Within five days the complaint is heard and ruled on by a five-member grievance committee that includes two wards as voting members. Grievants may call witnesses at the hearing and represent themselves or may choose another person to do so, who is not a lawyer.[80] Second, a grievant who is not satisfied with the hearing committee's decision may appeal it to the superintendent of the Holton School, who has five days to respond. Third, a grievant may appeal the superintendent's action to a special three-member review panel that incorporates a neutral third party and the principle of arbitration. One member of the panel is chosen by the grievant, the second by

e most advanced application of mal grievance principles is the ard Grievance Procedure" of California Youth Authority. e WGP model has been adopted adult prisons in New York, orado, and South Carolina.

the superintendent, and the third member is an outside professional mediator from the American Arbitration Association, who chairs the panel. Although the panel's advisory opinion is not binding on the administration, the position of the arbitrator carries considerable weight. It was responsible, for example, for modifying the Youth Authority's policy prohibiting inmates from wearing beards.

By August 1, 1974, after the WGP had been in operation for about 11 months at Holton, a total of 277 grievances had been filed. Of the 166 complaints heard by the grievance committee, 45 percent were fully upheld and 25 percent resulted in compromise solutions at the first level; 69 cases were appealed; and only 6 cases reached the three-member review panel. Significantly, less than 8 percent of the grievance committee hearings were divided along partisan lines and were unable to reach a majority decision. Only 12 percent of the 166 complaints were directed against specific staff members. The results were so encouraging and so beneficial to staff-inmate relations that the WGP was extended to all 16 Youth Authority institutions, including forestry camps, community houses, and reception centers.[81] The Ward Grievance Procedure, designated an "exemplary project" in 1976 by the LEAA, has since been emulated in New York, Colorado, and South Carolina, and there are plans to test it in California's adult prisons.

The Ombudsman

The ombudsman's employer

Originating in Sweden in 1809, the European *ombudsman* was a parliamentary officer who protected the rights of all citizens from the abuses and malfunctions of government agencies by investigating their complaints.[82] He used the enormous prestige of the unique office to cut through bureaucratic red tape in resolving disputes, and he made recommendations for institutional change in order to improve the delivery of consumer services. On the American correctional scene, the position of ombudsman affords a much less structured approach for settling inmate complaints than that of the formal grievance procedures described above. Operating largely on their own discretion, American ombudsmen may receive written or oral complaints from inmates, decide which ones to take action on, usually observe no time limits, investigate matters with as little formality as possible, and make recommendations to the appropriate official, on whose decision there is no appeal. Occasionally ombudsmen may be called on to provide services that go beyond officiating the grievances of individual prisoners.

The main determinants of the ombudsman's effectiveness are the personal qualities and qualifications of the individual who fills the position, his credibility with inmates and with staff, and the identity of his employer. To a large extent, the ombudsman's credibility with his constituency and his ability to perform his duties fairly and objectively rest on his independence from the system that he scrutinizes, criticizes, and corrects. In 1967 Hawaii became the first state in which the legislature appointed an ombudsman (patterned on the European model) to monitor the entire scope of governmental activities, which included receiving complaints from prisoners. At present only six states have ombudsmen who derive their mandate to investigate inmate grievances from the legislative branch and who are therefore independent of the correctional bureaucracy.* The California bill to create a correctional ombudsman responsible to the legislature was vetoed by the governor in 1971, owing largely to opposition from the Department of Corrections.[84] The much more common, yet controversial, arrangement is for ombudsmen to be hired by the warden or the Department of Corrections, as in Ohio. This situation may compromise their autonomy and jeopardize their credibility in the eyes of inmates, who tend to view such ombudsmen as paid appeasers for the establishment rather than as impartial free agents who will work to redress valid grievances.

The ombudsman in Minnesota

Having the ombudsman appointed by and reporting to the state (the governor or the legislature) is one of the most practical and promising ways for guaranteeing the officeholder's genuine independence, effectiveness, and credibility. Jurisdictionally, the Minnesota ombudsman is completely independent of the correctional bureaucracy, having been established by executive order of the governor in July 1972 and having been made a separate state agency by action of the legislature in July 1973. During its first two years of operation, the program handled 2,000 complaints, dismissed only 6 for being outside its jurisdiction, and disposed of virtually all complaints within one month. The issues directed to the ombudsman from all segments of the inmate population ranged from special diets for inmates with ulcers to visiting regulations governing displays of affection. The Minnesota ombudsman has been able to persuade the appropriate officials to accept half of his recommendations.[85] Among the significant prisoners' rights won by the Minnesota ombudsman was one that gave inmates a written explanation for denial of parole.

Independence of the ombudsman

Even when they do not owe their jobs to correction officials, ombudsmen who are appointed by the governor, the legislature, or another state agency may still be perceived as "company men" by inmates. The ideal solution to this problem is that the ombudsman be appointed by private groups outside the state bureaucracy, a practice that is difficult to implement. The chief obstacle to utilizing private employees as ombudsmen are the correction officials themselves, who find it difficult to get along with professional outside probers and critics over whom they have little

* As of 1975, the states in this category were Hawaii, North Carolina, Oregon, Nebraska, Iowa, and Delaware.[83]

A Minnesota ombudsman interviews an inmate at Stillwater. Ombudsmen are available in one-third of the nation's prisons.

control.[86] One of the notable exceptions to the private market's inability to act successfully as designated monitors of inmate complaints is Connecticut's outside ombudsman, who works for the Hartford Institute of Criminal Justice, a private employer. Despite the alleged "complete independence" of outside ombudsmen, however, the reality is that in one way or another all ombudsmen on the American correctional scene serve at the pleasure of the prison officials whose institutions they are permitted to enter and to remain in so long as they perform their duties discreetly. Indeed, there would probably be no Connecticut ombudsman at all if it were not for the progressive attitude of the commissioner of corrections, who pressed for the innovative position.

Regardless of the auspices under which they technically function, all correctional ombudsmen are restricted to investigating inmate complaints and making *recommendations* to state or correctional representatives, who then decide what action to take. If the ombudsman's powers of diplomacy and persuasion fail to make an impression on his superiors, his only recourse is the unspoken threat to expose the uncovered abuses or reprehensible conditions to high-level officials, politicians, the media, or the public. Notwithstanding the shortcomings of the American ombudsman, the mechanism does provide a channel for easing tensions within the prison, contributes to a more stable atmosphere, introduces a measure of flexibility in custodial institutions geared to regimentation, provides meaningful relief in individual cases, is a catalyst for changing obsolete and irrational prison policies, and is a humanizing element in an environment noted for inmate anonymity and depersonalization. The overall effect of the position of ombudsman has enough to recommend it that ombudsmen are available in one-third of the nation's prisons, and they are beginning to appear in jails and in juvenile facilities.[87,88,89] From the standpoint of most guards, almost any internal "concession" to the prisoners, whether achieved through the ombudsman or formal grievance procedures, would be better than having to live with inmate councils.

Inmate Councils

Inmate councils are devices for changing the custodial status quo by applying democratic and commercial principles of self-government and labor-management relations to a society of captives. Inmate groups (councils) representing the entire prisoner population meet regularly with prison management to discuss and negotiate their conditions of incarceration—the policies, procedures, and practices that regulate and determine their rights, the amount of freedom they will have, and the quality of their life. As such, inmate councils have the potential for upgrading the status of inmates, tearing down the walls between the keepers and the

e members of an inmate coun- meet at the Lorton Reforma- ry in Washington, D.C.

kept, altering the power base, and transforming totalitarian institutions into collaborative enterprises. The rationale behind inmate councils is the belief that the prisoners themselves should share the responsibility for resolving or avoiding problems, should participate in formulating rules and rights that are acceptable to both sides, and should contribute continuously to the administrative decision-making process. Self-government experience is also thought to contribute to rehabilitation and the capability of standing on one's own feet upon being released.

Washington's inmate council program

One of the more elaborate and highly publicized inmate council programs was begun at the Washington State Penitentiary in Walla Walla in 1970. Through direct negotiations between the Resident Government Council and prison administrators—negotiations that involved open meetings and secret ballots—mail censorship was ended, disciplinary procedures were brought into line with due process, and prisoners were allowed to grow beards and long hair, to wear their own clothes, and to decorate their cells as they wished. Except for matters that are governed by statute or statewide policy, virtually every facet of prison life was subject to exploration at community council sessions, although the superintendent retained veto power over the community council's majority vote. The value of inmate council programs in controlling violence was demonstrated when a rash of knifings broke out: the inmate council warned its constituents that such incidents jeopardized future benefits, and the assaults abruptly ceased.[90] As so often occurs with prison reform programs, however, the inmate council was terminated in 1978 after a conservative governor took office and a new warden—a former guard—was appointed warden of Walla Walla.[91]

For all of their accomplishments, their potential for penal reform, and their adoption by half of the nation's prisons, inmate councils are not without their share of problems and critics.[92] The most impassioned criticism of inmate councils by "law and order" advocates raises the question of who's running the prison. In many quarters, there is intense resentment at having to negotiate with criminals, at having to relinquish penal authority and discretion in the name of self-government, at being blackmailed into making excessive concessions to avoid riots, and at having to make prisons unsafe for corrections officers by sacrificing discipline. Many guards fear that inmate councils are the first step toward full-fledged inmate unions, under which the prisoners would run the prisons (see Close-up 15.3). And some administrators take the position that a prisoner who is capable and adjusted enough to give advice to the warden no longer belongs in prison.[93] Meanwhile, sociologists correctly point out that all prisons are operated with the implied consent or passive acquiescence of the confined, that the unacceptable alternatives to power sharing are open conflict and confrontation, and that prison officials still have the final word after listening to inmate councils.[94] Commenting on

Who's running the prisons?

Close-up 15.3 INMATE SELF-GOVERNMENT AT WALPOLE PRISON[a]

In one of the few situations where the principle of inmate self-government was fully implemented—involving the creation of an inmate union—the results were disastrous. From 1972 to 1975 administrators at Massachusetts' Walpole Correctional Institution gave official recognition and free reign to an inmate union, the National Prisoners Reform Association (NPRA). NPRA apparently took literally the new correction commissioner's conclusion that the only possible way to reform the maximum-security facility was "to tear the goddamn place down." The guards completely lost control of the prison, which *was* run by the inmate union leaders. During that period 15 inmates were murdered, hundred of guards and inmates were stabbed, and narcotics were easily smuggled into prison because of the liberalized visiting rules obtained by NPRA in negotiations with the administration. At one point, university students had to be called in to patrol the cellblocks. The situation culminated in a riot in January 1975 and the end of the inmate self-government experiment. Inmate sympathizers blamed the guards, who resented the inmates for "running the prison," for sabotaging the well-meaning efforts of NPRA. The guards, viewing the matter quite differently, claimed that NPRA was a "gang of ruthless thugs" who terrorized inmates and staff alike.

[a] *Source:* "Walpole Prison; After the Storm," *Corrections,* November/December 1975, pp. 49–50.

the role of inmate councils, one prison administrator observed, "If it means self-rule, that's an unreasonable expectation. I don't want to mislead the residents into thinking that decisions of institutional management will be made by majority vote. But if it means effective input by those affected by decisions, then we encourage it."[95] As for the gnawing question of who's running the prisons, the only uncontestable answer is the courts—to whom prisoners can turn if they are dissatisfied with the results of formal grievance procedures, the ombudsman, or inmate councils.

The future of prisoners' rights

The future of prisoners' rights may lie in the legislative adoption of specified maximum standards for operating custodial institutions by the individual states, steps which New York and Texas have already taken.[96,97] Should the states decide to recognize prisoners' rights by statute, there will be no shortage of comprehensive blueprints from which to choose.[98] Among them, the American Correctional Association's Commission of Accreditation for Prisons proposed 465 standards, including written policies for making unannounced searches of inmates and their cells, the use of sensor devices rather than body searches, the preparation of appetizing food, clean sheets and three showers a week, no more than one inmate per cell, a maximum of 500 inmates per prison, and specifications regarding the amount of training time for guards.[99] The ACA proposal would award accreditation to penal facilities that meet their guidelines, in the same way that hospitals and colleges are approved by their professional organizations; unaccredited institutions would risk losing financial support from the state legislature and the federal government. The practical significance of guaranteeing humane conditions of incarceration by statute would be that in the event they were not forthcoming, inmates would have a much clearer basis and an easier time of obtaining prisoners' rights through the courts.

SUMMARY

Until the mid 1960s, the courts adopted a strict hands-off policy toward involvement in correctional matters and the review of prisoner complaints concerning the conditions of incarceration. However, through a combination of factors, including the prospect of more riots like the one at Attica, the hands-off doctrine gradually made way for the prisoners' rights movement, which signaled that the Constitution had finally broken into jail. Significant prisoners' rights won through litigation include: access to the courts and counsel, correspondence with the general public, the free exercise of religion, protection against grossly inadequate medical services, and due process at prison disciplinary hearings. One lower court even recognized a qualified "right to escape" from prison to avoid being raped! Yet the hands-off doctrine continues to survive, as evidenced by a few recent Supreme Court decisions that give priority to the needs of institutional personnel and warn that the problems of prisoners "are not readily susceptible of resolution by decree." Although litigation has been the main route for securing prisoners' rights, nonjudicial means for achieving the same goals are emerging in the form of grievance procedures, the ombudsman, and inmate councils. The future of prisoners' rights may lie in statutory guarantees of humane and decent conditions of incarceration along the lines proposed by the American Correctional Association and other prison-reform groups.

DISCUSSION QUESTIONS

1. In terms of due process, what position would the Supreme Court probably take where an inmate was granted parole and committed

a serious disciplinary violation before the release date, which resulted in the parole board's rescinding the parole grant?

2. What reasons might there be for the courts' original refusal to override the decisions of correction officials concerning the conditions of incarceration, that is, for adhering to the hands-off doctrine?
3. Has the prisoners' rights movement gone too far in that its effect might be to reduce the deterrent objective of sentencing? Explain.
4. A guard is using too much force on a prisoner, and the prisoner's cellmate sees what is happening. Should the cellmate have the "right" to intervene and attack the guard in order to stop him from using excessive force?

Dues
To All Male & Female
Carry-Out
Beginning Feb 23rd
all urine
will be monitored
by the Program
Coordinator or
Dispensing Staff
The Typical

Chapter 16

COMMUNITY CORRECTIONS

Diversion

Formal diversion projects / Project Crossroads / The Manhattan Court Employment Project / Diversion by arbitration and conciliation / Youth Service Bureaus

Probation

Conditions of probation / Shock probation / Restitution / Revocation of probation: *Gagnon* v. *Scarpelli* (1973) / Volunteers in probation / California's probation subsidy law / Caseload size research / Community Resources Management Teams

Deinstitutionalization: The Massachusetts Experiment

Climate for change / Closing the training schools / Community corrections

Community-based Release Programs

Work Release

Eligibility for work release / Residential centers / Work release in action / Obstacles to work release

Education Release

Furloughs

Furlough eligibility / Problems with furloughs

Halfway Houses

Suitable locations for halfway houses / Criteria for participation / Effectiveness of halfway houses / The Minnesota Restitution Center / Halfway-in houses

Parole

Conditions of ex-carceration / Subsidies for released inmates / Restrictive license laws / Removing statutory barriers to employment

Close-up 16.1: Methadone Users Cannot Work for the New York City Transit Authority

The Fortune Society

The Parole Function
Revocation of parole: *Morrisey* v. *Brewer* (1972)
Aiding the Victims of Crime
Victim Compensation Programs
Victim Assistance Programs
Victim-Witness Assistance Programs
Close-up 16.2: The Federal Witness Security Program
Rape Crisis Centers
Summary

DIVERSION

The purpose of diversion is to give certain offenders a break by not making a formal arrest when the circumstances justify it, by suspending prosecution for arrested persons, or (less commonly) by placing on probation offenders who would ordinarily be incarcerated. Diversion is a relatively lenient, treatment-oriented, administrative procedure for handling and disposing of criminal cases, usually without a formal conviction. Police and prosecutors in particular exercise their discretion in deciding whether to divert cases rather than process them according to the book, which would invoke the full measure of the criminal justice system. Thus diversion is a means for settling criminal matters at a reduced level of involvement in the system and turning offenders away from reaching the next step in the justice hierarchy. Whenever more legalistic, severe, and impersonal action can be taken but is not, a case is said to have been diverted.

Diversion is not a new practice or resource in the criminal and juvenile justice system. The decision of a police officer to release a shoplifter with a tongue-lashing rather than make an arrest is an example of *informal* or *unofficial diversion.* An officer who decides to overlook a wife's minor assault on her husband and a prosecutor who nolles a case are both practicing informal diversion. Informal or unofficial diversion has always been an integral part of the administration of justice; it was usually based on individual decisions that tended to be personalized, standardless, uncontrolled, off the record, and inconsistent. Informal diversion had the appearance and substance of selective, random, double-standard law enforcement: low-visibility decisions regarding who should get what kind of consideration were based on the offender's race, age, socioeconomic status, demeanor, and attitude—and they were therefore highly subject to abuse of discretion.

Formal diversion projects

The President's Crime Commission was the first major group to use the term diversion in its modern sense. It recommended that *formal* or *official diversion* be extensively and systematically used whenever appropriate. The new form of official diversion endorsed in *The Challenge of Crime in a Free Society* was intended to be much more structured, aboveboard, objective, monitored and evaluated, and geared to treatment. Formal diversion operates within the framework of *diversion projects* and is a technique for improving the management of the justice system. The carrot-and-stick principle that underlies most diversion projects is the opportunity given offenders to be returned directly to the community, without a record, on a kind of informal probation. Those who fail on diversion face the prospect of being returned to the criminal justice system for standard processing and full prosecution.

The purposes of formal diversion and diversion projects are (1) to alleviate the overcriminalization of the criminal law, (2) to reduce systemwide overload and court backlog, (3) to provide early treatment before conviction or trial whenever appropriate, (4) to assure consistency and evenhandedness in selective enforcement of the law, (5) to allow the limited resources of the system to be used for more serious cases that are not ordinarily eligible for diversion, (6) to avoid the stigma of negative labels acquired by progressive and prolonged contact with the machinery of the justice system, (7) to select at each processing point the dispositions that least interfere with the offender's freedom and opportunity for reintegration into the community, and (8) to return responsibility for dealing with the crime problem to the community by having community volunteers serve on diversion projects in a variety of roles. Because most formal diversion occurs at the pretrial stage and especially at the prosecution level, modern diversion efforts are referred to as pretrial intervention or deferred prosecution programs. Project Crossroads and the Manhattan Court Employment Project were the first two major diversion projects to gain national attention and emulation.

Project Crossroads

The pioneer study of prosecutorial diversion of young adult offenders was Project Crossroads, conducted in the District of Columbia.[1] Project Crossroads was directed at unemployed and underemployed male and female first offenders 16–25 years of age charged with selected property offenses.* Regardless of the charge, drug addicts, alcoholics, and defendants with serious psychological disorders were ineligible. Upon a youth's agreeing to enter the program—which consisted of counseling, employment services, and education—the current charge was suspended for 90 days pending the outcome of treatment. At the end of three months the project staff recommended (1) that the court nolle the charges as a result of satisfactory performance, (2) that continuance of the case be extended

* For juveniles, the equivalent of employment deficiencies was "tenuous school enrollment or school dropout."

in order to give the staff more time to work with an individual whose performance has been marginal, or (3) that a defendant who failed on diversion be returned to the jurisdiction of the court for resumption of prosecution. Of the 750 offenders who had completed participation in Crossroads by September 1970, the court nolled the charges against 467; the remaining 283, who failed on diversion, were returned to court for resumed prosecution. Unfavorable project terminations were due to chronic uncooperativeness with the staff, the refusal to maintain employment, training, or school programs, and the commission of a new offense or absconding.

The Manhattan Court Employment Project

The Manhattan Court Employment Project (CEP) was developed by the Vera Foundation and operated under a $950,000 Department of Labor grant from November 1967 to November 1970.[2] CEP offered counseling by ex-offenders and career development services to drug-free male and female defendants charged with misdemeanors and nonserious felonies who were unemployed or marginal workers. The defendants' cases were adjourned for three months and they were released on recognizance to participate in the project. Defendants who did not make satisfactory progress in job placement or the training program, or who were arrested in the interval, were returned to court for a resumption of prosecution. Successful CEP participants had their cases dismissed. During the project's three-year demonstration period, the charges were dropped in 626 of the 1,300 cases accepted. The recidivism rate for the dismissed group (15 percent) was half that of those returned for prosecution and a control group (31 percent each).

In the Columbus Night Prosecutor Program, disputants resolve their problems at an informal hearing presided over by an arbitrator

Diversion by arbitration and conciliation

Perhaps the most innovative use of diversion has been its application in resolving interpersonal disputes in which there is no real legal issue to be litigated, the parties in conflict have a close continuing relationship, and the complainant is often at fault to some degree. Involving family members, neighbors, landlord and tenants, employees and employers, these cases of minor criminal matters are particularly inappropriate for effective disposition through standard criminal justice channels. Thus arbitration and conciliation projects have arisen as a diversionary alternative to handling them through the criminal process. As of 1980 there were over 100 projects in 28 states for resolving minor civil and criminal disputes nonjudicially, a figure which could increase considerably if Congress passes the Dispute Resolution Act.[3] In many places these mediation services are offered under the generic rubric and community auspices of "neighborhood justice centers."[4]

Begun in 1972, the Night Prosecutor Program (NPP) in Columbus, Ohio, typifies the arbitration approach to diversion.[5] The prosecutor screens all requests for arrest warrants that involve altercations between private citizens, identifying those suitable for diversion to the Night Prosecutor Program. The antagonistic parties are then given an opportunity to resolve their differences face to face, in an informal administrative hearing presided over by a neutral third party, the arbitrator. This hearing officer acts as a mediator, encouraging the disputants to work out a mutually satisfactory and permanent solution to their problems. In rare cases, witnesses and lawyers for both sides may attend the arbitration hearings, which are held in the evening (at "night") for the convenience of the citizens of Columbus. The hearings are conducted without regard for rules of evidence or other legal technicalities, and the hearing officer will suggest a solution if one is not forthcoming from the parties involved. If the matter cannot be settled through arbitration, the complainant may resume action through the regular criminal process. Of the 7,500 cases handled by the NPP in 1974, only 565 were finally disposed of through the filing of criminal complaints. The success of the arbitration diversion programs led to the expansion of their jurisdiction to include welfare fraud, forgery, shoplifting, and truancy and their adoption in cities throughout the country.[6]

Youth Service Bureaus

The President's Crime Commission also introduced the concept and the proposed treatment mechanism of the Youth Service Bureau (YSB). In the broadest terms, it described the Youth Service Bureau as a community-based delinquency prevention and control agency serving both delinquent and nondelinquent youth. However, the Youth Service Bureau's main function would be to divert youngsters already in trouble with the law from the juvenile justice system, as well as to handle juveniles on probation and parole (aftercare).[7,8] The need to avoid the stigma of the delinquency label and the destructive experience of incarceration in training schools and the need to have early treatment seemed particularly urgent

Youth Service Bureaus (this one is in New York) divert juveniles from the formal justice system to treatment in the community

in the case of minors. Accordingly, the President's Crime Commission foresaw the Youth Service Bureaus as offering individualized rehabilitation services through group and individual counseling, foster home placement, work and recreational programs, and special remedial and vocational programs. As a technique for preventing and responding to the early stages of delinquency, Youth Service Bureaus are becoming the hallmark of diverting children from the juvenile justice system. A large number of diversion projects of the YSB type have been funded by the LEAA, and the idea has been adopted in federal legislation under the name Youth Service Systems.[9]

Despite its apparently impressive results and enthusiastic endorsement, diversion's future as a permanent fixture or a mere fad in the administration of justice will depend on a number of factors. Coercive treatment in the name of diversion may be as repugnant as it was in the guise of prison rehabilitation. The legal status of diversion and the legal rights of diversioners have yet to be clarified—in particular, the propriety of making guilty pleas a condition of diversion and its impact on speedy trial.[10] Whether diversion actually reduces overload in the long run, simply shifts it to sources related and unrelated to the criminal justice system, or places new burdens on criminal justice personnel are all open questions.

PROBATION

Conditions of probation

Probation is the sentence most frequently imposed on convicted defendants. The granting of probation is still a matter of "grace," a part of the court's sentencing discretion, and a subject on which the statutes are usually silent. Consequently, there are practically no limits on the conditions of probation that can accompany the probation order.[11] The conditions of probation may be part of the probation department's standard rules that are applicable to all probationers, or they may stem from special conditions imposed by the court in individual cases. In either event, they can be successfully challenged only by proving that they are unreasonable, unrelated to any of the objectives of sentencing, or unconstitutional. For example, an appellate court invalidated a condition of probation requiring that the defendant wear his hair short, on the grounds that the stipulation violated First Amendment rights without being directly related to rehabilitation.[12] Similarly, it was considered unreasonable to insist that a chronic alcoholic on probation refrain from all alcoholic beverages or to grant probation on condition that the offender not become pregnant.[13,14] In a recent California case, the question of whether it was reasonable to make castration a condition of probation for two sex offenders (who faced life imprisonment as the alternative) was never settled, because no surgeon was willing to perform the operation.[15] Making sterilization a condition of probation, however, has been upheld by the appellate courts.[16]

Shock probation

One of the most unusual conditions of probation is that the offender serve a brief period in jail before being placed on probation in the community. Known as *shock probation,* or split sentencing, its theory is that a taste of prison life will be a sufficient jolt to deter first offenders and second offenders from recidivating or violating the conditions of probation. Probation with jail is also a feasible device for achieving two normally contradictory goals, community-based treatment and punishment. At the same time, it avoids the deleterious effect of long-term incarceration to which shock probationers might otherwise be sentenced, and it avoids adding to overcrowded prisons and their operating costs. In Ohio, for example, it costs $5,000 a year to maintain a person in prison compared with $500 for supervision on probation. In 1965 Ohio became the first state to authorize shock probation by statute. Since 1970, a number of states have passed shock probation laws, under which offenders may spend 30 days to six months in jail before being released to serve the regular probation portion of the sentence.

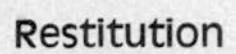

Restitution

One of the newer, more innovative, and widely endorsed conditions of probation is *restitution:* making the imposition of probation and fulfillment of sentence contingent on the offender's compensating the victim financially or donating his or her services to the community (service restitution). Fines go into the state coffer and leave the victims of crime unindemnified for their property loss or injuries. Financial restitution, however, goes directly to the victims, requires the offender to assume responsibility for the crime through reparations, is considered rehabilitative in nature, and provides a sensible and efficient alternative to the choice between straight probation and incarceration. From the victim's point of view, financial restitution is a much more meaningful penalty and a more constructive form of retribution than regular probation or incarceration, especially in the case of property offenses (where it is most commonly used) and where the victims are merchants.

fenders in Georgia work in a mmunity clean-up project to fill their service restitution sen-nce

In cases where offenders cannot afford financial restitution, it is impractical. In that event, and where the crime is against the public, the offender may be ordered to make restitution to the community by performing specified tasks or working a given period of time in designated places. Service restitution may consist of working in hospitals, health centers, charitable organizations, welfare agencies, or volunteer bureaus; counseling juvenile offenders; participating in community cleanup projects; repairing houses in depressed neighborhoods; transporting the elderly—virtually any worthwhile activity from which the community stands to benefit. Whenever possible, service restitution is made to relate to the crime involved. Thus courts may order juvenile vandals to work to repair damage done, and they may assign drunk drivers to work in detoxification centers.[17]

In cities throughout the country, the idea of cash or service restitution as a condition of probation is gradually becoming a reality through enabling legislation, formal restitution programs, and judicial discretion.* Courts in Minnesota make restitution a condition of probation in about 20 percent of adult felony and juvenile probation cases. The Georgia Restitution Program, begun in 1975 under a LEAA grant, functions as a diversionary alternative for probationers who would otherwise be incarcerated.[18] Program participants reside at "restitution centers," are helped to find jobs by the center's staff, and have a part of their earnings set aside for restitution purposes. In 1974, Iowa made restitution a requirement for probation or a deferred sentence and called for a court-approved restitution plan; similar legislation exists in Pennsylvania and Colorado.[19] The Court Referral Program in Alameda County, California, assigns minor offenders to serve as volunteers in nonprofit health and welfare agencies.[20] Washington was the first state to have a law requiring that juveniles designated minor offenders make restitution for property crimes and be diverted to a board of volunteers from the community.[21] The principle of restitution has also been adopted in pretrial intervention programs.[22] And the LEAA recently invested $2 million to implement and evaluate restitution programs in seven states.[23] The decision to turn offenders into "social workers" through financial and service restitution seems eminently fair, reasonable, and long overdue.

The conditions of probation are violated whenever a probationer is arrested for a new crime, fails to abide by the probation department's rules and regulations, or does not comply with the special conditions set by the court. When this occurs, the probation officer has the discretion to report the violation to the court, thereby setting in motion a process that may lead to the revocation of probation and the offender's commitment to prison. The probation officer does not have the authority to revoke probation; that decision falls within the realm of the court. The legal rights of probationers who face revocation were discussed in Chapter 15, where it was pointed out that, in *Gagnon* v. *Scarpelli* in 1973, the Supreme Court ruled that before probation can be revoked, the probationer is entitled to a dual revocation hearing that incorporates specified due process protections.†

Revocation of probation: *Gagnon* v. *Scarpelli* (1973)

Technically, the *Gagnon* decision provided for a bifurcated (two-stage) proceeding in revocation cases. At the time the probationer is taken into custody for violating the conditions of probation, there is an initial or preliminary hearing to determine whether there is probable cause to believe that the probationer actually violated probation conditions. If

* Restitution differs from victim compensation programs, which are discussed later in the chapter.

† In *Gagnon* the Supreme Court broke from its own precedent set in 1935, which said that probation revocation was not subject to constitutional requirements.[24]

there is a finding of probable cause, the probationer is entitled to a final, more comprehensive hearing at which the revocation decision is made. The constitutional safeguards established in *Gagnon* apply to both hearing stages. In recognizing due process for probationers in *Gagnon* (and for parolees in *Morrisey*) for offenders whose continued liberty interest would be jeopardized with revocation, the Supreme Court essentially applied the "grievous loss" test that it had enunciated in *Goldberg* v. *Kelly* in 1970.[25] (*Goldberg* was a civil case that involved the question of whether welfare recipients were entitled to a hearing before having their public assistance payments terminated.)

Volunteers in probation

One of the major obstacles that probation officers face are excessive caseloads, which apparently prevent them from providing effective supervision or treatment. That problem is compounded by the contradictory pressures of their having to function simultaneously as therapists and surveillance officers and the considerable social distance that exists between credentialed, white, middle class probation officers and their largely disadvantaged clients. To alleviate these interrelated problems (especially that of caseload size), citizen volunteers and paid indigenous community residents are being utilized by probation departments in unprecedented numbers as counselors, paraprofessionals, and case aides. The movement began in 1959 in Royal Oak, Michigan, where Judge Keith Leenhouts began a program called Volunteers in Probation.[26] By 1969, 250 volunteer "sponsors" were providing one-to-one services to 500 misdemeanant probationers, under the direction of the agency's professional probation officers.[27] Since then, the original VIP program has spread to cities throughout the country, its volunteers being students, businesspeople, ex-offenders, indigenous community residents, housewives, ministers, and virtually anyone who is able to establish a meaningful relationship with members of the client population.[28]

The use of volunteers in probation has of course expanded beyond the original Royal Oak model. The RODEO program of the Los Angeles County Probation Department uses residents of the community as probation aides who work in treatment teams; each team consists of two indigenous probation aides and a regular probation officer, who together supervise 30 juveniles.[29] In Columbia, Missouri, a Volunteer Supervisor Program was started with 15 citizens who agreed to spend at least six hours a week with juvenile probationers (regular probation officers spend only 15 minutes a week with juvenile probationers).[30] To relieve excessive caseloads and to test the feasibility of offering new career opportunities to minorities, the United States Probation Office began an experimental project in the Northern District of Illinois. Inexperienced indigenous paraprofessional assistants—probation officer case aides—were hired part-time at salaries far below that of professional probation personnel.[31] Overall, half of the case aides were ex-offenders. In the first phase of the project, a 26-month period that ended in May 1972, the case aides supervised 161 federal probationers and parolees in maximum caseloads of three. In their role as change agents, the aides counseled clients, provided direct services or made outside referrals, and helped clients to obtain training and jobs.

California's probation subsidy law

The most ambitious and best-known approach to reducing the caseloads of probation officers and improving the quality of probation services is California's probation subsidy law. The political organization of the criminal justice machinery in California consists of 58 independent counties that have the authority to commit local offenders to state-level correctional institutions. It was believed that the county governments, not having to assume the costs, were incarcerating many offenders who should have been placed on probation instead.[32] To discourage this practice, and to reduce the inmate population in the state's juvenile and adult institutions, the probation subsidy law was enacted in 1965. The law authorized the payment of state funds to counties for *not* committing cases to state institutions. Thus local (county) criminal justice systems were given a financial incentive to place offenders on probation who would ordinarily have been incarcerated in state facilities: for each case diverted to special, intensive treatment on probation, the county received up to $4,000.

In California, probation officers traditionally made presentence report recommendations that placed about 50 percent of the cases in the superior courts on probation.[33] Earlier studies in California were used to demonstrate the feasibility of safely increasing the number of probation grants instead of committing offenders to prison and the Youth Authority. These studies convinced the State Board of Corrections that at least 25 percent of new admissions to the state's institutional system could be safely retained in the community *if* adequate probation supervision and treatment programs were available. However, excessive caseloads and administrative matters prevented probation officers from providing meaningful supervision and treatment services.

Because the cases to be diverted were the more serious ones (those who would ordinarily have been committed), it was all the more necessary to offer high-quality probation services in the community. The California probation subsidy sought to achieve this goal in two ways: (a) for each case diverted from prison, the maximum $4,000 subsidy to the county was enough to cover the agency costs of supervising six newly diverted probationers, and (b) to be eligible for the subsidy, the county probation department had to agree to provide enriched services and innovative programs for both the diverted cases and the regular probationers already on their caseload. In this way, the California probation subsidy induced county government to reduce its reliance on institutional dispositions, to increase its use of probation, and to make concentrated efforts to upgrade probation standards, services, and treatment. Were it not for the state's probation subsidy, California's institutional population in 1972 would have been 37,000 instead of the actual 19,000.[34] As of March

1975, there were 19,000 subsidy probationers in special supervision programs, and probation officers were handling an average caseload of 30 offenders—less than the ideal caseload size of 35 recommended by the Standards and Goals Commission.[35] The program, however, was not popular with police chiefs and county sheriffs, who were jealous of the probation departments and who complained that the subsidy encouraged judges to place dangerous offenders on the street. Relentless campaigning against the program by law enforcement officials resulted in the 1978 repeal of the probation subsidy law and a new subsidy program designed to overcome their objections and to encourage a systemwide approach to reduce commitments.[36]

Caseload size research

The determination of the effect of reduced probation (and parole) caseloads on recidivism has been the subject of research beginning in the early 1960s in California and continuing today throughout the country. The general approach taken in caseload size research was to establish very high, average (typical), and small caseload conditions as part of an agency's actual operations. The hypothesis was that the "small" caseload would permit the probation officer to provide intensive supervision and treatment that would result in a lower recidivism rate than that of the comparison groups. Unexpectedly, the only clear conclusion to emerge from these studies was that the reduction of caseload size in and of itself, does not significantly reduce adult or juvenile probation recidivism. It appears that something more than smaller caseloads is needed to curtail recidivism. In this regard, several studies suggest that recidivism by probationers and parolees can be reduced through a combination of factors: smaller caseloads, differential treatment of each offender in the community according to the individual's specialized correctional needs, a suitable treatment setting, and an appropriate matching of the offender's personality with that of the prospective probation officer.[37]

Community Resources Management Teams

Traditional probation practice revolves around the probation officers' providing counseling to each of their probationers on a one-to-one basis. However, the changing picture of the offender's needs and the reformulation of the probation department's methods for meeting them point to an emerging new role for probation officers in the delivery of services: the Community Resources Management Team (CRMT).[38] The CRMT concept was introduced in 1975 and is being tested in ten probation and parole agencies in states west of the Mississippi River, under a grant from the National Institute of Corrections. Taking as its point of departure the Standards and Goals Commission recommendation that "the primary function of the probation officer should be that of community resource manager for probationers," the CRMT model is based on a team of probation officers who assume joint and specialized responsibilities in meeting the diverse needs of their pooled caseloads.[39] In a Des Moines probation agency, for example, after the seven-member CRMT staff decides what services a probationer needs, they are supplied by the appropriate team members. CRMT breaks new ground by casting the probation officer in the expanded role of a broker whose main responsibility is to deliver the necessary services to probationers. This may be accomplished entirely by the team itself, by tapping outside community resources, by contracting with the private business sector, or by referring cases to individual volunteers in probation.

DEINSTITUTIONALIZATION: THE MASSACHUSETTS EXPERIMENT

The belief that incarceration is inherently destructive, does not deter, and is an overreaction in the case of nondangerous offenders underlies the deinstitutionalization movement. Deinstitutionalization would remove juvenile and adult inmates from institutions by closing them down—by extraordinary means if necessary. As a step in the direction of depopulating adult facilities, in August 1975 Virginia became the first state to close its only maximum-security prison. Many of the inmates were transferred to work release centers, subcontracted to federal prisons, or sent to community correction centers.[40] The most ambitious, controversial, and best known example of large-scale deinstitutionalization has been taking place in the field of juvenile corrections; it is known as the Massachusetts Experiment.

Climate for change

The climate for change in the juvenile corrections system in Massachusetts began to develop in the 1960s, when the quality of care at the institutions fell to an all-time low.[41] Institution staff members relied increasingly on physical punishment to control the juvenile inmates, there was a series of "incidents" at the training (reform) schools, and the system's ineffectiveness was manifested in an 80 percent recidivism rate.[42] In every sense, juvenile offenders were treated like adult criminals in maximum-security prisons.[43] Criticism of the state's system of juvenile institutions reached a boiling point when the deteriorating situation was brought to the public's attention by the media and when several investigative reports on the conditions of incarceration in the training schools appeared. In response to the crisis, in October 1969 the governor appointed a reform-minded commissioner, Dr. Jerome Miller, to administer the institutions with a view toward improving the treatment of inmates.[44]

Dr. Jerome Miller closed juvenile institutions in Massachusetts and replaced them with community-based treatment

Miller's initial plan was to humanize the system of juvenile institutions by transforming them into therapeutic communities administered by retrained staff and "new blood" committed to rehabilitation, change, juvenile advocacy, and individualized treatment. In retrospect, Miller admitted, "it soon became very clear that the approach wasn't going to work. Everyone went wild; kids, staff, everyone took advantage."[45] After 15 months of disheartening progress that was thwarted by bureaucratic red tape, unsupportive state legislators, and entrenched staff opposition, Miller gave up trying to improve the system through gradualism and by working with the establishment. He concluded that juvenile institutions were so inherently brutalizing, antirehabilitative, and resistant to change that the only solution was to close them down completely and create new programs and alternatives within the community. In September 1970, Miller took the first step in this direction by closing the Bridgewater Correctional Institution, a maximum-security facility for hard-core offenders where Miller himself had observed staff members beating youngsters for trying to abscond.[46] The closing struck at the heart of the state's entire reform school regime because "if you take away the Bridgewaters, the whole system begins to crack."[47]

Closing the training schools

The major unresolved question was how to deinstitutionalize the majority of the remaining 700 inmates incarcerated in nine other facilities when any such large-scale move was certain to bring legislative intervention and organized opposition from the employees. The key to success depended on speed in removing the youths from the institutions in order to immobilize the opposition and to create a crisis atmosphere that would generate community solutions to the disposition of released delinquents. Accordingly, during the January 1972 legislative recess, Miller used his discretionary authority as commissioner to remove youths from the Shirley and Lyman institutions, in effect closing down the two major training schools. About 100 youngsters who could not be released immediately on aftercare (parole) were transferred to the University of Massachusetts at Amherst, ostensibly to participate in a one-month "conference" on the prevention of delinquency. The conference was actually a means for expediting deinstitutionalization before crippling opposition could develop, housing the juveniles on campus, and having college student advocates supervise the juveniles while arrangements were made for community placements.[48]

Community corrections

The swift, unannounced, and unexpected closing of the Shirley and Lyman schools symbolized the end of juvenile institutions in Massachusetts, signaled the arrival of a new era in juvenile corrections in the community, and offered the rest of the country a model for change. With the training schools closed, three approaches were developed to handle the deinstitutionalized youths and future offenders committed to the Department of Youth Services: (a) placing juveniles in nonresidential facilities rather than residential ones, in order to normalize the juvenile's presence and participation in community life; (b) sending juveniles to small, community-based homes instead of to larger, depersonalized living quarters; and (c) switching from a reliance on state-operated programs to the purchase of services from private community groups.

Ultimately, almost all of the deinstitutionalized children were placed in foster homes, group homes, boarding schools, halfway houses, day-care centers, social agencies, various community treatment programs, their own homes, or on parole (aftercare). About 35 potentially dangerous or severely troubled juveniles were sent to an "intensive care" unit of Roslindale that was operated by Andros, a community group of ex-offenders with a program geared to hard-core delinquents.[49] The Andros Program provided assurance to the court and the public that aggressive juvenile offenders were not simply returned to the streets unsupervised. Under the Massachusetts Experiment and the new system, not more than 5 to 10 percent of the cases committed to the Department of Youth Services required secure custody.[50] A six-month follow-up evaluation of the Massachusetts Experiment by the Center for Criminal Justice at Harvard found that the recidivism rate for the deinstitutionalized juveniles (24 percent) was half that of a comparison study of fully institutionalized youths released in the normal manner (49 percent).[51]

COMMUNITY-BASED RELEASE PROGRAMS

Prisoners not yet eligible for parole may be temporarily released from incarceration for limited periods of time and specific purposes under three prison programs that are based in the community: work release, education release, and furlough. These three forms of temporary release are intended to ease the transition from institutionalization to freedom on parole, to prepare inmates for successful adjustment as ex-offenders, to serve as a safety valve for the pressures that build up during uninterrupted confinement, to relieve overcrowding, to foster self-help rehabilitation, and to reduce the costs of operating jails and prisons. The movement toward community-based corrections for prisoners had its origin in work release.

Work Release

Three features of work release (WR) distinguish it from other correctional activities. (1) Jail and prison inmates are temporarily released into the community to work at jobs that await them or (less commonly) to seek employment. After work each day, the releasees are required to return to the parent institution, city or county jail, or halfway house in the community, where they are still considered inmates and remain under supervision and control. (2) Most states require work releasees to pay for their transportation costs and their room and board at whatever facility they return to after working hours. They may also have to pay family support, outstanding debts, and possibly restitution. The balance of inmates' earnings is set aside and distributed to them when they leave prison for good. (3) The pay and working conditions of releasees are expected to be the same as that of commercial employees holding the same positions.[52]

Work release had its origin in 1913 in Wisconsin's Huber Law, which allowed counties to release selected misdemeanants (and later felons) to work during the day and return to jail at night. Initially slow to catch on, WR for felons was first authorized by North Carolina in 1957;[53] by

1971, 43 states had statutes permitting WR for felons.[54] Most of the state enabling legislation contains no offense-related restrictions on eligibility for work release, or it offers guidelines so vague as to depend entirely on the discretion of corrections personnel (for example, choosing participants who are "not a high security risk" or are "likely to be rehabilitated by such programs"). As a practical matter, however, correction authorities often exclude from eligibility—or "scrutinize most carefully," as in Washington state—inmates convicted of violent crimes or sex offenses and "notorious" criminals.[55] Work release is geared to inmates who can derive the maximum long-range benefits of assuming employment responsibilities, having a degree of freedom, and putting their work experience to use—that is, inmates who are likely to be permanently released in the near future. For this reason, either by statute or by corrections policy, work release is invariably restricted to inmates who will be eligible for parole within a year (or less) or are serving the last year of hard time. Because work releasees perform the same jobs as commercial personnel and inadequate financial resources are a major barrier to success on parole, the wages and working conditions of releasees must usually meet commercial employment standards.

Eligibility for work release

Since most prisons are located in isolated rural areas far from urban WR sites, it is usually not feasible to transport work releasees back and forth to the parent institution on a daily basis. Instead, inmates who are released to work in metropolitan areas are housed in city and county jails, separate pretrial detention centers where available, halfway houses reserved for working inmates (WR centers), the YMCA, or a variety of

Residential centers

n inmate on work release awaits ansportation back to the Yard-le Correctional Center in New rsey community correction centers that may also contain parolees and probationers who have been diverted from prison. The ideal WR residential arrangement would be a network of relatively small centers located throughout the state, such as those Illinois, Florida, and North Carolina are developing.[56] This approach would increase the number of WR openings and employment options, and it would allow inmates with similar problems to benefit from living together. The groups would be small enough to afford effective counseling and differential treatment in connection with problems related to the releasees' jobs or their half-free status.

Releasees who violate any administrative or statutory rule governing their work responsibilities and housing requirements may be terminated from the program and returned to custody, and such violation may count against their chances for parole. A releasee who absconds may be prosecuted for escape. In theory, regardless of the specific housing arrangements, all releasees remain inmates in the custody of the state while they reside at the appropriate supervised facility; in practice, they are afforded a degree of dignity, independence, and permissiveness not to be found in the parent institution. This is functional in view of the emphasis of all three temporary release programs on facilitating the inmate's reentry into society.

Work release in action

For administrators the main attractions of WR are that it allows them to operate institutions more economically, alleviates the problems associated with overcrowding, makes it easier to comply with prisoners' rights, and makes the prisons more manageable. North Carolina has the largest such program in the nation, with more than 1,000 inmates on WR, down from a peak of 1,900 since a recession dried up many jobs.[57] In New Jersey, another leader in the field, about 400 inmates (including some convicted of violent crimes) leave each day for jobs in factories, restaurants, and other industries near the prison and return to the institution after work. Because the program is restricted by law to those serving the last six months of their sentences, most of the work releasees are chosen from the state's minimum-security camps.[58] Careful selection and good supervision may account for the fact that out of 1,900 inmates participating in the program during 1974, only 34 escaped and four committed new crimes. At the federal prison in Danbury, Connecticut, work releasees were earning upward of $80 a week in 1974, and one inmate was making about $600 a week as a steam fitter. The opportunity to earn real money and to be able to leave prison with some financial resources is so appealing that inmates occasionally request that they not be paroled at the earliest date, so that they may continue to accumulate savings through work release.[59]

Obstacles to work release

Despite enthusiastic endorsement of WR by administrators, most of the programs do not reach more than 2 to 5 percent of the total prison and jail population.[60] Various factors account for the limited use of work release. Perhaps the most important involve inbred bureaucratic conservatism, a refusal to take calculated risks in authorizing work release for the more serious offenders, public outrage over isolated crimes committed by releasees who are "supposed" to be behind bars, bona fide reports of program abuse, and political threats to terminate programs if caution is not exercised in selecting WR candidates. Thus the New York City WR program, in which some inmates were housed in a Brooklyn hotel, was canceled after it was revealed that half of the releasees had escaped or been returned to prison for disciplinary infractions, that some organized crime figures had bought their hotel placements, and that 70 percent of the absconders were arrested for committing new crimes.[61] In California, the WR program at Chino prison was terminated in March 1972, when it was discovered that some releasees were committing armed robberies instead of going to work, that inmates who were not in the program were giving themselves week-long passes out of prison, and that the inmates in charge of collecting room and board payments from releasees had embezzled most of the money.[62] Finally, the cautious utilization of WR may be due in part to unresolved questions about whether WR works: studies concerning WR's achievements in bringing about positive changes in attitude and reducing recidivism are contradictory and inconclusive.[63]

Education Release

A natural extension of the WR principle is education release (ER): permitting inmates to leave the institution in order to take college courses, adult basic education, and vocational or high school classes offered in the community. Begun in Connecticut in 1959, education (study) release was available in 40 states, the District of Columbia, and the Federal Bureau of Prisons by 1971. As with WR, many states require inmates to be in minimum-security custody in order to be eligible for education release. In comparison with the WR and furlough programs, the number of inmates who leave prison to go to school is very small: in 1971 there were about 3,000 prisoners in ER nationwide, of which 1,400 were attending vocational school and about 800 were in college.[64] In New York, the Ossining State Correctional Facility has one of the country's largest groups from a single institution enrolled in education release. Sixty prisoners who are within a year of parole or discharge take courses in Hostos Community College in integrated classes and are permitted to participate in extracurricular activities.[65] Twice a week a small group of inmates from Norfolk State Prison in Massachusetts attend classes in the community taught by faculty from Boston State College. Since the program began in 1971, a total of 116 inmates have participated and, upon graduating, the "students" receive associate degrees as human service technicians.[66]

In the federal system, California inmates from the minimum-security facility of Lompoc Camp may spend the last year of their sentence as students at the University of California at Santa Barbara. So far, the federal

ER program has been restricted to persons convicted of nonviolent crimes, the most trusted inmates, and those who have already had at least two years of college and need advanced courses not available at Lompoc to complete their baccalaureate degree. While assigned to the Santa Barbara campus, education releasees are supervised by a counselor, must observe curfews, are not allowed to drive, and cannot leave the campus area without permission.[67]

The specific housing needs and living arrangements for ER participants depend on the characteristics of each program. Inmates who are part-time students or who attend schools near the parent institution may commute daily; inmates at Lorton Prison in the District of Columbia, for example, are bused each day to the Federal City College. Other inmates may reside in the community at work release centers and may even participate in WR in their spare time and on days off from school, thereby making it possible for them to contribute to the costs of their education release. Because of the small number of inmates enrolled in ER, the strict eligibility criteria, the care exercised in choosing participants, and general public approval of continuing higher education for everyone, education release programs have not encountered the opposition that surrounds work release and furlough programs.

Inmates at the Lorton Reformatory prepare to leave the institution on furlough

Furloughs

The most recent and most controversial form of temporary release is the furlough: allowing inmates to make unsupervised trips into the community for a designated period of time in order to visit family and friends, to apply for a job or school, to make living arrangements in connection with an upcoming parole, to attend their children's wedding or graduation—for virtually any reason that correction officials consider rehabilitative in nature. Most furloughs (also called home visits) are for the purpose of visiting one's family, last 48 to 72 hours, and are taken on weekends.[68]

Whatever the formal reason for authorizing furlough, the general rationale for doing so is to allow inmates nearing the end of their prison stay to reinforce their ties with the outside world, to keep families intact, and to provide a measure of humanity by temporarily releasing inmates who are serving long-term sentences. In the federal system more than half of the annual 14,000 overnight furloughs are for "release transition"; that is, the furloughs are intended to help offenders maintain normal contact with their families and reorient themselves to noninstitutional life. By giving them something to look forward to besides parole, furlough programs foster compliance with prison rules, make rebellious inmates more manageable, and reduce the incidence of homosexual rape. In institutions without conjugal visiting, home visit furloughs with spouses serve the same purpose; and they are preferred by women inmates for the more dignified and natural settings for sexual contact that they provide.

Nonexistent before 1969, furlough programs were to be found in 44 states and the District of Columbia by 1974. Correction agencies ordinarily restrict furlough eligibility to those inmates in the final 6–12 months of incarceration who have not committed violent crimes. Other agencies, however, may make furloughs available to all inmates with minimum-security status and a clean disciplinary record, which may include inmates sentenced for violent crimes and persons who are several years away from parole eligibility (but sex offenders are invariably excluded). In Massachusetts, where first-degree murderers are eligible after five years incarceration, about 200 lifers annually leave the institution on unsupervised home visits, often several times a year. Since furlough programs are subject only to broad statutory eligibility criteria or are creatures of corrections policy, their features may vary considerably among institutions and corrections departments. To be eligible for furloughs in Pennsylvania, the inmate must have served half the minimum sentence and must be considered ready for community contact, and the institution's decision to grant furlough has to be approved by the sentencing judge.[69] The rules governing furloughs in the District of Columbia prison system—where virtually all offenders are sentenced for violent crimes—make any minimum-security inmate eligible for furloughs, regardless of the crime committed and the amount of time served.[70] In the federal system, inmates must be within six months of a firm release date, and even then they are limited to one furlough a month.

Furlough eligibility

Depending on the program, in the course of a year an individual inmate may be granted only one or dozens of furloughs. For example, the 1,000 inmates temporarily released from District of Columbia prisons in 1974 accumulated 38,000 furloughs. In the same year, 1,000 California inmates accumulated only 1,100 furloughs. And some states, such as Massachusetts, set a limit on the total number of furlough days an inmate may receive annually. Furlough programs reach a much larger number of inmates than work and education release combined, including serious offenders. However, the three programs are not necessarily mutually exclusive; in fact, half of the furloughs are granted to inmates residing in WR units and other community correctional centers. Overall, the escape rate of furloughees is about 5 percent. Technically, inmates who are late in returning to the release facility may be charged with escape and may face an additional sentence, but in practice their punishment consists of having their furlough privilege suspended or revoked. At this time, any conclusion regarding the effect of furloughs on reducing recidivism would be premature.[71]

Problems with furloughs

As with work release, highly publicized incidents of program abuse and serious crimes committed by prisoners on furlough may be responsible for the cancellation or curtailment of their scope by the imposition of tighter eligibility and screening requirements. In California, the furlough program that was begun in the mid 1960s with a few hundred select inmates rapidly and indiscriminately expanded to encompass thousands. After a furlough inmate killed a Los Angeles police officer in 1971 (a year in which there were 1,500 escapes) protests led to stricter eligibility conditions that reduced the annual number of participants from 14,000 just before the incident to 1,100 in 1974. Similar incidents in Illinois and Massachusetts were responsible for cutbacks in their furlough programs. Following the public outcry over a woman's murder, a rape, and a police killing committed by four work releasees in the New York program, the legislature refused to adopt the program on a permanent basis as Governor Hugh Carey had originally proposed. Instead the legislature authorized only a one-year extension under a new law that made inmates who had been sentenced for sex offenses, violent crimes, and the use of deadly weapons ineligible for work release.[72]

Furloughs, work release, and education release are chiefly devices for acclimating inmates about to be released to their new roles in the community and to the responsibilities associated with freedom. The principal goals of the three programs are "to build up a success pattern, so that when the inmate finally does leave the institution and goes back to society, it's nothing dramatic [traumatic] and all the ties are made and the transition is smooth. And we call that reintegration."[73] The programs also serve to test the inmate's readiness for permanent release, since inmate performance in the programs may weigh heavily with the parole board. Work release, education release, and furloughs are expressions of a distinct corrections philosophy: the best way to prepare inmates for eventual release, success on parole, and full reintegration is through a gradual return to society, in which they experience increasing degrees of freedom, responsibility, and contact with the community.

HALFWAY HOUSES

Halfway houses are residential facilities in the community to which inmates may be released in advance of parole eligibility or as a special condition of parole, and to which probationers may be sent as a condition of probation and an alternative to institutionalization. For inmates on their way out of jails and prisons, halfway houses are intended (a) to serve as a bridge between the institution and society for those nearing parole, (b) to make it possible for parole-eligible inmates without a job or private living quarters to be paroled, as well as offering paroled inmates who need it greater support in adjusting to a new environment than is provided in regular parole supervision, and (c) to function as a kind of decompression chamber in reintegrating the ex-offender into the community.

All the halfway houses share certain basic characteristics.

e nation's 400 halfway houses ovide an ideal means for reinte- ting offenders into the com- nity

They are related to corrections through court order, administrative authority, or legislative mandate.
Their context is that of a small, familylike group that stresses personal responsibility, a work and education ethic, and learning to make decisions.
The center's reason for being is to provide opportunities and preparation for contacts with the community, that is, reintegration.
The custodial trappings of institutions are absent.
Rules, regulations, and supervision give direction and structure to the program.
The primary aim is to offer a short, intensive, and transitional experience on the road to freedom.[74]

The early halfway houses were operated by religious and philanthropic groups.[75] The halfway house movement expanded rapidly in the 1960s with the formation of the International Halfway House Association, endorsement by Attorney General Robert Kennedy, the development of halfway house programs designed to treat drug addicts and alcoholics, and generous government support.[76] By July 1975, the LEAA had distributed $25 million in 348 grants to fund residential aftercare programs for pre-parolees and parolees.[77] A national survey of halfway houses conducted by Ohio State University in 1975–1976 found that there are about 400 halfway houses in the country, housing 10,000 offenders (about 25 residents per house) for an average period of three months.

Generally halfway houses develop an individualized treatment plan for each resident through a formal contract or an informal understanding. The primary emphasis is on interpersonal counseling, followed by vocational guidance and job placement. Residents are required to observe minimum security requirements (such as curfew), to perform house duties, to attend counseling and therapy sessions, to locate and maintain employment, to develop positive attitudes, to avoid socially undesirable behavior, and to contribute to their room and board when feasible.[78] Whenever possible, halfway houses have ex-offenders on staff as counselors or job placement officers, in order to increase rapport and credibility with residents and to provide new careers for former offenders.[79]

Suitable locations for halfway houses

All halfway houses face the critical problem of finding suitable facilities in a good neighborhood so that offenders can model their behavior after that of law-abiding citizens, can take advantage of the greater resources available, and can be reintegrated into legitimate society. Unfortunately, because of intense community opposition, halfway houses are often forced to locate in dilapidated facilities in ghetto areas that have the highest rates of crime and drug abuse. For example, most of the 12 halfway houses in the District of Columbia are located in the worst ghettos, efforts to establish them in middle class neighborhoods having been unsuccessful.[80] Florida is a pioneer in attempting to create a network of Community Correctional Centers to serve as work and study release centers. However, its plans to establish 40 centers accommodating 1,700 men and women inmates were delayed by fierce public resistance in some communities.[81] It took years of negotiations with community leaders throughout the state before New Jersey was able to open its first residential work release center, Newark House, in 1973 in a former old-age home. New Jersey has LEAA funds to open a second halfway house in Jersey City, but it has put off doing so because of stiff community resistance and the difficulty of finding a satisfactory facility.[82]

Besides their fear of crime, homeowners are apprehensive that the presence of group homes too close to their residences may decrease property values. While there is little evidence to justify such fears of depreciation, this concern is reinforced by zoning laws that prescribe single-family houses and city health standards that present stumbling blocks to halfway houses.[83] And at a time when rehabilitation is losing ground on all fronts, community treatment programs may be perceived as leniency or attempts to coddle criminals. Halfway houses for women always have an easier time finding adequate quarters than do men's houses. The halfway house for 11 women residents opened in Tallahassee in February 1973 is a two-story house leased by the state for $600 a month; it has the air of a college sorority as well as the full approval of the community. "People tend to think of 'a poor little girl in trouble.' Women inmates don't pose the threat that men do."[84] A men's halfway house with 50 residents that opened in Tallahassee at about the same time was located on the outskirts of the city; with its steel construction, it retains the look, feel, and stigma of an institution.

Criteria for participation

Inmates may be transferred to halfway houses usually within three to six months of parole eligibility or their expected parole date (sometimes sooner if the house is simply a residential vehicle for implementing work release), or inmates may be paroled to the house as a special condition of parole. Upon checking in at the house each day after work or school, residents are generally free to leave but must return by the stipulated curfew time or risk being considered an escapee. Either routinely or as a reward for satisfactory program performance, residents are granted family furloughs on weekends. In a few states they may have their parole dates advanced a month or two, and they might even be allowed to move out of the house on full-time furlough to a private residence.[85] Residents who are uncooperative, unable to find and hold a job, take drugs, or violate house rules may be sent back to prison or have their parole revoked.

Effectiveness of halfway houses

For many students of community-based corrections, the bottom line for halfway houses is the failure rate of their residents, as defined in terms of recidivism, escapes, and terminations from the program for disciplinary reasons. In its review of the existing literature, the national survey cautiously concluded that halfway houses are "just as" effective in preventing recidivism as alternative forms of institutional release. Stated another way, there is no reliable evidence that halfway houses either reduce or increase recidivism. According to this interpretation, the residents of halfway houses pose no extraordinary threat to society. And since the costs of operating the programs are a fraction of the costs of continued institutionalization, the national survey recommended increasing the occupancy rate of halfway houses to full capacity.* This would allow 30,000–40,000 inmates to be served each year instead of the current 10,000 (about 5 percent of the total prison population in the United States).

Other experts, taking a dimmer view of the program's failure to reduce recidivism, have drawn different conclusions concerning the value and the future of halfway houses.[86] Behind this harsher assessment of halfway houses is the position that their effectiveness should be measured by actual reductions in recidivism and that too many halfway houses have alarmingly high failure rates. In the District of Columbia, for example, one-third of 265 youths admitted to a halfway house either escaped, committed new crimes, or were returned to prison for unsatisfactory performance. To avoid situations like this, halfway house programs such as the Central City Community Center in Los Angeles, which has 35 men and women inmates all of whom are within five months of parole, have adopted rigorous screening procedures, including an "escape proneness" test. The Los Angeles program accepts only residents who have no history of drug involvement and a genuine interest in self-improvement, so that inmates will not exploit the halfway house opportunity as "just a way to get out of the joint."[87,88]

e Minnesota Restitution Center

The Minnesota Restitution Center is an innovative halfway house program, started in 1972 with LEAA funds, that has already generated spinoffs in Georgia and Iowa and may become the model for a second generation of halfway houses and a permanent feature of community-based corrections. The Minnesota Restitution Center is based on the principle that criminals should pay society back for their offenses rather than languish in a cell at society's expense. About 20 inmates who would normally have spent another two years in prison were, after four months, paroled to the Minnesota Restitution Center—quarters in the Minneapolis YMCA—where they live for a period of 4–12 months. Before being released from prison to the center, offenders must sign a formal parole contract in which they agree to get a job, to make regular restitution payments to their victims, to contribute $12.50 a week for their room and board, and to participate in therapy if they have drug, alcohol, or psychiatric problems. If the parole contract is broken, the center may request the parole board to revoke parole.[89] Service restitution is utilized where the individual victim suffers no financial loss, the victim is the community, or the victim refuses to cooperate.

The halfway houses discussed so far are technically halfway-*out*

* The national survey found that the occupancy rate ranged from 21 percent to 76 percent.

houses because their residents are pre-parolees and parolees who are on their way out of institutions and on the road back to the community. A less common but equivalent form of residential community facilities are the halfway-*in* houses to which juvenile and adult probationers are sent in lieu of confinement and as a special condition of probation. Halfway-in houses serve offenders who require greater supervision and a more structured living environment than is available under regular probation, but who do not need to be incarcerated. The Probationed Offenders Rehabilitation Training (PORT) project, which now has four centers, is a halfway-in house program begun in 1969 in Rochester, Minnesota, for adult offenders and juvenile delinquents who, without PORT, would have been confined.[90] In this way, halfway-in houses are an alternative to institutionalization. And residents whose performance is unsatisfactory may have their probation revoked and be committed to prison or juvenile training schools.

Halfway-in houses

Halfway-in houses (also called group homes) generally serve juveniles and young adults, first offenders, drug addicts, property offenders—individuals who are amenable to change, rehabilitation, and deterrence without doing time. Probation halfway houses often refuse to accept pre-parolees and parolees under any circumstances because doing so may expose the younger, less serious offender residents to the inmate subculture and the ways of more hardened criminals. There are also administrative problems involved in accommodating mixed offender groups.[91] Otherwise, the two types of halfway houses are virtually identical in their philosophy of community-based treatment, program content, and administration.

PAROLE

Inmates who leave prison through regular parole, mandatory release, and maxing out, as well as those paroled from halfway houses, face a variety of adjustment problems. The end of incarceration is often the introduction to conditions of ex-carceration that are in some ways as threatening, traumatic, and frustrating as confinement itself. The simplest of activities, minor obstacles, and temporary setbacks that the ordinary citizen takes for granted may become crisis situations for ex-offenders that could propel them to return to crime. Indeed, the recidivism rate is highest in the immediate postinstitutional period: within two years 50 percent or more of parolees are back in prison.[92] The conditions of parole are a further reminder that the ex-offender is not entirely free, and they are a constant source of potential friction between parolee and parole officer. "They tell you not to hang out with known criminals. But let's face it, almost everybody I know *is* a known criminal."[93]

Conditions of ex-carceration

The commonest and most serious hurdle faced by ex-offenders is that of economic insecurity and unemployment, which is a major factor in recidivism.[94] As a group, ex-prisoners are subject to legal barriers to employment that may bar them from government service, the army, obtaining occupational licenses, working in "sensitive" positions, and being bonded. A more insidious form of discrimination is practiced by employers who refuse to give ex-offenders a second chance regardless of their qualifications, their rehabilitation, and the degree to which their crime was job related. Several notable efforts have been made to improve the employment picture, economic plight, and ability of ex-offenders to become reintegrated and respectable citizens. Three of the more recent and most innovative steps involve changes in the laws that act as barriers to employment, "supported work" programs, and financial subsidies for newly released offenders.

Subsidies for released inmates

One of the first applications of the subsidy principle was sponsored by the Department of Labor and carried out in Baltimore in 1971–1974. Of 442 "high risk" offenders released from prison, one-fourth received a weekly stipend of $60 for 13 weeks, in addition to assistance in finding jobs. Comparisons of the subsidized experimental group with the control groups that had no financial assistance revealed that the subsidized men had a significantly lower recidivism rate two years later, that the most "disadvantaged" men benefited most from the subsidy, and that those who did return to crime had gone straight for a longer period than the controls who recidivated. There were also improvements in lifestyle, personal relationships, and general outlook as a result of the financial aid. Based on these encouraging findings, the Department of Labor and the LEAA recently launched a large-scale subsidy program in Georgia and Texas that will provide a more diversified population of released offenders with a stipend for up to 26 weeks.[95] Going one step further, the supported work program begun by the Vera Institute of Justice in 1970 places ex-addicts in well-paying jobs ($6,000 to $10,000 a year) maintaining parks and recreation areas, restoring city buildings, acting as messengers, running off-track betting offices, and working in a variety of other public service functions and in private industry. On the whole, the early results of the supported work experiment are favorable, and at least 12 cities plan to institute similar programs.[96,97]

Restrictive license laws

The most conspicuous and crushing obstacle to the employment of former offenders are the statutory provisions that restrict their entering licensed fields of work, the government-regulated private occupations in which seven million other Americans earn their livelihood. These laws either specifically exclude ex-offenders who have been convicted of a felony from licensed jobs or give licensing boards wide discretion to deny licenses on the basis of questionable moral character—which is presumed to characterize ex-offenders as a group and therefore to make them unfit for employment. This presumption was upheld by the Supreme Court in 1898 when it stated that "the record of a conviction may be conclusive evidence of . . . the absence of the requisite good character."[98] The restrictive license laws found throughout the nation prevent persons with a criminal record from becoming barbers, cosmetologists, electricians, elevator helpers, nurses, embalmers, apprentices, junk dealers, hairdressers, plumbers, waiters, and bar or nightclub employees. In theory, the restrictions are justified on the grounds of public protection: the need to exclude "undesirable elements" from positions in which they could undermine public health and welfare. But in practice many of the restrictions in these fields have less to do with the public's health and safety than with protecting the economic interests of those who control the occupations.

Removing statutory barriers to employment

Fortunately, there is an emerging trend toward lowering the license barriers, preventing the arbitrary denial of jobs in the private sector, and establishing a "right to work" for ex-convicts. The change is coming about through a combination of successful litigation by ex-offenders, statutory reform, advocacy, voluntary steps on the part of employers, and evidence that employment is the best protection against recidivism. Increasingly, the courts are taking the position that (a) a license may be denied ex-offenders only if the crime is job related, (b) the restrictions must bear a "rational relationship" between the qualifications of the ex-of-

Close-up 16.1 METHADONE USERS CANNOT WORK FOR THE NEW YORK CITY TRANSIT AUTHORITY

A job-related requirement test that applies to the hiring of ex-offenders may be read into two important Supreme Court decisions, *Schware* v. *Board of Bar Examiners of New Mexico* in 1957 and *Griggs* v. *Duke Power Co.* in 1971.[a] The Court, however, has not yet explicitly ruled that convicted felons, as a cognizable class, are entitled to equal employment opportunity unless their crimes are job-related.

The closest the Court has come to adopting a job-related test for determining the employment rights of ex-offenders was in *New York City Transit Authority* v. *Beazer* in 1979.[b] The Transit Authority has a blanket policy of refusing to employ persons who use narcotic drugs, including methadone. A class action suit was filed against the Transit Authority by two former employees who were dismissed because they were receiving methadone treatment, and by two applicants who were refused employment for the same reason. Relying on evidence purporting to show that the company's methadone policy discriminated against blacks and Hispanics and was not job related, the district court declared that the policy violated Title VII of the Civil Rights Act of 1964 and the Equal Protection Clause of the Fourteenth Amendment. The district court's con-

fender and the demands of the job, (c) licensing boards must presume that ex-offenders have good moral character unless proved otherwise, and (d) restrictive license laws are unconstitutional because they result in the kind of racial "discriminatory impact" prohibited by the Civil Rights Act.[99,100] However, efforts to establish a legal right to work for ex-offenders were jolted by the Supreme Court's most recent decision in this area, discussed in Close-up 16.1.

While in 1972 only California, Florida, and Illinois had enacted legislation to remove employment barriers for former felons, by June 1974 ten states had passed new laws, and bills were pending in many others. The revised statutory provisions generally follow the Florida law, which provides that a crime shall not be a disqualification for a license unless it is directly related to the occupations sought (job related), or the California legislation, which in effect requires the licensing board to presume that each applicant has good moral character.[101] The United States Civil Service Commission has relaxed its policy against hiring ex-convicts and is developing standards for determining whether the applicant's crime is job related.[102] Under the Federal Bonding Program, the Department of

stitutional holding was subsequently affirmed by the court of appeals.

In *Beazer,* however, the Supreme Court reversed the lower courts' rulings in an opinion that was a setback to the advancement of employment rights for ex-offenders, was compatible with the rationale behind restrictive license laws, and was an endorsement of the hands-off doctrine applied to the "conditions of ex-carceration." The Court disposed of the Title VII issue by succinctly noting that "even if it is capable of establishing a prima facie case of discrimination, it is assuredly rebutted by Transit Authority's demonstration that its narcotics rule (and the rule's application to methadone users) is 'job related.' " Sensitive to the public safety objective of the company's employment policy and to the cost of individualizing the decision to hire methadone users, the Court disposed of the equal protection issue by conceding that "No matter how unwise it may be for TA to refuse employment to individual car cleaners, track repairmen, or bus drivers simply because they are receiving methadone treatment, the Constitution does not authorize a Federal Court to interfere in that policy decision."

[a] *Schware* v. *Board of Bar Examiners of New Mexico,* 353 U.S. 232 (1957); *Griggs* v. *Duke Power Company,* 91 S.Ct. 849 (1971).
[b] *New York City Transit Authority* v. *Beazer,* No. 77-1427, Decided March 21, 1979.

Labor will purchase an insurance bond against employee dishonesty for any ex-offender who seeks a bond-related job and is unable to obtain coverage from a regular commercial source.[103] And the Department of Labor has funded the National Clearinghouse of Ex-Offender Employment Restrictions, operated by the American Bar Association, to coordinate the drive against occupational discrimination.[104]

The states invariably continue to make law enforcement off limits to felons, but the policy of excluding ex-convicts from private security work is starting to change. For example, an appellate court found unconstitutional a Connecticut statute that barred persons with felony convictions from receiving licenses to become security guards and private investigators. The state's argument that it could be *presumed* that convicted felons did not possess the moral character necessary to perform private security work was rejected by the court.[105] Despite the ruling, Pinkerton's Inc., which employs 40,000 private police, vowed that "our policy stands and our policy prohibits hiring anyone with a criminal record."

One of the most logical and meaningful areas of employment for ex-offenders is within the field of corrections itself. In this regard, 44 of the 52 corrections systems have dropped whatever blanket prohibitions they had against hiring ex-offenders, and probation and parole agencies are liberalizing their hiring policies.[106] An outstanding example of the latter is Ohio's Parole Officer Aid program, in which ex-parolees are hired as professional parole officers, are given six months of on-the-job training, are authorized to perform all parole officer duties except signing parole violation reports, and can earn promotion to full parole officer.[107]

The Fortune Society

In the struggle for equal employment, community acceptance, and the prevention of recidivism, few groups have been as dedicated and successful as the Fortune Society, a national organization of ex-convicts with headquarters in New York City. Founded by a nonoffender in 1968, the Fortune Society has a full-time paid staff of 15 ex-offenders who counsel, provide vocational training, obtain jobs, run programs for delinquents, and offer other forms of concrete services to 1,500 people a year. The Society also draws on 100 volunteers who do individualized tutoring, perform clerical tasks connected with advocacy, and serve as pen pals to 4,000 prisoners. The major overall objectives of the Fortune Society are to ease the practical problems that confront former inmates, to remove restrictive employment policies and laws, and to lobby for national prison reform by calling for the abolition of imprisonment.[108]

The Parole Function

Official responsibility for helping parolees with employment, resolving personal problems, obtaining community services, providing counseling, and preventing recidivism is that of the parole officer. However, a number of factors limit the parole officer's effectiveness, augur the creative use of volunteers, and suggest that a reorganization in delivering parole services may be in order.

1. Excessive caseloads, which may range from 40 to 150 per officer, make counseling an almost unattainable goal. Most of the agent's time is spent dealing with parole files and reports rather than with the parolees themselves. It is not uncommon for officers to have less than two hours of personal contact a month with each client.[109] To some extent, the use of volunteers can fill this gap and possibly overcome the cultural differences between clients and staff. Massachusetts, for example, began using volunteer community assistants, who were given a stipend of $15 a week to cover the expenses of making two contacts a week with their clients.[110]

2. Typically, the parole officer picks up the case and meets the client after the inmate has been released from the institution. Under this arrangement, they begin their relationship in the community as strangers; the agent's knowledge of the offender is limited to the prison record, and the offender does not believe that the officer is on his side. To remedy this situation, in 1974 the Massachusetts Parole Board started a pre-parole contact program in which the officer meets with the parole candidate several months in advance, develops a solid parole plan, and may function as an advocate for release at the parole hearing.[111] Vermont, which was able to cut its average caseload size from 80 to 65 with the money it saved by closing its maximum-security prison, may have been the first state in which parole officers have a continuing role throughout the inmate's incarceration.[112]

3. Beginning with the Special Intensive Parole Unit in California in 1952, caseload size research has failed to establish that small caseloads per se have any significant impact on reducing recidivism.[113] And to cut agency costs, states such as California have instituted a policy of discharging parolees early from active supervision if they have a clean record in the first year or two on parole.[114] However, early discharge from parole and caseload research findings do not indicate that parole supervision should be abolished completely. A recent study by criminologist Robert Martinson found that inmates released without parole supervision (maxed out) had higher recidivism rates than ex-offenders who received normal parole supervision, and this has significant implications for states that are considering flat sentence, no-parole release.[115]

4. In their traditional role, parole officers are passive, judgmental, and removed from clients, and they retain exclusive jurisdiction over their cases. In some places the conventional model for organizing the parole function is being replaced with a team approach that emphasizes specialization, group decisions, client advocacy, brokerage skills, and community outreach activities.[116]

5. The requirement that parole officers act as cops by enforcing the conditions of parole and as social workers whom parolees can trust may pose contradictory expectations and result in the worst of both worlds. To avoid such role conflict, Martinson has suggested turning social

workers into cops* by transforming parole supervision into a straightforward police function. Under Martinson's proposal, police officers would be assigned to provide rigorous surveillance of caseloads of three parolees who would not know the officers' identities.[118] Perhaps a more feasible immediate step toward reducing role conflict would be to make the administrative conditions of parole less restrictive and to encourage agents to seek parole revocation for technical violations less often. For it is not difficult for parole officers to find that a minor condition of parole has been violated, a substantial number of revocation actions are based on these technical violations, and parole agents enforce the technical rules selectively.[119] Consequently, the abolition of revocation for technical violations (except where absolutely necessary) would close the gap between the parole officer's dual roles and save money for the agency, which would process fewer technical violators. Ohio has established residential Parole Reintegration Centers, which are basically halfway houses to which technical parole violators are diverted in lieu of revocation and reincarceration.[120]

Revocation of parole: *Morrisey* v. *Brewer* (1972)

When a parole agent decides to initiate parole revocation for a technical violation or because the parolee has committed a crime, the parolee is entitled to the due process safeguards established by the Supreme Court in *Morrisey* v. *Brewer* in 1972 (as described in Chapter 15). The revocation decision itself is in the hands of the parole board, which often follows the parole officer's recommendation to reincarcerate the offender. *Morrisey* prescribed a two-stage revocation process, with the same due process protections applicable to both. The first stage is a preliminary hearing to determine whether there is probable cause to believe that the parolee violated the conditions of parole as specified. The hearing officer can be anyone who is not directly involved in the case, and it is often a parole administrator or the court. If probable cause is found, the parolee then has a final or revocation hearing before the parole board. Functioning like a court in this context, the parole board decides whether the parolee is guilty of the charges. If it finds the parolee guilty, the parole board may revoke parole and reincarcerate the offender, impose a less severe sanction, or give the violator another chance. Although the Supreme Court in *Morrisey* did not establish an absolute right to counsel at the revocation proceedings, 23 states had provided for state-supplied counsel for indigents by mid 1973.[121]

* Under the new model of parole supervision adopted by California in 1980, there are three categories of parole officers. Based upon the risk the parolee poses to the community, a point system determines whether the parolee is assigned to a minimum supervision, service, or control parole supervisor. The job of the control agent is strictly surveillance, acting as the personal police of parolees. Service agents, on the other hand, are only responsible for providing social services to their caseload. The single-hat theory behind California's new approach to parole is that parole officers cannot be expected to be all things to all ex-offenders and that parolees require a consistent, clear-cut type of supervision, rather than one which combines the conflicting roles of cop and counsellor.[117]

AIDING THE VICTIMS OF CRIME

Too often the victims of crime are twice traumatized, first by the offender and then by the criminal justice system. After years of neglect and indifference to the needs and the plight of victims, the picture is gradually beginning to change, partly through the LEAA's financial support of the victim assistance movements.

Victim Compensation Programs

The most direct method used to aid the victims of violent crime is the victim compensation program. Under victim compensation, the state compensates eligible victims for unreimbursed medical bills and for income lost as a result of the injuries incurred. In 1966, California became the first state to enact a victim compensation law.[122] In the second state to do so (in 1967), New York's Crime Victims Compensation Board (CVCB) is the largest such program in the country. Eligible victims of violent crime may receive from the CVCB a maximum of $20,000 for lost income, at the rate of up to $250 a week. (No limit is placed on reimbursing victims for out-of-pocket medical expenses.) In the case of victims who are killed, the Board pays $1,500 toward funeral expenses, and up to $20,000 may be awarded to the victim's survivors. To publicize the program's existence, starting in 1976 the police were required to give victims of violent crime a "reverse *Miranda* warning," informing them of

ew York City's Crime Victims ompensation Board Interviews a ctim their right to apply to the state board for compensation.[123] For New York victims of violent crime to be eligible for indemnification, they must report the crime to the police within 48 hours of its occurrence, they must not have "provoked" the assault, and they cannot be a relative of or live with the offender.

Specific eligibility requirements and coverage of victim compensation programs vary from one state to another. California, for example, limits its compensation for medical costs and lost income to $10,000 each;[124] some states may reduce rather than deny compensation to victims who "precipitate" the crime.[125] Because the financial needs of crime victims everywhere exceed the states' capacity to meet them out of general tax revenues, virtually all states currently restrict compensation programs to victims of violent crime. Only Hawaii permits financial awards for "pain and suffering."[126]

To defray the states' costs of operating compensation programs and to reach more victims, a congressional bill expected to become law by 1979 would provide $150 million to the states over a three-year period, thereby subsidizing 25 to 50 percent of the states' total outlay for victim compensation.[127] And the government's proposed new federal criminal code would compensate crime victims up to $50,000 for "pecuniary loss."[128] As of mid 1976, 14 states had victim compensation programs, and the number was expected to rise with the passage of the federal legislation.[129]

Victim Assistance Programs

Victim assistance programs provide crime victims with a variety of services that include counseling, referrals to various agencies, and information intended to help victims cope with the emotional, social, and practical consequences of crime. Referrals would of course be made to available victim compensation boards, and occasionally victim assistance programs may make nominal loans or gifts ($25–$50) to replace essential personal property (eyeglasses, canes) that was stolen or broken.

In St. Louis, Missouri, Aid to Victims of Crime counsels 350 victims a year and provides emergency food, clothing, and transportation as needed. Most of its services take the form of referring victims to welfare agencies, food stamp offices, social security, and hospitals. Volunteer staff members may arrange for legal services and child care, help get the victim's credit payments extended, persuade employers to hold open the victim's job until he or she has recovered, ask local hospitals for a reduction of the medical bills, assist in filing insurance claims, and help to replace or recover stolen items that are necessary to the victim's livelihood or physical well-being.[130] In some cases, the victim assistance program may try to obtain restitution from the offender, or it may request the court to make restitution a condition of probation.[131] The Victim Assistance Project in Fort Lauderdale, Florida, is sponsored by the police department, which assigns civilian "victim advocates" to provide services to victims of property crimes and violent crimes.[132] In Aurora, Colorado, Police and Citizens Together use women volunteers to help assault victims get through the traumatic post-crime period, remaining with the victim for support during police questioning and hospital examination.[133] A study released in 1976 by Marquette University—which found that one-third of the crime victims subsequently bought guns for protection—recommended that every county create an Office of Citizen Justice Advocates to represent the interests of victims and witnesses.[134]

Victim-Witness Assistance Programs

Concern for the witness goes hand in hand with helping the victim, especially since in many cases the state's main witness *is* the victim and many witnesses are reluctant to cooperate in prosecution. Victim-witnesses are often treated insensitively by the very system that is pledged to operate on their behalf and depends on their involvement for its success. Courtroom facilities are frequently physically inadequate. Witnesses incur financial burdens and receive low fees ($10 a day is the nationwide average) for doing their civic duty. Transportation may be a major problem for witnesses, and they are often not informed of judicial procedures and developments in their cases. Continuances and proceedings are scheduled with utter disregard for the witnesses' needs.[135]

Great strides toward correcting these deficiencies have been taken by the LEAA, which has distributed $30 million in grants to more than 100

The witness assistance center of the Vera Institute of Justice in Brooklyn offers witnesses a wide range of services

Close-up 16.2 THE FEDERAL WITNESS SECURITY PROGRAM[a]

To encourage lower echelon offenders and informers to testify against organized crime and to protect these witnesses against retaliation, the Justice Department established the Witness Security Program in 1970. There was no question about the need for such a program: in 150 narcotics-related cases where high-risk witnesses and informers were *not* protected by the program, there were 45 murders, nine attempted murders, nine death threats and numerous assults. So far, 3,500 witnesses have been the benefactors of the program at a government cost of $62 million. The program is operated by the U.S. marshals, who function much like FBI agents and are the nation's oldest law enforcement agency.

Initially, the type of assistance provided consisted of placing witnesses in "safe houses," which included residence within the grounds of federal prisons and on military bases. But when this arrangement proved inadequate, federal authorities agreed in 1975 to make relocation the core of the Witness Security Program. This involves moving informers and their families to different communities, and helping them to assume new identities and begin completely new lives. The relocated individuals are given name changes, living expenses, aid in finding work and, of course, continued protection.

Despite the program's laudatory objective, it has been marred by serious problems that were publicly revealed at Senate hearings on the subject in 1981. New social security cards, which protected witnesses need immediately to obtain employment, are often painfully slow in being issued; and credit is difficult to obtain. Fourteen states refuse to provide bogus birth certificates, documents that are essential for creating a credible new identity. Many of the marshals assigned to the program are not properly trained for their sensitive duties, sometimes disclosing the locations of their wards in casual conversation. Since the witnesses themselves are typically former hoods and convicted felons, they have difficulty in severing all ties with the underworld and few skills that are marketable to straight society. The program takes its greatest toll, though, on the 5 percent of witnesses who are respectable, law-abiding citizens confronted with erasing their past, starting from scratch, and hiding in plain sight.

Yet, no one wants to eliminate a program that is an invaluable law enforcement tool for convicting high-level crime figures and boasts that no witness under its protection has ever been killed. Accordingly, several steps have been taken to improve the Witness Security Program and avoid broken promises. Witnesses are now required to sign a 21-page memorandum of understanding that spells out in detail what services they can expect and the risks and sacrifices entailed. The training of marshals is being upgraded and becoming more specialized so that they can cope better with the diversified requirements of witnesses. Prosecutors must brief marshals on the particulars of the case as it relates to protected witnesses before placing witnesses in their custody. And more than 150 major companies are participating in a job pool for protected witnesses to provide more meaningful and stable livelihoods. With any luck, the revamped Witness Security Program may also prove to be an effective form of rehabilitation for a select group of ex-offenders who would not have otherwise repudiated their criminal lifestyle.

[a] *Source:* Transcript of "The Federal Witness Security Program," *20/20, ABC Television News,* October 2, 1980; "Life in Hiding," *Newsweek,* January 5, 1981, p. 42.

agencies in cities throughout the country to set up victim-witness assistance programs.[136] The two most prominent programs are those run by the Vera Institute of Justice in Brooklyn and the National District Attorneys Association, whose program is operated out of prosecutors' offices in eight cities. The programs offer witnesses a range of services intended to minimize the hardships associated with serving, to treat witnesses with dignity and as valued partners in effective prosecution, and to try to make their days in court as pleasant as possible. The services include

newly constructed reception centers that offer congenial surroundings for victims and witnesses waiting at the courthouse to testify (a children's center in the same building provides free child day-care supervision);
project staff, victim advocates, or paralegals who provide orientation by explaining what to expect while giving testimony, by clarifying legal jargon and the sequence of procedures, and by escorting witnesses to the proper courtroom;
transportation to and from court for the handicapped and elderly;
emergency repairs at the homes and businesses of burglarized witnesses;
hotline telephones for victims to report intimidation attempts by defendants or others;
a computerized notification system that reduces the number of witness appearances, continuances, and delays;
telephone or radio alert procedures that lessen the time spent waiting idly in court without knowing when or if the case will be reached;
plans for handling and returning the victim's recovered stolen property quickly while preserving its evidentiary value.[137]

A unique, highly specialized and controversial witness assistance system is described in Close-up 16.2.

Rape Crisis Centers

Rape crisis centers provide information, referral services, temporary shelter, and emotional support and counseling to rape victims. Their aid sometimes extends through the readjustment period after the trial has ended. Often operated by women who have themselves been sexually assaulted, crisis centers may provide staff to accompany the victim in reporting the offense and be present during police interrogation and court appearances. Although the treatment of rape victims is part of the victim assistance movement, its origins lie in the women's liberation movement and the severe dissatisfaction with the sexist, undignified, and insensitive treatment accorded rape victims by the police, prosecutors, and the courts.[138] Under a wide variety of auspices and generous LEAA funding, rape crisis centers and similar components within victim-witness assistance programs are found in cities across the country. As the problems of different groups of crime victims (such as the aged) become publicized and require special attention, the criminal justice system will face ever-increasing pressures to respond more adequately to the challenges presented by the victims of crime and by crime in a free society.

SUMMARY

Community corrections is an umbrella concept that covers all of the programs, statuses, and circumstances under which offenders are placed or released into the community, rather than being incarcerated or continuing to be confined without interruption. Diversion is the most recent example of community corrections; whether it is merely a fad or will become a permanent part of criminal justice administration remains to be seen. Probation, the original expression of community corrections, has taken on several new dimensions with shock probation, the growing use of restitution as a condition of probation, volunteers, the probation subsidy law, new roles for probation officers, and the due process safeguards made applicable to the revocation of probation in *Gagnon* v. *Scarpelli*. Few community corrections experiments have been as controversial, as closely watched, or so intensely welcomed by anti-prison advocates as the deinstitutionalization of juvenile training schools in Massachusetts. So far, the closest step taken to decarcerating adult institutions are three temporary prison release programs: work release, education release, and furlough. In comparison with the more limited purposes of these three programs, halfway-out houses are residential community centers that serve to reintegrate into society inmates who are nearing parole, while halfway-in houses are used for probationers as an alternative to institutionalization. The greatest obstacle faced by ex-offenders on parole and probationers is employment; significant developments to alleviate this problem include subsidies to released inmates, supported work programs, the removal of restrictive license laws applicable to offenders, and the growth of ex-offender advocacy groups such as the Fortune Society. In principle, anything that prevents returning parolees to prison for unwarranted reasons is in the long-run best interest of society, and this includes the due process requirements made applicable to the revocation of parole by *Morrisey* v. *Brewer*.

DISCUSSION QUESTIONS

1. What effect could diversion have on the certainty of punishment? How would diversion affect plea bargaining?
2. What are the differences between restitution, fines, and victim compensation programs?
3. What objections would you have to the location of a halfway house on your block?
4. Should the government make it illegal for private employers to refuse to hire ex-offenders? Why?
5. Could restitution and victim compensation programs ultimately eliminate the need for prisons?
6. What do the revocation of probation and parole have in common with the revocation of goodtime credit?
7. What are the factors behind deinstitutionalization?

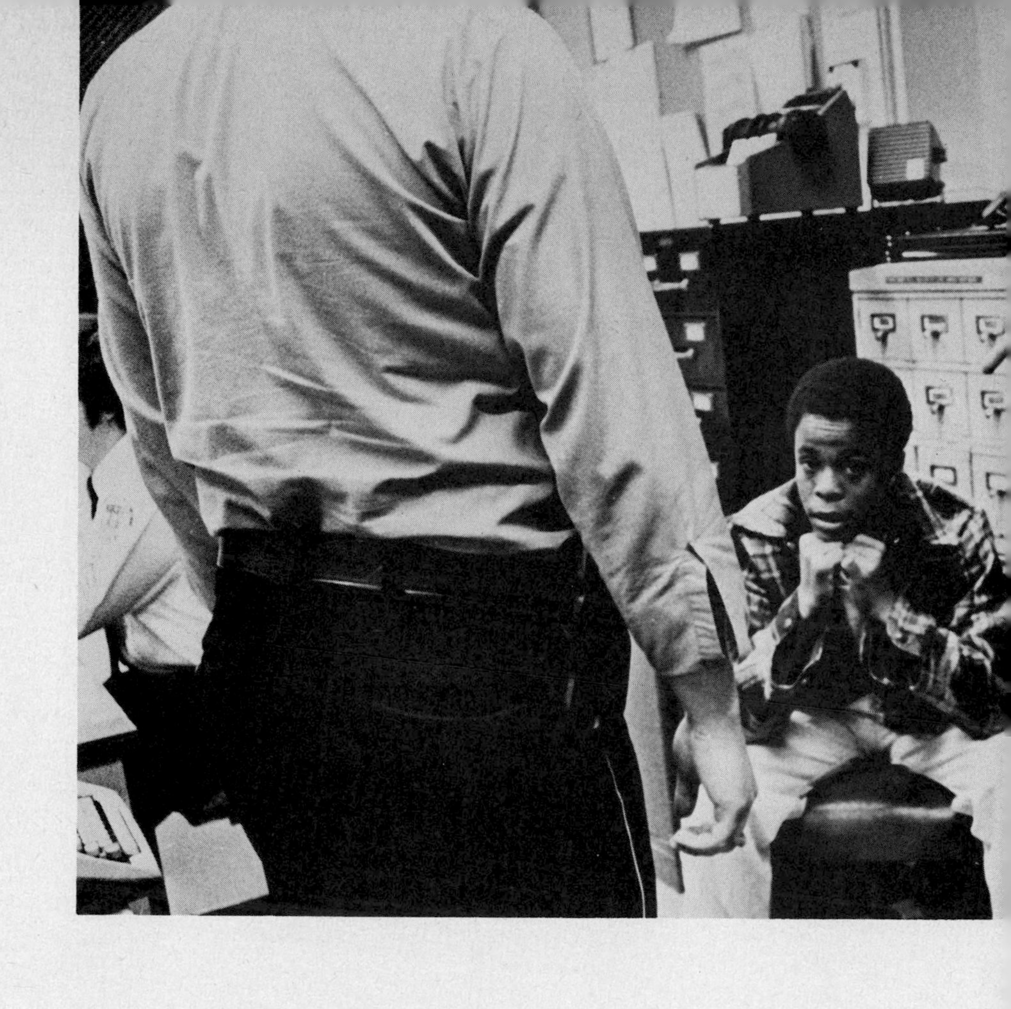

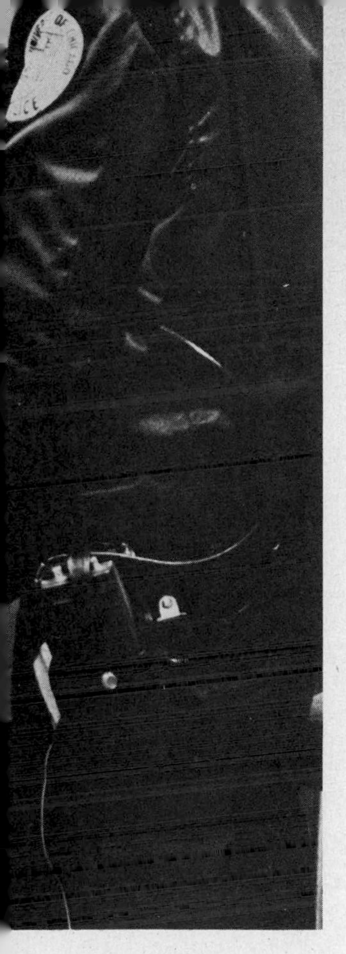

Chapter 17

THE JUVENILE JUSTICE SYSTEM

The Juvenile Court Until the 1960s
Grounds for creation of the juvenile court / Illinois Juvenile Court Act of 1899 / Adjudication hearings / Denial of constitutional rights to juveniles / Language differences / *Parens patriae*
Extending the Constitution to the Juvenile Court
Kent v. *United States* (1966)
Transfer of jurisdiction to criminal court / The Court's decision
In re Gault (1967)
Circumstances of the hearings / Rights for juveniles at adjudication hearings / Significance of the right to counsel / *Gault* and *parens patriae*
In re Winship (1970)
Standards of proof / The requirement of proof beyond a reasonable doubt
Breed v. *Jones* (1975)
The Contemporary Juvenile Court System
Jurisdiction / Referral of juveniles to intake
Intake
Screening and counseling / The social report / Court overload and diversion
The Adjudication Hearing
The Disposition Hearing
Use of the social report / Probation / Other types of disposition
Reforming the Juvenile Court
Getting tough with juveniles / The Juvenile Justice Standards Project
Summary

Crimes are committed by persons legally defined as adults. Adult status varies by state, but it ordinarily occurs between 16 and 18 years of age. The law refers to persons who are not adults as minors, children, youths, or juveniles. Juveniles can and do commit the same offenses as adults. As indicated in Chapter 1, they are responsible for a significant amount of recidivism, the crime count in the *Uniform Crime Reports,* and the crime rate.

THE JUVENILE COURT UNTIL THE 1960s

The hub of the juvenile justice system is the juvenile court. The juvenile court's mission is to act on behalf of children, to treat and rehabilitate rather than punish. A basic assumption of the juvenile court is that the interests of the state and the juvenile offender are identical and are never in conflict.

Grounds for creation of the juvenile court

Many factors contributed to the creation of the first juvenile court in Chicago in 1899, the juvenile court movement, and the framework for the juvenile justice system.[1]

A humanitarian concern for the special treatment of adolescents.

The rejection of punishment and deterrence as proper responses to juvenile misconduct and the adoption of treatment and rehabilitation in their place.

A desire to avoid the brutalizing effect on children of incarceration in reformatories and prisons with hardened criminals. Prior to the turn of the century, teenagers were held fully accountable for their crimes just as adults were; they were tried and convicted in adult criminal courts, were sentenced to prison (where they were treated like adult offenders), and were occasionally executed for their criminal acts.[2]

An emerging social welfare climate concerned with child labor legislation, compulsory school laws, women's suffrage, and poverty.

A belief in the need to divert juvenile offenders from the criminal justice system to a more appropriate agency for processing and responding to them.

A belief in the need to provide individualized justice within a framework of treatment and rehabilitation as the standard official response to delinquency.

A commitment to implementing treatment and rehabilitation through probation. Probation was the original form of community-based treatment; it was intended to replace (or at least to be the preferred alternative to) sending juvenile delinquents to institutions.

The central role of rehabilitation, care, and protection in responding to juvenile misconduct. The state's obligation was to act on behalf of and in the best interests of all children within its jurisdiction, regardless of who they were and what they had done.

Acceptance of the medical model as the basis for a proper response to delinquency. The medical model of crime was first applied to juveniles in trouble with the law. It seemed especially applicable to young offenders because the law and society have always recognized the doctrine of "reduced responsibility" in the case of juveniles. The obvious way to prevent crime among adults was by treating the ailment of criminality while it was still in the early and preventable stage of growth called childhood. The juvenile court judge was to be the wise and sympathetic doctor who would diagnose the juvenile's problems, select the most appropriate treatment, and have the prescription filled at the neighborhood drugstore—the probation department.

The belief that reform schools were no longer adequate to provide the necessary parental guidance for delinquent children.

The reformation of juvenile offenders and troubled youth would require new methods, facilities, personnel, and a new philosophy for responding to the crimes and problems of the young: it would require the creation of the juvenile court.

Illinois Juvenile Court Act of 1899

The first juvenile court legislation in the United States was passed in Illinois in 1899.[3] The Juvenile Court Act of 1899 gave the newly created juvenile court jurisdiction over persons 12 to 16 years of age. The act's definition of delinquency included not only criminal law violations (the equivalent of offenses listed in the *UCR*) but also such behavior as frequenting places where there were gambling devices, incorrigibility, growing up in idleness or crime, running away from home, loitering, and using profanity.[4] Such noncriminal violations that expose juveniles to the same jurisdiction and disposition by the juvenile court as children who commit crimes have come to be identified as *status offenses*. The purpose of the Juvenile Court Act was to treat and rehabilitate delinquents in the community and to use institutionalization only as a last resort. Treatment and rehabilitation were to be achieved by a unique combination of separate hearings from those conducted in criminal court, probation, and informal court procedures.

Adjudication hearings

Separate Hearings. The trial phase of the juvenile justice system is the *adjudication hearing*. The hearing is a judicial fact-finding inquiry to determine the validity of the charges against the juvenile. An adjudication means that the alleged offense or crimes have been proved to the court's satisfaction; the "guilty" child is adjudicated a delinquent or ward of the court. An adjudication empowers the court to take whatever action it considers to be in the best interest of the juvenile. It authorizes the state to assume responsibility for the juvenile's education, safety, and social and personal development—the implied goals to be accomplished through treatment and rehabilitation.[5] If the charges are not proven to the court's satisfaction, no adjudication is entered and the juvenile is dismissed or discharged (considered not guilty and released).

Probation. The initial juvenile court acts viewed probation as the single most important element. In principle, probation had existed prior to 1899 and was never limited to juveniles. In practice, however, its use was fragmented and infrequent until it became tied to the juvenile court through legislation. Probation was to become the primary tool of juvenile court disposition. The probation department, created as an arm of the court, would allow the judge an attractive disposition between incarceration and outright, unsupervised release. The main defect of the criminal court's treatment of children before 1899 was the absence of any midway disposition between doing nothing for the youth and the destructive impact of prison. In principle, the probation department would be able to utilize a wide variety of community resources in treating juvenile offenders. In theory, the probation officer would be able to match the child's individualized problems and needs with an equally individualized program of treatment. In 1899, Juvenile Court Judge Richard Tuthill described the character of the probation officer as being critical to the success of the court: they must be like "wise, patient, and loving parents." The first probation officers (social workers) were volunteers from the Chicago Women's Club and the Chicago Police Department.

Informal Court Procedure. The third critical element of the early juvenile courts was the informality of the hearing proceedings. Flexibility was required so that the court would be able to act in the best interest of the child and to select the most appropriate disposition. Informality at the hearing was considered essential to such flexibility. "Legal technicalities" were part of the adversary proceedings in the adult criminal court, where action was taken against defendants so that they could be punished for their acts and deterred from further crime. The juvenile court, however, was to be a judicial father figure dedicated to acting on behalf of and in the best interests of the youth. Given these objectives, legal technicalities (due process) would interfere with rehabilitation and the judge's discretion in deciding what was best for the child.[6]

The informal operation of the early juvenile courts set the pattern that the states would follow until the late 1960s.* Informality and numerous informal procedures were features of the operation of the juvenile court before 1966.

1. While the Illinois Juvenile Court Act gave juveniles a statutory right

* Informality in principle was abused in practice and became the basis for reforming the operation of the juvenile court in the mid 1960s.

to trial by jury, the juries had six members rather than 12. A six-person jury has traditionally been associated with a civil rather than a criminal proceeding; it is more difficult to avoid adjudication with the smaller jury. Most states have not yet provided juveniles with the statutory right to a jury trial.[7]

2. Proceedings in the juvenile court are initiated by a petition that is based on belief and unsworn testimony. The petition is filed by the probation officer on behalf of the child. (The criminal process is initiated by a formal complaint sworn under oath.)

3. The juvenile court used summary procedures instead of formal trial complete with due process, opposing counsel, adversary tactics, and strict rules of evidence. The nature of summary proceedings in the juvenile court meant that:

> the hearing was confidential (or only select outsiders were permitted to be present);
> notice of the charge was not provided in advance;
> the Fifth Amendment guarantee against self-incrimination was not observed, the theory being that complete truthfulness was the first step toward the child's rehabilitation;
> hearsay evidence was generally admissible;
> the strict procedural rules of criminal court were relaxed.

4. The outcome of an adjudication was guardianship by the state and the opportunity to treat the child, preferably through probation in the community rather than incarceration.[8]

5. The diversion philosophy of the juvenile court could be implemented after adjudication (by selecting probation instead of institutionalization) or at the intake stage, before a youth came to the attention of the juvenile court. Intake probation officers had the authority to initiate petitions for official hearings before the judge or to handle cases unofficially on their own.

6. From the outset, juvenile court acts defined their proceedings as civil rather than criminal. Juvenile court statutes, upheld by appellate court decisions, explicitly labeled the hearing as a civil proceeding. Up to the mid 1960s, this distinction encouraged juvenile courts throughout the country to deny Bill of Rights guarantees to children before the bench. The denial of due process was justified on the basis that legal rights for children were inappropriate because they would interfere with treatment and rehabilitation—the goals and philosophy that were the foundation of the juvenile court.

7. Defense lawyers were not welcome in the juvenile court. Since the proceedings were civil, nonadversary, and conducted on behalf of the child, there was no defense function to perform. Their presence could only antagonize the court and interfere with its humanitarian work. In summing up the prevailing attitude toward defense counsel, Juvenile

Court Judge Ben Lindsey said that lawyers should never be appointed to represent a child because "the court is their defender and protector as well as corrector."[9] Judge Lindsey's attitude became the norm for juvenile court judges until late in the 1960s, and it still exists in many jurisdictions.

8. Commitment to institutions was indeterminate, in keeping with the court's philosophy of rehabilitation and the medical model. Technically, the juvenile was committed until reaching adult status, when the juvenile court's jurisdiction over the child expired and the youth had to be released as a free adult. Incarceration for definite terms applied only to the criminal courts, where defendants were tried for specific criminal charges and punished for their acts.

Denial of constitutional rights to juveniles

How was it possible for reformers to create a specialized court of law for juveniles that directly and indirectly denied them the fundamental Bill of Rights guarantees?

First, most of the significant Bill of Rights protections applied only to criminal cases and to criminal prosecutions. Before the Supreme Court gave its attention to the juvenile courts in 1966, more than 40 state supreme courts upheld the denial of the Bill of Rights to juveniles on the ground that juvenile court proceedings were civil rather than criminal.[10] In this way, legislatures routinely deprived juveniles charged with offenses that carried the penalty of institutional commitment such constitutional protections as the right to a jury trial, the right to a public hearing, the right to notice of the charges in the petition, the right to defend themselves in person, the right to counsel, the right to confront their accusers, and the right to cross-examination.

Language differences

Second, different language was developed and used to describe the processing of juvenile offenders throughout the juvenile justice system. Technically, juveniles were (and still are) *taken into custody* rather than arrested. They are *petitioned* to appear before the bench rather than indicted. They are *adjudicated* rather than convicted (found to be in need of the state's guardianship rather than found guilty). Following adjudication, there is a *disposition* of the offender rather than a sentence. Those who cannot be placed on probation are committed to *training schools* rather than sentenced to prison. Juveniles committed to training school can be released at any time on *aftercare* rather than on parole. Thus the use of an entirely different vocabulary to describe their judicial and nonjudicial processing seemed to place juvenile offenders beyond the reach of the Constitution.

Third, it was not until the 1960s that the Supreme Court extended major Bill of Rights protections to adult suspects and defendants. Therefore, the extension of constitutional protections to children in juvenile court did not occur until the mid 1960s.

The fourth and most important reason for denying juveniles legal rights—particularly access to counsel—is what the juvenile court movement was all about: the decision by the state to respond to juvenile misconduct with treatment and rehabilitation rather than punishment and to treat juvenile offenders as children rather than as criminals.[11] The juvenile court was created and developed with the philosophy that the state had an obligation to protect all "dependent, neglected, and delinquent" children when their own parents could not do so. An adjudication meant that the state had officially assumed parental responsibilities over the juvenile and would act in the place of the youth's natural parents or guardian. This was the concept of *parens patriae*. Because juvenile crimes and status offenses were evidence that the natural parents were not providing the "care, custody, and discipline" to their children that they should, it became the responsibility of the state to intervene, enter an adjudication, and thereby officially become the youth's guardian. This was done to protect juveniles from incompetent parents, adverse social conditions, and themselves.

Parens patriae

Finally, for various reasons, appellate review of juvenile court adjudication and disposition was quite limited. The appellate courts had adopted a hands-off policy toward reviewing the decisions of juvenile court judges.[12]

EXTENDING THE CONSTITUTION TO THE JUVENILE COURT

Between 1966 and 1975, the Supreme Court reviewed five cases that involved delinquency and the juvenile court. All five became landmarks because they were the first juvenile court cases accepted by the Supreme Court and because they dealt with significant issues: the application of due process and the Bill of Rights to juveniles before the bench.

Kent v. *United States* (1966)

Sixty-six years after the enactment of the first juvenile court act, the Supreme Court accepted its first delinquency case, *Kent* v. *United States* in 1966. Morris Kent's first contact with the District of Columbia Juvenile Court came in 1959, when he was 14 years old. Apprehended for several housebreakings and an attempted purse snatching, he was placed on probation in the custody of his mother. The youth was interviewed periodically by juvenile court probation officers, who began compiling a social service file on him. On September 2, 1961, an assailant entered the apartment of a District of Columbia resident, took her wallet, and raped her. Fingerprints found at the scene by the police matched those of Kent, made when he was 14 years old, and Kent was taken into custody by the police on September 5, 1961. Kent admitted to the police that he was the intruder, and he "volunteered information as to similar offenses involving housebreaking, robbery, and rape." Because he was 16 years old at the time of the arrest, Kent was still subject to the exclusive jurisdiction of the juvenile court.

Transfer of jurisdiction to criminal court

The District of Columbia Juvenile Court had the discretion to transfer cases to the criminal court after it had conducted a full hearing. A *transfer of jurisdiction hearing* is a special proceeding in which the juvenile court judge decides whether to retain jurisdiction or to let the criminal court assume jurisdiction. In transferring the case of a juvenile charged with a criminal act to the criminal courts for prosecution, the juvenile court *waives* its jurisdiction and *certifies* the case for adult processing. The consequence of such a transfer is that the court will legally respond to the juvenile as an adult defendant. And this includes, in the event of conviction, the imposition of penalties associated with the crimes—even long-term imprisonment.

Ronald Zamora, 15 years old, was transferred from juvenile court to the adult criminal court to be tried for murder in 1977

The juvenile court transferred Kent's case to the criminal court. Kent was then indicted by a grand jury, convicted on six counts of housebreaking and robbery, and sentenced on each count to 5–15 years in prison, the sentences to run consecutively. Kent's full sentence, therefore, was 30–90 years imprisonment. Had Kent been retained within the jurisdiction of the juvenile court and adjudicated delinquent, he could have been confined for five years at most. Shortly after Kent's case was waived to the federal district court, Kent began the process of exhausting federal remedies in order to reach the Supreme Court.

The Court's decision

In 1966 the Supreme Court reversed Kent's conviction and vacated the sentence.[13] The Court's decision dealt entirely with procedural errors committed by the juvenile court judge with respect to his waiver of jurisdiction to the criminal court. Kent's lawyer argued, and the Court agreed, that the juvenile court's transfer of jurisdiction was invalid because (1) no waiver hearing was held, (2) no findings were made by the juvenile court, (3) no reasons were given by the juvenile court for the waiver, and (4) counsel was denied access to the social service file that the juvenile court apparently relied on in making its transfer decision. In setting aside Kent's conviction and sentence, the Supreme Court ruled that before a waiver order can be entered, the child must have an opportunity for a hearing on the issue of transfer. As part of this hearing, the child is entitled to counsel, and counsel is entitled to inspect the child's social record compiled by the probation department. The juvenile court must make a "full investigation" of the case. And it must accompany its waiver order with a statement of the reasons for the transfer decision, stated clearly enough to permit meaningful appellate review.

The practical effect of the *Kent* decision was minimal; only a handful of the more than one million delinquency cases that reach juvenile court judges each year are eligible or are considered for transfer to criminal court.[14] However, *Kent* was significant in that it was the first case to provide any constitutionally linked due process guarantees to juveniles at any stage of the juvenile court proceeding. Thus it set the tone and paved the way for the monumental decision that was handed down the following year, *In re Gault*.[15]

In re Gault (1967)

On June 8, 1964, Gerald Gault and another youth were taken into custody by the sheriff of Gila County, Arizona. Gault, who was on juvenile court probation at the time, was immediately placed in a detention home. At the time of the arrest, Gault's parents were both at work, and they were not notified of their son's custody or detention. The police acted on a complaint from a Mrs. Cook, a neighbor of the boys, who reported receiving an obscene telephone call.

Circumstances of the hearings

On June 9, 1964, an adjudication hearing was held in the chambers of Juvenile Court Judge McGhee. The complainant, Mrs. Cook, was not present; no one presented sworn testimony; no transcript, recording, or informal record of what transpired was made; no memorandum or record of the proceedings was prepared. Gault and his parents were not informed that he had a right to remain silent and a right to counsel. At the hearing, the probation officer filed a petition in juvenile court. The petition contained no specific charges; it merely concluded that "said minor is under the age of 18 years and in need of protection of this Honorable Court [and that] said minor is a delinquent minor." The petition was never served on the Gaults; they saw it for the first time two months later.

The hearing was continued on June 15, 1964. Mrs. Gault had requested that Mrs. Cook, the complainant, be present at the hearing "so she could see which boy done the talking, the dirty talking over the phone." The juvenile court judge replied that Mrs. Cook "didn't have to be present," and she was not. A referral report prepared by the probation officers and filed with the court listed the charge against Gault as "lewd phone calls." Although the report was formally filed with the court, it was not disclosed to Gault or his parents. At the conclusion of the June 15 hearing, the judge committed 15-year-old Gerald Gault as a juvenile delinquent to the State Industrial School "for the period of his minority [until 21], unless sooner discharged by due process of law." The judge's order stated that "after a full hearing and due deliberation the Court finds that said minor is a delinquent child."

After exhausting state remedies, Gault filed a writ of certiorari with the Supreme Court, which it granted. On May 15, 1967, five months after hearing oral arguments, the Court handed down its decision *In re Gault*.

Rights for juveniles at adjudication hearings

The Court ruled that in order to comply with due process, juveniles at an adjudication hearing that could result in commitment to a state institution must be granted certain constitutional rights.

In Gerald Gault's case, the Supreme Court extended to juveniles the right to counsel at the adjudication hearing

1. They must be given written notice of the charges against them in advance of the scheduled juvenile court hearing, in order that they will be able to prepare a defense.
2. They must be informed of the right to counsel and told that the state will provide counsel to juveniles who cannot afford their own lawyer. Thus the Sixth Amendment right to counsel was extended to juveniles. (The juvenile court judge had not advised Gault and his parents of either of these rights; he had conducted the hearings, labeled Gault a delinquent, and committed him to the industrial school without counsel being present.) The Supreme Court equated the seriousness of a delinquency hearing in which the juvenile might be incarcerated with that of a felony prosecution. Under these conditions, neither the probation officer nor the juvenile court itself can act as the juvenile's counsel.
3. They must be informed of the right to remain silent. And thus the Fifth Amendment protection against self-incrimination was extended to juveniles. (Gault had been adjudicated and institutionalized solely on the basis of uncounseled confessions he allegedly made to the arresting probation officers—who also functioned as police officers—and to the juvenile court judge at the two hearings. Without Gault's admitting to the lewd telephone calls, there was no case.) In *Gault,* the Court was emphatic that the right against self-incrimination could not be denied on the basis that juvenile court proceedings were classified by statute as *civil* proceedings and the Fifth Amendment's language refers to *criminal* cases. The Court would not permit the fate of juveniles to be determined on the flimsiness of labels; it noted sharply that there were no significant differences between an "industrial (training) school" for children and a prison for adults.
4. Sworn testimony must be presented at the adjudication hearing, and the juvenile's accusers must be present and available for cross-examination, as the Sixth Amendment provides. (The complainant in Gault's case was absent from the delinquency hearings that resulted in his adjudication and commitment.)

Procedural informality at the adjudication hearing had traditionally been justified on the theory that it was necessary if the juvenile court were to deal effectively with youthful misconduct. Given the accumulating evidence that the juvenile court was not accomplishing its purposes, there was little justification for continuing to deprive juveniles of the entire Bill of Rights. Among the constitutional rights applicable to post-*Gault* juveniles at adjudication, the right to counsel was central; it was the only way to assure that the welfare of the child remained the principal concern and was protected. The presence of counsel was the only way of avoiding the inherent conflict of interest in having probation officers and judges act as

Significance of the right to counsel

both prosecutors and protectors of the juvenile accused. The right to counsel was the only way to protect status offenders from their own parents who might petition the court to remove an "incorrigible" son or a "wayward" daughter from their household. Given the actual administration of juvenile justice, lawyers were to become the only persons whom juveniles in the arms of the law could trust—in principle—to protect their interests.

Gault and *parens patriae*

The recognition of select constitutional rights in cases of the *Gault* type was not intended by the Court to reduce any of the real advantages of *parens patriae*. "The observance of due process standards, intelligently and not ruthlessly administered, will not compel the States to abandon or displace any of the substantive benefits of the juvenile process." The Supreme Court emphasized the value of separate facilities for juvenile and adult offenders; pointed out that no constitutional rights had been given to juveniles at the disposition hearing; and grudgingly approved the classification of juvenile law violators as delinquents rather than criminals. *Gault* was a compromise between the denial of all constitutional rights at adjudication hearings and the imposition of the full adversary model of a criminal trial (whose hallmark is the right to counsel). The *Gault* decision was an effort to give juveniles before the bench the best of both worlds: select constitutional rights and *parens patriae*.

In re Winship (1970)

At an adjudication hearing in 1967, 12-year-old Stephen Winship was found guilty of illegally entering a locker and stealing $112 from a woman's pocketbook, a crime in New York. The juvenile court judge admitted that there may not have been sufficient proof to establish that Winship was guilty beyond a reasonable doubt; but this highest level of proof was irrelevant, the judge said, because the New York Family Court Act required only that guilt be established by the lower standard of proof based on a preponderance of the evidence. Winship's argument that the Fourteenth Amendment's due process clause required proof beyond a reasonable doubt to justify a determination of guilt was rejected at the adjudication hearing. At a later disposition hearing, Winship was committed to a training school for a period of 18 months, a term that could be extended annually until his 18th birthday. In effect, Winship had been found guilty and incarcerated for up to six years, based on a preponderance of the evidence.

After exhausting state remedies, Winship was granted certiorari by the Supreme Court. The case presented "the single, narrow question whether proof beyond a reasonable doubt is among the 'essentials of due process and fair treatment' required during the adjudicatory stage when a juvenile is charged with an act which would constitute a crime if committed by an adult."

Standards of proof

Proof based on a preponderance of the evidence is a belief that the accused is *probably,* but not *certainly,* guilty. A preponderance of the evidence is the probable cause standard used by police to arrest, by the lower courts to bind over felonies to trial court, and by the grand jury to indict.[16] Proof beyond a reasonable doubt means the *certainty*—having more than probable cause to believe—that the accused is guilty of the instant charges. Proof beyond a reasonable doubt has been the standard required in criminal court since 1798; the lower standard, a preponderance of the evidence, is used in civil court cases. Prior to *Gault,* the juvenile court and appellate criminal courts had accepted the preponderance standard in light of the legal classification of the adjudication hearing as a civil proceeding and its related differences from criminal trials.

Despite the fact that proof beyond a reasonable doubt had always been used at criminal trials, the Supreme Court had never ruled directly on the issue, even for adult defendants. The Constitution itself makes no reference to standards of proof in relation to guilt. Thus the Winship case had dual significance: it required the Supreme Court to comment directly on the two different burdens of proof used in the criminal and the juvenile courts, and it gave the Supreme Court the opportunity to decide whether to permit the continued common use of the lower standard in juvenile courts.

The requirement of proof beyond a reasonable doubt

In its decision *In re Winship* in 1970, the Supreme Court ruled that the standard of proof beyond a reasonable doubt was a vital part of criminal procedure, that it implemented the presumption of innocence and was a principle whose enforcement lay at the foundation of the administration of the criminal law.[17] "Lest there remain any doubt about the constitutional stature of the reasonable doubt standard, we explicitly hold that the Due Process Clause [of the Fourteenth Amendment] protects the accused against conviction except upon proof beyond a reasonable doubt of every fact necessary to constitute the crime with which he is charged." As in *Gault,* the Court in *Winship* rejected the civil-criminal distinction as a basis for depriving juveniles who face institutional commitment of a constitutional right enjoyed by adult defendants. Nonetheless, the Court's approval of individualized treatment—the cornerstone of juvenile court philosophy—remained intact. The decision, like *Gault,* applied only to juveniles who were charged with acts that would be crimes if committed by adults and who could be institutionalized if found guilty. The effect of the *Winship* decision was to move the adjudication stage one step closer to the requirements of criminal procedure in a trial and the full adversary model of criminal justice. However, in *McKeiver* v. *United States* in 1971, the Court refused to extend to juveniles the right to trial by jury, partly on the grounds that doing so might transform juvenile proceedings into a "criminal prosecution" and remove the need for a separate juvenile court system.[18]

Breed v. *Jones* (1975)

The Supreme Court's most recent decision, *Breed* v. *Jones* in 1975, extended to juveniles the Fifth Amendment protection against double jeopardy.[19] Jones, 17 years old, was adjudicated delinquent for committing an armed robbery. At a hearing following adjudication, the juvenile court judge declared that Jones was "unfit for treatment as a juvenile" and ordered that he be transferred to criminal court for prosecution as an adult. The Supreme Court found that requiring Jones to face trial twice for the same offense was a violation of the double jeopardy principle. The *Breed* decision does not preclude the transfer of juveniles to the criminal court; it simply requires that the transfer hearing be held *prior* to the adjudication hearing (trial) in order to avoid the double jeopardy involved in facing trial twice if the juvenile is transferred to the adult court.

THE CONTEMPORARY JUVENILE COURT SYSTEM

A judge who has the jurisdiction to hear cases involving juveniles *is* a juvenile court when sitting for that purpose. There are three types of juvenile courts.

Designated juvenile courts. Of the 2,975 juvenile courts nationwide, the vast majority consist of individual judges who spend most of their time functioning as criminal or civil courts.[20] Whenever one of these judges is designated to hear juvenile cases, that judge acts as the juvenile court in that jurisdiction.

Autonomous juvenile courts. Some of the larger states have a juvenile court system that is completely separate from the other courts. These judges spend full time on juvenile court matters.

Coordinated juvenile courts. Some juvenile courts are part of domestic relations courts or family courts.[21]

Regardless of their relationship to other courts, all juvenile courts have jurisdiction in delinquency cases. They also have jurisdiction over neglected and dependent children, situations in which the parents' or guardians' treatment of the child is in question.

Jurisdiction

The juvenile court's jurisdiction is further defined in terms of the youth's age and alleged offense. Typically, the maximum age of juvenile court jurisdiction is 18; in a few states, it is 16.[22] Minimum ages are rarely stated in juvenile court legislation. In effect, the juvenile court's jurisdiction in delinquency cases covers persons between 7 and 18 years of age. The juvenile codes of all 50 states define delinquent acts to include (1) criminal law violations, acts that are crimes when committed by adults and that are listed in the *Uniform Crime Reports*, and (2) status offenses.

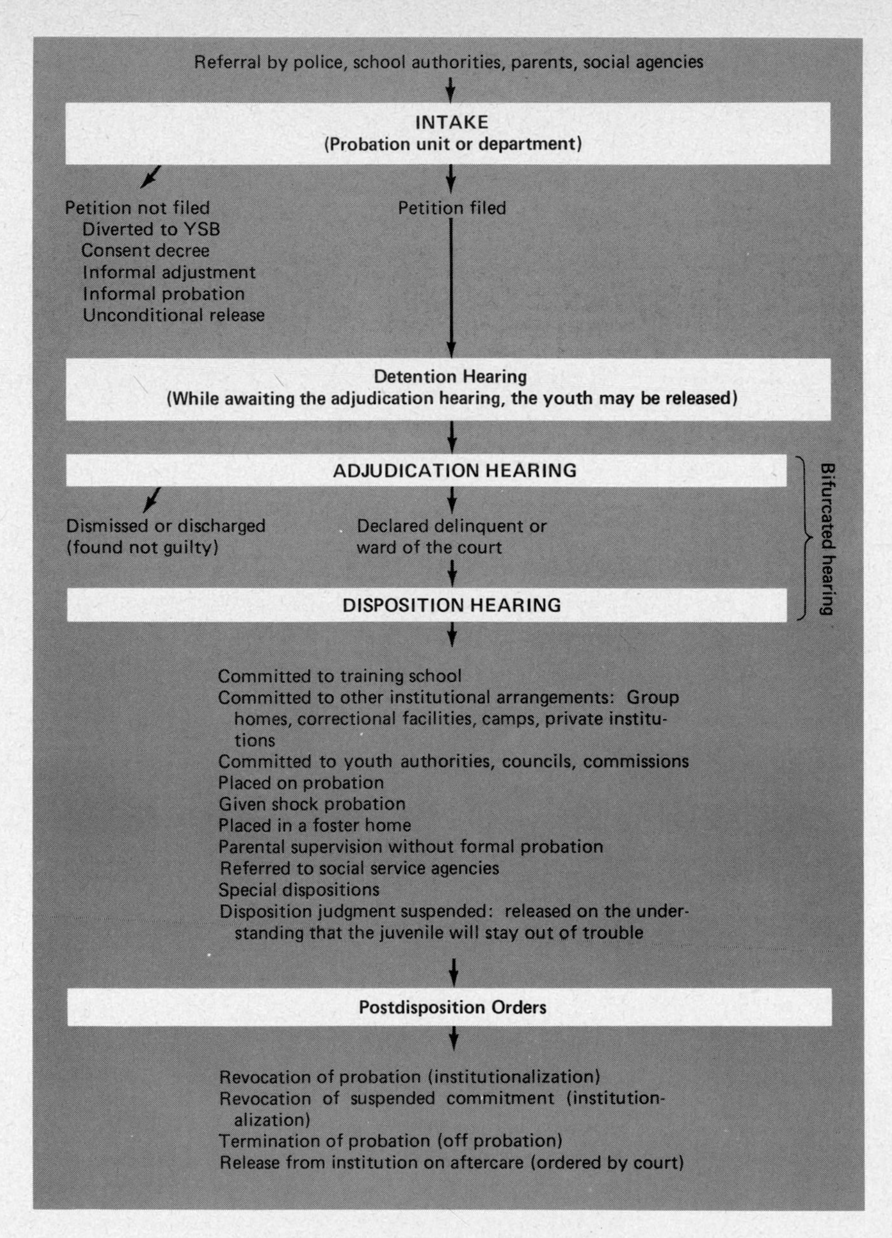

FIGURE 17.1 The processing stages of the juvenile court system.

Status offenses are specific acts or general behavior associated with and unique to the status of being a juvenile. They are acts (truancy, runaway) and conditions (incorrigibility, waywardness) that are defined as violations only for juveniles.

Three processing stages or phases constitute the modern juvenile court system: intake, the adjudication hearing, and the disposition hearing (see Figure 17.1). Each stage is characterized by the social work philosophy and relative procedural informality.

Referral of juveniles to intake

The overwhelming majority of juvenile cases that reach the juvenile court system are referred to intake by the police. For every 500 situations in which the police have the legal authority to arrest juveniles, only 100 arrests are actually made.[23] The remaining 400 contacts that police have with juveniles result in no official action being taken; the youths are warned or reprimanded on the spot, informally released to their parents, or simply told to move on. Some of the 100 arrested juveniles may be interviewed at the police station by a police juvenile officer, especially in larger cities that have the specialized police units. About half of the juveniles taken into custody are released by the arresting officer or the police juvenile specialist. Decisions by the police not to involve the youth with the juvenile court system constitute formal or informal police diversion from the juvenile court system. When the police decide that the juvenile offender requires more formal action than they are authorized to take, the youth is turned over to the intake officer of the juvenile court. For each 100 juveniles arrested, about 40 make their way to the intake stage.[24]

Intake

Screening and counseling

The intake unit is staffed by probation officers who usually have backgrounds in social work. All intake officers perform the four related roles of screening officer, hearing officer, counselor, and investigator. Their most important task is to screen out (divert) as many cases as possible from reaching the personal attention of the juvenile court judge. The intake hearing rarely lasts more than one hour; ordinarily, the intake officer reviews, hears, and disposes of the case within a few minutes. Off the record, intake officers admit that there is routine processing according to a mechanical formula.[25] But officially this is denied because all juvenile court personnel are supposed to operate on the principle of individualized treatment. As counselor, the intake officer attempts to provide advice, help, and sometimes therapy to juveniles and their families. In practice, counseling consists of lecturing the juvenile about his or her responsibilities "or trying to scare the hell out of him." This, the most common type of counseling and disposition by the intake officer, is referred to as CWR (counseled, warned, and released).[26]

In half of all the cases reviewed by intake, the intake officer will file a formal petition for an adjudication hearing before the juvenile court judge.[27] The decision by intake personnel to file a petition means that in their judgment (1) the juvenile requires the kind and degree of treatment that only the juvenile court judge is authorized to impose, (2) the juvenile is actually guilty of the charges and there is enough evidence to result in adjudication, and (3) the juvenile's present offenses, past record of crimes, and frequency of police contacts are so serious that deterrence and punishment may be required. In such cases the intake officer, or another probation officer in the intake unit, functions as an investigator. A *social report* is prepared, which will be used by the court at disposition in much the same way that presentence reports are used in criminal court.

The social report

The social report contains a description of the juvenile's social background, the circumstances of the present offense, and the juvenile's previous contacts with the juvenile justice system. In addition, the social report contains a disposition recommendation to the juvenile court. If the recommendation is that the juvenile not be institutionalized, a probation plan will be included. The probation plan is the recommended individualized treatment for the particular juvenile before the bench; it may include a recommendation that the juvenile enroll in a specific program, such as drug abuse education, or it may suggest that the youth be turned over to a public or private social agency for treatment.

Court overload and diversion

A common feature in the four related sets of activities that intake personnel perform is diverting (screening out) juveniles from court appearances. Intake officers are under great pressure to reduce the heavy caseloads of juvenile court judges, especially those in urban locations who must spend most of their time functioning in other capacities. Two-thirds of the country's judges who sat as juvenile courts in 1973 devoted less than one-fourth of their time to juvenile matters.[28] Only four statewide juvenile court systems require their judges to devote full time to juvenile matters. In 23 states, the requirement that juvenile court jurisdiction be a judge's full-time job varies with the population size of individual jurisdictions. Twenty-three other states have no such provision for juvenile judges in any of their counties.[29] Juvenile court judges also handle nondelinquency cases. The spiraling rate of juvenile crime has resulted in over one million delinquency cases being disposed of by the juvenile court each year. Together, these factors are responsible for the fact that almost 60 percent of juvenile offenders are screened out by probation officers at intake.

The Adjudication Hearing

The treatment philosophy of the juvenile court continues to be reflected in striking procedural differences between the adjudication hearing and trials in criminal court. Although a court of law, the juvenile court functions more like a social agency. Legally, the adjudication hearing is classified as a civil rather than criminal proceeding. It is still not considered an adversary proceeding; rather than *the state* v. *the defendant,* the juvenile court judge presides over a hearing conducted *on behalf of* the child. While the judge has to determine whether the juvenile actually committed the crime or status offense named in the petition, the purpose of that petition is not to litigate the specific legal elements of the offense alleged in it. Rather, the juvenile court uses the misconduct described in the petition as the basis and the opportunity for determining whether the youth is receiving the proper care, custody, and discipline from parents or guardian. And how closely juvenile courts adhere to the *Winship* requirement of proof beyond a reasonable doubt is not known.

The adjudication hearing continues to be confidential and is therefore closed to the public and the press.* Juveniles still have no constitutional right to be heard by a jury. Despite the Supreme Court's right to counsel ruling in *Gault,* lawyers are still not welcome in many juvenile courts. Status offenses are so vaguely defined (incorrigibility, waywardness, being stubborn) or so concretely defined (truancy, running away from home) that the establishment of guilt is not a significant issue. Procedures and terminology in the adjudicatory phase, as in the entire juvenile justice system, reflect an exclusive concern with the child's welfare, protection, and treatment. There is still no emphasis on the juvenile's legal rights, as there is on those of adult defendants at trial.

The Disposition Hearing

Disposition is the equivalent of the sentencing stage in the criminal court. Depending on the jurisdiction, the juvenile court may hold a single hearing, consisting of a fact-finding inquiry (the adjudication phase) immediately followed by disposition of the case, or it may hold adjudication and disposition hearings that are separated in time, disposition occurring a few weeks or more after adjudication. Jurisdictions that separate the determination of delinquency from the disposition of the juvenile are said to have a bifurcated hearing system. The reasons for combining adjudication and disposition in a single hearing are based on efficiency and the social work philosophy of the court. The reasons for separating the disposition and adjudication phases center on the legal rights of juveniles and especially on the content and use of the social report.

Use of the social report

The proper legal use of the social report is with disposition rather than adjudication. The social report, prepared by probation officers, contains

* The Supreme Court may have opened the door to allowing the publication of the names and pictures of juvenile offenders in 1977 in *Oklahoma Publishing Company* v. *District Court for Oklahoma County.* In this case the Court lifted the district court's order restraining the news media from disseminating the identity of a juvenile whose trial was pending.

information that is not legally verified; it presents hearsay evidence and unsworn testimony that would not be admissible at trial in criminal court. Thus the use of the social report by the juvenile court before or during adjudication is a violation of fundamental fairness in determining guilt or innocence. Only a few appellate decisions have permitted social reports to be used at the adjudication hearing. In each case, the appellate court justified such use on the basis of the *parens patriae* and social work procedures associated with the juvenile court.[30]

It is at the disposition stage that the juvenile court of the 1970s implements its historic philosophy of treatment and rehabilitation, *parens patriae,* individualized justice, and the rejection of punishment. In principle and in practice, the court's concern for the child's needs, education, and welfare—rather than the seriousness of the juvenile's criminal acts—determines the nature of the disposition.

Probation

There are several categories of disposition available to the juvenile court. The most common is probation, a formal court order in which the juvenile is granted conditional liberty under the supervision of a probation officer. The court has enormous discretion in imposing special conditions of probation; these conditions may include not associating with specified individuals, participating in a drug prevention project, receiving psychiatric treatment, even enrolling in college. The juvenile court has the authority to modify the conditions of probation whenever it feels that they are no longer serving their intended purpose.[31] Unlike the case with adult offenders, juvenile probation may be revoked and the youth committed to an institution with only minimal due process. The standard use of probation reflects the juvenile court's original disapproval of institutionalization as an appropriate response to youths in trouble with the law. Reliance on probation is also due to the limited number and types of available juvenile institutions and their already overcrowded facilities. For these reasons, even juveniles who commit serious criminal acts and are recidivists are commonly placed on probation.

The other categories of disposition that the juvenile court may invoke are:

Other types of disposition

Placement in residential treatment centers for emotionally disturbed children.

Commitment to minimum-security or "open" correctional settings that attempt to place youths in a normal, homelike environment (halfway houses, group homes, forestry camps, ranches, foster homes, farms).

Assignment of specialized dispositions. Delinquents may be ordered to make financial or service restitution; such dispositions may be part of the conditions of probation, or they may be separate from probation supervision. If they are not a part of probation, the juvenile's relationship to the court ends with the fulfillment of the disposition order.

Referral to public or private agencies. Juveniles who require more professional and individualized treatment than probation or institutionalization can provide may be referred to agencies that specialize in providing a range of services to "problem" children. The particular combination of services to be given to a referred delinquent will depend on the results of the agency's diagnosis and classification of the juvenile. The fact that the juvenile court refers rather than commits a delinquent to a public or private agency means that the court retains clear legal jurisdiction over the case, may revoke the referral at any time, and may select a more appropriate disposition.

Commitment to a state's youth authority or youth commission. Because youth authorities and commissions are a product of statute and a recent development, their authority and functions vary considerably. Statutes rarely require that the juvenile court dispose of any youths by committing them to the youth commission. When the court chooses to commit a delinquent to a youth authority, council, or commission, it (a) in effect reduces its operational jurisdiction over the case, (b) transfers the authority and responsibility for imposing a particular disposition to the youth authority, and (c) may be expressing a preference that the delinquent be institutionalized. These organizations in turn may decide that institutionalization is not required (if they have the statutory authority to make other dispositions). Or they may have the option or be required to commit the delinquent to the particular state institution under their jurisdiction from which the youngster is most likely to benefit.

Direct commitment to correction facilities (training schools). The juvenile court can commit youths directly to secure custody: training schools and other correction facilities. The primary interest lies in commitment to training schools; they are the counterpart of adult prisons, and almost all delinquents who are deprived of their liberty on more than a temporary basis are sent to training schools. All commitments to training schools and other custodial facilities are for an *indeterminate* period—from one day to the expiration of juvenile court jurisdiction (when the youth reaches legal age). There are no minimum terms for delinquents committed to correctional institutions. And regardless of how serious the crime, the juvenile court does not have to incarcerate the youth: there are no mandatory sentences. Institutionalized delinquents may be released on *aftercare* (the equivalent of parole) at any time, at the discretion of the school's director or appropriate professional staff.

REFORMING THE JUVENILE COURT

Getting tough with juveniles

As a consequence of the spiraling juvenile crime rate and the apparent failure of the juvenile court to rehabilitate, the present-day juvenile justice system is on the verge of the most radical changes since its origin in 1899.[32] In order to make some youths more answerable for their conduct, there are demands for more certain and severe punishment—longer and more definite commitments—for juveniles who commit violent crime and those who are repeated serious offenders. Such demands are consistent with the Supreme Court's "legalization" of the juvenile court (extending to juvenile delinquents and children the same rights as adult offenders in criminal cases) and with the increasingly legal treatment of minors who, in effect, are charged with crime. The most severe proposals involve the lowering of the maximum age of juvenile court jurisdiction. This would allow children who are presently handled within the juvenile justice system to be transferred to the criminal court for trial, to be treated as adult offenders, and to be punished as adult criminals. So long as they remain within the juvenile court's jurisdiction, both the child who steals a candy bar and the child who kills someone with a .45 during a holdup can be charged only with juvenile delinquency and can automatically benefit from the *parens patriae* philosophy and disposition structure of the juvenile court.[33]

To remedy this situation, states are taking action to reduce the age limit of juvenile court jurisdiction and are revising their juvenile codes to make room for punishment as a proper objective of disposition in certain cases. Washington state's Juvenile Justice Act of 1977 provides for "punishment commensurate with the age, crime, and criminal history of the juvenile offender."[34] New York's 1978 amendment to the penal code provides for treating 13, 14, and 15 year olds who commit designated acts as criminally responsible and subject to mandatory minimum prison terms.[35] Such legislation is intended to assure that young murderers, rapists, robbers, arsonists, and other violent offenders are not released from training schools within four to ten months. In 1973 Georgia authorized that capital felons could be tried in adult court at 13 years of age, and in 1975 New Mexico lowered the age at which juvenile defendants could be tried for first-degree murder in that state.[36] Other related efforts to implement deterrence and punishment for juveniles include reducing the age at which adjudicated delinquents can be sent to long-term custodial facilities run by the State Department of Corrections and transferring uncontrollable younger children accused of specified crimes to adult court directly or when they prove ungovernable in juvenile training schools.[37]

The Juvenile Justice Standards Project

A national commission to develop and implement comprehensive standards of juvenile justice was established in February 1971 by the Institute of Judicial Administration and the American Bar Association. The Commission's work centered around the Juvenile Justice Standards Project (JJSP). Judge Irving Kaufman, co-chairperson of the Joint Commission on Juvenile Standards, declared that "the rehabilitative ideal has proved a failure" and urged that the sentencing of juvenile offenders be geared to the gravity of the offense. His position was echoed by the president of the National Council of Juvenile Court Judges: "Sometimes the child's needs *are* determined by what a child has done."[38]

In 1977 the joint commission's recommendations were published in the 24 volumes of the *Juvenile Justice Standards Project.*[39] They included:

letting the punishment more closely fit the crime (as opposed to the juvenile court's traditional view of fitting the disposition to the needs of the child);
removing noncriminal status offenses from the jurisdiction of the juvenile court (truants, runaways, incorrigibles, and other status offenders would be diverted to Youth Service Bureaus);
removing the secrecy surrounding juvenile court proceedings and the sentencing process;
establishing clear criteria by which juveniles could be transferred from the jurisdiction of the juvenile court to that of the adult criminal court;
limiting the discretion of judges and abolishing indeterminate sentences;
removing from institutional authorities their discretion to decide when to release juveniles on aftercare;
permitting adjudicated delinquents to participate in selecting their own training and education programs (for a juvenile committed to a state institution, involvement in rehabilitation would be strictly voluntary);
having the prosecutor present at every proceeding in juvenile court, including the disposition hearing;
granting the right to a jury trial and allowing juveniles to direct their own defense.

The approach taken by the standards project in dealing with delinquency was a rational and measured response to a complex issue. The JJSP did not advocate eliminating consideration of the child's needs at disposition; even for the most violent offenses, the commission set two years as the maximum sentence. But it did break new ground in recommending that the seriousness of the crime, the degree of guilt, and the prior record should be included and reflected in the determination of sentence.[40] And by no longer allowing parole boards or institutional administrators to decide when to release youths, sentences would become more definite without being mandatory, the threat of punishment would be more believable, and incapacitation would be more effective.[41] In seeking to make juveniles legally more responsible for their actions, the 30-member commission formulated a single criminal code designed uniquely for juveniles. The commission's hope is that its guidelines will provide the basis for new and improved legislation on juvenile justice among the states, just as the Model Penal Code has for sentencing adults.[42]

SUMMARY

The origin and function of the juvenile court are rooted in diversion, rehabilitation, and *parens patriae*—features that permeate the entire juvenile justice system. Due process, lawyers, and legal technicalities were intentionally excluded from juvenile court proceedings on the theory that they would interfere with the court's achieving these goals. Beginning in the mid 1960s, however, the Supreme Court applied the Constitution to juveniles at the adjudication stage. The landmark decision, *In re Gault,* gave juveniles the right to remain silent, the right to counsel, and the right to be supplied with a lawyer if unable to afford their own. The basic structure of the contemporary juvenile court system consists of intake, the adjudication hearing, and disposition. The court's historic mission of rehabilitating rather than punishing juvenile offenders is reflected in its reliance on probation even for serious violators and the indeterminate nature of commitments to training schools. But dissatisfaction with abuses in juvenile court operation, the rising tide of juvenile crime, and the belief that punishment would be appropriate in some cases are responsible for an emerging "get tough" approach that includes greater reliance on institutionalization, more determinate commitments, and facilitation of the transfer of juveniles to the criminal courts.

DISCUSSION QUESTIONS

1. What changes are occurring in your community that concern the operation of the juvenile justice system?
2. What control do criminal courts have over juvenile offenders?
3. Why was a preponderance of the evidence, rather than proof beyond a reasonable doubt, the standard originally used in the juvenile court?
4. Should status offenses be removed from the jurisdicion of the juvenile court? Why?

References

Abbreviations Used in the Notes

ABS	*American Behavioral Scientist*
ACL	*American Criminal Law Review*
AJC	*American Journal of Correction*
CD	*Crime and Delinquency*
CJB	*Criminal Justice and Behavior*
CJR	*Criminal Justice Review*
CLB	*Criminal Law Bulletin*
Corrections	*Corrections Magazine*
JCC	*Journal of Criminal Law and Criminology*
JCJ	*Journal of Criminal Justice*
JCL	*Journal of Criminal Law, Criminology and Police Science*
JPS	*Journal of Police Science and Administration*
JRC	*Journal of Research in Crime and Delinquency*
LEB	*FBI Law Enforcement Bulletin*
LSR	*Law and Society Review*
PAR	*Public Administration Review*
Resolution	*Resolution of Correctional Problems and Issues*
Standards and Goals Commission	National Advisory Commission on Criminal Justice Standards and Goals
President's Crime Commission	President's Commission on Law Enforcement and Administration of Justice

Chapter 1

1. *Time,* June 30, 1975, p. 18.
2. Donald Cressey, *Crime and Criminal Justice* (Chicago: Quadrangle, 1971), p. 8.
3. *Crime in the United States—1979* (Washington, D.C.: U.S. Department of Justice), p. 35.
4. John F. Bordreau et al., *Arson and Arson Investigation: Survey and Assessment* (Washington, D.C.: Government Printing Office, October 1977), p. 17.
5. *Crime in the United States—1979* (Washington, D.C.: U.S. Department of Justice), p. 35.
6. Harry M. Shulman, "The Measurement of Crime in the United States," *JCL,* December 1966, p. 486.
7. Peter W. Greenwood, *An Analysis of the Apprehension Activities of the New York City Police Department* (New York: New York City Rand Institute, September 1970), pp. 18–19.

8. *Uniform Crime Reports 1974* (Washington, D.C.: Government Printing Office, 1974), Table 30 at p. 182 and Table 34 at p. 186.
9. Shlomo Shinnar and Reuel Shinnar, "The Effects of the Criminal Justice System on the Control of Crime: A Quantitative Approach," *LSR,* Summer 1975, p. 597.
10. *National Observer,* April 8, 1972, p. 6.
11. William L. Cahalan, "Certainty of Punishment," *Prosecutor* 9:9, p. 478.
12. Remarks of President to the California State Legislature, Press Secretary Release, September 5, 1975, p. 5.
13. *Boston Globe,* October 12, 1975, section 1, p. 7.
14. Richard L. Block, "Police Action as Reported by Victims of Crime," *Police,* November-December 1970, p. 43; Phillip H. Ennis, "Crime, Victims, and the Police," *Trans-action,* June 1967, p. 39.
15. *Crime in the Nation's Five Largest Cities: Advance Report* (Washington, D.C.: National Criminal Justice Information and Statistics Service, April 1974), p. v.
16. *Criminal Victimization in the United States: A 1973 Advance Report on the National Crime Panel Survey* (Washington, D.C.: National Criminal Justice Information and Statistics Service, May 1975), p. iv.
17. See John B. Cordrey, "Crime Rates, Victims, Offenders: A Victimization Study," *JPS,* March 1975, p. 110.
18. *Crime and Victims: A Report on the Dayton-San Jose Pilot Survey of Victimization* (Washington, D.C.: National Criminal Justice Information and Statistics Service, June 1974), Table 12 at p. 24.
19. Roland J. Chilton and Adele Spielberger, "Increases in Crime: The Utility of Alternative Measures," *JCL,* March 1972, p. 72; Michael J. Hindelang, "The Uniform Crime Reports Revisited," *JCJ,* Spring 1974, pp. 14–15.
20. Wesley Skogan, "Measurement Problems in Official and Survey Crime Rates," *JCJ,* Spring 1975, p. 25.
21. Cordrey, "Crime Rates," p. 110.
22. Standards and Goals Commission, *Criminal Justice System* (Washington, D.C.: Government Printing Office, January 1973), p. 205.
23. President's Crime Commission, *The Challenge of Crime in a Free Society* (Washington, D.C.: Government Printing Office, February 1967), pp. 50–51.
24. President's Crime Commission, *Crime and Its Impact–An Assessment,* p. 87.
25. *New York Times,* November 2, 1974, p. 36; *Wall Street Journal,* June 24, 1976, p. 1.
26. *LEAA Newsletter,* March 1974, p. 15.
27. See Kurt Weis and Michael E. Milakovitch, "Political Misuses of Crime Rates," *Society,* July–August 1974, p. 28.
28. "Fear of Crime Haunts the U.S.," *Newsweek,* September 29, 1980; *New York Times,* September 17, 1980, p. 5.
29. See Alan L. Otten, "The Shortening Odds on Murder," *Skeptic,* Special Issue no. 4, n.d., p. 10.
30. *Time,* June 30, 1975, p. 11.
31. Lawrence Mosher, "Fear by Day, Terror by Night," *National Observer,* January 13, 1973, p. 1.
32. *New York Times,* June 5, 1975, p. 41.

Chapter 2

1. Livingston Hall et al., *Modern Criminal Procedure* (St. Paul: West, 1969), p. 9.
2. Ibid., p. 10.
3. Ibid., p. 6.
4. *Coleman* v. *Alabama,* 399 U.S. 1 (1970).
5. Marvin E. Frankel and Gary P. Naftalis, *The Grand Jury: An Institution on Trial* (New York: Hill & Wang, 1977), pp. 18–19.
6. *Hamilton* v. *Alabama,* 368 U.S. 52 (1961).
7. *New York Times,* December 9, 1977, p. D1.
8. *Duncan* v. *Louisiana,* 391 U.S. 145 (1968).
9. President's Crime Commission, *Corrections,* p. 70.
10. "Justice on Trial," *Newsweek,* March 8, 1971.
11. Dan Freed, "The Nonsystem of Criminal Justice," in National Commission on the Causes and Prevention of Violence, *Law and Order Reconsidered* (Washington, D.C.: Government Printing Office, n.d.), pp. 265–284.
12. *Reform of the Federal Criminal Laws,* U.S. Congressional Hearings on June 13, 17, July 19, 22, 1974, p. 8102.
13. *Report of the National Advisory Commission on Civil Disorders* (Washington, D.C.: Government Printing Office, 1968), pp. 3, 5, 8, 81.
14. *NCCD News,* May–June 1965, p. 1.
15. Richard Harris, *The Fear of Crime* (New York: Praeger, 1971), p. 10.
16. Norval Morris, "Random Reflections on 'The Challenge of Crime in a Free Society,'" *LSR,* February 1968, p. 278.
17. *The Challenge of Crime in a Free Society* notes seven areas; I have combined the sixth and seventh points, which are substantively the same.
18. *Report of the National Advisory Commission,* p. 65.
19. Harris, *The Fear of Crime,* pp. 7, 18.
20. A large part of the material in this section is based on Gerald D. Robin, "The Emerging New Criminal Justice System," *Journal of Applied Behavioral Science,* July–August 1974, pp. 347–360.
21. Michael S. Serrill, "LEAA," *Corrections,* June 1976, p. 4.
22. *Criminal Justice Newsletter,* August 1970, p. 3.
23. *LEAA Newsletter,* November 1970, p. 5.
24. *Criminal Justice Newsletter,* October 8, 1979, p. 1.
25. *LEAA Newsletter,* December 1971, p. 2.
26. *Criminal Justice Newsletter,* June 9, 1980, p. 4.
27. *Criminal Justice Newsletter,* August 4, 1980, p. 1.

Chapter 3

1. James Q. Wilson, "Dilemmas of Police Administration," *PAR,* September–October 1968, pp. 407–417.
2. Roy R. Roberg, "The Current Police Role: Some Critical Implications of Patrol Work," in Roberg, *The Changing Police Role: New Dimensions and New Issues* (San Jose: Justice Systems Development, 1976), pp. 87–96.
3. Charles McDowell, "The Police as Victims of Their Own Misconceptions," *JCL,* September 1971, p. 435; James J. Teevan, Jr., and Bernard Dolnick, "The Values of the Police: A Reconsideration and Interpretation," *JPS,* September 1973, p. 368.
4. Egnon Bittner, *The Functions of the Police in Modern Society* (Rockville, Md.: NIMH Center for Studies of Crime and Delinquency, 1972), pp. 36–47, 112.

5. Thomas E. Bercal, "Calls for Police Assistance," *ABS,* May–August 1970, p. 682; Herman Goldstein, "Police Responses to Urban Crime," *PAR,* September–October 1968, p. 418.
6. Bittner, *The Functions of the Police,* p. 41.
7. Ibid.
8. Jack E. Whitehouse, "Historical Perspectives on the Police Community Service Function," *JPS,* March 1973, p. 92.
9. Jerome Skolnick, *Justice Without Trial* (New York: Wiley, 1966), pp. 42–70; idem., "Why Cops Behave The Way They Do," *New York Times Magazine,* October 23, 1966, pp. 12–14.
10. There is empirical support for the focal concern of patrol officers to danger. See Larry L. Tifft, "The 'Cop Personality' Reconsidered," *JPS,* September 1974, Table 1 at p. 270.
11. George L. Kirkham, "From Professor to Patrolman: A Fresh Perspective on the Police," *JPS,* June 1974, p. 136.
12. See James Q. Wilson, "The Police and Their Problems: A Theory," in Arthur Niederhoffer and Abraham S. Blumberg, *The Ambivalent Force* (San Francisco: Rinehart Press, 1973), pp. 293–307.
13. For a discussion of danger stress in relation to isolation, see Rodney W. Lewis, "Toward An Understanding of Police Anomie," *JPS,* December 1973, pp. 484–490.
14. Egnon Bittner, "Florence Nightingale in Pursuit of Willie Sutton," in Herbert Jacob, ed., *The Potential for Reform of Criminal Justice* (Beverly Hills: Sage, 1974), pp. 87–88.
15. John H. McNamara, "Uncertainties in Police Work," in David J. Bordua, *The Police: Six Sociological Essays* (New York: Wiley, 1967), Table 31 at p. 246.
16. Gerald W. Lynch, "Cooperation and Competition Among Police Officers," *JPS,* September 1973, p. 322.
17. William M. Kephart, *Racial Factors and Urban Law Enforcement* (Philadelphia: University of Pennsylvania Press, 1957), p. 107.
18. McNamara, "Uncertainties," pp. 194–195.
19. Robert C. Trojanowitz, "The Policeman's Occupational Personality," *JCL,* December 1971, Table 3 at p. 555.
20. Quinn Tamm, "Changes in Role Concepts of Police Officers: A Research Project," *Police Chief,* July 1972, p. 14; Martin Symonds, "Emotional Hazards of Policework," *American Journal of Psychoanalysis,* vol. 30, 1970, pp. 155–160.
21. David M. Rafky, "Police Race Attitudes and Labelling," *JPS,* March 1973, pp. 65–86, especially pp. 71–72; David H. Bayley and Harold Mendelsohn, *Minorities and the Police: Confrontation in America* (New York: Free Press, 1971), p. 144.
22. McNamara, "Uncertainties," Table 16 at p. 222, and p. 214.
23. C. E. Teasley III and Leonard Wright, "The Effects of Training on Police Recruit Attitudes," *JPS,* June 1973, pp. 244–245; Robert W. Balch, "The Police Personality: Fact or Fiction?" *JCL,* March 1972, pp. 106–119; Teevan and Dolnick, "Values of the Police," pp. 366–369.
24. Charles D. Reese, "Police Academy Training and Its Effects on Racial Prejudice," *JPS,* September 1973, pp. 257–268.
25. Kirkham, "From Professor," pp. 127–137; idem., "Doc Cop," *Human Be-*

havior, May 1975, pp. 16–23; idem., "A Professor's 'Street Lessons,'" *LEB,* March 1974, pp. 14–22.
26. *Standards Relating to the Urban Police Function* (New York: Institute of Judicial Administration, Approved Draft, 1973), pp. 19, 80, 93–94.
27. President's Crime Commission, *Police,* pp. 13–38; Standards and Goals Commission, *Police,* pp. 21–28.
28. Stephen A. Schiller, "More Light on a Low Visibility Function: The Selective Enforcement of Laws," *Police Law Quarterly,* July 1972, pp. 6–11; Albert J. Reiss, *The Police and the Public* (New Haven: Yale University Press, 1972), p. 76; Joseph Goldstein, "Police Discretion Not to Invoke the Criminal Process," in Abraham S. Goldstein and Joseph Goldstein, eds., *Crime, Law and Society* (New York: Free Press, 1971), p. 151.
29. Harvey G. Friedman, "Some Jurisprudential Considerations in Developing an Administrative Law for the Criminal Pre-Trial Process," *Journal of Urban Law,* February 1974, p. 442.
30. President's Crime Commission, *Police,* p. 7.
31. John C. Ball, "The Status of Criminological Research in the Federal Government," *Criminology,* May 1974, p. 6.
32. Gerald D. Robin, "Patterns of Department Store Shoplifting," *Crime and Delinquency,* April 1963, pp. 167–168.
33. Harold E. Pepinsky, "Police Patrolmen's Offense-Reporting Behavior," *JRC,* January 1976, p. 38.
34. Reiss, *Police and the Public,* p. 134.
35. William A. Westley, "Violence and the Police," *American Journal of Sociology,* July 1953, pp. 34–41.
36. Carl Wertman and Irving Piliavin, "Gang Members and the Police," in Bordua, *The Police,* pp. 56–98; Irving Piliavin and Scott Briar, "Police Encounters with Juveniles," *American Journal of Sociology,* September 1964, pp. 206–214; Richard J. Lundman, "Routine Police Arrest Practices: A Commonweal Perspective," *Social Problems,* October 1974, pp. 134–135; Albert Reiss, "Police Control of Juveniles," *American Sociological Review,* February 1970, pp. 74–75; Theodore N. Ferdinand and Elmer G. Luchterhand, "Inner-City Youth, The Police, The Juvenile Court, and Justice," *Social Problems,* Spring 1970, pp. 515–518; Larry J. Siegel, Dennis Sullivan, and Jack R. Greene, "Decision Games Applied to Police Decision Making," *JCJ,* Summer 1974, p. 141.
37. Nathan Goldman, *The Differential Selection of Juvenile Offenders for Court Appearance* (New York: National Council on Crime and Delinquency, 1963).
38. Ferdinand and Luchterhand, "Inner-City Youth," pp. 518–519.
39. Siegel, Sullivan, and Greene, "Decision Games," Tables 1, 2, and 3 at pp. 137–139.
40. Richard C. Smith et al., "Background Information: Does It Affect The Misdemeanor Arrest?" *JPS,* March 1976, pp. 111–113.
41. Joseph Goldstein, "Police Discretion," p. 151.
42. Siegel, Sullivan, and Greene, "Decision Games," p. 142.
43. Sanford H. Kadish, "Legal Norm and Discretion in the Police and Sentencing Process," *Harvard Law Review,* March 1962, pp. 904–931; Herman Goldstein, "Police Policy Formulation," *Michigan Law Review,* April 1967, pp. 1123–1146; Theodore K. Moran, "Judicial Administrative Control of

Police Discretion," *JPS,* December 1976, pp. 412–418; Jack B. Molden, "Management Reduction of Police Legal Discretion," *Police Law Quarterly,* October 1972, pp. 5–10.

44. The insightful remarks of Fred A. Wileman were helpful to me in preparing this section. Fred A. Wileman, ed., "Guidelines for Discretion: Five Models for Local Enforcement Agencies," (Madison: University of Wisconsin Institute of Governmental Affairs, mimeo., n.d.).
45. See James C. Zurcher and S. Betsy Cohen, "Officer Discretion: Limits and Guidelines," *Police Chief,* June 1976, pp. 38–40.
46. Schiller, "More Light," *Police Law Quarterly,* October 1972, p. 21.
47. Robert M. Igleburger, John E. Angell, and Gary Pence, "Changing Urban Police: Practitioners' View," in *Criminal Justice Monograph: Innovation in Law Enforcement* (Washington, D.C.: National Institute of Law Enforcement and Criminal Justice, June 1973), pp. 86–87.
48. Glenn Abernathy, "Police Discretion and Equal Protection," *South Carolina Law Quarterly,* Summer 1962, p. 475.
49. The five points are based on Schiller, "More Light," *Police Law Quarterly,* April 1973, p. 37.
50. Moran, "Judicial Administrative Control," p. 417.
51. James Q. Wilson, *Thinking About Crime* (New York: Basic Books, 1975), pp. 82–83.
52. S. James Press, *Some Effects of an Increase in Police Manpower in the 20th Precinct of New York City* (New York: New York City Rand Institute, October 1971), p. 2.
53. Jan M. Chaiken et al., *The Impact of Police Activity on Crime: Robberies on the New York City Subway System* (New York: New York City Rand Institute, 1974).
54. *Experiments in Police Improvement: A Progress Report* (Washington, D.C.: Police Foundation, n.d.), p. 36.
55. Edward M. Davis and Lyle Knowles, "An Evaluation of the Kansas City Preventive Patrol Experiment," *Police Chief,* June 1975, p. 25.
56. John C. Meyer, "The Reactive and Proactive Models of Information Search and Utilization by Police," *JPS,* September 1973, pp. 312–313.
57. Richard C. Larson, "What Happened to Patrol Operations in Kansas City?" *JCJ,* Winter 1975, pp. 267–297; Richard Ward, "Kansas City Patrol Experiments Raise Doubts," *Law Enforcement News,* September–October 1975, p. 2; Steven E. Fienberg, Kinley Larnzt, and Albert J. Reiss, "Redesigning the Kansas City Preventive Patrol Experiment," *Evaluation,* vol. 3, 1976, pp. 124–131; Davis and Knowles, "An Evaluation," p. 22; Harold Tytell, "Citizens, Patrol Commanders, and the Kansas City Preventive Patrol Experiment, *Police Chief,* November 1975, pp. 42–43.
58. George L. Kelling et al., *The Kansas City Preventive Patrol Experiment: A Summary Report* (Washington, D.C.: Police Foundation, 1974).
59. See Charles Bahn, "The Reassurance Factor in Police Patrol," *Criminology,* November 1974, pp. 338–345.
60. *Newsweek,* May 31, 1976, pp. 46–47.
61. "Justice on Trial," *Newsweek,* March 8, 1971.
62. Isaac Ehrlich, "Participating in Illegitimate Activities," in Gary S. Becker and William M. Landers, eds., *Essays in the Economics of Crime and Punishment* (New York: National Bureau of Economic Research, 1974), pp.

111–112; G. Swimmer, "The Relationship of Police and Crime," *Criminology,* November 1974, p. 313; Llad Phillips and Harold L. Votey, "An Economic Analysis of the Deterrent Effect of Law Enforcement on Criminal Activity," *JCL,* September 1972, pp. 330–342; Charles R. Wellford, "Crime and the Police," *Criminology,* August 1974, pp. 195–213; Lucius J. Riccio, "Direct Deterrence," *JCJ,* Fall 1974, pp. 207–217; John Tepper Martin, "City Crime," *CLB,* September 1973, pp. 557–604.

63. George F. Maher, "Organizing a Team for Hostage Negotiations," *Police Chief,* June 1976, pp. 61–62.
64. William L. Tafoya, "Special Weapons and Tactics," *Police Chief,* July 1975, pp. 70–74.
65. *Philadelphia Bulletin,* March 28, 1976, section 3, p. 1.
66. "The SWAT Squads," *Newsweek,* June 23, 1975, p. 95.
67. *Boston Globe,* July 27, 1975, section 1, p. 1.
68. "The SWAT Squads," p. 95.
69. *New York Times,* July 20, 1975, section 4, p. 7.
70. Capt. Patrick J. McGovern and Lt. Charles P. Connolly, "Decoys, Disguises, Danger—New York City's Nonuniform Street Patrol," *LEB,* October, 1976, p. 21.
71. Ibid., pp. 16–26.
72. "The Entrapment Game," *Newsweek,* November 15, 1976, p. 79.
73. *Newsweek,* February 28, 1977, p. 11.
74. *New York Times,* October 5, 1975, section 1, pp. 1, 62; *New York Times,* March 8, 1975, p. 27; *Target,* February 1977; "The Sting's the Thing," *Newsweek,* February 28, 1977, p. 11.
75. *U.S. News & World Report,* February 18, 1980, p. 19.
76. Joseph M. Livermore, "Enforcement Workshop: Abscam Entrapment," *Criminal Law Bulletin,* January–February, pp. 69–70; Stephen Gillers, "Entrapment, Where Is Thy Sting?" *The Nation,* February 23, 1980, p. 203.
77. *U.S.* v. *Harry P. Jannotti and George X. Schwartz,* U.S. Dist. Ct., Eastern Dist. of Penna., No. 80-166, November 26, 1980, p. 61.
78. *U.S.* v. *Russell,* 93 S. Ct. 1637 (1973).
79. *Target,* February 1977, cover page.
80. Michael Putney, "That Crime Computer," *National Observer,* June 30, 1973, p. 5.
81. *LEAA Newsletter,* May 1973, p. 11.
82. *New York Times,* September 5, 1975, pp. 27, 47; *Boston Herald Advertiser,* August 10, 1975, section 2, p. 28.
83. Gilbert Geis, *Not the Law's Business?* (Rockville, Md.: NIMH Center for Studies of Crime and Delinquency, 1972).
84. Alexander B. Smith and Harriet Pollack, *Some Sins Are Not Crimes* (New York: F. Watts, 1975).
85. "Tricks That Smugglers Use," *U.S. News & World Report,* March 14, 1977, pp. 52–54.
86. "San Francisco Mean Streets," *Newsweek,* December 20, 1976, p. 34; "Of Human Bondage," *Newsweek,* April 26, 1976, p. 35.
87. "Police: The Simple Steps to Corruption," *Psychology Today,* January 1975, p. 20; Ray R. Price, "Victimless Crime," *Social Work,* July 1974, p. 408.

88. *New York Times,* May 4, 1975, p. 42.
89. *New York Times,* April 4, 1976, section 1, p. 1.

Chapter 4

1. Albert J. Reiss, *The Police and the Public* (New Haven: Yale University Press, 1972), p. iii.
2. Albert J. Reiss, "Police Brutality—Answers to Key Questions," *Transaction,* July–August 1968, p. 17.
3. Reiss, *Police and the Public,* p. 53.
4. Reiss, "Police Brutality," p. 15.
5. Ibid., p. 18.
6. *U.S. News & World Report,* August 27, 1979, p. 27.
7. *Time,* August 27, 1979, p. 27.
8. Ibid.
9. *New York Times,* October 31, 1979, pp. 1, 18.
10. Bruce Cory, "The New Politics of Deadly Force," *Police Magazine,* March 1981, p. 10.
11. *Newsweek,* July 4, 1977, p. 24.
12. *Rizzo* v. *Goode,* 423 U.S. 362 (1976).
13. Catherine H. Milton et al., *Police Use of Deadly Force* (Washington, D.C.: Police Foundation, 1977), p. 41.
14. Robert N. Brenner and Majorie Kravitz, *A Community Concern: Police Use of Deadly Force* (Washington, D.C.: Superintendent of Documents, January 1979), p. 92; Arthur L. Kobler, "Police Homicide in a Democracy," *Journal of Social Issues,* v. 31, No. 1, 1975, pp. 164–165.
15. See Gerald D. Robin, "Justifiable Homicide by Police Officers," *Journal of Criminal Law, Criminology and Police Science,* June 1963, pp. 225–231.
16. Floyd R. Finch, "Deadly Force to Arrest: Triggering Constitutional Review," *Harvard Civil Rights—Civil Liberties Law Review,* v. 11, No. 2, Spring 1976, p. 365.
17. Nicholas John DeRoma, "Justifiable Use of Deadly Force by the Police," *William and Mary Law Review,* Fall 1970, p. 69.
18. See Kenneth R. McCreed and James L. Hague, "Administrative and Legal Aspects to Limit the Use of Firearms by Police Officers," *Police Chief,* January 1975, pp. 48–52.
19. *Model Penal Code* (Philadelphia: The American Law Institute, 1962), section 3.07, pp. 56–57.
20. For example, Ga. Code Ann. sec. 26-902, revised 1969; Ill. Ann Stat. ch. 38, sec. 7-5, 7-9, Smith-Hurd, 1964; La. Rev. Stat. Ann. sec. 14: 20, 1950; N.Y. Penal Law sec. 35.30, McKinney Supp. 1970.
21. *The Challenge of Crime In A Free Society,* p. 119.
22. Lowell Espey, "Permissible Use of Force to Effectuate An Arrest," *Criminal Justice Quarterly,* Fall 1974, pp. 216–218; Jerry W. Wilson, "Deadly Force," *Police Chief,* December 1972, pp. 44–46; "The Use of Force in Effecting or Resisting Arrest," *Nebraska Law Review,* v. 33, 1954, pp. 408–426.
23. Robin, p. 226.
24. Milton, p. 19.
25. Marshall W. Meyer, "Police Shootings at Minorities: The Case of Los Angeles," *Annals,* November 1980, pp. 102–103.

26. Paul Takagi, "A Garrison State In 'Democratic' Society," *Crime and Social Justice,* Spring–Summer 1974, p. 29.
27. John S. Goldkamp, "Minorities As Victims of Police Shootings: Interpretations of Racial Disproportionality and Police Use of Deadly Force," *Justice System Journal,* vol. 2, No. 2, 1976, pp. 169–183.
28. Takagi, "A Garrison State," p. 30; Editors, "The Management of Police Killings," *Crime and Social Justice,* Fall–Winter 1977, pp. 34–43; Clifton Rhead et al., "The Psychological Assessment of Police Candidates," in Arthur Niederhoffer and Abraham S. Blumberg, *The Ambivalent Force: Perspectives on the Police* (San Francisco: Rinehart Press, 1973), p. 58.
29. Richard W. Harding and Richard P. Fahey, "Killings by Chicago Police, 1969–1970: An Empirical Study," *Southern California Law Review,* March 1973, p. 311; Milton, *Police Use of Deadly Force,* p. 11.
30. Richard E. E. Kania and Wade C. Mackey, "Police Violence as a Function of Community Characteristics," *Criminology,* May 1977, p. 48.
31. Ibid.
32. Goldkamp, "Minorities As Victims," pp. 178–179.
33. George A. Hayden, "Police Discretion in the Use of Deadly Force: An Empirical Study of Information Usage in Deadly Force Decision-making," *Journal of Police Science and Administration,"* March 1981, pp. 102–107.
34. Arthur L. Kobler, "Police Homicide in a Democracy," *Journal of Social Issues,* vol. 31, No. 1, 1975, p. 165.
35. Milton, *Police Use of Deadly Force,* p. 10; Lawrence Sherman, "Enforcement Workshop: Restricting the License to Kill," *Criminal Law Bulletin,* November–December 1978, p. 583; Bruce Cory, "Deadly Force," *Police Magazine,* November 1978, p. 6.
36. Cory, Ibid., p. 8.
37. Ibid., p. 10.
38. James Q. Wilson, "Police Use of Deadly Force," *FBI Law Enforcement Bulletin,* August 1980, p. 20.
39. *New York Times,* March 15, 1981, p. 26.
40. James J. Fyfe, "Deadly Force," *FBI Law Enforcement Bulletin,* December 1979, p. 7.
41. Albert J. Reiss, "Controlling Police Use of Deadly Force," *Annals,* vol. 452, November 1980, p. 126.
42. *New York Times,* October 12, 1980, p. 61.
43. Fyfe, "Deadly Force," p. 8.
44. Cory, "Deadly Force," p. 8.
45. Cory, "The New Politics," p. 11.
46. Bruce Cory, "Police on Trial in Houston," *Police Magazine,* July 1978, p. 40.
47. Cory, "Deadly Force," pp. 12–13.
48. James J. Fyfe, "Administrative Interventions on Police Shooting Discretion: An Empirical Examination," *Journal of Criminal Justice,* Winter 1979, p. 316.
49. *Time,* August 18, 1980, p. 44.
50. Fyfe, "Deadly Force," p. 8.
51. Fyfe, "Administrative Interventions," pp. 319–320.
52. Meyer, "Police Shootings at Minorities," note 5 at p. 101; Reiss, "Controlling Police Use of Deadly Force," p. 126.

53. Cory, "The New Politics," p. 11. See also Lee P. Brown, "Reducing The Use of Deadly Force: The Atlanta Experience," in *Police Use of Deadly Force: What Police and the Community Can Do About It* (Washington, D.C.: Superintendent of Documents, 1979), pp. 20–27.
54. Paul Chevigny, *Police Power: Police Abuses in New York City* (New York: Vintage Books, 1969), p. 260; David P. Riley, "Should Communities Control Their Police?" in Anthony Platt and Lynn Cooper, eds., *Policing in America* (Englewood Cliffs, N.J.: Prentice-Hall, 1974), p. 193.
55. David H. Bayley and Harold Mendelsohn, *Minorities and the Police: Confrontation in America* (New York: Free Press, 1971), pp. 127–135.
56. Harold Beral and Marcus Sisk, "The Administration of Complaints by Civilians Against the Police," *Harvard Law Review,* January 1964, p. 511.
57. For a study of the police-citizen encounters leading to the filing of complaints with the Police Advisory Board, see James R. Hudson, "Police-Citizen Encounters That Lead to Citizen Complaints," *Social Problems,* Fall 1970, pp. 179–193.
58. Herbert L. Packer, "The Courts, the Police, and the Rest of Us," *JCL,* September 1966, p. 243.
59. James R. Hudson, "Police Review Boards and Police Accountability," *Law and Contemporary Problems,* Autumn 1971, pp. 525–538.
60. William H. Hewitt, "New York City's Civilian Complaint Review Board: Its History, Analysis and Some Notes," *Police,* September–October 1967, p. 23.
61. William H. Hewitt, "An Open Letter on Police Review Boards," *Police,* May–June 1966, pp. 33–35.
62. *The Challenge of Crime in a Free Society,* p. 103.
63. H.C. Zarislak, "The Citizen Complaint Process: More Than a Necessary Evil," *Police Chief,* March 1976, pp. 65–67.
64. James S. Hillgren and L.W. Spradlin, "A Positive Disciplinary System for the Dallas Police," *Police Chief,* July 1975, pp. 65–67.
65. Fred M. Broadaway, "Police Misconduct: Positive Alternatives," *JPS,* June 1970, pp. 210–218.
66. "Suing the Cops," *Newsweek,* October 6, 1975, p. 60.
67. "Police Officers Invading Constitutional Rights," *American Bar Association Journal,* October 1975, pp. 1263–1264.
68. *New York Times,* January 18, 1975, p. 28.
69. Michael Putney, "Police, Too, Have Malpractice-Insurance Woes," *National Observer,* November 6, 1976, p. 2.
70. Wayne W. Schmidt, *Survey of Police Misconduct Litigation 1967–71* (Evanston, Ill.: Americans for Effective Law Enforcement, 1974).
71. *AELE Law Enforcement Legal Liability Reporter,* sample issue, 1973, p. 5.
72. Wayne W. Schmidt, "Recent Developments in Police Civil Liability," *JPS,* June 1976, pp. 200–201.
73. Paul E. Smith and Richard O. Hawkins, "Victimization, Types of Citizen-Police Contacts, and Attitudes Toward the Police," *LSR,* Fall 1973, Table 1 at p. 137.
74. *Monroe* v. *Pape,* 365 U.S. 167 (1961).
75. Wayne W. Schmidt, "Recent Developments," p. 200.

76. *Monell* v. *New York City Department of Social Services,* 436 U.S. 658 (1978).
77. Henry C. Black, *Black's Law Dictionary* (St. Paul: West Publishing Co., 1979), p. 1179.
78. Candace McCoy, "Suing The Cops: The Demise of the Nuremberg Defense," *ACJS Today,* October 1980, no page number.
79. *Owen* v. *City of Independence, Mo.,* 100 S. Ct. 1398 (1980).
80. *Maine* v. *Thiboutot,* 100 S. Ct. 2502 (1980); *Scheuer* v. *Rhodes,* 416 U.S. 232 (1974); *Butz* v. *Economou,* 438 U.S. 478 (1977).
81. Robert L. Derbyshire, "Children's Perceptions of the Police," *JCL,* June 1968, pp. 183–190.
82. Robert Wasserman, Michael Paul Gardner, and Alana S. Cohen, *Improving Police/Community Relations* (Washington, D.C.: National Institute of Law Enforcement and Criminal Justice, June 1973), p. 1.
83. Eleanor Harlow, "Problems in Police-Community Relations: A Review of the Literature," *Information Review on Crime and Delinquency,* February 1969, p. 21.
84. Arnold Sagalyn, "The Riot Commission: Recommendations for Law and Order," *Police Chief,* May 1968, p. 45.
85. Harlan Hahn, "Cops and Rioters: Ghetto Perceptions of Social Conflict and Control," *ABS,* May–August 1970, p. 762.
86. President's Crime Commission, *Police,* p. 175.
87. William M. Kroes, Joseph H. Hurrell, and Bruce Margolis, "Job Stress in Police Administrators," *JPS,* December 1974, Table II at p. 383.
88. *San Francisco Chronicle,* December 6, 1967, p. 8.
89. Harold Mendelsohn, "The Police and Their Publics as Reflected in Attitude and Opinion Research," paper presented at the Symposium on Studies of Public Experience, Knowledge and Opinion of Crime and Justice, Washington, D.C., March 17, 1972, p. 7.
90. *The Challenge of Crime in a Free Society,* p. 99.
91. William McCord and John Howard, "Negro Opinions in Three Riot Cities," *ABS,* March–April 1968, p. 25; Burton Levy, "Cops in the Ghetto: A Problem of the Police System," *ABS,* March–April 1968, p. 32; Hahn, "Cops and Rioters," pp. 765–766; Ivan R. Gabor and Christopher Low, "The Police Role in the Community," *Criminology,* February 1973, p. 407; Llana Hadar and John R. Snortum, "The Eye of the Beholder," *CJB,* March 1975, Table 4 at p. 47; Sarah L. Boggs and John F. Galliher, "Evaluating the Police," *Social Problems,* February 1975, p. 393 and Table 2 at p. 401; Herbert Jacob, "Black and White Perceptions of Justice in the City," *LSR,* August 1971, p. 73; Fred I. Klyman and Joanna Kruckenberg, "A Methodology for Assessing Citizen Perceptions of Police," *JCJ,* Fall 1974, Table 3 at p. 227; Smith and Hawkins, "Victimization," p. 137.
92. Harlan Hahn, "Ghetto Assessments of Police Protection and Authority," *LSR,* November 1971, Table 2 at p. 189.
93. *The Challenge of Crime in a Free Society,* p. 100.
94. Gary A. Kreps and Jack M. Weller, "The Police-Community Relations Movement," *ABS,* January–February 1973, p. 406.
95. Gabor and Low, "Police Role in Community," p. 386.

96. James M. Erikson, "Community Service Officers," *Police Chief,* June 1973, pp. 40–46.
97. Henry A. Singer, "The Cop as a Social Scientist," *Police Chief,* April 1970, pp. 52–58; Robert F. Allen, Saul Pilnick, and Stanley Silverzweig, "Conflict Resolution," *JCL,* June 1969, p. 254.
98. Kreps and Weller, "Police-Community Relations," p. 407.
99. Hans Toch, "Change Through Participation," *JRC,* July 1970, pp. 198–206.
100. James H. Tenzel, Lowell Storms, and Harvey Sweetwood, "Symbol and Behavior: An Experiment in Altering the Police Role," *JPS,* March 1976, pp. 21–27; Tenzel and Victor Cizanckas, "The Uniform Experiment," *JPS,* December 1973, pp. 421–424.
101. Raymond Parnas, "Police Discretion and Diversion of Incidents of Intra-Family Violence," *Law and Contemporary Problems,* Autumn 1971, note 1 at pp. 540–541.
102. Raymond I. Parnas, "Judicial Response to Intra-Family Violence," *Minnesota Law Review,* January 1970, p. 594.
103. Morton Bard and Joseph Zacker, "How Police Handle Explosive Squabbles," *Psychology Today,* November 1976, p. 71.
104. Boggs and Galliher, "Evaluating the Police," Table 3 at p. 402.
105. Raymond I. Parnas, "The Response of Some Relevant Community Resources to Intra-Family Violence," *Indiana Law Journal,* Winter 1969, note 71 at p. 178.
106. Marvin E. Wolfgang, *Patterns of Criminal Homicide* (Philadelphia: University of Pennsylvania Press, 1958).
107. Raymond I. Parnas, "The Police Response to the Domestic Disturbance," in Leon Radzinowicz and Marvin E. Wolfgang, *The Criminal in the Arms of the Law* (New York: Basic Books, 1971), p. 213.
108. "Battered Wives: Now They're Fighting Back," *U.S. News & World Report,* September 20, 1976, pp. 47–48.
109. Martha A. Field and Henry F. Field, "Marital Violence and the Criminal Process: Neither Justice Nor Peace," *Social Science Review,* June 1973, p. 229.
110. Parnas, "Judicial Response," p. 594.
111. "Battered Wives," p. 48.
112. "The All-American Blood-Soaked Family," *Human Behavior,* February 1976, p. 35; Field and Field, "Marital Violence," pp. 231–232.
113. Raymond I. Parnas, "Prosecutorial and Judicial Handling of Family Violence," *CLB,* November 1973, pp. 735–736.
114. Parnas, "Judicial Response," pp. 614–616.
115. Donald A. Liebman and Jeffrey A. Schwartz, "Police Programs in Crisis Intervention: A Review," in John R. Snibbe and Homa M. Snibbe, *The Urban Policeman in Transition* (Springfield, Ill.: C. Thomas, 1973), p. 444; Allan Schor, Allen Berman, and Stanley I. Berger, *Training Police as Specialists in Family Crisis Intervention: A Preliminary Study* (Providence: Rhode Island Governor's Committee on Crime and Delinquency, December 1972), p. 7.
116. Morton Bard, *Training Police as Specialists in Family Crisis Intervention* (Washington, D.C.: Government Printing Office, May 1970); idem., "Fam-

ily Intervention Police Teams as a Community Mental Health Resource," *JCL,* June 1969, pp. 247–250; idem., "Alternatives to Traditional Law Enforcement," *Police,* November–December 1970, pp. 20–23; Bard and Zacker, "How Police Handle," p. 71; Bard and Katherine Ellison, "Crisis Intervention and Investigation of Forcible Rape," *Police Chief,* May 1974, pp. 68–74.

117. Bard, "Family Intervention Police Teams," p. 249.
118. For an excellent critique of Dr. Bard's project, methodology, and conclusions, see Liebman and Schwartz, "Police Programs," pp. 427–436; James M. Driscoll, Robert G. Meyer, and Charles F. Schanie, "Training Police in Family Crisis Intervention," *Journal of Applied Behavioral Science,* January–February 1973, pp. 65–66.
119. Myron Katz, "Family Crisis Training," *JPS,* March 1973, pp. 30–35; Driscoll, Meyers, and Schanie, "Training Police," pp. 62–68, esp. pp. 68, 73; *Target,* January 1977; Robert B. Murphy and Ed McKay, "Training Patrolmen to Become Crisis Intervention Specialists," *Police Chief,* December 1975, pp. 44–45.
120. Unless otherwise indicated, material in this section is based on "War on Crime by Fed-Up Citizens," *U.S. News & World Report,* September 29, 1975, pp. 19–21.
121. *LEAA Newsletter,* September–October 1973, p. 35.
122. *National Neighborhood Watch Program Newsletter,* vol. 2, No. 2, 1973; *National Observer,* April 24, 1976, p. 4.
123. August Gribbin, "Wanted by the FBI: Citizens to Fight Crime," *National Observer,* August 2, 1975, p. 4.
124. Robert K. Yin et al., *Patrolling the Neighborhood Beat: Residents and Residential Security* (Santa Monica: Rand, March 1976), pp. 1–2.
125. *Criminal Justice Newsletter,* August 1970, p. 3.
126. Standards and Goals Commission, *Community Crime Prevention,* p. 14.
127. Yin, *Patrolling the Neighborhood Beat,* p. 113.
128. Standards and Goals Commission, *Community Crime Prevention,* p. 14.
129. *New York Times,* November 30, 1974, p. 33.
130. Ron L. Willis, "Senior Citizen Crime Prevention Program," *Police Chief,* February 1976, p. 16.
131. Michael T. Klare, "The Boom in Private Police," *The Nation,* November 15, 1975, p. 487.
132. Clark Whelton, "In Guards We Trust," *New York Times Magazine,* September 19, 1976, p. 21.
133. Unless otherwise noted, material in this section is based on "Special Report: Terror in Schools," *U.S. News & World Report,* January 26, 1976, pp. 52–55.
134. *New York Times,* January 11, 1975, p. 18.
135. "Officials, Students Join to Combat Campus Crime," *U.S. News & World Report,* April 4, 1977, p. 45.
136. *National Observer,* December 23, 1972, p. 18; William B. Howard, "The Use of Paraprofessionals in Police Service," *Police Chief,* January 1977, pp. 52–56.
137. Marianne Stecich, "Keeping an Eye on the Courts: A Survey of Court Observer Programs," *Judicature,* May 1975, pp. 472–473.

138. "War on Crime by Fed-Up Citizens," p. 21.
139. James R. Dickenson, "If You Pay, Crime Won't," *National Observer*, January 27, 1973, p. 17.

Chapter 5

1. James Q. Wilson, *Varieties of Police Behavior* (New York: Atheneum, 1973).
2. James Q. Wilson, "Dilemmas of Police Administration," *PAR*, September–October 1968, p. 409.
3. Gene Stephens, "Criminal Justice Education: Past, Present, and Future," *CJR*, Spring 1976, pp. 93–98.
4. President's Crime Commission, *Police*, p. 109.
5. Ibid., p. 126.
6. Ibid., p. 123.
7. Ibid., p. 142.
8. George D. Eastman and James A. McCain, "Police Managers and Their Perceptions of Higher Education," *JCJ*, Summer 1973, p. 118.
9. P. Schwartz and Eugene O'Bryan, "Survey of Lateral Entry in Police Departments," *Police Chief*, November 1976, pp. 60–61.
10. William L. Tafoya, "Lateral Entry: A Management Perspective," *Police Chief*, April 1974, p. 60.
11. Donald E. Santarelli, "Education for Concepts—Training for Skills," *Police Chief*, August 1974, p. 20.
12. President's Crime Commission, *Police*, p. 127.
13. Standards and Goals Commission, *Police*, p. 369.
14. Ibid., pp. 378–379.
15. Ibid., pp. 362–365.
16. Roy R. Roberg, *The Changing Police Role* (San Jose: Justice System Development, 1976), p. 151.
17. James O. Finckenauer, "Higher Education and Police Discretion," *JPS*, December 1975, p. 451.
18. Alexander B. Smith, Bernard Locke, and Abe Fenster, "Authoritarianism in Policemen Who Are College Graduates and Non-College Police," *JCL*, June 1970, pp. 313–315.
19. Norman L. Weiner, "The Effects of Education on Police Attitudes," *JCJ*, Winter 1974, p. 318.
20. Ibid., p. 324; Robert E. Ford, James Meeker, and Richard Zeller, "Police, Students, and Racial Hostilities," *JPS*, March 1975, p. 14; see also A. Etzioni, "Human Beings Are Not Very Easy to Change After All," *Saturday Review*, June 1972, pp. 45–47.
21. Weiner, "The Effects of Education," p. 325.
22. Egnon Bittner, *The Function of the Police in Modern Society* (Rockville: NIMH Center for Studies of Crime and Delinquency, 1972), p. 86.
23. Lawrence W. Sherman et al., *The Quality of Police Education* (San Francisco: Jossey-Bass Publishers, 1978), pp. 3–9.
24. Thomas A. Reppetto, "Higher Education for Police Officers," *FBI Law Enforcement Bulletin*, January 1980, pp. 19–24; David G. Salten, "A Harsh Criticism of American Policing and Police Education," *Police Chief*, August 1979, pp. 22–26; George T. Felkenes, "Quality of Police Education," *Police Chief*, September 1980, pp. 22–23.

25. Standards and Goals Commission, *Police,* p. 380.
26. *The Challenge of Crime in a Free Society,* p. 112.
27. President's Crime Commission, *Police,* p. 175.
28. *Standards Relating to the Urban Police Function* (New York: Institute of Judicial Administration, Approved Draft, 1973) p. 207.
29. President's Crime Commission, *Police,* p. 138.
30. Ibid., pp. 63–67.
31. Samuel Laudenslager, "Providing Legal Assistance to Small and Rural Law Enforcement Agencies: The Regional Legal Advisor," *Police Chief,* August 1974, p. 53.
32. Stephens, "Criminal Justice Education," p. 99.
33. Walter E. Kreutzer, "The Elusive Professionalization That Police Officers Seek," *Police Chief,* August 1968, p. 27.
34. Dennis Catlin and Larry T. Hoover, "Role of Law Enforcement Training Commissions in the United States," *JCJ,* Winter 1973, p. 348.
35. "What the Police Need To Do a Better Job," *U.S. News & World Report,* December 16, 1974, p. 44.
36. *Project STAR: Project Summary* (Marina del Ray: American Justice Institute); Harry More, "Law Enforcement Education," *Criminology,* February 1973, pp. 505–507.
37. *Criminal Justice Update,* September 1974, p. 1.
38. *LEAA Newsletter,* August 1975, p. 7.
39. Ronald H. Sostkowski and William J. Nash, "Update on Accreditation," *Police Chief,* April 1981, p. 22.
40. Richard S. Allison, "Police Accreditation: A New Effort to Set Standards," *Police Magazine,* January 1980, p. 52.
41. Kenneth E. Joseph, "Law Enforcement Accreditation: Meeting Tomorrow's Challenges Today," *FBI Law Enforcement Bulletin,* October 1980, p. 9.
42. William T. Dean, "Accreditation for Law Enforcement Agencies," *Police Chief,* September 1980, p. 13.
43. President's Crime Commission, *Police,* p. 170.
44. Ibid., p. 171.
45. Standards and Goals Commission, *Police,* p. 330.
46. Anthony Balzer, "A View of the Quota System in the San Francisco Police Department," *JPS,* June 1976, p. 125.
47. Terry Eisenberg and Roger W. Reinke, "The Use of Written Examinations in Selecting Police Officers," *Police Chief,* March 1973, p. 25.
48. *Griggs* v. *Duke Power Co.,* 91 S. Ct. 849 (1971).
49. Elliott Abrams, "The Quota Commission," *Commentary,* October 1972, p. 56.
50. *Criminal Justice Newsletter,* June 11, 1973, pp. 4–5.
51. Abrams, "Quota Commission," p. 54.
52. David M. Rafky, "Racial Discrimination in Urban Police Departments," *CD,* July 1975, note 3 at p. 234; Arthur M. Jefferson, "Equal Employment Opportunity and Affirmative Action in Law Enforcement Agencies," *Resolution,* Summer 1975, p. 17.
53. *LEAA Newsletter,* November 1973, p. 24; *Criminal Justice Newsletter,* September 4, 1973, p. 4.

54. *Time,* January 19, 1976; *LEAA Newsletter,* February 1976, p. 3; *LEAA Newsletter,* January–February 1975, pp. 6–7.
55. Balzer, "View of the Quota System," p. 125; Rafky, "Racial Discrimination," note 3 at p. 234.
56. *Criminal Justice Newsletter,* February 25, 1974, p. 3.
57. *Poverty Law Reporter,* May 1974, p. 3.
58. Joseph T. Rouzan, "Positive Recruitment of Qualified Minorities," *Police Chief,* July 1976, pp. 50–52.
59. Gail Neumann, "Job Related Tests and Police Selection Procedures," *Police Chief,* February 1974, p. 43.
60. *National Observer,* March 25, 1968, p. 22; "Height Makes Right," *Human Behavior Magazine,* March 1974, p. 59.
61. D.P. Van Blaricon, "Recruitment and Retention of Minority Race Persons as Police Officers," *Police Chief,* September 1976, pp. 62–63.
62. *LEAA Newsletter,* December 1972, p. 3.
63. *LEAA Newsletter,* July 1973, p. 15.
64. *New York Times,* December 10, 1974, p. 22.
65. Balzer, "View of the Quota System," p. 129.
66. Dale T. Beerbower, "Equal Employment Opportunity v. Police Professionalism," *Police Chief,* May 1975, p. 65.
67. Roberg, *Changing Police Role,* pp. 219–220.
68. *American Bar Association Journal,* January 1976, pp. 111–112.
69. *Boston Herald American,* September 24, 1975, p. 36.
70. *New York Times,* August 10, 1975, p. 21.
71. *New York Times,* March 25, 1976, p. 29.
72. *Bakke* v. *Regents of the University of California,* No. 76-811 (Washington, D.C.: Bureau of National Affairs, June 28, 1978).
73. *United Steelworkers of America* v. *Weber,* 99 S. Ct. 2721 (1979).
74. Certiorari denied October 2, 1978, No. 77-1718; *United States* v. *City of Philadelphia,* Nos. 77-1707/77-1711 and 77-2140/77-2141.
75. *Fullilove* v. *Klutznick,* No. 78-1007. Decided July 2, 1980.
76. Peter Bloch, Deborah Anderson, and Pamela Gervais, *Policewomen on Patrol* (Washington, D.C.: Police Foundation, February 1973), forward.
77. Ibid., p. 3.
78. Lewis J. Sherman, "A Psychological View of Women in Policing," *JPS,* December 1973, pp. 384, 393.
79. Jude T. Walsh, "Some Questions In Re: 'Policewomen on Patrol,'" *Police Chief,* July 1975, pp. 20–22; see rejoinder by Peter B. Bloch, "Reply to Questions Raised In Re: 'Policewomen on Patrol,'" *Police Chief,* July 1975, pp. 22–23.
80. Anthony V. Bouza, "Women in Policing," *LEB,* September 1975, pp. 2–7.
81. *Boston Herald American,* October 20, 1975, p. 15; Bernard L. Garmire, "Female Officers in the Department," *LEB,* June 1974, pp. 11–13; William O. Weldy, "Women in Policing: A Positive Step Toward Increased Police Enthusiasm," *Police Chief,* January 1976, p. 47.
82. Balzer, "View of the Quota System," p. 124.
83. *New York Times,* September 14, 1976, p. 8.
84. Bouza, "Women in Policing," pp. 4–7.
85. *New York Times,* October 8, 1975, p. 45.

86. "Remarks of Congresswoman Martha W. Griffiths," Police Foundation Symposium on Women in Policing, May 29, 1974.
87. Glen Craig, "California Highway Patrol Women Officers," *Police Chief,* January 1977, p. 60; *Law Enforcement Journal,* April 1974, p. 5.
88. Virginia Armat, "Policewomen in Action," *Saturday Evening Post,* July–August 1975, p. 49.
89. Peggy E. Triplett, "Women in Policing," *Police Chief,* December 1976, p. 46.
90. Armat, "Policewomen in Action," p. 48.
91. Garmire, "Female Officers," p. 13.
92. *Miami Herald,* August 17, 1975, p. 4B.
93. "Remarks of Congresswoman Griffiths."
94. Susan Edmiston, "Policewomen: How Well Are They Doing a 'Man's Job'?" *Ladies Home Journal,* April 1975, p. 126.
95. "What the Police Need," *U.S. News & World Report,* p. 43.
96. "Spotlight Interview: Clarence M. Kelly," *CJR,* Spring 1976, p. 53.
97. *New York Times,* May 11, 1975, section 1, pp. 1, 42.
98. *Improving Police Productivity* (Washington, D.C.: National Commission on Productivity, no date).
99. Henry John Polis, "Police Administration: A Fresh Look," *Police Chief,* March 1976, p. 14.
100. Standards and Goals Commission, *Police,* p. 108.
101. *The Challenge of Crime in a Free Society,* p. 122.
102. Ibid., pp. 121–122.
103. "Police Department Merges," *Trial,* January–February 1971, p. 35; Dale G. Carson, "Consolidation of Police Departments," in *The Police Yearbook of 1970* (Washington, D.C.: International Association of Chiefs of Police, 1970), pp. 91–93.
104. Elinor Ostrom, "Institutional Arrangements and the Measurement of Police Consequences," *Urban Affairs Quarterly,* June 1971, p. 468.
105. Edward M. Davis, "Key to the Future of Policing," *Police Chief,* November 1976, p. 20.
106. George A. Lankas, "Central Services for Police," *JPS,* March 1974, pp. 66–76.
107. *New York Times,* December 28, 1976, p. 50.
108. Elinor Ostrom, Roger B. Parks, and Gordon P. Whitaker, "Do We Really Want to Consolidate Urban Police Forces?" *PAR,* September–October 1973, pp. 423–432; Elinor Ostrom and Dennis C. Smith, "Refuting the Case Against Small Police Departments," *Criminal Justice Newsletter,* May 26, 1975, pp. 4–5.
109. *New York Times,* August 13, 1975, p. 1.
110. *New York Times,* May 15, 1974, p. 47.
111. Ibid.
112. Gary B. Hirsch and Lucius J. Riccio, "Measuring and Improving the Productivity of Police Patrol," *JPS,* June 1974, pp. 176–177.
113. *Uniform Crime Reports 1975* (Washington, D.C.: Government Printing Office, 1975), Table 65 at p. 238.
114. George W. Greisinger, "The Use of Civilians in Police Work," *Police Chief,* July 1976, p. 30.

115. J.M. Morgan and R. Scott Fosler, "Police Productivity," *Police Chief,* July 1974, p. 28; James M. Erikson, "Where the Buck Stops," *Police Chief,* April 1976, p. 16.
116. *New York Times,* October 14, 1975, p. 42.
117. *New York Times,* January 7, 1977, p. 1.
118. O.W. Wilson, "One-Man Patrol Cars," *Police Chief,* May 1963, pp. 18–24.
119. *New York Times,* January 13, 1977, p. 34.
120. Wilson, "One-Man Patrol Cars," p. 24.
121. *New York Times,* September 19, 1976, section 1, pp. 1, 25.
122. Lucy N. Friedman, Samuel S. Herrup, and Hans Zeisel, "Saving Police Manpower Through Court Appearance Control," *JPS,* June 1973, p. 131.
123. Ibid., pp. 131–137.
124. *Standards Relating to the Urban Police Function,* p. 227.
125. Peter B. Bloch and David Specht, *Neighborhood Policing* (Washington, D.C.: Government Printing Office, December 1973); Lee P. Brown and Edgar E. Martin, "Neighborhood Team Policing," *Police Chief,* May 1976, p. 85.
126. Norman R. Knapp, "Coordinated Team Patrol," *LEB,* December 1975, p. 8.
127. Polis, "Police Administration," p. 14; Georgette Bennett Sandler and Ellen Mintz, "Police Organizations: Their Changing Internal and External Relationships," *JPS,* December 1974, p. 462.
128. Brown and Martin, "Neighborhood Team Policing," p. 84.
129. *The Challenge of Crime in a Free Society,* p. 118.
130. Standards and Goals Commission, *Police,* pp. 63–65.
131. Brown and Martin, "Neighborhood Team Policing," p. 84.
132. John E. Angell, "Organizing Police for the Future: An Update of the Democratic Model," *CJR,* Fall 1976; pp. 42–43.
133. Robert B. Koverman, "Team Policing: An Alternative to Traditional Law Enforcement Techniques," *JPS,* March 1974, pp. 18–19.
134. Thomas J. Sardino, "The Crime Control Team," *LEB,* May 1971, p. 19.
135. *LEAA Newsletter,* April 1975, p. 12; *Time,* March 22, 1976, p. 41.
136. Knapp, "Coordinated Team Patrol," p. 6; Bloch and Specht, *Neighborhood Policing,* p. 44.
137. Sardino, "Crime Control Team," p. 30; John T. O'Brien, "The Neighborhood Task Force in New Brunswick, New Jersey," *Police Chief,* June 1975, p. 49.
138. Joseph Maciejewski, "Team Policing Improves Teamwork," *Police Chief,* July 1976, p. 57; John Cordrey and Gary K. Pence, "An Analysis of Team Policing in Dayton, Ohio," *Police Chief,* August 1972, p. 48.
139. Knapp, "Coordinated Team Patrol," p. 8; Joseph S. Koziol, "Team Policing in a Small Department," *Police Chief,* July 1976, p. 15.

Chapter 6

1. Robert C. Finley, "The Appellate System," *Trial,* November–December 1971, p. 20.
2. *Zurcher* v. *Stanford Daily,* 98 S. Ct. 1970 (1978).
3. James R. Thompson and Gary L. Starkman, "The Citizen Informant Doctrine," *JCC,* June 1973, p. 163.

4. *Mincey* v. *Arizona,* 98 S. Ct. 23 (1978).
5. *Chimel* v. *California,* 395 U.S. 752 (1969).
6. *Ker* v. *California,* 374 U.S. 23 (1963).
7. Note, "Excluding the Exclusionary Rule: Congressional Assault on *Mapp* v. *Ohio,*" *Georgetown Law Journal,* July 1973, note 9 at p. 1454.
8. *Weeks* v. *United States,* 232 U.S. 383 (1914).
9. *Wolf* v. *Colorado,* 338 U.S. 25 (1949).
10. *Mapp* v. *Ohio,* 367 U.S. 643 (1961).
11. "Petition for Rehearing: *Mapp* v. *Ohio,*" *JCL,* November–December 1961, p. 439.
12. Theodore Souris, "Stop and Frisk or Arrest and Search—the Use and Misuse of Euphemisms," *JCL,* September 1966, p. 251.
13. William J. Cox, "The Decline of the Exclusionary Rule: An Alternative to Injustice," *Southwestern University Law Review,* Spring 1972, p. 76; "Trends in Legal Commentary on the Exclusionary Rule," *JCC,* September 1974, p. 381.
14. "Excluding the Exclusionary Rule," p. 1457.
15. Dallin H. Oaks, "Studying the Exclusionary Rule in Search and Seizure," *University of Chicago Law Review,* Summer 1970, pp. 665–757; "Trends in Legal Commentary," p. 383; James E. Spiotto, "Search and Seizure: An Empirical Study of the Exclusionary Rule and Its Alternatives," *Journal of Legal Studies,* January 1973, pp. 243–277.
16. Wayne R. LeFave, *Arrest: The Decision to Take a Suspect into Custody* (Boston: Little, Brown, 1965), pp. 437–489.
17. Robert Edward Mitchell, "Organization as a Key to Police Effectiveness," *CD,* October 1966, p. 349.
18. James Vorenberg, "A.L.I. Approves Model Code of Pre-arraignment Procedure," *American Bar Association Journal,* October 1975, p. 1214.
19. National Commission on the Causes and Prevention of Violence, *Law and Order Reconsidered* (Washington, D.C.: Government Printing Office, n.d.), p. 367.
20. Ferinez Phelps, "When Do Policemen Support the Courts?" *Police Chief,* September 1975, p. 49.
21. Sydney C. Cooper, *Dismissal of Narcotic Arrest Cases in the New York City Criminal Court, 1970* (New York: Rand Corporation, July 1973), Table 3 at pp. 10–11.
22. Frank G. Carrington, *The Victims* (New Rochelle, N.Y.: Arlington House, 1975), p. 260; Oaks, "Studying the Exclusionary Rule," p. 756; Fred P. Graham, *The Due Process Revolution* (Rochelle Park, N.J.: Hayden, 1970), p. 152.
23. *Haynes* v. *Washington,* 373 U.S. 503 (1963); Comment, "An Examination of the Right to a Voluntariness Hearing," *JCL,* March 1972, note 12 at p. 31.
24. *Ashcraft* v. *Tennessee,* 322 U.S. 143 (1944); *Watts* v. *Indiana,* 339 U.S. 49 (1949).
25. Gerhard O.W. Mueller, "The Law Relating to Police Interrogation Privileges and Limitations," *JCL,* May–June 1961, p. 9.
26. *Brown* v. *Mississippi,* 297 U.S. 278 (1936).
27. *McNabb* v. *United States,* 318 U.S. 332 (1943).

28. *Mallory* v. *United States,* 354 U.S. 449 (1957).
29. Harry W. More and F.M. Fabian, "The McNabb-Mallory Rule and Law Enforcement," *Police,* September–October 1964, pp. 42–48.
30. Bernard Weisberg, "Police Interrogation of Arrested Persons: A Skeptical View," *JCL,* May–June 1961, p. 31.
31. *Escobedo* v. *Illinois,* 378 U.S. 478 (1964).
32. Weisberg, "Police Interrogation," p. 29.
33. *Escobedo* v. *Illinois,* 378 U.S. 478 (1964).
34. Alan H. Shechter, *Contemporary Constitutional Issues* (New York: McGraw-Hill, 1972), pp. 94–95.
35. *Miranda* v. *Arizona,* 384 U.S. 436 (1966).
36. *Beckwith* v. *United States,* 425 U.S. 341 (1976).
37. *Schmerber* v. *California,* 384 U.S. 757 (1966).
38. *Rochin* v. *California,* 342 U.S. 165 (1952).
39. *In re K.W.B.,* 500 S.W. 2d 275 (1973), described in *Juvenile Court Digest,* May 1974, pp. 69–71.
40. James R. Thompson, "The Supreme Court and the Police: 1968?" *JCL,* December 1966, p. 421; Richard Harris, *The Fear of Crime* (New York: Praeger, 1971), pp. 45–47.
41. David W. Neubauer, "Confessions in Prairie City: Some Causes and Effects," *JCC,* March 1974, pp. 103–113; James W. Witt, "Non-Coercive Interrogation and the Administration of Criminal Justice: The Impact of Miranda on Police Effectuality," *JCC,* September 1973, pp. 320–332; Richard H. Seeburger and R. Stanton Wettick, "Miranda in Pittsburgh—A Statistical Study," *University of Pittsburgh Law Review,* October 1967, pp. 1–26.
42. Michael Wald et al., "Interrogations in New Haven: The Impact of Miranda," *Yale Law Journal,* July 1967, pp. 1519–1648; John Griffiths and Richard E. Ayres, "A Postscript to the Miranda Project: Interrogation of Draft Protestors," *Yale Law Journal,* December 1967, pp. 300–319.
43. Wald, "Interrogations," pp. 1532, 1536–1537, 1543, 1613.
44. Wayland D. Pilcher, "The Law and Practice of Field Interrogation," *JCL,* December 1967, pp. 476, 488.
45. Herman Schwartz, "Stop and Frisk," *JCL,* December 1967, note 15 at p. 436.
46. Evelle J. Younger, "Stop and Frisk: 'Say It Like It Is,'" *JCL,* September 1967, pp. 293–302.
47. Richard H. Kuh, "Reflections on New York's 'Stop and Frisk' Law and Its Claimed Unconstitutionality," *JCL,* March 1965, pp. 32–33.
48. *Terry* v. *Ohio,* 392 U.S. 1 (1968). The opinion consolidated four other cases, including *Peters* from New York.
49. *Model Rules for Law Enforcement: Stop and Frisk* (Washington, D.C.: Arizona State University and Police Foundation, May 1974), pp. 8, 40; John Dennis Miller, "Investigative Detention," *LEB,* December 1974, pp. 26–27.
50. Vorenberg, "A.L.I. Approves Model Code," p. 1214.
51. *Model Rules for Law Enforcement,* p. 7.
52. Kuh, "Reflections," p. 34.
53. William Gangi, "The Supreme Court, Confessions and the Counter-Revolution in Criminal Justice," *Judicature,* August–September 1974, p. 71.

54. *United States* v. *Calandra,* 414 U.S. 338 (1974).
55. *Stone* v. *Powell,* 428 U.S. 465 (1976).
56. *Allen* v. *McCurry,* No. 79-935. Decided December 9, 1980.
57. *Time,* July 19, 1976, pp. 43–44; *Newsweek,* July 19, 1976, p. 58.
58. *Jones* v. *U.S.,* 362 U.S. 257 (1960).
59. *U.S.* v. *Salvucci,* No. 79-244. Decided June 25, 1980.
60. *Simmons* v. *U.S.,* 390 U.S. 377 (1968).
61. *Rakas* v. *Illinois,* 439 U.S. 128 (1978).
62. Ibid.; *U.S.* v. *Payner,* No. 78-1729. Decided June 23, 1980; *Rawlings* v. *Kentucky,* 100 S. Ct. 2556 (1980).
63. Rebecca J. Lauer, "Fourth Amendment—The Court Further Limits Standing," *Journal of Criminal Law and Criminology,* Winter 1980, pp. 567–568.
64. *Harris* v. *New York,* 401 U.S. 222 (1971).
65. See also Charles A. Donelan, "The 'Harris to Hass to Hale' Combination," *LEB,* August 1976, pp. 25–31. *Hass* was a variation of the *Harris* case. *Oregon* v. *William Robert Hass,* 43 L.Ed.2d 570 (1975).
66. *Michigan* v. *Tucker,* 417 U.S. 433 (1974).
67. B.J. George, "From Warren to Burger to Chance: Future Trends in the Administration of Criminal Justice," *CLB,* May–June 1976, p. 265.
68. *Michigan* v. *Mosley,* 423 U.S. 96 (1975).
69. "The Miranda Doctrine on the Decline?" *American Bar Association Journal,* February 1976, p. 230.
70. *Oregon* v. *Mathiason,* 97 S.Ct. 711 (1977).
71. *Brewer* v. *Williams,* 97 S.Ct. 1232 (1977).
72. *New York Times,* October 4, 1976, p. 15; *New York Times,* December 16, 1975, p. 24.
73. *Rhode Island* v. *Innis,* No. 78-1076. Decided May 12, 1980.
74. *Adams* v. *Williams,* 407 U.S. 143 (1972).
75. "Stop and Frisk Revisited," *JCL,* December 1972, p. 525.
76. *United States* v. *Robinson,* 414 U.S. 218 (1973). The companion case was *Gustafson* v. *Florida,* 414 U.S. 260 (1973).
77. *Delaware* v. *Prouse,* 99 S. Ct. 1391 (1979).
78. George, "From Warren to Burger," pp. 256, 258.
79. *Ybarra* v. *Illinois,* 444 U.S. 85 (1979); *Brown* v. *Texas,* No. 77-6673. Decided June 25, 1979.
80. *Kirby* v. *Illinois,* 406 U.S. 682 (1972). See also Walter W. Steele, "*Kirby* v. *Illinois*: Counsel at Lineups," *CLB,* January–February 1973, pp. 49–58.
81. *Wade* v. *United States,* 388 U.S. 218 (1967).
82. *Cupp* v. *Murphy,* 412 U.S. 291 (1973).
83. *New York Times,* April 11, 1976, section 4, p. 9; *New York Times,* January 22, 1976, p. 21.
84. *New York Times,* April 11, 1976, p. 9; John P. MacKenzie, "The Lost Court," *Civil Liberties Review,* October–November 1976, p. 42.
85. *United States* v. *Ash,* 413 U.S. 300 (1973).
86. "Shifting Patterns in High Court," *U.S. News & World Report,* July 19, 1976, p. 59.
87. *United States* v. *Watson,* 423 U.S. 411 (1976).

Chapter 7

1. *North* v. *Russell,* 427 U.S. 328 (1976). See also Allan Ashman and Pat Cha-

pin, "Is the Bell Tolling for Nonlawyer Judges?" *Judicature,* April 1976, p. 417.
2. President's Crime Commission, *Courts,* p. 31.
3. Frank R. Prassel, *Introduction to American Criminal Justice* (New York: Harper & Row, 1975), p. 141.
4. Maureen Mileski, "Courtroom Encounters: An Observation Study of a Lower Criminal Court," *LSR,* May 1971, pp. 480–484.
5. *Wall Street Journal,* May 6, 1976, p. 27.
6. *New York Times,* October 30, 1974, p. 61; President's Crime Commission, *Courts,* pp. 29–35; *New York Times,* June 2, 1975, p. 16; "Rural Justice," *60 Minutes,* CBS-TV, February 22, 1976 (transcript).
7. President's Crime Commission, *Courts,* p. 34.
8. *A Guide to Court Systems* (New York: Institute of Judicial Administration, 1971), pp. 22–23.
9. Harold J. Grilliot, *Introduction to Law and the Legal System* (Boston: Houghton Mifflin, 1975), p. 42.
10. *Guide to Court Systems,* pp. 24–25.
11. Wesley Gilmer, *Cochran's Law Dictionary: Criminal Justice Edition* (Cincinnati: W.H. Anderson, 1974), p. 257.
12. *Guide to Court Systems,* p. 3.
13. Ibid., p. 13.
14. Mark W. Cannon, "The Federal Judicial System," *Criminology,* May 1974, pp. 16–17.
15. *American Bar Association Journal,* March 1973, p. 303.
16. *American Bar Association Journal,* March 1975, p. 304.
17. *National Observer,* November 11, 1972, p. 14.
18. Gilmer, *Cochran's Law Dictionary,* p. 143.
19. Peter Westen, "Threat to the Supreme Court," *New York Review of Books,* February 22, 1973, p. 29; *Guide to Court Systems,* Table A13.
20. *Report of the Study Group on the Caseload of the Supreme Court* (Washington, D.C.: Federal Judicial Center, December 1972), pp. A13, A14.
21. The 1,000 figure is from Arthur J. Goldberg, "Changing the Supreme Court," *Current,* March 1973, p. 6. A figure of 4,700 is cited in "How to Break Logjam in Courts," *U.S. News & World Report,* December 19, 1977, p. 22.
22. Ashman and Chapin, "Is the Bell Tolling," p. 417.
23. Lyman Ray Patterson, "Should Lawyers Judge the Judges?" *Judicature,* May 1976, p. 457.
24. Frank Greenberg, "The Task of Judging the Judges," *Judicature,* May 1976, p. 461.
25. "Now, the States Crack Down on Bad Judges," *U.S. News & World Report,* March 13, 1978, p. 63.
26. Jack E. Frankel, "Who Judges the Judges?" *Trial,* January–February 1975, p. 52.
27. *National Observer,* March 15, 1975, p. 6.
28. "States Crack Down," p. 65.
29. *New York Times,* January 22, 1978, p. 21.
30. *New York Times,* April 26, 1977, p. 43.
31. *New York Times,* October 2, 1975, p. 43.

32. *New York Times,* October 16, 1977, section 4, p. 14.
33. *New York Times,* February 15, 1978, p. A20.
34. Steven Flanders, "Evaluating Judges: How Should the Bar Do It?" *Judicature,* February 1978, p. 304.
35. "How to Break Logjam," p. 24.
36. Joseph Tydings, "Merit Selection for District Judges," *Judicature,* September 1977, p. 116.
37. "How to Break Logjam," p. 24.
38. George A. Beohm, "Help for Our Overburdened Courts," *Reader's Digest,* March 1976, p. 166.
39. *New York Times,* January 22, 1975, p. 18.
40. Barbara R. Schulert, "New York Governor Uses Panel to Screen Judicial Candidates," *Judicature,* April 1975, p. 450.
41. Dorothy W. Nelson, "Carter's Merit Plan: A Good First Step," *Judicature,* September 1977, p. 105.
42. *New York Times,* August 14, 1977, section 4, p. 5.
43. *New York Times,* February 18, 1977, p. A28.
44. Earl B. Hadlow, "Can Federal Merit Selection Work?" *Judicature,* February 1976, pp. 324–325.
45. Marvin C. Holz, "Judicial Education in Wisconsin," *Judicature,* October 1975, pp. 145–147.
46. David J. Saari, *Modern Court Management: Trends in the Role of the Court Executive* (Washington, D.C.: Government Printing Office, July 1970), p. 5.
47. Nesta M. Gallas, "Court Administration, a Discipline or a Focus," *PAR,* March–April 1971, p. 144.
48. Richard W. Gable, "Modernizing Court Administration: The Case of the Los Angeles Superior Court," *PAR,* March–April 1971, pp. 133–134.
49. Gerald C. Snyder, "The Conception, the Labor, and the Birth of the National Center for State Courts," *Judicature,* June–July 1972, pp. 17–23.
50. *Standards Relating to Court Organization* (New York: Institute of Judicial Administration, 1973), pp. 2–6.

Chapter 8

1. Caleb Foote, "The Coming Constitutional Crisis in Bail," *University of Pennsylvania Law Review,* May 1965, pp. 959–999, and June 1965, pp. 1125–1185.
2. *Stack* v. *Boyle,* 342 U.S. 1 (1951).
3. John De Cicco, "Pretrial Bail," *Criminal Justice Quarterly,* Spring 1973, p. 75.
4. H. Richard Uviller, "Bail, Preventive Detention and Speedy Trials," *Columbia Journal of Law and Social Problems,* Fall 1971, p. 7; John V. Ryan, "The Last Days of Bail," *JCL,* December 1967, pp. 542–550; *National Conference on Bail and Criminal Justice, Proceedings and Interim Report* (Washington, D.C.: Department of Justice and Vera Foundation, April 1965), pp. 156–157; Comment, "Pretrial Detention in the District of Columbia: A Common Law Approach," *JCL,* June 1971, pp. 194–204; Daniel J. Freed and Patricia M. Wald, *Bail in the United States: 1964* (Washington, D.C.: Department of Justice and Vera Foundation, May 1964).
5. Freed and Wald, *Bail in the United States,* p. 2.

6. Ibid., Patricia M. Wald, "The Right to Bail Revisited," in Stuart Nagle, ed., *The Rights of the Accused in Law and Action* (Beverly Hills: Sage, 1972), p. 179.
7. Ryan, "Last Days of Bail," p. 544.
8. President's Crime Commission, *Courts,* p. 37.
9. Frederic Suffet, "Bail Setting: A Study of Courtroom Interaction," in Richard Quinney, *Crime and Justice in Society* (Boston: Little, Brown, 1969), pp. 298–300.
10. Ryan, "Last Days of Bail," p. 544.
11. Michael R. Gottfredson, "An Empirical Analysis of Pre-Trial Release Decisions," *JCJ,* Winter 1974, pp. 293–294.
12. Freed and Wald, *Bail in the United States,* p. 23.
13. Lee S. Friedman, *The Evolution of Bail Reform* (New Haven: Yale University, Center for the Study of the City and Its Environment, n.d.), p. 55.
14. John E. Conklin and Dermot Meagher, "The Percentage Deposit Bail System: An Alternative to the Professional Bondsmen," *JCJ,* Winter 1973, p. 302.
15. Friedman, *Evolution of Bail Reform,* p. 60.
16. President's Crime Commission, *Courts,* p. 40.
17. Wald, "Right to Bail Revisited," p. 179.
18. National Commission on the Causes and Prevention of Violence, *Law and Order Reconsidered* (Washington, D.C.: Government Printing Office, n.d.), p. 437.
19. President's Crime Commission, *Courts,* p. 38.
20. Richard D. Hongisto and Carole Levine, "Workable Alternatives to the Present Bail System," *California State Journal,* November–December 1972, note 3 at p. 578.
21. President's Crime Commission, *Courts,* p. 39.
22. Ryan, "Last Days of Bail," p. 550.
23. *New York Times,* June 2, 1975, p. 16.
24. Patricia M. Wald, "Pretrial Detention and Ultimate Freedom: A Statistical Study," *New York University Law Review,* June 1964, p. 635.
25. Charles E. Ares, Anne Rankin, and Herbert Sturz, "The Manhattan Bail Project: An Interim Report on the Use of Pre-Trial Parole," *New York University Law Review,* January 1963, pp. 84–85.
26. Anne Rankin, "The Effect of Pretrial Detention," *New York University Law Review,* June 1964, Table 1 at pp. 641–642.
27. Herbert Sturz, "Experiments in the Criminal Justice System," Testimony presented before the Senate Subcommittee on Executive Reorganization, December 13, 1966.
28. Freed and Wald, *Bail in the United States,* p. 63.
29. Norman Johnson, Leonard Savitz, and Marvin E. Wolfgang, eds., *The Sociology of Punishment and Correction* (New York: Wiley, 1970), p. 159.
30. Freed and Wald, *Bail in the United States,* pp. 62–63.
31. *Bail and Summons: 1965* (Washington, D.C.: Department of Justice and Vera Foundation, August 1966), p. xiv; Friedman, *Evolution of Bail,* pp. 102–103.
32. Hank Goldman et al., *OEO Survey of Pretrial Release Programs* (Washington, D.C.: Office of Economic Opportunity, 1973), p. 1.

33. Tyce S. Smith and James W. Reilley, "The Illinois Bail System: A Second Look," *John Marshall Journal of Practice and Procedure,* Fall 1972, p. 33.
34. Solomon Forman, "Atlantic County Ten Percent Cash Bail Project," *Criminal Justice Quarterly,* Fall 1973, p. 185.
35. Hongisto and Levine, "Workable Alternatives," p. 580.
36. Very loosely based on Freed and Wald, *Bail in the United States,* pp. 75–77.
37. Peter S. Venezia, *Des Moines Community Corrections Project, Evaluation Report Number Two* (Davis, Calif.: NCCD Research Center, February 29, 1972), pp. 17–18.
38. "Plaudits in Des Moines, But Problems in Salt Lake," *Corrections,* September 1976, pp. 16–17.
39. Robert L. Bogomolny and Michael R. Sonnenreich, "The Bail Reform Act of 1966," *Arizona Law Review,* Summer 1969, pp. 203, 205.
40. *Law and Order Reconsidered,* p. 442.
41. Arthur L. Burnett, "Reform in the Law of Bail—A Magistrate's Viewpoint," *ACL,* July 1971, p. 198.
42. *Law and Order Reconsidered,* pp. 442–443.
43. Wald, "Right to Bail Revisited," p. 183.
44. Ibid., p. 184.
45. *Law and Order Reconsidered,* p. 446.
46. Bogomolny and Sonnenreich, "Bail Reform Act," pp. 216–217.
47. "Pretrial Detention in District of Columbia," p. 194.
48. Nan C. Bases and William F. McDonald, *Preventive Detention in The District of Columbia: The First Ten Months* (New York: Vera Institute of Justice and Georgetown Institute of Criminal Law and Procedure, March 1972), pp. 4–5.
49. Ibid., p. 69.
50. Ibid., p. 7; 60-day reference in Wald, "Right to Bail Revisited," p. 190.
51. Wald, "Right to Bail Revisited," p. 185.
52. *Law and Order Reconsidered,* p. 444.
53. Smith and Reilley, "Illinois Bail System," p. 36.
54. S. Andrew Schaffer, *Report on Bail and Parole Jumping in Manhattan* (New York: Vera Institute of Justice, August 1970), p. 28.
55. Conklin, "Percentage Deposit Bail System," p. 311.
56. Gottfredson, "An Empirical Analysis," p. 294.
57. *Law and Order Reconsidered,* p. 447.
58. Gottfredson, "An Empirical Analysis," Table IV at p. 294.
59. J. W. Locket et al., *Compilation and Use of Criminal Court Data in Relation to Pre-Trial Release of Defendants* (Washington, D.C.: Government Printing Office, August 1970), p. 2.
60. Paul B. Wice, "Bail Reform in American Cities," *CLB,* November 1973, Table 7 at p. 787.
61. *Law and Order Reconsidered,* p. 448.
62. *Chief Justice's Annual Report to the American Bar Association,* Houston, Texas, February 8, 1981.
63. Stuart Taylor, "Reviving 'Bail Reform': A Protection or Peril?" *New York Times,* October 4, 1981, p. 20.

Chapter 9

1. *Cox* v. *United States,* 473 Federal Reporter, 2nd No. 71-1384, January 29,

1973, discussed in Don J. Young, "Recent Appellate Cases," *Juvenile Justice,* May 1975, p. 53.
2. Comment, "Prosecutorial Discretion in the Initiation of Criminal Complaints," *Southern California Law Review,* Spring 1969, p. 524.
3. Frank J. Remington et al., *Criminal Justice Administration: Materials and Cases* (Indianapolis: Bobbs-Merrill, 1969), pp. 424–427.
4. Barbara J. Katz, "A Reason Crooks Go Free: Prosecutors Don't Prosecute," *National Observer,* May 9, 1977, p. 18.
5. David W. Neubauer, "After the Arrest: The Charging Decision in Prairie City," *LSR,* Spring 1974, pp. 497–499.
6. Lynn M. Mather, "Some Determinants of the Method of Case Disposition," *LSR,* Winter 1974, p. 192.
7. David S. Baime and Edward R. Rosen, "Prosecutorial Discretion," *Criminal Justice Quarterly,* Summer 1973, pp. 155–156.
8. *United States* v. *Falk,* 479 F.2d 616, 7th Cir. (1973). The landmark case was *Yick Wo* v. *Hopkins,* 118 U.S. 356 (1886). It applied the Fourteenth Amendment to persons of Chinese ancestry who had been denied licenses to operate a laundry in a wooden building, while non-Chinese applicants were granted permission to do so.
9. Joan E. Jacoby, "Case Evaluation: Quantifying Prosecutorial Policy," *Judicature,* May 1975, p. 487.
10. Ibid., p. 488.
11. *LEAA Newsletter,* November 1974, pp. 1, 4.
12. "Crime's Big Pay Off," *U.S. News & World Report,* February 9, 1976, p. 50.
13. Mario Merola and Eric Warner, "The Major Offense Bureau: A Blueprint for Effective Prosecution of Career Criminals," *Prosecutor,* vol. 11, no. 1, pp. 8–9.
14. Ibid., p. 13.
15. *LEAA Newsletter,* August 1975, p. 8.
16. *Powell* v. *Alabama,* 287 U.S. 45 (1932).
17. Jonathan Alpert, "The Right to Counsel at Lineup," *CLB,* September 1968, p. 386; Elias M. Schwarzbart, "The Scottsboro Case, a 'Lightning Flash,'" *New York Times,* January 25, 1975, p. 27.
18. *Gideon* v. *Wainright,* 372 U.S. 335 (1963).
19. *Betts* v. *Brady,* 316 U.S. 455 (1942).
20. *Argersinger* v. *Hamlin,* 407 U.S. 25 (1972).
21. *Faretta* v. *California,* 422 U.S. 806 (1975).
22. *New York Times,* June 22, 1975, p. 42; *Wall Street Journal,* February 24, 1975, pp. 1, 19.
23. Warren E. Burger, "Incompetence in the Courtroom," *Intellectual Digest,* April 1974, pp. 20–21.
24. Douglas R. Heidenreich, "Toward a More Competent Bar," *Judicature,* June–July 1976, p. 21.
25. *New York Times,* April 6, 1975, section 4, p. 8.
26. "Message for Bungling Lawyers," *U.S. News & World Report,* August 27, 1979, p. 57.
27. Charles E. Evans, "The Definition of Indigency," *St. Mary's Law Journal,* Spring 1972, pp. 34–47.

28. Paul B. Wice and Mark Pilgrim, "Meeting the *Gideon* Mandate: A Survey of Public Defender Programs," *Judicature,* March 1975, p. 406.
29. Sarah Grace Venable and Stephen Wells, "Providing Counsel for the Indigent Accused: The Criminal Justice Act," *ACL,* Spring 1975, p. 790.
30. Standards and Goals Commission, *Courts,* p. 257.
31. *LEAA Newsletter,* June 1974, p. 6.
32. Wice and Pilgrim, "Meeting the *Gideon* Mandate," p. 402.
33. Lewis R. Katz, "Gideon's Trumpet: Mournful and Muffled," *CLB,* December 1970, p. 543.
34. Wice and Pilgrim, "Meeting the *Gideon* Mandate," p. 402.
35. Nancy A. Goldberg, "Defender Systems of the Future: The New National Standards," *ACL,* Spring 1975, p. 724.
36. Katz, "Gideon's Trumpet," p. 535.
37. Herbert Jacob, *Justice in America: Courts, Lawyers, and the Judicial Process* (Boston: Little, Brown, 1972), p. 65.
38. Goldberg, "Defender Systems," p. 725.
39. Katz, "Gideon's Trumpet," p. 547.
40. Nancy B. Elkind, Milo L. Colton, and Francis L. Bremson, *Implementation of Argersinger: A Prescriptive Program Package* (Denver: National Center for State Courts, January 1974), p. 46.
41. Standards and Goals Commission, *Courts,* p. 263.
42. Goldberg, "Defender Systems," p. 721.
43. *New York Times,* August 8, 1975, p. 55.
44. "Recent Developments: The Right to Counsel, *Argersinger* v. *Hamlin,*" *CLB,* January–February 1975, p. 69.
45. Jacob, *Justice in America,* p. 66; Jerry L. Sumpter, "A Look Inside the 'Court Appointed Attorney' Situation," *Case and Comment,* July–August 1975, p. 22; Marshall Hartman and Nancy E. Goldberg, "Help for the Indigent Accused: The Effect of Argersinger," *National Legal Aid and Defender Association Briefcase,* July 1972, p. 206.
46. Goldberg, "Defender Systems," p. 723.
47. John Hersey, "Plea Bargaining in the Pit," *Skeptic,* Special Issue no. 4, n.d., p. 33.
48. Anthony Platt and Randi Pollock, "Channeling Lawyers: The Careers of Public Defenders," *Issues in Criminology,* Spring 1974, p. 19.
49. Jacob, *Justice in America,* p. 65; *Brady* v. *Maryland,* 373 U.S. 83 (1963); Herald Price Fahringer, "The Brady Rule: Has Anyone Seen Brady?" *John Marshall Journal of Practice and Procedure,* Fall 1972, p. 78.
50. "Justice on Trial," *Newsweek,* March 8, 1971.
51. Stephen R. Bing and S. Stephen Rosenfeld, *The Quality of Justice in the Lower Criminal Courts of Metropolitan Boston* (Boston: Lawyers Committee for Civil Rights Under Law, September 1970), p. 31.
52. Laurence A. Benner, "Tokenism and the American Indigent: Some Perspectives on Defense Services," *ACL,* Spring 1975, p. 679.
53. Wice and Pilgrim, "Meeting the *Gideon* Mandate," p. 404.
54. Benner, "Tokenism," p. 679.
55. Standards and Goals Commission, *Courts,* pp. 280–281.
56. Benner, "Tokenism," p. 680.
57. Wice and Pilgrim, "Meeting the *Gideon* Mandate," p. 405.

58. Benner, "Tokenism," p. 668; Goldberg, "Defender Systems," p. 715.
59. Benner, "Tokenism," p. 675.
60. Ibid., pp. 685–688. Pre-*Argersinger* cost and personnel projections made by Silverstein were much lower; see Lee Silverstein, "Manpower Requirements in the Administration of Criminal Justice," in President's Crime Commission, *Courts,* pp. 160–161.
61. Hartman and Goldberg, "Help for the Indigent," p. 204.
62. *Arizona Republic,* August 3, 1975, section B, p. 1.
63. Benner, "Tokenism," p. 677.
64. Ibid., p. 676.
65. "*Argersinger* v. *Hamlin:* An Unmet Challenge," *CLB,* January–February 1975, pp. 68, 74.
66. Steven Duke, "The Right to Appointed Counsel: *Argersinger* and Beyond," *ACL,* Spring 1975, p. 606.
67. *LEAA Newsletter,* June 1974, p. 6.
68. Barton L. Ingraham, "The Impact of Argersinger—One Year Later," *LSR,* Summer 1974, p. 623.
69. *"Argersinger* v. *Hamlin," CLB,* p. 75.
70. Benner, "Tokenism," p. 676.
71. Goldberg, "Defender Systems," p. 715; Ingraham, "Impact of Argersinger," p. 628.
72. *U.S. News & World Report,* June 6, 1977, p. 33.
73. Elkind, Colton, and Bremson, *Implementation of Argersinger,* pp. 58–60.

Chapter 10

1. Donald J. Newman, *Conviction: The Determination of Guilt or Innocence Without Trial* (Boston: Little, Brown, 1966), p. 3.
2. T. H. Hartnagel, "Plea Negotiations in Canada," *Canadian Journal of Criminology and Corrections,* January 1975, p. 46.
3. *CBS-TV Morning News,* October 28, 1975 (transcript).
4. *Criminal Justice Newsletter,* March 14, 1977, p. 1.
5. *New York Times,* January 27, 1975, p. 1.
6. *The Cost of Crime: The Plea Bargainers,* TV series by Peter Tufo, transcript, p. 10.
7. Albert W. Alschuler, "The Prosecutor's Role in Plea Bargaining," *University of Chicago Law Review,* Fall 1968, p. 55.
8. David Sudnow, "Normal Crimes: Sociological Features of the Penal Code in a Public Defender Office," in William J. Chambliss, *Crime and the Legal Process* (New York: McGraw-Hill, 1969), p. 245.
9. Alschuler, "Prosecutor's Role," p. 59.
10. Ibid.
11. "Justice on Trial," *Newsweek,* March 8, 1971.
12. David W. Neubauer, "After the Arrest: The Charging Decision in Prairie City," *LSR,* Spring 1974, p. 509; *Criminal Justice Newsletter,* March 14, 1977, pp. 1–2.
13. *National Observer,* May 9, 1977, p. 18.
14. Hartnagel, "Plea Negotiations," p. 51.
15. Milton Heumann, "A Note on Plea Bargaining and Case Pressure," *LSR,* Spring 1975, p. 525.
16. *Time,* November 22, 1971, pp. 69–70.

17. George F. Cole, "The Decision to Prosecute," *LSR,* February 1970, p. 340.
18. Sudnow, "Normal Crimes," p. 245.
19. Ibid., p. 246.
20. *Brady* v. *United States,* 397 U.S. 742 (1970).
21. *Santobello* v. *New York,* 92 S.Ct. 495 (1971).
22. *Blackledge* v. *Allison,* 97 S.Ct. 1621 (1977).
23. *Bordenkircher* v. *Hayes,* No. 76-1334. Decided January 18, 1978.
24. Jacqueline Cohen et al., "Implementation of the JUSSIM Model in a Criminal Justice Planning Agency," *JRC,* July 1973, p. 121.
25. Alschuler, "Prosecutor's Role," p. 50.
26. Ibid., p. 51.
27. William L. Cahalan, "Comments on the Court's Task Force Report," *Prosecutor,* vol. 9, No. 2, p. 126.
28. Donald J. Newman, "Reshape the Deal," *Trial,* May–June 1973, p. 12.
29. Wayne LaFave, "The Prosecutor's Discretion in the United States," *American Journal of Comparative Law,* vol. 18, No. 3, 1970, pp. 533–534.
30. Newman, "Reshape the Deal," p. 14.
31. Alan F. Arcuri, "Police Perceptions of Plea Bargaining: A Preliminary Inquiry," *JPS,* March 1973, p. 98.
32. Marshall Hartman, "Can Plea Bargaining Be Eliminated?" *Judicature,* June –July 1975, p. 9.
33. Alschuler, "Prosecutor's Role," p. 110.
34. Ibid, pp. 60–61; *New York Times,* February 24, 1975, p. 25.
35. *Alford* v. *North Carolina,* 89 S.Ct. 1306 (1969); Alexander E. Conlyn, "The Supreme Court's Changed View of the Guilty Plea," *Memphis State University Law Review,* Fall 1973, p. 85.
36. Robert Kroll, "The Plea Circus," *Student Lawyer,* January 1975, pp. 11, 52; Heumann, "Note on Plea Bargaining," p. 525.
37. Note, "Restructuring the Plea Bargain," *Yale Law Journal,* December 1972, p. 291.
38. Donald J. Newman, "The Agnew Plea Bargain," *CLB,* January–February 1974, pp. 85–90.
39. Alschuler, "Prosecutor's Role," p. 82.
40. Ibid., p. 57.
41. Alschuler, "Prosecutor's Role," p. 79.
42. Standards and Goals Commission, *National Strategy to Reduce Crime,* pp. 149–150.
43. "Restructuring the Plea Bargain," p. 286.
44. Kathleen Gallagher, "A Voluntary Trap?" *Trial,* May–June 1973, p. 25.
45. *Standards Relating to Pleas of Guilty* (New York: Institute of Judicial Administration, Approved Draft, 1968), pp. 11–12, 72–77.
46. President's Crime Commission, *Courts,* pp. 12–13.
47. "Why the Omnibus Hearing Project: A Panel Discussion," *Judicature,* May 1972, pp. 377–382; *New York Times,* May 16, 1976, p. 48.
48. Lynn M. Mather, "Some Determinants of the Method of Case Disposition: Decision-Making by Public Defenders in Los Angeles," *LSR,* Winter 1974, p. 190.
49. *New Haven Register,* November 26, 1976, pp. 1, 19.
50. "Restructuring the Plea Bargain," p. 311.

51. Raymond T. Nimmer, "Judicial Reform: Informal Processes and Competing Effects," in Herbert Jacob, ed., *The Potential for Reform of Criminal Justice* (Beverly Hills: Sage, 1974), p. 215.
52. "Why the Omnibus Hearing Project?" pp. 377–382.
53. *Miami Herald,* July 20, 1975, p. 9D.
54. John T. Putnam, "Municipal Plea Bargaining: Right or Wrong?" *Criminal Justice Quarterly,* Spring–Summer 1976, p. 74.
55. *Criminal Justice Newsletter,* July 21, 1975, p. 1.
56. *California Uniform Crime Charging Standards* (Sacramento: California District Attorneys Association, December 1974).
57. O.K. Armstrong, "How New Orleans Cracked Down on Crime," *Saturday Evening Post,* December 25, 1976, p. 40.
58. *New York Times,* July 12, 1975, p. 8.
59. Christopher T. Bayley, "Plea Bargaining: An Offer a Prosecutor Can Refuse," *Judicature,* December 1976, pp. 229–232.
60. Richard H. Kuh, "Plea Bargaining: Guidelines for the Manhattan District Attorney's Office," *CLB,* January–February 1975, pp. 48–61.
61. Armstrong, "How New Orleans," pp. 40, 108.
62. *Criminal Justice Newsletter,* July 21, 1975, pp. 3–4.
63. Bayley, "Plea Bargaining," p. 232.
64. *Miami Herald,* July 20, 1975, p. 9D.
65. Harold H. Greene, "Introduction: Toward Realizing the Promise of Effective Representation of the Indigent Defendant in the District of Columbia," *ACL,* Spring 1975, p. 783.
66. President's Crime Commission, *Courts,* p. 80.
67. *Philadelphia Inquirer,* March 5, 1972, p. 7A. I deducted six weeks from reported figures that included the sentencing period.
68. "Why Criminals Go Free," *U.S. News & World Report,* May 10, 1976, p. 38.
69. "New York's New Standards Attacks Court Backlogs," *Judicature,* January 1976, p. 305.
70. Lewis Katz, *An Analysis of Pretrial Delay in Felony Cases—A Summary Report* (Washington, D.C.: Government Printing Office, 1972), p. 1.
71. *Barker* v. *Wingo,* 407 U.S. 514 (1972).
72. Robert F. Olmert, "The Speedy Trial Act of 1974," *LEB,* November 1975, pp. 28–29.
73. "Speedy Trial Act of 1974," *CLB,* March–April 1975, p. 206.
74. *Time,* January 13, 1975, p. 51.
75. Statistics from *New York Times,* June 20, 1975, p. 32.
76. "Speedy Trial Act of 1974," *CLB,* pp. 208–209.
77. Leslie G. Foschio, "Empirical Research and the Problem of Court Delay," in *Criminal Justice Monograph: Reducing Court Delay* (Washington, D.C.: Government Printing Office, June 1973), pp. 37, 40.
78. Laura Banfield and C. David Anderson, "Continuances in the Cook County Criminal Courts," *University of Chicago Law Review,* Winter 1968, pp. 287–288 and Table 8 at p. 300.
79. "Speedy Trial Act of 1974," *CLB,* pp. 209–210.
80. *Speedy Trial Act of 1974,* 93rd Congress, 2d Session, Senate Report No. 93-1021, July 18, 1974, p. 9.

81. *Strunk* v. *United States,* 93 S.Ct. 2260 (1973).
82. *Speedy Trial Act of 1974,* 93rd Congress, pp. 16–17.
83. *New York Times,* October 2, 1975, pp. 1, 77; *New York Times,* October 5, 1975, p. 6.
84. *Time,* November 8, 1971, pp. 80–81.
85. *Boston Herald American,* November 13, 1975, pp. 1, 18.
86. Note, "Speedy Trial: A Constitutional Right in Search of Definition," *Georgetown Law Journal,* February 1973, p. 669.
87. *Time,* November 8, 1971, p. 81.

Chapter 11

1. *Duncan* v. *Louisiana,* 391 U.S. 145 (1968).
2. *Gannett* v. *DePasquale,* No. 77-1301. Decided July 2, 1979.
3. "Four Big Decisions," *Time,* July 14, 1980, p. 13; "The High Court's Grand Finale," *Newsweek,* July 14, 1980, p. 24.
4. Warren Weaver, "Burger's View on Report to Attend Trial," *New York Times,* August 11, 1979, p. 43; *New York Times,* November 21, 1979, p. 4; *New York Times,* September 9, 1979, p. 41.
5. *Richmond* v. *Virginia,* No. 79-243. Decided July 2, 1980.
6. *New York Times,* September 28, 1980, p. 61.
7. *Miami Herald,* July 20, 1975, p. 3E.
8. Millard C. Farmer, "Jury Composition Challenges," *Law and Psychology Review,* vol. 2, 1976, pp. 57, 60.
9. John P. Richert, "A New Verdict on Juror Willingness," *Judicature,* May 1977, pp. 498–499.
10. *Target,* May 1977; *National Observer,* June 5, 1976, p. 11.
11. *New York Times,* February 1, 1976, p. 30.
12. Gerald M. Caplan, "Improving Criminal Justice: A Consumer's Perspective," *Judicature,* February 1975, p. 347.
13. E. Patrick Healy, "Memoirs of a Manhattan Juror: An Adventure in Apathy," *American Bar Association Journal,* April 1976, p. 461.
14. *Mempha* v. *Rhay,* 389 U.S. 128 (1967).
15. *New Haven Register,* September 10, 1974, p. 40.
16. *New York Times,* October 26, 1975, p. 55.
17. *New York Times,* November 21, 1975, p. 1.
18. Morris J. Bloomstein, *Verdict: The Jury System* (New York: Dodd, Mead, 1968), p. 60.
19. *New York Times,* July 9, 1976, p. 11.
20. *New York Times,* July 29, 1975, p. 13.
21. *New York Times,* September 2, 1975, p. 24.
22. Michael J. Saks, "Social Scientist Can't Rig Juries," *Psychology Today,* January 1976, p. 49.
23. Jay Schulman, "Systematic Jury Selection," *Law and Psychology Review,* vol. 2, 1976, p. 31.
24. Paul G. Chevigny, "The Attica Cases: A Successful Jury Challenge in a Northern City," *CLB,* March–April 1975, p. 159.
25. "The Exclusion of Young Adults from Juries: A Threat to Jury Impartiality," *JCC,* June 1975, pp. 150–164.
26. *Boston Globe,* July 27, 1975, p. A1.
27. *Washington Post,* July 20, 1975, pp. A1, A4.

28. *National Observer,* November 15, 1975, p. 4.
29. Edwin Tivnan, "Jury by Trial," *New York Times Magazine,* November 16, 1975, pp. 30, 54.
30. Ibid., p. 30.
31. *Washington Post,* July 20, 1975, p. A4.
32. *New York Times,* July 24, 1975, p. 17.
33. Saks, "Social Scientists," p. 56.
34. *Williams* v. *Florida,* 399 U.S. 78 (1970).
35. *Ballew* v. *Georgia,* 98 S.Ct. 1029 (1978).
36. Julia Carlson Rosenblatt, "Should the Size of the Jury in Criminal Cases Be Reduced To Six?: An Examination of Psychological Evidence," *Prosecutor,* vol. 8, No. 4, p. 310.
37. Ibid.
38. *New York Times,* July 21, 1975, p. 10.
39. Ibid.
40. *New York Times,* June 27, 1973, p. 46.
41. Robert C. Cancilla, "The Size of Trial Juries Should Be Reduced," *Police Chief,* August 1973, p. 59.
42. Hans Zeisel, "And Then There Were None: The Diminution of the Federal Jury," *University of Chicago Law Review,* Summer 1971, p. 721.
43. Rosenblatt, "Should the Size," p. 313.
44. Hans Kalven and Harry Zeisel, *The American Jury* (Boston: Little, Brown, 1966).
45. Zeisel, "And Then There Were None," p. 716.
46. Ibid.
47. Tom C. Clark, "The American Jury: A Justification," *Valparaiso University Law Review,* Fall 1966, p. 3.
48. David J. Saari, "The Criminal Jury Faces Future Shock," *Judicature,* June–July 1973, p. 14.
49. Clark, "The American Jury," p. 4.
50. Rita James Simon and Linda Mahan, "Quantifying Burdens of Proof," *LSR,* Fall 1971, pp. 319–330.
51. Edward N. Beisner and Rene Varrin, "Six-Member Juries in the Federal Courts," *Judicature,* April 1975, pp. 425–433; William R. Pabst, "What Do Six-Member Juries Really Serve?" *Judicature,* June–July 1973, pp. 6–11.
52. "Jury Trial: *Williams* v. *Florida,*" *JCL,* December 1970, p. 530.
53. Rosenblatt, "Should the Size," p. 314.
54. *Johnson* v. *Louisiana,* 406 U.S. 356 (1972).
55. *Apodaca* v. *Oregon,* 406 U.S. 404 (1972).
56. Lloyd E. Moore, *The Jury* (Cincinnati: W.H. Anderson, 1973), p. 146.
57. Bloomstein, *Verdict,* pp. 31–32.
58. James A. Johnson, "Criminal Law—Jury," *Wisconsin Law Review,* no. 3, 1973, pp. 927–928.
59. Harry Kalven and Hans Zeisel, "Should All Jury Verdicts Be Unanimous?" *Current,* May 1967, p. 63.
60. Michael Masinter, "The Non-Unanimous Jury," *ACL,* Winter 1973, p. 543.
61. Keith Mossman, "Justice and Numbers," *Trial,* November–December 1974, p. 23.

62. Thomas E. Sims, "Teletest," *Judicature,* April 1976, pp. 434–436.
63. James L. McCrystal, "Videotape Trials: Relief for Our Congested Courts," *Denver Law Journal,* 1973, pp. 463–483.
64. Sherwood Allen Salvan, "Videotape for the Legal Community," *Judicature,* December 1975, pp. 222–224.
65. Michael J. Merlo and Howard C. Sorenson, "Video Tape: The Coming Courtroom Tool," *Trial,* November–December 1971, p. 56.
66. James L. McCrystal, "The Videotape Trial Comes of Age," *Judicature,* May 1974, p. 446.
67. Irving Kosky, "Videotape in Ohio," *Judicature,* December 1975, p. 232.
68. *National Observer,* September 28, 1974, p. 23B.
69. Robert H. Gebhardt, "Video Tape in Criminal Cases," *LEB,* May 1975, p. 7.
70. Salvan, "Videotape," p. 226; *New York Times,* March 11, 1977, p. D12.
71. Gerald A. McGill and James W. Thrasher, "Videotapes: The Reel Thing for the Future," *Trial,* September–October 1975, p. 43.
72. *Newsweek,* March 7, 1977, p. 67.
73. Jethro K. Liberman, "Will the Courts Meet the Challenge of Technology?" *Judicature,* August–September 1976, p. 90.
74. Gerald Miller, "Televised Trials: How Do Juries React?" *Judicature,* December 1974, pp. 242–246.
75. Francis J. Taiffeffer et al., *Video Support in the Criminal Courts: Executive Summary* (Washington, D.C.: Government Printing Office, October 1975), pp. 8–9.
76. Kosky, "Videotape in Ohio," pp. 237–238.
77. James L. McCrystal and James L. Young, "Pre-Recorded Videotape Trials —An Ohio Innovation," *Brooklyn Law Review,* Winter 1973, p. 561.
78. *Washington Post,* August 21, 1975, p. C3.
79. *New York Times,* July 8, 1976, p. 18.
80. *Newsweek,* October 20, 1975, p. 64; Gilbert J. Helwig, "The American Jury System: A Time for Reexamination," *Judicature,* October 1971, p. 99.

Chapter 12

1. Robert M. Carter, "It Is Respectfully Recommended," *Federal Probation,* June 1966, p. 41; Division of Probation, "The Selective Presentence Investigation Report," *Federal Probation,* December 1974, p. 48.
2. Note, "Procedural Due Process at Judicial Sentencing for Felony," *Harvard Law Review,* February 1968, p. 838.
3. *Standards Relating to Sentencing Alternatives and Procedures* (New York: Institute of Judicial Administration, Approved Draft, 1968), pp. 208–209.
4. Standards and Goals Commission, *Corrections,* pp. 186–187.
5. President's Crime Commission, *Corrections,* p. 18.
6. "Selective Presentence," p. 48.
7. *Standards Relating to Sentencing,* pp. 202–203.
8. Standards and Goals Commission, *Corrections,* p. 185; President's Crime Commission, *Courts,* p. 19; *Standards Relating to Sentencing,* p. 200; *Model Penal Code* (Philadelphia: American Law Institute, 1962), p. 118; *Model Sentencing Act* (Hackensack: Council of Judges of the NCCD, 1972).
9. *Mempha* v. *Rhay,* 389 U.S. 128 (1967).

10. Benson Schaffer, "The Defendant's Right of Access to Presentence Reports," *CLB,* December 1967, p. 674.
11. Robert M. Carter and Leslie T. Wilkins, "Some Factors in Sentencing Policy," *JCL,* December 1967, pp. 503–514.
12. Robert M. Carter, "The Presentence Report and the Decision-Making Process," *JRC,* July 1967, pp. 203–211.
13. *Standards Relating to Sentencing,* p. 211.
14. Maxim N. Bach, "The Defendant's Right of Access to Presentence Reports," *CLB,* April 1968, p. 161.
15. Willard D. Lorensen, "The Disclosure to Defense of Presentence Reports in West Virginia," *West Virginia Law Review,* February 1967, p. 160.
16. Bach, "The Defendant's Right," p. 161.
17. Comment, "Proposed Changes in Presentence Investigation Report Procedures," *JCC,* March 1975, note 60 at p. 64.
18. Schaffer, "The Defendant's Right," p. 674.
19. Lorensen, "The Disclosure," p. 162.
20. Note, "The Presentence Report: An Empirical Study of Its Use in the Federal Criminal Process," *Georgetown Law Journal,* February 1970, p. 474.
21. "Proposed Changes in Presentence Investigation," p. 60.
22. *Standards Relating to Sentencing,* p. 218.
23. President's Crime Commission, *The Challenge of Crime in a Free Society,* p. 145.
24. Daniel Katkin, "Presentence Reports: An Analysis of Uses, Limitations and Civil Liberties," *Minnesota Law Review,* November 1970, p. 25.
25. *United States* v. *Tucker,* 404 U.S. 443 (1972).
26. *Gardner* v. *Florida,* 97 S. Ct. 1197 (1977).
27. Marvin E. Frankel, *Criminal Sentences: Law Without Order* (New York: Hill & Wang, 1973), p. 18.
28. Whitney North Seymour, "1972 Sentencing Study for the Southern District of New York," *New York State Bar Journal,* April 1973, pp. 163–171.
29. "Sentencing Practices in the Federal Courts in New York City," *The Record,* December 1973, p. 877.
30. Keith D. Harries and Russell P. Laura, "The Geography of Justice: Sentencing Variations in the U.S. Judicial Districts," *Judicature,* April 1974, pp. 392–401; William James Zumwalt, "The Anarchy of Sentencing in the Federal Courts," *Judicature,* October 1973, p. 97; Julian C. D'Esposito, "Sentencing Disparity: Causes and Cures," *JCL,* June 1969, p. 183.
31. Committee on the Federal Courts, "The Second Circuit Sentencing Study," in U.S. Senate Hearings Before the Committee on the Judiciary, 94th Congress, June 13, 17, July 19, 22, 1974, pp. 8102–8132.
32. *National Observer,* September 14, 1974, p. 5.
33. Leonard Cargan and Mary A. Coates, "The Indeterminate Sentence and Judicial Bias," *CD,* April 1974, pp. 144–156.
34. Mark Berger, "Reducing Sentencing Disparity: Structured Discretion and the Sentencing Judge," *Case and Comment,* May–June 1977, p. 36.
35. Jack M. Kress, Leslie T. Wilkins, and Don M. Gottfredson, "Is the End of Judicial Sentencing in Sight?" *Judicature,* December 1976, p. 220.
36. "Sentencing Practices in the Federal Courts," p. 877; Edward Green, *Judicial Attitudes in Sentencing* (London: Macmillan, 1961).

37. Carter and Wilkins, "Some Factors," p. 514.
38. Frankel, *Criminal Sentences,* p. 62.
39. D'Esposito, "Sentencing Disparity," p. 185.
40. Frankel, *Criminal Sentences,* p. 67.
41. Talbot Smith, "The Sentencing Council and the Problem of Disproportionate Sentences," *Federal Probation,* June 1963, pp. 5–9; Richard F. Doyle, "A Sentencing Council in Operation," *Federal Probation,* September 1961, pp. 27–30.
42. Charles T. Hosner, "Group Procedures in Sentencing: A Decade of Practice," *Federal Probation,* December 1970, p. 25.
43. Peter B. Hoffman and Lucille K. DeGostin, "An Argument for Self-Imposed Explicit Judicial Sentencing Standards," *JCJ,* Fall 1975, p. 198.
44. Chris A. Korbakes, "Criminal Sentencing: Is the Judge's Sound Discretion Subject to Review?" *Judicature,* October 1975, p. 114.
45. Ibid.
46. Zumwalt, "Anarchy of Sentencing," p. 98.
47. *Standards Relating to Appellate Review of Sentences* (New York: Institute of Judicial Administration, Approved Draft, 1968), p. 3.
48. Standards and Goals Commission, *Corrections,* pp. 177–179.
49. *Standards Relating to Appellate Review,* p. 13.
50. Korbakes, "Criminal Sentencing," pp. 116–117.
51. Chris A. Korbakes, "Should the Judge's Sound Discretion Be Explained?" *Judicature,* November 1975, p. 187.
52. Gerald D. Robin, "Judicial Resistance to Sentencing Accountability," *CD,* July 1975, pp. 201–212; Joseph D. Tydings, "Ensuring Rational Sentences—The Case for Appellate Review," *Judicature,* August–September 1969, pp. 68–73; "Appellate Review of Primary Sentencing Decisions," *Yale Law Journal,* July 1960, p. 1454.
53. Korbakes, "Should the Judge's Sound Discretion," p. 191.
54. Ibid.
55. *New York Times,* March 18, 1976, p. 37.
56. *North Carolina* v. *Pearce,* 395 U.S. 711 (1969).
57. Sol Rubin, "Disparity and Equality of Sentences—A Constitutional Challenge," *Federal Rules Decisions,* vol. 40, 1966, p. 56.
58. *Standards Relating to Sentencing,* pp. 49–50.
59. Alfred P. Murrah and Sol Rubin, "Penal Reform and the Model Sentencing Act," *Columbia Law Review,* November 1965, p. 1167.
60. *Model Penal Code,* pp. 2–3.
61. "Penal Codes Revised," *CD,* October 1974, p. 427.
62. Model Sentencing Act.
63. *Rummel* v. *Estelle,* No. 78-6386. Decided March 18, 1980.
64. Milton G. Rector, "The Extravagance of Imprisonment," *CD,* October 1975, p. 326.
65. Robert W. Balch, "The Indeterminate Sentence and the Medical Model," *CD,* April 1974, pp. 128–129.
66. Richard A. McGee, "A New Look at Sentencing," *Federal Probation,* September 1974, p. 3.
67. Richard G. Singer and Richard C. Hand, "Sentencing Computation: Laws and Practices," *CLB,* May 1974, p. 324.

68. Ibid., p. 325.
69. American Friends Service Committee, *Struggle for Justice* (New York: Hill & Wang, 1971).
70. Thomas J. Bernard, "Individualization vs. Uniformity: The Case for Regulation in Criminal Justice," *Federal Probation,* December 1976, p. 19.
71. Singer and Hand, "Sentencing Computation," p. 323.
72. *New York Times,* May 2, 1976, p. 28.
73. *New York Times,* June 22, 1977, p. B2.
74. *LEAA Newsletter,* April 1975, p. 11. See also Andrew von Hirsch, "Giving Criminals Their Just Deserts," *Civil Liberties Review,* April–May 1976, pp. 31–33.
75. Kress, Wilkins, and Gottfredson, "Is the End," p. 222.
76. Bernard, "Individualization," p. 20.
77. S. 181, 95th Congress, 1st Session, January 11, 1977.
78. Edward M. Kennedy, "Criminal Sentencing: A Game of Chance," *Judicature,* December 1976, p. 213.
79. Walter A. Lunden, "Death Penalty Delays," *Police,* July–August 1963, p. 18.
80. Michael Meltsner, "Litigating Against the Death Penalty: The Strategy Behind *Furman,*" *Yale Law Journal,* May 1973, pp. 1112–1114.
81. *Newsweek,* July 18, 1977, p. 95.
82. *Time,* March 14, 1977, p. 57.
83. *Furman* v. *Georgia,* 408 U.S. 238 (1972).
84. *Weems* v. *United States,* 217 U.S. 349 (1910).
85. *Trop* v. *Dulles,* 356 U.S. 86 (1958).
86. "Statistical Evidence on the Deterrent Effect of Capital Punishment," *Yale Law Journal,* December 1975, p. 164.
87. Stephen Caswell, "Capital Punishment: Cementing a Fragile Victory," *Trial,* May–June 1974, p. 47.
88. Note, "Discretion and the Constitutionality of the New Death Penalty Statutes," *Harvard Law Review,* June 1974, pp. 1690–1719.
89. Caswell, "Capital Punishment," p. 51.
90. "Capital Punishment After *Furman,*" *JCC,* September 1973, p. 283.
91. *Model Penal Code,* pp. 128–133.
92. Abe Fortas, "The Case Against Capital Punishment," *New York Times Magazine,* January 23, 1977, p. 9.
93. *Gregg* v. *Georgia,* 428 U.S. 153 (1976); *Jurek* v. *Texas,* 428 U.S. 262 (1976); *Proffitt* v. *Florida,* 428 U.S. 242 (1976). The vote was 7–2 in each case.
94. Burger dissent in *Furman* v. *Georgia.*
95. Marlene W. Lehtinen, "The Value of Life: An Argument for the Death Penalty," *CD,* July 1977, p. 248; *New York Times,* June 14, 1981, p. 28.
96. "Death Penalty," *CD,* April 1973, p. 289.
97. *Woodson* v. *North Carolina,* 428 U.S. 280 (1976); *Roberts* v. *Louisiana,* 428 U.S. 325 (1976).
98. "Spreading Impact of a Historic Court Decision," *U.S. News & World Report,* July 12, 1976, p. 49.
99. Figures from *Time,* July 12, 1976, p. 35; *National Observer,* July 10, 1976, p. 2; *New York Times,* July 3, 1976, p. 1.

100. Charles L. Black, *Capital Punishment: The Inevitability of Caprice and Mistake* (New York: Norton, 1974), pp. 56–68.
101. *National Observer,* January 15, 1977, p. 3; *National Observer,* May 23, 1977, p. 2.
102. *New York Times,* May 9, 1977, pp. 1, 59.
103. *Curfew Davis* v. *State of Georgia,* 97 S.Ct. 399 (1976).
104. *Adams* v. *Texas,* No. 79-5175. Decided June 25, 1980.
105. *Witherspoon* v. *Illinois,* 391 U.S. 510 (1968).
106. *Roberts* v. *Louisiana,* 97 S.Ct. 1993 (1977).
107. *Coker* v. *Georgia,* 97 S.Ct. 2861 (1977).
108. *Lockett* v. *Ohio,* 98 S.Ct. 2954 (1978).
109. "Growing Enigma of the Burger Court," *U.S. News & World Report,* July 17, 1978, p. 24.
110. *Godfrey* v. *Georgia,* No. 78-6899. Decided May 19, 1980.
111. *New York Times,* May 20, 1980, p. 16.
112. *Estelle* v. *Smith,* No. 79-1127. Decided May 18, 1981.
113. *New York Times,* May 19, 1981, p. 1.
114. *The Hartford Courant,* May 19, 1981, p. 4.
115. *Bullington* v. *Missouri,* No. 79-6740. Decided May 4, 1981.

Chapter 13

1. Allan Ashman, "The Rhetoric and Reality of Prison Reform," *Judicature,* June–July 1972, p. 7; Herbert S. Miller, "The Lawyer's Hang-up: Due Process Versus the Real Issue," *ACL,* Fall 1972, p. 203.
2. Estimates of 3–4 million from Ronald L. Goldfarb and Linda R. Singer, *After Conviction* (New York: Simon & Schuster, 1973), pp. 85–86. Estimate of 5 million from Hans W. Mattick, "The Contemporary Jails of the United States: An Unknown and Neglected Area of Justice," in Daniel Glaser, ed., *Handbook of Criminology* (Chicago: Rand McNally, 1974), p. 795.
3. *The Nation's Jails: A Report on the Census of Jails from the 1972 Survey of Local Jails* (Washington, D.C.: National Criminal Justice Information and Statistics Service, May 1975); *Census of Jails and Survey of Jail Inmates, 1978: Preliminary Report* (Washington, D.C.: Law Enforcement Assistance Administration, February 1979).
4. *Survey of Inmates of Local Jails 1972: Advance Report* (Washington, D.C.: National Criminal Justice Information and Statistics Service, n.d.); *Profile of Jail Inmates: Sociodemographic Findings from the 1978 Survey of Inmates of Local Jails* (Washington, D.C.: Superintendent of Documents, October 1980).
5. LEAA's definition of *jails,* and therefore its survey, excluded facilities that retained persons for less than 48 hours (primarily "drunk tanks" and similar lockups), facilities used exclusively for juveniles, municipalities with less than 1,000 population, and state-operated jails such as those in Connecticut, Delaware, and Rhode Island.
6. The discussion here draws on the 1972 findings, but information has occassionally been taken from the 1970 report when it was not available in the 1972 National Jail Census.
7. According to the 1966 NCCD survey of jails, reported in Mattack, "Contemporary Jails," p. 799.

8. Based on the 3,319 jails in cities with 25,000 population.
9. Edith Elisabeth Flynn, "Jails and Criminal Justice," in Lloyd E. Ohlin, ed., *Prisoners in America* (Englewood Cliffs, N.J.: Prentice-Hall, 1973), p. 65.
10. In 79 of the 3,921 jails, juveniles and adults were customarily mixed.
11. The 1972 *Survey of Inmates of Local Jails* does not indicate the total number of convicted persons within the jail population of 141,600 inmates. Instead, the report focuses on comparisons between the 51,000 inmates awaiting trial and the 60,200 inmates serving jail sentences (the *minimum* number of convicted cases), relegating the remaining 30,500 cases to "other stages of adjudication." I obtained clarification on this point from inquiries to the LEAA, which supplied me with the 78,200 total conviction figure and its derivation: 60,200 inmates serving jail terms without appeals pending, 6,600 sentenced with appeals pending, and 11,300 awaiting sentencing.
12. Not all of the index offenses are defined as felonies by the states. However, the number of misdemeanor larcenies in the 20,000 figure may be offset by the number of inmates convicted of nonindex felonies.
13. The relatively small number of sentenced and detained inmates in jail for drunkenness/vagrancy is at odds with older studies that reported up to 50 percent of the commitments for intoxification. The difference may be explained in part by the definition of jail adopted in the National Jail Census, which excluded the voluminous number of facilities that retained persons for less than 48 hours (primarily "drunk tanks").
14. Ronald Goldfarb, *Jails: The Ultimate Ghetto* (New York: Anchor Books, 1976).
15. Ibid., p. 22.
16. Richard McGee, "Our Sick Jails," *Federal Probation,* March 1971, p. 3.
17. Mattack, "Contemporary Jails," p. 811.
18. The Illinois jail survey found that in only 3 percent of the city and 14 percent of the county jails were inmates given any work to do. Goldfarb, *Jails,* p. 9.
19. Vermont had four inmates in its four jails at the time of the 1972 census.
20. Ben H. Bagdikian, *The Shame of the Prisons* (New York: Pocket Books, 1972), p. 65.
21. Forty-seven according to the 1970 census.
22. Bagdikian, *The Shame of the Prisons,* p. 65.
23. Mattack, "Contemporary Jails," pp. 807–808.
24. 1970 National Jail Census.
25. Goldfarb, *Jails,* pp. 22–23.
26. "NIC to Establish National Jail Center," *AJC,* July–August 1977, p. 20.
27. Discussion based on consolidation from Mattick, "Contemporary Jails," pp. 777–843; Robert M. Carter, Richard A. McGee, and E. Kim Nelson, *Corrections in America* (Philadelphia: Lippincott, 1975), pp. 76–77; Flynn, "Jails and Criminal Justice," p. 62.
28. Except for federal correctional centers in San Diego, New York City, Chicago, and the small, remote Federal Detention Center in Florence, Arizona.
29. Goldfarb, *Jails,* pp. 19–20.
30. Ibid., p. 27.
31. A three-year study by the National Clearinghouse concluded that electronic surveillance of prisoners was generally less effective and much more expen-

sive than direct supervision by guards. Because of the enormous boredom and fatigue that results from watching a closed-circuit television screen, guards must be relieved every hour or so. Thus the costs are three to four times that of direct supervision. "TV Picture Not Too Bright for Prison Security," *AJC*, July–August 1975, p. 50.
32. *CD*, January 1974, p. 71.
33. Forty-six percent of the nation's jails allow some sentenced inmates to serve their time on weekends.
34. Sanford Bates, "How Many Years?" *CD*, January 1973, p. 17.
35. Standards and Goals Commission, *Corrections*, p. 292.
36. William G. Nagel, *The New Red Barn: A Critical Look at the Modern American Prison* (New York: Walker, 1973), p. 22.
37. Ibid., p. 29.
38. Flynn, "Jails and Criminal Justice," p. 59.
39. The material in this section is based on the footnoted sources in addition to information contained in other *New York Times* articles with details that I have interspersed, occasionally without citation.
40. *New York Times*, November 16, 1974, p. 23.
41. Jack Newfield, *Cruel and Unusual Justice* (New York: Holt, Rinehart & Winston, 1974), p. 66.
42. Bagdikian, *Shame of Prisons*, pp. 60, 63.
43. Ibid., p. 63.
44. Newfield, *Cruel and Unusual Justice*, p. 67.
45. Despite such assurances, the guards systematically clubbed prisoners with ax handles, baseball bats, and riot sticks on the day the revolt ended. And in January 1971, seven inmates involved in the riot were indicted on 50 separate counts of first-degree kidnapping. Newfield, *Cruel and Unusual Justice*, pp. 3, 67.
46. Bagdikian, *Shame of Prisons*, p. 63.
47. The unconstitutional conditions include: excessive use of maximum security, restrictions on visiting rights, excessive noise and heat, poor ventilation, inadequate staffing, and too few opportunities for exercise, recreation, and education. *New York Times*, December 3, 1974, p. 43.
48. *New York Times*, December 21, 1974, p. 34.
49. Judge Lasker's order was upheld by the U.S. Court of Appeals for the Second Circuit, which agreed that the Tombs conditions deprived inmates of "their fundamental constitutional rights." Significantly, because the Second Circuit's jurisdiction includes Connecticut and Vermont as well as New York, every jail in the three states was theoretically subjected to the minimum standards set forth in the federal appellate court's decision. The defunct Tombs was also used to give a group of juveniles heading for trouble with the law a "taste of jail," under a Department of Correction program designed to teach youngsters that crime does not pay. *New York Times*, September 14, 1977, p. B3.
50. *New York Times*, November 9, 1974, p. 35, and December 3, 1974, p. 43.
51. "Profile: The Adult Corrections System in New York City," *Corrections*, June 1976, pp. 30 ff.
52. *Time*, December 8, 1975, p. 10.
53. *New York Times*, January 7, 1976, pp. 1, 18.

54. *New York Times,* February 23, 1975, p. 33.
55. *New York Times,* May 8, 1977, section 4, p. 6.
56. The Board of Correction, at the time, was merely an advisory group that had no control over the Department of Correction, which operates all of the New York City correctional institutions.
57. Comparisons are ordinarily based on the first quarters of 1975 and 1974. *New York Times,* November 25, 1975, p. 31.
58. *New York Times,* May 8, 1977, p. 6.
59. Contact visiting rooms allow the prisoners to touch their visitors instead of having to use telephones or being separated from them by glass or partitions.
60. Many of the detainees preferred prison to jail. "We're not just in a hamster box here [at Sing-Sing]—a man is able to breathe better." Under a special contractual arrangement, city detainees were kept in a segregated cellblock in Sing-Sing and wore red uniforms to distinguish them from the "real" prisoners, who wear green. *New York Times,* January 7, 1976, pp. 1, 18. Quotation from "Profile: Adult Corrections System," p. 45.
61. *New York Times,* November 26, 1975, p. 1.
62. "Profile: Adult Corrections System," pp. 34, 37.
63. *Time,* December 8, 1975, p. 10.
64. *New York Times,* January 8, 1976, p. 35.
65. *New York Times,* February 23, 1975, p. 1.
66. *LEAA Newsletter,* April 1975, p. 12.
67. *New York Times,* February 22, 1975, p. 31, and January 8, 1976, p. 35.
68. *New York Times,* January 13, 1976, p. 36.
69. "Profile: Adult Corrections System," p. 47.
70. *New York Times,* December 4, 1977, p. 55.

Chapter 14

1. Michael S. Serrill, "Profile: California," *Corrections,* September 1974, p. 29.
2. Edgar May, "Profile: Arizona," *Corrections,* July–August 1975, pp. 46–47.
3. Serrill, "Profile: California," pp. 3ff.
4. May, "Profile: Arizona," pp. 40, 43–44.
5. Lauren Katzowitz, "Profile: Kentucky," *Corrections,* March–April 1975, pp. 18, 23–25.
6. Unless otherwise footnoted, the present statistical discussion of prison population growth is based on Steve Gettinger, "U.S. Prison Population Hits All-Time High," *Corrections,* March 1976, Rob Wilson, "U.S. Prison Population Sets Another Record," *Corrections,* March 1977, and Kevin Krajick, "Annual Prison Population Survey," *Corrections,* April 1981, pp. 16–20.
7. *Criminal Justice Newsletter,* August 3, 1981, p. 5.
8. *Transfer,* Special Issue (Champaign, Ill.: National Clearinghouse for Criminal Justice Planning & Architecture, n.d.).
9. Ibid.
10. Stephen Franklin, "The 'Law and Order' Backfire," *The Nation,* February 28, 1976, p. 242; "Prisons—A Target of Revolutionaries," *LEB,* September 1974, p. 13.
11. "Follow Up," *Corrections,* November–December 1975, p. 56.

12. Edgar May, "Prison Officials Fear Flat Time is More Time," *Corrections,* September 1977, pp. 43–46; Stephen Gettinger, "Three States Adopt Flat Time, Others Wary," *Corrections,* September 1977, p. 26.
13. *New York Times,* August 29, 1976, p. 5; "Alabama Under Strict Court Order to Upgrade Entire Prison System," *Corrections,* March 1976, pp. 18–19.
14. Franklin, "Law and Order," pp. 241–242.
15. Gettinger, "Three States Adopt," p. 9.
16. Wilson, "Prison Population Sets Record," p. 13.
17. *Corrections,* November–December 1975, p. 57.
18. William Hart, "Profile: New Mexico," *Corrections,* March 1976, p. 32.
19. *U.S. News & World Report,* March 1, 1976, p. 65; Gettinger, "Prison Population All-Time High," p. 16.
20. Gettinger, "Prison Population All-Time High," p. 16.
21. Wilson, "Prison Population Sets Record," pp. 12–13; *Time,* November 10, 1975, p. 43.
22. *New York Times,* October 24, 1975, p. 12.
23. *New York Times,* October 26, 1975, p. 67.
24. *Time,* October 21, 1974, p. 111.
25. Gettinger, "Prison Population All-Time High," p. 12.
26. *Criminal Justice Newsletter,* August 3, 1981, p. 2.
27. Franklin, "Law and Order," p. 242.
28. Norman A. Carlson, "A More Balanced Corrections Philosophy," *LEB,* January 1977, p. 23.
29. Wilson, "Prison Population Sets Record," p. 21.
30. Gettinger, "Prison Population All-Time High," p. 20.
31. *U.S. News & World Report,* March 1, 1976, p. 67.
32. Ibid., p. 65.
33. *New York Times,* October 26, 1975, section 4, p. 3.
34. *Criminal Justice Newsletter,* August 3, 1981, p. 5.
35. *New York Times,* July 24, 1981, p. 11.
36. "Alabama Under Strict Order," *Corrections,* pp. 18–19.
37. "Overcrowding," *CD,* January 1976, p. 100.
38. "Crisis in the Prisons: Not Enough Room for All the Criminals," *U.S. News & World Report,* November 28, 1977, p. 76.
39. *Holt* v. *Sarver,* 309 F.Supp. 362 (E.D.Ark, 1970); aff'd 442 F.2d 304 (8th Cir. 1971).
40. *Talley* v. *Stephens,* 247 F.Supp. 683 (D.C.E.D. Ark. 1965).
41. *Jackson* v. *Bishop,* 404 F.2d 571 (8th Cir. 1968).
42. Burton M. Atkins and Henry R. Glick, eds., *Prison, Protest, and Politics* (Englewood Cliffs, N.J.: Prentice-Hall, 1972), pp. 36, 38.
43. Ronald H. Rosenberg, "Constitutional Law—The Eighth Amendment and Prison Reform," *North Carolina Law Review,* October 1973, pp. 1542–1543; Stacy L. Moore, "Arkansas State Penitentiary Trangresses Constitutional Proscription Against Cruel and Unusual Punishment," *Seton Hall Law Review,* Fall 1971, p. 160.
44. *Gates* v. *Collier,* 349 F.Supp. 881 (N.D. Miss. 1971); 501 F.2d 1291 (5th Cir. 1974).
45. *Pugh* v. *Locke,* 406 F.Supp. 318 (M.D. Ala. 1976).
46. *James* v. *Wallace,* 406 F.Supp. 318 (M.D. Ala. 1976).

47. Charles S. Prigmore and Richard T. Crow, "Is the Court Remaking the American Prison System?" *Federal Probation,* June 1976, pp. 3–10.
48. *New York Times,* August 30, 1975, p. 13.
49. *CD,* January 1976, p. 100.
50. *Time,* January 26, 1976, p. 65.
51. *New York Times,* September 20, 1977, p. 29.
52. *Ruiz* v. *Estelle* 503 F. Supp. 1265 (1980).
53. Ibid., 1391.
54. Kevin Krajick, "U.S. Judge Calls Texas Prisons 'Malignant'" *Corrections,* February 1981, p. 46.
55. Ibid., p. 48.
56. Kevin Krajick, "A Federal Judge Comes Down Hard on Texas," *Corrections,* June 1981, p. 43.
57. *Ruiz* v. *McMillan,* U.S. Fifth Cir. Ct. of Appeals, June 26, 1981, No. 81-2224.
58. President's Crime Commission, *Corrections,* Table 15 at p. 197.
59. Barbara Goldstein, "Screening for Emotional and Psychological Fitness in Correctional Officer Hiring," American Bar Association paper, January 1975, p. 2.
60. "National Survey of State Correctional Officers," *Corrections,* December 1976, p. 35.
61. "Texas Offers Corrections Employees More Training," *AJC,* January–February 1974, p. 25.
62. Roan Conrad, "Profile: Connecticut," *Corrections,* January–February 1975, p. 66.
63. Lewis E. Powell and Michael S. Serrill, "Profile: Georgia," *Corrections,* November–December 1974, p. 71.
64. Edgar May, "Prison Guards in America," *Corrections,* December 1976, p. 44.
65. "Riots Behind Bars: A Search for Causes," *Connecticut Quarterly Journal of Criminal Justice,* Winter 1973–1974, p. 70.
66. William Hart, "Profile: Michigan," *Corrections,* September 1976, p. 61.
67. Anthony Astrachan, "Profile: Louisiana," *Corrections,* September–October 1975, p. 10.
68. Susan Sheehan, "Prison Life," *New Yorker,* October 31, 1977, p. 87.
69. William G. Nagel, *The New Red Barn* (New York: Walker, 1974), p. 48.
70. Ibid., p. 52.
71. Serrill, "Profile: California," p. 31.
72. *Minnick* v. *Cal. Dept. of Corrections,* No. 79-1213. Decided June 1, 1981.
73. Kathleen S. Claflin, "Women in Corrections," in Robert Brooks, *Demythologizing Corrections* (Cobalt, Conn.: Cottage Industries, 1976), pp. 16–21.
74. Ibid.
75. Joan Potter, "Should Women Guards Work in Prisons for Men?" *Corrections,* October 1980, pp. 30–35.
76. *New York Times,* April 5, 1977, p. 69.
77. Ibid., p. 36; *New York Times,* November 26, 1978, p. 56.
78. *Edward L. Kirland and Nathaniel Hayes* v. *New York State Department of Correctional Services,* Nos. 445, 449—September Term, 1974, U.S. Court of Appeals for the Second Circuit.

79. *Dothard* v. *Rawlinson,* 433 U.S. 321 (1977).
80. Charles S. Prigmore and John C. Watkins, "Correctional Manpower: Are We 'The Society of Captives'?" *Federal Probation,* December 1972, p. 13.
81. Anthony Astrachan, "Close-up: George Camp of Missouri," *Corrections,* March–April 1975, p. 35.
82. Conrad, "Profile: Connecticut," p. 69.
83. Anthony Astrachan, "Profile: Pennsylvania," *Corrections,* May–June 1975, p. 52.
84. "In Illinois, Guards Have a Wider Role," *Corrections,* December 1976, pp. 41–43.
85. Robert R. Smith, Lynda A. Hart, and Michael A. Milan, *Correctional Officer Training in Behavior Modification: An Interim Report* (Washington, D.C.: U.S. Department of Labor, May 1971).
86. Astrachan, "Close-up," p. 34.
87. *Philadelphia Bulletin,* March 8, 1972, p. 23.
88. "Our Prisons Are Powder Kegs," *Reader's Digest,* October 1974, pp. 184–188.
89. Anthony L. Guenther and Mary Guenther, "Screws and Thugs," *Society,* July–August, 1974, p. 43.
90. May, "Profile: Arizona," pp. 42–44.
91. Katzowitz, "Profile: Kentucky," p. 18.
92. "Jobs Behind Bars: Boon to Prisoners and Taxpayers," *U.S. News & World Report,* June 20, 1977, p. 60.
93. Serrill, "Profile: California," p. 35.
94. *New York Times,* August 29, 1976, section 4, p. 5.
95. Neil M. Singer, "The Value of Inmate Manpower," *JRC,* January 1976, pp. 3–4.
96. Serrill, "Profile: California," p. 36.
97. Singer, "Value of Inmate Manpower," p. 11.
98. "Jobs Behind Bars," p. 60.
99. Ibid.
100. Ibid.
101. Hart, "Profile: New Mexico," p. 35.
102. Serrill, "Profile: California," p. 35.
103. Ibid.
104. Michael S. Serrill, "Profile: New Jersey," *Corrections,* November–December 1974, p. 25.
105. Ronald H. Bailey, "Florida," *Corrections,* September 1974, p. 89.
106. Conrad, "Profile: Connecticut," p. 68.
107. May, "Profile: Arizona," p. 47.
108. Edward H. Dermitt, "Arkansas' New Graphic Communications Program Trains and Cuts Costs," *AJC,* March–April 1975, pp. 32–33.
109. "Michigan Prisons Ups Industry Production," *AJC,* January–February 1974, pp. 24ff.
110. Rachel Kamuf, "Public Saves Money, Correctional Workers Learn and Earn," *AJC,* May–June 1975, pp. 12–13.
111. Michael S. Serrill, "Profile: Minnesota," *Corrections,* January–February 1975, pp. 8–9.
112. "Lawbreakers' Financial Condition," *CD,* April 1975, p. 185.

113. "Canada Launches New Approach to Inmate Employment," *AJC,* November–December 1976, p. 10.
114. *Corrections Compendium,* October 1977, p. 4.
115. *New York Times,* April 19, 1975, p. 34.
116. *New York Times,* October 31, 1976, p. 40.
117. *New York Times,* August 29, 1976, p. 5.
118. *Analysis of Prison Industries and Recommendations for Change* (Washington, D.C.: Superintendent of Documents, June 1978).
119. Michael Fedo, "Free Enterprise Goes to Prison," *Corrections,* April 1981, pp. 5–15.
120. Analysis of Prison Industries, p. 21.
121. *Los Angeles Times,* February 4, 1979, p. 28.
122. Singer, "Value of Inmate Power," Table 1 at p. 5.
123. *Transfer,* no. 11, 1976, p. 1.
124. Ken Kerle, "Penal Education: United States and Europe," *Prison Journal,* vol. 53, Autumn–Winter 1973, p. 16.
125. "College Takes Over Inmate Education," *AJC,* March–April 1974, p. 29.
126. Astrachan, "Profile: Louisiana," p. 22.
127. R. V. Denenberg, "Profile: Washington State," *Corrections,* November–December 1974, p. 35.
128. Edgar May, "Profile: Missouri," *Corrections,* March 1976, p. 57.
129. John Irwin, "The Trouble With Rehabilitation," *CJB,* June 1974, p. 143.
130. Hart, "Profile: Michigan," p. 58.
131. May, "Profile: Arizona," pp. 42, 44, 47.
132. "College Takes Over Inmate Education," p. 29.
133. Denenberg, "Profile: Washington State," p. 39.
134. Steve Gettinger, "Profile: New York City's Adult Corrections System," *Corrections,* June 1976, p. 49.
135. Karl A. Slaikeu, "Evaluation Studies on Group Treatment of Juvenile and Adult Offenders in Correctional Institutions," *JRC,* January 1973, pp. 88–89.
136. Astrachan, "Profile: Pennsylvania," p. 52.
137. Norman S. Hayner, "Attitudes Toward Conjugal Visits for Prisoners," *Federal Probation,* March 1972, p. 48.
138. Michael S. Serrill, "Prison Furloughs in America," *Corrections,* July–August 1975, pp. 8–9.
139. George E. Dickinson, "Communication Policies in State Prisons for Adult Males," *Prison Journal,* Autumn–Winter 1972, p. 16.
140. Hayner, "Attitudes Toward Conjugal," p. 43.
141. *Martinez* v. *California,* No. 78-1268. Decided January 15, 1980.
142. *Prisoners in State and Federal Institutions on December 31, 1975,* National Prisoner Statistics (Washington, D.C.: U.S. Department of Justice, February 1977), Table 7 at p. 28.
143. Vincent O'Leary and Kathleen J. Hanrahan, *Parole Systems in the United States* (Hackensack, N.J.: National Council on Crime and Delinquency, 1976).
144. *Hartford Courant,* March 5, 1975, p. 1.
145. Theodore P. Fields, "Illinois Parole and Pardon Board Adult Parole Decisions," *Illinois Bar Journal,* September 1973, p. 21.

146. Serrill, "Profile: Minnesota," p. 12.
147. Hart, "Profile: Michigan," p. 65.
148. David T. Stanley, *Prisoners Among Us: The Problem of Parole* (Washington, D.C.: Brookings Institution, 1976), p. 38; Hart, "Profile: New Mexico," p. 49.
149. Rob Wilson, "Release: Should Parole Boards Hold the Key?" *Corrections,* September 1977, p. 48.
150. *Greenholtz* v. *Inmates of the Nebraska Penal and Correctional Complex,* No. 78-201. Decided May 29, 1979.
151. 18 *United States Code* 4230 (a).
152. Joseph E. Scott, "The Use of Discretion in Determining the Severity of Punishment for Incarcerated Offenders," *JCC,* June 1974, p. 219; Anne M. Heinz et al., "Sentencing by Parole Board: An Evaluation," *JCC,* March 1976, pp. 10–11.
153. Heinz, "Sentencing by Parole Board," p. 9.
154. William Parker, *Corrections Parole MDT Project, Resource Document #1: Parole* (College Park, Md.: American Correctional Association, May 1972), p. 27.
155. Standards and Goals Commission, *Corrections,* p. 411.
156. Daniel Glaser, *The Effectiveness of a Prison and Probation System* (Indianapolis: Bobbs-Merrill, 1964).
157. Scott, "The Use of Discretion," p. 222.
158. Robert O. Dawson, *Sentencing* (Boston: Little, Brown, 1969), pp. 296–298.
159. Astrachan, "Profile: Louisiana," p. 24.
160. Stanley, *Prisoners Among Us,* p. 40.
161. Ibid., p. 74.
162. Serrill, "Profile: Minnesota," p. 21.
163. Charles H. Percy, "An Overhaul of the Federal Parole System," *Case and Comment,* March–April 1973, p. 11.
164. Peter B. Hoffman and James L. Beck, "Salient Factor Score Validation—A 1972 Release Cohort," *JCJ,* Spring 1976, p. 69; Hoffman and James L. Beck, "Parole Decision-Making: A Salient Factor Score," *JCJ,* Fall 1974, p. 196.
165. William H. Mosley, "Parole: How It Is Working," *JCJ,* Fall 1977, Table 2 at p. 189.
166. Peter B. Hoffman and Lucille K. DeGostin, "Parole Decision-Making: Structuring Discretion," *Federal Probation,* December 1974, Tables 1 and 2 at p. 10.
167. William J. Genego, Peter D. Goldberger, and Vicki C. Jackson, "Parole Release Decisionmaking and the Sentencing Process," *Yale Law Journal,* March 1975, p. 894.
168. Wilson, "Parole Release," p. 52.
169. "Follow Up," *Corrections,* July–August 1975, p. 59.
170. Unless otherwise indicated, this section is based on Steve Gettinger, "Parole Contracts: A New Way Out," *Corrections,* September–October 1975, pp. 3–8, 45–50.
171. *The Mutual Agreement Program: A Planned Change in Correctional Service Delivery,* Parole Corrections Project, Resource Document #3 (College Park, Md.: American Correctional Association, 1973).

172. Allyn Sielaff, "Wisconsin Buys MAP Program," *AJC,* July–August 1977, p. 18.
173. Robert Bruce Rutherford, "Establishing Behavioral Contracts with Delinquent Adolescents," *Federal Probation,* March 1975, pp. 28–39; Edith Ankersmit, "Setting the Contract in Probation," *Federal Probation,* June 1976, pp. 28–33.
174. Bailey, "Florida," p. 91.
175. John R. Manson, "Determinate Sentencing," *CD,* April 1977, p. 204.
176. *Cicero* v. *Regan,* 75-2059-MEL, *New York Law Journal,* May 2, 1975.
177. California Senate Bill No. 42.
178. Mosley, "Parole," p. 193; M.G. Neithercutt, "Parole Legislation," *Federal Probation,* March 1977, p. 24.
179. Hart, "Profile: New Mexico," p. 50.
180. The number of jurisdictions with mandatory release and outright discharge laws was tabulated from case data presented in O'Leary and Hanrahan, *Parole Systems in the United States.*
181. *Prisoners in State and Federal Institutions on December 31, 1975,* Table 7 at p. 28.
182. Susan Sheehan, "Prison Life," *New Yorker,* October 24, 1977, p. 56.
183. George F. Cole and Charles H. Logan, "Parole: The Consumer's Perspective," *CJR,* Fall 1977, p. 74.
184. Kenneth J. Lenihan, "The Financial Condition of Released Prisoners," *CD,* July 1975, pp. 269–270.
185. Jimmy Hoffa, "Prison," *Saturday Evening Post,* October 1974, p. 45.
186. *News Fronts,* Autumn 1975, p. 5.
187. Nagel, *The New Red Barn.*
188. William G. Nagel, "On Behalf of a Moratorium on Prison Construction," *CD,* April 1977, pp. 154–171.
189. Nagel, *The New Red Barn,* p. 56.
190. *New York Times,* August 14, 1976, p. 33.
191. Frederic D. Moyer and Edith E. Flynn, *Correctional Environments* (Urbana: University of Illinois, National Clearinghouse for Correctional Planning and Architecture, 1971).
192. *Time,* May 17, 1976, p. 53.
193. Robert Martinson, "What Works?—Questions and Answers About Prison Reform," *Public Interest,* Spring 1974, pp. 22–54; Robert Martinson, Douglas Lipton, and Judith Wilks, *The Effectiveness of Correctional Treatment* (New York: Praeger, 1975).
194. Martinson, "What Works?" p. 25.
195. Ted Palmer, "Martinson Revisited," *JRC,* July 1975, pp. 133–152; Paul B. Klockars, "The True Limits of the Effectiveness of Correctional Treatment," *Prison Journal,* Spring–Summer 1975, pp. 53–64.
196. Seymour L. Halleck and Ann D. White, "Is Rehabilitation Dead?" *CD,* October 1977, pp. 372–382.
197. "Coed Prisons," *CD,* January 1974, p. 73.
198. Ibid.
199. "The Nondangerous Offender Should Not Be Imprisoned: A Policy Statement," October 1975, pp. 315–322.
200. Eugene Doleschal, "Public Opinion and Correctional Reform," *Crime and*

Delinquency Literature, August 1970, p. 470; *New York Times,* April 20, 1975, section 4, p. 6.

201. Paul K. Connolly, "The Possibility of a Prison Sentence Is a Necessity," *CD,* October 1975, pp. 356–359.
202. *New York Times,* September 16, 1977, p. A24.

Chapter 15

1. *Ruffin* v. *Commonwealth,* 62 Va. (21 Gratt, 1871), cited in David Paul Flint, "Judicial Response to Problems of Prison Administration," *Judicature,* June–July 1971, p. 25.
2. Neil P. Cohen and Dean Hill Rivkin, "Civil Disabilities: The Forgotten Punishment," *Federal Probation,* June 1971, pp. 19–25.
3. "A Symposium on Prisoners—A Target of Revolutionaries," *LEB,* September 1974, p. 13.
4. Ruggero J. Aldisert, "A Peculiar System: Federal Judges Hear State Prison Cases," *Resolution,* Spring 1975, pp. 4–5.
5. *Coffin* v. *Reichard,* 143 F.2d 443 (1944).
6. Gordon Hawkins, *The Prison: Policy and Practice* (Chicago: University of Chicago Press, 1976), pp. 139–140.
7. *The Emerging Rights of the Confined* (Columbia: South Carolina Department of Corrections and the Correctional Development Foundation, 1975).
8. *Cruz* v. *Beto,* 405 U.S. 319 (1972).
9. *Attica: The Official Report of the New York State Special Commission on Attica* (New York: Bantam Books, 1972); Tom Wicker, "The Men in D Yard," *Esquire,* March 1975, pp. 59ff.
10. Estimates vary from two-thirds, cited by the Attica Commission, to 85 percent, mentioned by other sources: "Attica: A Look at the Causes and the Future," *CLB,* December 1971, p. 817.
11. Tom Wicker, "A Time to Die," *Book Digest,* July 1975, p. 20.
12. Ronald Huff, "The Development and Diffusion of Prisoners' Movements," *Prison Journal,* Autumn–Winter 1975, p. 10.
13. *Johnson* v. *Avery,* 393 U.S. 483 (1969).
14. Sol Rubin, "The Administrative Response to Court Decisions," *CD,* July 1969, note 2 at p. 379.
15. *Younger* v. *Gilmore,* 404 U.S. 15 (1971).
16. *Gilmore* v. *Lynch,* 319 F.Supp. 105 (N.D.Cal. 1970).
17. *Wolff* v. *McDonnell,* 418 U.S. 539 (1974).
18. Hazel B. Kerper and Janeen Kerper, *Legal Rights of the Convicted* (St. Paul: West, 1974), p. 395.
19. *Procunier* v. *Martinez,* 411 U.S. 396 (1974).
20. *Fulwood* v. *Clemmer,* 206 F.Supp. 370 (1962).
21. *Cruz* v. *Beto,* 92 S.Ct. 1079 (1972).
22. Examples in this section are from William T. Toal, *Recent Developments in Correctional Case Law* (Columbia: South Carolina Department of Corrections, 1975), p. 17; *Emerging Rights of the Confined,* p. 16; *Cooper* v. *Pate,* 84 S.Ct. 1733 (1964).
23. *Lee* v. *Washington,* 390 U.S. 333 (1968).
24. Huff, "The Development and Diffusion," pp. 10–14; idem., "Unionization Behind the Walls," *Criminology,* August 1974, pp. 175–193; *Prisoners'*

Labor Union v. *State of Michigan,* Department of Corrections, 346 F.Supp. 697 (1972).

25. *Jones* v. *North Carolina Prisoners' Labor Union,* 97 S.Ct. 2532 (1977).
26. Unless otherwise noted, this section is based primarily on: Toal, *Recent Developments,* pp. 61–63; and *Emerging Rights of the Confined,* pp. 147–153.
27. David Gilman, "Courts and Corrections," *Corrections,* March 1977, p. 47.
28. *Estelle* v. *Gamble,* 429 U.S. 97 (1976).
29. Ronald H. Rosenberg, "Constitutional Law—The Eighth Amendment and Prison Reform," *North Carolina Law Review,* October 1973, p. 1540.
30. Beverly G. Toomey, Harry E. Allen, and Clifford E. Simonsen, "The Right to Treatment," *Prison Journal,* Autumn–Winter 1974, p. 46.
31. Donna E. Renn, "The Right to Treatment and the Juvenile," *CD,* October 1973, pp. 477–484.
32. Harry L. Miller, "The 'Right to Treatment': Can the Courts Rehabilitate and Cure?" *Public Interest,* Winter 1977, pp. 105–112.
33. *O'Connor* v. *Donaldson,* 95 S.Ct. 2486 (1975).
34. Jessica Mitford, *Kind and Unusual Punishment* (New York: Vintage Books, 1974), chapters 8 and 9; idem., "Experiments Behind Bars," *Atlantic,* January 1973, p. 68.
35. Alvin J. Bronstein, "Prisoners of Research," *Trial,* November–December 1975, pp. 16ff.
36. Ibid., p. 18.
37. Follow-Up: "FDA Bans Prison Drug Research," *Corrections,* December 1980, p. 47.
38. William E. Cockerham, "Behavior Modification for Child Molesters," *Corrections,* January–February 1975, p. 77.
39. James G. Holland, "Behavior Modification for Prisoners, Patients, and Other People as a Prescription for the Planned Society," *Prison Journal,* Spring–Summer 1974, pp. 25–27.
40. *Clonce* v. *Richardson,* 379 F.Supp. 338 (W.D.Mo. 1974).
41. *Washington Post,* August 7, 1975, p. A17.
42. Richard Speiglman, "Prison Psychiatrists and Drugs," *Crime and Social Justice,* Spring–Summer 1977, p. 33; Wayne Sage, "Crime and the Clockwork Lemon," *Human Behavior,* September 1974, p. 18.
43. Fred D. Hutchinson, "Procedural Due Process in the Involuntary Institutional Transfer of Prisoners," *Virginia Law Review,* February 1974, p. 356.
44. *Trop* v. *Dulles,* 356 U.S. 86 (1958).
45. The test established in *Weems* v. *United States,* 217 U.S. 349 (1910).
46. *Jordan* v. *Fitzharris,* 257 F.Supp. 674 (1966).
47. Robert Plotkin, "Recent Developments in the Law of Prisoner's Rights," *CLB,* July–August 1975, pp. 406–407.
48. *Morrisey* v. *Brewer,* 408 U.S. 471 (1972).
49. *Gagnon* v. *Scarpelli,* 411 U.S. 778 (1973).
50. *Wolff* v. *McDonnell,* 418 U.S. 539 (1974).
51. *Robert O. McDonnell* v. *Charles L. Wolff,* 483 F.2d. 1059 (1973).
52. David Gilman, "Developments in Correctional Law," *CD,* April 1975, pp. 163–165.

53. *Sostre* v. *Rockefeller,* 312 F.Supp. 863 (S.D.N.Y. 1970), reversed in part sub. nom. *Sostre* v. *McGinnis,* 442 F.2d 178 (2nd Cir. 1971); *Landman* v. *Royster,* 333 F.Supp. 621 (1971); *Clutchette* v. *Procunier,* No. 71-2357 (9th Cir., April 25, 1974).
54. *Meachum* v. *Fano,* 96 S.Ct. 2532 (1976).
55. Hutchinson, "Procedural Due Process," pp. 333–362.
56. *Jackson* v. *Bishop,* 404 F.2d. 571 (8th Cir. 1968).
57. Based on David Gilman, "Courts and Corrections," *Corrections,* September 1976, pp. 51–53.
58. *United States* v. *Bailey,* No. 78-990. Decided January 21, 1980.
59. *Jail Administration Law Bulletin,* Sample Issue, 76-1, n.d., pp. 6–7.
60. *In re Hoffman* (1968), unpublished opinion of Judge Barbieri, Court of Common Pleas, September 26, 1968.
61. Gary Wood, "Recent Applications of the Ban of Cruel and Unusual Punishments," *Hastings Law Journal,* April 1972, pp. 1116–1117.
62. *A Model Act for the Protection of Prisoners* (Hackensack, N.J.: National Council on Crime and Delinquency, May 1974), p. 12.
63. *Corrections Compendium,* October 1977, p. 4.
64. Stephen Gettinger, "Cruel and Unusual Prisons," *Corrections,* December 1977, p. 4.
65. *U.S. News & World Report,* January 19, 1976, p. 31.
66. Ibid., pp. 31–32; *New York Times,* December 24, 1975, p. 42.
67. *AJC,* May–June 1975, p. 39.
68. *Brenneman* v. *Madigan,* Civil No. C-70, 1911 AJC, U.S. Dist. Ct. N. Dist. Calif. (1971); *Jones* v. *Wittenberg,* 323 F.Supp. 93 (N.D. Ohio 1971); *Hamilton* v. *Love,* 328 F.Supp. 1182 (E.D.Ark. 1971).
69. *Hamilton* v. *Love,* 328 F.Supp. 1182 (E.D.Ark. 1971).
70. *Rhem* v. *Malcolm,* 371 F.Supp. 594 (D.D.N.Y. 1974), aff'd in relevant part 507 F.2d 333 (2d Cir. 1974).
71. *New York Times,* January 9, 1977, p. 28; *New York Times,* September 16, 1977, p. B3.
72. *New York Times,* April 24, 1977, p. 50.
73. *CD,* January 1976, p. 101.
74. *Bell* v. *Wolfish,* No. 77-1829. Decided May 14, 1979.
75. *Procunier* v. *Martinez,* 416 U.S. 396 (1974).
76. Virginia McArthur, "Inmate Grievance Mechanisms: A Survey of 209 American Prisons," *Federal Probation,* December 1974, Table 1 at p. 42.
77. Ibid., p. 43.
78. R. V. and Tia Denenberg, "Prison Grievance Procedures," *Corrections,* January–February 1975, pp. 38–41.
79. Ibid., p. 41.
80. George Nicolau, "Grievance Arbitration in a Prison: The Holton Experiment," *Resolution,* September 1975, pp. 11–16.
81. *Controlled Confrontation: The Ward Grievance Procedure of the California Youth Authority* (Washington, D.C.: Law Enforcement Assistance Administration, 1976), pp. 4–5.
82. *LSR,* November 1970, p. 300.
83. Edgar May, "Prison Ombudsmen in America," *Corrections,* January–February 1975, p. 46; McArthur, "Inmate Grievance," p. 43.

84. Fay Stender, "Wardens, Attorneys, and Prisoners," *Case and Comment,* September–October 1973, p. 14.
85. Randall K. Halvorson, "The Ombudsman for Corrections: A View of the Minnesota Experience," *Resolution,* Spring 1975, pp. 23, 25.
86. Linda R. Singer and J. Michael Keating, "The Courts and the Prisons: A Crisis of Confrontation," *CLB,* May 1973, p. 346.
87. McArthur, "Inmate Grievance Mechanisms," p. 42.
88. Rob Wilson, "Hongisto: A Very Different Sheriff," *Corrections,* December 1977, p. 32.
89. *CD,* October 1973, p. 585; *Morales* v. *Turman,* 364 F.Supp. 166 (1973); Linda R. Singer and J. Michael Keating, "Prisoner Grievance Mechanisms," *CD,* July 1973, p. 373.
90. R. V. Denenberg, "Profile: Washington State," *Corrections,* November–December 1974, pp. 39–40.
91. Gabrielle Tyrnauer, "What Went Wrong at Walla Walla?" *Corrections,* June 1981, p. 40.
92. McArthur, "Inmate Grievance Mechanisms," p. 44.
93. W. Lee Palmer, "Inmate Self-Government Is Fraught with Dangers: Fact or Fiction," in Robert J. Brooks, *Demythologizing Corrections* (Cobalt, Conn.: Cottage Industries, 1976), p. 36.
94. Hans J. Mattick, "The Prosaic Sources of Prison Violence," *Society,* November–December 1973, pp. 13ff.
95. Denenberg, "Profile: Washington State," pp. 33–34.
96. Sol Rubin, "Developments in Correctional Law," *CD,* April 1971, p. 221.
97. *New York Times,* March 27, 1977, p. 18.
98. *A Model Act for the Protection of Rights of Prisoners* (Hackensack, N.J.: National Council on Crime and Delinquency, 1974); "Tentative Draft of Standards Relating to the Legal Status of Prisoners," *ACL,* Special Issue, Winter 1977; Sheldon Krantz et al., *Model Rules and Regulations on Prisoners' Rights and Responsibilities* (St. Paul, Minn.: West, 1973).
99. *New York Times,* September 6, 1977, p. 23; "Principal Accomplishments of the ABA Corrections Commission 1971–1974," *AJC,* May–June 1975, pp. 14–16.

Chapter 16

1. Leon G. Leiberg, *Project Crossroads: Final Report* (Washington, D.C.: National Committee for Children and Youth, 1971).
2. *The Manhattan Court Employment Project: Final Report* (New York: Vera Institute of Justice, 1972).
3. Daniel McGillis, "Recent Developments in Minor Dispute Processing," private mimeo paper, no date, p. 1.
4. Royer F. Cook, Janice A. Roehl, and David I. Sheppard, *Neighborhood Justice Centers Field Test: Final Evaluation Report* (Washington, D.C.: National Institute of Justice, February 1980).
5. John W. Palmer, "The Night Prosecutor," *Judicature,* June–July 1975, pp. 23–27.
6. Janet Kole, "Arbitration as an Alternative to the Criminal Warrant," *Judicature,* February 1973, pp. 295–297; *Target* January 1977; *New York Times,* May 28, 1975, p. 45.
7. President's Crime Commission, *Juvenile Delinquency,* p. 19.

8. Ibid., pp. 19–21.
9. Robert J. Gemignani, "Youth Service Systems: Diverting Youth from the Juvenile Justice System," *Delinquency Prevention Reporter,* July–August 1972.
10. *Monograph on Legal Issues and Characteristics on Pretrial Intervention Programs* (Washington, D.C.: American Bar Association, 1974), pp. 1–13; Daniel L. Skoler, "Protecting the Rights of Defendants," *CLB,* July–August 1974, pp. 473–492.
11. Louis K. Polonsky, "Limitations upon Trial Court Discretion in Imposing Conditions of Probation," *Georgia Law Review,* Winter 1974, p. 468.
12. "Selected State Court Decisions," *CLB,* January–February 1972, p. 91.
13. Sol Rubin, "The Administrative Response to Court Decisions," *CD,* July 1969, p. 385.
14. Polonsky, "Limitations upon Trial Court," p. 470.
15. *New York Times,* February 15, 1976, p. 27.
16. Polonsky, "Limitations upon Trial Court," p. 484.
17. *U.S. News & World Report,* August 8, 1977, p. 66.
18. Anne Newton, "Aid to the Victim: Compensation and Restitution," *Crime and Delinquency Literature,* September 1976, p. 380; Bill Read, "How Restitution Works in Georgia," *Judicature,* February 1977, pp. 323–331.
19. Joe Hudson, Bert Galaway, and Steve Chesney, "When Criminals Repay Their Victims: A Survey of Restitution Programs," *Judicature,* February 1977, p. 313.
20. Sylvia Sullivan, "Convicted Offenders Become Community Helpers," *Judicature,* March 1973, p. 333.
21. "A Step Toward Determinancy for Juveniles," *Corrections,* September 1977, pp. 37–38.
22. Burt Galaway, "The Use of Restitution," *CD,* January 1977, p. 59.
23. *LEAA Newsletter,* February 1977, p. 7.
24. *Escoe* v. *Zerbst,* 295 U.S. 493 (1935).
25. *Goldberg* v. *Kelly,* 397 U.S. 254 (1970).
26. Keith J. Leenhouts, "Royal Oak's Experience with Professionals and Volunteers in Probation," *Federal Probation,* December 1970, pp. 45–46.
27. Elizabeth and James Vorenberg, "Early Diversion from the Criminal Justice System: Practice in Search of a Theory," in Lloyd E. Ohlin, ed., *Prisoners in America* (Englewood Cliffs, N.J.: Prentice-Hall, 1973), p. 164.
28. Joseph Ellenbogen and Beverly DiGregorio, "Volunteers in Probation Exploring New Dimensions," *Judicature,* January 1975, pp. 281–285; *New York Times,* March 13, 1977, p. 43.
29. Marguerite Q. Warren, *Correctional Treatment in Community Settings* (Rockville, Md.: National Institute of Mental Health, 1972), p. 14.
30. *Volunteer Courts: A Child's Helping Hand* (Washington, D.C.: Law Enforcement Assistance Administration, 1973).
31. Raymond D. Clements, *Para-Professionals in Probation and Parole* (Chicago: University of Chicago Law School, 1972).
32. See Thomas C. Neil, "Who Should Go and Who Should Stay: A Study of Prison Commitments," *Criminology,* May 1974, pp. 107–113.
33. Robert L. Smith, *A Quiet Revolution: Probation Subsidy* (Washington, D.C.: Government Printing Office, n.d.), p. 12.

34. Lawrence A. Bennett, "Should We Change the Offender or the System?" *CD,* July 1973, p. 337.
35. *California's Probation Subsidy Program: A Progress Report to the Legislature,* Report No. 3 (Sacramento: California Youth Authority, June 1976), p. i.
36. "Probation Subsidy: 'Behavior Modification' for Bureaucrats," *Corrections,* December 1980, pp. 19, 22.
37. Consolidated references to section on caseload research: Stuart Adams, "Some Findings From Correctional Caseload Research," *Federal Probation,* December 1967, pp. 48–57; Jerry Banks, Terry R. Siler, and Ronald L. Rardin, "Past and Present Findings in Intensive Adult Probation," *Federal Probation,* June 1977, pp. 20–25; William P. Adams, Paul M. Chandler, and M.G. Neithercutt, "The San Francisco Project: A Critique," *Federal Probation,* December 1971, pp. 45–53; Robert Martinson, "What Works—Questions and Answers About Prison Reform," *Public Interest,* Spring 1974, pp. 40–48; *Target,* September 1977; Marguerite Q. Warren, "Classification of Offenders as an Aid to Efficient Management and Effective Treatment," *JCL,* June 1971, pp. 239–258.
38. H. Ted Rubin, "New Directions in Misdemeanor Probation," *Judicature,* April 1977, pp. 435–441.
39. Standards and Goals Commission, *Corrections,* pp. 333–335.
40. *Boston Globe,* August 10, 1975, p. 29.
41. Yitzhak Bakal, "Viewpoint," *Criminal Justice Newsletter,* December 31, 1975, p. 4.
42. Brian Vachon, "Hey Man, What Did You Learn in Reform School?" *Saturday Review of Education,* October 1972, p. 69.
43. Lloyd E. Ohlin, Robert B. Coates, and Alden D. Miller, "Radical Correctional Reform: A Case Study of the Massachusetts Youth Correctional System," *Harvard Educational Review,* February 1974, pp. 81–82.
44. Yitzhak Bakal, *Strategies for Restructuring the State Department of Youth Services* (Washington, D.C.: U.S. Department of Health, Education and Welfare, n.d.), p. 4.
45. John M. Baer, "New Broom on the Cellblock," *Human Behavior,* June 1977, p. 42.
46. Andrew Rutherford, *The Dissolution of the Training Schools in Massachusetts* (Columbus, Ohio: Academy for Contemporary Problems, n.d.), p. 7. Rutherford's article is basically "reprinted" in Andrew Rutherford, "Facts and Fantasies Concerning Developments in Massachusetts," *Prison Journal,* Spring–Summer 1974, pp. 12–22.
47. Peter Schrag and Diane Divoky, "The New Juvenile Justice at Work," *Civil Liberties Review,* Summer 1975, p. 73.
48. *Overview of Changes in the Massachusetts Department of Youth Services* (Boston: Harvard Law School Center for Criminal Justice, September 1973), pp. 6–7.
49. Rutherford, *The Dissolution,* p. 16.
50. Yitzhak Bakal, "The Massachusetts Experience," *Delinquency Prevention Reporter,* April 1973, p. 5.
51. Lloyd Ohlin, Robert B. Coates, and Alden D. Miller, "Evaluating the Reform of Youth Correction in Massachusetts," *JRC,* January 1975, pp. 14–15.

52. Gordon P. Waldo, Theodore G. Chiricos, and Leonard E. Dobrin, "Community Contact and Inmate Attitudes: An Experimental Assessment of Work Release," *Criminology,* November 1973, p. 348.
53. Lawrence S. Root, "Work Release Legislation," *Federal Probation,* March 1972, p. 38.
54. Elmer H. Johnson and Kenneth E. Kotch, "Two Factors in Development of Work Release: Size and Location of Prisons," *JCJ,* March 1973, pp. 44–45.
55. Robert M. Carter, Cameron R. Dightman, and Malcolm W. Klein, "The Rate System Approach to Description and Evaluation of Criminal Justice Systems," *Criminology,* February 1974, p. 471.
56. Johnson and Kotch, "Two Factors," p. 48.
57. Michael S. Serrill, "Is Rehabilitation Dead?" *Corrections,* May–June 1975, p. 21.
58. Michael S. Serrill, "Profile: New Jersey," *Corrections,* November–December 1974, p. 28.
59. R. V. Denenberg, "Profile: Washington State," *Corrections,* November–December 1974, p. 42.
60. Kenneth J. Lenihan, *The Financial Resources of Released Prisoners* (Washington, D.C.: Bureau of Social Science Research, March 1974), p. 14.
61. *New York Times,* December 27, 1977, p. 24; *New York Times,* September 2, 1975, p. 23.
62. Michael S. Serrill, "California," *Corrections,* September 1974, pp. 39–40.
63. Waldo, Chiricos, and Dobrin, "Community Contact," pp. 345–381; James A. Beha, "Innovations at a County House of Correction and Its Effect upon Patterns of Recidivism," *JRC,* January 1977, p. 102; Robert Jeffery and Stephen Woolpert, "Work Furlough as an Alternative to Incarceration: An Assessment of Its Effects on Recidivism and Social Cost," *JCC,* September 1974, pp. 405–415; Alvin Rudoff, T.C. Esselstyn, and George L. Kirkham, "Evaluating Work Furlough," *Federal Probation,* March 1971, pp. 34–38; Alvin Rudoff and T.C. Esselstyn, "Evaluating Work Furlough: A Followup," *Federal Probation,* June 1973, pp. 48–53.
64. John M. Mckee and Michael A. Milan, "Study-Release Policies of American Correctional Agencies: A Survey," *JCJ,* Winter 1974, pp. 357–363.
65. *CD,* January 1974, p. 73.
66. *Boston Herald American,* August 12, 1975, p. 3.
67. *New York Times,* April 19, 1975, p. 38.
68. Unless otherwise noted, this section is based on Michael S. Serrill, "Prison Furloughs in America," *Corrections,* July–August 1975, pp. 3ff.
69. Anthony Astrachan, "Profile: Pennsylvania," *Corrections,* May–June 1975, p. 55.
70. Michael S. Serrill, "Profile: District of Columbia," *Corrections,* March–April 1975, p. 54.
71. But see Daniel P. LeClair, *The Effect of the Home Furlough Program on Rates of Recidivism* (Boston: Massachusetts Department of Correction, December 1977).
72. *New York Times,* August 26, 1977, p. B6; *New York Times,* May 6, 1977, p. B2.
73. Serrill, "Prison Furloughs," p. 55.

74. Oliver J. Keller and Benedict S. Alper, *Halfway Houses: Community-Centered Correction and Treatment* (Lexington, Ma.: Heath, 1970), p. 15.
75. Richard W. Nice, "Aftercare Treatment of the Released Offender," *Corrective Psychiatry and Journal of Social Therapy,* July 1966, p. 295.
76. James A. Beha, "Halfway Houses in Adult Corrections: The Law, Practice and Results," *CLB,* July–August 1975, p. 437.
77. Richard P. Seiter, *Halfway Houses: National Evaluation Program, Part I, Summary Report* (Washington, D.C.: Government Printing Office, January 1977), p. 1.
78. Serrill, "California," p. 42; Astrachan, "Profile: Pennsylvania," p. 58; "Massachusetts Adult Corrections System," *Corrections,* November–December 1975, p. 48.
79. "Massachusetts Adult Corrections," p. 48; Serrill, "Profile: District of Columbia," pp. 48–49; Earl L. Durham, "St. Leonard's House: A Model in the Use of Ex-Offenders in the Administration of Correction," *CD,* July 1974, p. 269.
80. Serrill, "Profile: District of Columbia," pp. 48–49.
81. Ronald H. Bailey, "Florida," *Corrections,* September 1974, pp. 89–90.
82. Serrill, "Profile: New Jersey," pp. 28–29.
83. "The Plight of Community Corrections," *Criminal Justice Newsletter,* March 25, 1974, pp. 4–5.
84. Bailey, "Florida," p. 90.
85. William Hart, "Profile: Michigan," *Corrections,* September 1976, p. 63.
86. Eugene Doleschal, "Criminal Justice Programs in Model Cities," *Crime and Delinquency Literature,* June 1972, pp. 307–311; James A. Beha, "Testing the Functions and Effect of the Parole Halfway House: One Case Study," *JCC,* September 1976, pp. 348–349; Beha, "Halfway Houses in Adult Corrections," pp. 462–475.
87. Serrill, "California," p. 42.
88. "Massachusetts Adult Corrections System," p. 48.
89. "The Minnesota Restitution Center," *Corrections,* January–February 1975, pp. 12–20.
90. Kenneth F. Schoen, "PORT: A New Concept of Community-Based Correction," *Federal Probation,* September 1972, pp. 35–40.
91. Keller and Alper, *Halfway Houses,* pp. 11, 116.
92. Paul Takagi, "Administrative and Professional Conflicts in Modern Corrections," *JCC,* September 1973, p. 314.
93. *Wall Street Journal,* October 6, 1975, p. 1.
94. Daniel Glaser, *The Effectiveness of a Prison and Parole System* (Indianapolis: Bobbs-Merrill, 1964).
95. Kenneth J. Lenihan, *Unlocking the Second Gate: The Role of Financial Assistance in Reducing Recidivism Among Ex-Prisoners* (Washington, D.C.: U.S. Department of Labor, 1977).
96. Sol Chaneles, "Project Second Chance," *Psychology Today,* March 1975, p. 45.
97. *Supported Work: An Alternative to the Revolving Door* (New York: Vera Institute of Justice, n.d.).
98. *Hawker* v. *New York,* 170 U.S. 189 (1898).
99. *Schware* v. *Board of Bar Examiners of New Mexico,* 353 U.S. 232 (1957); *Griggs* v. *Duke Power Company,* 91 S.Ct. 849 (1971).

100. "Recent Trends in the Criminal Law," *JCC*, December 1975, pp. 470–473.
101. James W. Hunt, James E. Bowers, and Neal Miller, *Laws, Licenses and the Offender's Right to Work* (Washington, D.C.: National Clearinghouse on Offender Employment Restrictions, 1974), preface, p. 13.
102. Thomas Kline, "Ex-Convict Civil Disabilities," *CLB*, January–February 1975, p. 39.
103. Mitchell W. Dale, "Barriers to the Rehabilitation of Ex-Offenders," *CD*, July 1976, p. 326.
104. Robert R. Smith, Larry F. Wood, and Michael A. Milan, "Ex-Offender Employment Policies: A Survey of American Correctional Agencies," *CJB*, September 1974, p. 243.
105. *New York Times*, November 9, 1977, p. D17.
106. Smith, Wood, and Milan, "Ex-Offender Employment," p. 234.
107. *Only Ex-Offenders Need Apply: The Ohio Parole Officer Aide Program* (Washington, D.C.: Law Enforcement Assistance Administration, April 1976).
108. "The Fortune Society: Championing the Ex-Offender," *Corrections*, May–June 1975, pp. 13–20.
109. Takagi, "Administrative and Professional," p. 318.
110. *The Massachusetts Community Assistance Parole Program* (Boston: Government Center, n.d.).
111. *The Massachusetts Impact Program* (Boston: Government Center, n.d.).
112. Michael Kiernan, "Profile: Vermont," *Corrections*, September–October 1975, p. 43.
113. Walter R. Burkhart, "The Great California Parole Experiment," *Federal Probation*, December 1976, pp. 9–14; C.H. Hudson, *An Experimental Study of the Differential Effects of Parole Supervision for a Group of Adolescent Boys and Girls: Summary Report* (Washington, D.C.: Law Enforcement Assistance Administration, March 1973).
114. Bennett, "Should We Change," p. 339.
115. Robert Martinson, "Save Parole Supervision," *Federal Probation*, September 1977, pp. 23–27.
116. Joseph Kleine, "Parole Comes to Life," *California Youth Authority*, Spring 1972, pp. 3–14.
117. Stephen Gettinger, "Separating the Cop From the Counsellor," *Corrections*, April 1981, pp. 34–38.
118. *People Magazine*, February 23, 1976, p. 21.
119. Paul Takagi and James Robison, "The Parole Violator: An Organizational Reject," *JRC*, January 1969, pp. 78–86.
120. *Target*, June 1977.
121. Vincent O'Leary and Kathleen Hanrahan, "Law and Practice in Parole Proceedings: A National Survey," *CLB*, May–June 1977, p. 209.
122. *New York Times*, May 30, 1976, section 4, p. 9.
123. *New York Times*, April 3, 1977, p. 22.
124. *Oakland Tribune*, August 4, 1974, p. 83.
125. Burt Galaway and Leonard Rutman, "Victim Compensation: An Analysis of Substantive Issues," *Social Service Review*, March 1974, p. 68.
126. Newton, "Aid to the Victim," p. 373.
127. *New York Times*, November 27, 1977, p. 54.
128. *National Observer*, May 16, 1977, p. 17A.

129. *Wall Street Journal,* June 24, 1976, p. 1.
130. Anne Newton, "Aid to the Victim: Victim Aid Programs," *Crime and Delinquency Literature,* December 1976, p. 509.
131. *National Observer,* March 13, 1976, p. 10; Mark R. Arnold, "Will Citizens Change the Judicial Process?" *Judicature,* August–September 1976, p. 77.
132. Leo F. Callahan, "The Victim Advocate," *Police Chief,* April 1975, pp. 50–51.
133. Newton, "Aid to the Victim: Victim Aid Programs," pp. 510–512.
134. "What Can Be Done for Victims?" *Police Chief,* June 1977, p. 18.
135. *New Haven Register,* April 30, 1975, p. 16.
136. *National Observer,* March 13, 1976, p. 10.
137. *U.S. News & World Report,* December 8, 1975, p. 43; *Judicature,* April 1975, p. 452; Newton, "Aid to the Victim: Victim Aid Programs," pp. 516–517.
138. Gerald D. Robin, "Forcible Rape: Institutionalized Sexism in the Criminal Justice System," *CD,* April 1977, pp. 136–153.

Chapter 17

1. Points very loosely based on Monrad G. Paulsen, "*Kent* v. *U.S.*: The Constitutional Context of Juvenile Cases," in Philip B. Kurland, ed., *The Supreme Court Review, 1966* (Chicago: University of Chicago Press, 1966), p. 169.
2. William O. Douglas, "Juvenile Courts and Due Process of Law," *Juvenile Court Judges Journal,* Spring 1968, p. 9.
3. Sanford J. Fox, "Juvenile Justice Reform," *Stanford Law Review,* June 1970, p. 1230.
4. As amended in 1907.
5. Mark M. Levin and Rosemary C. Sarri, *Juvenile Delinquency: A Comparative Analysis of Legal Codes in the United States* (Ann Arbor: University of Michigan National Assessment of Juvenile Corrections, June 1974), p. 11.
6. Robert M. Mennel, "Origins of the Juvenile Court," *CD,* January 1972, p. 78.
7. J. Lawrence Schultz, "The Cycle of Juvenile Court History," *CD,* October 1973, p. 466; Jim P. Manak, "The Right to Jury Trial in Juvenile Court," *Prosecutor,* vol. 4, no. 6, p. 328.
8. Manak, "Right to Jury Trial," p. 326.
9. Schultz, "Cycle of Juvenile Court," p. 467.
10. Paulsen, "*Kent* v. *U.S.*," pp. 174–175.
11. "The Philosophy and Theory of the Juvenile Court," *Juvenile Court Judges Journal,* Winter 1972, p. 4.
12. Points loosely based on, as point of departure, Fred Cohen, "A Lawyer Looks at Juvenile Justice," *CLB,* July–August 1971, pp. 517–518.
13. *Kent* v. *United States,* 383 U.S. 541 (1966).
14. Robert B. Keiter, "Criminal or Delinquent: A Study of Juvenile Cases Transferred to the Criminal Court," *CD,* October 1973, pp. 528–538.
15. *In re Gault,* 387 U.S. 1 (1967).
16. Thomas J. Gardner and Victor Manian, *Principles and Cases of the Law of Arrest, Search, and Seizure* (New York: McGraw-Hill, 1974), p. 17.
17. *In re Winship,* 397 U.S. 358 (1970).
18. *McKeiver* v. *Pennsylvania,* 402 U.S. 528 (1971).
19. *Breed* v. *Jones,* 421 U.S. 519 (1975).

20. *Time,* June 30, 1975, p. 24.
21. Robert C. Caldwell, "The Juvenile Court: Its Development and Some Major Problems," in Ross Giallombardo, *Juvenile Delinquency: A Book of Readings* (New York: Wiley, 1972), pp. 407–408.
22. Sanford J. Fox, *The Law of Juvenile Courts in a Nutshell* (St. Paul: West, 1971), pp. 22–23.
23. *Trial,* September–October 1971, p. 17.
24. Paul Nejelski and Judith La Pook, "Monitoring the Juvenile Justice System," *ACL,* Summer 1974, p. 14.
25. Donald R. Cressey and Robert A. McDermott, *Diversion from the Juvenile Justice System* (Ann Arbor: University of Michigan National Assessment of Juvenile Corrections, June 1973), p. 9.
26. Ibid., p. 10.
27. Nejelski and La Pook, "Monitoring the Juvenile," p. 14.
28. Kenneth Cruce Smith, "A Profile of Juvenile Court Judges in the United States," *Juvenile Justice,* August 1974, p. 33.
29. Levin and Sarri, *A Comparative Analysis,* p. 39.
30. Erwin G. Krasnow, "Social Investigation Reports in the Juvenile Court: Their Uses and Abuses," *CD,* April 1966, pp. 154–155.
31. Frank Miller et al., *The Juvenile Justice Process* (Mineola: Foundation Press, 1971), p. 1366.
32. "Coming: Tougher Approach to Juvenile Violence," *U.S. News & World Report,* June 7, 1976, pp. 65–67.
33. *New York Times,* October 17, 1974, p. 25.
34. State of Washington, House Bill No. 371, 45th Legislature, 1st Extraordinary Session, p. 35.
35. State of New York, S. 5-A—A. 43, July 14, 1978, Senate-Assembly Extraordinary Session, pp. 11–13.
36. *Newsweek,* September 8, 1975, pp. 70–71.
37. *New York Times,* March 21, 1975, p. 75, and May 14, 1975, p. 81.
38. *New York Times,* December 27, 1975, p. 17; *National Observer,* January 31, 1975, p. 22.
39. *Juvenile Justice Standards Project, Tentative Draft* (Cambridge: Ballinger, 1977).
40. *Juvenile Justice Standards Project: Standards Relating to Juvenile Delinquency and Sanctions,* pp. 37–48.
41. *New York Times,* December 15, 1975, p. 63.
42. Ibid.

Glossary of Terms

Acquittal A decision made by a judge or a jury that the defendant is not guilty of the criminal charges beyond a reasonable doubt.

Actus rea The conduct that constitutes a particular crime.

Adjudication hearing The trial (fact-finding) phase of the juvenile court, at which the judge decides whether the juvenile committed the alleged crimes or status offenses.

Administrative segregation Isolation from the general prison population for the inmate's own good, e.g., to protect homosexuals, child molesters, informers, those who owe gambling debts, and politically unpopular prisoners from assault by other inmates.

Affirm The decision by an appellate court to let stand the conviction obtained or the sentence imposed in a trial court.

Affirmative action Special efforts by police departments and other employers to recruit, hire, retain, and promote minority group members and to eliminate the sources and effects of past and present employment discrimination.

Appellate jurisdiction of the Supreme Court Discretionary authority of the Supreme Court to accept cases for review that involve a "substantial federal question," one that usually deals with an interpretation of the Constitution.

Arraignment The post-indictment stage at which the defendant is brought before a trial court, hears the charges in the indictment or prosecutor's information read, and is asked to enter a plea to each charge.

Arrest The act of being taken into custody to be formally charged with a crime. In a constitutional sense, an arrest is a seizure of the person.

Bail The financial or nonfinancial conditions under which defendants may be released while awaiting arraignment and the trial stage.

Bench trial A legal proceeding in which a decision regarding the defendant's guilt is made by the court sitting alone and is expressed in a "judgment."

Bifurcated hearing In juvenile cases, the practice of holding separate hearings for adjudication and disposition, rather than a single hearing that combines both functions.

Bind-over hearing Another name for the preliminary hearing, where probable cause is established and the case is bound over for grand jury action.

Brief A document submitted by defense counsel to an appellate court, stating why the conviction or the sentence should be reversed. Also the written arguments submitted by the prosecutor to an appellate court, explaining why the conviction or sentence should not be reversed.

Broken promises The state's failure to live up to its side of the plea bargain, a basis for appealing the conviction successfully. Broken promises were first prohibited by the Supreme Court in *Santobello* v. *New York* in 1971.

Career criminals Recidivists, violent offenders, professional criminals, and other serious violators whose success at avoiding punishment is at least partially responsible for their "careers" in crime.

Case law Procedural criminal law created by the courts in the context of their rulings on specific cases.

Cause for action A complaint that raises constitutional issues about which the courts can, and choose to, do something (such as provide effective "relief").

Challenge for cause The attempt by the prosecutor or defense counsel to remove a prospective juror during voir dire, by explaining why the juror in question is unfit to serve or would not be impartial.

Change of venue The holding of a trial in a different jurisdiction than the one in which the crime was committed, in order to guarantee that the defendant will receive a fair trial.

Charging the jury Verbal instructions given by the court to the jury, describing the principles of law that should guide the jury's deliberations and verdict.

Citation A written notice ordering the suspect to appear in court, usually used for specified petty offenses.

Civilianization Having police department jobs that do not require the attention of sworn police personnel performed by civilian employees.

Civilian review boards Civilian-dominated committees independent of the regular police bureaucracy, established for the sole purpose of facilitating, investigating, and hearing complaints from citizens against police officers.

Clearance rate The proportion of crimes reported to police that the police claim to have solved.

Common law crime Judicial creation and identification of crimes by the early English courts, before legislatures were in full operation.

Community corrections The conditions, sentences, and programs under which offenders are placed in the community rather than incarcerated: diversion, probation, parole, halfway houses, furlough, and work and education release.

Compensatory damages Damages levied by a civil court or jury against the defendant for actual financial losses incurred by the plaintiff because of the defendant's actions.

Concurrent sentence A prison sentence in which the separately imposed prison terms for each count are not added together but instead "run" at the same time. Thus, the sentence is the longest prison term imposed for the most serious count.

Conditional release on bail Nonmonetary release on bail of "higher risk" defendants. They are supervised while on bail and must observe the specified conditions of release.

Conditions of parole The rules and regulations that parolees must follow while on parole. Their violation may result in revocation of parole and reincarceration.

Conditions of probation The rules and regulations that probationers must follow. Their violation may result in revocation of probation and imprisonment.

Conjugal visits Family visiting programs that allow an inmate's spouse, children, and other family members to spend a day or two with the prisoner in private quarters.

Consecutive sentence Adding together the prison terms imposed for conviction on each of several separate crimes or criminal counts, to arrive at the total length of imprisonment.

Consolidation of police services An agreement between two or more jurisdictions to perform certain services jointly.

Contracting of police department services An arrangement in which smaller police departments purchase specific services from the private sector or from larger police departments.

Conviction A decision by a judge or a jury that the defendant is guilty of the criminal charges beyond a reasonable doubt; also a plea of guilty entered at arraignment.

Correctional institutions Jails and prisons.

Corrections A term that encompasses probation, institutions, and parole.

Court administrators Nonjudicial personnel who are trained to handle the administrative tasks involved in operating the courts.

Court unification Consolidation and centralization within and/or between jurisdictional levels, to facilitate the courts' functioning as a genuine system.

Crime Specific acts, or failures to act, that are a violation of the state's criminal statutes (penal code) or the acts of Congress.

Crime rate The number of index offenses per 100,000 total U.S. population.

Crimes cleared by arrest Crimes for which the police have identified the offender, have sufficient evidence to bring criminal charges, and have taken the suspect into custody. Crimes cleared by arrest are considered "solved" by the police, regardless of the outcome of the case.

Criminal statutes The law on the books (in the penal code) that defines those acts that are crimes and their penalties.

Criterion-related entrance tests Employment tests that are not culturally biased and that are related to external, objective measures of police performance on the job.

Critical stage Processing points and decisions made by criminal justice personnel that are so important that the Supreme Court has attached to them specified due process rights.

Dark figure of crime Crimes that victims do not report to the police.

Decriminalization Moderating harsh penalties for victimless crimes, especially abolishing lengthy incarceration and substituting fines.

Defense counsel The lawyer who represents defendants and convicted offenders.

Deinstitutionalization The movement to remove juvenile and adult inmates from institutions by closing down prisons and juvenile facilities or by resorting to other extraordinary means (such as "accelerated" parole) for emptying institutions quickly or reducing their populations.

Determinate, fixed, or flat sentence A prison sentence in which the convicted defendant is sentenced to a specific number of years.

Deterrence The threat or the actual imposition of punishment.

Disclosure of presentence report Making the content of the presentence report available to the defendant and defense counsel.

Discovery The process and procedures by which the prosecutor and defense counsel learn something about the legal strength of each other's case and their strategies for obtaining a conviction or an acquittal.

Discretion The exercise of judgment in deciding what to do in a concrete situation where any one of several decisions might be made. Individualizing the law on the books.

Dismissal Judicial termination of prosecution for lack of evidence.

Disproportionate impact The effect of a particular employment test or criteria that is discriminatory because a much larger proportion of minority group members than whites fail it and are denied employment.

Diversion Giving offenders a break by not making a formal arrest when the circumstances justify doing so, or by suspending prosecution for arrested persons. In general, a more lenient, treatment-oriented administrative procedure for handling and disposing of criminal cases, usually without a formal conviction.

Double jeopardy A constitutional safeguard contained in the Fifth Amendment that protects citizens from being exposed to punishment more than once for the same offense.

Downgrading of crime Classifying an offense as a less serious crime than it actually is, for the purpose of making the police look good by keeping the official crime count low.

Due process A legal means for guaranteeing citizens fair and proper treatment by the government officials who operate the criminal justice system. Due process is codified in the Fourteenth Amendment, which provides that no state shall "deprive any person of life, liberty, or property, without due process of law."

Education release Temporary release from prison for the purpose of pursuing educational opportunities in the community.

Entrapment Occurs when a person who is not predisposed to commit a crime does so because of police enticement, that is, is caused by the police to commit a crime.

Exhausting state remedies The requirement that appeals originating in the states can be carried forward in the federal court system only after the defendant or prisoner has unsuccessfully appealed his case to the highest state court.

Fear of crime A concept popularized by the President's Crime Commission, a phenomenon measured in victim surveys, and a term used to refer to the personal, social, and psychological consequences that crime has on its victims and on society in general.

Felony A crime punishable by death or incarceration in a state correctional institution, usually for one year or more.

Fine A sentence that demands financial recompense from the convicted defendant; the money goes to the state, not to the victim of the crime.

Flat sentence A prison sentence in which the convicted defendant is sentenced to a specific number of years.

Forfeiture Loss of cash bail deposited with the court as a penalty for failing to appear at trial.

Free will A legal philosophy that assumes that individuals have the capacity to choose between right and wrong, that their behavior is voluntary, and that they are accountable for their actions.

Frisk A pat-down of a suspect's outer clothing to discover objects that feel like or could be used as weapons.

Furloughs (home visits) Temporary release from prison, usually for 24–72 hours, for the purpose of visiting one's home, maintaining family ties, lining up a job for parole, or for any reason considered rehabilitative by correctional officials.

Gag order A court order that prohibits the publication of any incriminating evidence against the defendant. Because gag orders infringe on the First Amendment freedom of the press, they can only be used when all other means to control the effect of negative pretrial publicity have been exhausted and have failed.

General deterrence The effect that the punishment of offenders has on preventing law-abiding citizens from committing crime.

General preventive patrol Random motorized cruising by patrol officers when they are not responding to radio-dispatched calls. The basic crime control strategy of police departments, based on the theory that it will deter crime through the visibility of the police and their opportunity to apprehend offenders on the spot.

Good faith defense In a suit against the police, the defense that even though an arrest is illegal because the officer lacked probable cause as a matter of law, it was nonetheless reasonable for the officer to have acted as he or she did under the circumstances.

Goodtime credit laws Statutes that reduce the amount of time inmates must spend in prison before being eligible for parole, by deducting from the sentence a specified amount of time (1) for each month or year spent in prison, (2) for participating in prison industry, and (3) for being a model prisoner.

Grand jury A group of 16 to 23 citizens who decide whether there is probable cause to indict the defendant on the criminal charges contained in the bill of indictment prepared by the prosecutor. Defendants enter pleas at arraignment to the charges specified in the grand jury indictment.

Habitual offender statutes Special laws applicable to convicted defendants that provide extended imprisonment for persons with several prior felony convictions.

Halfway house Residential facilities in the community to which inmates may be released in advance of parole eligibility or as a special condition of parole, or to which probationers may be sent as a condition of probation in lieu of incarceration.

Hands-off doctrine The position followed by the courts until the mid 1960s, in which they refused to intervene in correctional matters by reviewing inmate complaints about the conditions of incarceration.

Hung jury A jury that is unable to reach a verdict, for lack of the number of votes required to convict or acquit.

Incapacitation The incarceration of offenders so that they will be physically restrained from committing crime while they remain a threat to society. Keeping dangerous offenders off the street through imprisonment.

Indeterminate sentence A prison sentence in which the convicted defendant is sentenced to a range of time, such as 2–5 years, 5–10 years, 10–20 years.

Index crimes Seven offenses, selected for their seriousness, frequency, and likelihood of being reported to the police, that serve as an indicator (index) of the amount, trends, and changes in crime nationwide. The seven index offenses are: willful homicide, forcible rape, robbery, aggravated assault, burglary, larceny-theft, and motor vehicle theft.

Indictment (1) A written accusation (bill) prepared by the prosecutor, charging the defendant with specified crimes. (2) The decision by the grand jury that there is probable cause to arraign the defendant on one or more of the criminal charges contained in the written accusation. When this occurs, the grand jury issues an indictment (a true bill), which is filed with the trial court.

Indigent defendant A defendant too poor to hire a lawyer and given free defense counsel in the form of court-assigned counsel or a public defender.

Informed consent The legal requirement that a prisoner's decision to participate in research experiments must be a genuinely voluntary one and not the product of coercion.

Initial court appearance The first processing stage after arrest, in which the defendant is taken before a magistrate; also called the presentment, first arraignment, or preliminary arraignment. Its purpose is to allow the court to inform defendants of their constitutional rights, to make arrangements to supply indigent defendants with free defense counsel, and to set bail.

In-presence requirement Some jurisdictions permit the police to make warrantless misdemeanor arrests only when the misdemeanor was committed in their presence. This is a higher standard than that of probable cause, which is applicable to warrantless felony arrests.

Involuntary confession A confession made without the suspect's having first been given the *Miranda* warnings or without a valid waiver of the *Miranda* rights having been obtained from the suspect.

Jail A local facility that houses pretrial detainees, misdemeanants serving sentences of one year or less, and a variety of miscellaneous groups.

Jailhouse lawyer Inmates without any formal legal qualifications who become self-taught in the law and who file petitions, for themselves and for other inmates, contesting the legality and conditions of incarceration.

Job-related tests Employment tests in which the applicant's performance on the test is related to actual performance on the job.

Judgment The decision made by a judge, at the conclusion of a trial, on whether the defendant is guilty or not guilty beyond a reasonable doubt.

Judicial discipline commission A commission established to investigate, control, and take action against judicial misconduct.

Jurisdiction The court's legal authority to preside over, handle, and decide the issues in specified kinds of cases.

Jury nullification A refusal or marked reluctance on the part of the jury to convict in capital cases because of the sentence involved.

Jury trial A legal proceeding in which the decision regarding the defendant's guilt is made by a group of 6 to 12 citizens (the petit jury) and expressed in a verdict.

Just deserts The revitalized theory that punishment should be a prime consideration in sentencing, that the punishment should fit the crime.

Lateral entry The opportunity to join police departments at an advanced rank (without starting at the bottom of the ladder) and to be given credit for prior service, experience, and achievement when applying for appointments in other agencies.

Law enforcement role of police The traditional crime control function of the police, as contrasted with their order maintenance role.

LEAA The Law Enforcement Assistance Administration, a federal agency created by the Safe Streets Act of 1968 to assist state and local governments to improve their criminal justice systems by distributing crime control funds to them.

LEEP The Law Enforcement Education Program, the component of the LEAA which provides grants to colleges to subsidize the higher education of preservice criminal justice students and inservice criminal justice practitioners.

Liberty interest The concept identified by the Supreme Court for determining whether and what due process safeguards are applicable to inmates at prison disciplinary hearings and to the revocation of parole and probation.

***Mala in se* crimes** Criminal acts that are considered wrong in themselves or inherently evil.

***Mala prohibita* crimes** Criminal acts that are "wrong" only because they are prohibited by law, that is, made wrong by legislation.

Mandatory release from prison Automatic release from prison after serving the maximum term minus goodtime credit, as required by statute (rather than as determined by parole board discretion).

Mandatory sentence A prison sentence whose imposition is required by penal code provisions upon conviction for a designated crime.

Mens rea "Guilty mind" or criminal intent, which is required in order to hold the offender responsible for criminal behavior; the state of mind at the time of the commission of the crime.

Merger of police departments When two or more smaller police departments pool or legally merge into a newly created, larger, unified, and centralized law enforcement agency.

Misdemeanor A crime punishable by a fine or incarceration in a local or county jail, usually for no more than one year.

Missouri Plan A procedure for selecting judges strictly on the basis of merit, in which a commission screens candidates and makes recommendations for appointment.

Multiple clearances The clearing of several crimes through the arrest of one person.

Multiple counts All of the criminal charges with which the defendant is charged, stemming from committing several different crimes during an uninterrupted sequence of illegal conduct or committing several different crimes at different times and places.

No bill The refusal of the grand jury to indict, which results in a dismissal of the case.

Nolle The decision by the prosecutor, subject to confirmation by the court, to terminate prosecution, which in effect results in a dismissal of the case.

Nolo contendere A plea of "no contest," whereby the defendant indirectly admits guilt but is protected from having the admission of guilt used in a civil court in the event the defendant is sued by the victim.

Nonsystem of criminal justice administration All of the obstacles that interfere with the personnel in different criminal justice agencies working together smoothly, effectively, and interdependently toward the common goal of reducing crime and delinquency.

Omnibus Crime Control and Safe Streets Act of 1968 Federal legislation, passed in the wake of the civil disorders of the 1960s, to assist state and local governments in improving their criminal justice systems. The Safe Streets Act created the LEAA to distribute crime control funds to the states.

Omnibus hearing A one-stop, formalized plea bargaining conference used in the federal system, in which the court does not directly participate.

Order maintenance role of police The non-law enforcement activities of the police, in which they provide immediate short-term relief in response to personal and interpersonal problems; also referred to as the social services, peacekeeping, or community service role of the police.

Original jurisdiction of Supreme Court Those cases that may be taken directly to the Supreme Court and the Court is required to accept them, that is, nondiscretionary Supreme Court jurisdiction.

Overcharging The prosecutor's charging the defendant with crimes that are virtually identical to each other or with crimes that cannot be proved in court.

Overcriminalization The belief that there are too many laws regulating too many activities, that victimless crimes should be decriminalized and ultimately legalized.

Overload When too many cases have to be handled by the available number of criminal justice practitioners, producing excessive caseloads throughout the criminal justice system.

Parens patriae The theory that sees the juvenile court acting in the role of parent to assure the care, custody, and proper social development of juveniles.

Parole board An autonomous administrative body, appointed by the governor, to which an inmate agrees to fulfill special goals in return for a definite parole.

Parole contract (Mutual Agreement Programming) An arrangement under which an inmate agrees to fulfill specified goals in return for a definite parole date's being set shortly after the offender arrives at the institution.

Parolee The legal status of an inmate who is released early from prison (or jail) after serving only a portion of the sentence inside.

Parole eligibility The earliest point at which the law authorizes early release from prison after an inmate has served only part of the sentence inside.

Parole guidelines project A research effort to provide a scientific means for arriving at the parole decision, thereby controlling excessive parole board discretion and unwarranted variation in granting parole.

Parole officer Corrections personnel responsible for supervising and counseling parolees, enforcing the conditions of parole, initiating the revocation of parole, and occasionally preparing presentence reports.

Parole plan The inmate's employment status or prospects, living arrangements, and treatment needs upon release.

Peremptory challenge The prosecutor or defense counsel's request for the removal of a prospective juror during voir dire without a reason for the request being given.

Plea The defendant's formal reply to the criminal charges (guilty, not guilty, or nolo contendere). To be considered valid, a guilty plea must be voluntary, intelligent, and informed, and the court determines this by questioning the defendant and pointing out the possible sentences. Defendants who refuse to plead to the charges (who stand mute) have a not guilty plea entered for them by the court.

Police brutality The excessive or unreasonable use of force by police in dealing with citizens, suspects, and offenders.

Preferred rights The expressive freedoms contained in the First Amendment: the right to the free exercise of religion, communication, and to petition the government for a redress of grievances. Because these rights are fundamental, and in recognition of their special status, they can be curtailed only on the basis of "compelling need" or "clear and present danger."

Preliminary hearing A hearing before a court, often held in felony cases, to protect the defendant against unwarranted prosecution and detention by requiring the state to establish probable cause that the defendant committed a crime.

Presentence report A comprehensive investigation of the convicted defendant that contains a nonbinding recommendation for disposition, prepared by the probation officer as a sentencing aid for the court.

President's Crime Commission A commission established by President Lyndon Johnson in 1965 to recommend changes and improvements in the administration of law enforcement and criminal justice. The commission's principal report, *The Challenge of Crime in a Free Society*, and its more detailed task force reports were released in 1967.

Presumptive sentence A system of standardized flat prison terms determined by the legislature, based entirely on the seriousness of the criminal behavior (just deserts), and subject only to slight variation, depending on the mitigating or aggravating circumstances surrounding the crime.

Pretrial conference A one-stop, formalized plea bargaining session, intended to avoid the worst aspects of informal plea bargaining as currently practiced.

Pretrial detainees Untried defendants who are confined in jail while awaiting trial because they are unable to raise the funds necessary for release on bail.

Pretrial motions Motions made to the court by defense counsel to suppress the introduction at trial of incriminating evidence because of the allegedly illegal manner in which it was acquired. Pretrial motions are often made to suppress evidence obtained by police conduct in violation of the Fourth and Fifth amendments.

Pretrial period The interval between arrest and the trial stage.

Preventive detention The jailing of untried defendants who the court believes would commit serious new crimes if released on bail during the pretrial period; achieved by setting excessively high bail that the accused cannot raise.

Prison A state-operated institution responsible for the secure custody and rehabilitation of sentenced felons.

Prisoners' rights The theoretical basis for attempts by inmates to obtain improvements in their conditions of incarceration through the courts and through nonjudicial means.

Proactive patrol A patrol strategy in which the police generate their own information and mobilize themselves to take action aimed at preventing crime or nipping it in the bud (as in "stop and frisk").

Probable cause Reasonable grounds to believe that a felony was committed and that the person arrested is the felon. Also the legal basis on which warrants are issued by the court and defendants are bound over from the preliminary hearing to the grand jury.

Probation A sentence of conditional liberty in the community.

Probation officer An officer of the court who is responsible for preparing presentence reports, supervising and counseling probationers, enforcing the conditions of probation, and initiating revocation of probation for those who violate the conditions of probation.

Procedural criminal law The law as contained in the Constitution and interpreted by the trial and appellate courts. The procedural criminal law safeguards the legal rights of citizens and regulates the conduct of criminal justice practitioners in performing their jobs.

Proof beyond a reasonable doubt The standard of proof required to obtain a conviction at trial (an adjudicated conviction) before a jury or a judge sitting alone. The state's burden of proving guilt beyond a reasonable doubt in court applies to each separate criminal offense with which the defendant is charged.

Prosecutor The state's legal representative whose primary responsibility is to convict offenders.

Prosecutor's information A written accusation prepared and authorized solely by the prosecutor and filed directly with the trial court, containing the criminal charges to which the defendant enters a plea at arraignment. Used more often with misdemeanors than felonies, this is the alternative method to accusation by a grand jury.

Punitive damages Damages levied by a civil court or jury against the defendant as a punishment for wrongful actions.

Punitive segregation Isolation from the general prison population in solitary confinement that is undertaken for disciplinary purposes.

Racial quotas Requirements by the courts that specified proportions of employees hired (and promoted) by police departments and other employers be minority group members.

Reactive patrol A patrol strategy in which the police respond to information received from sources outside the department, such as citizen-initiated calls for assistance, which the officer is dispatched to handle.

Reasonableness; the reasonable person The yardstick for much of the statutory and procedural criminal law; a frame of reference for determining the propriety and legality of conduct by citizens and criminal justice practitioners.

Recidivism A return to crime; repeated criminality; being arrested more than once.

Reduced charges Prosecution of an offender for a less serious crime than the offense(s) committed, in exchange for a guilty plea secured through plea bargaining.

Rehabilitation Efforts to change the offender through treatment.

Release on recognizance The nonmonetary release on bail of "good risk" defendants who are recommended for unconditional release, based on their social ties to the community, by Manhattan Bail-type projects.

Response time The time it takes for a police car to reach the scene of a reported crime or emergency.

Restitution A requirement that the convicted defendant "pay" for the crime by making financial compensation to the victim (cash restitution) or by performing work that will benefit the community at large (service restitution). Cash restitution differs from fines in that fines are paid to the state rather than to the victim.

Retribution The belief that the punishment should fit the crime; one of the objectives of sentencing currently receiving renewed attention under the theory of "just deserts."

Reversal The decision of an appellate court to overturn the conviction obtained or sentence imposed by the trial court.

Reverse and remand An appellate court's overturning the decision of a trial court and sending the case back (remanding it) to the trial court judge with instructions on what should be done to rectify the errors of law.

Reverse discrimination The "discrimination" against majority group members that occurs under affirmative action and racial quotas that give preference to the hiring and promotion of minority group members.

Revocation Taking away a present "liberty interest," with the result that the offender will probably or definitely be returned to prison or will have to spend more time in prison. The most important forms of revocation are probation revocation, parole revocation, and the revocation of goodtime credit.

Section 1983 of the Civil Rights Act A provision that permits *any* citizen —including prisoners—deprived of constitutional rights "under the color of state law" to file grievances directly with the federal courts. This was a tremendous tactical boost to the prisoners' rights movement.

Sentencing Upon conviction, the imposition of criminal penalties for violating the law.

Sentencing disparity Imposition of different sentences for the same crimes or offenses of comparable severity, differences that are not justified by the offender's previous record, personality, or specific deterrence results.

Set-off date The next time at which an inmate who has been turned down for parole will again be considered for parole.

Social report In effect, a presentence report used in juvenile cases as an aid to the judge at disposition. Like the presentence report, the social report contains a recommendation to the court.

Social ties to the community The factors used by the Manhattan Bail Project to recommend release on recognizance: residential stability, employment history, family contacts, and prior criminal record.

Special deterrence The effect that punishment has on discouraging offenders from recidivating.

Standards and Goals Commission The crime commission created in 1971 by the LEAA to carry forward the work of the 1965 President's Crime Commission, to recommend concrete benchmarks for controlling crime and delinquency, and to endorse the process of establishing standards and goals as prerequisites for improving the administration of criminal justice.

Stand mute A refusal of a defendant to plead to the charges at arraignment, in which case the court enters a not guilty plea.

Stare decisis The rule of precedent. Prior decisions on points of law are binding in future cases that are substantially the same, that is, where the totality of the circumstances does not vary.

State-supplied counsel Free defense counsel given to indigent defendants. The most common forms are public defenders and court-assigned private lawyers.

State-use laws Laws that protect the economic interests of the private sector against competition from cheap inmate labor by restricting the goods produced by prisoners to those used by the state and/or otherwise limiting prisoner-made commodities that can be sold to the public.

Status offenses Noncriminal violations of the juvenile code that expose juveniles to the same jurisdiction and disposition as children who commit crimes (acts named in the *Uniform Crime Reports*).

Statutory (substantive) criminal law Criminal statutes; the penal code.

Stop and frisk The police practice of stopping on the street persons whose behavior is suspicious, questioning them for identification purposes, and patting down the outer clothing of those whose answers or conduct arouse further suspicion or threaten police safety.

Strip cell A cell used for punitive segregation whose only furnishing is a hole-in-the-floor toilet that cannot be flushed by the inmate.

Substantive violation of probation and parole Committing a new crime while on conditional liberty.

Summons A written notice ordering the suspect to appear in court, usually used with specified petty offenses.

System of criminal justice administration Personnel in all of the different criminal justice agencies working together smoothly, effectively, and interdependently toward the common goal of preventing, controlling, and reducing crime and delinquency.

Target hardening Approaches designed to reduce the opportunity for successful crime commission.

Team policing A relatively democratic model of police organization that revolves around a team of officers who function as generalist-specialists and who are given fixed, continuous, and expanded responsibilities for providing all police services to a well-defined geographical area (the neighborhood).

Technical violation of probation or parole Failure to observe the administrative requirements or conditions of conditional liberty (for example, associating with known criminals, leaving the jurisdiction without permission).

Ten percent cash bail A bail reform program originated in Illinois that requires defendants to post ten percent of the bail set in order to be released (90 percent of the deposit is returned upon the defendant's appearing for trial).

Totality of the circumstances All the facts of a case, taken as a whole.

Training schools Secure facilities (reformatories) to which juvenile delinquents are committed; the counterpart for juveniles of prisons.

Transcript A written record of judicial or administrative proceedings, an important source of information in appealing convictions or sentences.

Trial The adversary method of proving in court, according to the rules of evidence, that the defendant is guilty of the criminal charges beyond a reasonable doubt.

Trial *de novo* A trial court's setting aside the decision of a court of limited jurisdiction and retrying the case anew, without regard for the previous trial.

Unfounded complaint A report to the police of a crime that police investigation reveals did not actually occur. Such false reports of crime are excluded from the *UCR* and index offenses.

Uniform Crime Reports A nationwide compilation of crime statistics based on information supplied by local police departments to the FBI and published annually. Its best-known feature is the national crime rate.

Valid guilty plea A guilty plea that the court determines is voluntary, informed, and made knowingly. The court questions the defendant to ascertain that he or she understands the nature of the charges and their possible consequences and informs the defendant of the sentences that may be imposed.

Venire The master list or population of potential jurors, from which jurors are ultimately chosen to serve in particular trials.

Verdict The decision by a petit jury, at the conclusion of a trial, that the defendant is guilty or not guilty beyond a reasonable doubt.

Victim assistance program A variety of services (but not financial compensation) provided to help victims of crime cope with the emotional, social, and practical consequences of crime.

Victim compensation State payments to the eligible victims of violent crime for unreimbursed medical bills and income lost as a result of injuries incurred.

Victimless crimes Crimes that cause no direct harm, injury, loss, or threat to anyone and in which there is no "victim" in the ordinary sense (as there is in index offenses).

Victim survey Social science research conducted to determine the actual amount of crime and the reasons that victims do not report crimes to the police. Victim surveys illuminate the "dark figure" of crime.

Victim-witness assistance programs Provisions for helping witnesses and improving their treatment by the criminal justice system.

Voir dire The questioning of prospective jurors by the prosecutor, defense counsel, and sometimes the court, in order to determine their fitness to serve in the trial in question and to eliminate jurors who would not be impartial.

Volunteered confession An admission of guilt that is not made in response to police-initiated questioning and is therefore not contingent upon custodial interrogation (which requires the *Miranda* warnings).

Waiver A defendant's or a convicted offender's decision to relinquish a legal right. Defendants often waive their right to a jury trial, to take their chances in a bench trial before a judge sitting alone.

Warrant An order from the court that directs the police to arrest the person identified in the warrant or authorizes them to search the place and area described "with particularity" in the warrant.

Warrantless arrest An arrest made by the police without prior authorization by the court. Police may make warrantless felony arrests on the basis of probable cause, but they are sometimes restricted to making warrantless misdemeanor arrests only when they themselves have observed the crime.

Work release Temporary release from prison for the purpose of taking employment in the community. Work releasees may reside at various facilities in the community, or they may commute daily from the parent institution to the work release site.

Writ of certiorari A petition requesting the Supreme Court to review the legality of a conviction or a sentence.

Writ of habeas corpus A writ used by defense counsel to bring the accused before a court to determine whether the defendant's detention and confinement are legal.

Glossary of Legal Cases

(All cases are Supreme Court decisions, unless otherwise indicated. Page numbers on which these cases can be found follow the description of each case.)

Adams v. *Williams* (1972)	Expansion of stop and frisk to situation where the officer's reasonable suspicion of criminal activity was based on an informant rather than personal observation. (190, 358)
Adams v. *Texas* (1980)	Pursuant to the Sixth Amendment, jurors cannot be excluded from jury service just because they are unwilling to take an oath that a mandatory death penalty would not affect their deliberations on any factual issues in the case. (358)
Alford v. *North Carolina* (1969)	Right of innocent defendant to enter a bartered guilty plea. (280)
Allen v. *McCurry* (1980)	Defendants cannot relitigate the issue of illegal searches in federal court by suing the police under Section 1983 of the Civil Rights Act, provided their Fourth Amendment claims were adequately reviewed by the state courts. (183)
Apodaca v. *Oregon* (1972)	Approval of nonunanimous verdicts. (316)
Argersinger v. *Hamlin* (1972)	Right to counsel in misdemeanors resulting in incarceration. (257, 264–266)
Bakke v. *University of California* (1978)	Upheld the principle of affirmative action but disapproved of racial quotas in the context of college admissions policy. Implications for the employment area are unclear. (145–146)
Ballew v. *Georgia* (1978)	The minimum number of jurors required in criminal trials is six. (313)
Barker v. *Wingo* (1972)	Balancing test for determining whether the right to speedy trial was violated. (289–290)
Beckwith v. *United States* (1976)	Noncustodial interrogation of a suspect on whom the investigation has focused does not trigger the Miranda safeguards. (176)
Bell v. *Wolfish* (1979)	The need to maintain order and security in detention facilities housing pretrial detainees justifies the imposition of various conditions and restrictions, such as placing two inmates in a room, body-cavity searches, not allowing inmates to receive outside packages of food and personal items, etc. (463–464)
Betts v. *Brady* (1942)	No right to counsel in all felonies. (257)
Blackledge v. *Allison* (1977)	Acceptability of plea bargaining and prohibition of broken promises. (277)
Bordenkircher v. *Hayes* (1978)	Prosecutors may seek reindictment on a more serious charge if defendants refuse to plead guilty to the less serious initial charge. (278)
Brady v. *United States* (1970)	First time Supreme Court indirectly accepted plea bargaining. (277)
Breed v. *Jones* (1975)	Protection against double jeopardy extended to juveniles. (527)

Brewer v. *Williams* (1977) — Unsuccessful attempt to overturn *Miranda* decision. (187)

Brown v. *Mississippi* (1936) — Confession secured through physical brutality is a violation of due process under the Fourteenth Amendment. (170)

Bullington v. *Missouri* (1981) — Pursuant to the double jeopardy clause, a defendant convicted of murder who is spared the death sentence under a bifurcated capital punishment structure cannot, upon retrial and conviction of the same charge, be sentenced to death. (362)

Burch v. *Louisiana* (1979) — Conviction by a six-person jury in nonpetty offenses must be based on a unanimous verdict, in order to comply with the substance of the right to jury trial guaranteed by the Sixth Amendment. (316)

Chandler v. *Florida* (1981) — States can permit the televising of criminal trials, even if the defendant objects to such coverage. (320)

Coker v. *Georgia* (1977) — Death penalty banned for rape of adult female. (358–359)

Coleman v. *Alabama* (1970) — The preliminary hearing is a "critical stage" at which the constitutional right to counsel applies. (38)

Cruz v. *Beto* (1972) — Accorded Muslim prisoners the same religious rights and opportunities as inmates of other religious faiths. (446)

Davis v. *Georgia* — If any prospective juror with "scruples" about capital punishment is excluded during voir dire because of such beliefs, the death penalty cannot stand. (358)

Delaware v. *Prouse* (1979) — Police cannot stop motorists at random to check their drivers' licenses, unless they have some objective reason to suspect that the driver has broken the law. However, states may develop methods for spot checks that do not involve the unconstrained exercise of police discretion, such as stopping all cars at road blocks. (191)

Dothard v. *Rawlinson* (1977) — Alabama's height and weight requirements for employment as a prison guard were struck down because they were not shown to be job related. But the state can prohibit women from holding contact posts in male institutions because the characteristics of Alabama prisons reduce a woman's relative ability to maintain security, which is the essence of an officer's duties there. (400)

Dunaway v. *New York* (1979) — Even when a confession follows a valid waiver of *Miranda* rights, the confession is inadmissible if it resulted from an illegal arrest. (173)

Duncan v. *Louisiana* (1968) — Right to jury trials restricted to crimes punishable by at least six months incarceration. (301, 325)

Durren v. *Missouri* (1979) — State laws which grant women automatic exemptions from jury service are unconstitutional because they deprive defendants of being tried by a fair cross section of the community. (214)

Escobedo v. *Illinois* (1964) — Right to counsel before custodial interrogation may take place. (172–174, 258)

Estelle v. *Gamble* (1976) — Deliberate indifference by prison personnel to serious medical needs of inmates constitutes cruel and unusual punishment. (449)

Estelle v. *Smith* (1981) — Before being questioned by a psychiatrist who might later testify against the accused at the penalty phase in a capital punishment case, the defendant must be informed of the right to remain silent and right to counsel. (359)

Fullilove v. *Klutznick* (1980) — Congress may allocate funds to the states for public works that involve racial quotas, without violating the Fourteenth Amendment. (147)

Furman v. *Georgia* (1972) — Death penalty is unconstitutional if administered improperly. (352–354)

Gagnon v. *Scarpelli* (1973) — Before probation can be revoked, certain due process safeguards must be accorded the probationer at an administrative hearing. (454, 484–485)

Gannett v. *DePasquale* (1979)	If the participants in the litigation agree to do so, pretrial hearings can be closed to the public and press in order to minimize the effects of prejudicial pretrial publicity. (302)
Gardner v. *Florida* (1977)	In capital cases, defendants have a due process right to full disclosure of presentence report. (335)
In re Gault (1967)	Landmark Supreme Court decision that extended to juveniles constitutional safeguards, especially the right to counsel. (523–525)
Gideon v. *Wainwright* (1963)	Right to counsel in felonies. (257)
Goldberg v. *Kelly* (1970)	Before welfare recipients can have their public assistance payments terminated (revoked), they are entitled to a hearing on the matter at which their grievous loss by such action must be considered along with the state's need for doing so. (485)
Godfrey v. *Georgia* (1980)	As an aggravating circumstance in murder cases, considering the offense "outrageously or wantonly vile, horrible and inhuman" is an insufficient basis, in itself, to justify imposition of the death sentence. (359)
Greenholtz v. *Inmates of Nebraska Penal and Correctional Complex* (1979)	Being considered for parole does not involve a "liberty interest" and, as such, the due process clause of the Fourteenth Amendment does not cover inmates at the parole grant hearing stage. (419–420, 458)
Gregg v. *Georgia* (1976)	Death penalty per se is constitutional. (354–356)
Griggs v. *Duke Power Co.* (1971)	Employment tests that discriminate against minority groups may only be used if they are job-related, that is, the test scores must correlate with on-the-job performance. (142–143, 502)
Hamilton v. *Love* (1971)	Arkansas district court ruling that since pretrial detainees are not "convicts" or "real" prisoners, they should not be subjected to *any* punishment as part of their conditions of incarceration. (463)
Hampton v. *United States* (1976)	If defendant has predisposition to commit crime, entrapment defense cannot be raised successfully, regardless of the involvement of government agents in the act. (79, 193)
Harris v. *New York* (1971)	Statements made in violation of *Miranda* warnings are admissible at trial if they are not used to show guilt but only to impeach the defendant's credibility as a witness. (185)
Holt v. *Sarver* (1970)	First appellate court decision to declare that overall conditions of incarceration made imprisonment per se in Arkansas facilities cruel and unusual punishment. (392–394)
Jackson v. *Bishop* (1968)	Appellate court ruling that whipping prisoners as a disciplinary measure was cruel and unusual punishment, which in effect put an end to corporal punishment in American prisons. (393)
James v. *Wallace* (1976)	Appellate court ruling that imprisonment per se in Alabama prisons was cruel and unusual punishment by virtue of the overall deplorable conditions of incarceration. (393–396)
Johnson v. *Avery* (1969)	Prison regulations cannot prohibit the activities of jailhouse lawyers unless the state provides other means for assisting inmates to access to the courts. (444–445)
Johnson v. *Louisiana* (1972)	Approval of nonunanimous jury verdicts. (316)
Jones v. *North Carolina Prisoners' Labor Union* (1977)	Prison officials have the right to prohibit the formation and activities of prisoner labor unions. (447)

Jones v. *United States* (1960) — Defendants charged with possessory crimes were automatically entitled to challenge the legality of the search leading to the criminal evidence used against them. This "automatic standing" doctrine was abandoned in 1980 in *United States* v. *Salvucci*. (183–184)

Jordan v. *Fitzharris* (1966) — A landmark federal court decision that solitary confinement as practiced in Soledad prison in California was cruel and unusual punishment. (453)

Kent v. *United States* (1966) — First case in which the Supreme Court applied the principle of due process and constitutional precepts to juvenile court procedures (in connection with a waiver of jurisdiction from juvenile court to the criminal court). (335, 521–523)

Kirby v. *Illinois* (1972) — No right to counsel at lineups that take place before indictment or before the adversary system begins to operate. (191)

Lee v. *Washington* (1968) — Ended racial segregation of prisoners. (447)

Lockett v. *Ohio* (1978) — Death penalty statutes cannot prevent judges from considering any and all relevant mitigating factors in passing sentence. (359)

McKeiver v. *Penn.* (1971) — Juveniles have no constitutional right to a jury trial. (526)

McNabb v. *United States* (1943) — Prompt arraignment required under the Federal Rules of Criminal Procedure. (171)

Mallory v. *United States* (1957) — Prompt arraignment required under the Federal Rules of Criminal Procedure. (171)

Mapp v. *Ohio* (1961) — Imposed the exclusionary rule on the states by declaring that evidence obtained in violation of the Fourth Amendment is inadmissible at trial. (163, 165–169)

Mastrian v. *Hedman* (1964) — No absolute right to be released on bail. (224)

Meachum v. *Fano* (1976) — The concept of a vested liberty interest is the key for determining whether and what due process safeguards are applicable to inmates at prison disciplinary hearings, and inmates have no rights with respect to their transfer to a less desirable institution. (454, 457–458)

Mempha v. *Rhay* (1967) — Established the defendant's right to counsel at sentencing. (333)

Michigan v. *Mosley* (1975) — Upheld renewed questioning of suspect in connection with a murder two hours after suspect excercised his *Miranda* warnings upon being arrested for a robbery. (186)

Michigan v. *Tucker* (1974) — Derivative evidence obtained in violation of the *Miranda* warnings can be used to convict a defendant. (185–186)

Miranda v. *Arizona* (1966) — Prior to custodial interrogation, defendants have the right to counsel and to remain silent. (163, 170, 174–177, 258)

Monroe v. *Pape* (1961) — Section 1983 of the Civil Rights Act of 1871 can be used to redress any deprivation by the states of the basic constitutional rights of *any* citizen. (440)

Morrisey v. *Brewer* (1972) — Before parole can be revoked, certain due process safeguards must be accorded the parolee at an administrative hearing. (453, 506)

Nebraska Press Association v. *Stuart* (1976) — Because of the need to protect the First Amendment guarantee of free speech, gag orders may be imposed only after employing less drastic means for curtailing the possible harmful effects of pretrial publicity. (307)

New York City Transit Authority v. *Beazer* (1979) — Policy of Transit Authority not to hire persons who use narcotic drugs (including methadone users) was upheld as being job-related and not being in violation of the Fourteenth Amendment's equal protection clause. (502–503)

North v. *Russell* (1976) — Lower court judges are not required to be lawyers. (199)

O'Connor v. *Donaldson* (1975)	A decision that, among other things, declined to establish a "right to treatment" for the institutionalized mentally ill. (450)
Oklahoma Publishing Company v. *District Court for Oklahoma County* (1977)	Supreme Court lifted a district court's order restraining the news media from disseminating the identity of a juvenile whose trial was pending. (531)
Oregon v. *Mathiason* (1977)	So long as defendant is not under arrest or otherwise significantly deprived of freedom, confession made to police officer without *Miranda* warnings is admissible at trial. (187)
People v. *Cahan* (1955)	Adoption of exclusionary rule by California Supreme Court. (169)
People v. *Lovercamp* (1974)	California Court of Appeals decision that recognized, under certain circumstances, a right to escape from prison to avoid being raped. (458–459)
Powell v. *Alabama* (1932)	Right to counsel in capital punishment cases. (256–257)
Procunier v. *Martinez* (1974)	Established prisoners' rights to uncensored general correspondence with the public. (445)
Rakas v. *Illinois* (1978)	Standing and access to the Fourth Amendment does not depend upon property interest but instead derives from privacy interests. (185)
Reid v. *Georgia* (1980)	The Drug Courier Profile used at the Atlanta airport by federal agents to stop and question passengers suspected of transporting narcotics is impermissible because it does not satisfy the requirements of reasonable suspicion. (192)
Rhode Island v. *Innis* (1980)	The Miranda safeguards are applicable whenever a person is subjected to express questioning or to its "functional equivalent": any words or actions by the police which they should have known were reasonably likely to elicit an incriminating response from the suspect. (188–190)
Rhodes v. *Chapman* (1981)	In and of itself, double celling does not violate the Eighth Amendment ban against cruel and unusual punishment. (390)
Richmond v. *Virginia* (1980)	The public and press have a strong constitutional right, derived from the First Amendement, to attend criminal trials, which may not be closed absent a showing of overriding interest. (302–304)
Roberts v. *Louisiana* (1977)	Mandatory death penalty for those convicted of killing police officers in line of duty is unconstitutional. (358)
Rochin v. *California* (1952)	Pumping a suspect's stomach to retrieve swallowed narcotics was a violation of the Fourteenth Amendment. (176)
Rouse v. *Cameron* (1966)	First case, by a federal court, to acknowledge a "right to treatment" for an institutionalized group of mentally ill. (450)
Ruiz v. *Estelle* (1980)	A federal court decision criticizing the Texas Department of Corrections for violating the constitutional rights of inmates and ordering unprecedented changes in the state's penal system. The decision is being appealed by the state. (396–397)
Rummel v. *Estelle* (1980)	Upheld the authority of the states to enact habitual offender laws providing for mandatory life imprisonment, even in the case of petty property offenses. (348)
Santobello v. *New York* (1971)	First time the Supreme Court explicitly approved plea bargaining through condemnation of broken promises. (277)
Schmerber v. *California* (1966)	No violation of Fourth or Fifth Amendments where a blood sample was involuntarily taken from a suspect. (176)
Scott v. *Illinois* (1979)	Supreme Court refused to extend the right to counsel to all cases in which incarceration is a possibility. (265)

Sherman v. *United States* (1958)	Overturned conviction of defendant for selling drugs to police informant because accused was not "predisposed" to commit the offense. (78)
Simmons v. *United States* (1968)	The prosecution is prohibited from using at trial a defendant's self-incriminating testimony made at a suppression hearing. (184)
Sorrell v. *United States* (1932)	First time the Supreme Court isolated "predisposition" to commit crime as the legal element on which the entrapment defense hinges. (79)
Sostre v. *Rockefeller* (1970)	Federal court decision that ordered improvements in the conditions of incarceration at Attica. (442)
Stack v. *Boyle* (1951)	Principle of right to bail upheld. (224)
Stone v. *Powell* (1976)	State prisoners cannot pursue their constitutional claims through federal habeas corpus, provided that their Fourth Amendment claims received a full and fair litigation at the state level. (183)
Strunk v. *United States* (1973)	Authorized dismissal of case for not providing speedy trial. (293)
Taylor v. *Louisiana* (1975)	State laws which discriminate against women serving on juries are unconstitutional because they deprive defendants of the right to a fair trial. (214)
Terry v. *Ohio* (1968)	Police may stop and frisk if they have reasonable suspicion to believe a crime is about to be committed and that the suspect is armed and dangerous. (179–181)
Trop v. *Dulles* (1958)	A sentence that transgresses the "evolving standards of decency" is cruel and unusual punishment and is therefore unconstitutional. (453)
United States v. *Bailey* (1980)	Defendants who escape from jail allegedly to avoid deplorable conditions of confinement are not entitled to have a defense of duress considered by the jury if the escapees did not make any effort to surrender to authorities. (459)
United States v. *Calandra* (1974)	Illegally obtained evidence is admissible at grand jury proceedings. (182)
United States v. *Robinson* (1973)	Full search of person incident to custodial arrest is permissible. (190–191)
United States v. *Russell* (1973)	"Predisposition" to commit crime invalidates the entrapment defense. (79, 193)
United States v. *Salvucci* (1980)	Abandoned the automatic standing doctrine and established a new and more stringent test for determining Fourth Amendment rights in third-party searches: Did the defendant have a "legitimate expectation of privacy" in the premises, place, or area searched?" (184–185)
United States v. *Tucker* (1972)	Sentence invalidated where it is based on erroneous information about prior convictions contained in the presentence report. (335)
United Steelworkers of America v. *Weber* (1979)	Private employers may voluntarily establish racial quotas for job training programs without violating Title VII of the Civil Rights Act. (146–147)
Wade v. *United States* (1967)	Defendant has the right to counsel at post-indictment lineups. (191)
Weeks v. *United States* (1914)	Adoption of exclusionary rule by the federal government. (165)
Weems v. *United States* (1910)	A sentence that "shocks the conscience" is cruel and unusual punishment. (352)
Williams v. *Florida* (1970)	First approval of six-person juries. (313–315)

In re Winship (1970)	Proof beyond a reasonable doubt rather than a preponderance of the evidence is the standard needed for an adjudication of delinquency. (525–526)
Wolf v. *Colorado* (1949)	Supreme Court refused to impose the exclusionary rule on the states. (165)
Wolff v. *McDonnell* (1974)	Accorded inmates facing the forfeiture of goodtime credit or solitary confinement certain due process rights at a prison disciplinary hearing. (455)
Younger v. *Gilmore* (1971)	Required states to make available to inmates adequate legal material in order to facilitate access to the courts. (445)

The Constitution of the United States

Selected Amendments Affecting Criminal Law

Amendment I [1791]

Congress shall make no law respecting an establishment of religion, or prohibiting the free exercise thereof; or abridging the freedom of speech, or of the press; or the right of the people peaceably to assemble, and to petition the Government for a redress of grievances.

Amendment II [1791]

A well regulated Militia, being necessary to the security of a free State, the right of the people to keep and bear Arms, shall not be infringed.

Amendment III [1791]

No Soldier shall, in time of peace be quartered in any house, without the consent of the Owner, nor in time of war, but in a manner to be prescribed by law.

Amendment IV [1791]

The right of the people to be secure in their persons, houses, papers, and effects, against unreasonable searches and seizures, shall not be violated, and no Warrants shall issue, but upon probable cause, supported by Oath or affirmation, and particularly describing the place to be searched, and the persons or things to be seized.

Amendment V [1791]

No person shall be held to answer for a capital, or otherwise infamous crime, unless on a presentment or indictment of a Grand Jury, except in cases arising in the land or naval forces, or in the Militia, when in actual service in time of War or public danger; nor shall any person be subject for the same offence to be twice put in jeopardy of life or limb; nor shall be compelled in any criminal case to be a witness against himself; nor be deprived of life, liberty, or property, without due process of law; nor shall private property be taken for public use, without just compensation.

Amendment VI [1791]

In all criminal prosecutions, the accused shall enjoy the right to a speedy and public trial, by an impartial jury of the State and district wherein the crime shall have been committed, which district shall have been previously ascertained by law, and to be informed of the nature and cause of the accusation; to be confronted with the witnesses against him; to have compulsory process for obtaining witnesses in his favor, and to have the Assistance of Counsel for his defence.

Amendment VII [1791]

In Suits at common law, where the value in controversy shall exceed twenty dollars, the right of trial by jury shall be preserved, and no fact tried by jury, shall be otherwise re-examined in any Court of the United States, than according to the rules of the common law.

Amendment VIII [1791]

Excessive bail shall not be required, nor excessive fines imposed, nor cruel and unusual punishments inflicted.

Amendment IX [1791]

The enumeration in the Constitution, of certain rights, shall not be construed to deny or disparage others retained by the people.

Amendment X [1791]

The powers not delegated to the United States by the Constitution, nor prohibited by it to the States, are reserved to the States respectively, or to the people.

Amendment XIII [1865]

Section 1. Neither slavery nor involuntary servitude, except as a punishment for crime whereof the party shall have been duly convicted, shall exist within the United States, or any place subject to their jurisdiction.

Section 2. Congress shall have power to enforce this article by appropriate legislation.

Amendment XIV [1868]

Section 1. All persons born or naturalized in the United States, and subject to the jurisdiction thereof, are citizens of the United States and of the State wherein they reside. No State shall make or enforce any law which shall abridge the privileges or immunities of citizens of the United States; nor shall any State deprive any person of life, liberty, or property, without due process of law; nor deny to any person within its jurisdiction the equal protection of the laws.

Section 5. The Congress shall have power to enforce, by appropriate legislation, the provisions of this article.

Index

Abortion, 69
Abscam, 80–82
Accountability for sentences, 343–344
ACLU. *See* American Civil Liberties Union
Actus rea, 2
Adams v. *Texas,* 358
Adams v. *Williams,* 190
Adjudication hearing, 528, 530–531
Adversary method of justice (*Duncan* v. *Louisiana*), 300–301, 324–325
Aetna Life and Casualty Co., 16
Affirmative Action Amendment, 142
Affirmative action and police personnel, 142–143, 146, 147
Alabama Highway Patrol, 144
Alabama Public Safety Department, 141
Alarm systems, 123
Alcoholics Anonymous, 448
ALERT (Automated Law Enforcement Response Team), 82
Alford v. *North,* 280
Allen v. *McCurry,* 183
American Bar Association, 68, 156, 282, 283, 285, 289, 332, 343, 534
  Commission on Standards of Judicial Administration, 304, 305
American Civil Liberties Union (ACLU), 100, 101, 352, 428, 451, 452
  National Prison Project, 441
American College of Trial Lawyers, 259
American Correctional Association, 426
  Commission of Accreditation for Prisons, 474
American Institute of Criminal Justice, 409
American Judicature Society, 344
American Justice Institute, 138
American Law Institute, 181, 346–347
Americans for Effective Law Enforcement, 104, 188
Andros Program, 490
Apodaca v. *Oregon,* 316
Appeals. *See* Trials
Appearance Control Project, New York, 155
Argersinger v. *Hamilton,* 257–258, 264–267, 286
Arizona Department of Corrections, 386
Arizona State Prison, 406
Arkansas Department of Corrections, 398, 408
Arraignment, 36, 43–45, 51, 247
  charge reduction of, 271
  delay in, 85
  efficient police procedures for, 155
  pleas in, 43–45
  prompt arraignment rule, 171–177
  temporal duration of, 292
Arrests, 5, 7, 252–253
  crimes cleared by, 19–20
  false, 104, 105
  in felonies, 33–36
  of juveniles, 21
  police behavior in, 34
    decisions, 70–71
    policewomen and policemen, compared, 148
  probable cause for, 5, 6, 34, 248, 273
  rates of, 19–21
  reasonableness of, 34, 36
  and stop and frisk, 177–181
  and warrants, 34, 167
Arson, 14–17
  antiarson programs, 16
  incidence of, 14–15
  and insurance, 15, 16
  reasons for, 15
Arson Warning and Prevention Strategy, 16
Assault, 13, 14, 68, 233
  fear of, 28
  incidence of, 18, 24, 26
  and plea bargaining, 275, 287
  and policewomen, 148
  pretrial detention for, 231
  in series crime, 249
  of taxi and truck drivers, 78
  in victim survey, 24, 26
Assembly line justice, 282–283
Atlanta Police Department, 72, 99, 145
Attack sessions in prisons, 413
Attica Correctional Facility, riot at, 441–444
Attorneys. *See* Counsel, right to; Defense counsels
Authoritarianism
  defined, 66
  origins of, 67
  of police, 66–67
    and education, 135
Automated Law Enforcement Response Team (ALERT), 82
Automatic standing doctrine (*United States* v. *Salvucci*), 184–185

Bail, 36–37, 224–243
  administration of before 1960s, 225–228

Bail (*Continued*)
criticisms of, 225–226
and bondsperson, 227–228
commercialization of, 227–228
and conditional release, 236–243
with services (RWS), 236–237
current perspective on, 240–242
excessive, 9
and jail conditions, 254
Manhattan Bail Project, 231–235, 241–243
nonmonetary, 226
and pleas, 224
and preparation of defense (*Stack* v. *Boyle*), 224
and pretrial detention, 228–231
and preventive detention, 226–227, 229–241
Reform Act of 1966, 227–240, 242
conditions of release in, 237–238
inadequacies of, 238–240
reform of, proposals, 241–242
and release on recognizance, 232–236
right to, 224–225
and state proceedings (*Mastrian* v. *Hedman*), 224
ten percent cash, 235–236
Bakke, Allan, 146
Bakke v. *Regents of the University of California,* 145–147
Ballew v. *Georgia,* 313
Bard, Morton, 117, 118
Barker v. *Wingo,* 289–290
Bazelon, David, 4
Beckwith v. *United States,* 176
Bedford Hills Correctional Facility, 400, 409
Behavior modification in prisons, 413, 451
Bell v. *Wolfish,* 463–464
Berrigan, Philip, 315
Betts v. *Brady,* 257
Beyond a reasonable doubt standard, 248, 270, 272, 273, 526
Bill of Rights, 43
and juveniles, 519, 520, 524
Blackledge v. *Allison,* 277
Black Liberation Army, 306
Black Panthers, 183
Blacks. *See* Race and minorities
Blending approach to crime control, 76–78
Body language, 323
Bondsperson and bail, 227–228. *See also* Bail
Bordenkircher v. *Hayes,* 278
Boston State College, 493
Boston University Center for Criminal Justice, 265
Boy Scouts, 448
Brady v. *United States,* 277
Brazelton, David, 450
Breed, Allan, 466–467
Breed v. *Jones,* 527
Brewer v. *Williams,* 187–188, 190
Bribery, 81, 254
parole guidelines on, 424
Bridgewater Correctional Institution, 489
Bronx House of Detention, 380
Bronx Major Offense Bureau (MOB), 252–255
Brown v. *Mississippi,* 170
Bullington v. *Missouri,* 362
Burch v. *Louisiana,* 316–317
Burger, Warren, 145, 182, 183, 188, 194, 242, 259
Burglary, 13, 14, 150, 187
incidence of, 18, 24, 26
parole guidelines on, 424
and plea bargaining, 275
second-degree, sentencing guidelines for, 342
in series crimes, 249
in victim survey, 24, 26

California Correctional Training Facility, 453
California Department of Corrections, 399, 445–446, 469
California District Attorneys' Association, 16
California Highway Patrol, 144, 149–150
California State Board of Corrections, 486
California State Prison at San Quentin and Folsom, 385
California Training Facility, 406
California Youth Authority, 466–468, 486
Capital punishment. *See* Death penalty
Careers in Crime program, 21
Carey, Hugh, 496
Carter, Jimmy, 58, 59
Carter, Robert M., 333
Case law, 6
Casper, Jonathan D., 282
CCHF (Computerized Criminal History File), 21
CCRB (Civilian Complaint Review Board), 102–103
Central Arizona College, 412
Challenge of Crime in a Free Society, The, 54, 55, 479
Challenges for cause, 308–310
Chandler v. *Florida,* 320–321
Chicago Police Department, 106, 112–113, 143, 518
Chicago Women's Club, 518
Child molesters, 451
Christie, Richard, 311
Citizen patrols, 120–123
Citizens for Law and Order, 126
Civil disorders, 53–55. *See also* Riots
and police-community relations, 108–111
police control of, 76
Civilian Complaint Review Board (CCRB), 102–103
Civilianization of police departments, 153–154
Civilian review boards of police, 100–103
Civil Rights Act
of 1871, 104, 106, 440
of 1964, 92, 140–143, 145, 146, 149–151, 159, 400, 502–503
of 1965, 439, 440, 448
Cleveland Police Department, 150
Cocaine, 192

Coker v. *Georgia,* 358–359
Coleman, Wayne, 360
Coleman v. *Alabama,* 38
Commission on Accreditation for Law Enforcement Agencies, 139–140
Commission on Law Enforcement and Administration of Justice. *See* President's Crime Commission
Commission on Peace Officer Standards and Training (POST), 132, 138
Common law, 11–13
  on deadly force, 93–94
Community Relations Unit, 101
Community Release Board, 429
Community Resources Management Team (CRMT), 487–488
Community Service Officer (CSO), 111–112, 131, 132, 144
Community Service Units, 111–112, 131–132, 144
Computerized Criminal History File (CCHF), 21
Computers in crime control, 82–83
Conditional release on bail, 236–243
Confessions and interrogations, 9, 169–177, 361
  blood samples, mandatory (*Schmerber* v. *California*), 176
  brutality (*Brown* v. *Mississippi*), 170
  circumstances of (*Oregon* v. *Mathiason*), 187
  counsel and indigency (*Michigan* v. *Tucker*), 185–186
  definition of (*Rhode Island* v. *Innis*), 188–189
  and delay (*Mallory* v. *United States, McNabb* v. *United States*), 171–172
  focus-test (*Beckwith* v. *United States*), 176
  and functional-equivalent test, 189–190
  permanent immunity from (*Michigan* v. *Mosley*), 186–187
  and prompt arraignment rule, 171–177
  and right to counsel (*Brewer* v. *Williams, Escobedo* v. *Illinois*), 172–174, 187–188, 190
  self-incrimination (*Miranda* v. *Arizona*), 174–177, 181, 182, 185–190, 194
  and shock of conscience (*Rochin* v. *California*), 176
  and stop and frisk, 177–181
  and trustworthiness of statements (*Harris* v. *New York*), 185
  voluntary and involuntary, 169–170, 173
  and waiver of *Miranda* (*Dunaway* v. *New York*), 172
Consciousness raising in prisons, 413
Consecutive sentences, defined, 44
Conspiracy, 81
Constitution of the United States, selected Amendments, 615. *See also specific amendments and principles of*
Cornell University, 125
Correctional institutions. *See* Jails; Prisons
Corrections, defined, 366. *See also* Rehabilitation
Corrections officers. *See* Prisons
Counsel, right to, 188, 256–259, 524–525. *See also* Confessions and interrogations; Prisoners' rights
  as due process (*Powell* v. *Alabama*), 257, 258
  in felonies (*Betts* v. *Brady, Gideon* v. *Wainwright*), 257, 258, 263, 264
  and grand jury system, 42
  in misdemeanors (*Argersinger* v. *Hamilton*), 257–258, 264–267
  and postindictment photographic identification, 193
  pre-trial, 191
  scope of (*Scott* v. *Illinois*), 265
Court Referral Program, 484
Courts, 198–220. *See also* Juvenile court system; System of criminal justice
  and bail setting, 224
  excessive continuances of, 291–292
  initial appearance in for felonies, 36–37
  overload and diversion of, 530
  and plea bargaining, 285–286
  and racial quotas, 143–144, 146
  and speedy trial, 288–296
Court watchers, 125–126
Crime
  actus rea, 2
  blending approach to, 76–78
  case law on, 6
  classification of, 11–13
    felonies and misdemeanors, 12–13
    mala in se, 11
    mala prohibita, 11
    statutory and common law, 11–12
  cleared by arrest, 19–20
    national rates of, 19–20
  community prevention of, 119–126
    citizen patrols, 120–123
    court watchers, 125–126
    crime watches, 119
    police auxiliaries, 123
  criminal intent, 68
  and failure to act, 2
  fears of, 27–29
  and free will, 3
  and legal action and discretion, 7–9, 11
    limits to, 9
  medical model of, 517
  mens rea, 2–3, 10, 78, 80
  and necessary defense (*Regina* v. *Dudley, State* v. *Wooten, United States* v. *Holmes*), 460
  procedural law on, 5–7, 9

Crime (*Continued*)
and reasonableness of law, 9–11
recidivism in, 21–23, 254, 422
and jail inmates, 369
on parole, 487
and selective prosecution, 251
in schools, 124–125
series of, 249
statutory law on, 5–7
in subways, 74
victimless, 69
decriminalization of, 84–86
and victim precipitation, 276
Crime Victims Compensation Board (CVCB), 507
Criminal Code Reform Act of 1976, 351
Criminal Justice Act, 259, 260, 288
Criminal Sentences: Law Without Order (Frankel), 336
CRMT (Community Resources Management Team), 487–488
Cross-examination of witnesses, 37, 453, 524
Cruel and unusual punishment
and death penalty, 351–354, 357, 358, 363
excessiveness (*Weems* v. *United States*), 352
and prisons. *See* Prisoners' rights
and reasonableness, 9
and standards of decency (*Trop* v. *Dulles*), 352
Cruz v. *Beto,* 446–447
CSO (Community Service Officer), 111–112, 131, 132, 144
Cummins Farm Unit, 392–393
Custodial convenience, principle of, 375
CVCB (Crime Victims Compensation Board), 507

Davis v. *Georgia,* 358
Deadly force
common law on, 93–94
control of, 98–99
and police, 93–100
state laws on, 94
Death penalty, 95
banned for rape (*Coker* v. *Georgia*), 358–359
constitutionality of (*Gregg* v. *Georgia*), 352, 354–363
as correction, 366
as cruel and unusual punishment (*Furman* v. *Georgia*), 351–354, 357, 358, 363
and defendant right to silence and counsel (*Estelle* v. *Smith*), 359, 361
and double jeopardy (*Bullington* v. *Missouri*), 359
guided discretion on, 353–354
and jury (*Adams* v. *Texas, Davis* v. *Georgia, Witherspoon* v. *Illinois*), 311, 312, 358
for killing police officer (*Roberts* v. *Louisiana*), 358
mitigating factors in (*Lockett* v. *Ohio*), 359
opinion on of jurors, 311, 312
and plea bargaining, 357
and presentence report, 335
Decoys, police, 76–78, 87
Decriminalization
forms of, 84
rationale for, 85–86
Defense counsels, 256–267
and bail, 226
court-assigned, 259–267
delaying tactics of, 254
law students as, 266
and plea bargaining, 271
and caseloads, 275
and disclosure, 284, 286
and economic advantages, 274–275
incentive for, 274
public defenders, 256–267, 282
deficiencies of, 262
at sentencing hearing (*Mempha* v. *Rhay*), 333
Deinstitutionalization, Massachusetts experiment on, 488–490
Delaware v. *Prouse,* 191
Demonstration for peace, 104
Depersonalization, 471
Determinate sentences, defined, 46
Deterrence as objective of sentencing, 329–330, 362
Dewer, Leroy, 442
Discovery in preliminary hearing, 37–38
Disorderly conduct, 68
Disposition hearing, 528, 531–532
Dispute Resolution Act, 481
District attorneys, 253. *See also* Prosecutors
and plea bargaining, 272, 276, 277
District of Columbia Bail Agency, 238
District of Columbia Court Reform and Criminal Procedure Act, 240–243
Diversion, 478–482, 512
by arbitration and conciliation, 481
formal, 479
informal (unofficial), 478
Domestic disturbances
incidence of, 112–113
police intervention in, 64, 112–119
policewomen, 149
Dothard v. *Rawlinson,* 401–402
Double jeopardy, 362, 527
Draper Correctional Center, 401–402
Driving, drunkenness, 103–104
Drug abuse, 79, 80, 479–480
and bail release, 239
Drug Courier Profiles, 192
Drug Enforcement Administration, 192
Drunkenness, 69, 103–104
Due process, 6, 9, 165, 170, 206, 215, 257, 320, 525, 526
and disclosure, 335
and entrapment, 82
in parole, 419–420, 484
and plea bargaining, 278–279, 281
and prisoners, 448, 457
revolution in, 194, 278–279
and right to counsel, 257, 258
Duke University, 124

Dunaway v. New York, 172
Duncan v. Louisiana, 301, 324
Durham, Monte, 4
Durham rule, 4, 5

Economic Development Administration, 16
Education release (ER), 493–494
EEOC (Equal Employment Opportunity Commission), 140, 142–145, 159, 400
Effectiveness of prosecutors, 274
Efficiency
  of law enforcement, 8–9, 150–155
  of prosecutors, 246, 271–272
Eighth Amendment, 9
  and bail, 224, 225, 242, 351
  and death penalty, 348, 351, 352, 354, 359
  and prison conditions, 390, 391, 396
  and prisoners' rights, 440, 449, 453, 462
  and quality of punishment, 393
Electroshock treatment in prisons, 451, 452
Embezzlement, 14
  parole guidelines on, 424
  in series crime, 249
Emergency calls (911), 83, 150
Encounter groups in prisons, 413
England, abolishment of grand juries in, 41
Entrapment, 78–82
  and criminal intent (*Sherman* v. *United States*), 78–80
  in drug sales (*Hampton* v. *United States*), 79, 80
  and due process, 82
  and fairness and shock (*United States* v. *Russell*), 79, 80
  and police role (*Sorrells* v. *United States*), 79
Equal Employment Opportunities Act, 142
Equal Employment Opportunity Commission (EEOC), 140, 142–145, 159, 400
Equal protection, 6, 72–73, 250, 502
Erdmann, Martin, 274
Erie County Department of Central Police Services, 153
Ervin, Sam, 290, 292
Escobedo, Danny, 172–174
Escobedo v. *Illinois*, 172–174, 258
Espionage, parole guidelines on, 424
Estelle v. *Gamble*, 449
Estelle v. *Smith*, 359, 361
Estes, Billy Sol, 320–321
Estes v. *Texas*, 320–321
Exclusionary rule, 82, 163–169
  applicability of (*Weeks* v. *United States*, *Wolf* v. *Colorado*), 165
  as deterrent (*People* v. *Cahan*), 169
  entry and search (*Mapp* v. *Ohio*), 163, 165–169
  and grand juries (*United States* v. *Calandra*), 182
  inflexibility of, 167
  intent of (*Allen* v. *McCurry*), 183
  modification of, 182–185
  and prisoners (*Stone* v. *Powell*), 183
  third party searches (*Jones* v. *United States*), 183–184
  viability of, 166–169
Expert testimony, 5

Failure to act, 2
False arrest, 104, 105. *See also* Arrests
Family Crisis Intervention Unit (FCIU), 117–119
FCIU (Family Crisis Intervention Unit), 117–119
Federal Bonding Program, 503
Federal Bureau of Investigation (FBI), 13, 14, 16–18, 24, 29, 80, 81, 99
Federal Bureau of Prisons, 391, 393, 399, 433
Federal Judicial Center, 336
Federal Metropolitan Correctional Center, 374, 463–464
Federal Prison Medical Center, 452
Federal Rules of Criminal Procedure, 171, 225
Federal Youth Center, 411–412, 433
Felonies
  arrests in, 33–36
  and beyond a reasonable doubt standard, 248
  classification of, 12–13
  fleeing rule on deadly force, 93–98
  forcible rule on deadly force, 94
  parole guidelines on, 424
  and plea bargaining, 270–272, 287
  and processing stages of, 33–49
  and release on bail, 229
  rights of defendants, 301
  sentences for, 257, 258, 263, 264, 347, 348
    guidelines on, 341–343
  and trial delays, 289
  and work release, 490–491
Feminism, 399
Fifth Amendment, 9
  and double jeopardy, 362, 527
  and exclusion of evidence, 45
  and interrogations, 174–175
  and self-incrimination, 170, 174–176, 186, 194, 519, 524
  and testimony, 41
Figgie Report on Fear of Crime, 28
Fines for victimless crimes, 84
Firearms possession, 72, 105
First Amendment, 104
  and prisoners' rights, 440, 444–448
  and public access to trials, 301–304, 307
Fleeing felon rule on deadly force, 93–98
  and race, 96–98
Flood, Daniel, 317, 318
Florida Community Correctional Centers, 498
Florida State University, 135

Food and Drug Administration, 451
Forcible felony rule on deadly force, 94
Ford, Gerald, 251, 292
Fordham University, 121
Forgery, 278, 481
  parole guidelines on, 424
Fort Grant prison, 385
Fort Grant training center, 408, 412
Fortune Society, 504, 513
Fourteenth Amendment, 162
  and affirmative action, 147
  and bail, 224
  and due process, 6, 9, 165, 170, 206, 215, 257, 320, 525, 526
  and equal protection, 6, 72–73, 250, 502
  and interrogation, 177
  life, liberty, property protections of, 193
  and prison conditions, 396
  and prisoners' rights, 448–449, 453–457, 462
Fourth Amendment, 9, 104, 163, 176
  automatic standing doctrine, 184–185
  as binding on states, 165
  and evidence, exclusion of, 45, 79, 163–165, 167–169, 180, 191
  and warrants, 194
Frankel, Marvin E., 336
Fraternal Order of Police, 101
Fraud, 14
  parole guidelines on, 424
  welfare, 481
Free Venture program, 409–411
Free will and crime, 3
Frisks, police, 177–181
FTA bail rates, 241
Fullam, John P., 82
Fullilove v. *Klutznick,* 147
Fulwood v. *Clemmer,* 446
Functional-equivalent test of interrogations, 189–190
Furloughs, 494–496
  eligibility for, 495, 496
  problems with, 495–496
Furman v. *Georgia,* 351–354, 357, 358, 363
Fyfe, James J., 96, 97, 99

Gagnon v. *Scarpelli,* 484–485, 512
Gallup public opinion polls, 28
Gambling, 69
Gannett Company, 301
Gannett v. *DePasquale,* 301–304
Gardner v. *Florida,* 335
Gault, Gerald, 523–525
Georgia State Prison, 406
Gideon, Clarence, 257, 258
Gideon v. *Wainwright,* 257, 258, 263, 264
Gilmore, Gary, 358
Godfrey v. *Georgia,* 359
Goldberg v. *Kelly,* 485
Goode, Alvestus, 93
Good faith defense, 106, 107
Goodtime credit laws, 417–418
Grand juries, 38–43, 45, 247
  criticism of, 41–43
  and exclusionary rule (*United States* v. *Calandra*), 182
  improper composition of, 45
  and indictments, 39–43
Greenholtz v. *Inmates of Nebraska Penal Complex,* 419–420, 454, 456–457
Gregg v. *Georgia,* 352, 354–363
Grievance procedures of prisoners, 464–468
Griggs v. *Duke Power Co.,* 142, 143, 502
Grigson, James, 361
Guardian Angels, 121–123
Guided group interaction in prisons, 413
Guilt beyond reasonable doubt, 9–10
Guilty plea. *See* Pleas, guilty

Habeas corpus, writ of, 172, 182–183, 210–211, 439
Habitual offender statutes and plea bargaining, 287–288
Halfway houses, 496–500, 512–513
  criteria for participation in, 498
  effectiveness of, 498–499
  suitable locations for, 497–498
Hamilton v. *Love,* 463
Hampton v. *United States,* 79, 80, 193
Hands-off doctrine, 439
Hanrahan, Kathleen J., 418
Harassment, police, 104, 105, 110
Harris, Emily, 309
Harris, William, 309
Harrisburg Seven defense team, 315
Harris public opinion polls, 28
Harris v. *New York,* 185
Hartford Institute of Criminal Justice, 470
Harvard University Center for Criminal Justice, 490
Hayden, 96
Hearst, Patricia, 309
Heroin use and sale, 185, 190–191, 205, 307, 370
Hijacking, parole guidelines on, 424
Hinson, Richard, 103–104
Holt v. *Sarver,* 392–394
Homicide, 13, 324
  arrests for and racial discrimination, 96, 97
  and bail, 241
  incidence of, 24, 99
  parole guidelines on, 424
  and plea bargaining, 275, 276, 287
  and police misconduct litigation, 104, 105
  in victim survey, 24
Homosexuality, 69
  in police, 151
  in prisons, 453
Hostos Community College, 493
Hotline (911), 83
House of Detention for Men (HDM), 378–380
Houston Police Department, 99

Huber Law, Wisconsin, 490
Human relations training laboratory, 112
Human Rights Commission, 395–396

IACP (International Association of Chiefs of Police), 251
Illinois Juvenile Court Act, 517–519
Illinois Law Enforcement Commission, 350
Immunity. *See* Sovereign immunity doctrine
Incapacitation as objective of sentences, 329–330, 362
Indeterminate sentences, 348–349, 427–428
  defined, 46
Indictment
  and grand jury system, 39–43
  multiple counts on, 249
  and right to attorney, 191
  temporal duration of, 292
Indigency, 6
  and counsel, 260, 454–455
Informed consent on treatment of prisoners, 451
Inmate councils, 465, 471–474
Inmate Grievance Commission (IGC), 465–466
In re Gault, 523–525, 531, 536
Insanity defense, 3–5
  product test in, 4
Institute of Contemporary Corrections and Behavioral Science, Sam Houston University, 398
Institute of Judicial Administration, 534
Insurance and arson, 15, 16
Intake officers in juvenile court system, 529–530
International Association of Chiefs of Police (IACP), 13, 104, 113, 119, 137, 150
  Annual Conference of, 251
International Halfway House Association, 497
Interrogations. *See* Confessions and interrogations
Iowa State Penitentiary, 411

Jackson, Bruce, 397
Jackson Community College, 412
Jackson State Prison, Michigan, 412
Jackson v. *Bishop,* 393
Jacksonville Police Department, 153
Jails, 366–381. *See also* Prisons
  conditions of, 105
    and bail, 254
  defined, 48
  dehumanization and degradation in, 370–371
  inadequate facilities in, 371, 463
  local administration of, 371–373
    standards for, 372–373
  national survey of, 367–370, 381
    on personnel, 368, 370
    on populations and facilities, 367–370
  and prisons, 366–367
  rights in (*Bell* v. *Wolfish, Hamilton* v. *Love, Rehm* v. *Malcolm*), 462–464
  riots in, 377–380
  security in, 374–376
  state-operated, 375–376
James v. *Wallace,* 393–396, 400, 434
Jaycees, 449
JJSP (Juvenile Justice Standards Project), 534, 535
John Jay College of Criminal Justice, 117, 413
Johnson, Frank, 392, 393, 395
Johnson, Lyndon B., 54
Johnson v. *Avery,* 444–445
Johnson v. *Louisiana,* 316, 318, 325
Joint Commission on Correctional Manpower and Training, 398
Joint Commission on Juvenile Standards, 534
Jones v. *North Carolina Prisoners' Labor Union,* 447–448
Jones v. *United States,* 183–184
Jordan v. *Fitzharris,* 453
Judd, Orrin, 380
Judges, 51. *See also* Courts
  and bail, 238
  and court watchers, 125–126
  and death penalty, 360–361
  personality and philosophy of, 6
  and plea bargaining, 277–278, 284–285
  and prisoners' rights, 439
  and sentences, 340–350
Judicial activism, 439–440
Judicial Conference of the United States, 304
Judiciary Act of 1789, 225, 237, 240
Juries. *See also* Grand juries
  charging of, 323–324
  and death penalty (*Adams* v. *Texas, Davis* v. *Georgia, Witherspoon* v. *Illinois*), 358
  and evidence in homicide cases, 276
  fact-finding of, 300–301
  impartiality of, 9, 358
  instruction of, 45–46
  juvenile right to (*Mckeiver* v. *United States*), 526
  nonunanimous verdicts of (*Apodaca* v. *Oregon, Burch* v. *Louisiana, Johnson* v. *Louisiana*), 316–318, 325
  payment of, 305
  peremptory challenges of, 308, 310, 311
  selection of, 304–313
    abbreviated service, 305–306
    exclusion and discrimination, 306
    exemptions, 304–305
    pool for, 305
    scientific, 310–313
    venire and venue, 304–306, 308, 311, 324–325
    voir dire, 308–313
  six-person (*Ballew* v. *Georgia,*

Juries (*Continued*)
Williams v. *Florida*), 313–314, 325
research on, 315–316
size of, 12, 313–316, 325
Justice, William W., 396
Juvenile court system, 516–536
adjudication hearings, 517–520, 523–524
denial of constitutional rights in, 520
double jeopardy (*Breed* v. *Jones*), 527
grounds for creation of, 516–517
investigatory guarantees in (*Kent* v. *United States*), 521–523
jurisdiction of, 427, 429
jury trials (*Mckeiver* v. *United States*), 526
procedural rights in (*In re Gault*), 523–525, 531
processing stages in, 528–533
adjudication hearing, 528, 530–531
disposition hearing, 528, 531–533
intake, 528–530
probation, 532
reform of, 533–535
standards of proof in (*In re Winship*), 526
types of, 527
Juvenile Justice Act, 534
Juvenile Justice Standards Project (JJSP), 534, 535

Kaiser, 146
Kansas City Experiment, 74–76, 86–87
Kansas City Police Department, 82, 103, 318
Karl Holton School, 467
Kaufman, Irving, 534
Kennedy, Edward, 351, 362–363
Kennedy, Robert, 55, 497
Kent, Morris, 521–523
Kentucky Department of Correction, 386
Kentucky State Reformatory at La-Grange, 386
Kent v. *United States,* 335, 521–523
Kerner Commission, 108–109
Kidnapping, 174
parole guidelines on, 424
and plea bargaining, 287
King, Martin Luther, Jr., 55
Kirby v. *Illinois,* 191
Knievel, Evil, 44
Kohlberg, Lawrence, 414

Lake Butler Prison, Florida, 389
Lakewood Plan, 153
Lantana Correctional Institute, 414
Larceny, 239. *See also* Theft
parole guidelines on, 424
and pretrial detention, 231
Lasker, Judge, 380
Law Enforcement Assistance Administration (LEAA), 25, 32, 56–59, 62, 76, 77, 83, 111, 119, 120, 138, 139, 143, 144, 158, 159, 248, 251, 252, 259, 319, 336, 367–370, 373, 374, 376, 381, 398, 409, 423, 426, 468, 482, 484, 497–499, 509, 512
Law Enforcement Education Program (LEEP), 32, 56–58, 133
LEAA. *See* Law Enforcement Assistance Administration
Leenhouts, Keith, 485
LEEP. *See* Law Enforcement Education Program
Lee v. *Washington,* 447
Legal Aid Society, 261, 266, 274, 377
Legalistic style of policing, 130
Libel, 105
Lindsay, John V., 101
Lindsey, Ben, 520
Lineups, police, and right to attorney, 191
Little, Joan, 310–312, 324, 325, 352
Lockett v. *Ohio,* 359
Lompoc Camp, 493
Lorton Prison, 494
Los Angeles Central City Community Center, 499
Los Angeles County Probation Department, 485
Los Angeles County Sheriff's Department, 153
Los Angeles Police Department, 76, 99, 119, 139, 153
Louisiana State Penitentiary, 411
Lyman institution, 489

McCall v. *Clemens,* 318
MacDonald, Colette, 294
MacDonald, Jeffrey, 294, 295
Mckeiver v. *United States,* 526
McNabb v. *United States,* 171, 172
Major Offense Bureau, 252–255, 293
Mala in se crimes, 11
Mala prohibita crimes, 11
Mallory v. *United States,* 171–172
Mandatory sentences, defined, 44, 47
Manhattan Bail Project, 231–235, 241–243
results of, 233–234
significance of, 234–235
Manhattan Court Employment Project, 479–480
Manhattan House of Detention (Tombs), 377–381
Mann Act and parole guidelines, 424
Manpower Development Training Act, 408
Manslaughter, 312
and plea bargaining, 275
sentencing guidelines for, 342
MAP (Mutual Agreement Programming), 425–428
Mapp, Dolree, 165
Mapp v. *Ohio,* 163, 165–169, 194
Marathon sessions in prisons, 413
Marijuana use, 69, 72, 318
and decriminalization, 84
parole guidelines on, 424
Marquette University, 144, 509

Martinson, Robert, 433, 505–506
Massachusetts Correctional Institution, 457
Massachusetts Department of Youth Services, 489
Mastrian v. *Hedman*, 224
Mathiason, Carl, 187
Meachum v. Fano, 454, 457
Medical model of crime, 517
Medical services, prisoners' rights to, 447–448
Mempha v. *Rhay*, 333
Memphis Police Department, 98
Mens rea, 2–3, 10, 78, 80
Mental competency hearings, 292
Methadone use and employment, 502–503
Michigan Department of Corrections, 408
Michigan Reformatory, Ionia, 398
Michigan State University, 125
  National Center for the Study of Police Community Relations, 112
Michigan v. *Mosley*, 186–187
Michigan v. *Tucker*, 185–186
Midwest Research Institute, 318
Miller, Jerome, 488, 489
Minnesota Restitution Center, 499
Minnick v. *Cal. Dept. of Corrections*, 399
Miranda v. *Arizona*, 163, 170, 174–177, 181, 182, 185–190, 194, 207
Miranda warnings, 172, 301, 319, 507
Misdemeanors, 12–13, 38, 40, 51, 233
  classification of, 12–13
  and counsel, 265–266
  and plea bargaining, 270–272
  and prisoners' rights, 257–258, 264–267
  trials for, 301
Mississippi State Prison, 389
Mitchell, John, 57
M'Naghten, Daniel, 3, 4
M'Naghten Rule, 4, 5
Model Cities Program, 112
Model Penal Code, 4, 95, 99, 535
  on deadly force, 94, 95
  on pretrial detention applied to sentence, 230
  on sentencing, 346–347, 362
Model Rules on Stop and Frisk, 181
Model Sentencing Act, 347–348
Monell v. *Department of Social Services of New York City*, 106–107
Monroe v. *Pape*, 106, 440
Moore, Sara Jane, 292
Morrisey v. *Brewer*, 453–455, 506, 513
Multiple Offender Act, Louisiana, 288
Murder, 11, 125, 171, 254, 310–313
  and death penalty, 355–358
  fear of, 28
  incidence of, 18
  and plea bargaining, 276
  in series crime, 249
  and trial delay, 289–290
Murton, Thomas, 394
Mutual Agreement Programming (MAP), 425–428

NAACP Legal Defense Fund, 352, 356, 359
Narcotic Addiction and Rehabilitation Act (NARA), 414, 450
Narcotics. *See* Heroin use and sale
National Advisory Commission on Civil Disorders, 62, 91, 108, 109, 140
National Advisory Commission on Criminal Justice Standards and Goals, 57, 290
National Advisory Commission on Higher Education for Police Officers (Sherman Report), 136, 137
National Board of Trial Advocacy, 259
National Center for State Courts, 319
National Clearinghouse for Correctional Planning and Architecture, 432
National Clearinghouse for Criminal Justice Planning and Architecture, 373
National Clearinghouse of Ex-Offender Employment Restrictions, 504
National Commission on Reform of Criminal Laws, 460
National Council of Juvenile Court Judges, 534
National Council on Crime and Delinquency, 347, 423
National Crime Panel (NCP), 25–27
National Defender Survey, 259, 262, 265
National District Attorneys Association, 188, 511
National Fire Protection Association, 14
National Institute of Corrections, 487
National Institute of Justice, 96, 372
National Jail Census, 367–370, 381
National Jail Center, 372
National Legal Aid and Defender Association, 259
National Neighborhood Watch Program, 119
National Opinion Research Center (NORC), 23–24, 26, 27, 110
National Planning Association, 139
National Prisoners Reform Association (NPRA), 473
National Rifle Association (NRA), 323
National Sheriffs' Association, 119
National Strategy to Reduce Crime, A, 58
NCP (National Crime Panel), 25–27
Nebraska Press Association v. *Stuart*, 307
Neighborhood crime watches, 119
Neighborhood team policing, 155–158
Newark House, 498

New Jersey State Police, 149
New Mexico State Penitentiary, 407
New York Board of Corrections, 378, 380
New York City Police Department, 73, 98, 114, 117, 149, 154
New York City Probation Department, 234
New York City Rand Institute, 19, 74
New York City Transit Authority, 121, 502–503
New York City Transit Authority v. *Beazer,* 502–503
New York Civilian Complaint Review Board, 102–103
New York Housing Authority, 120
New York Municipal Police Training Council, 138
New York Street Crime Unit, 77
New York Times, 76
Night Prosecutor Program (NPP), Columbus, 480, 481
Nixon, Richard, 181, 240, 311
Nolle prosequi, 248–249
Nolo contendere, 44
NORC (National Opinion Research Center), 23–24, 26, 27, 110
Norfolk State Prison, Massachusetts, 493
North Carolina Prisoners' Labor Union, 447–448
Northern Arizona University, 385, 408
Northwestern University, 124
Not guilty plea. *See* Pleas, not guilty
NPP (Night Prosecutor Program), 480, 481
NPRA (National Prisoners Reform Association), 473
NRA (National Rifle Association), 323

O'Connor v. *Donaldson,* 450
Office of Citizen Justice Advocates, 509
Officer Friendly, 107
Ohio State University, 497
Oklahoma Publishing Company v. *District Court for Oklahoma,* 431
O'Leary, Vincent, 417, 418
Ombudsmen and prisoners' rights, 464–465, 468–471
Omnibus Crime Control and Safe Streets Act, 55
Omnibus hearings in federal cases, 286
Operation Handshake, 107
Operation Identification, 123
Operation Whistlestop, 123–124
Order maintenance, police role in, 62–63
Oregon v. *Mathiason,* 187
Ossining State Correctional Facility, 493
Oswald, Russell, 442, 444
Overcriminalization
  defined, 69
  and prosecutors, 247
Owen v. *City of Independence,* 107

PAB (Police Advisory Board), 101, 102
Parens patriae doctrine, 521, 525, 532, 534, 535
Parole, 8, 47–50
  abolition of, 427–428
  boards for, 48, 51, 52
    membership on, 418–419
    plan for, 421
    procedures of, 421–422
  conditions for ex-carceration, 500–510
  contracts for, 425–427
  due process in (*Greenholtz* v. *Inmates*), 419–420, 484
  eligibility for, 48, 417
  and employment (*Griggs* v. *Duke Power Co., New York City Transit Authority* v. *Beazer, Schware* v. *Board of Bar Examiners of New Mexico*), 502–503
    licensing laws, 501–503
    statutory barriers, 502–504
  function of, 504–506
  guidelines table for, 422–425
  hearings for, 419
  officers, 48–51
    caseloads of, 49, 85, 487, 505
    effectiveness of, 50, 52
  plan for, 421
  prosecutor opposition to, 247
  and recidivism, 487
  and rehabilitation, 428
  revocation of (*Gagnon* v. *Scarpelli, Morrisey* v. *Brewer*), 453–455, 484–485, 506
  rules for, 48
  and sentences, 351
  subsidies for released inmates, 501
  violations of, 49
Parole-Corrections Project, 426
Parole Decision-Making Guidelines Project, 422
Parole Officer Aid program, Ohio, 504
Parole Reintegration Centers, 506
Participant observation, 112
Patrolmen's Benevolent Association, 102
PCR (Police-community relations), 108, 109, 112, 119. *See also* Police
PCR Units (Police Community Relations Units), 111, 112, 147
Peel, 3, 4
Penal code, 5
People Magazine, 433
People v. *Cohan,* 169
People v. *Lovercamp,* 458–459
Percy, Charles, 410
Peremptory challenges of juries, 308, 310, 311
Perley, 4
Philadelphia Police Department, 93, 99, 146
Pike, Joseph, 4
Plea bargaining, 38, 250–253, 270–288, 296. *See also* Pleas
  approval for (*Brady* v. *United States*), 277

broken promises in (*Blackledge* v. *Allison*), 277
case against, 280–281
case for, 279–280
and death penalty, 357
defined, 271
due process in, 278–279, 281
and felonies, 270–272, 287
guilty pleas (*Alford* v. *North*), 280
and habitual offender status, 287–288
process of, 275–279
and reindictment threats (*Bordenkircher* v. *Hayes*), 278
restructuring of, 283–288, 296
pretrial conference, 284–286
scope, 286–288
and sentences (*Santobello* v. *New York*), 277, 285–287, 296
and speedy trial, 295–296
Pleas, 51. *See also* Plea bargaining
in arraignment, 43–45
and bail setting, 224
guilty, 44–45, 202, 204, 224, 275–277, 280–282, 285, 301
and counsel, 265
and right of appeal, 246
and sentences, 270, 271, 280–281, 332
nolo contendere, 44
not guilty, 44, 45, 224, 270, 273, 295
Police, 51
arrest behavior of, 34
auxiliaries, 123
brutality of, 90–93, 104, 105, 109, 110, 126, 193
physical, 90–91
verbal, 91
civilian employment, 153–154
civilian review boards of, 100–103, 126
and community crime prevention, 119–126
community relations of, 107–112
community review board, 100–103, 126
and community service officer, 111–112
goals of, 111
origins of idea, 108–109
and race, 108–110
and Constitution, 161–194
custodial interrogation and confessions, 169–177
exclusionary rule, 163–169
stop and frisk, 190–191
street interrogation, 177–181
and crime control, 73–83
effectiveness and efficiency in, 76
preventive patrol, 73–74
proactive patrol, 74
special approaches to, 76–83
and deadly force, 93–100
fleeing felon rule on, 93–98
and police safety, 99–100
and racial discrimination, 95–98
decisions to file charges, 248
decoys, 76–78, 87
discretion of, 67–73
control of, 71–73, 98–99
in decision to arrest, 70–71
selective enforcement, 68–70
and domestic crisis intervention, 64, 112–119
dangers in, 113
policewomen, 149
and entrapment, 78–80
entry level positions of, 131–133
lateral entry, 132–133
harassment by, 104, 105, 110
homosexuals as, 151
human relations work of, 64
injuries of, 99–100
internal review of, 100–101
and law enforcement, 62–65
and order maintenance, 62–64
paramilitary organization of, 155–156
patrol strategies of, 154–156
private, use of, 123–124
professionalization of, 129–159
and college education, 130–137
and efficiency of departments, 150–155
and minorities, 130, 140–147, 159
and neighborhood team policing, 155–158
and policewomen, 130, 147–150
and training, 130, 137–140
and race and minorities, 91, 93, 95–98, 130, 140–147
role conflict of, 63–65
suing of, 103–107
evidence in, 105–106
and good faith defense, 106, 107
and sovereign immunity, 106
types of civil suits, 105
team policing, 156–158
effects of, 158
training of, 98
and community relations, 112
typology of policing, 130
undercover operations of, 78
and victimless crime, 84–86
working personality of, 65–67
and authority and isolation, 65–66
and danger, 65
and police subculture, 66
prejudice and authoritarianism, 66–67, 135
Police Advisory Board (PAB), 101, 102
Police Agent, 131
Police and Citizens Together, 509
Police-community relations (PCR), 108, 109, 112, 119. *See also* Police
Police Community Relations Units (PCR Units), 111, 112, 147
Police Foundation, 74, 95, 103, 147, 149, 150, 181
Police Officer, 131
Polygraph, 171
PORT (Probated Offenders Rehabilitation Training), 500
POST (Commission on Peace Officer Standards and Training), 132, 138
Powell v. *Alabama,* 257, 258
Prejudice of police, 66–67
Preliminary hearing, 51, 247
discovery in, 37–38

Preliminary hearing (*Continued*)
probable cause in, 37, 38
waiving of (*Coleman* v. *Alabama*), 38
Presentence report, 47, 328, 332–335
and death penalty (*Gardner* v. *Florida*), 335
disclosure in, 333–335
erroneous information (*United States* v. *Tucker*), 335
fundamental fairness in, 334–335
as mandatory, 333
recommendation in, 333
uses of, 332–333
President's Crime Commission (Commission on Law Enforcement and Administration of Justice), 23, 25, 27, 32, 54–55, 57–59, 62, 95, 102–103, 108–111, 131, 137, 140, 152, 153, 158, 159, 229, 230, 283, 285, 289, 332, 334, 335, 479, 481, 482
Pretrial phase, bail conference, 284–286
Preventive detention and bail, 226–227, 239–241
Preventive patrol, 73–74
Prisoners' rights, 7, 392, 438–474. *See also* Confessions and interrogations; Counsel, right to; Prisons
attorneys without fees (*Johnson* v. *Avery*), 444–445
and conditions of incarceration (*Sostre* v. *Rockefeller*), 438–444
detainees (*Bell* v. *Wolfish, Hamilton* v. *Love, Rehm* v. *Malcolm*), 462–464
extant liberty (*Greenholtz* v. *Inmates of Nebraska Penal Complex*), 454, 456–458
indigency and counsel (*Gagnon* v. *Scarpelli*), 454–455
labor unions (*Jones* v. *North Carolina Prisoners' Labor Union*), 447–448
law book availability (*Younger* v. *Gilmore*), 445
mail censorship (*Procunier* v. *Martinez*), 445–446
medical services (*Estelle* v. *Gamble*), 448–449
nonjudicial means for, 464–474
formal grievance procedures, 464, 468
inmate councils, 465, 471–474
ombudsmen, 464–465, 468–471
nontreatment, 451–452
parole revocation hearings (*Morrisey* v. *Brewer*), 453–455
prison conditions (*Ruiz* v. *Estelle*), 396–397
rehabilitative treatment (*O'Connor* v. *Donaldson, Rouse* v. *Cameron*), 449–450
religion (*Cruz* v. *Beto, Fulwood* v. *Clemmer*), 446–447
safety (*People* v. *Lovercamp, United States* v. *Bailey*), 458–461
severe punishment (*Holt* v. *Sarver, Jackson* v. *Bishop, Wolff* v. *McDonnell*), 392–394, 454–457
solitary confinement (*Jordan* v. *Fitzharris, Trop* v. *Dulles*), 453
transfer (*Meachum* v. *Fano*), 454, 457–458
Prisons, 384–434. *See also* Jails; Prisoners' rights
corrections officers, 6
custodial staff of, 398–404
education and training of, 398
guard roles, 401–404
physical qualities (*Dothard* v. Rawlinson), 400–402
race, 398–399
women in, 399–401
defined, 48
education in, 411–413
future of, 431–434
coed facilities, 433–434
design and location, 432
rehabilitation, 432–433
and jails, 366–367
mandatory release from, 430–431
overcrowding of (*Rhodes* v. *Chapman*), 387–392
administrative responses to, 389–391
causes of, 387–389
judicial response to, 392
new construction, 391–392
and parole decision, 416–431
rehabilitation in, 428, 432, 433
treatment in, 413–416
and conjugal visits, 415–416
impediments to, 413, 415
types of, 384–387
classification of, 386–387
and Department of Corrections, 385–386
security levels in, 385–386
vocational training in, 405–411
Privacy, rights to, 165
Proactive patrol, 74
Probable cause
for arrests, 5, 6, 34, 248, 273
at preliminary hearing, 37, 38
Probation, 47, 250
community resources management for, 487–488
conditions of, 482–483
and juvenile court system, 518, 524–525, 532
officers, 47, 50, 51
and juveniles, 524–525
reports of, 246, 432–434, 484, 486
as restitution, 483–484
revocation of (*Gagnon* v. *Scarpelli*), 47, 484–485
shock, 483–484, 512
state subsidy of, 486–487
and sterilization, 482–483
violation of, 367
volunteers in, 485–486
Probationed Offenders Rehabilitation Training (PORT), 500
Procedural criminal law, 5–7, 9
Procunier v. *Martinez*, 445–446
Project Crossroads, 479–480
Project Star (Systems and Training Analysis of Requirements

for Criminal Justice Participants), 138–139
PROMIS (Prosecutor's Management Information System), 252
Prosecutors, 34–36, 37, 51, 246–255, 266–267
and arresting officers, 252–253
and beyond a reasonable doubt standard, 248, 270
burden of proof on, 246, 270
and career criminal program, 251
case-evaluation systems of, 251
and certainty of punishment, 250–251
in criminal justice system, 247
and death penalty, 357
and decision to prosecute, 247–248
and dropping multiple counts, 249–250
effectiveness of, 274
efficiency of, 246, 271–272
and grand jury system, 40–42
legal strength of cases of, 248
and *nolle,* 248–249
opposition to parole of, 247
and overcriminalization, 247
and plea bargaining, 271, 275, 284, 285
and disclosure, 284, 286
and discretion, 271
incentive for, 271–274
prosecution on reduced charges, 249
selective prosecution of, 251, 254
sentence recommendations on, 249, 250
Prosecutor's Management Information System (PROMIS), 252
Prostitution, 69
Psychosurgery in prisons, 451, 452
Psychotherapy in prisons, 413
Public Advocates Inc., 143
Public defenders. *See* Defense counsels, public defenders
Public Defender Service, 261
Punishment. *See also* Cruel and unusual punishment
capital. *See* Death penalty
certainty of, 250–251
corporal, 11, 458
imprisonment as, 331–332
and rehabilitation, 331–332

Quotas, racial, for police personnel, 143–144, 146

Race and minorities, 193–194
and fear of crime, 27
hiring and selection (*Bakke* v. *Regents of the University of California, Fullilove* v. *Klutznick, Griggs* v. *Duke Power Co., United Steel Workers of America*), 142–147
and jury selection, 306, 311
and police-community relations, 108–110
and police personnel, 91, 93, 95–98, 130, 140–147
and prison custodial staff (*Minnick* v. *Cal. Dept. of Corrections*), 398–399
segregation in prison (*Lee* v. *Washington*), 447
and sentences, 343
Race Relations Information Center, 145
Rape, 11, 13–14, 125, 171–172, 174, 185–186, 257, 306, 307, 321, 358–359, 428, 521–523
crisis centers for, 512
and death sentence, 358–359
fear of, 28
incidence of, 18, 24, 26
and plea bargaining, 279, 287
of prisoners, 458–459
self-defense against as defense, 311
in series crimes, 249
in victim survey, 24, 26
Rap sessions in prisons, 413
Reality therapy in prisons, 413
Reasonableness
of arrests, 34, 36
beyond a reasonable doubt, 248
changing standards of, 11
and Constitution, 9–11
and cruel and unusual punishment, 9
of evidence, 312
in good faith defense, 106
and police use of deadly force, 95
principle of, 7
of searches, 191–193
of trial delays, 291–292
Reckless driving, 3
Regina v. *Dudley,* 460
Rehabilitation
and parole, 428
in prisons, 428, 432, 433
and punishment, 331–332
and sentences, 329–330, 349, 362
as treatment, 449–450
Rehabilitation-Research Foundation, 401–402
Rehm v. *Malcolm,* 463
Rehnquist, William H., 82, 360
Reid v. *Georgia,* 192
Reiss, Albert J., 70, 90, 91, 109
Release on recognizance (ROR), 232–236, 238, 240
and failure-to-appear (FTA), 234
Release with services (RWS) on bail, 236–237
Religion, prisoner rights to, 446–447
Retribution as objective of sentencing, 329–330, 362
Return of the Sting operation, 80
Reverse discrimination, 145–146
Revolving-door justice, 85
Rhode Island v. *Innis,* 188–189
Rhodes v. *Chapman,* 390–391
Richmond Newspapers, Inc., 302
Richmond v. *Virginia,* 302–304
Riots, 53–54
in jails, 377–380
and police-community relations, 108–111

Riots (*Continued*)
police control of, 76
and prisoners' rights, 441–444
Rizzo, Frank, 91
Rizzo v. *Goode,* 193
Robbery, 13, 14, 324, 521–523
armed and unarmed, 2, 331
disparate sentences for, 337
fear of, 28
incidence of, 18, 24, 26
and pretrial detention, 231
sentencing guidelines for, 342
in series crime, 249
of taxi and truck drivers, 78
in victim survey, 24, 26
Roberts v. *Louisiana,* 358
Rochin v. *California,* 176
Rockefeller, Nelson, 444
RODEO program, 485
Role playing, 112
Rouse v. *Cameron,* 450
Ruiz v. *Estelle,* 396–397
Rummel v. *Estelle,* 348

Safe Streets Act, The, 56, 59, 82, 110
St. Louis County Police Department, 319
Sam Houston University, 398
San Diego Police Department, 131
San Diego State University, 125
Sandifer, Jawn, 380
San Francisco Police Department, 143, 149, 151
San Jose Police Department, 99
San Quentin Six, 309
Santobello v. *New York,* 277, 296
Saxbe, William, 251
Schmerber v. *California,* 176
Schools, crime in, 124–125
Schware v. *Board of Bar Examiners of New Mexico,* 502
Scientific method in jury selection, 313
Scott v. *Illinois,* 265
Search and seizure, 5, 9, 51, 79, 191. *See also* Fourth amendment; Stop and frisk
and exclusionary rule, 163–165
reasonableness of, 191–193
third party, 183–184
and warrants, 164–169
Search warrants. *See* Warrants
Selective law enforcement, 68–70, 72, 87
Self-help in prisons, 413
Self-incrimination, 170, 174–176, 186, 194, 519, 524
Selman, Terry, 359
Sensitivity training, 112
Sentence Review Division, Connecticut, 345
Sentences, 7, 12, 46–47, 51, 328–363. *See also* Punishment
appellate review of, 343–346, 351
and accountability, 343–344
obstacles to, 344, 346
structures for, 344, 345
capital punishment. *See* Death penalty
and certainty of punishment, 250–251
concurrent, 250
consecutive, defendant awareness of, 44
councils on, 340–341
and court watchers, 125–126
determinate, 46, 349–350
and prison overcrowding, 389
as deterrence, 329–330, 362
discretion in, 46–47
disparity in, 335–339
evidence of, 336
and individualized justice, 338–339
negative consequences of, 336–338
problems of, 339
and domestic disturbances, 115, 116
and felonies, 257, 258, 263, 264, 347, 348
guidelines on, 341–343
and guilty pleas, 270, 271, 280–281, 332
indeterminate, 46, 348–349, 427–428
institutes on, 340
life imprisonment, 417
mandatory (*Rummel* v. *Estelle*), 47, 348, 350–357
Model Penal Code on, 346–347, 362
Model Sentencing Act, 347–348
objectives of, 329–332
deterrence, 330–331, 362
incapacitation, 330–331, 362
rehabilitation, 331–332, 362
retribution, 329–330, 362
and parole, 351
and plea bargaining, 277, 285–287, 296
and presentence reports, 246, 332–335
pretrial detention applied to, 229–231
legal consequences of, 230–231
as punishment, 230
prosecutor recommendations on, 249, 250
and race, 343
and rehabilitation, 329–330, 349, 362
U.S. Sentencing Commission bill, 351
weekend, 375
of young adults, 533, 535
Service style of policing, 130
Sex discrimination suits, 149–150
Sexual molestation, 187–188. *See also* Rape
Sheppard, Sam, 307
Sherman Report, 136, 137
Sherman v. *United States,* 78–80
Shirley institution, 489
Shock probation, 483–484, 512
Shoplifting, 193, 481
Simants, Erwin, 307
Simonson, Archie, 338
Sing-Sing prison, 380
Sixth Amendment
and nonunanimous verdicts, 316
and number of jurors, 313
and police restraint, 173
and public access to trials, 301, 302, 304, 307
and right to counsel, 170, 188, 256–257, 524–525

and right to trial of, 323
and speedy trial, 288, 300
and witness cross-examination, 524
60 Minutes, 433
Slander, 105
Sliwa, Curtis, 121, 122
Social report, 528, 530–532
Solitary confinement in prisons, 453
Sorrells v. *United States,* 79
Sostre v. *Rockefeller,* 442
Southeastern Community College, 411, 412
Southern Ohio Correctional Facility, 390
Southern Poverty Law Center, 143–144, 312, 352
Sovereign immunity doctrine
good faith defense of local governments (*Owen* v. *City of Independence*), 107
local governments and litigation (*Monnell* v. *Department of Social Services of New York City*), 106–107
searches (*Monroe* v. *Pape*), 106
SPA (State Planning Agency), 56–58
Special Intensive Parole Unit, California, 505
Special Narcotics Squad, 168
Special Treatment and Rehabilitative Training Project (START), 452
Special Weapons and Tactics (SWAT), 76, 87
Speedy trial, 288–296, 300
balancing process (*Barker* v. *Wingo*), 289–290
dismissal as remedy (*Strunk* v. *United States*), 293–294
obstacles to, 289
and plea bargaining, 295–296
rights to, 45
Speedy Trial Act of 1974, 289–296
Stack v. *Boyle,* 224
Standards and Goals Commission, 57–59, 62, 72, 133, 152, 158, 259, 261, 263, 264, 283, 289, 290, 296, 332, 343, 376, 487
Standards Relating to Speedy Trial (ABA), 289
Stanford University prison experiment, 402–403
STAR (Systems and Training Analysis of Requirements for Criminal Justice Participants), 138
Stare decisis, 6
START (Special Treatment and Rehabilitative Training project), 452
State courts. *See* Courts
State Law Enforcement Training Commissions, 138
State Planning Agency (SPA), 56–58
State Prison Diagnostic Center, Lake Butler, 389
State Troopers, Alabama, 144
State v. *the Accused,* 6
State v. *Wooten,* 460
Statute of limitations, 45
Statutory criminal law, 5–7
Sterilization and probation, 482–483
Stillwater Data Processing, 410
Sting operation, 80, 83
Stone v. *Powell,* 183
Stop and frisk, 75, 194
and arrests, 177–181
and basis for suspicion (*Adams* v. *Williams*), 190
conditions for, 180–181
expansion of, 182, 190–191
justifications for (*Terry* v. *Ohio*), 179–181, 190
in traffic violations (*United States* v. *Robinson*), 190–191
Strunk v. *United States,* 293
Subculture of police, 66
Subway crime, 74
Suicide of offender, 19
Supreme Court, U.S.
Burger court, 181–194
and classification of crime, 12–13
Warren court, 162–181, 215
SWAT (Special Weapons and Tactics), 76, 87
Symbionese Liberation Army, 309
Synanon, 413
System of criminal justice, 31–59
administration as system and nonsystem, 49–53
arraignment in, 36, 43–45, 51, 247
arrest in, 33–36, 51
components of, 50–51
correctional institutions in, 48, 50, 51
division of labor in, 50, 51
grand jury in, 38–43, 45, 247
initial court appearance in, 36–37, 51, 247
jurisdictional and operational problems in, 52–53
parole in, 48–50, 51, 247
people problems in, 53
preliminary hearing in, 37–38, 51, 247
pretrial motions in, 45
probation in, 47, 51
prosecutors in, 247
roles and goals in, 52–53
sentencing in, 46–47, 51, 247
state and local systems, federal role in, 53–58
and LEAA, 56–58
President's Crime Commission on, 54, 57–58
and riots, 53–55
and Standards and Goals Commission, 57–59
substantive issues in, 53
trial in, 45–46, 51, 247
Systems and Training Analysis of Requirements for Criminal Justice Participants (STAR), 138–139

Task Force on Violent Crime, 242, 391
Tax evasion, 336
parole guidelines on, 424

Taxi-Truck Surveillance Unit, 78
Taylor, Richard, 302, 303
Tennessee State Prison, 445
Terry v. *Ohio,*179–181, 190, 194
Texas Department of Corrections, 396–398, 411
Theft. *See also* Larceny
  larceny-theft, 13, 14
    incidence of, 18, 24, 26
    in victim survey, 24, 26
  motor vehicle, 13, 14
    incidence of, 18, 24, 26
    in victim survey, 24, 26
  parole guidelines on, 424
  and plea bargaining, 275
Therapeutic community in prisons, 413–415
Thirteenth Amendment and involuntary servitude of prisoners, 406
Training Center for Men, Moberly, 411
Trials, 51, 247, 300–325
  adversary model of, 45–46, 300–301
  appeals of, 6–7, 343–346
  delays of, 291–292
  and jury selection, 304–313
  pretrial publicity (*Gannett* v. *DePasquale*), 301–304, 306, 307
    gag on, 307
  public access to, 301–304, 307
    gag orders (*Nebraska Press Association* v. *Stuart*), 307
    rationale for (*Richmond* v. *Virginia*), 302–304
  six-person juries for, 313–316
  speedy. *See* Speedy trial
  videotapes for, 300, 318–323
Trop v. *Dulles,* 352, 453
Truancy, 481, 531
Tucker Reformatory, 392–394
Tuthill, Richard, 418

UCR. See Uniform Crime Reports
Undercover police operations, 78
Uniform Arrest Act, 181
Uniform Crime Reports (*UCR*), 13, 17, 18, 23, 24, 26–29, 55, 119, 517, 527, 529
Union Correctional Institution, 408
Unions, labor, and prisoner rights, 447–448
United States Board of Parole, 422
United States Bureau of the Census, 25, 26
United States Civil Service Commission, 503
United States Department of Education, 58
United States Department of Justice, 55, 91–93
United States Department of Labor, 480, 501, 503–504
United States Fire Administration, 16
United States Probation Office, 485
United States v. *Bailey,* 459, 461
United States v. *Calandra,* 182
United States v. *Holmes,* 460
United States v. *Robinson,* 190–191
United States v. *Russell,* 79, 80, 193
United States v. *Salvucci,* 184–185
United States v. *Tucker,* 335
United Steelworkers of America v. *Weber,* 146, 147
University of California, 125, 493–494
University of Georgia, 398
University of Massachusetts, 489
University of Michigan, 124
University of Minnesota Law School, 266
University of Wisconsin, 124

Vagrancy, legal vagueness on, 7
Vandalism of schools, 124
Venire and venue, 304–308, 311
Vera Institute of Justice (Vera Foundation), 231–232, 234, 238, 501, 509, 511
Verdict. *See* Juries
Victim Assistance Project, Fort Lauderdale, 508
Victimless crime, 69
  punishment of, 84–86
Victims
  assistance programs for, 508–509
  compensation program for, 507–508
  financial restitution of, 483–484
  and plea bargaining, 279
  precipitation by, 276
  race of, 97
  surveys and statements of, 23–29, 332
  victim-witness assistance programs, 509–511
Videotapes
  in police training, 98
  for trials (*Chandler* v. *Florida, Estes* v. *Texas*), 300, 318–323
Vienna Correctional Center, 401
"Violence and the Police" (Westley), 70
VIP (Volunteers in Probation) program, 485–486
Vocational training in prisons, 405–411, 418
Voir dire, 308–313
Vollmer, August, 131
Volunteers in Probation (VIP) program, 485–486
Volunteer Supervisor Program, 485

Wade v. *United States,* 191
Wallace, George, 395
Ward Grievance Procedure (WGP), California, 466–468
War on crime, 240
Warrants, 164–169, 183–184
  and arrests, 34, 167
  nonrequirement of, 194
  and search and seizure, 164–169
Warren, Earl, 78, 162, 163, 181, 194, 215
Washington Corrections Center, 411

Washington, D.C. Metropolitan Police Department, 147–148
Washington State Penitentiary, 413, 472
Washington State University, 413
Watchman style of policing, 130
Watergate, 311
Watts riot, 76
Wayne State University, 124
Weapons possession, 233
  and pretrial detention, 231
Weber, Brian, 146
Weeks v. *United States,* 165
Weems v. *United States,* 352
Welfare, revocation of (*Goldberg* v. *Kelly*), 485
Westley, William A., 70
White, Byron, 353
Wife battering, 113–116. *See also* Domestic disturbances
Wilkins, Leslie T., 333
Williams, Harrison, 81
Williams, Robert, 187–188
Williams v. *Florida,* 313–314, 325
Wilson, James Q., 130
Winship, Stephen, 525–526
Witherspoon, William, 309
Witherspoon v. *Illinois,* 358
Witnesses
  cross-examination of, 37, 524
    prisoner flights for, 453
  immunity of, 41–42
Witness Security Program, Federal, 510–511
Wolff v. *McDonnell,* 454–457
Wolfgang, Marvin, 21
Wolf v. *Colorado,* 165
Work release (WR), 490–493
  obstacles to, 492–493

Yardville Correctional Center, 407, 491
Younger v. *Gilmore,* 445
Youthful Offender Act, 271
Youth Service Bureau (YSB), 481–482, 535

Zeitlin, Maurice, 122
Zimbardo, Philip, 135, 402

84 85 86 9 8 7 6 5 4 3 2